Cognitive Psychology and Instruction

FIFTH EDITION

Roger H. Bruning
University of Nebraska–Lincoln

Gregory J. Schraw
University of Nevada–Las Vegas

Monica M. Norby
University of Nebraska–Lincoln

Boston   Columbus   Indianapolis   New York   San Francisco   Upper Saddle River
Amsterdam   Cape Town   Dubai   London   Madrid   Milan   Munich   Paris   Montreal   Toronto
Delhi   Mexico City   Sao Paulo   Sydney   Hong Kong   Seoul   Singapore   Taipei   Tokyo

Vice President, Editor in Chief: *Paul A. Smith*
Editorial Assistant: *Matthew Buchholz*
Marketing Manager: *Joanna Sabella*
Production Editor: *Paula Carroll*
Editorial Production Service: *Element*
Manufacturing Buyer: *Megan Cochran*
Electronic Composition: *Element*
Cover Designer: *Central Covers*

Credits and acknowledgments borrowed from other sources and reproduced, with permission, in this textbook appear on appropriate page within text.

Library of Congress Cataloging-in-Publication Data
Bruning, Roger H.
   Cognitive psychology and instruction / Roger H. Bruning, Gregory J.Schraw,
   Monica M. Norby. — 5th ed.
      p. cm.
   Includes bibliographical references and index.
   Previous ed. cataloged under title.
   ISBN-13: 978-0-13-236897-1
   ISBN-10: 0-13-236897-8
 1. Learning. 2. Cognitive psychology. 3. Cognitive learning. 4. Instructional systems—Design.
 I. Schraw, Gregory J. II. Norby, Monica M. III. Cognitive psychology and instruction. IV. Title.
   LB1060.B786 2011
   370.15'23—dc22

                                    2010032890

10 9 8 7 6 5 4 3 2 1   RRD-VA   14 13 12 11 10

www.pearsonhighered.com

ISBN-10: 0132368978
ISBN-13: 9780132368971

ABOUT THE AUTHORS

Roger Bruning is Velma Warren Hodder Professor of Educational Psychology and co-directs the Center for Instructional Innovation at the University of Nebraska-Lincoln (UNL). A graduate of UNL, his teaching and research examine applications of cognitive principles to teaching and learning, especially in literacy, science, and mathematics.

Gregg Schraw is Barrick Distinguished Professor of Educational Psychology at the University of Nevada, Las Vegas. His work has concentrated on implicit beliefs about intelligence and knowledge and on methods for developing critical thinking. He is a graduate of the University of Utah.

Monica Norby is Assistant Vice Chancellor for Research at UNL. Drawing on her background as a plant geneticist and scientific writer, her current efforts are focused on research supporting processes of scientific inquiry and on best practices for educating students in science and mathematics. She is a graduate of UNL.

BRIEF CONTENTS

CONTENTS

PREFACE

Cognitive Psychology and Instruction, Fifth Edition, is the latest revision of a text first published in 1990. This book, like the earlier editions, is aimed at giving educators a solid grounding in cognitive psychology and helping them tie important principles from cognitive psychology to instruction. It is directed at those who are interested in understanding the principles of cognitive psychology and in applying them to instruction and curriculum design.

New to This Edition

The original book had a simple two-part structure; the first part laid out the basic principles of cognitive psychology, and the second part concentrated on school-based applications of a cognitive approach. We subsequently added two new sections, one reflecting the growing emphasis on the importance of beliefs in cognition and a second describing new approaches to problem solving, critical thinking, and reflective thought. We also added a chapter on technology to reflect new developments in this important area.

As in previous editions, this fifth edition reflects the dynamic nature of our field of cognitive psychology and how it is being applied to educational practice. Among the major revisions in this edition are the following:

- Part I of the text has again been significantly revised by updating and further integrating the information in Chapters 1 through 5. The result is that this section now provides a more comprehensive framework for the entire book, including the motivation and subject-area chapters.
- Chapter 2, "Sensory, Short-Term, and Working Memory," has been extensively revised to reflect important new developments. Chapter 2 is key in that it introduces readers to the most recent research on memory and explains memory's central role in learning and cognition. This edition also includes a new section on neuropsychology and its increasing importance for understanding memory processes.
- Each chapter includes a new section focusing on assessment. These sections clearly show the increasing impact of cognitive and motivational theory on assessment. They provide state-of-the-art examples of cognitively oriented measures on topics ranging from working memory to mathematics and science learning. They also alert readers to significant controversies about educational standards and assessment methods and point to ways that cognitive principles can inform decisions about assessment.
- The latest cognitive and motivational research has been carefully reviewed for every chapter topic and incorporated into this revision. The chapters thus reflect the newest developments in cognitive and motivational theory and an up-to-date perspective on how that research applies to teaching and learning in the content areas. New citations are included in all of the chapters and mirrored in the extensively updated references list.

■ The *Implications* sections that are included in every chapter have been extended to reflect new developments in cognitive and motivational research.

■ The Glossary, which provides concise definitions of key terms, has been revised to include new concepts that have become prominent in the cognitive and motivational literature since the last edition.

Organization of This Edition

Cognitive Psychology and Instruction, Fifth Edition, begins with an introduction to cognitive psychology in Chapter 1, which explains how cognitive psychology developed into its current position of dominance. Part I, "Information Processing Theory," describes key elements of a cognitive model in Chapters 2 through 5. Chapter 2, "Sensory, Short-Term, and Working Memory," has been substantially revised and rewritten. It presents the modal memory model and describes the latest research and theory on sensory, short-term, and working memory. It also includes a new section on neuropsychology, an area that has rapidly grown with the availability of new imaging technologies. Chapter 3, "Long-Term Memory: Structures and Models," is devoted to long-term memory and identifies the key concepts that have guided cognitive research since the beginning of the cognitive era. Chapters 4 and 5, "Encoding Processes" and "Retrieval Processes," provide detailed accounts of how encoding and retrieval affect the nature and quality of cognitive processes.

Models of cognition now incorporate variables related to learner beliefs, choices, and motivation. These variables are of great interest to educators, and Part II, "Beliefs and Cognition," focuses on them. Chapter 6, "Beliefs About Self," examines motivational issues of special importance to educators, including Bandura's social cognitive theory, attribution theory, and issues of student autonomy and control. Chapter 7, "Beliefs About Intelligence and Knowledge," shows how students' beliefs about their own abilities and the nature of knowledge are critical determinants of what they choose to do and what they achieve.

The three chapters in Part III, "Fostering Cognitive Growth," extend the basic cognitive model as they describe the nature and development of higher-level cognitive processes in school settings. Chapter 8, "Problem Solving and Critical Thinking," translates research from these two vital areas into practical applications for teaching and learning. Chapter 9, "Classroom Contexts for Cognitive Growth," provides an integrated view of how educators can design environments based on cognitive principles that will stimulate cognitive growth, reflection, and self-regulation. Chapter 10, "Technological Contexts for Cognitive Growth," describes research in a thriving new area of application for cognitive principles. It links cognitive and motivational theory to technology use and highlights some of the most innovative ways that cognitively oriented educators are using technology to promote cognitive growth.

Part IV, "Cognition in the Classroom," presents research that shows how cognitive perspectives have profoundly affected our views of schooling. Three of the five chapters in this section focus on literacy and its development. Chapter 11, "Learning to Read," and Chapter 12, "Reading to Learn," are detailed accounts of linguistic and cognitive processes in beginning and later reading. Chapter 13, "Writing," illustrates how cognitive analyses are applied to writing and writing instruction. Chapter 14, "Cognitive Approaches to Mathematics," and Chapter 15, "Cognitive Approaches to Science," show how cognitive theory has altered the conceptions of learning and teaching in mathematics and science.

Philosophy of This Text

As we have stated in earlier editions, we do not argue that cognitive psychology is the only psychological viewpoint that can inform education. We remain strongly committed, however, to the belief that cognitive psychology provides an important perspective for better understanding educational goals and processes. There are few educational decisions to which the cognitive issues of memory, thinking, problem solving, and motivation are not relevant. Also, in the years since the fourth edition was published, cognitive psychology has been anything but static. The field continues to be extraordinarily dynamic and we expect its evolution to continue into the foreseeable future.

ACKNOWLEDGMENTS

Many individuals were involved in making this latest edition a reality. Kevin M. Davis served as our editor for the second, third, and fourth editions and helped set us on the path to this fifth edition. We owe him a debt of gratitude for his wise counsel on matters great and small. Paul A. Smith, Vice President and Editor in Chief at Allyn & Bacon Education, now serves as our editor. We are deeply appreciative of Paul's having assumed this role and grateful for his perceptive insights, capable guidance, and considerable patience. We also wish to express appreciation to two past editors: Chris Jennison, who first encouraged our author group when we began this project years ago, and Robert Miller, then an acquisitions editor for Merrill, who provided us with much-appreciated support and counsel. We are also grateful to a very capable group of reviewers of this edition: Joyce Alexander, Indiana University; Radhi Al-Mabuk, University of Northern Iowa; Steven Condly, University of Central Florida; Vanessa Dennen, Florida State University. Their perceptiveness and suggestions led us to once again reexamine the content of the book and prompted many positive changes. We also wish to acknowledge reviewers of previous editions: Robert L. Benefield, Louisiana State University, Shreveport; Michael L. Bloch, University of San Francisco; Martha Carr, University of Georgia; Linda D. Chrosniak, George Mason University; Wallace Hannum, University of North Carolina; Mary Lou Koran, University of Florida; Raymond W. Kulhavy, Arizona State University; Michael S. Meloth, University of Colorado; S.J. Samuels, The University of Minnesota; Robert Tennyson, University of Minnesota; Charles K. West, University of Illinois; and Karen Zabrucky, Georgia State University. We especially wish to thank N for her very able service as Project Coordinator for this edition, our copyeditor N , and Production Editor N. We have come away from our interactions with them with great admiration for their professional skills and dedication and with gratitude for their assistance in improving this text.

We again dedicate this edition to Royce R. Ronning, whose personal qualities and scholarly excellence still continue to inspire us and energize our efforts, and to his wife, Ruth, who always has supported our efforts with characteristic warmth and generosity of spirit. We are deeply grateful to both Royce and Ruth for their roles in our lives and work.

Roger Bruning
Gregory Schraw
Monica Norby

1 Introduction to Cognitive Psychology

A Brief History ■ **Cognitive Themes for Education** ■ **Summary** ■
Suggested Readings ■

This book is about cognitive psychology and its implications for education. Cognitive psychology is a theoretical perspective that focuses on understanding human perception, thought, and memory. It portrays learners as active processors of information—a metaphor borrowed from the computer world—and assigns critical roles to the knowledge and perspective that students bring to their learning. What learners do to enrich information, in the view of cognitive psychology, determines the level of understanding they ultimately achieve.

The cognitive psychology we describe has become the major force in American psychology over the past half century. Cognitive psychology has provided many powerful concepts, each with considerable explanatory value for education. Among these concepts are **schemata** (sing., schema), the idea that there are mental frameworks for comprehension; **levels of processing,** the notion that memory quality is a by-product of the kind of processing that information receives; and **constructive memory,** the view that knowledge is created by learners as they confront new situations. Now, as cognitive psychology has matured, it emphasizes social influences on cognitive development; connections among cognition and motivation, as well as between self-awareness and cognitive strategies; and the growth of subject matter expertise in such areas as mathematics and science. It also has begun to seek connections between cognitive and neurological processes (e.g., Anderson, Douglass, & Qin, 2004; Katzir & Paré-Blagoev, 2006; Posner, 2004; Ward, 2006), the latter made more accessible by new brain-imaging technologies. The major emphasis of this book is to describe and elaborate these concepts and themes of cognitive psychology and relate them to education.

A Brief History

The Associationist Era

Each of us has his or her own view of the world, a "world hypothesis" (Pepper, 1942/1961), that guides our observations, actions, and understanding of our experience. Any theoretical perspective in psychology similarly rests on a particular view of the world; it counts some things as evidence but not others, organizes that evidence, and leads to hypotheses about how evidence is interrelated and what it means. Cognitive psychology is one such theoretical perspective; it makes the claim that the purpose of scientific psychology is to observe *behavior*—the observable responses of individuals—in order to make inferences about unobservable, underlying factors that can explain the actions we see. In cognitive psychology, observations are used to generate inferences about such factors as thought, language, meaning, and imagery. The field of cognitive psychology seeks to construct formal, systematic explanations about the nature and functions of our mental processes.

For much of the 20th century, however, the world of psychology in the United States was dominated by a theoretical perspective of an entirely different sort—*behaviorism*. Learning, in this view, involves associating or linking a *stimulus* (e.g., a flashing light on a panel or an English word) with a *response* (e.g., a bar pressed by a lab animal or saying the foreign language equivalent of the English word). The general goal of this approach to psychology was to derive elementary laws of behavior and learning and extend those laws to more complex settings. Inferences about these laws were closely tied to observed behavior. Animals, as well as humans, were suitable objects of study; investigations of learning and memory in "lower organisms" were fueled by a faith that the laws of learning were universal and that work with laboratory animals could be extrapolated to humans. Especially during the period from 1920 to 1970, behaviorism was *the* American psychology. There was no real alternative to it in the United States (Glover & Ronning, 1987), even though other, more cognitive, perspectives were flourishing in Germany, Britain, France, and Canada (Mandler, 2002a).

Among the clearest formulations of behavioral principles of learning were those made by Clark Hull (1934, 1952) and his colleague Kenneth Spence (1936, 1956). Reasoning from the data of numerous experiments with laboratory animals, Hull and Spence derived equations based on hypothesized variables, such as strength of habits, drive, and inhibition, which enabled predictions to be made about behavior in laboratory settings. Elementary laws of learning captured in equations such as these could account for many phenomena, such as animals learning to make simple distinctions (e.g., choosing a circle instead of a square button when pressing the circular button was followed by the offer of a food pellet) or learning by **trial and error** (Hull, 1952).

Behaviorism fits within the general theoretical framework of *associationism,* which emphasized the nature and strength of associations—principally between stimuli and responses—and their role in learning. The associationistic perspective provided a natural bridge between psychologists studying animal learning and those more interested in human learning. Especially in the United States, the study of memory, thinking, and problem solving was dominated by associationism, almost to the exclusion of other perspectives (Mandler, 2002a). Most research in memory during this period focused on rote, or nonmeaningful, learning. Following a tradition begun by Hermann Ebbinghaus well before 1900, many researchers studied subjects' memory for individual items, most commonly nonsense syllables (e.g., KAJ, WUV, and XJC) and individual words. They assumed that understanding learning and memory for these simple materials would lead to principles that could explain complex learning and memory phenomena.

Among preferred research methods were **serial list learning,** in which one item cues the next item in the list, and **paired associate learning,** in which a response must be linked with a stimulus. These methods allowed the development of associations to be most clearly predicted and studied. As this research was refined further, tables of norms were developed in which nonsense syllables and words were calibrated for their "meaningfulness"; that is, they were rated for the likelihood that they could elicit associations from learners. Knowing these characteristics of words and syllables permitted researchers to precisely manipulate features of their materials (see Noble, 1952, and Underwood & Schultz, 1960, for examples). Like the aims of Hull and Spence's work with animals, the goal was to develop basic principles from research using simple materials in highly controlled settings that would apply to broader contexts such as learning and recall of materials in school.

A fundamental difficulty, however, was that as experimental psychologists made finer and finer distinctions in their laboratory research on animal trial-and-error learning and studies of human memory, their findings seemed to have few applications (Mandler, 2002a) and to become less and less relevant for education. The search for general laws of learning that crossed all species and settings was failing. Although experimental methodologies for studying learning and memory were becoming highly refined and experiments more internally valid (Campbell & Stanley, 1963), they were becoming less valid externally. Even though many studies had very sophisticated methodologies, their findings could not be easily generalized. As elucidated by experimental psychology in the United States, the laws of learning seemed to be described more properly as the "laws of animal learning," the "laws of animals learning to make choices in mazes," or the "laws of human rote memory" rather than as the universal learning principles associationists sought (but see Dempster & Corkill, 1999, for an argument for the relevance of associationist learning principles to a variety of domains, including school learning).

Near the end of the behavioral–associationistic period, the so-called radical behaviorists, led by scientist-philosopher B. F. Skinner, made a strong impact on both psychology and education. Skinner's views were strongly environmental, in the tradition of the early behaviorist John B. Watson (see Watson, 1913). Learners were seen as coming to learning *tabula rasa,* as blank slates ready to be conditioned by their environment. Like Watson, Skinner rejected the idea that the purpose of psychology was to study consciousness; the goal of a scientific psychology, he asserted, was to predict and control behavior. What organisms do, Skinner contended, is largely a function of the environment in which they are placed and their learning histories (Skinner, 1938, 1953). By managing the antecedents and consequences for behavior, prediction and control can be achieved. Consequences for behavior are particularly critical, he argued. By providing positive consequences for behavior and by arranging the schedule by which these consequences were delivered, behavior could be shaped and controlled.

In his research, Skinner demonstrated that laboratory animals indeed are exquisitely sensitive to manipulations of both antecedents and consequences of their actions. Skinner and his associates showed that animals' patterns of responding (e.g., rats pressing a bar or pigeons pecking) were predictable from the ways consequences such as food or drink were delivered (see Ferster & Skinner, 1957). Skinner also demonstrated that by working backward from consequences to the behaviors preceding them, very complex sequences or chains of behaviors could be developed.

By the mid-1960s, behaviorism as guided by Skinner's views had become such a potent force in American psychology that, in many settings, consciousness was discredited as a respectable topic for research and theory (Baars, 1986). Part of the reason for the extraordinary influence of Skinner's behavioral approach was that he and his students saw the potential utility of behavioral principles in human learning and began to apply them successfully in a variety of settings. Initial applications were in residential treatment facilities for persons with mental disabilities, where standardizing learning environments and carefully specifying behavioral goals was shown to be very useful for treating a wide range of problems. Extensions of behavioral principles to education soon followed, appearing in such technologies as classroom management (e.g., Baer, Wolf, & Risley, 1968) and teaching machines (Holland & Skinner, 1961; Skinner, 1968). Teaching machines, Skinner contended, could provide the key elements of learning: frequent responding, progress in small steps, shaping, and positive reinforcement. By the early 1970s, as the cognitive movement was just beginning to emerge in American psychology, behavioral principles were being applied to a wide range of therapeutic and educational settings.

Education today still reflects behaviorism's influence. For instance, behavioral theory is recognizable in such familiar educational approaches as the use of rewards, instructional objectives, and performance-based accountability systems. All evolved out of a behavioral philosophy of learning specifying that desired responses must be explicitly stated, made overtly, and rewarded. Many of these interventions based on behavioral principles arguably have helped make education more effective and accountable. Particularly in special education settings, behavioral principles have provided possibilities for instruction that did not exist before.

At about the same time Skinner's behaviorism was being widely applied to education, the American psychological community was growing dissatisfied with the ability of strict associationistic psychologies to provide an adequate account of human thought and memory. For instance, the radical behaviorists' concentration on only observable activity was considered by many to be too limiting, even by those who saw careful observation as the *sine qua non* of any scientific enterprise (e.g., Bandura, 1969). Others decried what they believed to be behaviorism's mechanistic view of human beings as controlled by their environments. A few voiced fears that behavioral principles would be misused by those with totalitarian goals.

Many psychologists who were interested in mental processes were increasingly frustrated as they attempted to use associationist theoretical frameworks and behavioral concepts to describe the complexity of human memory, thinking, problem solving, decision making, and creativity (Mandler, 2002a). Trying to explain this vast array of mental processes within a stimulus/response framework seemed neither to satisfy nor to contribute greatly to our understanding of human cognition. Even as researchers employed ever more sophisticated methodologies in their research, their explanatory system, associationism, did not seem to produce generalizable principles.

Adding to the growing perception that behavioral–associationistic explanations of human functioning were too narrow were objections from nonpsychologists to behavioral-based explanations of language development. For instance, Skinner's publication of *Verbal Behavior* in 1957 prompted immediate reactions from linguists and set off a heated debate about the adequacy of behavioral explanations of language development. In Skinner's judgment, language was acquired largely through processes of imitation, shaping, and reinforcement. Linguists disagreed strongly, citing developments in linguistic theory (e.g., Chomsky, 1957, 1965) and research (e.g., Brown, Cazden, & Bellugi, 1968; Ervin, 1964) showing qualitative differences in child and adult speech and less-than-theoretically expected levels of imitation. Their persuasive arguments weakened behaviorism as a generally applicable theory of language development.

The Cognitive Era

No single event signaled an end to the behavioral era and the beginning of a cognitive one in American psychology. Early on, the cognitive revolution was a quiet one. Certainly, the time was right, as many American psychologists grew frustrated with behavioral theory and methods. As mentioned, research by linguists on the nature of language development supplied evidence against the behaviorists' strongly environmentalist perspective. Another prominent factor was the emergence of computers, which provided both a credible metaphor for human information processing and a significant tool for modeling and exploring human cognitive processes.

Beyond these general trends, the work of many individuals clearly was pivotal in creating a cognitive revolution. Some point to the publication of Ulrich Neisser's *Cognitive Psychology* in 1967, which provided early definition to the new area of cognitive psychology or, even earlier, to the work of Jerome Bruner (Bruner, Goodnow, & Austin, 1956) or David Ausubel (Ausubel, 1960; Ausubel & Youssef, 1963), which emphasized mental structures and organizational frameworks. Others would nominate G. A. Miller's still frequently cited article "The Magical Number Seven, Plus-or-Minus Two: Some Limits on Our Capacity for Processing Information" (1956) or his founding, with Jerome Bruner, of the Center for Cognitive Studies at Harvard in 1960 (Baars, 1986). Many cite J. J. Jenkins's 1974 *American Psychologist* article in which he contrasted the fundamental differences among the mass of rote learning research that he and others had done for a generation and their work within the new cognitive paradigm. Still others would cite Marvin Minsky's 1975 "frames paper," which outlined the necessary features of a vision system that could recognize simple objects. This article highlighted the critical role of mental structures in human thinking and decision making, a theme echoed by others in the related concepts of schemata (Rumelhart, 1975) and **scripts** (Schank & Abelson, 1977).

Today, cognitive psychology is mainstream American psychology, and the cognitive perspective no longer is considered revolutionary. In education, however, its applications continue to be discovered and explored (see, e.g., Bransford, Brown, & Cocking, 2000; Bransford et al., 2006; Carver & Klahr, 2001; National Research Council, 2005; van Merrienboër & Kirschner, 2007). What we attempt to do in this text is present many of cognitive psychology's important concepts and points of view. We do this by organizing our thinking around several key themes in cognitive psychology that we see as most potent for educational practice.

Cognitive Themes for Education

Cognitive psychology now encompasses an enormous body of research on a wide range of theoretical and applied topics (see Anderson, 2005; Baddeley, 2007; Dowd, 2004; Eysenck & Keane, 2005) and in the related and fast-growing fields of cognitive science and cognitive neuroscience. Not all of this research has relevance for education, and our strategy in this text is to organize the information around eight powerful themes that we hope will help you judge cognitive psychology's relevance for teaching and learning.

1. *Learning is a constructive, not a receptive, process.* Most cognitive psychologists see learning as the product of the interaction among what learners already know, the information they encounter, and what they do as they learn. Learning is not so much knowledge and skill

acquisition as it is the *construction of meaning* by the learner (Prawat, 1996). Knowledge is not simply acquired; it is created and re-created on the basis of previous learning. What motivates learning is the "search for meaning."

The old adage "You get out of it only what you put into it" aptly describes a cognitive perspective. Some students approach learning in passive or "shallow" ways, either failing to engage fully or relying heavily on rote memorization. Both cognitive research and our experience as educators tell us that the resultant learning is likely to be both superficial and transitory. In contrast, other students' attempts at learning are clearly aimed at deeper understanding; they relate new information to what they already know, organize it, and regularly check their comprehension.

2. *Mental frameworks organize memory and guide thought.* Among the most compelling concepts of cognitive psychology is the concept of schemata. Schemata are mental frameworks we use to organize knowledge. They direct perception and attention, permit comprehension, and guide thinking. The concept of schemata appeared at about the same time under different labels in the work of several theorists, including Minsky (1975), Rumelhart (1975), Schank and Abelson (1977), and Winograd (1975). Clever experimental demonstrations soon showed how much these mental structures affected perception, learning, and memory.

Pichert and Anderson (1977), for example, asked individuals to read a passage describing a house from the perspective of either (1) a prospective home buyer or (2) a burglar. They hypothesized that these contrasting perspectives would activate different frameworks for comprehending the passage (activate different schemata) and result in different recall patterns. As predicted, their readers did recall significantly more information relevant to their own perspective (e.g., "home buyers" were more likely to recall a leaking roof, information important to a prospective home buyer) than information relevant to the other perspective (e.g., remembering three parked 10-speed bikes, a detail the "burglars" noticed).

Experiments like these shifted the attention of many researchers away from the abstract phenomenon of learning to *learners themselves*—to their prior knowledge and frames of reference, to the activities they undertook and the strategies they used as they learned, and to their role in creating new knowledge. Soon, cognitive psychologists (e.g., Anderson & Pearson, 1984; Brown & Palincsar, 1982) were suggesting instructional approaches based on these ideas. They suggested methods encouraging students to describe what they already knew and how they felt about it, to link new information with old, to use analogies and metaphors as tools for understanding, and to create their own structures for organizing new information. As we will show later, ideas like these have had a significant impact on thinking about instruction in virtually every area of the curriculum.

3. *Extended practice is needed to develop cognitive skills.* The old adage "practice makes perfect" is equally as true for cognition as it is for physical skills. Although we typically think of cognitive psychology as emphasizing meaning and thought, the other side of cognition—automated processes—is equally important. Automated processes in attention, perception, memory, and problem solving allow us to perform complex cognitive tasks smoothly, quickly, and without undue attention to details. Because skilled readers' word recognition and understanding of language structures are rapid and automatic, for example, they can concentrate on the meaning of what they are reading.

Becoming an expert depends on building large repertoires of automated cognitive processes, and there really are no shortcuts to acquiring them. In virtually any domain—from reading or quilting to baseball or beekeeping—developing the underlying automatic processes on which expertise depends can require literally thousands of hours of practice. Thus, in upcoming chapters, we often stress the need for repetition and practice in helping our students increase their cognitive capabilities.

4. *Development of self-awareness and self-regulation is critical to cognitive growth.* Cognitive psychology has consistently promoted the idea of a self-directed, strategic, reflective learner. This idea has been supported by a large body of research on **metacognition,** which generally refers to two dimensions of thinking: (1) what students know about their own thinking and (2) their ability to use this awareness to regulate their own cognitive processes. As students progress through their school years, they typically develop along both dimensions, becoming (1) *more aware* of their own abilities to remember, learn, and solve problems and (2) *more strategic* in their learning and better able to manage their own learning, thinking, and problem solving. For instance, younger students often have little sense of their ability to remember and tend not to use such cognitive strategies as rehearsing or organizing information to help them do so. Older students, however, typically will try at least some strategies to assist them in comprehension and recall.

One of the most important educational implications of metacognitive research has been the growing recognition that acquiring knowledge and skill is only a part of cognitive growth. Although knowledge and skills are important, students' learning strategies and their ability to reflect on what they have learned—to think critically—may be even more important. Unless learners monitor and direct their cognitive processes, they are unlikely to be either effective learners or flexible, effective problem solvers (see, for example, Pressley & Harris, 2006).

5. *Motivation and beliefs are integral to cognition.* Cognitive psychology's scope has expanded greatly as it has matured. Early cognitive research stressed memory, thinking, and problem-solving processes and their applications to instruction. Newer conceptions of cognitive psychology include not only the "purely cognitive" variables of memory and thought but also learners' motivational and belief systems (e.g., Perry, Turner, & Meyer, 2006; Schunk & Zimmerman, 2006). How confident, for instance, are students in their ability to perform certain actions, and what outcomes do they believe will result if they are successful? How do they analyze their successful and unsuccessful performances? What are learners' typical goals? What beliefs do they hold about the nature of knowledge, their own abilities, and their intelligence?

Research on questions such as these has shown the importance of learners' goals, beliefs, and strategies for motivating and regulating learning. For instance, theory and research focusing on such constructs as self-efficacy, outcome expectancy, and self-regulated learning (see Anderman & Wolters, 2006; Pintrich & Schunk, 2002; Schunk & Zimmerman, 2006) have shown that individuals constantly judge their own performances and relate them to desired outcomes. These judgments are an integral part of whether the learner will attempt, complete, and repeat activities. Similarly, cognitive researchers have shown that how individuals explain their successes and failures—their attributions (Graham & Weiner, 1996; Weiner, 1995, 2000)—also have important consequences for learning, as do the kinds of goals they seek (Ames & Archer, 1988). Still other researchers have stressed beliefs that people hold about the nature of knowledge (e.g., Duell & Schommer-Aikins, 2001), intelligence (e.g., Dweck, 2000), and literacy (e.g., Schraw & Bruning, 1996; White & Bruning, 2005).

This very active area of research demonstrates that both cognitive and motivational variables should be considered in accounting for student learning. Successful learning involves not only comprehending content but also learning to become an active, motivated, and self-regulated learner. Cognitive activity occurs within a framework of learners' goals, expectancies, and beliefs, all of which have important consequences for determining what students choose to do, how persistent they are, and how much success they enjoy.

6. *Social interaction is fundamental to cognitive development.* Cognitive psychology's evolution has led to another important understanding—the role of social interactions in cognitive development. Cognitive psychology has helped us see that, like other traits, "ways of thinking" and "ways of knowing" need to be nurtured in a supportive social context.

Educators traditionally have stressed individual study as the route to cognitive growth. Cognitive research, however, has shown that social-cognitive activities, such as well-managed cooperative learning and classroom discussions, stimulate learners to clarify, elaborate, reorganize, and reconceptualize information (e.g., Cazden & Beck, 2003; O'Donnell, 2006). Interacting with peers gives students the opportunity to encounter ideas and perceptions that differ from their own; new knowledge can be constructed out of these exchanges. Collaborative efforts seem to have special potential for cognitive development, affording students the opportunity to observe others, express ideas, and get feedback. As they work on meaningful tasks with others, students begin to internalize modes of thought and expression that lead to higher levels of cognitive activity (Greeno & van de Sande, 2007).

7. *Knowledge, strategies, and expertise are contextual.* Throughout its history, cognitive psychology's dominant metaphor has been the computer. Information enters the human information processing system, is processed and stored, and can be recalled. In short, the mind is machinelike.

From cognitive psychology's earliest beginnings, however, another worldview—*contextualism*—was strongly voiced. The contextualist perspective in cognitive psychology emphasizes history and situation (Gillespie, 1992). Events are inherently situational, occurring in contexts that include other events and taking some or even much of their meaning from those contexts (Gauvain, 2001; Lave & Wenger, 1991; Rogoff, Bartlett, & Turkanis, 2001).

Contextualist views underlie many of the most fertile ideas of cognitive psychology. In early experimental demonstrations, Bransford and his colleagues (Bransford, Barclay, & Franks, 1972; Bransford & Franks, 1971) clearly showed that memory was strongly affected not only by experimental manipulations but also by participants' knowledge of relations and events. Other work (Hyde & Jenkins, 1969; Jenkins, 1974; Tulving & Thompson, 1973) showed that memory was strongly influenced by the actions of learners as they attempted to encode information. Learning and memory are not, it seems, so much a product of machinelike input and output as they are something learners construct in a social context from their prior knowledge and intentions, and the strategies they use (e.g., see Gauvain, 2001).

Today, this viewpoint underlies a strong interest in cognitive strategy instruction and self-regulated learning. The goal is to help students manage their own learning. Research generally shows that for learners to successfully use strategy and self-regulation requires attention not only to the strategies themselves but also to metacognitive knowledge—knowledge about how, when, and why to use particular strategies (e.g., Israel, Block, Bauserman, & Kinnucan-Welsch, 2005; Pressley & Harris, 2006; Schunk & Zimmerman, 2006). Effective strategy use and self-regulation, in short, are thoroughly contextual; they need to be used at the right time and place and be grounded in learners' understanding of themselves and their social worlds.

8. *A cognitive approach to teaching implies new approaches to assessment.* Educators always hope that what is being assessed in any classroom or school will mirror the aims of instruction. In cognitively-oriented instruction, we would expect important cognitive concepts, principles, and goals to be reflected in assessment practices (e.g., see Shepard, 2000, 2005). This in fact is the case; cognitive psychology is affecting assessment in several important ways.

First, although assessing basic knowledge hasn't been abandoned, many newer assessments place more emphasis on higher mental processes such as knowledge application, problem solving, and critical thinking. Cognitive psychology also suggests new assessment dimensions. Reflecting the cognitive concepts of *metacognition* and *situated cognition,* for instance, newer measures tend to emphasize knowledge in context—that is, not only determining *whether* students possess key information but know when, where, and how to apply it. As cognitive psychology has broadened to include attitudes, beliefs, goals, and motivations, assessment approaches have expanded to include such qualities as *self-efficacy* (behavioral confidence), *goal orientation* (the types of goals students seek), and *beliefs about intelligence* (whether they believe their ability is fixed or changeable)—dimensions of cognition that research has shown to be important for teaching and learning.

Our experience tells us that if we describe the concepts of cognitive psychology well and organize them thematically, you will see their considerable power for education. They not only can help you conceptualize your goals for education in cognitive terms but also should aid you in developing highly motivated and capable students. We also know that the cognitive concepts and principles described in this book fit well with many educators' core beliefs: a sense of students as whole human beings; advocacy of active, not passive, learning; and valuing of diversity. We believe that you will find yourself drawn to this perspective, and the "cognitive view" will begin to affect your thinking about your students and your beliefs about how best to teach them.

An Example

To help you get a better sense of the direction in which cognitive psychology will likely take you, think for a moment about one student—Kari, a 15-year-old girl in her first year at Southeast High School. It is midway through the fall semester, and, all in all, Kari has made a reasonably good transition from middle school to high school. Her grades are holding up fairly well, with one exception—a history class with the dreaded Mr. Bergstrom. But, at this point, no one in the class has higher than a B anyway. Kari's immediate concern, however, is an assignment for Ms. Lawrence's Citizenship Issues class. Printed on a half-sheet of photocopied paper, the assignment reads:

> Produce a first draft of a two-page paper on the issue YOU consider to be the most critical issue facing American youth today. Please type your draft and double-space it. As we have done in the past, you need to make four copies. As usual, plan to read it in your small group and to get written comments from each member. This draft is due Friday, the 13th. Final drafts are due a week from Friday, the 20th. P.S. Papers with lines shorter than four inches in length are NOT acceptable. This means you, Bobby!

We next see Kari the following Thursday before school in the computer lab. As she pulls the assignment from her notebook, she mulls over her choices: "Hmmm . . . a two-pager . . . problems facing youth. Let's see, what should I pick? Jobs? Stress and suicide? Drugs? AIDS? Gangs?"

"Jobs . . . much too dull," she thinks. "Stress and suicide? I've been reading about that, but writing about that would be so depressing. Drugs? Maybe . . . AIDS? It'd be good, but I'm not going to write about it for Lawrence. Gangs, well . . . maybe. Hey, there were articles about drugs in the paper last Sunday; I could go look at those." She smiles at Ms. Lawrence's instructions to Bobby.

Twenty minutes later, Kari has yet to type a word, but we see her visiting with her class-mate and friend Hannah, who has come into the lab on a similar mission. They chat a bit, look-ing at a CNN.com article on Kari's computer and sharing some ideas about what Ms. Lawrence *really* wants. By the half-hour, Kari is typing busily, checking the CNN article and occasionally looking into two books from the school library. Ten minutes before the hour ends, we see suc-cess: The printer is humming away, and a second page emerges—with six-inch lines, no less.

In many ways, Kari's assignment is a straightforward one, not much different from those given millions of times each day by teachers in schools across the United States and elsewhere around the world. In each of them, a directive motivates a set of actions—the need to recall earlier events, make decisions, gather and use information, and create a product. Most are sim-ple assignments, yet all are very rich from a cognitive perspective. For Kari to be successful (and we presume she will be), she needs to engage in and guide herself in cognitive operations as diverse as extracting meaning from written instructions; translating her thoughts and implicit knowledge about how school works into plans of action; searching for and organizing information; generating words and sentences from stored and newly acquired information; and, of course, just making the computer and printer work. When all of these dimensions are considered, the array of cognitive functions required seems almost so complex as to defy understanding.

In Kari's sequence of activities, however, we can see certain basic elements. To succeed, she must understand what the task requires her to do. She needs to draw on a body of knowl-edge in memory and guide her mental activities by directing her attention toward some things and away from others. She must make sense of the details she encounters and get information in and out of her memory. She must use language to express this information and, to finish the assignment successfully, monitor her progress and make appropriate decisions about whether the emerging document "solves the problem," that is, meets the assignment criteria.

We chose Kari as an example not because she is unique but because the cognitive resources on which she draws and the actions she takes show many features of cognitive psy-chology. Her actions, though thoroughly familiar, illustrate key elements of human cognitive functioning—perception, attention, short- and long-term memory, associative processes, problem solving, and decision making. They represent motivated and self-directed cognitive activity in school, which is the most important social context supporting students' formal learning. At the same time, they raise the following important questions about our information-processing capabilities:

- How do learners focus their attention on certain elements in the world "out there" while ignoring others, and what are the limits of learners' capacities for "paying attention"?
- How do learners acquire information, make sense of it, store it in memory, and retrieve it? Then, once information is stored, how is it organized, what makes it more or less available when it is needed, and what role does it play in cognitive processes? In other words, why do we sometimes remember and sometimes forget, sometimes understand and sometimes not?

- How does cognition change and develop? How are later cognitive, self-regulation, and motivational processes related to the early learning experiences, habits, and predispositions of young children?
- What role do learners' goals play in cognition and how important are the beliefs that students hold about their capabilities? Are they confident in their abilities? How do students learn to become self-regulated and autonomous?
- How do learners use their cognitive processes in solving problems and what kinds of social contexts, learning tasks, educational practices, and assessments are likely to foster reflective thought?

In Part I of this text, "Information Processing Theory," we begin to examine these questions. Chapter 2, "Sensory, Short-Term, and Working Memory," provides a general model of information processing, describes what happens as we encounter new information, and relates features of sensory and working memory to education. Chapter 3, "Long-Term Memory: Structures and Models," focuses on a topic of concern to all educators—how information is organized and stored in memory. We examine the research and theory on the nature and organization of long-term memory and relate key findings to education. Chapter 4, "Encoding Processes," expands our discussion of memory. It describes how the activities that take place during learning affect memory. In the last chapter of this first section, Chapter 5, "Retrieval Processes," we explore factors controlling recognition and recall as we retrieve information from memory.

By the time you have completed the first part of this text, you should have a clear sense of the basic concepts and perspectives of cognitive psychology and a feel for what it has to offer education. Part II, "Beliefs and Cognition," tracks the evolution of cognitive psychology as it has expanded into important new areas, such as learning strategies, self-regulated learning, motivation, and the role of beliefs in learning. Part III, "Fostering Cognitive Growth," links cognitive psychology with the processes that many educators would place highest among their goals for students—the ability to think critically about issues, reflect wisely on them, and choose effective solutions for problems. The general perspective of this section is the contextual nature of cognition, as we emphasize roles that classroom processes and well-designed technology can play in nurturing "ways of thinking." Part IV, "Cognition in the Classroom," first closely examines the key cognitive skills that apply across all subject areas—language use, reading, and writing—and then how cognitive psychology has begun to transform mathematics and science instruction.

New to this edition, we have included a section in each chapter that ties concepts in the chapter to assessment. The sections address assessment issues and give examples of assessments based on the chapter's ideas. We hope that they provide a valuable bridge between your growing understanding of cognitive concepts and principles and the many assessment-related decisions that are part of educators' lives today.

Summary

For much of the past century, associationism was *the* American psychology. Working within this tradition, American psychologists attempted to derive basic laws governing learning and memory by studying these phenomena in simplified, rigorously controlled experimental settings. As this research became more and more focused, however, much of it seemed to lose its relevance.

Researchers could not find the general laws they were seeking. Nonetheless, one branch of associationistic psychology—behaviorism, which focused on observable responses and environmental design—had a powerful impact on education that continues today. Behaviorism generally has de-emphasized the need to understand learners' mental processes, instead concentrating on the relationships between environmental stimuli and learners' responses.

In psychology itself, however, was a growing dissatisfaction with stimulus–response theories, which increasingly were judged deficient for understanding complex mental events. Memory researchers were frustrated as they attempted to use associationistic theory and experimental studies of rote learning to explain the complexities of human memory, especially meaningful learning. The behavioral perspective was attacked by linguists, who questioned its accounts of language development, and by others who criticized the idea of behavioral control and feared a technology of behavior management.

Today, American psychology is cognitive. Cognitive psychology portrays humans as information processors. The computer metaphor is reflected both in the theorizing and methods of many cognitive psychologists. Drawing on contextualist as well as more mechanistic perspectives, cognitive psychology stresses the importance of learners' activities, strategies, and mental structures in comprehending and creating meaning. As cognitive psychology matures, it increasingly is focusing on the interplay among beliefs, goals, and cognition and how cognition develops in such social contexts as families, classrooms, and communities.

Although cognitive views are now dominant in psychology, their application to education still is only partially realized. Our goal, therefore, is to present the concepts, principles, and perspectives of current cognitive psychology in detail and to help you explore their implications for educational practice.

SUGGESTED READINGS

Anderson, J. R. (2005). *Cognitive psychology and its implications* (6th ed.). New York, NY: Worth.
> This is the sixth edition of a textbook by John R. Anderson, a widely respected cognitive researcher and theorist. First published in 1980 and updated extensively since then, Anderson's book provides a good overview of cognitive psychology and its evolution over time, covering important cognitive concepts such as attention, perception, problem solving, and reasoning.

Eysenck, M. W., & Keane, M. (2005). *Cognitive psychology: A student's handbook* (5th ed.). New York, NY: Psychology Press.
> This well-written, comprehensive introduction to cognitive psychology provides summaries of cognition's multiple levels, ranging from basic perceptual processes through higher-level cognitive functions such as problem solving, decision making, and creativity. It includes information on how advances in cognitive neuroscience, brain imaging, and computer modeling are deepening our understanding of cognitive psychology.

CHAPTER
2
Sensory, Short-Term, and Working Memory

The Modal Model ■ Sensory Memory and Perception ■ The Role of Knowledge and Context in Perception ■ Attention ■ Short-Term and Working Memory ■ Cognitive Neuroscience and Working Memory ■ Assessment of Working Memory ■ Implications for Instruction: Guiding and Directing Attention ■ Summary ■ Suggested Readings ■

Humans have always been fascinated by memory. The scientific study of memory is a relatively recent matter, however, tracing back more than 125 years to the pioneering work of Hermann Ebbinghaus (1850–1909), *Uber das Gedächtnis,* first published in 1885. Ebbinghaus's genius was to reduce the study of memory to its most elemental forms—lists of so-called nonsense syllables (e.g., *FOH* and *TAF*). Ebbinghaus carefully tested his learning of syllables at regular intervals, noting how much he remembered and forgot and how easy it was to relearn forgotten information.

The tradition of memory research begun by Ebbinghaus dominated the study of memory for nearly a century (MacLeod, 1988). Today, our conception of what constitutes the valid study of memory has broadened considerably. Memory research has transcended the painstaking study of how words and isolated facts are remembered and focuses instead on memory of complex chunks of information, such as the gist of a newspaper article or a technical chapter, like the one you are reading now.

Memory research now also has developed several distinct branches. One of these focuses on memory performance during the act of learning. Most researchers refer to this as **working memory.** This chapter examines this research and its implications for learning in detail. A second branch of research focuses on the contents and functioning of permanently stored information, often referred to as **long-term memory,** examined in Chapter 3. A third branch of research focuses on the relationship between memory and brain physiology. Although fascinating and important, much of this research lies beyond the scope of this book.

In this chapter, we introduce a general model of memory that we refer to as the **modal model** (Healy & McNamara, 1996). The modal model includes several different memory components, each of which performs a specific task, much as different gears perform different tasks in an automobile. Our goal is to provide an overview of the modal model and why it is important to the study of learning. Next, we discuss **sensory memory,** the initial memory component that perceives, recognizes, and assigns meaning to incoming stimuli. Then, we consider **short-term memory,** the so-called mental workbench, and describe how the concept of short-term memory has been supplanted by the concept of working memory. Finally, we consider the practical implications of working memory research for learning.

This chapter focuses on sensory memory and short-term memory. We believe that three obstacles stand in the way of effective learning. One is the information bottleneck that occurs in sensory and short-term memory. Because these two dimensions of memory are limited-capacity, brief-duration systems, only a small amount of information can be processed at one time. The second is acquiring and organizing a knowledge base in long-term memory, which holds a large amount of information indefinitely. Third is constructing metacognitive knowledge (knowledge about the contents and regulation of memory) that enables learners to use their memory efficiently. This chapter focuses on the first of these problems, Chapter 3 on the second, and Chapters 4 and 5 on the third.

The Modal Model

Memory researchers traditionally have divided memory processes into stages of acquisition, storage, and retrieval. For a memory to be made, new information somehow must be acquired and brought into the system. Information must also be stored within the system and retrieved when it is needed. In the 1950s, cognitive scientists began creating models that acknowledged these stages; their models also clearly reflected the increasing influence of the computer as a metaphor for human cognition. The models came to be known collectively as **information processing models** (e.g., Atkinson & Shiffrin, 1968; Waugh & Norman, 1965) and their common features as the modal model. Although new memory models continue to evolve, the modal model provides a useful organizer for thinking about memory.

Figure 2.1 presents a schematic diagram of the modal model. The main assumption of the model is that information is processed via a series of discrete memory systems, each serving a specific function. Although this view dates back to William James's distinction between primary and secondary memory, it did not achieve central importance in information

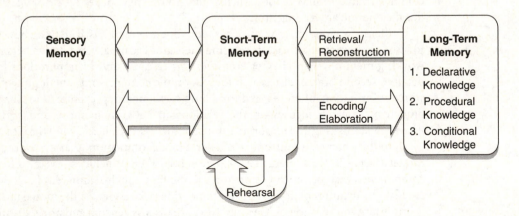

FIGURE 2.1   The Modal Model.

processing theory until the publication of George Miller's (1956) landmark article "The Magic Number Seven, Plus-or-Minus Two." **Sensory memory** in this framework refers to initial perceptual processing that identifies incoming stimuli. Information that has been processed in sensory memory is then passed to short-term memory, where it receives additional meaning-based processing. Information that is relevant to one's goals is then stored indefinitely in long-term memory until it is needed again.

Clarifying the role of different memory systems is only part of our goal. We also want to understand how information is transferred between the memory systems. It turns out that skilled learners use a variety of information processing strategies to move new information from short-term to long-term memory. These processes, collectively known as *encoding processes,* are discussed in detail in Chapter 4. Similarly, processes used to access information in long-term memory for use in short-term memory are known as *retrieval processes* and are discussed in Chapter 5.

Recent versions of the information processing model have added more components. One addition is that short-term memory has been replaced by working memory (Baddeley, 2001, 2007), which makes an important distinction between subprocesses in short-term memory that passively maintain versus actively process information. A second addition is a loop connecting long-term and sensory memory. This loop enables information in permanent memory to influence initial perceptual processing. A third addition is metacognition, which guides the flow of information through the three "lower" memory systems. These components are important because they allow us to use what we already know to learn new information, a phenomenon known as top-down processing. In the model's original version, information processing was bottom-up because none of the "higher" components of memory, such as long-term memory and metacognition, affected initial processes in lower components, such as sensory memory. In the revised model, initial sensory processing is affected by short-term, long-term, and metacognitive processes simultaneously.

It may be helpful to consider some of the main assumptions of contemporary information processing theory that pertain specifically to sensory and short-term memory.

1. *Memory systems are functionally separate.* All information processing accounts of cognition postulate two or more global memory systems that perform specific functions. These systems originally were assumed to be metaphorical in nature; that is, they corresponded neither to specific neurological regions in the brain nor to specific neurobiological processes. Recent research on humans and other animals suggests that the functional distinctions proposed by information processing theorists may have biological analogues as well (Barrett & Kurzban, 2006).

2. *Attention is limited.* The ability to perform mental work is limited in several ways. One is **attention,** or the mental energy used to perceive, think, and understand. Although individual differences exist, everyone's attentional capacity is extremely limited (Just & Carpenter, 1992; Treisman, 2006). Cognitive psychologists refer to this phenomenon as *limited processing capacity.* It is important to note, however, that the limits of information processing can be stretched in amazing ways by using "capacity-saving" strategies such as chunking, categorization, and elaboration (Ericsson, Chase, & Faloon, 1980; Radvansky, 2006).

3. *Cognitive processes are both automatic and controlled.* Skilled cognition is the result of using one's limited resources efficiently. Some tasks require more resources than others, in part because of the complexity of the task but also because of how automatic one is at performing it. **Automaticity** refers to performing any cognitive activity (e.g., retrieving word meanings, driving a car) in an automatic fashion. Automated processes require very little attentional capacity; thus, we get something for nothing when we are automated (Barrett, Tugade, & Engle, 2004; Stanovich, 2000; Sweller, 1999).

In contrast with automated processes, **controlled processes** require some portion of our limited attentional resources. One assumption is that controlled processing can only be allocated to higher-order tasks (e.g., constructing inferences when reading) when basic cognitive processes (e.g., decoding words and grammatical parsing) are automated. One of the best examples of a controlled process is selective attention, or the process by which we allocate all of our limited resources to the most important information before us.

4. *Meaning is constructed.* Information processing is more than just translating information from physical stimuli to a symbolic mental representation. Almost all information is transformed in the process (Kintsch, 1998). Meaning is constructed on the basis of prior knowledge and the context in which the task occurs. Even though the construction of meaning is supported by all components of the information processing system, much of it takes place in short-term memory. Research suggests that once meaning is constructed and forwarded to long-term memory, much of the original form of information is lost.

The modal model has proved highly useful to researchers and educators for several reasons. First, the model helps us better understand the specific role of different memory components. Second, the model has generated massive amounts of research that contribute to theory and practice. Indeed, many ongoing changes in the modal model are a result of this research. Third, the modal model makes an important distinction between memory *structures,* such as short-term memory, and memory *processes,* such as encoding and retrieval, that enable us to move information around in memory.

The modal model also has critics. One criticism is that the model proposes three separate structures in memory corresponding to sensory, short-term, and long-term memory. Many researchers question this assumption for theoretical and empirical reasons. A better assumption is that memory consists of many small interrelated parts. A second criticism is that the modal model implies that information flows through memory in a linear, unidirectional manner. That is, information enters sensory memory, proceeds to short-term memory for additional processing, and then proceeds to long-term memory. In fact, research indicates that information processing is much more dynamic. Information in long-term memory often influences initial processing, and there is reason to believe that information is processed simultaneously in short-term and long-term memory (Neath & Surprenant, 2003). A third criticism is that the modal model does not correspond to the neurological structure of the brain. Recent theories have opted for an entirely different metaphor in which memory is viewed as one integrated network of connected neurons. These theories are referred to as connectionist models and discussed in Chapter 3.

Despite these criticisms, we believe the modal model has great utility as a metaphor for understanding different aspects of memory. Keep in mind that the modal model is just one way to think of memory and that many alternative models could also be proposed.

Sensory Memory and Perception

The modal model portrays memory as a collection of holding systems. Sensory memory is a system that briefly holds stimuli in sensory registers so that perceptual analyses can occur before that information is lost. The first step in this process is **perception,** which enables us to detect incoming perceptual stimuli by allocating attention to them. The next step is **pattern recognition,** which enables us to associate perceptual information with a recognizable pattern. Once stimuli are perceived and recognized, they are forwarded to short-term memory for additional processing. Research on sensory memory attempts to answer three main questions: how we perceive incoming stimuli, how we recognize those stimuli, and how we allocate our attention during perception. We explore each of these questions in more detail in the following discussion.

Think for a moment about what is required for perception to occur. First, some stimulus in the environment has to be detected—seen or heard, but not necessarily understood—by the person. That stimulus then somehow must be transformed and held. This process usually is referred to as **storage.** Next, a body of knowledge has to be available and brought to bear on the stimulus in the process referred to as **pattern recognition.** Finally, some decision has to be made regarding its meaning. This process is referred to as **assignment of meaning.**

The very common phenomenon of identifying the letter *a* seems far more complex when we consider what may happen during the process of perception. One important observation is that perception takes time. The fact that perception requires time and effort leads to a problem of sorts. Because environments may change rapidly (e.g., when watching a film or driving a car), a stimulus could stop being available before a meaning was assigned. Without being able to "hold" that stimulus for a while, our perceptual processes would stop in midstream (Fisher, Duffy, Young, & Pollatsek, 1988). The experience of watching a movie, for example, would be terribly frustrating if stimulus after stimulus disappeared before we could interpret their meanings. Our experience, however, tells us that such breakdowns in our perceptual processes occur infrequently. This is because our cognitive systems are equipped with sensory registers.

Sensory Registers

One of the wonders of our cognitive system is that the system can temporarily retain environmental information after it has disappeared (DiLollo & Dixon, 1988; Treisman, 2006). Even though each of our senses has this ability—a **sensory register**—research has focused almost entirely on vision and hearing. Here, we discuss the visual and auditory sensory registers to give you a flavor of this research.

Visual Registers   The classic work on the visual registers was performed a half-century ago by George Sperling (1960). Sperling was engaged in basic perception research, attempting to identify the nature of the visual registers. As a part of his study, he showed subjects slides depicting arrays of letters, such as the one shown in Figure 2.2.

Sperling noted that when subjects were shown this kind of array for less than 500 milliseconds (i.e., 0.5 second), they could recall about four of the letters. This number did not

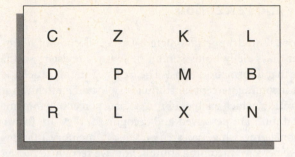

FIGURE 2.2   Stimulus Array Similar to That Used by Sperling.

change, regardless of whether Sperling altered the length of time subjects saw the array (from 15 to 500 ms) or altered the number of letters they saw from 4 to 12. He developed two hypotheses that could account for his results. One hypothesis was that it was possible that only the four letters reported by subjects were registered; that is, subjects saw only 4 letters and could recall no more because they had never registered. The second hypothesis was that all 12 letters were registered but somehow were lost before they could be reported.

To test these hypotheses, Sperling developed what has come to be called the *partial report method*. He reasoned that if subjects had more information available than they could report, he could sample their knowledge. So, rather than ask subjects to report all they saw, he asked them to recall only one of the rows of letters in the arrays they were shown (see Figure 2.2).

Sperling's partial report procedure was quite clever. Participants were told that after the array of letters disappeared from the screen, they would hear a tone. If the tone was of high pitch, subjects were to recall the top row. If the tone was of middle-range pitch, they were to recall the middle row. If the tone was of low pitch, they were to report the bottom row. Because the subjects had no way of knowing which row they would be asked to recall until after the array disappeared from view, the number of letters they recalled could be used as an estimate of the total number of letters they actually had available when they began their recalls. By varying the delay between the disappearance of the array and the tone, Sperling was able to estimate how long such information was retained.

The results of Sperling's study are summarized in Figure 2.3. When the tone occurred immediately after the array was terminated, the subjects were able to remember about three of the four letters in the row for which they were cued. The longer the tone was delayed, however, the fewer letters were recalled. This decrease was very rapid. After only a 0.5-second delay, subjects recalled an average of slightly more than one letter per row overall, indicating that about four letters were available.

The data supported Sperling's second hypothesis; all or most of the letters in the arrays were registered, but most were lost before they could be reported. Apparently, Sperling's subjects were able to hold visual information for about 0.5 second. After that time, it no longer was available, having decayed in sensory memory.

The answer to Sperling's question was clear: People register a great deal of the information they see in brief presentations. After the information is removed from sight, however, it is

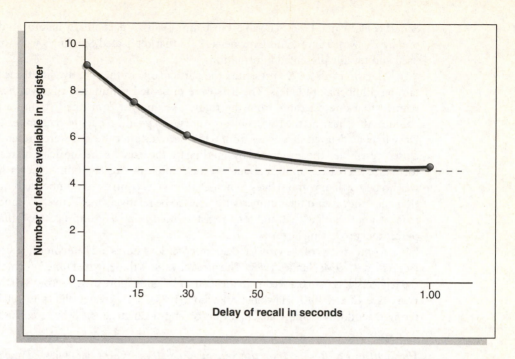

FIGURE 2.3   Results of Sperling's 1960 Experiment. This graph, which is based on that presented by Sperling, represents recall without sampling by the dashed line.

available only briefly—about 0.5 second. By the time Sperling's subjects could say the letters from one row (e.g., *c*, *z*, and *k*), the rest of the information was gone.

Another question that Sperling addressed in his 1960 article was whether meaning had been assigned to information in the visual sensory register, also called the **icon.** To examine this question, Sperling (see also Sperling, 1983; Von Wright, 1972) presented arrays, such as the one in Figure 2.2, containing both numbers and letters. Participants in the study then were given cues indicating that they were to recall either numbers or letters. Such cues would work only if meaning (number or letter) had been assigned to the information in the array. The results indicated that unlike the location cues described earlier, number/letter cues were ineffective. This outcome strongly suggests that the information in the icon is held with relatively little processing. Had the arrays been processed (if meaning had been assigned), then the number/letter cues would have made a difference.

Collectively, these findings suggest that visual sensory memory is very limited. Only seven to nine pieces of information are processed at any given time, and much of that decays rapidly. Information held in visual sensory memory receives only limited processing.

Auditory Registers   Although the majority of research on sensory registers has centered on the icon, considerable work also has been devoted to understanding the auditory register (for reviews, see Deutsch, 1987; Handel, 1988; Hawkins & Presson, 1987; Scharf & Buss, 1986;

Scharf & Houtsma, 1986; Schwab & Nusbaum, 1986). A particularly helpful study in the area is one by Darwin, Turvey, and Crowder (1972) that replicated Sperling's work on the icon but used auditorily presented information.

Darwin et al. (1972) presented the participants in their study with three brief lists containing numbers and letters. The lists were presented simultaneously over headphones so it seemed that one list came from the right, a second list from the left, and a third list from behind. After hearing the lists, subjects were given position cues to remember one of the lists. Darwin et al. delayed these cues from 0 to 4 seconds after the lists were presented. The results closely resembled those reported by Sperling for the icon. As the cue delay increased, recall performance decreased, until, at about 3 seconds after the presentation, subjects' recall with cues was no better than without cues. When Darwin et al. contrasted number/letter cues with position cues, they found the number/letter cues to be relatively ineffective. So, much like with the icon, it appears that that auditory registers hold relatively unprocessed information while perceptual processing begins.

Comparisons of the visual and auditory sensory stores indicate some interesting differences (see Ashcraft, 1994; Handel, 1988). The most obvious is the length of time information is stored in the registers: less than 0.5 second in the icon and slightly more than 3 seconds in the auditory registers (see Chase, 1987; Hawkins & Presson, 1987). This greater ability to retain information received auditorily seems related to the processing of language (see Schwab & Nusbaum, 1986).

Implications of Research on the Sensory Registers   Our brief review of research on the sensory registers suggests some direct implications for teaching. First, there are limits to the amount of information that can be perceived at any one time. The short duration of memory in the sensory registers should remind us of the need for teachers to limit the amount of information they present to students. Further, some work on developmental differences in cognition (e.g., Case, 1985) suggests that the size of the sensory registers increases with age. Children's sensory registers have more stringent constraints than those of adults. Especially with early elementary-age children, teachers must be aware of the need to manage the amount of information that children are expected to perceive at any one time.

Second, there may be real benefits to presenting information both visually and auditorily. Given the limits of students' ability to hold information in their sensory registers, we would expect that information presented both visually and auditorily would have a higher likelihood of being perceived than information presented in only one format. Using visual aids for auditory presentations and discussing visual materials seem to be reasonable approaches to increasing the likelihood that instructional materials will be perceived. It is also reasonable to assume that stimulation of the senses of touch, taste, and smell may also enhance learning.

The Role of Knowledge and Context in Perception

Prior knowledge directly influences perception, pattern recognition, and the assignment of meaning (Cowan, 2005). Knowing what we see (or hear) and even how to look (or listen) depends on the knowledge we have (see McCann, Besner, & Davelaar, 1988). An expert chess player, for example, perceives the pieces of a chess game in progress very differently from a person who has never played the game. The expert immediately recognizes that a king is in check, that a certain style of defense is being played, and so on, whereas a non-player merely perceives pieces she or he may not even be able to name on a checkerboard playing surface.

Knowledge also influences how we look for things to perceive. For example, an accomplished baseball fan knows the need to watch the shortstop's behavior to determine whether the pitcher is going to throw a fastball, curveball, or slider. A nonfan may have no inkling why the shortstop takes steps right or left as soon as the pitcher releases the ball. Similarly, an accomplished debater understands what to look for in evaluating other debaters, much as an expert welder knows what to examine in judging another welder's work.

It is clear, then, that knowledge permits perception to occur and guides our perception of new information (see Mandler, 1984). As is shown in Chapter 3, one compelling way to envision our knowledge is by means of **schemata** (sing. **schema**). Schemata are domain-organized knowledge structures in long-term memory that contain elements of related information and provide plans for gathering additional information (Anderson, 1984; Mandler, 1984). Schemata incorporate prototypes, feature analyses, and structural descriptions. For example, a person's schema for "tree" will contain not only its structural description but also information about the nature of trees (they take in carbon dioxide and give off oxygen), where trees are found (not above certain elevations or in areas that are too dry or cold), and the care of trees (they must be pruned and watered).

In some situations, appropriate schemata seem to be activated because of the results of pattern recognition processes. For example, if you are sitting quietly in your living room and smell smoke, schemata for reacting to that situation are activated by the data (a fire!). Activation of the schemata results primarily from the analysis of an environmental event. In such instances, schemata allow us to make sense of what we encounter and prepare us for continued analyses of the environment.

Context affects what we look for and perceive as well. Consider the following sentences:

The man walked into the quiet *wood*.
The man threw the *wood* into the fire.
The man got good *wood* on the ball.
The man was made of *wood*.

In each instance, the word *wood* is understood differently because of the sentence context. Research indicates that skilled readers automatically retrieve the appropriate meaning of a word without being distracted by inappropriate meanings, provided that the context is sufficiently rich.

Now look at Figure 2.4. In this case, what first appears as the letter *B* turns out to be an equally acceptable *13* in a different context. Most readers probably have no difficulty understanding the appropriate meaning in either case, even though the physical stimulus is identical in both settings. The moral to this story is that perception is a relative, rather than an absolute, phenomenon. Different people can interpret the same stimulus in more than one way, depending on what they know and the context in which they encounter a stimulus!

A BC   12 13 14

FIGURE 2.4   Context Effects in Perception.

Attention

Interwoven with perception is **attention**—a person's allocation of cognitive resources to the task at hand. In general, the research on attention shows that human beings are severely limited in the number of things they can pay attention to at a given time (e.g., Muller & Krummenacher, 2006; Spear & Riccio, 1994). This phenomenon is usually referred to as *limited processing capacity*. Although there are individual differences in this regard, most people cannot do more than one or two things at the same time. Multitasking has a downside: Eventually, a person can try to do too much at once and wind up doing everything poorly.

Attention is the mind's most valuable resource, with the possible exception of knowledge. Attention is the fuel on which the mind runs. Thinking about attention as a kind of mental fuel reveals that there are three ways to improve learning: increasing the amount of attention at one's disposal, decreasing the amount of attention each task consumes, or allocating one's limited attention as carefully as possible to the most important information one needs to learn.

Because students must learn a large amount of information in school, they need to select what they attend to. Sixth graders might begin to pay careful attention to their teacher's explanation of an arithmetic problem but then shift their attention to a whispered conversation across the aisle. Their attention then might wander to the aroma drifting into the room from the cafeteria and later to the sight of the snow falling outside. As a result, the explanation for how to work the new set of mathematics problems may not be remembered.

Research on attention has a long, contentious history. The main debate focuses on how learners allocate their attention. Various theories suggest that attention is allocated early or late in information processing and contradictory findings in the research literature make it difficult to construct a clear understanding of the allocation process. However, researchers eventually realized that different experiments led to different results because attention allocation is highly sensitive to the type of task being performed. This led several researchers to distinguish between what are known as resource-limited and data-limited tasks (Norman & Bobrow, 1976; Nusbaum & Schwab, 1986).

In this context, **resource-limited tasks** are those in which performance will improve if more resources are shifted to them. For example, if you are watching television as you read this chapter, the chances are good that you will not be allocating enough of your attention to understanding the chapter's main points. Turning off the television and concentrating on the book should improve learning greatly!

Data-limited tasks are those in which performance is limited by the quality of data available in the task. Above some minimal amount of resources needed to perform the task in the first place, allocating more resources to a data-limited task will not improve performance. Trying to make sense of a poor-quality recording is an example of a data-limited task. If the recording is bad, after a certain amount of resources have been assigned to the task, no amount of additional effort will help. For many students, following complicated instructions or "analyzing" Shakespearean sonnets may fit into the category of data-limited tasks; no matter how many resources they assign, performance will not improve. Most serious, however, is when the data to complete a task do not exist—for example, when the first-semester calculus student has little prior knowledge of key mathematical concepts from algebra and trigonometry.

Resource-limited tasks are difficult if we do not have enough attention to allocate to them. For example, remembering three numbers such as 7, 3, and 5 is easy, unless you also are asked to count backwards by 3s from 102 while trying to remember them! Each of these tasks is relatively easy in isolation, but once combined, we do not have ample resources to do both. In contrast, data-limited tasks are difficult regardless of how much attention we allocate. For example, sometimes car radio reception is just too poor for us to make out the voice we hear in the distant night.

The important point to carry away from this discussion is that attention is allocated differently depending on situational demands. Skilled learners become adept at allocating the right amount of attention to a learning task at the right time. When information is important, skilled learners selectively attend to it (Fisher et al., 1988; Muller & Krummenacher, 2006) and rely on many automated skills to conserve resources.

Automatic Processes

One of the major themes of this text is the importance of automatic cognitive processes (see Chapter 1). Because automatic cognitive processes require fewer resources than nonautomated processes (Unsworth & Engle, 2007), learners need fewer resources to perform tasks where their skills are automated than those tasks requiring conscious attention and thought. The notion of automatic processes, or **automaticity,** was first conceived of by Neisser (1967) and elaborated by LaBerge and Samuels (1974), Shiffrin and Schneider (1977), Neves and Anderson (1981), and Nusbaum and Schwab (1986). Although opinions differ concerning the specifics of automatic processes, it is generally agreed that they (1) require little or no attention for their execution and (2) are acquired only through extended practice.

The existence of automatic processes helps us explain why people can carry out complex tasks and perform different tasks simultaneously. Examples of automatic processes are decoding by good readers, changing lanes by accomplished drivers, punctuating sentences by skilled writers, and finger placement on strings or keys by expert guitar or piano players. Processes such as being able to change lanes while also talking to a passenger and a musician's playing her instrument while singing appear to require few cognitive resources and little or no conscious attention.

It is easy to see how automatic processes are related to how students allocate their attention to tasks. For example, if a student could not perform most of the processes of multiplication automatically, resources could not be applied to making estimates and evaluating. Similarly, good readers can devote their attention to reading for meaning because word decoding no longer requires much in the way of cognitive resources. Poor readers, in contrast, may have trouble with meaning because many of their resources are used for decoding words, not because they lack comprehension skills (Stanovich, 2000). Perhaps you have experienced this yourself when reading in a second language.

Research on development of automaticity has shown that in the beginning, performance of any cognitive activity will be awkward and slow. As learning proceeds knowledge of facts can become knowledge of *how to use those facts.* This "proceduralized knowledge" is much more readily and quickly available for use and greatly reduces the demands on our limited processing resources during routine tasks such as reading.

In fact, there is a startling consistency in research findings on skill acquisition in a wide range of tasks. Although performance initially may be halting, it soon improves to a reasonable level of competence. Amazingly, in most areas in which expertise has been investigated, performance continues to improve even after hundreds or even thousands of hours of practice! Such findings have been shown in studies as diverse as Crossman's (1959) classic investigation of cigar rolling (in which performance continued to improve over almost 3 million trials and 2 years!), the reading of inverted text after hundreds of pages (Kolers, 1975), and the continued learning of a card game after hundreds of hands (Neves & Anderson, 1981). Consider students' efforts to improve their skiing, learn a new video game, or develop fluency in a new language. Careful examination of their performance, even after many hours of practice, reveals continuing skill improvement.

Summary of Sensory Memory Processes

Sensory memory briefly processes a limited amount of incoming stimuli. Visual registers hold about seven to nine pieces of information for about 0.5 second. Auditory registers hold about five to seven pieces of information for up to 4 seconds. Incoming stimuli are first perceived, then matched to a recognizable pattern, and then assigned a meaning. How much information we can process depends on two things: (1) the complexity of the information and (2) our available resources. Resource-limited tasks can be improved if we selectively allocate more attention to them. Data-limited tasks are difficult no matter how much attention we allocate because the information itself is deficient. Automated tasks are easy to perform because they require fewer attentional resources.

Short-Term and Working Memory

Short-term memory refers to the place where information is processed for meaning. In the modal model (see Figure 2.1), information is assumed to enter short-term memory once it has received initial processing in sensory memory. Like sensory memory, short-term memory is limited with respect to capacity and duration. Researchers have also investigated how information is accessed from short-term memory. More recently, the very notion of short-term memory as a unitary system has been questioned. Many researchers now prefer the name **working memory,** which consists of three component subsystems, each performing a highly specialized function (see Baddeley, 2007; Swanson & Kim, 2007).

Capacity and Duration

The first serious discussion of short-term memory as a separate cognitive entity was George Miller's (1956) classic article "The Magic Number Seven, Plus-or-Minus Two: Some Limits on Our Capacity for Processing Information." Miller argued that information processing is constrained by a severe "bottleneck" in the memory system. Under most circumstances, people can hold no more than seven or so **chunks** (meaningful units of information) in memory at one time. One way to process information more efficiently, according to Miller, is to increase the size of chunks of information. For example, although the number *4727211* may be meaningless to you and therefore remembered as seven chunks of information, we remember it as the main switchboard number at one of our universities, usually as three chunks: *472, 72,* and *11.* The most provocative part of Miller's article, however, was that short-term memory is sensitive only to the number of chunks, not their size. As a result, people can hold large amounts of information in memory and therefore improve information processing dramatically simply by chunking information into larger and larger units of meaning. Numerous studies over many decades have supported this view. Some have shown that ordinary people can be taught to use chunking strategies to improve the capacity of short-term memory (Ericsson et al., 1980).

Another important aspect of short-term memory is the duration of information. Early studies by Peterson and Peterson (1959), using what is now known as the *Brown–Peterson paradigm,* showed that information is quickly forgotten from short-term memory. Peterson and Peterson asked college adults to study a list of three unrelated syllables and then to count backward from a number by threes (i.e., *90, 87, 84,* ...). When tested after 3 seconds, people already had forgotten about half of the information. After 18 seconds, almost everything had been forgotten. Originally, forgetting in short-term memory was attributed to decay—that is, information fading from memory as a function of time. Subsequent studies revealed that forgetting was less a result of the passage of time than of *interference* caused by other information (Cowan, 2005). For example, Waugh and Norman (1965) varied the amount of intervening information within a fixed time interval after studying the target list. Their results confirmed that the amount of information that intervened increased forgetting regardless of time. This result and others like it led researchers to conclude that forgetting is a result of interference rather than of time-related decay.

Taken together, many early studies suggested that the capacity of short-term memory is limited to seven or so chunks, as Miller had predicted. Information is also forgotten quite rapidly, particularly when new information follows it in the information processing cycle. Thus, although evidence suggests that information decays in short-term memory, strong evidence supports the idea that forgetting typically is a result of interference and capacity overload.

Accessing Information

Researchers soon began to address how we search through information that is held temporarily in short-term memory. In a now-famous set of studies, Saul Sternberg (1975) asked people first to learn a short list of unrelated letters (e.g., *BVGK*) and then to identify whether a target letter matched any of the letters included in the original list. The rationale of this technique was that letters included in the list should be judged faster than those not in the list. Sternberg addressed two specific questions related to subjects' decision making. The first was whether letters in the list were searched in a *serial* (one by one) or *parallel* (simultaneously) manner. The second was whether search was *self-terminating* (the search ended when the letter was found in the list) or *exhaustive* (the entire list was searched even when the letter was found prior to the end of the list). Contrary to intuition, Sternberg argued that people search the contents of short-term memory in a serial, exhaustive fashion. The main evidence on which Sternberg relied was that decisions took longer when the size of the original list increased, regardless of where the target letter was located in the list. Sternberg argued that self-terminating, parallel searches, which at face value appear much more efficient, are impossible because of (1) the speed at which decisions are made and (2) the fact that the entire search process is completely automated and not under conscious control.

Working Memory

By the 1970s, researchers were becoming increasingly disenchanted with the idea of short-term memory. The main complaint was that many different kinds of activities were attributed to short-term memory without specifying how these activities occurred. To illustrate, imagine that you are given the letters *I, N, R,* and *U* and are asked to decide whether they form a meaningful word. After a few moments, you retrieve the word *ruin.* But what does it take to perform these relatively simple mental operations in short-term memory? On the one hand, you need to store the letters *inru* temporarily while, on the other, you permute these letters to determine whether they match lexical entries elsewhere in memory. Of course, to do so, you evoked general knowledge about the structure of words and subsequently searched lexical memory (memory for words) in a highly strategic fashion (e.g., alphabetically). The point of this exercise is that you did several very different kinds of activities just to perform a simple lexical decision task in short-term memory.

The complexity of operations in short-term memory led a number of theorists, most notably Baddeley (1986), to propose a model of **working memory.** Baddeley's model included three main components, shown in Figure 2.5. The *executive control system* is assumed to be a limited capacity control system that governs what enters short-term memory. A second important function is selecting strategies necessary to process information—for instance, deciding to search lexical memory alphabetically. The central executive also controls two "slave systems," the *visual-spatial sketch pad* and the *articulatory loop.* The former enables us to hold visual-spatial information in short-term memory and perform a variety of computations on that information (e.g., mental rotation of an object). The latter is the verbal analog to the sketch pad. It enables us to hold acoustic information temporarily via rehearsal, usually for 2 to 4 seconds. Together, these three subsystems perform the mental operations usually assigned to short-term memory.

The working memory model proposed by Baddeley and Hitch (1974) and developed more fully by Baddeley (1986, 2001, 2007) makes assumptions about the three subsystems previously described. One assumption is that each of the three subsystems has its own limited attentional resources. This means that, under normal information processing loads, each subsystem can perform mental work without taxing the resources of the remaining subsystems. A second assumption is that the central executive regulates the activities of the two slave systems. Presumably, the more purposeful and strategic the central executive is, the more efficient the slave systems.

Questions remain, however, about the exact nature of the working memory system (Hulme & Mackenzie, 1992). One question is the degree to which the three subsystems have access to their own unique pool of resources or compete for a shared pool. A second question is the specific role of the central executive, which at times appears to take on the duties usually performed by the lower slave systems. A third question is the extent to which information in the articulatory loop is stored temporarily with or without some kind of elaborative rehearsal.

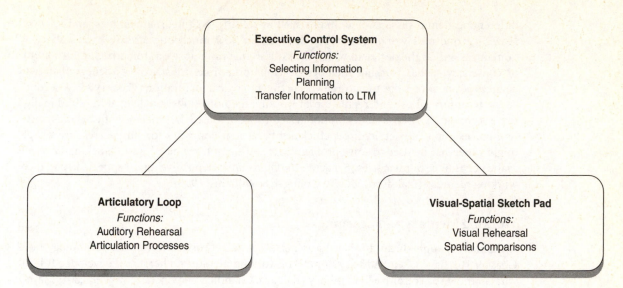

FIGURE 2.5   A Model of Working Memory.

Meanwhile, more and more models of working memory have appeared in the literature (e.g., MacDonald & Christiansen, 2002). Some of these models are similar to Baddeley's three-component model shown in Figure 2.5, and some are not. Experts also have invested a great deal of time developing tests of working memory (Daneman & Merikle, 1996; Miyake, 2001). Some of these tests involve memory for random numbers (e.g., *4, 3, 7, 1, 8*) or letters (e.g., *D, X, Z, P*). Others involve what is known as digit or letter recoding, in which an individual hears a string of random digits and then recalls them in ascending numeric order. More recent tests involve counting objects, pointing to a designated square, or judging whether complex sentences are grammatically acceptable. Tests of working memory generally are good predictors of learning and are correlated with academic achievement and intelligence test scores. Some experts have even argued that working memory is the key factor in intelligence (Ackerman, Beier, & Boyle, 2005; Engle, Kane, & Tuholski, 1999).

Despite the ongoing debate about the structure and importance of working memory, there are a number of points that most experts agree on (Miyake, 2001; Miyake & Shah, 1999). One is that working memory is not a physically separate component in the cognitive system, as suggested by Baddeley's model (2001) and Figure 2.1. Research indicates that working memory is closely tied to long-term memory and is greatly affected by it; thus, what we already know has a direct impact on current processing. A second point of agreement is that working memory is responsible for active information processing rather than strictly passive short-term maintenance of information. Said differently, working memory is the place where meaning is made in the information processing system. A third point is that working memory is essential for skilled self-regulation of learning and memory, a point discussed further in Chapter 6. A fourth point is that working memory is best viewed as a domain-specific rather than domain-general phenomenon. That is, working memory is not equally efficient across different academic subjects or domains such as reading, writing, mathematics, and science. How well one uses working memory depends on how much one already knows about a domain, as well as the degree to which the skills in that domain are automatized. A fifth point of consensus is that working memory develops over time. Most experts believe that two changes occur. One is due to naturally occurring biological maturation (Case, 1985). A second is due to improved use and regulation of working memory skills (Engle et al., 1999). Finally, there is growing consensus that emotional factors play a role in the efficiency of working memory. For example, anxiety reduces efficiency because it competes for limited resources that might otherwise be used to solve problems. Negative emotions may lead to blocking or traumatic persistence of memories (Schacter, 2001). In contrast, positive mood appears to enhance working memory (Oaksford, Morris, Grainger, & Williams, 1996).

Working Memory and Learning

A number of applied educational researchers, especially those working with technology (see Chapter 10), have taken Baddeley's model of working memory to heart and developed it into what is known as **cognitive load theory** (Kalyuga, Chandler, Tuovinen, & Sweller, 2001; Mayer & Chandler, 2001; Rikers, 2006; Sweller, 1999; Sweller, van Merriënboer, & Paas, 1998; van Merriënboer & Sweller, 2005). Cognitive load theory assumes that some learning environments impose greater demands than others and, as a consequence, create a higher information processing load for the limited cognitive resources in working memory (van Merriënboer & Sweller, 2005). Cognitive load may vary due to intrinsic or extraneous demands. According to cognitive load theory, **intrinsic cognitive load** is caused by the inherent properties of the to-be-learned information and is unalterable other than by schema acquisition, whereas **extraneous cognitive load** results from how the information to be learned is presented or from activities required of the learner. Intrinsic cognitive load cannot be changed because it is due to the complexity of the information itself. In contrast, extraneous cognitive load can be changed in a variety of ways, such as using adjunct aids, providing specific learning instructions, or enhancing the organization of to-be-learned information.

In essence, cognitive load theory states that there are three constraints on the efficiency of learning. The first includes *characteristics of the learner,* especially working memory capacity, task-relevant conceptual knowledge in long-term memory (i.e., schemata), and the extent to which the learner has automatized basic learning processes. Research suggests that individuals who are automated and knowledgeable in a domain use their working memory resources efficiently. A second constraint is the *complexity of the to-be-learned information.* Information that includes concepts that can be learned in isolation imposes a smaller cognitive load than information consisting of concepts that must be learned simultaneously. A third constraint is the *instructional environment.* Learning can be enhanced by providing helpful instructions, segmenting a learning task so that it reduces load or enables the learner to manage the load more efficiently, or by providing adjunct aids such as advance organizers, notes, and summaries. In addition, learning improves when information processing is distributed across two modalities, such as verbal and visual, in working memory. For example, Mousavi, Low, and Sweller (1995) found that students solved geometry problems more efficiently when they involved words and pictures rather than just words or just pictures. Increased efficiency was attributed to the fact that utilizing both the verbal and spatial slave systems in working memory increases total processing capacity.

Mayer and Moreno (2003) have used cognitive load theory to distinguish between three different types of cognitive demands during learning. *Essential processing* refers to cognitive processes that are absolutely necessary in order to understand the information. These include understanding main ideas, generating inferences that link these ideas together, and relating them to related information in memory. *Incidental processing* refers to information processing that is not absolutely necessary even though it may enhance understanding. For example, a student may take detailed notes of a passage she already understands quite well. *Representational holding* refers to temporarily holding information in memory while other information is being processed. For example, it may be necessary for a reader to look back at information in order to understand a graph she is studying.

Mayer and Moreno (2003) suggest that learning is most efficient when individuals focus all of their resources on essential learning and few or none of their resources on incidental learning and referential holding. They have described several scenarios in which additional incidental learning or referential holding lead to cognitive overload and poor learning. One overload situation occurs when an individual is forced to do too much essential processing simultaneously. One possible solution is *segmenting*, in which the learner is allowed time between successive presentations to manage the information more efficiently. Another solution is *pretraining*, in which the individual receives instruction designed to automate essential skills.

A second overload scenario occurs when the individual is overloaded with some combination of essential and incidental processing. One solution is *weeding*, in which the learner eliminates all but essential processing through either instructional guidance or periodic feedback. A third overload scenario occurs when individuals are forced to hold information in memory while engaged in some other information processing task. One solution is providing *adjunct spatial displays* such as pictures or diagrams that eliminate the need for representational holding. An alternative is *synchronizing*, or tying information and tasks together, which enables the learner to reduce the amount of information or time that information is held in memory while other cognitive processing takes place.

Research on working memory has made a tremendous contribution to our understanding of learning from both theoretical and practical perspectives. Experts agree on a number of important points, including the ideas that working memory has limited capacity, oversees a variety of different learning activities, and is closely involved in self-regulated learning. Cognitive load theory has enabled educators to apply working memory theory to the design of instruction. Students find it difficult to learn because they lack knowledge, the to-be-learned information is too difficult, or the instructional environment does not adequately support learning. Cognitive load theory has increased our awareness of problems due to redundancy, divided attention, and information complexity.

Cognitive Neuroscience and Working Memory

Cognitive psychology has expanded its horizons greatly in the past 3 decades. Until the mid-1970s, the study of human cognition focused mainly on underlying cognitive structures and processes, such as working memory and encoding. During the 1970s and 1980s, scholars in other disciplines, such as linguistics, information science, and philosophy, collaborated with cognitive psychologists to establish the field of **cognitive science.** More recently, researchers interested in the biological and neurological underpinnings of memory and cognition have helped establish the study of **cognitive neuroscience** (Freberg, 2006).

Cognitive neuroscientists focus on the structure and workings of the *brain,* whereas cognitive scientists tend to focus on the presumed structure and workings of the *mind.* Ideally, cognitive neuroscience can offer us a plausible description of both brain and mind and, more important, how the brain and mind work in unison. There are many reasons for the late addition of neuroscience to cognitive psychology, but two are worth noting in particular. One is the specialized training required to understand the detailed workings of the physical brain. A second reason is that research methods in neuroscience were hindered by the lack of equipment that enabled researchers to address important research questions in relatively noninvasive ways.

Cognitive neuroscientists often distinguish between two different organizational levels for understanding and studying the brain: the neuronal and cortical levels. These levels correspond to the cellular level of brain activity tied to the transmission of electrochemical signals and the larger structural units that control complex cognitive activity.

The Neuronal Level

The neuron is the basic unit of electrochemical activity in the brain (Freberg, 2006; Radvansky, 2006; Ward, 2006). There are between 100 and 150 billion neurons in a healthy adult brain. Each neuron is connected to up to 10,000 other neurons, giving rise in the 1980s to "connectionist" theories of memory. Humans appear to lose some neurons after birth, especially if the brain is not cognitively stimulated. **Pruning** refers to a process in which neurons that are linked to a consistent cognitive activity thrive, whereas neurons that fall into disuse are "pruned" away. Debate continues as to whether it is possible to generate or regenerate neurons after the onset of adulthood. Conventional wisdom once held that we are born with a finite set of neurons and lose them regularly throughout life. However, researchers now believe that we are capable of generating and regenerating neurons through rigorous mental activity and through drug therapies.

A neuron can be subdivided into three essential parts: a nucleus, dendrites, and an axon. One useful analogy is to think of a neuron as an airport, with the nucleus serving as the control tower, the dendrites representing a network of runways for incoming flights, and the axon representing a runway for an outgoing flight. In a neuron, incoming and outgoing traffic consists of electrochemical information. In the neuron cell body, the cell nucleus contains the genetic code that regulates the uptake and distribution of chemical neurotransmitters, such as dopamine and acetylcholine, which regulate the inhibition and excitation of the neuron. The dendrites connect the cell body to adjacent neurons and are responsible for receiving the neuron's incoming electrochemical signals. The number and type of dendrites on the cell body depend in part on the neuron's location in the brain and the degree to which the neuron is routinely involved in brain activity. It is thought that dendrites increase with increased intellectual and brain activity (Freberg, 2006). Unlike the dendrites that receive information, the axon is responsible for sending information to other neurons through interfacing terminal buttons.

Neurons are connected at the synapse where terminal buttons on one neuron interface with dendrites on another neuron. Electrochemical signals are passed through the synapse to active surrounding neurons by neurotransmitters. The strength of the signal determines the neuron's action potential. High action potential creates a stronger signal and is assumed to create a large fan effect of synaptic activation with surrounding neurons (Ward, 2006). There are a variety of important neurotransmitters, including acetylcholine (affecting learning and memory), dopamine (affecting planning and movement), serotonin (affecting mood), and norepinephrine (affecting arousal and vigilance). Disruption in the normal functioning of neurotransmitters due to chemical imbalance, drugs, or alcohol can have a major impact on cognitive functioning.

The Cortical Level

The **cerebral cortex** consists of folded grey matter that can be divided into four functional areas, including the frontal, temporal, parietal, and occipital lobes. The frontal lobe is located directly behind the forehead and is associated with emotional and affect regulation, executive regulation of learning, and long-term memory functions. The frontal lobe appears to be particularly active in the organization and coordination of information in working memory. Damage to the frontal lobe can seriously disrupt emotion and cognition processing. An infamous example is the case of Phinias Gage, who had a heavy iron rod shot through his skull during a railroad accident, destroying much of his frontal lobe (Ward, 2006). Gage's accident transformed him from a polite, hard-working railroad foreman into a profane, dissolute wanderer. Similar effects could be seen during the era when frontal lobotomies were conducted to control unruly behavior in individuals with mental retardation. The frontal lobe also includes the primary motor cortex, which helps to regulate motor movement and coordination, and the primary auditory cortex, which controls the processing of sound.

The temporal lobe is located in the midregion of the brain in the lower part of the cortex and controls transfer of information from short-term memory to long-term memory, and assists in the regulation of memory processes. Several types of amnesia have been traced to neurological insults to the temporal lobe. Oddly, problems associated with remembering past events (i.e., retrograde amnesia) or new events (i.e., anterograde amnesia) may have no effect on other types of memory, personality, and executive cognitive regulation. The temporal lobe also has been linked to autobiographical memory. Another important brain structure for memory is the hippocampus, which is located adjacent to the temporal lobe but actually is part of the brain's limbic system rather than the cerebral cortex. The hippocampus is involved in remembering both verbal and spatial information, although these functions seem to utilize separate processes. The hippocampus also helps regulate encoding and retrieval of information from long-term memory.

The parietal lobe is located near the rear and crown of the head and is associated with visual and spatial reasoning in working memory, and constructing mental images and spatial maps. The parietal lobe includes the primary somatosensory cortex, which helps control body temperature and its senses, including touch and pain sensation.

The occipital lobe is located in the rear part of the brain and is involved in any perceptual processing occurring in sensory memory. The occipital lobe processes basic incoming "bits and pieces" of information, such as perceptual features (Radvansky, 2006). It also includes the primary visual cortex, which helps us to organize and make sense of general visual information. There is evidence that neurons in the primary visual cortex are highly specialized, with some devoted solely to detecting vertical or horizontal lines, and others devoted to detecting shape.

One important concept that is implicit in our review of the cerebral cortex, and brain structure in general, is the notion of **modularity** (Barrett & Kurzban, 2006). Modularity refers to the fact that the brain has specialized physical regions, such as the primary visual cortex, that perform specialized functions. Further specialization occurs even within these regions, such as feature detectors devoted exclusively to vertical versus horizontal movement. There is strong evidence that specific cognitive processes are located in specific parts of the brain. One example is Broca's area, which regulates word recognition, retrieval, and phonological processing. If this part of the brain is injured, such as from an accident or stroke, some or all of these language functions can be lost and very difficult to recover.

Although the brain is modular in nature, in children prior to age 12 or so, there fortunately is a high degree of plasticity, enabling functions to migrate to other parts of the brain if part of the brain is damaged. But this ability of specialized cognitive skills to migrate or recover quickly fades after the onset of puberty. Despite the brain's modular nature, there is vigorous debate about the extent to which human cognition is subject to functional modularity, as opposed to structural modularity. Some critics worry that it is easy to adopt a view of human cognition in which processes are viewed as innate, functionally separate from other processes, and perhaps unchangeable (Barrett & Kurzban, 2006; Sperber, 2005). For example, Howard Gardner's (1993) theory of multiple intelligences suggests that there may be as many as 10 different types of intelligence that are separate from each other, whereas most other theories assume that there are only 1 or 2 main components (Ackerman & Lohman, 2006). The point of contention is this: Even though the brain has modules, this does not imply that all cognitive functions are separate from each other. Indeed, the majority of cognitive psychologists assume that all of the brain's separate functions are integrated into a single entity we call the "thinking mind."

Neurological Evidence for Working Memory Functions

Do neuroscientific research findings support the cognitively oriented models and explanations of working memory described in this chapter? The answer is overwhelmingly yes. Many studies conducted on the brain are providing evidence that is quite consistent with theories of cognition. For example, neuroscientific research has identified activity in the frontal lobe during learning related to executive planning in working memory (Morrison, 2005; Ward, 2006). Research has strongly supported the notion of functional specialization and modularity, particularly in the frontal cortex, where many complex memory storage and executive processes are located (Freberg, 2006). Nevertheless, debate continues among cognitive and neuroscience-oriented researchers on such issues as the precise structure of working memory, the roles that different areas of the cerebral cortex and limbic system play in memory, and the extent to which some functions are strictly modularized versus being distributed across different parts of the brain.

Assessment of Working Memory

Researchers who study working memory experience great challenges collecting data because many cognitive processes occur rapidly, usually in 0.5 second or less. George Sperling, who developed the partial report paradigm described earlier, is famous to this day as much for his innovative research methods as for his theoretical contributions to memory research. Often, major discoveries by cognitive scientists in memory research are due in part to new and clever ways of measuring elusive memory processes. This also has become true in cognitive neuroscience. In the past decade, neuroscientists' innovative use of imaging technologies, such as magnetic resonance imaging (MRI), for studying the structure and electrochemical activity of the brain has contributed greatly to our understanding of what parts of the brain are active in cognitive activities.

The past 3 decades have seen a great deal of research on working memory, particularly on working memory span, which is assumed to reflect the amount of storage and active processing occurring in working memory at a single point in time. Individuals with larger memory spans are assumed to be faster and more efficient information processors.

Two span tasks are used widely in the working memory research literature. The **reading span task,** developed by Daneman and Carpenter (1980), is arguably the best-known cognitive measure. This method requires individuals to perform two tasks simultaneously: reading a list of sentences and remembering the last word from each sentence at recall. In one version of the task, individuals judge whether a sentence is grammatically correct, and they also remember a word associated with the sentence. After the list of sentences is checked for appropriateness, the individual must recall the words that followed each sentence. This task presumably measures both a basic storage and central executive processing mechanism in working memory (Swanson, 2004). A variation of the reading span called the *operation span task* was developed by Turner and Engle (1989); it requires a person to read aloud a two-step math problem such as $(3 \times 3) = 9$, judge whether the given answer is correct, view a single word after each problem, and then recall as many words as possible after the problem set is over. A large number of studies have investigated the reading span and operation span tasks over the last quarter of a century. Both are considered to be excellent measures of working memory (Daneman & Merikle, 1996).

Using span tasks is a relatively straightforward way to measure working memory capacity. These tasks are predictive of a wide variety of related cognitive measures, such as intelligence, reading comprehension, and problem solving (Ackerman et al., 2005; Unsworth & Engle, 2007). Yet a span task tells us nothing about physical activities in the brain. For this reason, researchers interested in the neurobiology of memory have developed different methods for examining working memory processes.

Neuroscientists rely on both *structural* and *functional imaging techniques* (Ward, 2006). Structural imaging uses procedures such as computerized tomography (CT) and magnetic resonance imaging (MRI) that provide a "map" of the brain's physical properties. Functional imaging, in contrast, uses technologies to study electrochemical activity in the brain as it occurs. The two most common functional imaging techniques are positron emission tomography (PET) and **functional magnetic resonance imaging (fMRI).** Both types of imaging are important, but functional techniques enable researchers to examine in detail what parts of the brain are involved in different cognitive activities and the degree to which they are involved.

Implications for Instruction: Guiding and Directing Attention

The information presented in this chapter, given its highly theoretical nature, might seem to some readers to be unrelated to educational practice, yet it has a number of important implications for learning and instruction, explained in the following pages.

   1. *Information processing is constrained by a "bottleneck" in sensory and short-term memory.* Because there are rather severe limits on sensory and short-term memory, students need to selectively focus on the most important information. Students who do so remember more important information and spend less time and effort studying (Reynolds, 1993). Highlighting important information for students before they begin studying helps focus their attention. Having prior knowledge also improves a student's selective attention. Students who know more about a topic find it easier to identify and focus on important information. Presenting examples and texts that provide the most important information can greatly facilitate learning.

2. *Automaticity facilitates learning by reducing resource limitations.* Automatic processes allow students to use fewer cognitive resources in completing a task. Teachers need to remember and students need to be reminded that cognitive processes become automatic only after extensive practice. Achieving true automatic processing even on simple skills requires hundreds of hours of practice. Practice conditions should also be varied. For example, you would not want to practice driving only in your driveway under ideal conditions.

3. *Perception and attention are guided by prior knowledge.* What we already know greatly affects the stimuli we perceive, how easily we recognize them, and even what meaning we give them. Students should be encouraged to use what they know to help themselves process new information. One way to do so is to provide preteaching that activates existing knowledge (see Chapter 4). Another approach is to allow students to share knowledge in small-group discussions prior to beginning a new and possibly unfamiliar task.

Teachers should also carefully match instructional activities with students' current levels of knowledge. Perception is apt to be no better than the knowledge base that supports it. When sophisticated perceptions are the goal (e.g., noting subtle differences in chemicals or hearing when a clarinet is slightly out of tune), an extensive knowledge base combined with extensive practice is crucial.

4. *Perception and attention are flexible processes.* The key for teachers is to understand that perception and attention ultimately need to be under learners' control. Therefore, any method that helps a student learn to manage these processes is a step toward independent learning. Although our ability to process new information has limits, skilled learners are able to overcome these limits in a number of ways. One way is practicing tasks to the point of becoming automatic. Automaticity increases the rate at which information is processed because perception and attention require fewer cognitive resources. In a sense, automaticity is equivalent to increasing the flow of water through a garden hose of fixed capacity; we cannot increase the diameter of the hose (processing capacity), but we can accelerate the flow of water (information). A second way to enhance processing flexibility is learning to attend selectively to what is important. A third way is distributing the information processing load strategically across visual and auditory channels, for example, by using visual materials to augment lectures and discussion.

Although students clearly have physiological differences in their ability to process information, these seem to us to be less important than strategic differences (see Brody, 1992, for alternative views). Educators can do very little about differences in innate ability, but we often can have a substantial impact on the way students use their cognitive resources. Learners are remarkably adaptive and help from parents, peers, and teachers can aid learners in using the resources they have more strategically.

5. *Resource and data limitations constrain learning.* Not all learning tasks are the same. Sometimes we are limited by our cognitive resources. Even the best driver lacks sufficient cognitive resources to talk on a cell phone and skillfully drive through rush hour traffic. Similarly, tasks can be too demanding for some students to master all at once; these students may lack the cognitive resources to process the amount of information they are expected to learn. If you suspect that a student lacks the necessary resources for a learning task, try breaking it into smaller, more manageable parts; providing an easier task; or making some kind of peer-tutor assistance available to the student.

Learning can also be limited by the quality of data or information available for learning a task. Data-limited tasks are those in which performance is limited by the quality of data available in the task. Above some minimal level of resources needed to perform the task in the first place, allocating more resources to a data-limited task will not improve performance. For instance, textbooks often omit information that is important or even essential. When this happens, students may be forced to find this information themselves or perhaps not even realize that critical information is missing. Unfortunately, many students in this situation simply give up because they cannot cross the gulf created by insufficient data. We encourage teachers to examine carefully what students are expected to learn and the resources that are provided to ensure that too much or too little information does not create a problem.

6. *All students should be encouraged to "manage their resources."* Good learners are self-regulated, a concept discussed in more detail in Chapter 4. Being self-regulated requires that learners have appropriate knowledge and strategies to perform required tasks, and the motivational will to apply their knowledge and strategies. At the heart of self-regulation is the willingness and ability to manage one's limited cognitive resources in the most strategic way possible. Research suggests that even college students fail to manage their resources effectively, in part because they lack knowledge and in part because they lack the desire to do so (Wade, Trathen, & Schraw, 1990). In our judgment, helping students be more strategic, identify important information, and use their prior knowledge is essential to effective teaching.

7. *Information processing is easier when to-be-learned information is distributed in working memory.* Baddeley's three-component model of working memory suggests that visual and auditory information are processed separately in working memory. Presenting some information to one modality may reduce the burden on another (Mousavi et al., 1995). By using their working memory systems more efficiently, students can learn more with less stress.

Summary

This chapter reviews the processes of perception and attention. Perception is the assignment of meaning to incoming stimuli. Attention is the allocation of cognitive resources to the tasks at hand.

Perception begins with the sense receptors. Each of our senses apparently has a sensory register, but most research has focused on the visual sensory register (icon) and the auditory sensory register. The sensory registers are where incoming stimuli—unprocessed information—is briefly stored and the perception process begins.

Research indicates that attention is allocated in a flexible manner. Skilled learners selectively focus on what is important to learn. Some tasks are difficult because they are resource-limited; that is, we may not have adequate resources to allocate to them. Other tasks are difficult because they are data-limited; that is, the information is degraded or insufficient.

Like sensory memory, the capacity and duration of short-term memory are quite limited. Miller (1956) suggested that we can hold approximately seven pieces of information in working memory at a time. This information is forgotten quickly because of interference, decay, and replacement by new information.

We also described the transition from short-term memory to working memory. The latter includes a central executive, articulatory loop, and visual-spatial sketch pad. The central executive coordinates the two so-called slave systems, which are responsible for maintenance of verbal and spatial information. Research suggests that each subsystem possesses some unique resources that enable information processing load to be distributed among them.

Cognitive load theory has built on Baddeley's model of working memory to better understand learning. Cognitive load theory states that learning is constrained by limited processing capacity. The higher the cognitive load of to-be-learned information, the harder it is to learn. Researchers have considered a number of ways to reduce cognitive load, either through the better design of learning materials or through instructional methods that enable learners to use limited resources more efficiently.

We discussed cognitive neuroscience, the study of the biological and neurological underpinnings of memory and cognition. Cognitive neuroscientists focus on the structure and workings of the brain, while cognitive scientists tend to focus on the presumed structure and workings of the mind. Cognitive neuroscientists distinguish two organizational levels in the brain, the neuronal and cortical levels. These correspond to the cellular level of brain activity that controls the transmission of electrochemical signals, and larger structural units that control complex cognitive activity. Neuroscientists' innovative use of imaging tools, such as magnetic resonance imaging, has enabled noninvasive methods for studying the brain. Neuroscientific research findings are supporting the cognitively oriented models and explanations of working memory we described in this chapter. For example, neuroscientific research has identified activity in the frontal lobe during learning related to executive planning in working memory.

SUGGESTED READINGS

Barrett, H. C., & Kurzban, R. (2006). Modularity in cognition: Framing the debate. *Psychological Review, 113,* 628–647.
    This review provides a comprehensive summary of modularity theory, including its strengths, weaknesses, and fit with a wide variety of empirical data in cognitive psychology.

Cowan, N. (2005). *Working memory capacity.* New York, NY: Psychology Press.
    This book provides an up-to-date, comprehensive review of the working memory literature, as well as a comparison among competing models of working memory.

Greene, R. (1992). *Human memory: Paradigms and paradoxes.* Mahwah, NJ: Erlbaum.
    This book continues to provide an extremely well-written overview of memory research.

Mayer, R. E., & Moreno, R. (2003). Nine ways to reduce cognitive load in multimedia learning. In R. Bruning, C. Horn, & Lisa PytlikZillig (Eds.), *Web-based learning: What do we know? Where do we go?* Greenwich, CT: Information Age.
    This chapter nicely summarizes cognitive load theory, describes a variety of scenarios that create cognitive overload, and discusses ways to reduce overload.

van Merriënboer, J. J. G., & Sweller, J. (2005). Cognitive load theory and complex learning: Recent developments and future directions. *Educational Psychology Review, 17*(2), 147–177.
    This article provides a detailed overview of cognitive load theory and its implications for complex learning.

3

Long-Term Memory: Structures and Models

A Framework for Long-Term Memory ■ The Building Blocks of Cognition ■ Another Dimension of Long-Term Memory: Verbal and Imaginal Representation ■ Evolving Models of Memory ■ Assessment of Long-Term Memory Functions ■ Implications for Instruction ■ Summary ■ Suggested Readings ■

In Chapter 2, we presented a model that portrays how information enters memory, is stored, and is retrieved. We focused especially on the first two parts of the model: sensory memory and working memory. In this chapter, we turn our attention to the third part of the model, **long-term memory (LTM).**

When we talk about sensory and working memory, we are typically examining events recently experienced or currently in consciousness. LTM, in contrast, involves memory traces developed over periods of days, weeks, months, and years. LTM is the permanent repository of the lifetime of information we have accumulated. Also encoded in our LTM is the memory that lets us recognize familiar people and objects, drive a car, brush our teeth, or type a letter.

Constant rehearsal and repetition, so crucial for keeping information in working memory, are less critical for LTM. For instance, we can state our uncles' names, name a large city on the East Coast, or easily give examples of large, hairy animals without having to rehearse any of this information—despite the fact that we may not have thought of these topics for months or even years. More important for LTM are meaning and organization. Recall depends on our understanding what information means and being able to find it.

When you consider our first theme for cognitive education, that learning is a constructive process where knowledge is created and re-created on the basis of previous learning, the importance of LTM to learning becomes clear. Understanding how LTM works allows us to find ways to help students access and use their prior knowledge to create new knowledge. Just as cognitive research has helped us understand a great deal about how information initially enters our cognitive systems, it also has given us a vast amount of knowledge about how the information we process is organized, stored, retrieved, and used.

This chapter is the first of three devoted to the topic of LTM. In this chapter we begin by presenting a general framework that represents how different kinds of knowledge are organized in LTM. We then describe several units that cognitive theorists have proposed as "building blocks of cognition," highlighting features that qualify each as a useful way of thinking about memory and thought, including the role of imagery. A description of important new developments in memory research follows, and in the final section, we lay out the implications of long-term memory research for education.

A Framework for Long-Term Memory

Cognitive psychologists have found it useful to distinguish between the types of knowledge in memory (Radvansky, 2006). The classifications they make have both a common sense and a neurophysiological base (e.g., see Eichenbaum, 1997). Perhaps the most basic distinction is the one between declarative knowledge and procedural knowledge (Anderson, 1983a, 1993; Chi & Ohlsson, 2005; Schraw 2006). **Declarative knowledge** is factual knowledge, "knowing what." Some examples of declarative memory are recalling that Sakhalin is an island off the coast of Siberia, that Ebbinghaus studied memory by using nonsense syllables, and that you had Oat Squares for breakfast. **Procedural knowledge,** in contrast, is "knowing how" to perform certain activities. Our procedural knowledge allows us to make coffee, drive a car, use a computer, and perform a host of other actions. A young child who has learned how to unlock a door, turn on a faucet, brush her teeth, and open a book is demonstrating her recall of procedural knowledge.

A third category of knowledge—conditional knowledge—is increasingly grouped with declarative and procedural knowledge (see Figure 3.1) and emphasized as a vital goal for learning. **Conditional knowledge** is "knowing when and why" to use declarative and procedural knowledge. For example, students may have learned basic concepts of algebra (e.g., representing

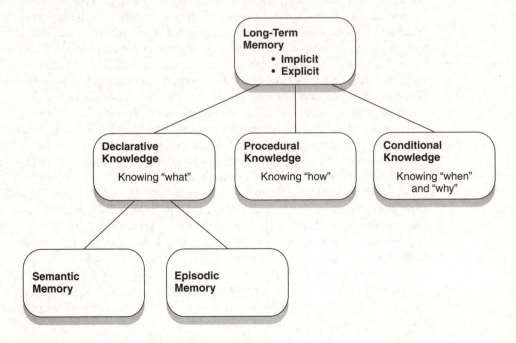

FIGURE 3.1   The Knowledge in Long-Term Memory.

numbers by letters and expressing numerical relationships by algebraic expressions) and be able to reliably perform certain procedural operations (e.g., simplifying an algebraic expression) but still be unable to apply this knowledge to real-world problems, such as figuring out driving time on a trip or buying the right amount of tile for a bathroom floor. Conditional knowledge is needed to help students make effective use of their declarative and procedural knowledge.

Most learning involves interplay among declarative, procedural, and conditional knowledge. A concert pianist learning a new song by Domenico Scarlatti, for instance, may search her memory for declarative knowledge about that composer's preferred method of executing certain embellishments, such as the *appoggiatura, mordent,* and *trill*—declarative knowledge that will be used in the development of procedural and conditional knowledge. Her procedural and conditional knowledge about performing, in turn, give substance to the declarative knowledge she possesses (e.g., "Scarlatti intended for the mordents to be played according to the basic tempo of the passage. That would mean there should be thirty-second notes here") and allow her to use this knowledge in her performance.

The declarative–procedural–conditional knowledge distinction is valuable for helping educators think about our goals for student learning. Novice students in a teacher education program, for instance, may memorize and recite a principle of cooperative classroom learning (e.g., "Establish an atmosphere of shared decision making and trust") as declarative knowledge but have little or no notion of how, why, and when actually to use this principle in the classroom (i.e., they lack procedural knowledge and conditional knowledge). As important as declarative knowledge is, we almost always will benefit from thinking beyond it to include both procedural and conditional knowledge goals.

For example, one of the most important aims of education is to help students develop relatively large, stable, and interrelated sets of declarative knowledge. As educators, we expect students to be "knowledgeable" in domains as diverse as mathematics, science, literature, and history. Yet we also need to place a considerable premium on knowing "how," "when," and "why." The reason is that almost all learning combines declarative, procedural, and conditional elements. No matter what the content domain, declarative knowledge—although a basic building block of all expertise—is most valuable when linked appropriately to actions. In settings ranging from elementary students reading and writing to students in the professional schools of journalism, architecture, teaching, business, and medicine, procedural and conditional knowledge are critical outcomes of the educational process.

Beginning in Chapter 4, with our introduction of the concepts of *metacognition* and *learning strategies* and continuing throughout the remaining chapters, we frequently revisit and elaborate on the importance of conditional knowledge. Here, however, we focus primarily on the role of declarative and procedural knowledge in cognition. We begin by discussing two subcategories of declarative knowledge, semantic and episodic memory.

Semantic and Episodic Memory

Within the category of declarative knowledge, Tulving (1972, 2002) has distinguished further between memory for general knowledge, called semantic memory, and memory of personal experiences, called episodic memory.

Semantic memory refers to memory of general concepts and principles and the associations among them (Radvansky, 2006). Semantic memory contains such information as the facts that lemons are yellow and that computers contain chips. Also in semantic memory is the organized knowledge we have about words and concepts and how they are associated. For instance, areas such as English literature and American history represent vast networks of semantic information that we encode, organize, and have available for retrieval. Recalling word meanings, geographic locations, and chemical formulas requires searches of semantic memory.

Episodic memory refers to storage and retrieval of personally dated, autobiographical experiences (Tulving, 1983, 1985). Recalling childhood events, recollecting the details of a conversation with a friend, and remembering what you had for dinner last evening all fall within the realm of episodic memory. Episodic memories are retrieved using "personal tags," associations with a particular time or place linked to the memory. Obviously, a great deal of what we must recall to function effectively in our personal lives is episodic.

An ongoing disagreement exists among psychological researchers about the distinction between semantic and episodic memory. Some researchers, such as McKoon and Ratcliff (1986), Howe (2000), and Craik (2000) believe that there is no division between the two; rather each simply is a different type of remembering. Others, such as Squire (1987), see the distinction as reflecting separate memory systems in the brain. Work with amnesics who have lost their episodic memory and studies using functional neuroimaging of brain activity have supported the two-system theory (Tulving, 2002). Other studies have shown that semantic and episodic memory systems are not absolutely separate but sometimes work in tandem (Klein, Cosmides, Tooby, & Chance, 2002). Certainly the two-system distinction is useful for helping us think about the types of information we—and our students—must remember and the cognitive procedures that learners use (Roediger, 1990). On the one hand, we need a broad knowledge base to think and reason effectively. On the other hand, our episodic memories must function well enough for us to locate ourselves in time and space and to have a reasonably accurate picture of our experiences.

The recent interest in episodic memory has in part been rekindled by research on the topic of **implicit memory,** an unintentional, nonconscious form of retention, such as that underlying playing a piece on the piano or tying your shoes (e.g., see Roediger, 1990; Schacter, 1993, 1996; Schacter & Cooper, 1993).

Implicit Memory: Retention Without Remembering

When we think of memory, we usually think about bringing a past experience to mind. Whether the memory is voluntary (a conscious search for information) or involuntary (thoughts pop into our heads), we recognize it as corresponding to some past event. This kind of memory, involving conscious recall or recognition of previous experiences, is called **explicit memory.** Explicit memory has been studied for many decades by memory researchers; it usually is tested by recall and recognition tasks that require intentional information retrieval.

Yet often the record of our earlier experience is not available to our consciousness, but still affects our behavior. This kind of memory is called **implicit memory.** Implicit memory is an unintentional, nonconscious form of retention in which our actions are influenced by a previous event but without conscious awareness (Jacoby & Witherspoon, 1982). Many of our daily performances, for example, reflect prior learning but resist conscious remembering. In skills as diverse as using computers, tying our shoes, and driving a car, conscious remembering seems to play little part. In fact, when a person tries to reflect on how these skills are being performed, performance often deteriorates (Roediger, 1990).

Memory researchers dating back to Ebbinghaus have recognized the phenomenon of implicit memory, but systematic research on the topic dates back only to the 1980s (Graf & Schacter, 1985; Jacoby, 1983; Jacoby & Witherspoon, 1982). Since the early 1990s, this topic has moved from obscurity to a position of central importance in cognitive psychology (Litman & Reber, 2005; Ratcliff & McKoon, 1996; Roediger, 1990; Schachter & Cooper, 1993).

Interest in the topic of implicit memory first developed among cognitive neuroscientists working with *amnesics,* individuals with certain forms of brain injury that make them unable to remember verbal materials, such as words or names, for more than a very brief period. Other functions, however, such as perceptual abilities and motor skills, remain intact.

The early conclusion was that the inability of such individuals to transfer verbal materials from STM to LTM played a critical role in their amnesia. That view proved to be too simple, however, as researchers demonstrated that some kinds of long-term verbal memory in amnesics were not impaired at all. Instead, the crucial dimension was whether explicit or implicit memory was being tested.

A representative early experiment by Jacoby and Witherspoon (1982) comparing amnesic and normal subjects provides an excellent example of the experimental procedures that have been used to contrast explicit and implicit memory performance. They used homophones (e.g., *read/reed*) as their experimental materials. In Phase 1, all subjects were asked questions (e.g., Name a musical instrument that employs a *reed*) to bias the interpretation of the target homophones toward their less frequent interpretation. Hearing the word in isolation, most subjects would think of *read*, not *reed*. The question prompts the less frequent choice. In Phase 2, subjects were asked to spell words, a task that for the subjects seemed totally unrelated to Phase 1. The list of words to be spelled, however, contained some homophones previously presented and some not. Although the experimenters made no connection between Phases 1 and 2, how subjects chose to spell the homophones was the key measure of effects of earlier encounters with some of the homophones. If the prior presentation influenced later interpretation, the lower probability spelling (e.g., *reed*) would be more likely for the homophones encountered earlier. As Jacoby and Witherspoon (1982) pointed out, an influence of memory on spelling does not necessarily require awareness of remembering. Awareness, however, was indeed necessary in a recognition task presented in Phase 3 of the experiment, which required subjects to indicate whether they had seen words before. Words from Phase 1 were mixed into the set of words in Phase 3.

Predictably, the probability of correctly recognizing whether they had seen a word before (the Phase 3 measure) was much lower for amnesics (.25) than for normal controls (.76). As expected, amnesics' explicit memory was very poor. But the amnesics' spelling performance was startling. It revealed very strong effects of their earlier encounters with the words primed by the questions even though they had no awareness of the impact; that is, the spellings they chose (e.g., *reed*, not *read*) reflected their implicit memory from encountering the words in the questions they answered in Phase 1. In fact, although both groups showed the influence of implicit memory, their probability of choosing the low-frequency spelling was even higher than that of normal controls (.63 vs. .59)!

Since that time, implicit memory effects have been demonstrated in both amnesic and normal subjects by using a variety of experimental methods. These have been as diverse as better performance on completion tasks, in which subjects are shown partial stimuli and asked to complete them (e.g., having seen the word *flower* before, guessing the word FLOWER more easily when shown –L–WER), and decision tasks, in which subjects make more favorable judgments (e.g., of liking or preference) about individual members of pairs to which they earlier had been exposed. Researchers also have demonstrated that effects of implicit memory extend to nonverbal materials, such as novel visual patterns and shapes (see Schacter & Cooper, 1993).

For memory theorists, two aspects of implicit memory research have been especially intriguing. First was the emergence of unequivocal evidence that behavior can be influenced by memory of past events even without conscious awareness. Second, and even more exciting for many theorists, was the fact that implicit and explicit memory tasks sometimes elicit **functional dissociations,** in which implicit and explicit memory performances are unrelated. In Jacoby and Witherspoon's (1982) research, for instance, explicit memory performance as demonstrated by word recognition greatly favored normal subjects, but implicit memory performance on the spelling task did not. Weldon and Roediger (1987; see also Roediger, 1990) similarly showed a dissociation between explicit and implicit memory tasks. When a mixed list of pictures and words was studied and subjects' recall was tested later in explicit free recall, the names of the pictures were better recalled than the words. On an implicit word-fragment completion test (see the preceding example), in which some fragments corresponded to presented words and some to names of pictures, prior study of words produced far greater effects than study of pictures.

Findings of dissociations like these are extremely interesting to memory theorists, some of whom (e.g., Squire, 1987) have proposed distinct memory systems to account for them. These theorists, who tend to be those working in the neuroscience tradition, argue that the declarative memory system is responsible for performance on explicit tests of retention, whereas the procedural system underlies implicit memory. Other theorists, such as Roediger and Jacoby, assert the more straightforward explanation that explicit and implicit memory tasks require different cognitive operations. They contend there is no need to propose different memory systems. As yet, however, neither the multiple memory systems nor the processing accounts (Litman & Reber, 2005) have proven wholly satisfactory in explaining all of the experimental results.

What has been learned nonetheless has been quite remarkable. Researchers have explored systematically a completely new class of memory tasks and acquired much basic knowledge about how implicit memory affects behavior. The finding that implicit and explicit memory can be dissociated from each other may have important implications for understanding memory performance in special groups, such as very young children and the elderly. Research examining developmental patterns for implicit and explicit memory (see, e.g., Drummey & Newcombe, 1995; Hayes & Hennessy, 1996) likely will continue to produce revisions of our theories of memory development. Similarly, we will better understand memory processes associated with aging or memory loss due to injury because of the empirical and theoretical advances in this area.

The Building Blocks of Cognition

One challenge for the science of cognition is to find the most meaningful "units" for describing cognitive operations. In the previous section, we presented a framework for describing the contents of LTM. In this section, we elaborate on that framework by describing five concepts proposed by theorists as "building blocks of cognition" that make up the information stored in LTM. These concepts have common features, but each of them represents a somewhat different view of how best to conceptualize the information stored in memory. Three of them—*concepts, propositions,* and *schemata*—have been related most closely to declarative knowledge (see Figure 3.1) and, though equally relevant for understanding episodic memory, have been studied most extensively in the context of semantic memory. The fourth and fifth concepts—*productions* and *scripts*—have been used primarily to explain procedural knowledge. Each of the five illuminates somewhat different aspects of LTM and is important in thinking about memory and cognition.

Concepts

One major way we deal with the bewildering array of information in the world is to form categories (Medin & Rips, 2005). In science, for example, Chi, Slotta, and de Leeuw (1994) have proposed that students' concepts about science fall into three primary categories: *matter* (e.g., *animals* and *minerals*), *processes* (e.g., *osmosis* and *acceleration*), and *mental states* (e.g., *curiosity* and *doubt*). Our language in general reflects conceptual categories: The words *grandfather, exercise, bird, psychology, blue, dog,* and *cheerful* each represent a category meaningful to most of us. **Concepts** are the mental structures by which we represent meaningful categories. Particular objects or events are grouped together on the basis of perceived similarities; those that "fit" the category are examples, or instances of the concept; those that do not fit are nonexamples. The similar features across examples of a concept (e.g., all oceans contain water and are large) are called **attributes;** features essential to defining the concept are called **defining attributes.** Learning a concept involves discovering the defining attributes and discovering the rule or rules that relate the attributes to one another.

Rule-Governed Theories of Conceptual Structure   There is a rich tradition of psychological research on how we identify and acquire concepts. One such tradition, exemplified by the early work of Bruner, Goodnow, and Austin (1956), focused on concept identification. Bruner et al. presented students with an array of simple objects or stimuli, such as triangles and squares, for which there were only four defining features: number, size, color, and form. The task was to discover the unknown concept.

The experimenters had predetermined the rules defining the concepts, which could be either relatively simple (e.g., "All green objects are examples") or quite complex (e.g., "Either green patterns or large patterns are examples"). A single stimulus (e.g., a green triangle) within the array was specified as a positive instance of the unknown concept to be discovered. On the basis of that example, the subjects were asked to formulate their best guesses—their hypotheses—about the unknown concept. They then were allowed to pick another stimulus from the array and to ask whether it was a positive or negative example of the concept, to which the experimenter responded truthfully. The procedure continued until subjects were confident they could identify the concept.

Bruner et al.'s (1956) work showed quite clearly that most individuals quickly formulate hypotheses about relevant attributes and choose stimuli accordingly. A sizable number of individuals adopt what is called a **conservative focusing strategy** to test their hypotheses where their first hypothesis is quite global. Here is a protocol:

This is a single large, green triangle. I can't rule out any of these things. But I can rule out examples with two and three objects, small- and medium-size objects, red and blue objects, and circles and squares. Now, I'll pick a new example that differs in one and only one attribute from the first; in that way, I'm guaranteed to get new information.

Others adopt a strategy called **focus gambling,** in which they vary more than one attribute of a stimulus at once. In this strategy, subjects may shortcut the methodical steps of conservative focusing but also run the risk of getting no information at all by their selection. Still others use **scanning strategies,** in which they attempt to test several hypotheses at once, a technique that puts some strain on subjects' ability to remember and process information.

The early work of Bruner et al. (1956) and others (e.g., Haygood & Bourne, 1965; Neisser & Weene, 1962) showed that individuals typically solve concept identification problems by trying to discover the rules relating the concept attributes. In general, concepts with more difficult rules are more difficult to learn. The simplest rules involve affirmation (e.g., any green object) and negation (e.g., any object that is not green), which apply if only one attribute is being considered. But most concepts involve more than one relevant attribute and require more complex rules. Among the most common are **conjunctive rules,** in which two or more attributes must be present (e.g., any triangle that is green), and **disjunctive rules,** in which an object is an example of a concept if it has one or the other attribute (e.g., either a triangle or a green object).

Bourne's work (e.g., Bourne, 1982) has represented the clearest statement of rule-governed conceptual structure. In his view, concepts are differentiated from one another on the basis of rules such as the above. These rules can be learned either through instruction or through experience with instances that either are members of the class (positive instances) or are not (negative instances). One learns to classify a set of animals as birds or nonbirds by acquiring rules for combining characteristic attributes of birds (e.g., wings, bills, and feathers). Using these rules one can unambiguously classify a new instance as either a bird or a nonbird. This works fine with a very simple classification, where a new instance either is a bird or not a bird. But such a rule-based conceptual system is not always adequate.

Most natural or real-world concepts are "fuzzier" and differ qualitatively from those studied in the laboratory. Consider the concept of *furniture*. We would all quickly agree that tables, chairs, sofas, and floor lamps are furniture, and we can describe many rules that differentiate articles of furniture from other objects. But some of our attempts at rule formation quickly run into trouble. Presence of legs? What about some floor lamps? What about a table or a desk? Is a rug furniture? Some would say it is but would wish to include a qualifying statement, or **hedge;** it is like furniture but not exactly like it. What is the set of rules that unambiguously determines which objects are members of the concept class *furniture*?

Logical efforts to determine such sets of rules mostly have been unsuccessful, especially with ambiguous examples such as a rug. Rosch and Mervis (1975), dissatisfied both with the artificiality of laboratory work on concept formation and with the difficulties of classifying concepts with rule-governed approaches, proposed an alternative view based on "degree of family resemblance" to a **prototype**—a highly typical instance of the concept.

Prototype Theories of Conceptual Structure   Prototype theories of concepts, in contrast with rule-governed theories, do not assume an either–or, member–nonmember process of concept identification. Instead, prototype theorists (Rosch, 1978; Rosch & Mervis, 1975) have

TABLE 3.1   Typicality of Members in Six Superordinate Categories

Item	Furniture	Vehicles	Fruits	Weapons	Vegetables	Clothing
1	Chair	Car	Orange	Gun	Peas	Pants
2	Sofa	Truck	Apple	Knife	Carrots	Shirt
3	Table	Bus	Banana	Sword	String beans	Dress
4	Dresser	Motorcycle	Peach	Bomb	Spinach	Skirt
5	Desk	Train	Pear	Hand grenade	Broccoli	Jacket
6	Bed	Trolley car	Apricot	Spear	Asparagus	Coat

Source: Adapted from "Family Resemblance: Studies in the Internal Structure of Categories," by E. Rosch and C. B. Mervis, 1975, *Cognitive Psychology, 7,* 573–605. Copyright 1975 by Academic Press, Inc. Reprinted by permission.

argued that conceptual class membership is determined by the degree to which an example is similar to a known instance in memory—one that seems to best exemplify the concept. As stated in Chapter 2, this line of reasoning is similar to that employed by perception theorists in accounting for pattern recognition in perception. Wattenmaker, Dewey, Murphy, and Medin (1986) have suggested that the majority of "natural," or real-world, concepts are structured in terms of sets of typical features.

Particular instances of concepts in the real world do not have all the defining features but rather have a family resemblance. So, for North Americans, robins or blue jays often are proto- types of birds. We also might classify animals such as emus or penguins as "birds," but with less assurance. In those instances, we frequently hedge or qualify, what we say with a statement such as "Well, they are birds, but not the best examples of birds." The hedge is necessary because the emu and the penguin do not exhibit a particularly strong family resemblance to robins or blue jays, yet they do have some resemblance. Rosch (1978) and others have provided evidence that young children learn category memberships for prototypical and near-prototypical instances (see Table 3.1) before they learn the less typical ones.

Both rule-governed and prototype conceptual theories correctly classify many simple, naturally occurring phenomena, but both have difficulty developing clear categorizations for abstract concepts, such as *wisdom, justice,* and *equality.* What are the rules for defining a partic- ular act as "wise" or "just"? Most of us find making such distinctions quite difficult because, in most cases, we can only categorize whether an act fits these categories if we understand the con- text in which the act occurred. As a result, theorists have suggested that both rule-governed and prototype theories of concepts are inadequate. They propose a *probabilistic* view, in which a suf- ficient number of attributes must be present to reach a "critical mass"—the number sufficient to make a category judgment. This view incorporates some characteristics of rule-governed approaches but retains the "naturalness" of prototype views.

Probabilistic Theories of Conceptual Structure   Some theorists (e.g., Tversky, 1977; Wattenmaker et al., 1986) have suggested that concept learning involves weighing probabili- ties. When faced with a new instance, the learner searches it for characteristic, but not neces- sarily defining, attributes (e.g., observing flying and singing in an animal that looks like a bird). Whether it is a bird is determined by the summing of evidence for category membership against criteria stored in memory. If a particular instance reaches a critical sum of properties consistent with category membership, it is classed as an example of that concept. The emu, though it does not fly or sing melodiously, lays and hatches eggs, feeds its young in "bird-like" ways, and in general looks like a bird. It exhibits enough characteristics to be classified as a bird.

In general, the greater the sum beyond the critical value, the quicker the classification. On the one hand, robins and blue jays are identified quickly as birds and not mammals because they have many characteristics of birds and relatively few of mammals. On the other hand, emus and penguins have comparatively fewer bird characteristics and so are less likely to be identified quickly as birds. These expectations are similar to those of prototype theory. Note that the "critical sum" approach also has some characteristics of rule-governed conceptual behavior because the learner must have a "rule" for determining when a set of features reaches the critical value.

We emphasize that the greater difficulty of categorizing emus and penguins as birds is probably, at least in part, because of our lack of familiarity with these animals. Nevertheless, probabilistic models emphasize that those exotic birds exhibit sufficient attributes common to birds that they are so classified. In the same way, a rug, though not exactly like "a piece of furniture," can be classified as furniture by virtue of its uses, presence in homes, and so on.

Summary of Concepts   Using concepts is one way we structure the huge amount of information that we acquire and store in our LTM. This structuring of knowledge is one of the important cognitive themes for education we outlined in Chapter 1. Whether concepts are conceived of in terms of rules, prototypes, or probabilistic judgments, each of the theories of concept learning suggests that different cultures may define concepts in different ways, depending on the set of properties used to characterize the concept. For instance, Schwanenflugel and Rey (1986) compared Spanish- and English-speaking individuals on prototype tasks similar to those Rosch used and found clear cultural differences even in such simple tasks as determining prototypical birds. One would expect even greater differences in classifying abstract concepts, in which the relevant attributes are much less obvious. Classifications of abstract concepts such as *just* or *wise* could be expected to reflect strongly the cultural context in which they are used.

Medin, Wattenmaker, and Hampson (1987) suggest that simple rule-governed or prototype conceptual sortings are common in memory and are used widely when conceptual categorizations are easy to make. But when objects contain attributes from multiple categories or are influenced heavily by the context within which they occur (e.g., "ethical behavior"), people may make categorizations probabilistically. It should be clear that no unambiguous evidence exists supporting a single view of the nature of concepts. Some consensus, however, appears to be emerging concerning a probabilistic view.

Propositions

Suppose you read the following sentence:

> The trainer of the Kentucky Derby winner Alysheba was Jack Van Berg, who always wore a brown suit.

How can its meaning be represented in LTM? The most common way cognitive psychologists have represented declarative knowledge, especially linguistic information, is by propositions

(J. R. Anderson, 1996; Kintsch, 1974; Rumelhart & Norman, 1978). A **proposition** is the smallest unit of meaning that can stand as a separate assertion. Propositions are more complex than the concepts they include. Where concepts are the relatively elemental categories, propositions can be thought of as the mental equivalent of statements or assertions about observed experience and about the relationships among concepts. Propositions can be judged to be true or false (J. R. Anderson, 2005).

Propositional analysis has been used extensively in analyzing semantic units such as sentences, paragraphs, and texts. When we analyze the sentence again for instance, we see that it can be broken into the following simpler sentences, or "idea units":

1. Jack Van Berg was the trainer of Alysheba.
2. Alysheba won the Kentucky Derby.
3. Jack Van Berg always wore a brown suit.

These simple sentences are closely related to the three propositions underlying the complex sentence. Each represents a unit of meaning about which a judgment of truth or falsity can be made. If any of these units of meaning are false, then of course the complex sentence is false. Propositions are not the sentences themselves; they are the meanings of the sentences. Memory contains the *meaning* of information, not its exact form.

Now examine the following two sentences without looking back. Have you seen either of them before?

1. The Kentucky Derby was won by Alysheba.
2. Jack Van Berg always wore a blue suit.

Most individuals readily will reject having seen sentence 2; after all, we have just read that Jack Van Berg always wore a brown, not blue, suit. But if some time has passed between reading and recognition, many will "recognize" sentence 1, even though they have not seen it either. We remember the sense of oral and written statements; the meaning of propositions is what is preserved. In contrast, the surface structure of the information (e.g., whether the first sentence above read *Alysheba won the Kentucky Derby* or *The Kentucky Derby was won by Alysheba*) usually is lost quickly unless we make a special effort to attend to it.

Propositions usually do not stand alone; they are connected with one another and may be embedded within one another (see J. R. Anderson, 1996). Kintsch (1986, 1988) has shown that texts can be viewed as ordered lists of propositions. In Kintsch's formal system of analysis, each proposition consists of a predicate and one or more arguments. Several examples are written below, using Kintsch's notation, in which predicates are always written first and propositions are enclosed in parentheses:

1. John sleeps. (SLEEP, JOHN)
2. A bird has feathers. (HAVE, BIRD, FEATHERS)
3. If Mary trusts John, she is a fool. IF, (TRUST, MARY, JOHN) (FOOL, MARY)

Kintsch and others have done propositional analyses of many texts, transforming them into **text bases,** which are ordered lists of propositions. Using such propositional analyses,

Kintsch has shown that the reading rates in expository texts are directly related to the number of propositions in the texts. Moreover, Kintsch and others (e.g., Kintsch, 1988; Meyer & Rice, 1984) also have demonstrated experimentally that free recall patterns reflect the hierarchical propositional structure of the text (see Chapter 12 for a detailed discussion of Kintsch's theory of comprehension).

What implications do propositions have for LTM? Cognitive theorists have hypothesized that propositions sharing one or more elements are linked with one another in **propositional networks.** As is shown, the notion that ideas—whether concepts, propositions, or schemata—are linked in large networks is very useful for thinking about how information is stored in and retrieved from memory. Students' ability to comprehend information and to use it effectively in cognitive operations such as problem solving hinges on the quality of the networks they create.

Schemata

Many cognitive theorists are interested in how memory is organized and how knowledge is used to interpret experience (Mayer, 2008; Radvansky, 2006). One of the most productive theories is that of **schemata**—mental frameworks that we use to organize knowledge. Schema theorists have proposed that knowledge is organized into complex representations called schemata (sing., schema) that control the encoding, storage, and retrieval of information (Mayer, 2008; Rumelhart, 1984; Seifert, McKoon, Abelson, & Ratcliff, 1986).

As described by Rumelhart (1981), schemata are hypothesized data structures that represent the knowledge stored in memory. Schemata are presumed to serve as "scaffolding" (Anderson, Spiro, & Anderson, 1978; Ausubel, 1960; Rumelhart, 1981) for organizing experience. Schemata contain **slots,** which hold the contents of memory as a range of slot values. In other words, knowledge is perceived, encoded, stored, and retrieved according to the slots in which it is placed. Schemata are fundamental to information processing. Some schemata represent our knowledge about objects; others represent knowledge about events, sequences of events, actions, and sequences of actions.

Whenever a particular configuration of values is linked with the representation of variables of a schema, the schema is said to be **instantiated** (Rumelhart, 1981). Much as a play is enacted whenever actors, speaking their lines, perform at a particular time and place, so schemata are instantiated by concepts and events. A "teaching" schema may be instantiated when you view a situation where enough of the requisite values—a teacher, some students, and a transaction between them—are present to activate the schema. Once schemata are instantiated, they are part of our long-term memory, and their traces serve as a basis of our recollections (Rumelhart, 1981).

Before 1970 or so, the notion of schemata was an obscure one in experimental psychology, appearing in historical perspective in the early work of Bartlett (1932) and in the work of the 18th-century philosopher Immanuel Kant, who referred to the "rules of the imagination" through which experience was interpreted. But by the mid-1970s many leading cognitive theorists and researchers (e.g., Bobrow & Norman, 1975; Minsky, 1975; Rumelhart, 1975; Rumelhart & Ortony, 1977; Schank & Abelson, 1977; Winograd, 1975) had become tremendously interested in schema theory. Why did this perspective assume such importance?

In our judgment, the reason schema theory came to the fore so rapidly had to do with its extraordinary power to explain memory and other cognitive phenomena. To get a better feel for the power of schemata, consider the following paragraph. Read it carefully a time or two.

Death of Piggo

The girl sat looking at her piggy bank. "Old friend," she thought, "this hurts me." A tear rolled down her cheek. She hesitated, then picked up her tap shoe by the toe and raised her arm. Crash! Pieces of Piggo—that was its name—rained in all directions. She closed her eyes for a moment to block out the sight. Then she began to do what she had to do.

Think now about some of the things you need to know in order to comprehend this passage, one with fairly simple sentence construction, no rare words, and dealing with a topic—piggy banks—familiar to most. Let's start with piggy banks. What do we know about them? A short list follows. Piggy banks

- are representations of pigs
- hold money
- usually hold coins
- have a slot to put the money in
- are hard to retrieve money from
- have fat bodies
- are not alive
- usually are made of brittle material
- can be shattered by dropping or a blow
- look friendly
- usually are smaller than real pigs
- once broken, usually stay that way
- etcetera

This list of "piggy bank facts" could be continued almost indefinitely. Note that the list does not define the concept of *piggy bank* (a piggy bank is . . .) but rather is a partial description of our overall conception of piggy banks—how they look, work, and so on. Our overall mental representation, or schema, of even a single concept like *piggy banks*, we discover, is an immensely complex array of information and its interrelationships. Within and related to this global schema are embedded many other schemata—for instance, schemata for "tap shoe," "striking something with a hard object," "saving money," and so on.

If you turn again to "Death of Piggo" and examine it closely, you quickly see the vital role your schemata for piggy banks and many other objects and events played in comprehending this paragraph. The notions that piggy banks hold money, that they can be shattered, that shattering is necessary to retrieve their contents, and that they are friendly looking—*none of this information actually is stated in the passage*. Yet, all of it must have been activated automatically as you read, or else you could not have understood what you read. You somehow "filled in" the information.

In Rumelhart's terms, the slots in your schemata had default values assigned to them when they were activated. Although specific information actually was not presented on the piggy bank containing money or its brittleness, we assumed these to be true from our general knowledge of piggy banks. Even the simplest event or message has an enormous number of features that could be attended to. Yet as was shown in Chapter 2, only a few of these actually become a part of memory. One critical function of schemata is guiding attention. Pichert and Anderson's (1977) "home buyer" and "burglar" study (described in Chapter 1) shows this guiding function. "Home buyers" tended to recall information about a picture of a house that was relevant to their perspective, such as number of bedrooms, newly painted rooms, and a nursery. "Burglars" showed significantly better recall for such details as the presence of 10-speed bicycles in the garage, a valuable painting, and a color television. Pichert and Anderson (1977, p. 314) commented on their findings as follows:

> The striking effect of perspective on which elements of a passage were learned is easily explained in terms of schema theory. A schema is an abstract description of a thing or event. It characterizes the typical relations among its components and contains a slot or placeholder for each component that can be instantiated with particular cases. Interpreting a message is a matter of matching the information in the message to the slots in a schema. The information entered into the slots is said to be subsumed by the schema.

Because "home buying" and "burglary" represent quite different schemata, information more likely to instantiate important variables in one was less likely to instantiate the other. The information individuals paid attention to and subsequently recalled was that most consistent with their currently activated schema. Schemata play several other critical roles, including guiding interpretation. For example, given sentence 1 below, most people later will recall sentence 2.

1. The paratrooper leaped out the door.
2. The paratrooper *jumped* out of the plane.

Or, to take a second example, the first sentence below often is recalled as the second one.

1. The student spoke to the department chair about her instructor's sexist comments.
2. The student *complained* to the department chair about her instructor's sexist comments.

Recall is transformed, often subtly, by schemata. Especially if information is general or vague, instantiation molds it into familiar form, as demonstrated by the following passage, used in early research by Bransford and Johnson (1972, 1973) and Dooling and Lachman (1971):

> The procedure is actually quite simple. First you arrange items into different groups. Of course one pile may be sufficient depending on how much there is to do. If you have to go somewhere else due to lack of facilities that is the next step; otherwise, you are pretty well set. It is important not to overdo things. That is, it is better to do too few things at once than too many. In the short run this may not seem important but complications can easily arise. A mistake can be expensive as well. At first, the whole procedure will seem complicated. Soon, however, it will become just another facet of life. It is difficult to foresee any end to the necessity for this task in the immediate future, but then, one never can tell. After the procedure is completed one arranges the materials into different groups again. Then they can be put into their appropriate places. Eventually they will be used once more and the whole cycle will then have to be repeated. However, that is part of life. (Bransford & Johnson, 1972, p. 722)

Most individuals asked to read and recall Bransford and Johnson's passage have poor comprehension and subsequent recall. But simply adding the title "Washing Clothes" improves both comprehension and recall significantly by adding an appropriate context for the information. When schemata are not or cannot be activated during learning, new knowledge cannot be assimilated easily.

Schema theory provides an explanation for several memory phenomena (McVee, Dunsmore, & Gavalek, 2005). Because the contents of memory consist of representations of knowledge, rather than exact copies of it, encoding will vary according to the schemata activated at the time of encoding. In this way, schema theory supports a constructivist view of learning and an explanation for the effect of context in memory storage, two of the major cognitive themes we discussed in Chapter 1. Recall is seen as a reconstructive activity, with schemata providing frameworks that direct the recall process (e.g., "Who *is* the author of *The Polar Express*? Let's see, wasn't that book a Caldecott Medal winner? That guy also wrote *Jumanji*. Just give me a minute; I'll think of his name!"). Recall is not simply remembering stored information but rather is *re-creating* information and events. Memory, in this view, is not so much reproductive as constructive and reconstructive.

Because it emphasizes the application of what learners already know, schema theory has been tremendously appealing to both cognitive theorists and educators. It helps us understand that many recall and recognition "errors" are not so much errors as they are constructions logically consistent with the learner's mental structures. In general, schema theory portrays learners in a dynamic, interactive way. Although schema theory has been criticized for its generality and vagueness (Alba & Hasher, 1983), cognitive research (see, e.g., Mayer, 2008, for examples) has continued to reflect schema-based conceptions of perception, memory, and problem solving.

Productions

Whereas concepts, propositions, and schemata are ways of representing declarative knowledge, productions and scripts are ways of representing procedural knowledge. **Productions** can be thought of as condition–action rules—if/then rules that state an action to be performed and the conditions under which that action should be taken (Anderson, 1983a, 1993). The idea of productions can be illustrated by the following set of instructions and actions for unlocking a car door:

Production A: If car is locked, then insert key in lock.
Production B: If key is inserted in lock, then turn key.
Production C: If door unlocks, then return the key to vertical.
Production D: If key is vertical, then withdraw key.

In general, productions are seen as having the capability of "firing" automatically: If the specified conditions exist, then the action will occur. Memory for productions ordinarily is implicit memory, discussed earlier in this chapter. Conscious thought typically is not involved. Outcomes of productions supply the conditions, as in the example above, to trigger other productions in a sequence of cognitive processes and actions.

The idea of productions has been a useful one. It not only captures the automatic nature of much of cognition but also lends itself to modeling many cognitive processes on the computer. Productions and the rules they embody can be specified formally as instructions in computer programs that operate on data and simulate cognitive processes. In reading, for example, Just and Carpenter (1987) incorporated the idea of productions in a computer model (READER) designed to simulate various aspects of reading. In this model there are productions such as the following:

If the word *the* occurs, assume a noun phrase is starting.

If READER encountered the word *the* in a text it was analyzing, this production would fire (an instruction is triggered in READER), leading READER to "infer" that it currently was processing a noun phrase.

Like propositions, productions are organized in networks called **production systems.** In a production system, multiple productions may be active at a given time. Outcomes of the productions modify memory and activate knowledge, which in turn may activate new productions and new knowledge. Cognition moves ahead from state to state until its ultimate goal is accomplished.

Production systems enable us to represent the dynamic, changing aspects of cognitive processes. For instance, conceptualizing certain cognitive processes as production systems nicely captures the "automatic side" of reading. In reading, as in many of our other cognitive functions, we do not necessarily think about what we are doing; we simply do it, an example of the "automaticity" described in Chapter 2. Similarly, Anderson (1993, 1996; Lovett & Anderson, 2005) has used production systems and the concept of **production rules** in modeling automatic processes in tasks as diverse as list learning and problem solving (see the discussion of Anderson's theory later in this chapter; see also Chapter 8). Knowledge, once in production form, is seen as applying much more rapidly and reliably. In Anderson's view, the critical productions of problem solving are those that recognize general goals and conditions and translate them into a series of subgoals.

Scripts

Just as schemata organize our declarative knowledge, *scripts* provide the underlying mental frameworks for our procedural knowledge. Simply, **scripts** are schema representations for *events*. In proposing the concept of scripts, Schank and Abelson (1977) were attempting to account for our comprehension of commonplace events such as going to a restaurant or a movie. When actions such as these are done repeatedly, the researchers argued, our knowledge becomes encoded in script-like mental structures. These mental structures contain not only action sequences and subsequences but also the actors and objects characteristic of that setting. In a restaurant, for example, one typically enters, orders, eats, gets and pays the bill, and leaves. As predicted by script theory, people's knowledge, inferences, and recall do closely conform to stereotypical patterns of activity.

Another Dimension of Long-Term Memory:
Verbal and Imaginal Representation

"A picture is worth a thousand words." Although the validity of this aphorism may be debatable, there is little doubt that humans have extraordinary capabilities for remembering visual information. For example, Standing, Conezio, and Haber (1970), in an early study of visual recognition memory, showed subjects 2,500 slides for 10 seconds each. Recognition, estimated from a test on a subset of these slides, was over 90%! In another study by Standing (1973), participants viewed an even larger number of pictures—10,000—over a 5-day period. From the test performance, Standing estimated subjects' memory at 6,600 pictures, remembered in at least enough detail to distinguish these pictures from ones they had not seen before. Given evidence such as this, there is little doubt that pictorial information can be represented in our memories quite well. Most of us can easily conjure up images of a book, a soaring bird, a train wreck, or a walk in the woods.

One major contribution of cognitive psychology has been a revitalization of interest in mental imagery. Once largely banished from experimental psychology as subjective, mentalistic, and therefore unscientific (Watson, 1924), imagery has come to play a significant role in cognitive theory and research.

Alan Paivio (1971, 1986a) has proposed that information is represented in two fundamentally distinct systems: one suited to verbal information and the other to images. The **verbal coding system** is adapted for linguistically based information and emphasizes verbal associations. According to Paivio, words, sentences, the content of conversations, and stories are coded within this system. In contrast, nonverbal information, such as pictures, sensations, and sounds, are stored within an **imaginal coding system** (Paivio, Clark, & Lambert, 1988).

Paivio's theory has been called a **dual coding theory,** because incoming information can be coded within one or both of the systems. Information that can be coded into both systems will be more easily recalled than information coded only in the verbal or imaginal system. In Paivio's view, the verbal and nonverbal codes are functionally independent and "contribute additively to memory performance" (1986a, p. 226). Paivio has also hypothesized that image-based memory traces generally are stronger than verbal memories. More recently, Paivio and colleagues have argued that all information encoded in long-term memory retains concrete qualities in addition to more abstract, verbally based conceptual qualities (Krasny, Sadoski, & Paivio, 2007).

Much of Paivio's early work demonstrated the effects of the abstractness of materials on their memorability and relating these results to dual coding theory. For instance, some words (e.g., *bird, star, ball,* and *desk*) have concrete referents and presumably are highly imaginable. When presented with such words, both the verbal (e.g., the linguistic representation of the word *bird,* its pronunciation, and its meaning) and the imaginal (e.g., an image of a bird soaring) representations are activated simultaneously. Other, more abstract words (e.g., *aspect, value,* and *unable*), are far less readily imaginable and activate the nonverbal system only minimally. In Paivio's view, memory for abstract materials should be poorer because such materials are represented only within a single system. Pictures, because they tend to be labeled automatically and are dual coded, should be more memorable than words (Paivio, 1986a).

Words, even concrete ones, are not necessarily automatically imaged (see also Svengas & Johnson, 1988). In many experimental studies, Paivio and his associates (e.g., Paivio, 1971; Paivio & Csapo, 1975; Paivio, Yuille, & Madigan, 1968) demonstrated beneficial effects of imagery on learning and memory that were consistent with his predictions. Words that are rated high in imagery also are better remembered in free recall, serial learning (i.e., a series of words recalled in order), and paired-associate learning (i.e., the "associate" of a word must be recalled when the word is presented). Also, when subjects are instructed to form images, their memory is enhanced.

Although considerable debate has surrounded the exact mechanisms by which imagery functions (e.g., Intons-Peterson, 1993; Kosslyn, 1994; Pylyshyn, 1981), there is little doubt that imagery is important to memory and cognition. In reading and text recall, for example, effects of concreteness and imagery are well-documented (e.g., Goetz, Sadoski, Fatemi, & Bush, 1994; Sadoski, Goetz, & Rodriguez, 2000). A large body of evidence shows that materials high in imagery are more memorable and that learners instructed to create images will enhance their learning. As educators, the distinction between verbal and imaginal information should remind us not to rely too heavily on verbal instruction. Just as in Chapter 2, when we discussed the use of auditory and visual material to enhance working memory, we should remember the potential that visual images hold for storage and recall in LTM.

Evolving Models of Memory

Through the 1960s and well into the 1970s, the prominent model of memory was the modal model, exemplified by the "stage" models of Waugh and Norman (1965) and Atkinson and Shiffrin (1968). As shown in Chapter 2, these models portray human cognition as computer-like and emphasize sequential steps in information processing. Information moves from the sense receptors and sensory registers into short-term/working memory and, depending on the success of the processing there, into long-term memory (Lewandowsky & Heit, 2006).

The importance of the distinction between short-term/working memory and LTM has diminished as memory models shifted from a "storage" to a "processing" emphasis (e.g., Collins & Loftus, 1975; Craik & Lockhart, 1972; Jenkins, 1974; see also Ericsson & Kintsch, 1995). This processing emphasis is retained in most current models (see Anderson, 1993, 1996; Collins, Gathercole, Conway, & Morris, 1993). As discussed in Chapter 2, rather than being conceived of as a "place" where information is held for brief periods, the concept of STM has broadened into the idea of **working memory** (Baddeley, 2007), which better reflects the many ways in which we process and transform information. For example, J. R. Anderson's ACT model, discussed later in this chapter, incorporates a working memory and a long-term memory. These two are not emphasized as "separate places" but rather as closely interrelated. The current contents of consciousness set up a pattern of activation in LTM; this activation of LTM, in turn, "reverberates" back into working memory.

Obviously, all components of memory—sensory memory, working memory, and long-term memory—are highly interactive. Although information plainly does move through sensory memory and working memory to LTM, the contents of LTM simultaneously are exerting a powerful influence on what we perceive, pay attention to, and comprehend (Ericsson & Kintsch, 1995; Kintsch, 1998). Although the modal model has been useful in drawing our attention to important dimensions of our memory systems, it should not be taken as implying that cognition is neatly separable into a set of sequential steps. The "early" process of perception, for instance, plainly is guided by semantic memory from the supposedly "later" stage of LTM. Also, many cognitive activities are highly automatic, driven by the information coming in, and seem to depend only minimally on "central processing."

Researchers have continued to develop new models aimed at better portraying the active, dynamic nature of cognition and its ability to interpret and restructure incoming information. Memory models continue to evolve, with earlier models contributing key elements to those that follow. In this section we describe three of the most prominent of these models—the network model, the ACT model, and the connectionist model—and their evolution.

Network Models

In **network models** of memory, knowledge is represented by a web or network, and memory processes are defined within that network (J. R. Anderson, 1983b, 1993, 1996). In most such models, the networks are hypothesized to consist of **nodes,** which consist of cognitive units (usually either concepts or schemata), and **links,** which represent relations between these cognitive units.

Quillian (1968) and Collins and Quillian (1969) proposed an early network model, called the **Teachable Language Comprehender (TLC),** as a model for semantic memory. Devised as a computer program, TLC was based on the assumption that memory could be represented by a semantic network arranged into a hierarchical structure. In this hierarchy, the nodes are concepts arranged in superordinate–subordinate relationships. Properties of each concept are labeled **relational links,** or pointers going from the node to other concept nodes. An example of such a network is presented in Figure 3.2.

Quillian proposed five kinds of links: (1) superordinate (ISA) and subordinate links, (2) modifier (M) links, (3) disjunctive sets of links, (4) conjunctive sets of links, and (5) a residual class of links. These links can be embedded in one another. In Figure 3.2, the links from *are fast, are agile,* and *are gentle* to *quarter horses* are **M** (modifying) links; the links between *quarter horses* and *horses* and between *horses* and *mammals* are **ISA** (superordinate) links. In general, properties particular to a concept were assumed to be stored along with the concept (e.g., *are gentle* is stored with *quarter horses*). Those not unique to that concept (e.g., *have manes* and *have hooves*), however, are assumed to be stored with more general concepts higher in the hierarchy.

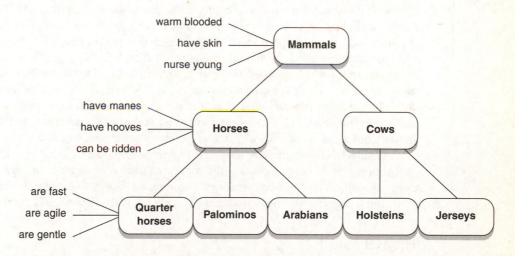

FIGURE 3.2   A Network Model of Memory.

Source: This sample of a network is modeled after those developed by Collins and Quillian (1969).

When memory is searched, activation moves along the links from the node that has been stimulated (say, by reading the word *horse*). This **spreading activation** constantly expands, first to all the nodes directly linked with the concept (in our simple model, from *horses* to the superordinate concept of *mammal* and to the subordinate concepts of *Arabians, palominos,* and *quarter horses*) and then to the nodes linked with these nodes and so on (Collins & Loftus, 1975). As activation moves forward through the nodes, an activation tag is left at each. When a tag from another starting node is encountered, an *intersection* has been found. By tracing the tags backward from the intersection to their sources, the path linking the starting nodes can be reconstructed. The question *Are quarter horses mammals?* would trace a path in the network from the starting nodes *quarter horses* and *mammals* through the node for horses.

According to this model, language comprehension consists of path evaluation to see whether it is consistent with the constraints imposed by language. For instance, the starting point in comprehending the question *Are quarter horses mammals?* is activation of the paths from *quarter horses* to *horses* and from *horses* to *mammals*. The memory search is presumed to begin at the concepts included in the input question (*quarter horses, mammals*). Beginning with the concept of quarter horses, this search would arrive in one step (link) at the properties *are fast, are agile,* and *are gentle* and at the superordinate concept of *horses*. A second step takes the search to *mammals*. If the relationship between the two nodes is permitted by the syntax and context of the question, the question can be comprehended.

Collins and Quillian tested a number of hypotheses based on their model, including the hypothesis that the more links needing to be traversed in accessing memory (e.g., deciding whether a Holstein is a mammal vs. deciding whether a cow is a mammal; see Figure 3.2), the longer the process will take. This prediction usually was borne out, although, like all models, Collins and Quillian's model had trouble accounting for some results, such as familiarity effects (e.g., deciding whether a palomino is a horse is easier than deciding whether a tarpon is a horse simply because most of us are more familiar with palominos than tarpons). To account for such findings and their own accumulating data, Collins and Loftus (1975) extended the model, including several assumptions to make the model less "computer-like" and more "human." (Quillian's original theory was developed as a program for the computer, which imposed constraints that he thought were unrealistic.) Spreading activation remained a key assumption, but with activation decreasing over time. In addition, Collins and Loftus proposed the existence of a separate **lexical network,** in which concept names were stored. Links in this lexical network could serve as an alternative source of entry into memory (e.g., "words that sound like *horse*"). Collins and Loftus's revised network model accounted for results from a variety of studies and dealt with many criticisms of the original model.

Collins's network models, although superseded by other models in recent years, have contributed key concepts, especially the conceptualization of memory as organized into networks of nodes and links and the idea of spreading activation, to current theories and models of memory. Arguably the most prominent of these is J. R. Anderson's ACT model.

The ACT Model

Perhaps the most comprehensive current model of memory and cognition is the ACT model (J. R. Anderson, 1976, 1983a, 1983b, 1993, 1996). Growing out of an early model called *human associative memory* (*HAM*) (J. R. Anderson & Bower, 1973), ACT is broader than the models of Collins and Quillian (1969) and Collins and Loftus (1975). In formulating and revising ACT, Anderson's ambitious intention has been to provide a unifying theoretical framework for all aspects of thinking, one that includes initial encoding of information and then information storage and retrieval and encompasses both declarative and procedural knowledge.

In the latest version of ACT, called *ACT-R* (J. R. Anderson, 1996; Anderson et al., 2004; Lovett & Anderson, 2005), declarative knowledge is represented by schema-like structures or chunks that encode the category and contents of the information. Procedural knowledge, such as the ability to solve mathematics problems, is represented by productions. Production rules specify the conditions and actions of productions—that is, the conditions under which the action will take place and the outcome of the production, which can include creating new declarative information. Production rules respond to goals of the situation (e.g., the need to solve a word problem in algebra), often by creating subgoals (e.g., converting linguistic information in the word problem into symbolic representations).

In ACT-R, declarative and procedural knowledge are intimately connected. Production rules specify how chunks are transformed and apply only when a rule's conditions are satisfied by the knowledge available in declarative memory. In short, declarative knowledge provides the context in which cognitive processes, as represented by production rules, take place.

As in most other network models, the concept of *spreading activation* is a key feature of ACT. Spreading activation is seen as determining the level of activity in long-term memory. Of course, activation must begin somewhere; the points where activation begins are called **focus units.** Once focus units are activated—either externally from perception (e.g., by reading a sentence) or from working memory (e.g., by thinking about what has been read)—activation spreads to associated elements. When you read the word *hot,* elements for *cold, warm, water,* and other related items likely would be activated automatically. Any item's activation is a function of prior experience—the extent to which an item has been useful in the past—and the odds that it will be useful in the current context. In Anderson's words, "The mind keeps track of general usefulness and combines this with contextual appropriateness to make some inference about what knowledge to make available in the current context" (1996, p. 360). Attention determines the continued activation of the network; when the source of activation for the focus unit drops from attention, activation decays.

Because working memory and LTM overlap extensively, activation spreads easily from working memory to associated elements in LTM. From there, activation can "reverberate back" to nodes in the network. If Node 1 activates Node 2, then activation from Node 2 also can spread to Node 1. Retrieval occurs when focus units are reactivated. Activation is cumulative: The more units activated, the more likely an item will be retrieved. In the classroom, a student who may not be able to recall a fact when first questioned may remember the information if the teacher rephrases the question or supplies "hints" that activate additional pathways, stimulating recall.

In ACT, well-learned concepts are seen as producing more activation and so are more easily retrieved than less well-learned concepts. Well-learned information has wide-ranging activation and many associations that permit access through multiple routes. Also, the ACT model implies that more activation occurs on paths leading to stronger nodes. Anderson's model would predict that students who are helped to relate new information to existing, well-learned knowledge will have superior recall.

The ACT model has generated a great deal of research. Because of its breadth, ACT has been adapted not only to the study of memory but also to modeling high-level cognitive processes, such as problem solving and decision making (Anderson, 1996; Anderson et al., 2004). Because it can account for a wide variety of data and addresses many important aspects of cognition, this model is likely to play an important role in directing cognitive research in the foreseeable future.

Connectionist Models

Throughout much of its history, cognitive psychology has been dominated by a computer metaphor. Human cognition, cognitive scientists have argued, is computer-like. Information is taken in, processed in a single central processor of working memory, and stored in and retrieved from long-term memory. The computer metaphor has generated models of memory (e.g., Atkinson & Shiffrin, 1968), knowledge representation (e.g., Kintsch, 1986, 1988), and problem solving (e.g., Newell & Simon, 1972). Beyond providing a metaphor for cognition, computers have provided a mechanism for simulating cognition and for testing cognitive theories.

Most computer architecture requires sequential or **serial processing.** Computer programs typically are a series of instructions the computer executes very rapidly, one after the other. One serious problem in modeling cognition is that this kind of serial information processing is not very "brain-like." Where digital computers are quick and precise, executing millions and even billions of operations in sequence per second, human information processing is far slower. Yet although our brains are slower, they are much better suited and far more powerful than computers for most kinds of "messy" everyday cognitive tasks, such as recognizing objects in natural scenes, understanding language, searching memory when given only fragmentary information, making plans, and learning from experience.

Also in contrast with most computer programs, our cognitive systems can operate under multiple constraints. Although some cognitive tasks require serial processing, many require **parallel processing,** with processing occurring simultaneously along several dimensions. For instance, in a famous example from Selfridge (1959), the interpretation of the middle letter in the words CAT and THE is determined by the context in which it appears. Similarly, we have little trouble identifying the words in Figure 3.3 even though parts of key letters are obscured. Our perceptual system somehow explores possibilities simultaneously without committing itself to one interpretation until all constraints are taken into account. The identity of each letter is constrained by all the others. Most cognitive tasks, including physical performances (e.g., hitting a ball, typing, playing a piano) and language use (e.g., oral language comprehension, reading and understanding stories), involve resolving multiple constraints.

FIGURE 3.3   Examples of Information Processing with Multiple Constraints.

Given the characteristics of the brain and its tremendous adaptability, some cognitive theorists (e.g., McClelland, McNaughton, & O'Reilly, 1995; McClelland, Rumelhart, & Hinton, 1986; Rumelhart & Todd, 1993) have proposed replacing the computer metaphor with a "brain metaphor," a so-called **connectionist model of memory,** or **parallel distributed processing (PDP) model.** The reason human beings are better than conventional computers at many tasks, they contend, is that the brain has an architecture that better fits natural information processing tasks. What humans do so exceedingly well, far better than any computer, is to consider many pieces of information simultaneously. Processing occurs in *parallel,* along many dimensions at the same time. Although any single bit of information may be imprecise or ambiguous, the system's parallel processing capabilities make it possible to make judgments and decisions with a high level of confidence.

According to McClelland (1988), the major difference between connectionist models and other cognitive models is that, in most models, knowledge is stored as a static copy of a pattern. When access is needed, the pattern is found in long-term memory and copied into working memory. In a connectionist model, however, the units themselves are not stored. What is stored are the connection strengths among simple processing units. These connection strengths allow the patterns to be re-created when the system is activated. Figure 3.4, from McClelland et al. (1995), contrasts a connectionist network with a semantic (propositional) network of the type traditionally used to model the organization of knowledge in memory. Note the close correspondence of the semantic network with the Collins and Quillian (1969)

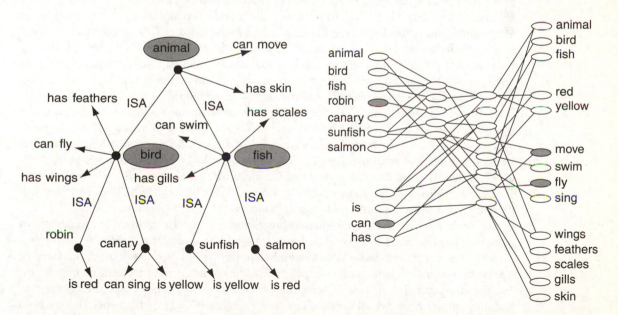

FIGURE 3.4   Contrast Between Network (left) and Connectionist (right) Models of the Knowledge in LTM.

Source: Adapted from "Why There Are Complementary Learning Systems in the Hippocampus and Neocortex: Insights from the Successes and Failures of Connectionist Models of Learning and Memory," by J. L. McClelland, B. L. McNaughton, & R. C. O'Reilly, 1995, *Psychological Review, 102,* 419–457. Copyright 1995 by the American Psychological Association. Used by permission.

model presented in Figure 3.2. In the connectionist model, a subset of one used by Rumelhart (1990) to "learn" the relationships in the semantic network, inputs consist of concept-relation pairs and activation spreads from left to right. Over time, the network can be "trained" to turn on all of the output units (those on the right side) that are correct completions of the input pattern. The network learns connection weights linking inputs and outputs.

Because processing is parallel in connectionist models, it can proceed along many dimensions at the same time. In reading, for instance, the cognitive processes are not portrayed as moving through steps from "lower levels," such as decoding, to "higher levels," such as comprehension. Instead, processing moves ahead on many levels at once; as we read, we simultaneously depend on feature extraction processes (e.g., recognizing lines, curves, and angles in letters), letter and word recognition processes, syntactic assignment processes (e.g., is *feature* a noun or a verb?), and schema activation. These processes trigger and inhibit one another as processing moves forward. Top-down, bottom-up, and interactive (a combination of top-down and bottom-up) processing all can occur within such a system (McClelland et al., 1995). As is shown in Chapters 11 and 12, this conception of reading seems to fit well with the data.

Another key concept in connectionist models is that of **distributed representation** (Bechtel & Abrahamsen, 2002). As we have indicated, in a connectionist model, knowledge is stored in the strengths of connections between processing units, not in the units themselves. Researchers such as McClelland and his associates argue that connectionist models can provide a better account of how semantic networks, such as that in Figure 3.4, are acquired and can help us understand how knowledge is transferred. Knowledge of any specific pattern (e.g., oaks, trees, plants, and living things) does not reside in a special processing unit reserved just for that pattern, but instead is distributed over the connections among a very large number of simple processing units. Our understanding of *bark* in the sentence "Marty's dog let out a loud *bark!*" arises through activation of connections among a host of processing units, including those for letter perception, word meanings, and syntactic roles and those relating to the context in which the sentence was uttered. We comprehend automatically that *bark* is something Marty's dog did, not what covers the oak tree outside our window.

In connectionist models, processing units are roughly analogous to neurons or assemblies of neurons, and the connections by which units are linked are seen as roughly analogous to synapses. These parallels make them particularly attractive in helping researchers understand brain structures and functions (see, e.g., McClelland et al., 1995; McClelland & Seidenberg, 2000). When stimulated by the environment, input units cause other units to be activated via their connections—the familiar spreading activation from Collins and Quillian's early network model. Eventually, activation spreads to those units associated with responses.

"Brain-like" models of information processing now are appearing more frequently in computer hardware and software. The computer world has long recognized that the conventional, single-central-processor design has inherent limitations. Because instructions must be operated on serially, a bottleneck eventually will occur in the central processor no matter how fast the computer. The newest supercomputers are based on parallel distributed processing and may contain hundreds of dedicated processor systems linked by a high-speed network—a brain-like, connectionist system that enables these computers to do advanced simulations and modeling not possible with serial processing.

Connectionist models continue to have some intriguing applications in cognitive psychology. Because of their higher degree of correspondence to brain characteristics and their

TABLE 3.2   Three Models of Knowledge Representation in Long-Term Memory

	Network	Production System	Connectionist
Type of architecture	Hierarchical	Non-hierarchical production rules	Non-hierarchical distributed neural networks
Important components	Nodes, properties, and relational links	Production rules and systems of rules	Units (explicit and hidden), weighted connections, and neural networks
Important processes	Spreading activation	Spreading activation	Activation and forward and backward propagation
Strengths	Good job of modeling the hierarchical relationship of declarative knowledge	Models procedural knowledge and explains development of expertise	Modeled after brain physiology, can be tested using computer simulations, and generalizes to other life forms
Weaknesses	Does not distinguish procedural, conceptual, or self-regulatory knowledge	Mechanistic, places strong emphasis on experience and practice rather than reflection	Highly data driven, removes the mind from learning

ability to match more closely aspects of human cognition, including learning, they seem likely to make a major contribution to cognitive psychology and to the understanding of human learning and memory.

A Comparison of the Three Types of Models

Models continue to evolve that attempt to explain the representation of knowledge in long-term memory (Mayer, 2008; Reed, 2006a). Nevertheless, three general families of models exist, including networks, production systems, and connectionist models. Table 3.2 provides a comparison of these models. Networks models focus on how declarative knowledge might be represented. Production models extend this approach in two ways, first by describing the representation of procedural knowledge and second by relating declarative and procedural knowledge. Connectionist models propose a radically different cognitive architecture modeled on the human brain, rather than a computer. Each of the three models has strengths and weaknesses.

Assessment of Long-Term Memory Functions

The study of long-term memory has a rich tradition in cognitive psychology. Early theories postulated a holistic LTM system without distinguishing between important subcomponents such as declarative and procedural knowledge. Models proposed after 1970 have made finer- and finer-grained distinctions between different subcomponents of LTM, such as Tulving's

(1972) comparison of semantic and episodic memory systems and his suggestion that these systems may be located in different regions of the brain. More recently, but especially with the rise of connectionist models of LTM described earlier, researchers have investigated the relationship between functional aspects of LTM such as procedural memory and the neurological basis of those memories in both humans (Anderson, Fincham, Qin, & Stocco, 2008) and animals (Tse et al., 2007). One critical issue is whether hypothesized functions such as semantic memories can be linked to a specific region of the brain. Being able to make this link would lend credibility to the argument that hypothetical psychological constructs such as semantic memory have a neurological basis.

A great deal of research over the past 2 decades has focused on the biological underpinnings of cognitive functions. Much of the contemporary research has relied on functional magnetic resonance imaging (fMRI), a noninvasive neuroimaging technique used to scan the brain that does not rely on harmful radiation and is sensitive to ongoing neurological activity. In a recent representative study, Anderson et al. (2008) investigated the link between four important functional skills (i.e., procedural execution, goal setting, controlled retrieval from declarative memory, and construction of imaginal representations) and cortical regions of the brain. They found that each of the four cognitive activities was associated with increased neurological activity in a different cortical region of the brain. For example, controlled retrieval from declarative memory was associated with increased activity in the prefrontal region of the brain. These findings help to make a convincing argument for discrete cognitive functions such as complex declarative learning (Chi & Ohlsson, 2005) as well as support the idea that different cognitive functions reside in different regions of the brain.

Debate continues about the utility and accuracy of fMRI techniques for understanding human cognition. One common criticism is that evidence of increased neurological activity does not indicate why the increase occurred or how it should be interpreted. Nevertheless, the fact that activation of declarative information appears to stimulate one region of the brain, while activation of a complex procedure activates a different part of the brain, suggests important differences. Taken collectively, researchers can use fMRI data to validate hypothetical cognitive functions such as encoding and retrieval, as well as structural components of memory such as semantic and episodic memory. We believe that neuroimaging methods provide a valuable assessment tool for researchers and that, in general, data from these studies match well with the claims of cognitive psychologists regarding hypothesized cognitive processes and memory structures.

Implications for Instruction

The models of memory and the memory-related concepts we have explored provide us with several powerful conceptions about the nature of learning and memory. These have important implications for educators.

1. *Recognize that the starting point of learning is what students already know—their prior knowledge.* Students understand what they read, hear, and see through the filters of their experiences in their families and cultures. The models of memory we have examined in this chapter all stress the role of prior knowledge in information processing and memory. What can be learned depends substantially on what learners already know. In the modal model, for instance, we see knowledge from LTM affecting perception and attention. Schema research has dramatically illustrated how knowledge structures guide information processing and influence what we learn and remember. As discussed in Chapter 1, learning is a constructive process. A beginning point of instruction should be the recognition that much of what students learn is constructed from the prior knowledge in their long-term memory.

2. *Help students activate their current knowledge.* Having relevant knowledge is one thing; using it in new learning is another. From a schema theory standpoint, new information needs to be instantiated within learners' schemata. From an instructional perspective, this implies that teachers need to ensure that students have activated relevant knowledge. Using the framework of ACT-R, we can see that knowledge activation provides more and stronger links for embedding new declarative and procedural knowledge within existing networks. As teachers, we need to take maximum advantage of the relationship between prior and new knowledge. Stimulating students' recall of related information, providing analogies and schema activation, and probing both intellectual and emotional reactions to materials and activities are only a few of many ways in which what students already know can be acknowledged and used to improve instruction.

3. *Help students organize new information into meaningful "chunks."* As shown in Chapter 2, the research on STM/working memory highlighted our ability through organization to increase the size of information "chunks" and so hold more information in memory. Organization may play an even more critical role in LTM. Organizing and linking information makes units of memory larger and more meaningful. When students are helped to discover relationships, to group related concepts and ideas, and to see how information can be used in their lives, comprehension increases and recall is enhanced.

4. *Aid students in proceduralizing their knowledge and linking it to conditional knowledge.* A frequent challenge to educators is to make knowledge useful for students. Although it is important that we build students' declarative knowledge, particularly organized declarative knowledge, we usually want to go well beyond this. We hope the knowledge that students acquire will become a vital, working part of their lives. In J. R. Anderson's view (1993), declarative knowledge needs to be **proceduralized,** which is a function of practice. Solving mathematics problems is an example. Once a student knows the steps to solving a problem (the knowledge is proceduralized) and understands when and where it can be used (conditional knowledge), this knowledge can be applied rapidly and reliably across a variety of situations. We can help students develop working knowledge by providing experiences in which they use information to solve real-life problems and integrate their skills in complex performances.

5. *Provide opportunities for students to use both verbal and imaginal coding.* Most classroom transactions are verbal: Teachers and students spend their days talking, listening, reading, and sometimes writing. Images—generated by pictures, touch, activities, and imagination—are less often the focus of classroom processes. When we exclude images, we may be neglecting some of the most important tools and goals for learning. Imagery can be a powerful factor in improving memorability of information that students need to acquire, as Paivio and others have shown. It also is a key to creative imagination.

Summary

Memory is one of the most important concerns of cognitive psychologists, playing a major role in two of our cognitive themes in education: that learning is a constructive process and that mental structures organize memory and guide thought. The earliest scientific studies of memory were experimental investigations of rote learning and set the course of memory research for most of the 20th century. This changed with the advent of cognitive psychology, as memory theorists made immense strides in describing the encoding, storage, and retrieval of meaningful information in real-life settings.

The basic or modal model of memory, which was introduced in Chapter 2, portrays memory as composed of three major components: sensory memory, STM or working memory, and LTM. LTM, the focus of this chapter, is the permanent repository for information and seems to have virtually unlimited capacity. LTM represents the prior knowledge that is used for constructing much of our learning. As cognitive theorists have shifted to studying meaningful learning, they have made distinctions that are useful for educators. These include contrasts between declarative and procedural knowledge, episodic and semantic memory, implicit and explicit memory, and verbal and imaginal representation. They also have defined mental structures and cognitive units—such as concepts, propositions, schemata, productions, and scripts—that organize memory and guide thought. These units are the building blocks in comprehensive models of memory, such as Anderson's ACT model.

Early models of memory that were based on a computer metaphor have evolved, as has computer science itself, from a stepwise, serial processing-type model to a more brain-like connectionist models. Connectionist models offer a closer match to aspects of human cognition, especially learning, and may suggest new ways to enhance our students' abilities to learn and to recall and use their knowledge.

SUGGESTED READINGS

Anderson, J. R. (1993). Problem solving and learning. *American Psychologist, 48,* 35–44.
    This early article is a readable description of J. R. Anderson's ACT model (ACT* version) and its potential for understanding the phenomenon of problem solving.

Anderson, J. R., & Matessa, M. (1997). A production system theory of serial memory. *Psychological Review, 104,* 728–748.
    This review article provides a good description of the ACT-R (adaptive control of thought-rational) version of J. R. Anderson's theory and applies it to an area long studied by memory researchers, serial list learning (e.g., learning to say items in a list in order). Although somewhat technical, the review nicely shows how the assumptions and procedures of a theoretical perspective are applied to a specific domain of memory research.

Anderson, J. R., Fincham, J. M., Qin, Y., & Stocco, A. (2008). A central circuit of the mind. *Trends in Cognitive Science, 12*(4), 136–143.
    This article illustrates the growing connection between cognitive psychology and cognitive neuroscience. It reveals interesting convergences between the cognitive framework proposed by the ACT-R model and fMRI data showing model-consistent activation of brain regions connected to performance of certain cognitive tasks.

Tulving, E. (2002). Episodic memory: From mind to brain. *Annual Review of Psychology, 53,* 1–25.
    This review article gives an excellent, easily understandable overview of episodic memory, how it has changed since its inception, criticisms of it, and new supporting evidence of its existence as a separate memory system. The new evidence provided by memory-impaired patients and the recent work in neuroimaging is intriguing.

4   Encoding Processes

Encoding Simple Information ▪ Encoding More Complex Information ▪ Metacognition: Thinking About Thinking ▪ Assessment and Encoding ▪ Implications for Instruction ▪ Summary ▪ Suggested Readings

In Chapter 2, we reviewed perception, attention, and working memory and noted how all three are powerfully affected by people's knowledge of the world. In Chapter 3, we introduced the topic of long-term memory and how knowledge is stored. The topic of this chapter is the process involved in placing information into long-term memory. This process is usually referred to as **encoding** (see Figure 2.1). As you might expect, encoding has a major impact on other cognitive processes, such as *storage* (how information is kept in memory) and *retrieval* (how information is retrieved from memory). Chapter 5 addresses retrieval and its relationship to encoding and storage. In this chapter, we focus on strategies that help us encode information.

Not all of the information we want to learn is the same. Some is straightforward, such as the capital of Nebraska, the atomic structure of hydrogen, or the names of the oceans. But much of what we encounter and need to learn is more complex and inferential. For example, if you are using this text as part of a course, you could be expected to read this chapter and take a test on it. You might need to know specific facts and technical terms. More important, however, is understanding what the chapter means in both a theoretical and an applied sense. Presumably, a theory for understanding encoding is presented in this chapter. Your task is to comprehend it, identify its component parts, understand the relationships among these parts, and apply them to your everyday and professional life.

Educators traditionally have distinguished between simpler and more complex forms of learning. For example, learning to link states with their capitals or Civil War battles with their dates does seem much simpler than explaining why state capitals are often not located in major cities or arguing whether social or economic factors were more important in causing the Civil War. The former examples seem more a matter of associating and acquiring terms through rehearsal, while the latter involve understanding, reasoning, and critical thinking.

Much early research on cognitive processes involved experimental studies of the simpler kinds of learning and identifying strategies students could use to better encode and retrieve information. Recent applications of cognitive theory, however, have tended to focus on helping students better *understand* concepts and ideas and use them to reason and solve problems. Strategies for acquiring simple information actually turn out to be quite useful in helping students master more complex cognitive tasks but need to be combined and used thoughtfully.

Reflecting these applications of cognitive theory, this chapter is organized in five parts. In the first part, we discuss research-based strategies that have proven useful for encoding and making simpler kinds of information more memorable. In the second part, we focus on encoding complex information and the role meaning plays in enabling students to comprehend and use what they learn. The third section begins a detailed discussion of conditional knowledge with the introduction of the concept of *metacognition*—the knowledge that students have about their own thought processes. We show that the more students are aware of their own cognitive strategies for encoding information, the more likely they will be to understand and use what they learn. The two final sections summarize the relationship of assessment and encoding and the implications of encoding theory for instruction.

Encoding Simple Information

How we encode to-be-remembered information makes a huge difference in how well we remember it. One important dimension of encoding is rehearsal. To closely examine rehearsal, consider two sixth graders studying for a spelling test. Assume that the two children are of equal ability, but differ in how they rehearse the spelling words. Anna starts at the top of the list, reads the first word, and spells it to herself over and over *("familiar—f, a, m, i . . .")*. She does this six times for each of the 25 words on the list and then sets the list aside. Carlita also starts by reading the first word on the list, but she rehearses the information differently, by breaking the words into smaller words and syllables she already knows how to spell *("familiar—fam, i, liar.* That's *fam—f, a, m; i—I,* and *liar—l, i, a, r")*. Carlita also cycles through her list six times for each word.

If we give Anna and Carlita a test of the spelling words after they finish studying, the odds are high that Carlita will obtain a better score than Anna. The reason for this difference is obvious to us, if not to the sixth graders: The way the information was rehearsed influenced its memorability.

The kind of rehearsal Anna engaged in has been called **maintenance rehearsal** (Bunce & Macready, 2005; Craik, 1979). Maintenance rehearsal is the direct recycling of information in order to keep it active in short-term memory. It is the sort of rehearsal we perform when we look up a telephone number and want to retain it just long enough to dial the number (e.g., repeating 472–2225 over and over until the number is dialed). When maintenance rehearsal is interrupted, however, information can be easily lost. For example, have you ever repeated a telephone number to yourself until you dialed it, obtained a busy signal, been distracted a bit, and then had to look up the number again?

The virtue of maintenance rehearsal is that it helps us retain information for a short time without heavily taxing our cognitive resources. For example, you can cycle 472–2225 over and over while looking for a pencil and a pad of paper, picking up the telephone, and thinking about what you are going to say once you reach the person at 472–2225. Maintenance rehearsal also can enhance some kinds of long-term memory, such as recognition (see Lockhart, 2002), but for the majority of long-term memory tasks involving meaning, elaborative rehearsal is the better choice.

Elaborative rehearsal is any form of rehearsal in which the to-be-remembered information is related to other information (Lockhart, 2002). Later in this chapter, we discuss *levels of processing* (Craik, 2002; Craik & Lockhart, 1986), which refers to the ways information can be encoded. In terms of the levels-of-processing framework, elaborative rehearsal amounts to deeper or more varied encoding activities, while maintenance rehearsal can be seen as shallow encoding.

Carlita's rehearsal of the spelling words is a clear example of elaborative rehearsal. Rather than merely spelling words over and over, she broke them into components and elaborated (related) the to-be-remembered information to what she already knew. Carlita's encoding activities are much more likely to lead to better recall than Anna's.

Another example of elaborative rehearsal in the learning of spelling words can be seen in how the fourth-grade daughter of one of the authors learned to spell *respectfully*. While getting ready to study her spelling, she heard an old rock song in which the word *respect* is spelled out in the lyrics to a very strong beat. Later, when her father walked by, the fourth grader had her spelling list turned out of sight and was mimicking the singer's lyric line: *r, e, s, p, e, c, t, fully*.

Research suggests that elaborative rehearsal is superior to maintenance rehearsal for long-term recall but that it tends to use considerably more of a person's cognitive resources than maintenance rehearsal (Craik, 1979). It also suggests that maintenance and elaborative rehearsal might be thought of as representing opposite ends on a continuum of rehearsal. At one extreme of the continuum would be the minimal processing needed to repeat a term over and over; at the other end would be more robust, meaning-oriented encoding activities (Lockhart, 2002) in which the to-be-learned information is linked with several bits of information already in memory.

One implication of research on rehearsal is that different types of rehearsal are appropriate for different tasks. When long-term memory is desired (e.g., when a student will be tested over content or when the information will be important for later understanding), some form of elaborative rehearsal should be employed. As you might suspect, many encoding strategies employ elaborative rehearsal, and we review several of them in the next few pages.

Mediation

One of the simplest elaborative encoding strategies is **mediation.** Mediation involves tying difficult-to-remember items to something more meaningful. The original research on mediation in memory was based on the learning of paired nonsense syllables (e.g., BOZ and BUH). Although we hope none of what we teach is at the level of nonsense syllables, the strategy has some implications for instruction.

In early research on mediation (Montague, Adams, & Kiess, 1966), it became apparent that subjects who used mediators in committing pairs of nonsense syllables to memory outperformed subjects who used no mediators. When subjects could devise a mediator such as *race car* when faced with a pair of nonsense syllables (e.g., *RIS-KIR*), they were able to tie their memory for the meaningless information to something meaningful and ease their memory task.

Although mediation is a simple and easily learned technique that enhances memory for a limited range of information, it is congruent with the theme of this chapter; what people do with to-be-learned information determines how it will be remembered. Even at its simplest levels, learning proceeds better as a constructive, than as a receptive process. Mediation results in deeper, more elaborated encoding than does simple repetition of new content.

Imagery

Our emphasis up to this point has been on the encoding of verbal information. One powerful adjunct to verbal encoding is the use of imagery. (See Chapter 3 for a discussion of imagery and Paivio's dual coding theory.) Consider the fourth grader who conjures up an image of an emperor complete with rich robes, a crown, and a jewel-encrusted scepter when trying to learn the meaning of the word *czar*. Or the chemistry student who shuts her eyes and visualizes a three-dimensional picture of the bromination of benzene as she studies for a quiz. In each of these examples, imagery is an important part of encoding information.

As shown in Chapter 3, the presence of imagery usually leads to better memory performance, but some conditions can affect its usefulness. One is that some materials have higher imagery value than others. For example, the word *toboggan* leads much more easily to an image than does the word *truth*. Similarly, the word *feather* would prompt a clear picture, while *freedom* might not.

Easily imaged words tend to be remembered more readily than hard-to-image words, even in the absence of instructions to use imagery (Paivio, 1986a, 1986b). When subjects are instructed to use imagery, the difference is even more pronounced. Even subjects' memory for nonsense syllables is enhanced when they use imagery in learning.

Imagery value should not be thought of as being restricted to individual words. The idea can be extended to the imagery value of concepts (e.g., compare internal combustion to entropy), people (e.g., compare Theodore Roosevelt with Calvin Coolidge), and whole segments of information (e.g., compare *Macbeth* with 99% of the situation comedies ever produced). Simply, some sets of information are easier to image than others.

A second issue to be considered when we discuss imagery is the likelihood of individual differences among students in their ability to image information (e.g., Kozhevnikov, Kosslyn, & Shepard, 2005; Scruggs, Mastropieri, McLoone, Levin, & Morrison, 1987). Results suggest that some students are better able to employ imagery than others and that these differences can lead to differences in memory performance. Unfortunately, no evidence indicates whether ability to image can be improved with practice. Still, even students who score very low on measures of ability to image do show improved memory performance when they employ imagery (Scruggs et al., 1987).

A third factor associated with imagery concerns the nature of the images that people conjure up. Many memory experts have argued that the best images are bizarre, colorful, and strange. For example, if you wanted to remember that one of J. P. Morgan's characteristics was greed, you could imagine J. P. Morgan as a hog wearing a business suit with a watch fob, chomping on a large black cigar, and fighting with other industrialists for a share of the spoils. Similarly, if you wanted to remember that the word *peduncle* refers to the stem bearing a flower, you could imagine a garish flower being carried by its stalk with the word *peduncle* pictured on each side of the stalk.

Research on the value of bizarre imagery, however, has been inconclusive. Early work (e.g., Collyer, Jonides, & Bevan, 1972) sometimes found no advantage for bizarre imagery, as opposed to mundane imagery (e.g., trying to remember *peduncle* by picturing a daisy) and sometimes found it to be valuable (Furst, 1954). More recent studies (e.g., Clark & Paivio, 1991; Macklin & McDaniel, 2005; McDaniel, Einstein, DeLosh, & May, 1995) have revealed the complexity of the effects of bizarre imagery effects. Outcomes are affected by variables such as whether bizarre and nonbizarre images are encountered mixed together or alone, with mixed conditions favoring the effectiveness of bizarre imagery. Also, when conditions of recall are varied, bizarreness effects have been noted with free recall measures but not with cued recall or recognition.

In general, however, imagery has considerable value in helping make information memorable. When used in conjunction with a group of memory-enhancing techniques called *mnemonics,* imagery can be a powerful tool for improving memory performance.

Mnemonics

Mnemonics (nih-MAH-niks) are memory strategies that help people remember information by creating more elaborate coding of new materials and stronger memory traces. Typically, mnemonics involve pairing to-be-learned information with well-learned information in order to make the new information more memorable. Mnemonics help us learn new information by making it easier to elaborate, chunk, or retrieve it from memory.

Mnemonic techniques include the use of rhymes ("*i* before *e,* except after *c*"), sayings ("thirty days hath September, April, June, and November"), gestures (the "right-hand rule" in physics is a mnemonic for determining the flow of a magnetic field around an electrical current—putting the thumb of the right hand in the direction of the current and the curl of the fingers around the conductor will show the direction of the magnetic field), and imagery. Teachers have long used mnemonics as a part of their instruction. For example, music teachers may instruct students in the use of "Every Good Boy Does Fine" to help them remember the lines of the treble clef and "FACE" to remember the spaces. Students report that they often use mnemonics without being instructed to do so (Schneider & Pressley, 1997). As might be expected, some mnemonics are more effective than others (Levin, 1993), and different mnemonics seem especially suited to specific forms of learning. In the remainder of this section, we examine several mnemonic techniques and see how they may be implemented in instruction.

The Peg Method   In the **peg method,** students memorize a series of "pegs" on which to-be-learned information can be "hung" one item at a time. The pegs can be any well-learned set of items, but the most popular approach involves the use of a set of very simple rhymes, each related to an easily imagined concept (e.g., bun, shoe, etc.).

One is a bun.
Two is a shoe.
Three is a tree.
Four is a door.
Five is a hive.
Six is sticks.
Seven is heaven.
Eight is a gate.
Nine is a pine.
Ten is a hen.

The key to the success of the peg method is thoroughly learning the pegs. For example, students who have mastered this rhyme can use it to learn lists of items, such as the names of authors, politicians, or terms in a social studies course. The technique is simple and effective. Its use can be seen, for example, in the learning of the following grocery list: pickles, bread, milk, oranges, and light bulbs.

In using the rhyme, the first step is to construct a visual image of the first item on the to-be-learned list interacting with the object named in the first line of the rhyme. For instance, to remember pickles, we could imagine a very large pickle stuffed into the center of a bun. Next, a loaf of bread could be imagined shoved into a shoe as it sits in the closet. The third item, milk, could be visualized as a milk tree—a large tree with quarts of milk, rather than fruit, hanging from it, and so on through the entire list. After each item on the list has been carefully imagined interacting with the corresponding item in the rhyme, the learner is finished until time for recall. At recall, the learner simply recites the rhyme. Each image is retrieved as the recitation proceeds, and so recall of the list follows.

When it is well learned, the peg method has been shown to be effective for learning word lists of various sorts (Bugelski, Kidd, & Segmen, 1968). It also has been shown to be helpful in learning written directions (Glover, Harvey, & Corkill, 1988) and learning steps in complex procedures (Glover, Timme, Deyloff, Rogers, & Dinnel, 1987). Interestingly, the peg method can be used over and over without losing its effectiveness.

The Method of Loci   One of the best-known mnemonic procedures dates back to the ancient Greeks. According to Bower (1970) and Schacter (1996), the **method of loci** got its name from an event in which the poet Simonides was attending a banquet and was called outside. While Simonides was outside, the roof of the banquet hall collapsed, killing everyone left inside. The tragedy was especially cruel because the bodies were so badly mangled that not even the victims' loved ones could identify them. Simonides, however, was able to remember each person on the basis of where the person sat at the banquet table. Hence, the name "method of loci" came from Simonides's use of location to recall information.

To use the method of loci to learn new information, a very imaginable location, such as one's home or the path one walks to school, must be learned flawlessly. The location then is practiced so that the person can easily imagine various "drops" in the location, such as the sofa, coffee table, window, television, and armchair in a living room. These drops must be learned such that they are recalled in exactly the same order each time.

Once the location and its drops have been overlearned, the system is ready for use as a mnemonic. Suppose a student must recall five famous poets: Spenser, Keats, Sand, Dickinson, and Eliott. We could imagine Spenser sitting on the sofa, Keats with his boots propped up on the coffee table, Sand looking out the window, Dickinson changing channels on the television, and Eliott sitting in an armchair. If our list were longer, we could continue to place people in locations until we completed the list.

At the time of recall, we would take our mental walk back through the location, and each drop would lead to the image of the to-be-remembered person. As with the peg method, the method of loci can be used over and over for a variety of information without losing its effectiveness. Both methods, however, exact a price—the effort required to learn the original "base" on which the mnemonic depends. Students sometimes balk at giving the effort needed to develop one of these mnemonics, but they almost always report that the effort was well worth it after they begin using them (Kilpatrick, 1985).

The Link Method Relatively little research has been done on the link method. Memory experts have reported using it (e.g., Neisser, 1982), and it has the advantage over the method of loci and the peg method of not needing an external system or previously learned set of materials.

In the **link method,** which is best suited for learning lists of things, the student forms an image for each item in a list of things to be learned. Each image is pictured as *interacting* with the next item on the list so that all of the items are linked in imagination. For example, if a student needed to remember to bring her homework, lab notebook, chemistry text, goggles, lab apron, and pencil to class tomorrow, she could imagine a scene in which the homework papers were tucked inside the lab notebook. The lab notebook then could be placed into the textbook, with her goggles stretched around it. Next, the total package could be wrapped up in the lab apron, with the ties of the apron wrapped around a pencil to make a nice bow. The next morning, when she is thinking about what she must take to class, she can recall the image and mentally unwrap it. The interactive image makes it probable that recalling any item on the list will cue recall of the others.

Stories Another simple mnemonic is the use of **stories** constructed from a list of words to be remembered. In this method, the to-be-learned words in a list are put together in a story such that the to-be-learned words are highlighted. Then, at recall, the story is remembered, and the to-be-remembered words are plucked from the story.

For example, let's suppose a student is expected to remember to bring scissors, a ruler, a compass, a protractor, and a sharp pencil to school. He could construct the following story to help her or him remember these items: "The king drew a *pencil* line with his *ruler* before he cut the line with *scissors*. Then he measured an angle with a *protractor* and marked the point with a *compass*."

The story method is simple but effective. An early study by Bower and Clark (1969) gave experimental subjects in two conditions 12 lists of 10 words each. The subjects in one condition were asked merely to learn the words in each list, as they would be tested over the words at a later point. Subjects in the other condition, however, were asked to construct stories around each list of 10 words. Holding study time equal in the two conditions, Bower and Clark tested for recall after each list was presented and found no difference in recall between the two conditions. When they tested subjects for recall of all 120 words on completion of the entire experiment, however, there was a very large difference indeed: Subjects in the story condition recalled 93% of the words, whereas subjects in the control condition recalled only 13%.

The First-Letter Method A mnemonic that students often use spontaneously is the **first-letter method** (Boltwood & Blick, 1978). This method is similar to the story mnemonic, except that it involves using the first letters of to-be-learned words to construct acronyms, words, or sentences, which then function as the mnemonic. At recall, students recall the word or sentence and then, using it, retrieve the items on the list.

For example, let's suppose a high school student is trying to remember that borax is made of boron, oxygen, and sodium. The student could take the first letter of each component and construct a word, *bos,* as a mnemonic. Then, when she or he attempts to recall the constituents of borax on a test, she or he would remember the word *bos* and generate the constituents from the first letters. Similarly, if we asked you to remember a grocery list consisting of cheese, ham, eggs, radishes, razor blades, and yogurt, the word *cherry* could be constructed from the first letter of each item on the list. Then, when you visit the store, if you remember the mnemonic *cherry,* you should be able to use the letters in the word to reconstruct the items in your list.

As straightforward as first-letter mnemonics might seem, results of experimental research on first-letter mnemonics have been mixed (Boltwood & Blick, 1978). Nonetheless, it remains popular and evaluations of its use in such areas as the teaching of psychology (e.g., Lakin, Giesler, Morris, & Vosmik, 2007; Stalder, 2005) show that students both like first-letter mnemonics and remember more when they are provided (e.g., being given the acronym *CoED* to remember three types of research—Correlational, Experimental, Descriptive—or HOMER for recalling steps in the scientific method—Hypothesize, Operationalize, Measure, Evaluate, and Replicate/Revise/Report). Using variations on the first-letter mnemonic is also a staple of medical education (e.g., remembering the nasal cavity components, Nares [external], Conchae, Meatuses, Nares [internal], and Nasopharynx, by recalling a sentence that mirrors their first letters, "**N**ever **C**all **M**e **N**eedle **N**ose!").

The Keyword Method   Of all the mnemonic techniques, probably the most flexible and powerful is the **keyword method** (Carney & Levin, 2000, 2003; Fontana, Scruggs, & Mastropieri, 2007; Levin, 1993). This method was developed originally to facilitate vocabulary acquisition, but it has many other uses. As in the link method, the method of loci, and the peg method, imagery is critical to the effectiveness of the keyword method, but how imagery is used in the keyword method is quite different.

The keyword mnemonic consists of two separate stages—an acoustic link and an imagery link. In vocabulary learning, for example, the first stage—the acoustic link—requires the identification of a "keyword" that sounds like a part of the to-be-learned vocabulary word. It furnishes the acoustic link necessary to the method. The second stage—the imagery link—requires the learner to imagine a visual image of the keyword interacting with the meaning of the to-be-learned vocabulary word. At the time of recall, the original vocabulary word on a test should evoke the interactive image in memory, allowing for recall of the word's meaning.

An example will clarify these stages. A sixth grader has the assignment of learning 10 vocabulary words in a language arts unit. Among these words is *captivate*. Although our sixth grader has a fine vocabulary, *captivate* is not in it, so she decides to use the keyword method to help remember this word. First, she searches for a keyword within the to-be-learned word and settles on *cap*, which she can readily picture in imagination. She then links her keyword with an image—in this case, her Uncle Bill, who always wears a cap and holds everyone's attention with outrageous stories whenever he visits. So the student's image linked to the word's meaning is of her Uncle Bill captivating her with a story. If all goes well, when she has her test and sees the word *captivate,* she will remember her keyword, *cap,* and remember her image of Uncle Bill and the word's meaning.

The keyword method does not depend on a perfect match of the keyword with the vocabulary word. For example, the word *exiguous* does not contain an easily located keyword. With a little Kentucky windage worked in, however, the keyword *exit* (rather than *exig*) can be selected. Then, if you imagine an extremely tiny exit (ours is in a darkened movie theater with red neon letters spelling out *exit* on a mouse-sized sign above it), you should have a workable interactive image. Next time you see *exiguous,* find the *exig* or *exit* and recall the image of the miniature exit. This should be all you need to remember that *exiguous* means "small" or "meager."

The keyword method was developed originally for the acquisition of foreign-language vocabulary (Atkinson, 1975). Consider, for example, the Spanish word *caballo,* which means "horse." The keyword *ball* can be picked out easily, and an image of a horse balancing on a ball readily comes to mind. Alternatively, the keyword *cab* could be chosen, and the interactive image could be of a horse driving a cab on Chicago's Wabash Avenue.

In the years since Atkinson's early work, a great deal of research has been done on the keyword method. In general, results have been positive among students of all ages (Fontana et al., 2007; Levin, 1986, 1993; Pressley, Levin, & Delaney, 1982) and across several languages (e.g., Atkinson & Raugh, 1975; Pressley, 1977; Wyra, Lawson, & Hungi, 2007). The keyword method has been effective in improving the learning of students with mild retardation and learning disabilities (Mastropieri & Scruggs, 1989; Scruggs & Mastropieri, 2004). The method has also been shown to be valuable for enhancing memory for facts other than vocabulary (Levin, 1993), for increasing learning from text (Mastropieri & Scruggs, 1989), and even for matching artists with their paintings (Carney & Levin, 2000).

Although study after study has shown the benefits of the keyword method, recommendations for its use are typically not part of most teaching-method textbooks. The method is easy to teach and readily learned by even the youngest children, and students generally enjoy using it. Because students generate their own keywords and images, probably the major challenge for teachers is to help students learn to use the keyword method flexibly and apply it to new situations (Levin, 1993).

Summary of Mnemonics Mnemonics are rhymes, sayings, and other procedures designed to make new material memorable. They help generate more elaborate encoding of new materials and strong memory traces. The peg method and the method of loci both depend on a well-learned base to which to-be-learned information is related. The link and story methods put to-be-learned items together in a list and rely on the recall of the overall image or story to facilitate recall. The first-letter mnemonic chains items together by forming a word or acronym from the first letters of the words in a to-be-learned list. The most powerful and flexible mnemonic is the keyword method, which employs interactive imagery to form an acoustic and a visual link.

Encoding More Complex Information

Even though mnemonics have a fairly wide range of applications, their use largely has been limited to learning vocabulary items, related facts, or steps in a skill (although see Carney & Levin, 2000, 2003, for research indicating that higher-order learning can benefit from better lower-order learning enhanced by mnemonics). Many of our instructional goals are broader in scope, such as helping students learn about John Steinbeck's portrayal of human nature, Isaac Newton's laws of physics, or American foreign policy trends in the past 20 years. Cognitive psychologists have given a great deal of thought to how students' encoding of such complex materials can be facilitated and a general consensus has been emerging during the past 2 decades.

In the following sections, we discuss ways students can elaborate on and enrich complex information. Consistent with a key theme of this text, our perspective is that effective learning needs to be active, not receptive. The sheer bulk of information that learners must cope with—whether from texts, media, the Internet, or a teacher's presentation—requires them to focus selectively on what is most important, grasp its meaning, make inferences from main ideas, and represent this information in long-term memory. Of course, meaning may be constructed in many ways. Effective learners use a variety of approaches to organize, enrich, and add to new information. Here, we review three general frameworks and associated methods for improving active learning: activating prior knowledge, guided questioning, and levels of processing.

Activating Prior Knowledge

Activating prior knowledge refers to various methods designed to stimulate students' relevant knowledge in preparation for a learning activity (Pearson, 1984). For instance, before a lesson on internal combustion engines, seventh-grade students can be asked to describe the characteristics of model cars or airplanes, their parents' cars or lawn mowers, and city buses in order to activate relevant concepts and schemata. Similarly, high school students preparing for a unit on the Holocaust can be asked to talk about their own experiences with prejudice, racism, and scapegoating in order to activate relevant schemata. Fourth-grade students, as another example, can be led in a discussion of various animals they have seen in their neighborhood to introduce a lesson on the characteristics of mammals. The central idea underlying knowledge activation is that new learning always builds on prior knowledge. A foundation of well-understood information will help students comprehend new information and will guide their thinking about the new topic.

Methods using prior knowledge activation are based on the assumption that students at any age will have some relevant knowledge to which new information can be related. For example, a class of fourth graders we know, for example, began to learn about heat conduction and the relationship of density to heat conductivity by first thinking of examples of objects that carry heat (e.g., the handle of a metal frying pan, the outside-facing wall of a room on a cold day, and the end of a burning match). The students then performed a simple experiment in which several rods of the same length and diameter, but made of different materials (e.g., iron, glass, and wood) were put into a flame. The students then discussed why some rods rapidly became warm, while others seemed to remain cool, and related the results of the experiment to their own experiences. One girl camped out frequently and knew that a metal frying pan over a fire very quickly would become too hot to touch, while even a burning stick would remain comfortable to the touch at the nonburning end. One boy noted how his metal cup filled with hot chocolate would burn his lips, but the same hot chocolate in a ceramic cup would not.

With their schemata for "heat conduction" presumably activated, the students weighed the various rods on a balance and recorded the masses, noting next to each whether it had become hot rapidly or slowly. Then, the students were asked to guess why some of the rods conducted heat more readily than others. Finally, the teacher helped them summarize what they had learned about density, heat conduction, and the relationship of the two.

The relationship of density to heat conduction is, of course, a fairly sophisticated concept that many adults do not clearly understand. By carefully activating her students' prior knowledge, the teacher in our example was able to help her students learn and remember a difficult concept.

Prior knowledge activation is a general procedure for enhancing students' encoding of new information by connecting it to what they already know. It can involve having students describe examples from their experiences, perform experiments, review previous learning, or use the context in which new material is presented. Overall, any teaching procedure that helps students form conceptual bridges from what they already know to what they are to learn involves some form of knowledge activation.

Guided Questioning

Asking and answering questions about a text or teacher-presented information can greatly improve comprehension, especially when those questions prompt students to think about and discuss material in specific ways, such as comparing and contrasting, inferring cause and effect, evaluating ideas, explaining, and justifying (King, 1994, 2007; King, Staffieri, & Adelgais, 1998; McNamara, 2004; McNamara, O'Reilly, Rowe, Boonthum, & Levinstein, 2007; Rosenshine, Meister, & Chapman, 1996). Comprehension presumably improves because asking and answering such questions helps learners build elaborated and integrated links among the ideas in the materials, making their mental representations more durable and providing more cues for recall. In research by King and her associates (King, 1994; King & Rosenshine, 1993), for example, students were taught a procedure called **guided peer questioning.** Working in pairs, students were trained both to ask and answer specific thought-provoking questions on the material to be learned (e.g., "What causes . . .?", "What could happen if . . .", and "How does . . . tie in with what we learned before?"). When they used this procedure, their learning was significantly enhanced.

As King et al. (1998, p. 135) have pointed out, this approach to structuring peer interaction is successful because it "ensures that partners carry out specific cognitive activities known to promote learning, such as rehearsing orally, accessing prior knowledge, making connections among ideas, elaborating ideas, assessing accuracy of responses, and monitoring metacognitively." In general, guided questioning is seen as prompting the inferences and self-explanations that help learners make connections both within and beyond the text (King, 2007). The goal is deep comprehension based on an integrated, coherent mental representation that not only includes the text information but also its relationships to the world outside.

Levels of Processing

A third general framework for thinking about how encoding activities influence memory was developed by Craik and Lockhart. In a paper that has been cited literally thousands of times since its publication, Craik and Lockhart (1972) proposed a constructivist view of learning, arguing that memory depends on what learners do as they encode new information.

In their **levels of processing** view, memory for new information is seen as a by-product of the perceptual and cognitive analyses learners perform on incoming information. On the one hand, if the semantic base or meaning of the new information is the focus of processing, then the information will be stored in a semantic memory code and will be well-remembered. On the other hand, if only superficial or surface aspects of the new information are analyzed, the information will be less well-remembered. In Craik and Lockhart's terms, memory depends on *depth* of processing. *Deep processing* is seen as that processing centered on meaning. *Shallow processing* refers to keying on superficial aspects of new material.

These two levels of processing may be seen in two common classroom assignments. In the first, students are asked to find and underline a set of vocabulary words in a brief essay. In the second, students are asked to read the same essay and be prepared to tell the class about it in their own words. If the students follow directions, the first assignment is a clear example of shallow processing; all they have to do is find the words in the essay and underline them. They do not have to think about the meaning of the essay and perhaps not even the meaning of the words. Not surprisingly, if we tested these students for their understanding of the contents of the essay, the odds are they would remember relatively little.

In contrast, if the students asked to explain the essay to their classmates followed instructions, we would likely see a very different outcome. Putting an essay into one's own words requires thinking about the meaning of the content and carefully analyzing and comprehending the material. If we were to surprise these students with a test measuring their understanding of the essay, they almost certainly would remember far more of its contents than the group that underlined vocabulary words.

The two assignments described above might be given for different instructional purposes. In fact, the vocabulary word group might remember more vocabulary words (but probably not their meanings) than the group asked to read and explain the materials. In this instance, students' recall would fit with the type of processing in which they engaged, a topic we examine in more detail a bit later. In any event, students in the underlining group engaged in an activity almost guaranteed not to result in memory for the essay.

Another example of levels of processing can be seen in an *incidental learning paradigm*— where individuals are not directed to learn material but in which their memory for that material is checked unexpectedly. Suppose that one group of students is asked to count the number of *i*'s in a list of words (e.g., "festive," "colic," and "delight"), and another group is asked to rate the pleasantness of the same words on a scale of 1 to 5. If, after both groups finish their tasks, we give them a surprise quiz and ask them to recall as many words on the list as possible, the probability is high that the group that rated the pleasantness of the words will recall more than the group that counted the number of *i*'s. The reason for this difference in performance is quite simple: Rating the pleasantness of words requires students to think about the words' *meanings,* requiring deep processing. In contrast, counting the number of *i*'s merely requires a superficial analysis (see Hyde & Jenkins, 1969).

The levels-of-processing framework is intuitively appealing and has led to a great deal of research emphasizing educationally relevant applications (see Andre, 1987b, for an extensive review). The "levels" position, however, has been criticized on the grounds of not having an independent measure of "depth" and the apparent circularity of its depth formulation (Baddeley, 1978; Loftus, Green, & Smith, 1980); that is, saying that something is well remembered because it was deeply processed doesn't really tell us how we can ensure deep processing in students.

In response to these criticisms, Craik and his associates developed two variants of their original "levels" perspective: distinctiveness of encoding (Jacoby & Craik, 1979; Jacoby, Craik, & Begg, 1979) and elaboration of encoding (e.g., Craik & Tulving, 1975). By the late 1980s, the elaboration position clearly was dominant (see Walker, 1986, for a critical discussion), but both are useful in considering the applications of the levels framework. We examine each of these positions next, as well as an alternative position offered by Bransford and his associates.

Distinctiveness of Encoding   The **distinctiveness of encoding** position states that the memorability of information is determined, at least in part, by its distinctiveness (Craik, 2002; Jacoby & Craik, 1979; Jacoby et al., 1979). In a series of experiments in which distinctiveness was defined by the difficulty of decisions required of students during various learning episodes, with more difficult decisions equated with more distinctive encoding, Jacoby et al. (1979) found that materials requiring more difficult decisions at the time of encoding were better recalled than materials requiring less difficult decisions.

The experiments conducted by Jacoby et al. (1979) led to a series of studies focusing on distinctiveness of encoding in reading and mastering various learning tasks (Benton, Glover, Monkowski, & Shaughnessy, 1983; Glover, Bruning, & Plake, 1982; Glover, Plake, & Zimmer, 1982). These studies were designed to determine how students' decision making during reading affected recall and to examine the possibility that an independent means of specifying depth of processing (or, in this case, distinctiveness) could be developed. In general, requiring students to make decisions about what they read leads to greater recall than when decisions are not required. Also, when students were asked to make more difficult decisions, they recalled more than if their decisions were easier. In other words, as students make more complex and difficult decisions during encoding, they remember the content better.

Elaboration of Processing   The **elaboration of processing** perspective was outlined first by Craik and Tulving (1975) and specified further by Anderson and Reder (1979), Anderson (1983a), and Walker (1986). Anderson and Reder described elaboration of processing as follows:

> The basic idea is that a memory episode is encoded as a set of propositions. This set can vary in its richness and redundancy. At the time of recall, only a subset of these propositions will be activated. The richer the original set, the richer will be the subset. Memory for any particular proposition will depend on the subjects' ability to reconstruct it from those propositions that are active. This ability will in turn depend on the richness of the original set and hence the amount of elaboration made at study. (Anderson & Reder, 1979, p. 388)

Considerable research has been performed on the acquisition of educationally relevant material, showing generally that as the elaborateness of students' encoding of information increases, so does their memory for the content (see McDaniel & Einstein, 1989, for a review). Elaborate processing is not merely reprocessing the same information, but rather encoding the same content in different but related ways. For example, in an explanation of how to solve a specific type of problem, students are more likely to remember the explanation if different examples are given than if the same example merely is restated. Similarly, when students read about a famous person, their ability to recall information about that person is strongly related to the number of details provided (Dinnel & Glover, 1985).

Transfer-Appropriate Processing   Morris, Bransford, and Franks (1977) reacted to the original levels perspective by offering an alternative. In their view, differences in memory are the result of what is contained in various semantic memory codes and whether what is encoded matches or can be transferred to the retrieval context (see Roediger, Gallo, & Geraci, 2002, and Lockhart, 2002, for commentaries on transfer-appropriate processing). From a transfer-appropriate processing perspective, for example, shallow processing does not lead to the encoding of the image of the letter *i* if people are seeking the number of *i*'s in a passage. Instead, a semantic memory is produced (e.g., "forty-three *i*'s were in the passage"), but one that does *not* contain information about the meaning of the content. In Morris et al.'s view, deep processing differs from shallow processing primarily because the semantic memories formed in deep processing contain the meaning of the content that students encounter (e.g., the main idea in a paragraph).

Transfer-appropriate processing is an interesting alternative to the original levels perspective, and it seems clear that students' memories for to-be-learned information almost inevitably are semantic. For instance, in the example we first used to show the difference between deep and shallow processing, one group of students read to find key words and another group read to be able to explain the contents of the material. In the original levels perspective, differences in memory performance between these two groups are a result of different kinds of memory codes brought about by different levels of analysis. In contrast, transfer-appropriate processing holds that both groups of children form semantic memory codes. The differences in memory are a result of the contents of those memories; the vocabulary group's codes likely would contain little more than some of the words, whereas the "explanation" group's codes would contain information about the topic of the reading passage.

Summary of Encoding Processes

In this and the previous sections, we reviewed several frameworks for encoding simple and more complex information. Rehearsing, categorizing, and using special mnemonic techniques are helpful ways to encode new information that is important but not yet particularly meaningful. As you have seen, most mnemonics rely on distinctive visual images or auditory processes. We also considered the encoding of more complex information. Much of the research conducted in this area is related to the theoretical frameworks of prior knowledge activation and levels of processing. Both of these strongly emphasize the importance of what students *do* while encoding information. To the extent that students are helped to use their prior knowledge and required to deal with the meaning of content, their memories improve. Tasks focusing on superficial or surface aspects of to-be-learned materials are unlikely to result in understanding or long-term recall.

Our discussion suggests a variety of ways to encode information at deeper levels. One is to relate new information to background knowledge at the time of encoding, another is to ask and answer questions relating to meaning, a third is to increase its distinctiveness and elaborate its meaning as much as possible. Also, we should keep in mind that techniques such as rehearsing information and creating images, although most often researched and discussed earlier in connection with simpler forms of learning, also are applicable for more complex forms of learning. Rehearsal is needed to make processing more automatic and to build stable memories for new vocabulary and concepts. Similarly, the ability to generate images can aid in the comprehension of text materials (e.g., Sadoski, Goetz, & Rodriguez, 2000).

In the next section, we turn our attention specifically to the roles learners themselves play in managing their encoding, storage, and retrieval. As we have seen, what learners do as they encode information is very important to their understanding and recall. The question we now address is how to help them learn to guide their own cognitive processing effectively. The starting point is for learners to become aware of their own strengths and weaknesses as learners. The goal is for learners to have the conditional knowledge required to use powerful encoding strategies when needed in any learning situation. Both of these abilities fall under the general framework of metacognition—the knowledge that people have about their own thought processes and how to manage them effectively.

Metacognition: Thinking About Thinking

Metacognition refers to knowledge people have about their own thought processes. A teacher who knows she does not remember names well, for example, and has her new students wear nametags for several days, is showing metacognitive knowledge about her memory. Similarly, a student is revealing his metacognition when he listens to a teacher's explanation of how to solve a problem and takes notes only on those points he thinks will be difficult. Still another example is a student asking a teacher whether an upcoming test will be essay or multiple-choice. Each example shows the person's awareness of her or his own cognition and either shows or hints at a strategy for managing learning based on this awareness.

Since the concept was first introduced some 40 years ago, metacognition has been viewed as an essential component of skilled learning because it allows students to control a host of other cognitive skills. In a way, metacognition is like the "mission control" of the cognitive system. It enables students to coordinate the use of extensive knowledge and many separate strategies to accomplish learning goals, just as a real mission control coordinates the many operations necessary for a successful space flight. This does not imply a single place in our minds where metacognition takes place; rather, we simply want to suggest that metacognition is a part of our cognition that controls other cognitive functions, such as perception and attention.

One of the clearest descriptions of metacognition has been that of Ann Brown (1980, 1987). In her view, metacognition includes two related dimensions: *knowledge of cognition* and *regulation of cognition*. The former refers to what we know about our memory and thought processes; the latter refers to how we regulate them. **Knowledge of cognition** usually is assumed to include three components (Brown, 1987; Jacobs & Paris, 1987). The first involves *declarative* knowledge about ourselves as learners and knowing what factors influence our performance. For example, most adult learners know the limitations of their memory and can plan accordingly for a task based on this knowledge. The second component is *procedural*, knowledge about cognitive strategies. For instance, most older students possess a basic repertoire of useful reading comprehension strategies, such as taking notes, slowing down for important information, skimming unimportant information, using imagery, summarizing main ideas, and using periodic self-testing. The third component is *conditional* knowledge, knowing when or why to use a strategy. One example of this kind of conditional knowledge would be studying differently for essay versus multiple-choice tests; another would be "overrehearsing" the key points that you want to make in a talk, because you realize you may be a bit nervous and distracted.

Ann Brown argued that knowledge of cognition is usually statable and late developing. Research suggests that these assumptions are reasonable when considering the metacognitive activity of older students but probably not for preadolescents (Flavell, 1992; Garner & Alexander,

1989). For example, research by Paris and colleagues (Paris, Cross, & Lipson, 1984; Paris & Jacobs, 1984) found that instructional training programs enhance the development and use of metacognitive knowledge among elementary-age children, who ordinarily cannot recognize and describe their metacognitive abilities. Studies comparing expert performance among adults, however, are consistent with Brown's assumptions (cf. Glaser & Chi, 1988).

Regulation of cognition also typically is seen as including three components: planning, regulation, and evaluation (Jacobs & Paris, 1987; Kluwe, 1987). *Planning* involves selecting appropriate strategies and allocating resources. Planning frequently includes setting goals, activating relevant background knowledge, and budgeting time. *Regulation* involves monitoring and self-testing skills necessary to control learning. Making predictions, pausing while reading, sequencing activities, and selecting appropriate repair strategies also belong in the category. *Evaluation* involves appraising both the self-regulation processes and the products of one's learning. Typical examples are reevaluating one's goals, revising predictions, and consolidating intellectual gains.

Brown has contended that regulation of cognition, unlike knowledge of cognition, often is not conscious in many learning situations. One reason is that many of these processes are highly automated, at least in adults. A second reason is that some of these processes have developed without any conscious reflection and therefore are difficult to report to others. In addition, Brown has drawn an important distinction about the relationship of age to metacognitive regulation and abstract reflection, arguing that regulatory mechanisms, such as planning, are independent of age, whereas reflection is not (Brown, 1987). Thus, like metacognitive knowledge, conscious use of regulatory processes may be more limited by one's ability to reflect than one's ability to regulate.

Research on Metacognitive Processes

A wealth of research on metacognition and on instructional practices aimed at developing metacognitive strategies has been conducted since the mid-1970s (e.g., see Block & Pressley, 2002; Boekaerts, Pintrich, & Zeidner, 2000; Fuchs & Fuchs, 2007; Graesser, 2007; Harris & Graham, 1996; Harris, Graham, & Deshler, 1998; Kendeou, van den Broek, White, & Lynch, 2007; Pressley & Harris, 2006; Zito, Adkins, Gavins, Harris, & Graham, 2007). A number of important findings have appeared. One is that metacognition is late developing. In a variety of studies, children between kindergarten and sixth grade consistently show an inability to monitor their comprehension accurately and, just as important, to describe their own cognition (Baker, 2002). Even skilled readers often are unable to see inconsistencies in text materials (Markman, 1979), especially if pieces of inconsistent information are not adjacent to each other (Oakhill, Hartt, & Samols, 2005). Older students and adults, however, are better able to describe their own cognitive processes.

Recognizing the need to remember information also develops slowly throughout childhood (Pressley & Schneider, 1997; Schneider & Pressley, 1997). While preschoolers may have to be told to remember certain things, older children have learned that some information is likely to be important to recall (e.g., directions for where to meet a friend and tips for assembling a bicycle). By the time students reach high school, most know a great deal about what should be remembered and are very selective about what they will and will not try to remember. Developmental trends also are seen in the ability to assess the difficulty of various memory tasks.

As adults, we understand that the sheer amount of material to be remembered makes a difference. For instance, we know that learning 1 telephone number is far less demanding than committing 10 new telephone numbers to memory. Similarly, we know that learning 5 new psychological terms will take less effort than learning 30. In contrast with adults and older children, younger children typically have only a rudimentary knowledge of the factors influencing task difficulty. Their diagnostic skills are immature and develop slowly (Alexander et al., 1995; Pressley & Schneider, 1997). Teachers still can make an important difference in children's diagnostic skills by providing instruction in how to make estimates of task difficulty, prompting children to make such estimates, and providing practice in making diagnoses.

Monitoring skills also improve as children mature (Butler & Winne, 1995). These changes presumably reflect important differences in *how* one monitors, as well as increased knowledge about *what* to monitor. This is not to say that adults are skilled monitors or have conscious access to metacognitive knowledge. Even college students have much difficulty monitoring their performance prior to a test (Schraw & Dennison, 1994). Although college students are better able to monitor their test performance during or after the test, it still is far from perfect (see Chapter 11).

The reason for poor monitoring among adults is becoming increasingly clear. Monitoring accuracy appears to be related to two dimensions of performance: *task difficulty* and *prior knowledge*. When a task is difficult, students are more likely to be overconfident in their performance (Schraw & Roedel, 1994). Although you might expect monitoring accuracy to improve as prior knowledge increases, the opposite appears to be true. Glenberg and Epstein (1987) found that music majors monitored their performance more poorly after reading a passage about music than one about physics. A subsequent study by Morris (1990) clarified this relationship further. Prior knowledge aids performance, but it does not contribute to more accurate monitoring. Thus, older students monitor accurately when they possess enough knowledge to perform well; in turn, performing well reduces overconfidence.

Metacognitive monitoring also appears to be unrelated to aptitude. For example, Pressley and Ghatala (1988) found that college students of different verbal ability levels monitored with similar accuracy. Swanson (1990) reported that metacognitive knowledge as measured on a verbal self-report interview was not limited by intellectual aptitude. On the contrary, metacognitive awareness sometimes compensated for lower levels of ability in that low-aptitude/high-metacognitive-knowledge students outperformed high-aptitude/low-metacognitive-knowledge students with respect to the number of moves necessary to solve pendulum and fluid combination problems. Overall, low-aptitude/high-metacognition students required 50% fewer moves. These students also used fewer domain-specific problem-solving strategies than high-aptitude/high-metacognition students, suggesting that domain-specific knowledge alone could not account for the low-aptitude/high-metacognition group's performance.

Many instructional studies suggest that metacognition can be improved by direct instruction and modeling of metacognitive activities. For example, Paris and colleagues' *Informal Strategies for Learning Program* (ISLP; Paris et al., 1984; see also Jacobs & Paris, 1987) is designed to help children learn about and use metacognitive reading strategies in several ways. Gains during an academic school year were particularly impressive with respect to reading awareness and evaluating the effectiveness of reading strategies.

Delclos and Harrington (1991) examined fifth and sixth graders' ability to solve computer problems after assignment to one of three conditions. The first group received specific problem-solving training, the second group received problem-solving plus self-monitoring training, and the third group received no training. The self-monitoring problem-solving group solved more of the difficult problems than either of the other groups and took less time to do so.

These studies suggest several general conclusions about metacognition. First, younger students may have only a limited amount of metacognitive knowledge at their disposal. This knowledge improves performance; moreover, metacognitive knowledge appears to be trainable even in younger students. Second, aptitude and knowledge constrain metacognitive knowledge far less than one might expect. Thus, rather than reserve metacognitive training for more advanced students, teachers should make a special effort to provide training to students who appear to lack it, regardless of relative achievement level. Third, evidence suggests that metacognitive awareness can compensate for low ability and insufficient knowledge. Developing metacognitive skills should be particularly helpful for students attempting to learn unfamiliar content.

Research on Strategy Instruction

Research clearly shows that the strategic use of knowledge, rather than merely having it, improves learning. Using strategies not only produces learning gains but also empowers students psychologically by increasing their self-efficacy (see Chapter 6). Pressley and Wharton-McDonald (1997) suggest that strategy instruction is needed before, during, and after the main learning episode. Strategies that occur before learning include *setting goals* and *determining how much information to learn, how new information relates to prior knowledge,* and *how the new information will be used.* Strategies needed during learning include *identifying important information, predicting, monitoring, analyzing,* and *interpreting.* Strategies typically used after learning include *reviewing, organizing,* and *reflecting.* Good strategy users should possess some degree of competence in each of these areas to be truly self-regulated.

Educational researchers have been studying strategy instruction for more than 25 years. Analyses of this research (e.g., Hattie, Biggs, & Purdie, 1996; Pressley & Harris, 2006; and Rosenshine et al., 1996) generally support the following claims.

- *Strategy instruction is typically moderately to highly successful, regardless of the strategy or instructional method.* This means that students usually benefit from strategy instruction, whether on single strategies or combinations of strategies. Strategy instruction appears to be most beneficial for younger students, as well as for low-achieving students of all ages. One reason may be that younger and lower-achieving students know fewer strategies and therefore have far more room for improvement.
- *Programs that combine several interrelated strategies are more effective than single-strategy programs* (Hattie et al., 1996; see also Pressley & Harris, 2006). One reason may be that no single strategy is enough to bring about a substantial change in learning, because most learning is typically complex. A repertoire of four or five strategies that can be used flexibly, however, can be quite effective. Interested readers are referred to Pressley and Harris (2006) and to R. Brown and her colleagues (Brown, 2008; Brown, Pressley, Van Meter, & Schuder, 1996) for detailed descriptions of a successful multi-strategy program, *Transactional Strategies Instruction,* developed by Pressley and his associates.

- *Strategy instruction programs that emphasize the role of conditional knowledge are especially effective.* One explanation is that conditional knowledge enables students to determine when and where to use the newly acquired strategy.
- *Newly acquired strategies do not readily transfer to new tasks or unfamiliar domains.* We often overestimate our students' abilities to use strategies in new situations. It is almost always a good idea to teach specifically for transfer of strategies (Pressley & Harris, 2006). Two ways of accomplishing this are to help students make the link between strategies and their application (Duffy, 2002) and have them practice applying strategies in a variety of settings (Mayer & Wittrock, 2006). Research also indicates that the more automatic a strategy, the more likely it is to transfer (Cox, 1997).

Another question of interest is what kinds of strategies are most important to teach. Hattie et al. (1996) compared rank orderings for approximately 25 learning strategies across three cultures (Japanese, Japanese–Australian, and Australian). Results indicated that a handful of general learning strategies were rated as most important among all cultures. These included, in order of importance, self-checking, creating a productive physical environment, goal setting and planning, reviewing and organizing information after learning, summarizing during learning, seeking teacher assistance, and seeking peer assistance. Not surprisingly, most of the commonly used strategy instruction programs incorporate these skills (see Pressley & Harris, 2006, and Pressley & Wharton-McDonald, 1997, for excellent reviews of strategy instruction and summaries of programs).

Becoming a Good Strategy User

Interest in metacognition and its relationship to strategies soon gave rise to the concept of a good strategy user. What might such a student look like? Pressley, Borkowski, and Schneider (1987) suggested five criteria: (1) a broad repertoire of strategies; (2) metacognitive knowledge about why, when, and where to use strategies; (3) a broad knowledge base; (4) ability to ignore distractions; and (5) automaticity in the four components described above.

Regarding the first of these five criteria, Pressley et al. distinguished between two types of strategies. The first of these is a *domain-specific strategy* (e.g., applying the quadratic formula), which is of little or no use outside that domain. A second type of strategy is a *higher-order strategy,* which is used to control other strategies. One example is how a skilled reader sequences strategies while reading—perhaps skimming before beginning to read, then selectively attending to important information, then monitoring, and finally reviewing. Having knowledge about how to orchestrate related strategies enables good strategy users to regulate their learning efficiently.

The second criterion described by Pressley et al. emphasizes a key theme of our text—that cognitive ability is enhanced by self-awareness and the ability to self-regulate. As has been shown, knowing *how* to do something is of little practical good if you do not have the conditional knowledge of knowing *when* or *where* to use it. For example, you can study for a test for several hours and still do poorly if you do not focus on the information that appears on the test. Being able to size up a test in advance, to determine what it will include and how you can best prepare, illustrates nicely the value of conditional knowledge.

By this point, we hope that we also have convinced you that the third criterion—*a broad knowledge base*—is one of the most important components of learning. Pressley et al. have argued that encoding and representing new information in memory without some prior knowledge as an anchor makes efficient learning almost impossible. But prior knowledge also is important because it promotes strategy use and, at times, compensates for lack of strategies. For example, elementary-age children have been found to learn categorizable lists without using strategies because of their ability to activate knowledge about the category (e.g., *kitchen utensils* include *spoons, forks,* and *knives*).

The fourth criterion of a good strategy user is what Pressley et al. refer to as *action control*. This means that students are able to motivate themselves, tune out distractions, and correctly attribute their progress to effort rather than to ability (see Chapter 7). Even very young children show signs of controlling their learning and directing their attention (Alexander et al., 1995), although there is steady improvement into early adulthood.

The fifth criterion is that good strategy users accomplish all of these things *automatically*. As shown in Chapter 2, automaticity depends heavily on practice and is the ability to activate knowledge or perform a task with minimum drain on our limited processing resources. Becoming automatic is essential to good strategy use because, without it, we are unable to allocate our resources to higher levels of learning. In fact, nonautomated students allocate many of their resources to trying to select and manage strategies, in addition to such basic cognitive tasks as perception, attention, and accessing information from long-term memory. In contrast, good strategy users accomplish these basic tasks with much less cognitive load, freeing up valuable resources for constructing meaning and overseeing their learning.

Assessment and Encoding

A recurring theme of this chapter is that encoding activities strongly affect what is learned and remembered. As we review the chapter's content, we see two major dimensions of this theme that connect to assessment-related decisions, whether in the classroom or in selecting measures used to satisfy external demands for information.

The first of these is the levels-of-processing framework, which clearly points to the benefits of deep processing. Although deep processing is often effortful, the student's learning outcomes are typically exactly what we seek—deep understanding and ability to use knowledge flexibly. Presumably we want our assessments to fit within a framework supporting deep learning and leading to such outcomes as understanding, analysis, application, and evaluation. The importance of these was anticipated many years ago by Bloom, Englehart, Furst, Hill, and Krathwohl's (1956) *Taxonomy of Educational Objectives* and Gagne's (1965) hierarchical framework of learning goals. What is different now is modern cognitive psychology's conceptions of learning and assessment and their relationship. Instead of targeting highly sequenced, hierarchical bits of knowledge with objective tests, modern cognitive approaches generally promote a much more holistic view in which assessment is central to teaching and learning (Shepard, 2000, 2005). In this perspective, the ideal is ongoing, dynamic assessment closely tied to student learning, with assessments designed with special attention to what students already know, to enhancing student–teacher interactions, and to providing rich feedback.

A second encoding dimension of encoding with significant implications for assessment is the growing emphasis on learning strategies. Whereas content-related outcomes were once viewed as the primary if not only valid goal for instruction, learning strategies are now increasingly seen as important in their own right. McNamara et al. (2007) point, for example, to the recent inclusion of reading strategies in the College Board's Reading Comprehension Standards as evidence of strategies' growing importance. Extensive research showing strategies' applicability to many learners (e.g., disabled learners, college students) and content areas (e.g., writing, math) gives further indication of their value.

In our view, the upshot of an emphasis on strategies is that assessment—like instruction itself—increasingly should target strategic as well as content-related outcomes. Assessment is expanding to include such areas as ability to set learning goals, make connections to relevant information, find and organize information, interact effectively with others, and control study time and effort. In this same vein, it should be noted that computer-based environments increasingly are being seen as tools for developing strategic skills (e.g., Azevedo, 2005; McNamara et al., 2007), based on the possibility for prompting, assessing, and giving feedback on a variety of student activities and decisions.

Currently, teachers and researchers wishing to assess learning strategies often rely on self-report scales measuring general study-related metacognitive and strategic variables. Among the most widely used are Pintrich and associates' *Motivated Strategies for Learning Questionnaire* (MSLQ, see Duncan & McKeachie, 2005), Schraw and Dennison's *Metacognitive Awareness Inventory* (MAI, see Schraw & Dennison, 1994), and *Weinstein's Learning and Study Strategies Inventory* (LASSI, see Weinstein, 1996). All have been used extensively in research and in the classroom. They tap a variety of motivational and strategic dimensions, including categories of student thoughts, attitudes, and beliefs shown to relate to successful learning and behaviors such as use of rehearsal, elaboration and organizational techniques, general self-regulation, and even help-seeking.

Implications for Instruction

Encoding is more than simply the starting point of learning. As you have seen, how information is encoded determines what it means to learners, whether it can be recalled when needed, and how useful it will be. The following guidelines offer suggestions for encoding information in ways that help make learning more productive.

1. *Match encoding strategies with the material to be learned.* This chapter describes many strategies for encoding both simple and more complex information. Students should match their strategies to the materials, goals of learning, and types of evaluation as much as possible. For example, learning a list of five recent American presidents for a recognition test is a much different learning goal for students than using this knowledge in an essay contrasting the presidents' relative emphases on foreign and domestic policy.

Our goal should be to help students be as *strategic* and *flexible* as possible when encoding information. Sometimes this means using maintenance rehearsal rather than deep processing, although usually it means the opposite. Encouraging content-appropriate processing should be a goal of every teacher. Of course, to do so successfully requires students to possess a repertoire of strategies, as well as the metacognitive knowledge to use them.

2. *Encourage students to engage in deeper processing.* The deeper students' processing, the better their understanding and memory. One way students can process information more deeply is to make connections to their prior knowledge and the learning context. Encouraging affective responses is another way to promote deeper processing. A third way—having students answer questions about to-be-learned information or generating questions themselves—clearly facilitates inferential processing of that information.

3. *Use instructional strategies that promote elaboration.* Teachers can do much in the classroom to promote elaborative encoding. Most important is that teachers encourage students to give meaning to what they are learning in terms of their own knowledge, goals, and uses of information. Making students more active in this way and helping them take responsibility for their learning will do more than anything else to improve learning.

One structured technique for teachers to use is *prior knowledge activation,* which refers to finding ways of activating what students already know—such as preteaching, class discussions, brainstorming, and clarifying salient concepts. Another method is to encourage students to categorize and organize new information. A third method is to promote knowledge construction through cooperative social practices. This topic is discussed in detail in Chapter 9.

4. *Help students become more metacognitively aware.* Having declarative and procedural knowledge is only part of effective learning; knowing one's own cognitive strengths and weaknesses and using knowledge strategically are equally important. Educational psychologists have been intensely interested in metacognition since it became evident that good learners are knowledgeable about their own thinking and memory and use this information to regulate their learning. Their knowledge includes the *how, why,* and *when* of learning. Teachers should make a special effort to model their own conditional knowledge for their students. A second component is regulation of cognition. Students need to learn basic regulatory skills such as planning and monitoring and, most important, how to coordinate them.

The first step is to make students aware that metacognition is vital to good learning. Metacognitive skills should be taught and discussed in every classroom (Brown, 2008; Pressley & Harris, 2006; Pressley & Schneider, 1997). These discussions should be between students and other students, as well as teachers. Peer tutoring or small cooperative learning groups are especially effective methods for sharing and developing metacognitive knowledge and strategies (see Chapters 6 and 9).

The second step is acquiring some level of basic automaticity with metacognitive skills. One way to do so is to use monitoring checklists in which students check off component steps in monitoring one's learning (Schraw, 1998). The following checklist provides an example:

1. What is the purpose for learning this information?
2. Do I know anything about this topic?
3. Do I know strategies that will help me learn?
4. Am I understanding as I proceed?
5. How should I correct errors?
6. Have I accomplished the goals I set for myself?

Studies that have used checklists and related methods such as cue cards report favorable findings (King, 1994; King et al., 1998), especially when students are learning difficult material. We recommend that a variety of prompts for using strategies be used consistently until students become automatic at using them.

5. *Make strategy instruction a priority.* We recommend that teachers target age-appropriate strategies at each grade by thinking about their most and least successful students. Successful students likely rely on strategies that struggling students do not use. Incorporating these strategies into your instruction will, no doubt, enhance the ability of all your students to learn more effectively.

Helping your students become good strategy users demands a fair amount of dedication and diligence. For students to use strategies independently and capably requires that they not only use strategies well and automatically but also believe in their value and know when and where to apply them. The instructional sequence that follows, which aims at these goals, draws heavily on strategy research by Palincsar and Brown (1984), Pressley and his associates (Brown, 2008; Brown et al., 1996; Block & Pressley, 2002), Poplin (1998), and Harris and Graham (e.g., Graham, 2006; Harris et al., 1998; Pressley & Harris, 2006) in addressing these issues. Much, if not most, of this instruction can occur as students work in groups (O'Donnell, 2006), with members using the strategies to construct meaning jointly.

STEP 1. *Discuss and explain the value of strategies.* Students should understand why they are being asked to learn strategies, what instruction will be like, and how they will use the strategies. In addition to understanding the obvious benefits for learning, students need to know that strategies can help them overcome lack of prior knowledge and domain-specific ability. Another reason is that strategies positively affect their self-confidence and expectations (see Chapters 7 and 8).

STEP 2. *Introduce one or at most a very few strategies at a time.* Students can be overwhelmed easily. The best chance of teaching students strategies that are useful to them is to limit their number to perhaps two or three (e.g., summarization, creating mental images, and generating questions) over a several-week period of instruction. A single strategy can usually be taught in 10 hours or less, including time to practice applying it (Pressley & Woloshyn, 1995), but students need the time and opportunity to use it in a variety of situations before the strategy is really "theirs" and they can use it flexibly.

STEP 3. *Continue practice over an extended period.* Teachers should plan on 6 to 10 weeks for instruction, modeling, and practice of a new strategy. Effective strategy instruction occurs throughout the school year; ideally, it should even continue across school years (Pressley & Woloshyn, 1995). Periodic follow-ups also are helpful to ensure that the strategy has been maintained.

STEP 4. *Explain and model strategies extensively.* Even when students understand why they are learning a strategy and how to use it, they need to see strategy use modeled by a teacher or another expert. Modeling should include at least two components: (1) how the strategy is used in a variety of settings to accomplish different learning objectives and (2) when and why the teacher uses the strategy. The former will convey declarative and procedural knowledge to the student; the latter conveys conditional knowledge. Of course, teachers are not the only models for using strategies. Students also should be coached to model strategy use for each other—for example, thinking aloud as they read or prepare to write.

STEP 5. *Provide feedback to students about strategies* (Butler & Winne, 1995). One way for teachers to share their expertise with students is to provide feedback on which strategy works best for which task. Feedback helps students apply the strategy in the best way and evaluate its effectiveness, that is, whether it has improved performance or increased efficiency.

6. *Look for opportunities to help students transfer strategies.* A common failing of strategy instruction is that students do not use strategies they've learned in new settings. Among ways to combat this problem are teachers' modeling flexible strategy use, thinking aloud as they do (Duffy, 2002), and providing opportunities for students to practice strategies across the curriculum (see Mayer & Wittrock, 2006, for a review). In our view, it is better to teach fewer strategies and have students practice using them in every content area than it is to bombard them with new strategies in every class. For older students, of course, this approach will require coordination among different content instructors.

7. *Encourage reflection on strategy use.* Students become metacognitively aware and self-regulated by thinking and talking about their learning. All students, no matter how young, should be encouraged to do so. Older students should be given regular time in school to reflect on using strategies by means of small-group discussion, journals, and essays. Younger students should be helped to understand how older students and adults think about their learning. Careful teacher modeling helps accomplish this goal, along with coaching students to ask questions, use strategies, and express their ideas.

Summary

This chapter focuses on encoding and how effective learners adopt strategies relevant to the kind of information they are learning. Some strategies have been studied extensively in relation to learning simpler kinds of information, such as vocabulary, lists of things, and procedural steps. Others typically are applied to more complex information.

Rehearsal, mediation, mnemonics, and use of imagery are examples of strategies that often are used in acquiring simpler kinds of information. A distinction is made in this chapter between maintenance and elaborative rehearsal. Maintenance rehearsal refers to the recycling of information for brief periods of time to keep it ready for use, such as when a person repeats a telephone number over and over while getting ready to dial. Elaborative rehearsal, in contrast, is the recycling of information in ways that relate it to other, previously learned knowledge. In general, elaborative rehearsal results in superior memory performance, but both types of rehearsal have distinct uses. One form of elaborative rehearsal involves mediation, in which difficult-to-remember items are converted into something more meaningful and easily remembered.

Mnemonics are memory aids designed to help people remember information. They include the peg method, the method of loci, the link method, stories, first-letter mnemonics, and the keyword method. The various mnemonics differ, but all use familiar information to facilitate remembering unfamiliar information. Most use imagery in one form or another. Mnemonics are generally easy to teach, and students enjoy using them. In our view, mnemonics are best seen as adjuncts to regular classroom methods.

This chapter introduced three general frameworks for understanding complex information: prior knowledge activation, guided questioning, and levels of processing. All three of these perspectives hold that what students already know and what they do while encoding determine the quality of what they remember. Activities that focus students on the meaning of to-be-learned information almost always result in better memory performance than activities that center on superficial aspects of to-be-learned materials.

The nature of the materials students encounter also influences memory. Well-organized materials tend to be better recalled than poorly organized ones. In the absence of organization, students impose their own organization on to-be-remembered information. Complex materials are best encoded by using meaning-oriented procedures that help students relate new information to what they know already.

Finally, we considered the role of metacognition in learning and saw that skilled students are aware of their mental processes and have the conditional knowledge to regulate their learning. Metacognitive abilities can help students compensate for low domain knowledge and a limited strategy repertoire.

Metacognition can improve with instruction; an example is teaching students to use learning strategies. We explored what it means to be a good strategy user and how to make strategy instruction more effective. We observed that good strategy users possess more strategies, use them more flexibly, are more automatic, and control their motivation to learn. Because these skills are teachable and improve substantially with practice, all students have the potential to become good strategy users if they are helped to use them consistently.

SUGGESTED READINGS

Pressley, M., & Harris, K. R. (2006). *Cognitive strategies instruction: From basic research to classroom instruction.* In P. A. Alexander & P. H. Winne (Eds.), *Handbook of educational psychology* (2nd ed.) (pp. 265–286). Mahwah, NJ: Erlbaum.
　　This handbook chapter by two leading strategies researchers, Michael Pressley and Karen Harris, contains a comprehensive discussion of strategies instruction and how it can be applied in the classroom.

Siegler, R. S., & Alibali, M. W. (2004). *Children's thinking* (4th ed.). Upper Saddle River, NJ: Prentice Hall.
　　This text, by Robert Siegler and Martha Alibali, includes an excellent discussion of how children's approaches to encoding and remembering become more strategic over time.

CHAPTER

5

Retrieval Processes

In Chapters 3 and 4, we examined the nature of memory, its structure, and the processes involved in encoding. Our focus in this chapter is on retrieval, the process of accessing and placing into consciousness information from long-term memory (see Figure 2.1). Retrieval processes arguably are even more important than those of encoding and storage. As Roediger (2000) has pointed out, the reason for this can be derived from an analogy to perception. Just like the world outside contains an enormous amount of information and we perceive only a small portion, our brains contain vast amounts of encoded and stored information accessible only through the processes of retrieval. Somehow, in retrieval, we sort through our past experience and convert it into conscious experience. As we will see in this chapter, variables such as which cues are present at retrieval and how learners have practiced retrieving information have powerful effects on what is remembered and utilized.

We begin our discussion of retrieval processes by illustrating some common retrieval phenomena through the following story:

Mrs. Thompson has just finished handing out her American history test. Most students begin writing immediately, but Ronald reads the first question and feels a cold shiver run up his spine. Not only can he not remember the answer, but he also cannot even remember that the topic was ever talked about. He gulps and proceeds to the next question.

Laura, in contrast, reads the first question and smiles to herself, remembering a joke Mrs. Thompson told on the day she covered the material. Laura starts to write her answer and finds that the words come easily. For Laura, the question is a perfect cue for remembering.

Aisha, meanwhile, writes part of the answer and then stops. She knows that she knows the rest of the answer, but somehow the words do not come to her. She raises her hand, and Mrs. Thompson drifts over to Aisha's desk. Mrs. Thompson briefly clarifies the question. After hearing just a sentence from her teacher, Aisha has a powerful "aha!" feeling, and she returns to her writing, confident that she can answer Mrs. Thompson's question.

Across the room, Alejandro is having trouble remembering the answers to the test. Finally, he flips the test over and scratches out the outline he used to organize his studying the night before. Then he uses his outline to help him remember what to say. Mrs. Thompson watches Alejandro, bemused because he often seems to provide his own cues for her tests.

The experiences of the four students in Mrs. Thompson's history class were varied, but the probability is high that we have all shared similar ones. Sometimes our retrieval processes seem ineffective and, like Ronald, we draw a blank. At other times, we marvel at our own abilities to retrieve information in great detail. At still other times, we retrieve the information we need only after a struggle.

Research on human memory has focused extensively on understanding encoding and storage, but many important issues related to retrieval are coming to light in recent years. One of these is the phenomenon that has come to be known as encoding specificity.

Encoding Specificity

From our discussion of encoding, you have seen that the organization of material and the context in which it is learned have considerable influence on how well the material is remembered. For years, psychologists have wondered whether this organization is important only at the time of encoding, only at the time of retrieval, or at both times. In an important early study, Tulving and Osler (1968) addressed this question.

Tulving and Osler divided their group of subjects into two conditions. In one condition, the subjects merely were presented a 24-item word list to learn. In the second condition, the subjects received the same word list, but in this instance each of the 24 to-be-learned words (e.g., boy) was paired with a weak associate (e.g., boy–child; a strong associate pair would be boy–girl). Then, when the subjects were tested for their ability to remember the words, the two conditions were divided further. Half of the subjects in both original conditions simply were asked for free recall of the 24 words. The other half also were asked to recall the 24 words, but these subjects were given the 24 weak associates that originally were given only to the subjects in the weak-associates condition. In this way, Tulving and Osler constructed four groups: (1) word list to learn without associates, test without associates; (2) word list to learn without associates, test with associates; (3) word list to learn with associates, test without associates; and (4) word list to learn with associates, test with associates.

Results of the study indicated that the weak associates or cue words facilitated memory performance only when they were available to the subjects *both* at encoding and at retrieval. Having cues present at encoding only or at retrieval only did not enhance memory performance. The conclusion is that cues indeed make a difference in memory performance but only when cues present at encoding are reinstated at retrieval. The phenomenon that Tulving and Osler observed in their experiment is known as **encoding specificity,** and it has become one of the basic principles for understanding memory.

The gist of the encoding specificity principle is that remembering knowledge is enhanced when conditions at retrieval match those present at encoding. We thus can see that it is closely related to the concept of *transfer-appropriate processing*, discussed in Chapter 4. If such a match occurs, contextual cues help individuals perform an efficient search of memory. More often, however, our goal is to broaden the range of cues linked to both encoding and retrieval so that learners can retrieve and use what they know in the widest possible range of situations. When retrieval cues differ substantially from those present at encoding, an efficient search of memory may be impossible. A number of studies have investigated encoding activities designed to create a richer context for retrieval. These studies include research on the *generation effect, elaborative interrogation, guided peer questioning,* and *state-dependent learning.*

The **generation effect** refers to the finding that verbal material self-generated at the time of encoding is better remembered than material that students merely read at encoding (see our discussion of distinctiveness of encoding in Chapter 4). For example, Rabinowitz and Craik (1986) presented subjects with 56 words to learn. Each word in the list was paired with an associated item. Half of the to-be-learned or target words merely were read by the subjects. The remaining target words had letters deleted from them that were replaced with blanks. As the subjects encoded these words, they had to generate the missing letters from memory. At the time of the test, half of the target words subjects read were cued by the original associates; the other half were cued by different words that rhymed with the target words. The target words that students had to generate also were split at the time of testing so that half received the original cue and half got a rhyming cue.

Results were striking. As Rabinowitz and Craik had predicted from the generation effect literature (see Jacoby, 1978; McElroy & Slamecka, 1982; Slamecka & Graf, 1978; Slamecka & Katsaiti, 1987), a large generation effect was observed. Students remembered far more words for which they had to generate missing letters than words they merely read. The generation effect only worked, however, when the cues present at encoding also were present at recall. Apparently, even one of the most durable phenomena known to memory researchers—the generation effect—is governed by the principle of encoding specificity.

Other studies have investigated the effect of generation on implicit and explicit memory (Segar, 1994). In Chapter 3, we learned that implicit memory occurs when individuals remember information without conscious awareness (Roediger, 2003). A wide variety of studies have shown that shallow processing can affect implicit memory without any corresponding effect on explicit memory (e.g., see Berry & Dienes, 1993). In contrast, generating information typically has a positive effect on explicit memory and transfer of information to new settings (Toth, Reingold, & Jacoby, 1994).

Still other researchers have examined whether the generation effect occurs when reading longer texts and in classroom discussions. For example, Pressley and his colleagues and others (e.g., Dornisch & Sperling, 2006; Martin & Pressley, 1991; Pressley, Symons, McDaniel, Snyder, & Turnure, 1988; Willoughby, Waller, Wood, & McKinnon, 1993) have investigated the technique of **elaborative interrogation,** in which students are asked to answer "why" questions about information they have just read. As discussed in Chapter 4, work by King and her associates (e.g., King, 1994, 2007; King, Staffieri, & Adelgais, 1998) has shown that the related technique of **guided peer questioning**—having students ask each other thought-provoking questions about class content—significantly enhances their learning and recall. Studies consistently have shown that these approaches improve learning for text and teacher-presented information, especially when they prompt learners to activate relevant prior knowledge and to carry out other cognitive activities (e.g., connecting ideas and metacognitive monitoring) known to promote learning.

The research on elaborative interrogation and guided peer questioning answers some questions about why the generation effect occurs. One explanation is that learners are more apt to integrate new information with what they already know, making elaborated information easier to store in memory. A second is that elaboration helps students "enrich" incoming information in a variety of ways. Information is learned better not only because elaboration assimilates it into existing mental structures (Mandler, 2002b) but also because it can be reconstructed in ways that make it more meaningful.

An instance of research on encoding specificity can be seen in a study by Corkill, Glover, and Bruning (1988) that focused on factors that make for an effective advance organizer. Advance organizers are materials given to students prior to reading that are designed to tie the to-be-learned material in an upcoming passage to what students already know (see Chapter 12). In their Experiment 3, Corkill et al. sorted students into conditions based on whether they read an advance organizer prior to reading a chapter on astronomy. Then, at recall, Corkill et al. examined the effects of presenting advance organizers as cues for retrieval. In contrast with no cue conditions and other conditions (in which other types of cues were furnished to students at time of retrieval), giving readers the advance organizer as a retrieval cue led to significantly greater levels of recall of the passage content. However, presenting the advance organizer as a retrieval cue worked only if the students had read the advance organizer prior to reading the chapter on astronomy. Students who merely read the chapter without an advance organizer obtained no benefit from having the advance organizer presented to them at the time of retrieval. Apparently, even the recall of long reading passages can be facilitated when students are given cues at retrieval that were present when they first activated schemata about the material.

The type of cues used in studies of encoding specificity seems to make little difference as long as the cues are present both at encoding and at retrieval. Tulving and his associates (Sloman, Hayman, Ohta, Law, & Tulving, 1988; Tulving, 1983) examined encoding specificity with both semantic and episodic elements of memory (see Chapter 3). As you recall, *semantic memory* refers to memory for general knowledge (e.g., that canaries are yellow and that Greenland has an ice cap) *not* tied to a specific occurrence in a person's lifetime. In contrast, *episodic memory* refers to our memories for specific events in our lives (e.g., this morning, one of the authors had wheat toast for breakfast). Apparently, both semantic and episodic information may be used as effective retrieval cues. For example, a teacher could construct an item that used episodic information as a cue (e.g., "As you recall from our class demonstration in which Sharmar bent the glass tubes . . .") or an item that used semantic information (e.g., "As you recall, many historians have argued that Hoover actually laid the groundwork for recovery from the Depression. What were the . . ."). Either of these kinds of retrieval cues presumably could facilitate retrieval as long as it is present at the original encoding and encoding is deep enough to tie episodic details to each other and to important semantic representations (Craik, 2002).

One interesting aspect of the encoding specificity principle is its wide applicability. For example, researchers have shown that retrieval is more efficient when it matches encoding conditions even when unusual affective or psychological states are involved. This phenomenon often is referred to as **state-dependent learning** (Overton, 1985; Schramke & Bauer 1997). In one study, Bower (1981) found that students who learned information when they were sad recalled that information better when they were in a similar state versus when they were happy. Godden and Baddeley (1975) found similar differences when individuals learned information on land or under water! These results suggest a strong relationship between the conditions—or states—at encoding and those at retrieval. The more these match, the more likely retrieval will be successful.

Results from encoding specificity studies are important for educators because they underscore the importance of context to memory. In these studies, the context for retrieval is varied by the presence or absence of cues available to students at encoding. Yet the effects of context on retrieval go beyond the presence or absence of study cues. Smith (1986) and Smith, Vela, and Williamson (1988), for example, showed that even the general environmental context in which encoding and retrieval occur influences memory. It turns out that students' memory for information depends not only on study cues but even on the classroom in which students study. When students were tested in the same room in which they studied, their memory performance was better than if they were tested in a room different from the one in which they studied.

Studies of the influence of context on retrieval and the principle of encoding specificity have become integral to our understanding of memory. They help us think about how success in retrieving information relates strongly to the match between study and retrieval conditions. They also can help us think about the study and learning conditions most likely to give students the best opportunity to apply and use what they have learned.

The principle of encoding specificity also is important because it highlights the relationship between different stages of information processing. We now know that activities that improve the encoding of information will also improve retrieval. Although it is convenient at times to distinguish among encoding, storage, and retrieval, it is even more important to remember that all memory functions are closely tied.

Encoding specificity also helps us explain everyday memory experiences. For example, all of us have had the experience of hearing a certain song on the radio and then remembering things we have not thought of in years (recall our discussion of episodic memory). Similarly, most of us have experienced a rush of memories we thought were forgotten when we meet a friend from our childhood or high school days. In these examples, the music or the sight of the friend reinstates cues present when we encoded information. Without the cues, retrieval may be difficult, such as when we run into a work acquaintance "out of context"—say, at the supermarket—and initially fail to recognize the person.

Encoding specificity emphasizes the situated nature of our cognitive processes (Lave & Wenger, 1991; Wortham, 2001) and the importance of context in cognition. Students' memories do not function like DVD players; events are not simply replayed at their choosing. Instead, retrieval depends on the quality of memory cues available to them, based on the degree of match between encoding and retrieval contexts. A rich context providing multiple, rich cues for retrieval almost always will lead to better memory performance, while a context with weak or few retrieval cues is apt to give us little indication of what students actually know.

One way that context at retrieval may be varied is by the demands we place on students at the time of assessment. For instance, on the one hand, we could provide students with some information and ask them whether they recognize it, such as when a simple multiple-choice or true–false item is used. On the other hand, we could ask that students supply information from memory, such as when we ask them to discuss two important domestic consequences of the Iraq War. In the latter context, we are asking students to recall and utilize information. A good deal of attention has focused on how recognition and recall operate. In the following section, we review each of these approaches to retrieving information from long-term memory.

Recognition and Recall

Imagine that you are preparing to take a midterm examination for a course. Your understanding is that the exam will be multiple-choice (recognition), and so you work hard readying yourself to recognize pertinent ideas on the test and to discriminate important facts from other material. You finally finish studying at 4:00 in the morning—exhausted, but happy in the knowledge that you seem to have mastered the content. Unfortunately, your happiness lasts only until you walk into the testing room and see that you were mistaken. The test is not multiple-choice. Instead it is an essay exam, which requires you to *recall* information, not just *recognize* it. Not only is this situation likely upsetting but probably will negatively impact your performance, given the differences between recognizing and recalling information.

There is empirical evidence tying students' test preparation strategies to their performance. In laboratory settings, students who expect recall tests tend to focus on the organization of material, while those who anticipate recognition tend to emphasize discriminating items from each other so that they can pick out the relevant items from the distracters on the test (Kintsch, 1986). These different methods of preparation lead to test-taking performances shaped to the type of test expected. Students who are tested in a manner consistent with their expectations for testing far outperform students who receive a type of test they did not expect (Glover & Corkill, 1987).

Students' actual study habits bear out the laboratory work. Typically, students prepare differently for essay tests than for recognition tests. They report that when they study for an essay examination, they emphasize organizing content, relating important ideas to each other and practicing the recall of information. In contrast, when students prepare for a recognition test, they report focusing on becoming familiar with the material and discriminating the to-be-learned information from other materials. They also recall studying harder for essay tests than for recognition tests. This latter difference makes especially good sense because laboratory studies indicate that recognition is easier than recall. In almost all situations, students' performance is better on recognition tests than on recall tests (Hamilton & Ghatala, 1994; Mitchell & Brown, 1988).

Despite the overwhelming array of circumstantial evidence indicating important process differences in recall and recognition, the exact nature of these differences has been elusive (see Nilsson, Law, & Tulving, 1988). An early hypothesis offered to account for differences in recall and recognition was put forward by McDougall (1904) over a century ago. This "threshold" hypothesis held that both recognition and recall performance depend on the strength of information in memory. Further, the hypothesis held that a bit of information must have a specific strength before it can be recognized, the so-called **recognition threshold.** The threshold hypothesis also held that a greater amount of strength is necessary for information to be recalled, the **recall threshold.**

The implications of the threshold hypothesis were clear and seemed to account for most data from studies that contrasted recognition and recall. This hypothesis predicted that some bits of well-learned information would be both recognized and recalled because the strength of that information in memory would be above both the recognition threshold and the recall threshold. When information was poorly learned, however, it would be neither recalled nor recognized because its strength in memory was below both thresholds. The threshold hypothesis also predicted that some information would be recognizable, but not recallable, because its strength was above the recognition threshold but below the recall threshold.

As appealing as the threshold hypothesis once was, it no longer is accepted by cognitive psychologists. It was abandoned for two reasons. First, it is quite possible for some items in memory to be recalled but not recognized. The threshold hypothesis would imply that this is not possible. Second, the threshold hypothesis never offered an explanation for how recall or recognition operated. Instead, it was a hypothesis to account for why recall seemed more difficult than recognition.

The threshold hypothesis has been replaced by more contemporary perspectives. One, typified by the work of Tulving and his colleagues (e.g., Nilsson et al., 1988; Tulving, 1983, 1985), argues that differences in recall and recognition are a part of larger contextual phenomena in memory akin to encoding specificity; that is, the match of the encoding and retrieval operations determines performance. Tulving's argument is less of an attempt to examine the processes involved in recall and recognition than it is an attempt to explain performance differences in recall and recognition. A second perspective on recall and recognition is referred to as the **dual process model of recall.** This view holds that recall and recognition essentially are the same, save that a much more extensive memory search is required in recall than in recognition (see Greene, 1992, for a further discussion).

To illustrate how recall and recognition searches differ (see Chapter 3 for a detailed discussion of memory searches), Figure 5.1 shows an example of a propositional network based on J. R. Anderson's view of how related propositions can be represented (Anderson, 2005). It represents the information that Monroe was president after Madison. Consider, for example, the following two questions:

1. Who was president after Madison?
2. Was Monroe the president after Madison?

The first question (*"Who was . . ."*) is a recall question; the second (*"Was Monroe . . ."*) is a recognition question. The recall question gives students *Madison* as a point of access from which to begin a memory search. From Anderson's perspective, such a question requires that

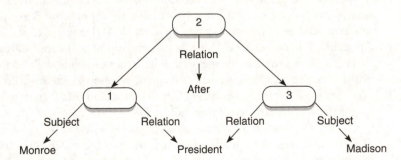

FIGURE 5.1   A Propositional Network. The figure illustrates a propositional network of the information that Monroe followed Madison as president of the United States.

Source: Based on similar figures in *Cognitive Psychology and Its Implications* (5th ed., p. 150), by J. R. Anderson, 2000, New York, NY: Worth.

readers enter memory at *Madison* and search to *Monroe*. To accomplish this, a student first would activate the *Madison* node and have activation spread until it reached *Monroe*. If, however, the link between the second and third proposition were weak or if it could not be sufficiently activated, then recall would fail.

In contrast with the recall question, the recognition question provides two points of access in memory from which activation could spread: *Madison* and *Monroe*. Presumably, if students cannot activate the appropriate link from *Madison*, they might do so from *Monroe*. Thus, the recognition question provides more ways to enter and search memory.

A full theoretical analysis of potential differences between recall and recognition is beyond the scope of this text. Our brief discussion of these processes might seem to imply that if students are given the proper cues, retrieval is a matter of searching for the appropriate memory, finding it, and then just reading it off. If you were to sit down to take a test over this content, it might seem that all you need to do is find where you stored your memories in order to successfully recall the content. This view would be incorrect, because it presumes that the entire content of a memory event (e.g., the results of studying this chapter) is stored and that it is all stored in the same spot. It also assumes that all that must be done is to locate the memory event and retrieve it. If memory were stored in this way, each of us would need a warehouse to hold all of our separate memories. We simply encounter far too much information during our lives to allow for such massive storage.

Reconstruction

If retrieval is not just a straightforward reading out of memory, what is it? Considerable evidence suggests that retrieval is **reconstructive memory** (e.g., Craik, 2002; Greene, 1992; Mandler, 2002b), just as encoding is constructive memory. In other words, rather than the entirety of a memory event, only key elements of an episode are stored, guided by schemata (see Chapter 3). At retrieval, we bring up these key elements and put them together with general knowledge (both domain-specific and general) to reconstruct what we encountered. This process allows us to "handle" far less information than if we encoded and retrieved all of the information we encounter.

For example, suppose you were to witness an automobile accident this afternoon. Later, when a police officer asks you to tell what happened, you probably would retrieve some key elements of the event and reconstruct the rest. For instance, you might recall clearly that an old pickup truck broadsided a new Mercedes in the intersection. You also recall that you were waiting for the "Walk" sign to come on, but you may not actually have been in a position to see the traffic lights. So, to describe which vehicle ran the red light, you work from what you actually did see and recall to reach the conclusion that the pickup's driver must have ignored a red light. For all you know, though, the traffic lights could have been stuck so that both vehicles had green lights.

Mistakes spawned by reconstructive memory, such as which vehicle ran a light, are common in retrieval. Students make similar errors when recalling what they read and hear. They may write about George Washington having been elected the first president of the United States and that John Adams ran with him as vice president. In fact, Adams finished second in the race for president and so became vice president. The election laws that set up our current system of "running mates" for president and vice president were not formulated until well after Washington's time. In this instance, students recall who was president and who was vice president, but reconstruct how the vice president came to office. A similar phenomenon often occurs when psychology students describe John B. Watson's famous study of Little Albert. As you know, Watson conditioned a fear response in the child Albert by pairing a loud noise with white objects until the white objects themselves elicited the fear response. However, we have seen several students who went on to state that Watson then "unconditioned" Little Albert and removed the fear response. In fact, there is no report of this happening. Students use their knowledge of contemporary approaches to psychology research to reconstruct a plausible ending for the story.

As can be seen from our examples, a reconstructive memory system should be far less demanding of memory "space" than a "readout" system. Only key elements need be remembered about a memory event when other knowledge is used to reconstruct events. Of course, a reconstructive system also will be open to far more errors that lead to improper reconstruction. In fact, errors of just this type have convinced most cognitive psychologists of memory's reconstructive nature (see Ceci & Bruck, 1993; and Welch-Ross, 1995, for reviews).

Two classic studies performed in the 1930s have been central to arguments for the reconstructive nature of human memory. Each has been replicated several times, and results remain consistent (see Schwartz & Reisberg, 1991). In a study reported in his book, *Remembering* (1932), Bartlett, an English psychologist, had subjects read a brief story titled "The War of the Ghosts." This story was an abstraction of a North American Native legend that was firmly grounded in that culture. Bartlett's subjects, however, were British and had little, if any, cultural preparation for understanding for the story. For them, it was very unusual.

After the subjects read the story, Bartlett assessed their recall at differing time intervals. Bartlett noted that recall for the passage was poor even at short intervals. More important, Bartlett observed that subjects seemed to recall only the gist or theme of the story. From this gist, they constructed a reasonable story that made a kind of sense out of the information recalled. Not surprisingly, the reconstructed stories often contained errors and distortions that made the story fit the general cultural knowledge possessed by the British subjects (see Box 5.1).

In the same year Bartlett's book was published, Carmichael, Hogan, and Walter (1932) reported quite different but similarly convincing evidence for reconstructive processes. In their experiment, which involved memory for drawings, all of Carmichael et al.'s subjects were shown a set of line drawings similar to those pictured in Figure 5.2. The subjects were grouped into three conditions on the basis of the labels they received with the drawings. The subjects in the control condition received no labels; they merely were shown the drawings. The subjects in one experimental condition received the labels shown in List A in Figure 5.2. The subjects in the second experimental condition were provided the labels pictured in List B in Figure 5.2. For example, the subjects in one experimental condition saw the two circles connected by a straight line labeled as "dumbbell," whereas the subjects in the other condition saw this drawing labeled as "eyeglasses."

When the subjects in Carmichael et al.'s study were asked to draw the figures from memory, interesting differences appeared among the conditions. The subjects in the control condition most accurately depicted the drawings as originally shown. Members of the experimental group given the labels in List A tended to bias their drawings systematically so that they fit the labels. In a classroom demonstration in which we repeated the Carmichael et al. experiment, one student drew nosepieces and bands on the "eyeglasses." Similarly, the subjects shown the labels in List B also biased their reproductions to fit the labels they saw. In our use of these materials, we have seen students who drew a cowboy hat for "hat" and another who put grips on the handle of the "trowel."

BOX 5.1

Bartlett's Story "The War of the Ghosts" and One Student's Protocol

The War of the Ghosts

One night two young men from Egulac went down to the river to hunt seals, and while they were there it became foggy and calm. Then they heard war cries, and they thought: "Maybe this is a war party." They escaped to the shore, and hid behind a log. Now canoes came up, and they heard the noise of paddles, and saw one canoe coming up to them. There were five men in the canoe, and they said:

"What do you think? We wish to take you along. We are going up the river to make war on the people."

One of the young men said: "I have no arrows."

"Arrows are in the canoe," they said.

"I will not go along. I might be killed. My relatives do not know where I have gone. But you," he said, turning to the other, "may go with them."

So one of the young men went, but the other returned home.

And the warriors went on up the river to a town on the other side of Kalama. The people came down to the water, and they began to fight, and many were killed. But presently the young man heard one of the warriors say: "Quick, let us go home: that Indian has been hit." Now he thought, "Oh, they are ghosts." He did not feel sick, but they said he had been shot.

So, canoes went back to Egulac, and the young man went ashore to his house, and made a fire. And he told everybody and said: "Behold, I accompanied the ghosts, and we went to fight. Many of our fellows were killed, and many of those who attacked us were killed. They said I was hit, and I did not feel sick."

He told it all, and then he became quiet. When the sun rose he fell down. Something black came out of his mouth. His face became contorted. The people jumped up and cried. He was dead.

Student's Protocol

Two youths were standing by a river about to start seal-catching, when a boat appeared with five men in it. They were all armed for war.

The youths were at first frightened, but they were asked by the men to come and help them fight some enemies on the other bank. One youth said he could not come as his relations would be anxious about him; the other said he would go, and entered the boat.

In the evening he returned to his hut, and told his friends that he had been in a battle. A great many had been slain, and he had been wounded by an arrow; he had not felt any pain, he said. They told him that he must have been fighting in a battle of ghosts. Then he remembered that it had been queer and he became very excited.

In the morning, however, he became ill, and his friends gathered round; he fell down and his face became very pale. Then he writhed and shrieked and his friends were filled with terror. At last he became calm. Something hard and black came out of his mouth, and he lay contorted and dead.

From *Remembering: A study in experimental and social psychology* by F. C. Bartlett, 1932, Cambridge, England: Cambridge University Press, pp. 23–26.

Although Bartlett's and Carmichael et al.'s studies clearly demonstrated that memory is reconstructive, their explanations for how reconstruction operated were vague and not well-accepted. Not until schema theory began to be generally accepted did more sophisticated theoretical accounts of reconstructive memory appear. In general, a current view of reconstructive processes in memory emphasizes students' assimilating new information into existing memory structures. Rather than remember all of the details in an episode, students remember the gist of an event (e.g., Washington and Adams were the first president and vice president) and then use their general knowledge about similar events (e.g., students' schemata for "presidential elections") to reconstruct the information at the time of test. The rarity with which we see

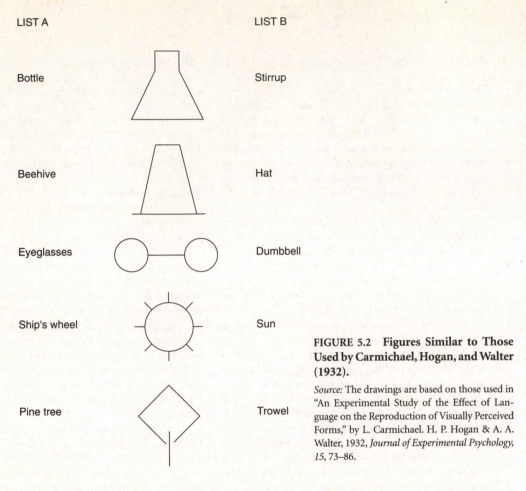

LIST A   LIST B

Bottle   Stirrup

Beehive   Hat

Eyeglasses   Dumbbell

Ship's wheel   Sun

Pine tree   Trowel

FIGURE 5.2   Figures Similar to Those Used by Carmichael, Hogan, and Walter (1932).

Source: The drawings are based on those used in "An Experimental Study of the Effect of Language on the Reproduction of Visually Perceived Forms," by L. Carmichael. H. P. Hogan & A. A. Walter, 1932, *Journal of Experimental Psychology, 15,* 73–86.

reconstructive memory in recitations of information committed to rote memory (e.g., the Pledge of Allegiance and Hamlet's soliloquy) also suggests that reconstructive memory is most likely when students are learning and recalling meaningful information—information for which knowledge structures are readily available.

Recalling Specific Events

The previous discussion indicates that people tend to reconstruct the meaning of a story when they retrieve that information from a general knowledge store—something like semantic memory described in Chapter 3. But what happens when we try to remember specific events that have happened to us? These events probably are retrieved from a different representational schema in memory—something like episodic memory.

Among the questions that researchers have studied are whether episodic events are easier to retrieve and whether they are reconstructed to the same degree as semantic information. Most of us believe that we can retrieve specific events from memory with a great deal of ease and accuracy. For example, many older Americans remember exactly where they were and what they were doing when President John F. Kennedy was assassinated. Others have similar memories regarding the death of Beatle John Lennon or the loss of the space shuttles *Challenger* and *Columbia*. The images of the World Trade Center tragedy now are fixed in virtually everyone's mind. Memories of highly specific events of this kind often are referred to as **flashbulb memories** (Brown & Kulik, 1977). Memories for a traffic accident you witnessed or for your sister's wedding also would fall into this category.

Researchers have discovered startling things about flashbulb and other episodic memories. Flashbulb memories are not as accurate as one might think, and in most cases certainly are not "photographic." Loftus and Loftus (1980), who examined the accuracy of testimony, found that eyewitness testimony is often highly inaccurate and that, like all memories, can be affected by conditions imposed at retrieval. For instance, asking a witness to recall how fast the car was traveling when it *smashed* into the other car is more likely to elicit an overestimate than a more neutral word such as *struck*. These findings strongly suggest that information is subject to serious distortion at retrieval not only because of learner-induced reconstruction but by retrieval cues as well.

Studies of flashbulb memories report similar findings. McCloskey, Wible, and Cohen (1988) asked college students to fill out a questionnaire about events surrounding the explosion of the space shuttle *Challenger* 3 days after the disaster. McCloskey et al. reported that shortly after the accident, most individuals had strikingly vivid memories of where they were, what they were doing, and how they felt. Interviews with the same individuals 9 months later, however, revealed many inaccuracies between initial and delayed memory for the event, with only about 65% of subjects' reports matching their original versions. Schmidt (2004) similarly reported low memory consistency between college students' recall of their 9/11 experiences immediately after the event and their recollections 2 months later.

Studies like these show that retrieval is not as straightforward as one might expect, even for vivid and emotionally charged information. Retrieval errors fall into two categories: (1) those that are self-induced, as in Bartlett's study, (2) those that are situationally induced, such as a lawyer's "leading questions" in a courtroom. These errors occur because of our storing as little information as we need, which makes for a much more efficient and versatile cognitive system but opens memory to the possibility of reconstructive errors.

Most reconstructive errors are of little importance, although a few may lead to serious consequences. For example, erroneous eyewitness testimony in a courtroom setting may have significant consequences for victims and the accused. Most adults are far less accurate than they suspect when monitoring their own memories (Johnson, Hashtroudi, & Lindsay, 1993). Memory monitoring is even less accurate when it comes to autobiographical memories, in part because most people can be quite overconfident when assessing their own memory ability. Children are especially poor in this regard (Ceci & Bruck, 1993), often failing to distinguish between actual events that happened versus events that were suggested by credible adults and peers.

Relearning

At times, information we once knew fairly well seems forgotten forever. One of the authors, for example, had 3 years of college French and some 20 years later stated that he remembered only *un peu*. Apparently, 3 years of study had disappeared somewhere, as recognition and recall of the French language from that distant vantage point seemed impossible. When the author later visited Montréal, however, he found himself rapidly relearning basic French—at least to the point that he was able to shop, ask simple directions, and get the gist of a baseball story in *La Presse*. Apparently, his knowledge of French only *seemed* to be lost because the relearning was far easier than the original learning had been.

Most cognitive scientists agree that the most sensitive measure of memory is not recall, recognition, or the ability to reconstruct events. Instead, it is the memory savings that people experience when relearning information (MacLeod, 1988). The relearning method was the favorite of the pioneer memory researcher Hermann Ebbinghaus (1885). In Ebbinghaus's use of the approach, he first practiced a list of nonsense syllables until he obtained one error-free recitation. Then, after varying delays, Ebbinghaus would relearn the materials to the same criterion. He determined the level of memory savings by comparing the number of trials he needed in the first and second learning sessions. The existence of any savings (if fewer trials were required on the second than on the first session), even when recognition or recall was not possible, indicated that some of the information had been remembered between the first and second learning sessions.

Even though the memory savings approach is the most sensitive measure of memory and still occasionally employed by researchers studying second language vocabulary learning (e.g., Hansen, Umeda, & McKinney, 2002), the method is seldom used by psychologists. A major reason is that it isn't particularly suitable for complex stimulus materials. While a criterion of one error-free verbatim recall might seem reasonable for a list of nonsense syllables or foreign language vocabulary, it hardly seems workable for the contents of a chapter on American history, a lecture on basic genetics, or recounting the gist of *The Grapes of Wrath*. Generally, after-the-fact attempts to measure savings in learning are extraordinarily difficult and rarely attempted.

In two of these infrequent attempts, Nelson (1985) and MacLeod (1988) developed variations on Ebbinghaus's classic procedure. In their studies, individuals learned a list of paired associates, with nouns paired with numbers. Initially, they worked until they attained one error-free pass through the list in which they elicited the nouns paired with the provided numbers. After a lengthy delay (weeks or months in Nelson's work), a second session was conducted. This second session had two phases. The first was a test of recall in which individuals were given the numerical cues and attempted to remember as many nouns as they could. In the second phase, subjects were asked to relearn the unrecalled items and an equivalent number of previously unseen items on a single trial. Differences then seen in the immediate recall of previously studied and new items were taken as indications of memory savings.

What is clear both from the early and more recent relearning research is that we retain memory traces of far more than we are able to recall, recognize, or even reconstruct. Exactly how relearning differs from original learning is a topic for future research, but one factor known to affect both initial learning and relearning is the type of practice in which one engages (Ericsson, 1996). **Distributed practice** refers to regular periods of practice (e.g., daily piano practice). **Massed practice** refers to irregular periods of intense practice (e.g., cramming for a test). Distributed practice appears to be more efficient than massed practice (Ashcraft, 1994). For example, learning five new words each day for 30 days requires less learning time than learning those same 150 words in a 3-day interval. Distributed practice appears to be more beneficial when learning declarative, rather than procedural, knowledge (Mumford,

Costanza, Baughman, Threlfall, & Fleischman, 1994). Distributed practice also facilitates learning higher-order concepts, which typically require more time or effort to learn than simple facts.

Assessment and Retrieval: Testing as Retrieval Practice?

Traditionally we think of test-taking primarily from the perspective of assessment. Tests are to measure what students know. Recently, however, research by Roediger, McDaniel, and their associates (e.g., Chan, McDermott, & Roediger, 2006; Karpicke & Roediger, 2007; McDaniel, Anderson, Derbish, & Morrisette, 2007; Roediger & Karpicke, 2006a, 2006b) has renewed interest in the **testing effect**—that taking tests or quizzes on materials being studied improves learning and retention on a final test.

While we all appreciate that students can learn something from being tested, recent laboratory and classroom research on the testing effect has produced some interesting and even counterintuitive findings. It shows that, under certain conditions, taking a test over material can have an even greater effect on its future retention than taking that same amount of time to restudy it. This effect appears even when test performance is not perfect and even when no feedback is given on missed information (although feedback, if available, is beneficial). In other words, as far as ultimate test performance is concerned, after initially studying the materials, it may be better to use your time being repeatedly quizzed (or quizzing yourself) than to spend it repeatedly going over the materials.

In a representative study of the testing effect (Roediger & Karpicke, 2006a, Experiment 2), college students interacted with the materials in prose passages in four 5-minute blocks. They either studied the passage once and took three tests (STTT group), studied it three times and took one test (SSST group), or studied the passage four times (SSSS group). Those taking tests were given sheets of paper with the passage title and told each time simply to write down what they remembered and not to be concerned with exact wording or order. No feedback was given on these tests. A final test was given 5 minutes after learning or 1 week later and scored for number of idea units recalled.

As predicted, on the tests given 5 minutes after learning activities concluded, the SSSS group was best; the massed practice of repeated study was beneficial. On the 1-week test, however, both the STTT and SSST groups recalled considerably more than the SSSS group (61 and 56% recall, respectively, vs. 40% recall). These data are quite dramatic, especially considering that the STTT students read the passage only 3.4 times on average (during their one study period), while students in the SSSS group read it an average of more than 14 times!

In general, this and related research on the testing effect has shown that taking a test tends to be a better learning activity than just continuing to study material (Karpicke & Roediger, 2008; McDaniel et al., 2007). Why might this be? One explanation could be that testing allows for more processing and learning, but that doesn't explain why effects are more prominent in long-term than immediate recall. A better reason, according to Roediger and Karpicke (2006b) is that the benefits are related to the retrieval process itself. Testing gives students a chance to practice retrieval skills they will use later. A related factor is that, much like initial deep processing producing more elaborated traces (see Chapter 4), the so-called *desirable difficulty* (Bjork, 1999) of test-induced retrieval increases elaboration and promotes better long-term recall. Also, the close correspondence between retrieval practice and the retrieval context of the final test illustrates transfer-appropriate processing, which we know is tied to improved retention.

The educational community to this point mostly has paid little attention to the potentially beneficial effects of testing. Many teachers and other educators view testing in a less-than-positive light, perhaps because of the heavy emphasis on standardized tests with little or no connection to classroom learning processes or because of the effort involved in preparing and scoring tests. But with a number of well-controlled studies demonstrating testing's worth as a learning tool, perhaps it is time, as these researchers argue, to include testing more systematically in the design of our instruction. With anecdotal reports indicating positive student acceptance of frequent assessment (e.g., see Roediger & Karpicke, 2006b), the practice of quizzing students at spaced intervals not only may increase the odds of later retrieval, but also prove valuable for assuring both students and teachers that learning is occurring.

Implications for Instruction

This chapter has suggested ways that information retrieval can be made more effective. One way is to provide a match between encoding and retrieval conditions, including offering retrieval practice as part of learning. A second way is to provide relevant cues at retrieval. A third way is to use prior knowledge to reconstruct missing information. Implications of these three retrieval strategies follow.

1. *Encoding and retrieval are linked.* The literature on encoding specificity clearly indicates that students' ability to remember information is related strongly to their ability to encode it in a meaningful fashion. When information is elaborated at encoding and when information present at encoding is used to prompt retrieval, students remember better than if "encoding-specific" information is not present. An example is the use of an advance organizer given to students prior to reading a chapter, and then presenting the organizer again as a retrieval cue.

At a broader level, the concepts of encoding specificity and transfer-appropriate processing reaffirm the highly interactive nature of our cognitive system. Learning and retention of information do not occur in isolated acts of "encoding," "storage," or "retrieval" but rather result from all of these processes. We need to bear in mind the continuous, interactive nature of learning when planning instruction. This requires us to plan ahead so that our instructional activities include effective review and retrieval practice. Even more important, we need to ask whether our classroom encoding and retrieval activities match the contexts in which our students ultimately will need to retrieve and *use* what they have learned.

2. *Learning always occurs in a specific context that affects encoding and retrieval.* One way to improve learning is to situate it in a context that provides students a useful structure (see Lave & Wenger, 1991), such as specifically telling them the purpose of the learning task. Another useful strategy is to activate students' prior knowledge or to provide a schematic framework prior to instruction (see Chapter 4). Finally, information should be presented and worked with in ways that reflect how students will be asked to use it in their everyday lives.

3. *Retrieval is state-dependent.* Few teachers or students think about their ability to remember information depending on their emotional state or physical location. Nevertheless, a large body of research indicates that recall is related to our mood and the conditions under which we learned that information. One implication is that assessment conditions should match learning conditions. Taking students to an unfamiliar room at a different time of day than their regular class may negatively affect their performance. Conducting final exams at a new time or location, as is often done at universities, may also be ill-advised. One way that teachers can help students is to teach them to prepare for important tests, such as the SAT, under conditions likely to approximate those of the actual test.

4. *Memory is reconstructive.* Retrieval is more than playing back an event from memory. Students often retrieve main ideas and use them and their general knowledge to construct a reasonable response. Overall, it seems that increasing the richness and number of cues at retrieval produces more accurate processes of reconstruction. Regardless of how supportive a retrieval context is provided, recall will vary from student to student on the basis of their world knowledge. Two students with the "same" amount of learning may write about a topic quite differently, not because one knows more than the other, but because of the knowledge available to support reconstruction.

Recalling a key theme of this text, we should never lose sight of the fact that learning is a highly constructive process. In Chapters 3 and 4, we saw how learners construct meaning by elaborating it with respect to their prior knowledge or processing it at a deeper level. The analog to constructive processes at encoding is reconstructive processes at retrieval. Some teachers look at constructive and reconstructive processes in a negative light, perhaps assuming that students should focus on explicit facts and concepts instead of making their own meaning. We disagree strongly with this view. Research has consistently shown that students learn more and remember it better when they are active (constructive) learners (see Chapter 12). Although constructing or reconstructing meaning may seem to lead to more errors than a verbatim translation of to-be-learned material, these errors are usually insignificant, whereas the cost paid for rote approaches to learning is high.

5. *Learning increases when students generate their own contexts for meaning.* Research on the generation effect, elaborative interrogation, and guided peer questioning consistently has shown that learning improves when students make, rather than take, meaning. For example, generating an antonym to the word *stop* (e.g., *go*) will improve memory for the word *go* compared with simply reading it from a list or seeing it paired with *stop*. Answering questions about to-be-learned information (e.g., using methods such as elaborative interrogation, guided peer questioning, and the testing effect) also will improve remembering. One explanation is that students are more apt to remember what they've learned if they've also created conditions at the time of encoding that will be favorable to later retrieval. Although cues provided by the text or teacher can be useful, those generated by students themselves are more likely to be available and effective.

6. *Recall and recognition are not the same.* Evidence suggests that recall and recognition tests generate different retrieval processes and elicit different study patterns. Because of this, students' retrieval performance is best when they know in advance what form the assessment will take. Students expecting a multiple-choice test will perform best on a multiple-choice test; students who have prepared for a true–false test will perform best on a true–false test; and so forth. Knowing the kinds of performances expected on assessments also helps students study more effectively.

7. *Retrieval is fallible.* Retrieval is subject to error under the best of circumstances. A frequent reason for poor retrieval is that information was not encoded adequately in the first place, but errors in reconstruction also occur. Although one might expect this to be less of a problem when retrieving specific facts or events, reconstructive errors are common even for highly memorable events such as flashbulb memories. Some reconstructive errors happen because of our inclination to "bend" information to make it fit our existing schemata, whereas others are a result of new cues not available at encoding. Reconstructive errors are more likely to occur when either the context or cues present at encoding are unavailable or have been changed.

8. *Distributed practice is more efficient than massed practice.* Spaced practices help students learn declarative knowledge more efficiently and appear to be most effective when they are trying to organize that information. Ericsson (1996) also has argued that distributed versus massed practice is more likely to positively affect motivation for performing a task.

Summary

Retrieval contexts have a powerful influence on memory performance. Generally speaking, the most effective cues at retrieval are those that were present at the time of encoding. A major implication of the principle of encoding specificity is that contexts for learning should match those likely to be present when information needs to be retrieved and used. In most school settings, various assessments are important contexts for retrieval. In general, students will perform better on recognition measures, but it should be kept in mind that performance is best when there is a match between the type of assessment actually given and how students expect to be assessed. The more important goals, however, are for students to understand what they have learned and to have their knowledge and skills available for use in the widest possible range of contexts. This goal is best accomplished by helping them encode and practice retrieving what they learn in as many ways as possible with the broadest range of cues.

SUGGESTED READINGS

Nairne, J. S. (Ed.) (2007). *The foundations of remembering: Essays in honor of Henry L. Roediger, III.* New York, NY: Psychology Press.
   Mirroring many of the emphases in Henry Roediger's long and distinguished career as a memory researcher, this collection of essays honoring his work focuses on the variables affecting retrieval processes.

Lave, J., & Wenger, E. (1991). *Situated learning: Legitimate peripheral participation.* New York, NY: Cambridge University Press.
   This classic book addresses contextual constraints on thinking and learning and identifies many principles central to the constructivist view of memory.

Roediger, H. L. III, & Karpicke, J. D. (2006). The power of testing memory: Basic research and implications for educational practice. *Perspectives on Psychological Science, 1*(3), 181–210.
   This readable article traces early and recent research on testing effects on memory in building an argument for using systematic assessment as an integral part of the learning process.

6

Beliefs About Self

Bandura's Social Cognitive Learning Theory   Attribution Theory   Autonomy and
Control   Assessing Beliefs   Summary   Suggested Readings

This chapter examines three perspectives on why students succeed and fail in the classroom: Bandura's social cognitive theory, attribution theory, and the role of student control and autonomy. The first of these theories considers how self-confidence to perform a specific task such as writing or algebra problem solving affects academic learning. The second examines how students explain their academic success and failure to themselves based on their internalized explanations. The third considers how students' and teachers' expectations create a controlling or autonomy-producing environment in the classroom.

These perspectives are by no means exhaustive, although we believe that they provide a sound basis for understanding why some students succeed and others do not. One reason we selected these particular theories is that they are comprehensive and cover most aspects of life in the classroom. These theories also have attracted a great deal of empirical research over a 30-year period, so they are conceptually and empirically sound. We believe that most everyday motivational issues of special importance to teachers can be addressed by these theories.

Bandura's Social Cognitive Learning Theory

Most of us realize that self-confidence is essential to success in any discipline, yet few of us have thought carefully about what self-confidence is, where it comes from, or how it can be improved. Albert Bandura (1986, 1997) has developed an extensive theory that has examined people's self-confidence in a variety of settings, how confidence develops, and how it affects behavioral outcomes, such as persistence and effort.

At the heart of Bandura's theory is the idea of reciprocal determinism (Bandura, 1997; Schunk, 2008). As the name implies, **reciprocal determinism** suggests that learning is the result of interacting variables. Figure 6.1 shows the relationship among three basic components described by Bandura: personal, behavioral, and environmental factors. Personal factors include beliefs and attitudes that affect learning, especially in response to behavioral and environmental stimuli. Behavioral factors include the responses one makes in a given situation—for

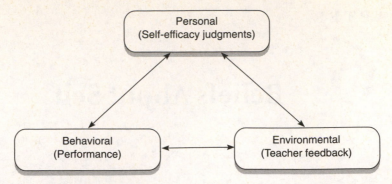

FIGURE 6.1   Bandura's Model of Reciprocal Determinism.

Source: Adapted from *Social Foundations of Thought and Action: A Social Cognitive Theory,* by A. Bandura, 1986, Upper Saddle River, NJ: Prentice Hall. Adapted by permission.

example, whether one responds to a poor test score with anger or with increased effort. Environmental factors include the roles played by parents, teachers, and peers.

The idea of reciprocal determinism suggests that personal factors, such as self-beliefs, affect behaviors and the interpretation of environmental cues. One way that personal factors are related to behaviors and environmental cues is through **mediated responses**—how events are interpreted cognitively before responding. For example, poor performance on a test may elicit anxiety in one student and increased effort in another because the same event (a poor grade) is interpreted differently.

The fact that beliefs and attitudes affect behaviors and environmental cues gives special importance to personal factors in Bandura's model. Two personal factors provide especially powerful influences on behavior. One factor is **self-efficacy,** or the degree to which an individual possesses confidence in her or his ability to achieve a goal. Self-efficacy has been related to many behavioral outcomes that we explore in greater detail later in this section. A second factor is outcome expectancy, or the perceived relationship between performing a task successfully and receiving a specific outcome as a consequence of that performance.

Consider the plight of African American baseball players prior to 1946, the year that Jackie Robinson became the first African American player to play in the major leagues. Prior to this time, two particularly talented African American players—Satchel Paige and Josh Gibson—were excluded from the all-White major leagues. Both of these players undoubtedly had very high degrees of self-efficacy concerning their baseball skills. In fact, both eventually were elected to the Hall of Fame, long after their active careers were over. Neither, however, had high outcome expectancies for playing in the major leagues during their careers because, as a result of racial bias, no amount of talent would guarantee admittance. We return to the topic of self-efficacy in greater detail later in this section. First, however, let's examine how learning is portrayed in Bandura's model.

Enactive and Vicarious Learning

Learning occurs in two ways, according to Bandura (1997). The first—**enactive learning**—occurs when one learns something by doing it. Bandura has argued that enactive attainments are the most important form of learning because they provide direct feedback about one's performance. Performing a task successfully over many occasions gives rise to a high level of self-efficacy that is unaffected by occasional failures. The second type of learning—**vicarious learning**—occurs when one learns about a task by observing others perform or discuss it.

Both types of learning appear to be extremely important. Enactive learning enables us to develop the basic procedural knowledge necessary to perform a task, whereas vicarious learning allows us to observe the subtle nuances of expert performance long before we are capable of such performance ourselves. Vicarious learning, especially when it involves a skilled model, is useful for several reasons (Bandura, 1997). First, observing a model allows us to allocate all of our resources to learning about the task rather than to performing it. Second, vicarious learning enables us to see expert strategies performed without interruption. Third, observing others provides motivation to less skilled observers.

Schunk (2008) has identified three influences on the effectiveness of learning and performance. One is the developmental status of the individual. For example, students differ with respect to reasoning skills and working memory capacity at different ages. Children may also lack the physical ability or knowledge base to perform a task modeled by a skilled adult. A second influence is the prestige of the model. Models with a high functional value (those judged to be more credible) exert a stronger influence on learning. The effects of model prestige also extend to other skills in which the model is not necessarily expert. For instance, some aspiring basketball players may be more apt to eat a particular breakfast cereal because Kobe Bryant's picture is on the front of the cereal box. A third influence is one's ability to set an attainable goal, often with standards provided by a model. Goals do not necessarily improve learning but rather offer incentives to students. Goals that are specific, of moderate difficulty, and attainable within a limited amount of time appear to provide the greatest incentives (Usher & Pajares, 2006).

Self-Efficacy

Self-efficacy should not be confused with general self-esteem. According to Bandura (1997), self-efficacy is a judgment of one's ability to perform a task within a specific domain. High efficacy in one setting does not guarantee high efficacy in another. Within a specific domain, however, self-efficacy is linked reciprocally with behavioral outcomes and environmental cues (see Figure 6.1). High self-efficacy positively affects performance, and good performance, in turn, positively affects one's sense of self-efficacy. Self-efficacy also indirectly affects future learning by predisposing students to engage in challenging tasks and to persist longer despite initial failures (Lodewyk & Winne, 2005; Maddux, 2002; Pajares, 2003).

Judgments of self-efficacy differ along three dimensions related to performance. One dimension is the level of task difficulty. Even students with high efficacy in a domain may be reluctant to take a challenging graduate class. The general level of expertise in such a class may be much higher than what the students are used to, or students may lack the prior knowledge or strategies necessary to do well in the class.

A second dimension is the generality of one's self-efficacy. Some individuals feel able to perform well in almost any academic setting. Others feel confident in only one or two settings. Still others have very little self-efficacy in any domain. Generally speaking, self-efficacy in one domain is unrelated to efficacy in another domain. This does not mean that some individuals do not have high self-efficacy in general. Rather, it suggests that they have reason to believe they can perform competently in many domains. In some cases, self-efficacy may generalize from one domain to another. Shell, Colvin, and Bruning (1995) found that elementary and high school students with high self-efficacy in reading also had high self-efficacy in writing.

A third dimension is the strength of one's efficacy judgments. Weak perceptions of efficacy are more susceptible to disconfirming evidence (observing someone else fail at a task) or to poor performance. Individuals with strong senses of self-efficacy persevere in the face of disconfirming evidence and poor performance. Two people may receive the same low grade on a chemistry test, with very different effects on their efficacy. All other things being equal, the student with the higher efficacy will be more inclined to persist and to maintain self-confidence than the student with lower efficacy.

Research by Bandura and colleagues (see Bandura, 1993; Goddard, Hoy, & Hoy, 2000; Pajares, 1996; Schunk & Zimmerman, 2006; and Woolfolk-Hoy, Davis, & Pape, 2006, for reviews) indicates that self-efficacy is linked closely with initial task engagement, persistence, and successful performance. Bandura (1986) has identified four influences on the level, generality, and strength of self-efficacy. One influence is enactive information acquired during the performance of a task. Successful performance leads to higher self-efficacy; failure leads to lower efficacy. A second influence is observation of others, which often improves efficacy, especially when the model is judged to be similar in ability to the observer. Vicarious influences are strongest when observers are uncertain about the difficulty of the task or their own ability. A third influence is verbal persuasion. Although the effect of persuasion often is limited, it may facilitate engagement in an otherwise forbidding task that, in turn, leads to enactive feedback. Self-efficacy is judged, in part, by a fourth influence—one's psychological state. Sleepiness or physical fatigue often lower efficacy even though they may be unrelated to the performance of a task. Strong emotional arousal also often reduces efficacy, chiefly by invoking fear-inducing thoughts.

Research on Student, Teacher, and School Self-Efficacy

Bandura's social cognitive theory has attracted much attention from educational and psychological researchers. One reason is that self-efficacy is a concept that applies to successful task engagement and performance in any domain, whether mathematics, history, waterskiing, or social events. Virtually all of this research reports the same findings so we will focus our attention on research most relevant to educators.

Student Efficacy   The most important and consistent finding in the research literature is that student self-efficacy is strongly related to critical classroom variables such as task engagement, persistence, strategy use, help seeking, and task performance. High self-efficacy is associated with greater flexibility, resistance to negative feedback, and improved performance (Lodewyk & Winne, 2005; Pajares, 1996).

For example, Collins (reported in Bandura, 1993) examined the way children used mathematics skills. She compared mathematics performance across high-, average-, and low-ability students who exhibited either high or low self-efficacy. Students with high self-efficacy at each level discarded unproductive strategies more quickly than their low-efficacy counterparts. High-efficacy students also were more likely to rework problems they missed originally. High-efficacy students at each level outperformed their low-efficacy counterparts. The finding that self-efficacy positively affects performance has been replicated many times in the last 20 years in domains as diverse as reading, writing, mathematics and science (Schunk, 2008; Schunk & Zimmerman, 2006).

The collective self-efficacy literature highlights two important conclusions. First, efficacy improves performance and strategy use among students even when their ability level is controlled. Second, low-ability students may have the same degree of self-efficacy as some high-ability students. When they do, they tend to perform as successfully as their high-ability/low-efficacy counterparts. When they do not, they perform significantly lower than higher-ability students (Rimm-Kaufman & Sawyer, 2004; Usher & Pajares, 2006).

The collective self-efficacy literature also suggests that self-efficacy is related to perceived control of one's environment. Higher self-efficacy was positively related to two kinds of control. The first concerns the belief that control can be achieved through effortful use of one's skills and resources. The second addresses the degree to which the environment can be modified. Those with higher efficacy were more apt to feel greater control and, in turn, persist in the face of performance failures.

Higher levels of self-efficacy have also been linked with the way individuals explain their success and failure in a particular situation (causal attributions). Self-efficacious individuals are more likely to attribute their failure to low effort than to low ability, whereas low-efficacy individuals attribute their failure to low ability.

Research reviewed by Bandura (1993), Pajares (1997), and Woolfolk-Hoy et al. (2006) points to other ways that self-efficacy may help students. One way occurs when students have high self-efficacy for controlling their own thoughts. Students who believe that they have control are less likely to experience stress, anxiety, and depression when goals have not been met. Another way occurs when students demonstrate a strong sense of self-efficacy for coping with anxiety-producing situations in the classroom or at home. Students who believe that they cope well are less apt to engage in avoidant behaviors.

Recent research indicates important consequences of self-efficacy on classroom behavior and performance (Murdock & Anderman, 2006; Woolfolk-Hoy et al., 2006). One consequence is that self-efficacious students are better goal setters, in part because of their willingness to set "close" rather than "distant" goals. Another is that self-efficacious students are better at setting their own goals. Ironically, the ability to set one's own goals has been shown to enhance self-efficacy!

Teacher Efficacy   Teachers' expectations and behaviors also are affected by self-efficacy judgments (Calderhead, 1996; Woolfolk-Hoy and Burke-Spero, 2005). Teachers appear to evaluate their performances by using two independent efficacy assessments (Woolfolk & Hoy, 1990). One assessment is **teaching efficacy,** which refers to the belief that the process of education affects students in important ways. The second is **personal teaching efficacy,** which refers to the belief that the teacher can enact significant change in her or his students. Woolfolk and Hoy (1990) found that the relationship between teaching efficacy and controlling attitudes among teachers is negative; that is, teachers high on this dimension are more likely to value student control and autonomy. This is true especially when teachers also show high personal teaching efficacy.

Other studies have investigated teacher efficacy by using only a single dimension similar to what Woolfolk and Hoy (1990) refer to as "personal teaching efficacy." A review of these studies by Kagan (1992) found that self-efficacious teachers were more apt to use praise, rather than criticism, to persevere with low-achieving students; to be task oriented; to be more accepting of students; and to raise their achievement levels. In contrast, low-efficacy teachers devoted less class time to class-related activity, spent more time criticizing students, and gave up on "problem students" more quickly. Studies by Poole, Okeafor, and Sloan (1989) and Smylie (1988) also found that self-efficacious teachers were more likely than low-efficacy teachers to use new curriculum materials and to change instructional strategies. These results have been replicated closely over the past 2 decades by a variety of researchers (Woolfolk-Hoy et al., 2006).

Since the early 1990s, teacher efficacy has become something of a touchstone. A number of reviews have appeared (Goddard et al., 2000; Herbert, Lee, & Williamson, 1998; Tschannen-Moran, Woolfolk-Hoy, & Hoy, 1998), and more attention has been focused on ways of improving teacher efficacy (Alderman, 2004, Coladarci & Breton, 1997; Guskey & Passaro, 1994). Researchers have also focused on better ways to measure teacher efficacy (Brouwers & Tomic, 2001; Henson, Kogan, & Vacha-Haase, 2001; Rich, Smadar, & Fischer, 1996; Zhang & Burry-Stock, 2003) that suggest that as teachers' efficacy improves, teacher decision making and students' efficacy (Schoon & Boone, 1998) improve as well. Similarly, Caprara, Barbaranelli, Steca, and Malone (2006) found that teachers' self-efficacy was related to their job satisfaction and retention, which in turn was related to student academic achievement.

Alderman (2004) provides an excellent summary of attitudes and practices associated with high and low teacher efficacy, as well as ways to improve it. High-efficacy teachers possess a greater sense of personal accomplishment, convey more positive expectations to their students, and are more likely to take personal responsibility for their choices and decisions (Egyed & Short, 2006; Ghaith & Yaghi, 1997). High-efficacy teachers also teach more strategies to their students. There is higher student accountability and more time focused on academic learning. High-efficacy teachers also show more confidence in working with parents.

Alderman (2004) suggests several ways to increase teacher efficacy. One is social support, which includes support from the administration as well as a close personal relationship with other teachers. A second category is teacher planning, which includes seeking feedback from other teachers and using this information to state goals, plan, and evaluate in a systematic fashion. One particularly important way to enhance teacher efficacy is to encourage teachers to maintain ongoing assessment of student progress.

One disturbing finding, however, is that the number of years teachers spend in the classroom negatively affects their efficacy (Brousseau, Book, & Byers, 1988). Research suggests that experienced teachers are more likely to adopt a custodial view of classroom control in which rigid rules and standards are used to maintain discipline. In contrast, teachers with fewer years of experience or those who maintain high self-efficacy regardless of years of experience are more inclined to adopt a humanistic view of control in which student individuality and classroom diversity are used.

School Efficacy   Research reviewed by Bandura (1993) suggests that schools differ with respect to self-efficacy. School communities that collectively judge themselves powerless to improve student learning negatively affect both students and teachers. Within this context, individual teachers with low self-efficacy appear to lower the efficacy of their students, especially when students view themselves as having low ability. Factors that appear to affect school efficacy negatively are the stability of the student body and their relative socioeconomic status. The length of teaching experience of the teaching staff is negatively related to school efficacy as well, although it is positively related to students' academic achievement. Not surprisingly, students' prior academic achievement is positively related to school efficacy.

Modeling

Modeling is demonstrating and describing component parts of a skill to a novice. It is an extremely important component in the development of self-efficacy. Bandura (1997) proposed that positive instances of modeling are effective because they can raise expectations that a new skill can be mastered, provide motivational incentives, and provide a great deal of information about how a skill is performed. Not all models are the same, however. Peer models are usually the most effective because they are most similar to the individual studying the model. For example, third-grade mathematics students will not be convinced they can develop mathematical competence just by observing a teacher solve difficult mathematics problems. They are most likely to improve their self-efficacy vicariously when observing a student who is similar in age and perceived ability (Schunk, 2008; Schunk & Zimmerman, 2006).

This is not to say that teachers are not important classroom models. Often, the teacher is the only person in the classroom who can model a complex procedure adequately. One of the most effective ways to do so is through **cognitive modeling** (Meichenbaum, 1977; Schunk, 2008), which includes the following six steps:

1. *Create a rationale for the new learning skill.* Explain to students why acquisition of this skill is important. Provide examples of how, when, and where this skill will be used (establish outcome expectancies).

2. *Model the procedure in its entirety while the students observe.* For example, a piano teacher plays an entire piece of music without interruption.

3. *Model component parts of the task.* If the task can be broken into smaller parts (e.g., using the "integration by parts" method in a calculus class), model each part by using different problems or settings.

4. *Allow students to practice component steps under teacher guidance.* For example, a music student may practice only the first eight measures of a piece of music, receiving feedback on each occasion from her piano instructor.

5. *Allow students to practice the entire procedure under teacher guidance.* Component steps eventually are merged into a single, fluid procedure that is performed intact.

6. *Have the students engage in self-directed performance of the task.* Research suggests that modeling is a highly effective way to improve simple and complex skills learned in the classroom. New skills may be modeled in many ways other than teacher-directed instruction. One method is reciprocal teaching, in which two to four students work in cooperative learning groups (Schraw, Crippen, & Hartley, 2006). A variety of other methods are described in Schmuck and Schmuck (1992).

Regardless of which method is used, feedback should be an essential part of the modeling process, using either face-to-face or computer-administered feedback (Denton, Madden, Roberts, & Rowe, 2008; Shute, 2008). Recall that Bandura's model of reciprocal determinism postulates a strong relationship between performance and environmental cues and learning. Feedback provided to students directly from the teacher improves both performance and self-efficacy. Feedback provided to students from other students appears to be equally effective in many situations. Perhaps the most effective type of feedback is self-generated by students when they make reflective judgments about their own performance. Self-generated feedback is important because it enables students to self-regulate their performance without teacher or peer-model assistance (Butler & Winne, 1995).

Previous research indicates that different types of feedback exert different influences on performance (Hogarth, Gibbs, McKenzie, & Marquis, 1991; Shute, 2008). **Outcome (performance-oriented) feedback** provides specific information about performance and has little effect on initially correct or subsequent test performance (Lhyle & Kulhavy, 1987). **Cognitive (informational-oriented) feedback,** which stresses the relationship between performance and the nature of the task, appears to exert a more positive influence on subsequent performance by providing a deeper understanding of how to perform competently (Balzer, Doherty, & O'Connor, 1989). In a study by Schraw, Potenza, and Nebelsick-Gullet (1993), outcome feedback did little to improve students' comprehension monitoring, whereas incentives to use self-generated cognitive feedback improved both monitoring accuracy and performance. Shute (2008), in a comprehensive review, concluded that formative feedback (i.e., specific, immediate feedback about performance) increases student self-efficacy and engagement, and typically has a positive effect on subsequent performance.

Self-Regulated Learning Theory

Since the early 1990s, researchers have attempted to integrate the key components of Bandura's learning theory with findings from other areas of cognitive psychology. These attempts have led to the development of **self-regulated learning theory** (Perry, Turner, & Meyer, 2006; Pintrich, 2000b; Schunk & Zimmerman, 1994, 2006; Winne & Perry, 2000; Zimmerman, 2000). Self-regulated learning refers to the ability to control all aspects of one's learning, from advance planning to how one evaluates performance afterward.

Most theories of self-regulation include three core components: metacognitive awareness, strategy use, and motivational control (Zimmerman, 2000). In Chapter 4, we discussed how metacognition includes knowledge about, and regulation of, cognition. These different kinds of knowledge enable students to select the best strategy for the occasion and to monitor its effectiveness with a high degree of accuracy. An especially important part of metacognition is what we refer to as the planning sequence, in which students set goals, plan how to reach those goals, and periodically assess the extent to which goals were achieved. Students who engage in effective planning generally do quite well (Pintrich, 2000b; Zimmerman, 2000).

Strategies are an essential part of self-regulation because they provide the means by which learners encode, represent, and retrieve information (see Chapters 4 and 5). Skilled learners choose strategies selectively and monitor their effectiveness throughout the learning process (Zimmerman & Martinez-Pons, 1990). In turn, strategies enable skilled learners to use their limited resources as efficiently as possible. Randi and Corno (2000) provide a comprehensive list of study strategies that is consistent with those discussed in Chapter 4. These include planning, focusing one's resources on important goals, persistence, emotional control, effective use of available external resources, and seeking help when needed.

Motivational control refers to the ability to set goals, evoke positive beliefs about one's skills and performance, and adjust emotionally to the demands of studying and learning. Skilled learners understand the role of effort and strategies in learning and are less likely than unskilled learners to attribute poor performance to uncontrollable causes, such as ability and luck. Skilled learners also are more adept at blocking out disturbances while studying (Pressley, Borkowski, & Schneider, 1987; Pressley & Harris, 2006,).

Self-regulated learning represents an important step forward in understanding how learners develop intellectual independence. Randi and Corno (2000) describe four aspects of teaching that help students achieve their best. One is providing students with choice that facilitates autonomy (Flowerday & Schraw, 2000; Ryan & Deci, 2000). A second is community building, with a special emphasis on collaborative instruction. A third is explicit scaffolded instruction that carefully models complex skills and provides teacher support during the acquisition of new skills (Schraw et al., 2006). A fourth is ongoing assessments that include teacher and peer feedback to students, as well as regular performance-based assessments of critical learning skills.

Research suggests that students who receive quality instruction are motivated to learn and succeed. Teachers help encourage self-regulation through modeling and efficient instruction. Students also observe other students engage in self-regulated learning. Teachers and other students model self-efficacy and strategy use for less regulated students (McInerney, 2000; Shell & Husman, 2008). Students also benefit from feedback. Collectively, students become self-regulated because of skilled teachers and other students who demonstrate critical skills which, in turn, are incorporated into their own learning repertoire.

Implications for Instruction: Improving Self-Efficacy

Research indicates that self-efficacy is affected by self-assessments, behavioral feedback, and environmental cues. Self-efficacy strongly influences many classroom behaviors, including task engagement, performance, anxiety, stress, persistence, and use of academic or social coping strategies. Because self-efficacy can be changed, teachers and parents bear a special responsibility for providing an environment conducive to improving efficacy. Several suggestions for doing so follow:

   1. *Increase students' awareness of the self-efficacy concept.* Many teachers and students underestimate the importance of self-efficacy. Emphasizing the positive consequences of high efficacy, describing how efficacy develops and deteriorates, and promoting positive efficacy messages in the classroom are goals every teacher should adopt. Teachers may wish to communicate to parents the role of efficacy to help promote an efficacy-producing environment at home.

   2. *Use expert and intermediate-level modeling.* Self-efficacy is domain-specific. One way to improve efficacy is by exposing students to expert and intermediate-level models. The former provide examples of expert performance that are motivational and informative. The latter illustrate that expertise develops slowly and is attainable through effort and use of strategies. Peer models appear to be especially effective in many settings.

3. *Provide feedback.* Behavioral and environmental feedback are two of the most important influences on self-efficacy. Students should be helped to evaluate their own performance. Teachers should also provide prompt, in-depth "performance" and "cognitive" feedback. For example, teachers should emphasize not only whether a strategy succeeded or failed but also why it did. The most effective kind of feedback relates performance outcomes to activities that cause those outcomes.

4. *Build self-efficacy rather than reduce expectations.* Bandura (1993) has stressed the importance of improving self-efficacy by incorporating efficacy-increasing experiences in the classroom rather than by decreasing task difficulty (see also Stevenson & Stigler, 1992). Decreasing task difficulty may actually decrease efficacy if students perceive that the teacher has little confidence in them. Teachers should consider ways in which class content can be challenging yet attainable. One effective method is to incorporate small, cooperative groups. Another is to allow ample time for students to achieve mastery of the material.

5. *Encourage self-regulation.* Educators should be mindful that teaching individual skills, such as metacognitive awareness and strategies, is only one aspect of the educational process. A more important aspect is to help students integrate all of these skills in a manner that enables them to become self-regulated learners once they leave school. Doing so presents a tremendous challenge to parents, teachers, and society. Although no easy paths lead to this goal, careful planning and reflection on what it means to be self-regulated no doubt will benefit students and teachers alike.

Attribution Theory

Every day, events take place in our lives that can be interpreted in several ways. Consider two college students who receive the same mediocre score on a history test. One student becomes angry and decides to drop the class because, according to her, the professor is a poor teacher who has written an unfair test. The second student resolves to work harder to learn the material. Clearly, these students have interpreted their experiences in very different ways despite similar levels of performance.

But what separates these two students? Why does one drop the class, whereas the other increases her effort? One explanation is that the two students have made different attributions about their poor test performance. The first student attributes her poor showing to the teacher, although she secretly may believe that it is because of her own lack of ability. The second student attributes her poor performance to lack of effort.

Attribution theory is the study of how individuals explain events that take place in their lives. An **attribution** is a causal explanation of an event. Attribution theory provides a framework for understanding why people respond so differently to the same outcomes (for reviews see Eccles & Wigfield, 2002; Peterson & Schrieber, 2006; Rudolph, Roesch, Grietemeyer, & Weiner, 2004; Stipek, 1996). Some of these causal explanations may predispose individuals to negative emotions or decrease the likelihood of future task engagement. Other explanations may provide individuals with reasons to persist or to work even harder.

In this section, we describe some main assumptions of attribution theory. To do so, we must consider what causes people to make certain kinds of attributions, what the most common attributions that people make are, what kinds of affective responses attributional judgments elicit, and how attributional judgments affect our behavior. We refer to these steps as the *attributional process*, described in the following section.

The Attributional Process

One way to think about the attributional process is the model shown in Figure 6.2. Four components are included in this model. One is *outcome evaluation*, the process by which we assess whether an outcome (e.g., a test score) is favorable or unfavorable. The second is *attributional responses*, in which we attribute this outcome to a particular cause. The third is some kind of *affective response*, in which the attributional response elicits an emotional reaction. The last is a *behavioral response*, in which we respond to the outcome in a particular way.

The key aspect of Figure 6.2 is that events do not elicit behavioral reactions *directly*, but do so only after being *mediated* by some form of cognitive interpretation. This model is similar in many regards to the basic assumptions of Bandura's social cognitive learning theory. One important difference, however, is that self-efficacy judgments pertain to future events, whereas attributional judgments pertain to past events (Graham & Weiner, 1996; Rudolph et al., 2004).

Outcome Evaluation   Outcome evaluations are made by using several criteria. One is the individual's prior history with similar outcomes. For example, if a student consistently performs poorly in history class, even an average grade on an essay test may seem favorable. A more important constraint is performance feedback. Typically, performance that falls below

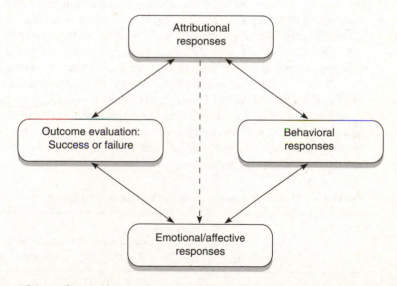

FIGURE 6.2   The Attributional Process.

Source: Adapted from *Learning and Instruction: Theory into Practice* (2nd ed.), by M. E. Gredler, 1992, Upper Saddle River, NJ: Merrill/Prentice Hall. Adapted with permission.

a preestablished standard is viewed unfavorably. Whether an outcome is viewed favorably also depends on the characteristics of the person, such as the need for achievement, the perceived importance of the task, and the expectations of others. Finally, outcomes are evaluated, in large part, on the basis of cues from others. For example, students who usually do quite well in class may be chided by instructors for submitting an average paper, while other students performing the same level of work may be praised because instructors expect less from them.

Attributional Responses   Attributional responses vary along three causal dimensions (Weiner, 1986, 1995). The first dimension is **locus of control,** which defines the cause of an outcome as either internal or external to the individual. Mood, for example, is an internal cause even though it may be affected by external variables. In contrast, parents and teachers are external causes of success or failure. The locus of control dimension frequently is linked with the kind of affective responses individuals experience after an outcome. For example, pride and confidence are associated with internal causes of academic success, such as ability, expert knowledge, and effort. Shame and anxiety are associated with external causes, such as unsolicited teacher help.

The second dimension described by Weiner is **stability.** Some causes of success, such as ability, usually are assumed to be stable, although considerable debate surrounds this issue (see Chapter 7). Other causes, such as effort, are less stable. Still other external causes, such as luck, are completely unstable. The stability dimension usually is linked with a person's success expectancy. If success is attributed to a relatively stable trait, such as ability or knowledge, it seems reasonable that past success would be repeated. In contrast, if success is attributed to a highly unstable cause, such as luck, there is little reason to believe that success will occur again.

The third dimension is **controllability.** Some causes of success, such as effort and strategy use, are highly controllable; others, such as ability or interest, are not. Uncontrollable factors, such as task difficulty and luck, obviously fail to promote confidence in one's ability to succeed again. The controllability dimension often is related to the amount of effort and persistence an individual devotes to a task. Outcomes viewed as uncontrollable often promote anxiety and avoidance strategies, while those under control lead to increased effort and persistence.

The three dimensions described above can be used to create a locus (stability) controllability matrix that is shown in Table 6.1. As this table reveals, causal attributions must be categorized along all three dimensions simultaneously because two different causes, such as effort and ability, may share two common dimensions but differ along a third. According to Weiner (1986), the unique configuration of each attributional cause elicits different emotional and behavioral responses in people.

TABLE 6.1   Three Dimensions of Weiner's Attribution Theory

	Internal		External	
	Stable	*Unstable*	*Stable*	*Unstable*
Controllable	Typical effort	Specific effort	Teacher responses	Help
Uncontrollable	Ability	Interest	Task difficulty	Luck

Affective Responses   Different attributional configurations give rise to different, though highly predictable, affective responses (Peterson & Schrieber, 2006; Weiner, 1990). Positive affective responses, such as pride and confidence, are most likely to occur when an event is attributable to an internal, controllable, and stable factor, such as general effort. This is especially true for average- and low-achieving students because effort allocation is under their direct control, whereas ability and task difficulty are not. Other positive emotions, such as gratitude, are most likely to occur when an event is attributable to an external, uncontrollable, and unstable factor, such as help from individuals who are not expected to provide it.

Negative emotions, such as anger, are most likely when an event has external, controllable, and stable causes. In contrast, humiliating emotions, such as shame, guilt, and embarrassment, have internal causes that vary along other dimensions. For example, students are most likely to feel shame when an outcome (e.g., low mathematics performance) is caused by an internal, uncontrollable, and stable trait (e.g., low mathematics ability). By the same token, pity is most apt to be elicited from others under the same conditions, wherein observers view the individual as helpless. Emotions such as guilt are most likely to occur when a cause is internal, controllable, and unstable, such as failing to complete one's homework or engaging in occasional inappropriate behavior.

Behavioral Responses   One basic tenet of attribution theory is that the interpretation of an outcome (causal attribution) will determine the kind of behavioral response an individual makes. As we have seen, attributions in which stability is the critical dimension frequently give rise to higher success expectancies and, in turn, higher levels of task engagement, challenge seeking, and performance. Attributions in which controllability is the critical dimension lead to greater effort and more persistence. Attributions in which internal locus of control is critical lead to feelings of confidence, satisfaction, and pride, whereas an external locus results in positive responses, such as help seeking, as well as negative reactions, such as helplessness, avoidance, and lack of persistence (Graham, 2005; Schunk, 2008).

Attributions in the Classroom

Studies have examined the kind of attributions that students make and why they make them. One of the most important findings from this literature is that different students make very different kinds of attributions. Some differences are related to gender; others are related to students' perceptions of ability. Still others are related to the ways teachers respond to students (Stipek, 1993).

A review by Peterson and Schrieber (2006) found that students' negative attributional styles (e.g., attributing failure to ability and teachers) are related to low grades, less help seeking, vaguer goals, poorer use of strategies, and lower performance expectations. Studies focusing on help-seeking behaviors in particular have reported that many students do not seek help because doing so provides an explicit low-ability cue to one's peers. In other words, a student's help seeking can be interpreted as evidence that he or she lacks ability.

A number of studies have found that help seeking among college students was positively related to global self-esteem but negatively related to the perceived psychological risk of help seeking (Peterson & Schrieber, 2006). One plausible explanation of these findings is that high-self-esteem students were more likely to attribute their success to controllable causes, including asking competent individuals for help. In addition, students who were more likely to seek help tended to use cognitive and metacognitive learning strategies even after the effect of perceived risk was controlled statistically.

Newman and Goldin (1990) reported similar findings in a study of elementary-age children. One interesting outcome was that children were more reluctant to seek help from peers, compared with adults (including teachers), because they were afraid to "look dumb" in the eyes of their classmates. Girls were more concerned about public appearances than boys, especially in mathematics classes, compared with reading classes. Help seeking was related also to academic achievement in that low achievers sought less help. Finally, the more the children thought help seeking would benefit them, the more likely they were to ask.

These studies suggest that low-achieving students are less likely to seek help because doing so provides a low-ability cue. A series of seminal studies by Barker and Graham (1987) and Graham and Barker (1990) has investigated low-ability cues in more detail. Barker and Graham (1987) found that teachers transmitted low-ability information to other students by way of the type and amount of praise and/or blame. Students praised for average achievement were judged by other students as having lower ability than students praised only for outstanding performances. Similar results were found when teachers blamed students for mistakes on simple versus complex tasks.

Graham and Barker (1990) extended these findings to teachers' offers of help in the classroom. Students who were quick to be helped by teachers were judged as having lower ability. The amount of teacher help also provided a low-ability cue. These cues were most apt to be detected among older (12-year-old) versus younger (5-year-old) students, although cues were salient at times even among the youngest students.

Together these studies suggest that teacher–student interactions provide a great deal of unintended information to other students (Schunk, 2008). Several studies indicate that reluctance to seek help is caused by low-ability cues provided inadvertently by teachers! Ironically, students labeled as low ability may be less likely to solicit teacher help in the future. They may try to decline help even when it is offered spontaneously by teachers despite the fact that seeking help is related to improved performance and higher academic achievement.

Attributional Retraining

Attributional retraining refers to helping individuals better understand their attributional responses and develop responses that encourage task engagement. A review by Försterling (1985) found that the majority of attributional retraining programs are quite successful. The general sequence is as follows: (1) Individuals are taught how to identify undesirable behaviors, such as task avoidance, (2) attributions underlying avoidant behavior are evaluated, (3) alternative attributions are explored, and (4) favorable attributional patterns are implemented.

Försterling reported that most programs emphasize a shift in "unfavorable" attributions based on ability to "favorable" attributions based on effort. Shifting attributions from ability to effort appears to be effective because effort is a controllable variable, whereas ability is not. Programs adopting this strategy frequently report an increase in task persistence and achievement levels.

In a series of studies by Schunk and colleagues (Schunk, 1983, 1987; Schunk & Cox, 1986), attributional feedback provided to students while they were engaged in a task increased self-efficacy and performance. Feedback about effort frequently improved task persistence, especially when it was given early in the learning cycle. To be effective, however, attributional feedback must be credible.

In contrast, Schunk (1984) found that sometimes feedback about ability has a stronger effect than feedback about effort. One group of students in this study received effort-only feedback, a second group received ability-only feedback, and two other groups received either effort-ability or ability-effort feedback. Schunk found that those who received ability feedback before effort feedback performed better and reported higher self-efficacy than those who received effort-only feedback or those who received effort feedback prior to ability feedback. Apparently, information regarding ability is linked more closely with one's sense of efficacy than is information about effort.

These findings suggest that attributional training should not focus exclusively on effort. In some cases, students may need to be reminded that their success is a result of high ability. In other cases, especially when students lack basic skills necessary for task completion, emphasizing the role of effort may increase persistence and task performance.

In addition, attributional training programs may be more effective for some individuals than others. Perry and Penner (1990) found that college students with an external orientation (those who perceived their success as having external causes) benefited more from attributional retraining than students with an internal orientation. Externally oriented students receiving the training earned higher achievement scores in coursework than externally oriented students without training and all internally oriented students. Hall et al. (2007) found that attributional retraining was beneficial for college students who engaged in written summaries of classroom success. Writing enhanced performance cognitions as well as course improvement.

Overall, the attributional retraining literature provides clear evidence that increasing students' awareness about the attributions they make and helping them make more favorable attributional responses improve self-efficacy and learning while reducing achievement-related anxiety (Alderman, 2004; Rudolph et al., 2004). For this reason, we believe that teachers should discuss the role of attributions in learning and provide some degree of retraining for students who make inappropriate attributions.

Implications for Instruction: Improving Student Attributions

1. *Discuss attributions and their effects with students.* Teachers can help students better understand the learning process by explaining what attributions are and the effects they have on learning. Research indicates that some students struggle unnecessarily because they incorrectly attribute failure to ability rather than to lack of effort or undirected effort. Explaining these subtle differences to students is not time-demanding or difficult and may greatly improve learning and confidence.

Studies also reveal that children younger than age 10 often do not distinguish between different attributional responses to the same extent as older children, adolescents, and adults (Schunk, 2008). For this reason, younger students may need explicit instruction to help them understand and redirect their attributional responses.

2. *Help students focus on controllable causes.* Most attributional retraining programs attempt to shift emphasis from ability to effort judgments. Attributing success or failure to effort is not as damaging psychologically because effort is controllable. In general, emphasizing controllable factors in the learning process increases task engagement, persistence, and performance. Emphasizing uncontrollable causes, such as ability, mood, task difficulty, luck, and characteristics of other students, increases anxiety and decreases challenge seeking.

3. *Help students understand their emotional reactions to success and failure.* Attribution theory provides a framework for understanding not only how we explain success and failure but also how we feel about it. Students who make certain types of attributions after failure experience predictable types of emotional responses. For instance, attributing failure to ability elicits some degree of humiliation in most students, whereas attributing failure to lack of effort leads to embarrassment. Clearly, some emotions are interpreted as more denigrating than others. Parents and teachers can do students a great service by helping them understand their emotional reactions to success and failure. More important still, students can be shown how to change these emotions by redirecting their attributional thinking.

4. *Consider alternative causes of success and failure.* Most attributional studies investigate a core set of responses, including ability, effort, teacher help, and luck. Curiously, many students struggle in class for different reasons, but especially because they lack prior knowledge, appropriate strategies, monitoring skills, and automaticity. Fortunately, all of these factors are controllable (changeable) even though it may take some time to change them. Students should recognize that many difficulties in the classroom are attributable to these factors, instead of to low ability or lack of effort. Doing so may help remove blame from students for poor performance or for difficulty mastering new information.

5. *Be mindful of inadvertent low-ability cues.* Sometimes teachers unintentionally provide low-ability cues about students. Unfortunately, some of these cues are transmitted while teachers are engaged in otherwise positive activities, such as praising and helping students. We recommend that teachers carefully consider the kind of information they communicate to their class by the way they offer help and praise and the way they reprimand students. Offering praise or help privately or through written feedback may be more beneficial for low-achieving students or for students who are prone to low self-esteem. Similarly, praising high-achieving students privately for normatively high performance may reduce the number of performance-oriented expectations they impose on themselves.

Autonomy and Control

The question of student autonomy is an important one, particularly as it pertains to real and imagined success in the classroom. **Self-determination theory** has argued that autonomy and control are essential components for well-being and academic achievement (Levesque, Zuehlke, Stanek, & Ryan, 2004). To examine this question in more detail, we first consider what it means to be motivated and how motivation affects behavior and a student's sense of control. In this section, we review current frameworks for understanding motivation, examine how motivation is related to behavior, and explore how controlling versus noncontrolling environments affect motivation.

One way to think of motivation is to distinguish between internal and external constraints on behavior. **Intrinsic motivation** refers to behaviors that are engaged in for their own sake (Ryan & Deci, 2002; Vansteenkiste, Lens, & Deci, 2006). When an individual is intrinsically motivated, tasks are performed for internal reasons, such as joy and satisfaction, rather than for external reasons, such as reward, obligation, or threat of punishment. Thus, a student is intrinsically motivated when she or he solves unassigned math problems simply out of interest. **Extrinsic motivation** refers to behaviors that are performed to achieve some externally prized consequence, not out of interest or a personal desire for mastery. Solving mathematics problems that one does not enjoy because they were assigned as homework is an example.

Studies have shown that even young children distinguish between intrinsic and extrinsic sources of motivation (Deci, Vallerand, Pelletier, & Ryan, 1991). Gottfried (1990) found that intrinsic motivation at age 7 was correlated with intrinsic motivation 2 years later, was positively related to intellectual ability, predicted current and future academic achievement, and was positively correlated with students' grades. Vallerand, Blais, Briere, and Pelletier (1989) reported that high intrinsic motivation was related to school satisfaction and more positive emotions in the classroom. More recent research has replicated this effect with older students up through college students (Black & Deci, 2000; Reeve, 2002).

At first glance, one might conclude that promoting intrinsic motivation would be sufficient for high levels of task engagement, persistence, and satisfaction. Unfortunately, the relationship between intrinsic motivation and classroom success is not as straightforward as it seems. Deci and Ryan (1985, 1987) have argued that a more fundamental distinction can be made between actions that are **self-determined** and **controlling.** The former actions include behaviors that individuals choose to engage in for intrinsic reasons. The latter are behaviors that individuals engage in because of internal or external pressure to conform to a set standard or to meet a particular expectation. For example, one student may choose to complete her homework because she enjoys the topic and takes pleasure in learning the material. Another student may choose to complete the same assignment to avoid a failing grade or because failure to complete the assignment would jeopardize his eligibility on the swim team. Although both students technically "choose" to complete the assignment, the degree of choice clearly is not the same.

According to Deci and Ryan, the distinction between autonomous and controlling actions is an important one because the degree of perceived choice determines one's behavioral response within a particular context. To be autonomous, a behavior must be chosen without pressure and be self-determined. In contrast, a controlling behavior may be chosen, but it will never be self-determined. As the example provided above illustrates, the same behavior in two individuals may be autonomous or controlling, depending on each person's understanding of why the behavior is performed and what the internal and external consequences are for performing or not performing the behavior. The subjective perception of why an action takes place is referred to as its **functional significance.** Individuals may attach different functional significance to the same event because "a person's perception of an event is an active construction influenced by all kinds of factors" (Deci & Ryan, 1987, p. 1033).

Control in the Classroom

Deci and Ryan have identified two types of environments: autonomy-supporting and controlling. A growing body of research has investigated some factors that promote autonomy and control, as well as their effects on task engagement, persistence, and learning (Burton,

Lydon, D'Alessandro, & Koestner, 2006). The most important of these factors are the nature of the to-be-learned materials, task constraints, teacher expectations, student expectations, evaluation, and rewards. We examine in the following sections how each of these factors affects intrinsic motivation and a variety of other behavioral measures.

Nature of the Materials   One of the most important motivational characteristics of materials is their difficulty. Materials that are too difficult for students promote a controlling environment, reduce intrinsic motivation, and create resistance to the task in many students. Materials may be difficult for several reasons, ranging from their grammatical complexity to their relative unfamiliarity. Information that students know little about typically will require more time and effort to learn and be more difficult to remember because they lack existing background knowledge.

Another important dimension is how interesting materials are. Research suggests that students find it easier to learn and remember more when they are interested in what they are studying. This is true especially of children and adolescents (Ainley, Hidi, & Berndorff, 2006; Chen & Darst, 2002; Durik & Harackiewicz, 2007). For example, Guthrie et al. (1996) found that high intrinsic motivation and interest were correlated with strategy use (.80) among fifth- and seventh-grade students. One reason is that interesting materials may increase intrinsic motivation to learn. A second reason is that interesting materials are more likely than uninteresting materials to be familiar to students. Not all interesting materials improve learning, however. Garner, Gillingham, and White (1989), for example, found that seductive details (information that was highly interesting but unrelated to the main topic of the story) interfered with learning main ideas. Lehman, Schraw, McCrudden, and Hartley (2007) reported that seductive details attract a great deal of readers' attention that would be spent more profitably on nonseductive main ideas.

Surprisingly, some studies suggest that individuals may regulate how much interest they have in materials. Sansone and colleagues (Sansone & Thoman, 2006; Sansone, Weir, Harpster, & Morgan, 1992) found that college students conceptually redefined boring tasks (e.g., copying information in different typefaces) that were viewed as important to complete. It remains to be seen whether younger students similarly spontaneously adopt strategies to make boring tasks more exciting and intrinsically rewarding. In a study by Schraw and Dennison (1994), students read a story from one of two assigned perspectives. Information relevant to the assigned perspective but not to the other unassigned perspective was judged as more interesting and remembered better.

In general, materials are most apt to promote autonomy and to be remembered when they are student selected or generated, of moderate difficulty, personally interesting, and familiar. Research also has shown that relating newly learned material to real-life experiences increases interest in that material, facilitates learning, and promotes autonomy.

Task Constraints   The nature of the task affects whether individuals perceive it to be autonomy producing or controlling. One obvious constraint frequently overlooked is whether the purpose of the task is clearly understood. Research suggests that low-achieving elementary-age children often do not understand purposes of many tasks. Although higher-achieving students within the same age-group have a better understanding of the immediate purpose, they lack broader knowledge of the task, such as what skills the task will help them develop and how successful task performance is related to performance outside school.

Another factor is the task's difficulty. Tasks of moderate difficulty appear to be the most challenging and satisfying for students. For this reason, accelerating the difficulty of a task to keep abreast of student development has a beneficial effect on learning and motivation. Non-accelerated tasks have been shown to promote within-class performance comparisons that, in turn, adversely affect intrinsic motivation.

One problem that teachers often face, however, is how to increase task difficulty in a heterogeneous group. Alderman (2004) describes several strategies for meeting this challenge. One strategy is to divide a class into smaller groups based on course achievement or task expertise. A second strategy is to use individual mastery programs in which students work at a pace that is comfortable for them until each has mastered the core material included in a unit. Learning centers where students work individually or in small groups are good examples. A third strategy is using peer tutors (including parents and volunteer aides) from either the same class or other classes. Research reveals that peer tutoring leads to higher motivation and learning in both tutors and those being tutored.

The pace and variability of tasks also is important. Tasks that require active student participation tend to increase intrinsic motivation and learning. Question-asking activities before, during, and after class discussions are one avenue for involving students. Similarly, encouraging students to use deeper, more elaborative strategies, such as those described in Chapter 4, leads to more active learning.

Varying the types of tasks to which students are exposed increases interest and learning. Tasks that require students to engage in problem solving, to consider unusual applications, or to think divergently about material not only encourage more active processing but also give students autonomy by allowing them to self-regulate their goals and strategy use.

Finally, research suggests that responses to different types of classroom tasks may depend on expectations established prior to beginning the task. Sansone, Sachau, and Weir (1989) found that students responded more favorably to instruction when it matched students' perceived academic goals. In this study, Sansone et al. emphasized either skill acquisition or fantasy while learning a computer game. Students in the skill-acquisition condition responded more favorably to instruction intended to facilitate skill acquisition, whereas the reverse was true of the fantasy condition. These findings suggest that responses to a learning task, as well as receptivity to instruction, depend, in part, on student- and teacher-imposed expectations.

Teacher Expectations   Teachers create either an autonomy-producing or controlling environment in the classroom by their actions and responses to students (Reeve, 2002; Reeve, Bolt, & Cai, 1999; Vansteenkiste, Simons, Sheldon, & Deci, 2004). Studies have revealed some ways teachers intentionally or unintentionally affect student motivation. Providing enjoyable and challenging tasks, making favorable attributional responses that emphasize the role of effort and strategies while minimizing the role of ability, and evaluating in a nonthreatening manner, are all ways that teachers promote intrinsic motivation and autonomy (Black & Deci, 2000; Rubie-Davies, 2007).

Research suggests that it is not so much what a teacher does but *how* she or he does it that matters most to students. For example, different "lesson-framing statements" can promote either an autonomous or a controlling environment. Statements that emphasize performance aspects of the task, such as "I want you to learn this material so that you will do well on the test," are more apt to decrease intrinsic motivation, compared with statements that emphasize learning aspects of the task, such as "Reading this passage will really help you understand the concept better." In one study, Williams and Deci (1996, p. 767) reported that "students who perceived their instructors as more autonomy-supportive became more autonomous."

Grolnick and Ryan (1987) studied different lesson-framing statements. Students in the controlling condition were told that they would take a test after reading a passage and that they were expected to do well on it. Other students read the same passage after being told to read however they wanted to read. Students in the controlling group reported greater interest in the passage and outperformed the noncontrolling group on a measure of conceptual learning. These effects also were observed 1 week later.

In another study, Flink, Boggiano, and Barrett (1990) investigated the effect of teacher pressure on student performance. Teachers were either pressured to maximize student performance or encouraged to teach in a style comfortable to them. Students of pressured teachers also were more pressured, compared with students taught by nonpressured teachers. The nonpressured students outperformed their pressured counterparts. In addition, pressured teachers made fewer personal disclosures and laughed less.

Another way teachers promote autonomy or control in the classroom is by the type of feedback they give students. **Performance-oriented feedback** emphasizes how well a student has performed in relation to other students. **Information-oriented feedback** emphasizes how performance can be improved. Studies indicate that informational feedback leads to greater intrinsic motivation, task engagement, and persistence than performance feedback. Written informational feedback has been found to be especially effective.

In addition, teachers elicit very different student responses based on their expectations. Teachers form expectations based on factors that include in-class performance and behavior, information provided by other teachers, and contact with siblings (Alderman, 2004). In general, the more controlling a teacher's expectations, the more likely it is that students will have low intrinsic motivation. Ironically, performance expectations communicated to students in a controlling manner tend to lower student performance rather than improve it (cf. Flink et al., 1990).

Good and Brophy (2007) have provided a useful framework for understanding teacher expectations. *Proactive* teachers do not allow their expectations to interfere with student interactions. Instead, they communicate beliefs and expectations openly, provide opportunities to all students, incorporate accelerated tasks, and offer genuine praise. *Reactive* teachers, however, are more likely to act on erroneous beliefs about students and to impose controlling expectations. Research surprisingly indicates that proactive teachers set performance standards that are as high as or higher than those of reactive teachers even though they provide students with more choices and options for achieving those standards. Proactive teachers also seem less likely to establish teacher's pets (Tal & Babad, 1990).

Jussim and Eccles (1992) asked whether teachers' expectations cause students to behave in a manner consistent with those expectations. Contrary to many earlier studies (e.g., Rosenthal & Jacobson, 1968), Jussim found that teachers' expectations tended to be quite accurate and showed little evidence of creating a "self-fulfilling prophecy." Of course, this does not mitigate the effect of some teachers' controlling behaviors and expectations. Jussim and Eccles (1992), for instance, reported that teachers' expectations were unrelated to standardized test performance but were related to systematic bias in the grades they gave to students. Thus, it appears that teachers' expectations may affect their views of students and influence students' motivation negatively by affecting students' expectations. This does not mean, however, that a teacher's expectations actually cause a student to act in accord with those expectations.

Finally, teachers' expectations are shaped in part by ability and gender variables (for a review see Eisenberg, Martin, & Fabes, 1996). Oakes (1990) reported that teachers of low-ability classes put less emphasis on basic concepts, complex problem-solving skills, and preparation for future coursework in the same area. In contrast, teachers of high-ability classes attempted to provide students with more in-class control and greater autonomy. Similarly, Kimball (1989) reported that females receive less teacher contact in middle school and high school settings despite similar numbers of student-initiated interactions. Females also received less praise and more criticism than males.

Student Expectations   Students create their own autonomous and controlling environments by the expectations they hold for themselves. Bandura (1993) identified two ways that beliefs promote autonomy. One way concerns the strength of personal self-efficacy. As efficacy increases, individuals feel a greater sense of control, which leads to less anxiety, greater persistence, more task-related effort, and better use of feedback. A second way pertains to the modifiability of the environment. Individuals with low self-efficacy are more likely to view their environment (as well as personal traits) as fixed rather than as changeable. This belief has been associated with a greater sense of futility, lower aspirations, and less ingenuity.

Other researchers have distinguished between a desire for control and perceived control. Desire for control among older students is related to increased effort, challenge seeking, persistence, and positive attributional response patterns, such as attributing success to effort rather than to luck (Vansteenkiste et al., 2004). Perceived control is positively related to academic achievement. Skinner, Wellborn, and Connell (1990) found that beliefs of elementary-age students were related to task engagement and grades. One type of belief pertained to *capacity*—that is, whether a student has the resources to accomplish a challenging goal. A second type of belief pertained to *control*—that is, whether a student could control her or his own academic progress. Skinner et al. reported that both capacity and control beliefs were significantly related to engagement and grades. In addition, teacher ratings of students' task engagement were significantly related to students' grades.

Boggiano, Main, and Katz (1988) investigated whether children's perceptions of academic control were related to academic competence and intrinsic interest. As predicted, children with a greater sense of personal control in the classroom reported more intrinsic interest in school activities, more academic competence, and a greater preference for challenge. These findings closely mirror those reported by other researchers (see Chapter 6 in Stipek, 1993, for a review of this area).

Classroom factors can increase intrinsic motivation as well. One factor is to provide students with a choice of materials and in-class tasks. Students allowed to choose relevant and pleasurable tasks usually select more challenging tasks and engage in them for longer periods of time. Setting personal learning goals also has a positive effect on motivation and learning. Studies show that **proximal goals** (short-term goals that can be achieved within several learning sessions) increase intrinsic motivation, provide more feedback, and increase feelings of competence and personal control compared with **distal goals** (long-term goals that require a great deal of time and effort to achieve).

Students also feel a greater sense of control when they are active participants in learning and classroom management. Teachers who allow students to set rules and choose appropriate consequences for violating those rules experience fewer behavioral problems. Similarly, when students generate their own materials, select learning strategies they feel most comfortable with, and ask questions of other students and teachers, they are more likely to persist and to report greater interest in a task.

Evaluation   One area of academic life that imposes a strong perception of control is testing and evaluation, but not all types of evaluation elicit the same reactions in students. **Norm-referenced evaluation** (students compete against other students) often reduces intrinsic motivation for average and low-achieving students. In contrast, **criterion-referenced evaluation** (students compete against a predetermined standard) may increase intrinsic motivation. Achieving a preestablished standard is especially motivating when the standard is related to the student's personal goals, signifies improvement, and is reached through effort rather than through normatively high ability.

Research further indicates that written evaluation serves a very useful function and frequently increases intrinsic motivation and performance. Comments that provide formative and/or diagnostic information help students identify the source of their errors, the nature of the errors, and how to correct them in subsequent assignments. In contrast, controlling feedback, such as negative remarks; excessive amount of red ink; or, worst of all, a poor grade without any comments, unequivocally reduces intrinsic motivation, task engagement, and persistence.

Another aspect of evaluation that strongly affects motivation is how teachers deal with errors. In a performance-oriented class, errors reduce motivation. Emphasizing the informational value of errors through written feedback or conferences, however, increases intrinsic motivation. Studies indicate that errors need not undermine performance, provided teachers believe that errors are potentially useful (Poplin, 1988). Using errors to evaluate the "process" rather than the "product" components of performance is helpful. Moreover, praising correction of errors frequently increases intrinsic motivation because it rewards student effort. One helpful rule of thumb for increasing intrinsic motivation is to allow students, whenever possible, to redo work containing errors.

Teachers also should consider the relative merits of private versus public evaluation. Most motivation theorists do not advocate public evaluation because it orients students to normatively high performance, rather than to improvement, and typically benefits only the top 15 to 20% of students. If public evaluation is used, teachers must ensure that all students are capable of competing with other students for high grades.

Private evaluation has important advantages from a motivational perspective. One advantage is that private evaluation does not provide ability cues to other students in the class. A second is that private evaluation is more apt to encourage students to engage in challenging assignments. It also enables students to track their progress actively by using charts and records in journals.

Rewards   Rewards have been part of classroom life since education began, and they continue to spark tremendous debate among practitioners and theorists (Cameron & Pierce, 1994; Cameron, Pierce, Banko, & Gear, 2005; Eisenberger & Cameron, 1996; Kohn, 1996; Patall,

129

Cooper, & Robinson, 2008). Unfortunately, from our perspective, the most commonly used types of rewards are for compliant behavior or normatively high performance. Many teachers and parents use rewards on a regular basis to motivate students. Indeed, many school programs use token economies and other complex reward systems to encourage learning and good behavior. Others rely on the first cousin of rewards—some form of threat or punishment. Many teachers give students in-class choices as a reward (Flowerday & Schraw, 2000; Patall et al., 2008; Schraw, Flowerday, & Reisetter, 1998).

But how effective are rewards at motivating students and improving performance? Deci and colleagues (Deci & Ryan, 1985, 1987; Deci et al., 1991) have identified two kinds of rewards: **informational** and **controlling.** Rewards that provide useful information or feedback to students generally increase intrinsic motivation and learning, whereas rewards that attempt to shape or control student behavior and performance generally decrease it. Moreover, controlling rewards invariably lead to poorer performance and reduced task engagement and interest *once they are terminated* (see Kohn, 1996, for a book-length review). In contrast, in a review that evaluated 41 studies of choice in the classroom, Patall et al. (2008) found that noncontingent choices increased intrinsic motivation and feelings of self-competence.

The potentially deleterious effects of rewards have been observed in a wide variety of settings. Newby (1991) found that first-year teachers' use of rewards and threats was negatively correlated with on-task behaviors, while confidence-building strategies, such as verbal encouragement, explicit instruction with examples, and favorable comments about mistakes, were positively correlated with the same behaviors. Hennessey and Amabile (1988) found that rewarding children for artistic performance had little immediate effect on the quality of artistic productions. When rewards were curtailed, however, students reported less interest in artistic endeavors and produced lower quality artistic productions. Similar negative effects were found when students were given strong criticism, received controlling rather than informational feedback, or were forced to compete with other students. In many cases, mere surveillance was sufficient to reduce intrinsic motivation and impair performance (Deci & Ryan, 1987).

The "reward withdrawal" effect described above seems universal in scope. Rewards decrease intrinsic motivation even though they do increase extrinsic motivation when intrinsic motivation is lacking. For this reason, rewards should be used only when individuals are *not* intrinsically motivated to perform a task. When rewards are used, negative effects are most likely to occur when they are expected, salient, and contingent on engagement, rather than when individuals are expected to meet a criterion-referenced performance standard. Curiously, providing a reward after the fact, when it is not expected, has few negative effects on motivation and performance. Thus, the *anticipation* of the reward, rather than the reward itself, seems to impair motivation.

For those who prefer to use limited rewards, the following tips may be helpful. First, use rewards sparingly. Rewards help motivate students, albeit extrinsically, in many tasks they would not engage in otherwise because of indifference or anxiety. Second, make sure all students are capable of meeting the criteria for earning the reward. Third, eliminate rewards once they are no longer needed, while simultaneously modeling positive, intrinsic reasons to engage in tasks (e.g., reading is relaxing and entertaining). Finally, avoid threats, deadlines, and other constraints that could be construed as punishments. Often punishments fail to elicit compliance and may impair performance and reduce intrinsic motivation.

Implications for Instruction: Fostering Student Autonomy

Research reveals many ways to promote either an autonomy-producing or controlling environment. Alderman (2004), Deci et al. (1991), and Schunk (2008) are good references on this topic. The following are some main points to consider when trying to promote student autonomy.

1. *Let students make meaningful choices.* The more options students are given, the more likely they will be to engage in, persist in, and enjoy a task. Parents and teachers should provide students with at least some choice regarding the materials, tasks, and kinds of evaluations used in the classroom. Allowing students to help select the tasks they undertake, to establish rules democratically, and to set appropriate consequences for violating rules helps promote better classroom discipline.

2. *Scrutinize teacher and student expectations.* Students often are unaware of teachers' and their own expectations. Taking some time at the beginning of the school year and periodically throughout the year to clarify expectations may be helpful. Low expectations or those that intentionally or unintentionally impose control have been shown to affect the performance of everyone in the classroom in negative ways. Teachers' expectations are especially important because students may form self-expectations based on these messages.

3. *Minimize extrinsic rewards.* Extrinsic rewards should be used thoughtfully and sparingly. Intangible rewards, such as genuine praise and attention, usually have a positive influence on students *provided* they are genuine, not overused, and accessible to all students. Tangible rewards, such as money, tokens, gifts, and free time, may reduce intrinsic motivation and interest in tasks while they are being performed and frequently decrease task engagement, persistence, and quality of performance once they are curtailed. Both tangible and intangible rewards, however, can promote task engagement when intrinsic motivation is low.

For these reasons, extrinsic rewards should be used only when students have no other reason to engage in the task. Using rewards as a long-term motivator may be disastrous unless the rewards are continued indefinitely. Using threats, punishment, or surveillance also is ill-advised because these methods rarely accomplish their purpose and may lower intrinsic motivation. In particular, essential academic skills, such as reading, writing, and mathematics, should never be used as punishments (e.g., writing essays after school for being late). Doing so gives students many reasons not to be intrinsically motivated in these activities in the future.

One final point: Rewards can be used effectively without any of the negative consequences described previously, provided that they are not contingent on some type of performance outcome. Rewards offered spontaneously—when they are not expected—as a rule do not reduce intrinsic motivation and performance.

4. *Incorporate criterion-referenced evaluation.* Evaluation that reduces the amount of direct competition while increasing the amount of informational or cognitive feedback to students usually increases intrinsic motivation and other task-engagement variables. In most instances, criterion-referenced evaluation satisfies these constraints more readily than does norm-referenced evaluation. Examples of the former include mastery learning, in which students work toward a preestablished standard that does not depend on the performance level of other group members; multiple-choice and essay tests that allow students to revise or justify their responses to improve their grade; portfolio assessment; and most forms of ongoing (formative) evaluation.

5. *Provide intrinsically motivating reasons for performing a task.* Providing students with an explicit or implicit rationale for engaging in an activity is a powerful instructional technique. Teachers who read more and model their own intrinsic enjoyment of reading to their students usually have students who read more in and outside class. Similarly, explicitly highlighting positive aspects of reading may help offset some students' feelings of low self-efficacy or anxiety.

Assessing Beliefs

This chapter addresses different types of motivational beliefs. One special problem regarding student and teacher beliefs is that they are unobservable, and therefore difficult to conceptualize and measure. Researchers often refer to abstract, unobservable psychological phenomena such as beliefs as *latent constructs*. A great deal of progress has been made over the past 30 years, however, in terms of conceptualizing and measuring the unobservable beliefs of students and teachers. For example, there are several widely used measures of teacher self-efficacy, as well as a large number of student assessments for self-efficacy in reading, mathematics, science, and writing. These instruments usually include 10 to 15 statements that require respondents to indicate whether she or he strongly agrees or strongly disagrees with statements such as "I can learn to solve algebra problems with a high degree of accuracy" or "I can plan a semester long science curriculum for my students."

The Teachers' Sense of Efficacy Scale (TSES) was developed by Tschannen-Moran and Woolfolk-Hoy (2001) to measure preservice or in-service teachers' sense of self-efficacy to teach. The TSES includes 24 items that measure three different aspects of teacher self-efficacy, including efficacy for student engagement, efficacy for using effective classroom strategies, and efficacy for classroom management. Although these three dimensions are part of the broader latent construct of teacher self-efficacy, they also represent somewhat different (and important) components of classroom instruction. The development of self-report instruments that assess teachers' beliefs has been extremely helpful because they enable researchers to test theories about the number and interrelationships between beliefs such as engagement, strategies, and management; and to determine the extent to which each of these beliefs is an important predictor of student engagement and achievement. For example, it may be the case that instructional strategies determine in large part whether students are successful learners in the classroom. In contrast, it may be the case that all three components measured by the TSES are equally important.

Self-report instruments such as the TSES undergo a sophisticated validation process to ensure that they measure what they claim to measure. The general validation strategy is to administer the pilot instrument to a large number of individuals of interest (e.g., 250 in-service teachers). The correlations between and among different items on the self-report instrument are used to determine whether the instrument measures one latent construct (e.g., general teaching efficacy) or two or more different constructs such as the engagement, strategies, and management traits proposed by Tschannen-Moran and Woolfolk-Hoy (2001). Next, researchers attempt to determine if teachers' scores on each of the measured scales (e.g., classroom strategies) are related to important classroom behaviors and achievement. Finally, researchers also correlate scores on the instrument of interest (e.g., teacher self-efficacy) to other related measures such as teacher motivation, years of experience, and educational background to determine how self-efficacy is related to a broader set of variables.

We believe that assessment of student and teacher beliefs is every bit as important as assessing students' academic achievement. Teachers and parents alike want students to succeed academically, but they also realize that it is important to identify factors that contribute to student achievement, including curriculum planning, teacher knowledge and adequate educational funding. In addition, understanding the role of beliefs and attitudes, and factors that affect beliefs and attitudes, is equally important. Conceptualizing and measuring these beliefs has become an important component of educational research. This research has led to a richer understanding of the complex relationships among beliefs, curricula, teacher knowledge, and student achievement.

Summary

This chapter describes three frameworks for understanding self-beliefs and how they can affect self-determination in the classroom. Bandura's learning theory emphasizes the reciprocal relationship among self-beliefs, performance, and environmental feedback. We focused in detail on one type of belief—self-efficacy—which is related to task engagement and academic achievement. Self-efficacy is domain-specific and subject to change through modeling, feedback, and self-statements.

Whereas self-efficacy beliefs are judgments about future events, attributions are judgments about past events. Attributions are causal explanations of our success and failure experiences in the classroom. Attributions vary along three dimensions: locus of control, stability, and controllability. Each dimension is associated with a particular type of emotional response. Research indicates that students' attributional patterns strongly affect their task engagement, persistence, and achievement. Undesirable attributional patterns can be changed with the help of attributional retraining programs.

We also considered the role of student autonomy in the classroom and how intrinsic motivation promotes feelings of autonomy. Students who feel a sense of control are more likely to seek challenge, persist at difficult tasks, and perform better than teacher-controlled students. Teachers who experience a sense of control also interact with students more favorably. Factors were discussed that affect students' sense of control, including classroom materials, task constraints, teacher and student expectations, evaluation strategies, and the use of rewards. Providing choices to students is an important means for increasing feelings of control and intrinsic motivation. Using extrinsic rewards, such as money or praise, generally decreases intrinsic motivation.

SUGGESTED READINGS

Alderman, M. K. (2004). *Motivation for achievement: Possibilities of teaching and learning* (2nd ed.). Mahwah, NJ: Erlbaum.

This book covers all the topics discussed in Chapters 6 and 7. Alderman focuses on day-to-day educational implications of motivation research.

Bandura, A. (1993). Perceived self-efficacy in cognitive development and functioning. *Educational Psychologist, 28,* 117–148.

This review provides an excellent summary of self-efficacy theory from its developer.

Eccles, J. S., & Wigfield, A. (2002). Motivational beliefs, values, and goals. *Annual Review of Psychology, 53,* 109–132.

This article reviews research on motivation, including self-efficacy, self-regulation, and attributional research.

Reeve, J. (2002). Self-determination theory applied to educational settings. In E. L. Deci & R. M. Ryan (Eds.), *Handbook of self-determination research* (pp. 183–203). Rochester, NY: University of Rochester Press.

This article describes implications of self-determination theory in the classroom.

Schunk, D. H., & Zimmerman, B. J. (2006). Competence and control beliefs: Distinguishing means and ends. In P. A. Alexander & P. H. Winne (Eds.), *Handbook of educational psychology* (2nd ed., pp. 349–368). Mahwah, NJ: Erlbaum.

This chapter provides an informative review of five contemporary theories of student and teacher motivation.

Shute, V. J. (2008). Focus on formative feedback. *Review of Educational Research, 78,* 153–189.

This article provides an up-to-date review of different types of feedback, especially formative feedback, and how to provide feedback in the classroom to improve learning and achievement.

Woolfolk-Hoy, A., Davis, H., & Pape, S. J. (2006). Teacher knowledge and beliefs. In P. A. Alexander & P. H. Winne (Eds.), *Handbook of educational psychology* (2nd ed., pp. 715–737). Mahwah, NJ: Erlbaum.

This chapter provides a comprehensive overview of teacher beliefs and their relationship to student academic achievement.

7 Beliefs About Intelligence and Knowledge

This chapter examines the role that beliefs about intelligence and knowledge play in thinking and problem solving. Often we are unaware that we hold these beliefs even though they predispose us to respond or think in a certain way. Research suggests that individuals who reflect on their beliefs are more apt to change them. Reflection can occur in a variety of ways, including collaborative dialogue, written reflection, journals and diaries, and most importantly, in-class discussions (Murphy & Mason, 2006).

The beliefs we hold, whether they are implicit or explicit, affect our behavior in many ways. In Chapter 6, we found that individuals with high self-efficacy are more willing to try a difficult task. By the same token, people who hold certain beliefs about the changeability of intelligence are more likely to persist when faced with difficulty, and those who view knowledge as certain only within a particular context are more likely to engage in skilled reasoning than those who view knowledge as absolutely certain. Before we discuss beliefs about intelligence and knowledge in more detail, let's first look at implicit beliefs.

Understanding Implicit Beliefs

What makes us think and act the way we do? At some point, most of us find ourselves voicing opinions that at another time and upon reflection we do not agree with. Sometimes, we realize quite unexpectedly that we are not sure what we believe about a controversial issue; at other times, we may articulate strong beliefs about important social topics without having any conscious awareness of where these beliefs came from or why we believe them. Researchers are beginning to understand that much of our behavior is shaped by unconscious beliefs about key aspects of learning, such as intelligence and knowledge. Beliefs of this type often are referred to as **implicit beliefs** because they represent unconscious, personal beliefs about the world that evolve slowly over time (see Chapter 3 for a discussion of implicit memory). No one is certain how or when these beliefs begin to develop. There is considerable agreement, however, that implicit beliefs have a significant effect on the way we view ourselves as learners and how we operate in the classroom (Dweck, 2000; Hofer, 2001; Schraw, 2000; Sinatra, 2001).

Implicit beliefs often give rise to an **implicit theory;** that is, a set of tacit assumptions by a person about how some phenomenon works. To illustrate, let's compare two typical students in a beginning algebra class. Imagine that they are talking after a difficult test and Akira says, "It doesn't surprise me that I'm no good in math. Nobody in my family was good at it either!" Presumably, Akira believes (at least implicitly) that success in a mathematics class is, in large part, attributable to genetic inheritance; otherwise, his family's mathematics ability should have nothing to do with his own success or failure. Now compare Akira with Alonzo, who responds, "At first, I struggled in this class, but then I went to the math lab, and the work I did there really helped me improve!" Alonzo appears to believe that his success in a mathematics class is attributable more to effort than to ability. Of equal importance, Alonzo implicitly endorses the view that his ability to learn mathematics is changeable.

Alonzo seems to hold a different view about his ability than does Akira about his. Their beliefs about their abilities form the basis of "theories of intelligence." These theories almost certainly are implicit. If Akira and Alonzo were asked to state their "theories of intelligence" explicitly, they would find it difficult to do (Schraw & Moshman, 1995). Moreover, the theory that each actually describes may be at odds with the implicit beliefs echoed in their conversation.

Although at first glance the study of implicit theories may appear to have little to do with effective learning and teaching, a good argument can be made that understanding and clarifying students' implicit theories may be just as important as providing basic content knowledge or strategy instruction. One reason is that research has shown that students with differing implicit beliefs differ in their willingness to use strategies while learning (Ames & Archer, 1988; Murphy & Mason, 2006; Roeser, Peck, & Nasir, 2006). Another reason is that students with differing implicit beliefs appear to think and reason in different ways, some of which are far more conducive to effective learning (Kardash & Scholes, 1996; Kuhn & Weinstock, 2002).

At this point, you may be asking yourself what kinds of implicit beliefs you have and how they affect your learning. The answer to this question is that all of us have many implicit beliefs, or in some cases explicit beliefs, about all kinds of everyday intellectual phenomena. Consider your attitudes about intelligence. What is intelligence? Do you believe that your intellectual aptitude is fixed and that no amount of effort, strategy use, or metacognitive awareness will improve it, or do you believe, as does Sternberg (2005), that intelligence is changeable by improving the kinds of intellectual skills that are necessary for classroom success?

Now, consider your views on creativity. Are some people born creative, whereas others are not? Is creativity teachable and, if so, to whom? Next, consider knowledge. Is there an ultimate, knowable truth in the universe that humans eventually will discover? Is knowledge relative? Does "truth" exist, and if it does, is it fixed and certain?

These examples illustrate the scope and importance of implicit beliefs about thinking and learning. The chances are good that you found these questions difficult to answer. The chances also are good that you have spent little time trying to reach definitive answers to these questions. Nevertheless, the "hidden assumptions" that underlie our thinking and behavior exert a very powerful influence.

Understanding implicit beliefs is an important first step in becoming self-regulated. Let's begin by examining some specific implicit beliefs in greater detail.

Beliefs About Intelligence

Dweck and colleagues (Dweck, 2000; Dweck & Leggett, 1988) proposed a highly influential social-cognitive model of motivation based, in large part, on the kinds of implicit theories that people hold about intelligence. Two types of implicit theories are proposed in their framework. The first is referred to as an **incremental theory,** due to the assumption that intelligence is changeable and improves incrementally. In contrast, individuals holding an **entity theory** of intelligence tend to believe that intelligence is fixed and unchangeable. According to Dweck and Leggett, most individuals can be characterized by one of these basic belief orientations. Individuals holding incremental and entity theories view the world in different ways that affect how they react to challenging situations.

One interesting aspect of the Dweck and Leggett model is that incremental and entity views of intelligence seem to be independent of a person's true intellectual ability (Dweck, 2000; Anderman & Wolters, 2006). Many studies support this view, indicating that high-ability students are no more likely than low-ability students to adopt incremental theories (Wolters, 2003, 2004). This finding holds promise for educators because it suggests that students' beliefs about intelligence need not be compromised on the basis of their true ability. Even those who struggle in the classroom can change the way they think about intelligence, which in turn may have a positive effect on their classroom achievement and beliefs (Braten & Stromso, 2005).

Holding either incremental or entity views also appears to have important consequences for personal academic goals. Incremental beliefs give rise to the development of **learning goals** (also commonly referred to as *mastery goals*), in which individuals seek to improve their competence. Entity beliefs give rise to **performance goals,** in which individuals seek to prove their competence. Research indicates that children and adolescents attuned to learning goals persist longer in the face of task difficulty; are more likely to attribute success to internal, controllable causes, such as strategy use and effort; and have an overriding concern for personal mastery (Greene & Miller, 1996; Harackiewicz, Barron, Tauer, Carter, & Elliot, 2000; Kaplan & Maehr, 1999). Children attuned to learning goals also show a preference for challenge and risk taking (Ames, 1992) and spend more time on-task (Midgley, Kaplan, & Middleton, 2001). In contrast, individuals attuned to performance goals are more apt to become frustrated and defensive when confronted with a challenging task; tend to attribute failure to external, uncontrollable causes, such as luck or teachers, or to internal, uncontrollable causes, such as lack of ability; and show an undue concern for demonstrating high performance, compared with others (Anderman & Wolters, 2006).

More recently there has been debate about the specificity of performance goals (Urdan & Mestas, 2006). Researchers have distinguished between performance-approach and performance-avoidance goals (Lau & Nie, 2008; Midgley et al., 2001; Pintrich, 2000b; Wolters, 2004). Performance-approach goals are those in which a student willingly approaches a task to prove his or her competence and high ability. Performance-avoidance goals are those in which a student attempts to avoid a task in which he or she looks incompetent. Urdan and Mestas (2006) found that high school students adopted different combinations of these goals for a variety of different reasons, including pressure from parents, pleasing peers, and proving to themselves that a goal could be accomplished. Pintrich (2000a) suggests that performance-approach goals may facilitate adaptive behaviors such as strategy use and positive feelings over and above the effects of mastery goals. In contrast, Midgley et al. (2001) suggest that performance-approach goals do not facilitate learning and achievement. Although the jury is still out on this debate, all of the relevant research on goal orientations agrees that learning goals facilitate learning and achievement and that performance-avoidance goals interfere with them. Interestingly, the same approach-avoidance framework for mastery and performance goals appears to apply to social settings (i.e., social goal orientation and interaction patterns) (Horst, Finney, & Barron, 2007).

Table 7.1 presents some important characteristics of individuals with learning and performance goals. Individuals with learning orientations tend to be most interested in academic improvement and, as a consequence, may be more apt to focus on the *process,* rather than on the *products,* of learning (Stipek & Gralinski, 1996; Urdan, Midgley, & Anderman, 1998). These students enjoy learning for its own sake and feel comfortable asking for help when they do not understand something. Another important characteristic of learning-oriented students is that they enjoy intellectual challenge and usually will work harder when they encounter challenging materials. When students with learning goals fail a quiz, they correctly recognize that many reasons can account for failure and that most of these reasons are changeable. They do not tend to attribute failure to low ability, as do students with strong performance goals. This characteristic, more than any other, may give learning-oriented students a distinct advantage because academic challenge or even failure may increase their motivation.

Students with learning goals differ from those with performance goals in several other important ways. One difference is that learning-oriented students are more likely to adopt more complex strategies once they begin to fail at a task, whereas performance-oriented students resort to inappropriate strategies (Elliot & Thrash, 2001; Midgley, 2002). A second difference is that individuals characterized by a learning orientation are more apt to engage in adaptive behaviors, such as persistence, focusing attention, and appropriate help seeking (Anderman & Wolters, 2006). For example, Nichols and Miller (1993) found that college students characterized by a strong learning orientation were significantly more likely to persist when confronting difficult material in an introductory statistics class. One explanation of this finding is that students with learning orientations maintain a higher sense of self-efficacy while engaged in a difficult task (Bandura, 1993).

TABLE 7.1   Characteristics of Learning- and Performance-Oriented Students

Learning Orientation	Performance Orientation
Improving competence	Providing competence
Seeks challenge	Avoids challenge
Persists	Quits
Attributes success to effort	Attributes success to ability
Positive response to failure	Negative response to failure
Uses strategies effectively	Uses inappropriate strategies
Self-regulated	Helpless

Source: From "A Social-Cognitive Approach to Motivation and Personality," by C. S. Dweck and E. S. Leggett, 1988, *Psychological Review, 95,* 256–273. Copyright 1988 by the American Psychological Association. Adapted by permission.

In contrast, performance-oriented students often adopt a maladaptive response pattern to failure. One type of maladaptive response occurs when students assume that they do not have the ability to succeed and refuse to continue working on a difficult task once they begin to fail (Solmon, 1996; Urdan, 1997). A second maladaptive response occurs when performance-oriented students become verbally defensive after experiencing difficulty on a task: These students may change the focus of conversation unexpectedly and describe in detail their competence at skills totally unrelated to the task at hand. For example, after failing a mathematics task, a performance-oriented student may boast about his or her skill at singing. A third behavior occurs when individuals refuse to engage in a task on the assumption that they will fail. In some cases, **learned helplessness** is a defense against perceived incompetence (Dweck & Leggett, 1988).

In general, individuals with performance orientations often seem overly concerned with doing better than others and may show far greater concern for the grade they receive than for the amount of information they learn. These students see their success or failure as the direct consequence of their intellectual ability yet do not see their ability as controllable. Performance-oriented students do not enjoy challenge to nearly the same degree as their mastery counterparts. For this reason, they may be less likely to show interest in topics they know little about or may fail at. They also may be less willing to try new strategies or to investigate novel solutions to a problem. One particular concern is that performance-oriented students are more likely to quit when faced with a difficult task.

As you might expect, students with learning and performance goals also differ noticeably in the types of attributions they make for academic success and failure. Results of a correlational study conducted by Ames and Archer (1988) are presented in Table 7.2. In this study, approximately 200 middle school and high school students were classified according to their goal orientations (see Roedel, Schraw, & Plake, 1994, for a similar study using college students). Students with learning and performance orientations were compared on several dimensions, including self-reported strategy use, responses to task challenge, and attributions for classroom success and failure. Results of the Ames and Archer study suggest some important and startling differences, which are summarized in Table 7.2. According to this study, students with learning goals tend to attribute their success in the classroom to effort, strategy use, and teachers.

TABLE 7.2   Attributions for Classroom Success and Failure for Students with Learning and Performance Orientations

	Learning Orientation	Performance Orientation
Reasons for success	Effort (.37)	Effort (.14)
	Strategy use (.22)	Strategy use (.24)
	Teacher assistance (.47)	
Reasons for failure	Teachers (−.29)	Low ability (.21)
		Task difficulty (.29)
		Lack of strategy use (.16)

Note: Numbers in italics indicate statistically significant correlations.

Source: From "Achievement in the Classroom: Student Learning Strategies and Motivational Processes," by C. Ames and J. Archer, 1988, *Journal of Educational Psychology, 80,* 260–267. Copyright 1988 by the American Psychological Association. Adapted by permission.

Learning- and performance-oriented students also differ with respect to academic self-efficacy and self-regulation (Midgley, 2002; Midgley, Anderman, & Hicks, 1995). A large number of studies have reported that K–12 students with strong learning goals are more efficacious (see Anderman & Wolters, 2006; and Schunk, 2008, for reviews). Roedel, Schraw, and Plake (1994) reported similar findings among college students. Bouffard, Boisvert, Vezeau, and Larouche (1995) found that college students who reported strong learning and performance goals attained the highest levels of academic self-regulation. These findings have since been replicated (Wolters, 2003, 2004).

Learning-oriented students also appear to have better relationships with teachers compared with performance-oriented students. In fact, of all the variables considered in the pivotal Ames and Archer (1988) study, learning-oriented students considered teachers to be of greater importance to academic success than ability, effort, or strategy use! Performance-oriented students, however, saw no relationship between teacher assistance and academic success. One important consequence of this difference is that learning-oriented students may be more inclined to ask for help from teachers or other students when they begin to struggle.

An examination of performance-oriented students reveals a rather different picture. Although these students appropriately attribute classroom success to effort and strategy use, they also view failure as the consequence of low ability, task difficulty, and poor teacher–student interactions. This pattern of attributions captures the essence of performance goals—the belief that success and failure in the classroom depend, in large part, on one's ability rather than on effort, strategy use, or teachers. Ironically, students with performance goals are more apt to quit when faced with a difficult task, on the assumption that they lack the ability needed to succeed even though they do not differ in ability, compared with students with learning goals.

Constraints on Classroom Behaviors

One might ask at this point what classroom factors, if any, are known to affect students' goal orientations positively. The work of Dweck (2000) and other researchers (Church, Elliot, & Gable, 2000; Harackiewicz et al., 2000; Midgley et al., 2001; Pintrich, 2000a; Urdan et al., 1998) suggests two important components: situational factors, such as classroom climate or home environment, and dispositional factors, such as basic personality makeup. Unfortunately, little is known about the relative contribution of each of these factors, although many researchers working in this area believe that the type of goal orientation a student adopts depends on a complex interaction between the two (Cain & Dweck, 1989). The work of Dweck and colleagues generally places a greater emphasis on dispositional factors that the student brings to the classroom. Ames and Archer (1988), however, have argued that learning and performance orientations are largely the result of classroom structure. Most recent writings have emphasized the effect of environmental factors as well, including school, teachers, and classmates (Perry, Turner, & Meyer, 2006; Wolters, 2004). Studies using sophisticated statistical modeling approaches suggest that classroom goal structures strongly impact both mastery and performance goals of students (Lau & Nie, 2008). Classes that place normatively high emphasis on ability and performance within the classroom peer group appear to promote a performance orientation among the majority of students, whereas classes that place high value on improvement, strategy use, persistence in the face of difficulty, and effort may promote learning goals even among students who are otherwise rather performative. From a practical viewpoint, all theorists agree that goal orientations are changeable, given careful consideration on the part of the teacher and students' awareness of the consequences of adhering to different types of goals.

Clearly, educators should think carefully about the kind of environment they create in their classrooms because situational factors are known to affect interest and motivation (Durik & Harackiewicz, 2007; Hidi & Renninger, 2006). Careful consideration also should be given to the role of ability, effort, and strategy use in successful learning. Emphasizing daily academic improvement and de-emphasizing the importance of ability is central to establishing a learning-oriented environment. The results of Sansone and Thoman (2006) also suggest that instruction is most effective when skill acquisition is emphasized from the onset.

Is Intelligence Changeable?

The work of Dweck and colleagues (Dweck, Chiu, & Hong, 1995; Dweck & Leggett, 1988; Elliott & Dweck, 1988) has raised interesting questions about the controllability of such traits as intelligence and personality. Attribution theorists such as Weiner (1986) suggest that intelligence is defined as an internal, stable, and uncontrollable trait, a view quite consistent with the beliefs of entity theorists (see Chapter 6). In contrast, other theorists believe that intellectual ability is changeable and therefore partially under the control of the learner (Ackerman & Lohman, 2006; Perkins, 1995).

The idea that one's intelligence is controllable may seem foreign to some readers. Whether intelligence is controllable and, if it is, to what extent it can be changed, remains hotly debated. Some experts working in the area of human intelligence support the entity view (Jensen, 1992); others, such as Robert Sternberg (1986), have proposed theories consistent with an incremental theory. In Sternberg's view, individuals can improve their intellectual performance in any given situation by adapting to the demands of the situation as strategically as possible.

Ultimately, whether intelligence is fixed or changeable depends on how one defines intelligence. If *intelligence* means "the ability to adapt successfully to an environment," then surely it is changeable. In Chapter 4, for instance, we described helpful learning strategies that are known to improve learning by helping individuals use their cognitive resources more efficiently. In Chapter 6, we described the many ways that academic performance and reasoning ability are improved by a concomitant change in self-efficacy (see Bandura, 1993, for a further discussion of changeable ability). Our own view is that successful learning depends far more on how one uses one's resources than on how many resources one has. Although it is unknown whether the amount of resources one has can be changed, it is well known that how effectively one uses them can be changed quite dramatically.

Guidelines for Fostering Adaptive Goals

Dweck and Leggett's (1988) theory suggests that individuals with learning orientations are more likely to feel comfortable and to succeed in an academic setting. This suggestion raises the question of how teachers and parents can create an environment conducive to the development of learning goals. We offer the following suggestions.

1. *Promote the view that intellectual development is controllable.* The basic distinction made in Dweck and Leggett's framework is between individuals who believe that intelligence is fixed or changeable. Those who believe that it is changeable report more satisfaction with school and persist longer on a difficult task without succumbing to frustration. Promoting the view that intellectual performance is controllable may lead to the kinds of adaptive behaviors described earlier.

2. *Reward effort and improvement while de-emphasizing native ability.* Students clearly differ in ability. Basing class grades or recognition on ability, however, may promote a performance orientation, especially if carried to an extreme. In contrast, rewarding effort and improvement emphasizes the incremental nature of learning.

3. *Emphasize the process, rather than the products, of learning.* Focusing on the process of learning highlights its incremental nature, whereas focusing on the products emphasizes the outcome of that process. Research suggests that feedback acquired about the process of learning is especially important to learners.

4. *Stress that mistakes are a normal (and healthy) part of learning.* Everyone makes mistakes when learning a new skill. How teachers respond to these mistakes sends a powerful message to students. When mistakes are viewed positively, receive corrective attention, and are used to provide feedback to students, students learn more than when mistakes are viewed in a negative light (Poplin, 1988). Using mistakes constructively also highlights the incremental nature of learning, a view consistent with a learning orientation.

5. *Encourage individual, rather than group, evaluative standards.* Much of the evaluation that occurs in education, especially among high school and college students, is **norm-referenced** (each student's performance is compared with the group's average performance). Group-based grading may lead to the adoption of a performance orientation, given that each student is compared directly with the group norm. In contrast, encouraging individual standards (e.g., portfolio evaluation) is more likely to promote the development of a learning orientation.

Beliefs About Knowledge

Our discussion thus far has focused on the classroom consequences of implicit beliefs about intelligence. Researchers also have discovered that students' beliefs about the nature of knowledge have important consequences for academic performance and critical thinking (Bendixen & Rule, 2004; Braten & Stromso, 2005; De Jong & Ferguson-Hessler, 1996; Farnham-Diggory, 1994; Hofer, 2004). Historically, beliefs about the origin and nature of knowledge, or **epistemological beliefs,** have been of interest since the Greek philosophers (Packer & Goicoechea, 2000; Ponterrotto, 2005). Recent studies of epistemological beliefs have attempted to isolate more precisely the consequences of holding particular beliefs (Cunningham & Fitzgerald, 1996; Hofer & Pintrich, 1997; Joram, 2007; Marra, 2005). This research has investigated the developmental sequence that individuals pass through on their way to mature reasoning about knowledge (Kuhn & Weinstock, 2002; Valinides & Angeli, 2005), as well as how these changes are related to academic performance (Cano, 2005).

One of the earliest educators to investigate this phenomenon was Perry (1970), who proposed a model in which students pass through several distinct, ordered stages in the development of beliefs about knowledge. In the early stages, students adopt what Perry refers to as a *dualist* perspective, in which knowledge is viewed as either right or wrong. Students in this stage tend to view knowledge as being absolute, universally certain, and accessible only to authorities. Individuals at this level of reasoning may assume, for example, that only prominent theologians have a true understanding of life's basic truths. Rather than question this authority, dualists accept these truths on the assumption that understanding such matters is beyond their intellectual grasp and must be accepted on faith. In later stages, however, students progress beyond the dualist mode of thinking to a more relativist stage, in which knowledge is viewed as uncertain and relative. *Relativists* hold the view that knowledge must be evaluated on a personal basis by using the best available evidence.

Ryan (1984) provided an experimental test of Perry's basic framework and concluded that relativists not only hold different beliefs from dualists but also approach learning in a more sophisticated way. To test the dualist–relativist distinction, Ryan first grouped college students into the two categories described above. Next, he asked them to describe the strategies they used to monitor their comprehension while reading. Finally, he tracked students through a semester-long psychology class and recorded their final grades.

Results of this study suggest some important findings. First, dualists do not do as well as relativists when final grades are considered. An analysis of comprehension-monitoring standards suggests why: Dualists tend to search for fact-oriented information while studying, whereas relativists tend to search for context-oriented information. Dualists generally rely on remembering information reported explicitly in the text, whereas relativists are more likely to construct a meaning from the text, to paraphrase, or to create an overall framework that summarizes the main ideas presented in the chapter. Surprisingly, these differences were found even when academic aptitude (SAT scores) and academic experience were taken into consideration. These latter findings suggest that the performance differences observed between dualists and relativists are attributable to beliefs about knowledge and how these beliefs affect study strategies.

Responses to Ryan's work have been mixed, however. Schommer (1990) argued that Ryan's dichotomous view is too simple to describe accurately the complexity of epistemological beliefs. To test this view, Schommer developed a self-report inventory in which students responded to 62 true–false questions on their beliefs about the nature of knowledge. Three of the questions included in this instrument are "Truth is unchanging," "Scientists can ultimately get to the truth," and "Successful students learn things quickly."

Schommer's study suggests that people hold extremely complex beliefs about knowledge that vary across four separate dimensions. The first dimension, *simple knowledge,* refers to the belief that knowledge is discrete and unambiguous. Students who score high on this dimension believe that learning is equivalent to accumulating a vast amount of factual knowledge in an encyclopedic fashion. Schommer's second dimension, *certain knowledge,* pertains to the belief that knowledge is constant: Once something is believed to be true, it remains true forever. The third dimension is *fixed ability;* that is, the belief that one's ability to learn is inborn and cannot be improved through either effort or strategy use. Like Dweck and Leggett's (1988) entity theorists, these individuals may believe that intelligence is fixed and personally uncontrollable. The final dimension, *quick learning,* refers to the belief that learning occurs quickly or not at all. Students scoring high on this dimension assume (inappropriately) that limited failure is tantamount to permanent failure. If a problem cannot be solved within 10 minutes, for example, it will never be solved. A number of recent studies have replicated these dimensions (Hofer, 2000; Schraw, Bendixen, & Dunkle, 2002).

Schommer's work is unique in that it is among the first to examine closely the underlying complexity of beliefs about knowledge. After identifying the four component beliefs just described, she next investigated their relationship to socioeconomic variables and information processing skills (for reviews see Schommer, 1994; and Schommer-Aikins, 2002). One of the more interesting findings is that the amount of higher education that students receive is inversely related to their belief in certain knowledge. All other things being equal, the longer students attend college, the more likely they are to believe that knowledge is tentative and subject to personal interpretation. One important implication of this finding is that better educated people may be more willing to adopt a constructivist approach to learning because believing that knowledge is certain should rarely lead one to question the legitimacy of that knowledge. This finding also suggests that encouraging individuals to further their education beyond high school may have a profound effect on their beliefs about knowledge (Baxter-Magolda, 1999, 2002; Kuhn, Cheney, & Weinstock, 2000). A similar effect has been found in research that investigated continuing education in pre- and in-service teachers (Brownlee, 2004), as well as studies that investigated graduate students' discussions of their epistemological beliefs (Marra, 2005; Olafson & Schraw, 2002).

Another interesting finding is that females are more likely to believe that learning is gradual rather than quick. This belief may lead females to stick with a difficult -to- learn subject longer than males and to feel less frustrated when an answer does not occur immediately. Quick learning was related as well to other socioeconomic indicators: the student's year in school, the father's educational level, and how much independent discussion was allowed at home. Those with less education were more apt to believe that acquiring new knowledge occurs in an all-or-nothing fashion; those with more college experience tended to view knowledge as tentative. Simple knowledge was related to the strictness of the home environment: Stricter standards led to the belief that knowledge is unambiguous, whereas greater tolerance led to the belief that knowledge is complex and subject to interpretation. Encouragement toward independence in the family structure also had positive effects on beliefs about simple knowledge and quick learning.

An analysis of the relationship between beliefs about knowledge and information processing strategies showed that quick learning predicted oversimplified conclusions when students were asked to provide a written conclusion to a chapter on theories of aggression. Prior knowledge also was related to the type of conclusions students drew in that more knowledge about the topic was associated with broader conclusions. A belief in quick learning also led to poorer performance on a summative mastery test of the material, as well as greater overestimation of understanding of the passage.

A number of studies have reported that beliefs in simple knowledge negatively affected complex problem solving. As beliefs in complex, incremental knowledge increased, problem solving improved. Jehng, Johnson, and Anderson (1993) found that epistemological beliefs differ across academic disciplines among college undergraduate and graduate students. Students in "soft" disciplines, such as the humanities, were more likely to believe that knowledge is uncertain than students in "hard" disciplines, such as physics. Compared with undergraduates, graduate students were more likely to believe that knowledge is uncertain and develops incrementally (they did not believe in quick learning). Bendixen, Schraw, and Dunkle (1998) found that epistemological beliefs were related to moral reasoning among adults. Individuals adopting beliefs in complex, incremental knowledge reasoned at a higher level on the Defining Issues Test. Kardash and Scholes (1996) reported that beliefs in certain knowledge were associated with lower scores on the Need for Cognition Scale and in written measures of cognitive reasoning.

Kuhn and colleagues (Kuhn 1991, 1992; Kuhn et al., 2000) found that epistemological beliefs are related to one's ability to argue persuasively. In this study, individuals were classified as an *absolutist* (one who believes that knowledge is absolutely right or wrong), a *multiplist* (one who believes that knowledge is completely relative), or an *evaluative* theorist (one who believes that knowledge, though relative, is constrained by situational factors such as commonly accepted rules) on the basis of their beliefs about the certainty of knowledge. Evaluative theorists were more likely than absolutists to provide legitimate evidence in support of an argument. In addition, compared with absolutists, evaluative theorists generated a greater number of plausible alternative theories and provided better counterarguments.

Elsewhere, Schoenfeld (1983) investigated consequences of quick learning. Schoenfeld reported that even experienced students who were asked to solve mathematics problems gave up after 5 to 10 minutes on the assumption that if they failed to solve the problem during this time, the problem could not be solved. One interesting question raised by this research is whether students who are prone to quit after a brief period are more likely to hold entity theories of learning that predispose them to failure avoidance.

Together, these studies indicate that beliefs about knowledge and the knowing process affect the way one reasons, how long one persists at a difficult task, the degree to which one is metacognitively engaged in self-regulatory activities, and perhaps what academic discipline one enters (Muis, 2008; Schraw, 2001). They also indicate that epistemological beliefs are affected by home environment and, in particular, by educational level. More education seems to translate into a more relativist viewpoint—a fact that has not escaped the attention of some civic and religious leaders who view universities suspiciously as bastions of "secular humanism" (cf. Moshman, 1981). Ironically, when using objective criteria such as amount and kind of evidence at one's disposal, virtually all studies indicate that relativist thinking leads to better reasoned conclusions (see Kuhn, 1991; and Kuhn & Weinstock, 2002, for a review).

Teachers' Epistemological Beliefs

Researchers have begun investigating teachers' epistemological beliefs in the past decade. Many of these researchers have argued that teachers' epistemological beliefs influence teaching practices (Brownlee & Berthelsen, 2006; Chan & Elliott, 2004; Haney & McArthur, 2002; Ozgun-Koca & Sen, 2006; Yang, 2005). For example, teachers with more sophisticated epistemological beliefs and worldviews were more likely to endorse student-centered instructional practices that emphasize critical reasoning. In contrast, teachers with less sophisticated beliefs were more likely to focus on traditional curriculum, student testing, and mastery of basic science concepts. Kang and Wallace (2004) reported similar findings when examining the relationship between epistemological beliefs and laboratory activities in American high school science classrooms. Lidar, Lundqvist, and Ostman (2005) found that teachers with more sophisticated personal epistemologies used a greater number of *epistemological moves* in their science classrooms, where moves consisted of cognitive activities designed to promote deeper learning and reflection, including generating, constructing, and reconstructing. They also reported that the relative success of different epistemological moves depended in large part on contextually specific factors such as student knowledge, complexity of activity, and sophistication of students' conceptual understanding.

Teachers' epistemological beliefs may also have an impact on student epistemological development and learning (Johnston, Woodside-Jiron, & Day, 2001; Lidar et al., 2005; Louca, Elby, Hammer, & Kagey, 2004; Marra, 2005). In their study of two contrasting classrooms, Johnston et al. (2001) found that students held different views of what it meant to be competent in literacy, and that students' literacy-related epistemologies can be traced from teacher to student.

The development of teachers' epistemological beliefs is another area of study within the field. Brownlee (2004) found that preservice teachers who were enrolled in a program based on relational pedagogy experienced more growth in sophisticated epistemological beliefs as compared with preservice teachers in a tutorial group. Marra (2005) reported similar findings in a study of how constructivist instruction affected the development of graduate student teachers at a university. Teachers reported a variety of changes after the course, but especially changes in epistemological and pedagogical beliefs (Gill, Ashton, & Algina, 2004). One key finding was that teachers were much more likely to adopt constructivist beliefs that emphasized the role of student interactions (Olafson & Schraw, 2006).

Reflective Judgment

Another framework for studying beliefs about knowledge and how they affect behavior is that of Kitchener and King (2004) and King and Kitchener (1994, 2002). The focus of this research is somewhat different from Perry's in that it emphasizes examining differences in the way people resolve dilemmas rather than differences in their beliefs per se. In their initial study, Kitchener and King (1981) developed a seven-stage developmental model of *reflective judgment*. Table 7.3 presents the characteristic reasoning processes and assumptions of each of these stages.

Reflective judgment is a term used by Kitchener and King (1981, 2004) to refer to one's ability to analyze critically multiple facets of a problem, reach an informed conclusion, and justify one's response as systematically as possible. Previous research suggests that reflective judgment depends on a set of epistemological assumptions that develop slowly in a predictable, developmental sequence (Kitchener, 1983; Kitchener & King, 1981). For example, abandoning the belief that knowledge can be known with absolute certainty appears to improve the quality of one's reasoning (Kitchener & Fischer, 1990). Other studies reveal that reflective judgment develops throughout early adulthood (Kitchener & King, 1981) and is related to age and education (King, Wood, & Mines, 1990) and critical thinking ability (King et al., 1990) but is independent of measures of cognitive ability, such as verbal fluency (King & Kitchener, 1994).

Kitchener and King (1981) identified seven developmental stages of reflective judgment that can be distinguished on the basis of three criteria. One criterion is the *certainty* of a knowledge claim (King et al., 1990). Individuals in Stages 1 through 3 of the taxonomy believe that knowledge is certain and permanent even though knowledge may be known to only a select few. Individuals in Stages 4 and 5 view knowledge as almost totally uncertain. Individuals in Stages 6 and 7 view knowledge as context-dependent; some things are knowable, at least temporarily, even though one's views on a particular topic may change in the light of new information or a different set of evaluative criteria.

TABLE 7.3   Stages in Kitchener and King's Reflective Judgment Model

Stage 1	Knowledge is unchanging, absolute, and accessible.
	• Beliefs are based on personal observation.
	• Knowledge exists absolutely and concretely.
Stage 2	Knowledge is certain but may not be accessible to everyone.
	• Knowledge is certain.
	• Knowledge is accessible only to authorities.
Stage 3	Knowledge is certain, though it may be accessible to anyone.
	• Knowledge exists absolutely.
	• There is no rational way to justify beliefs.
Stage 4	Knowledge is uncertain and idiosyncratic.
	• Truth varies from person to person.
	• Knowledge is interpreted subjectively.
Stage 5	Knowledge is uncertain, though contextually interpretable.
	• Objective knowledge does not exist.
	• Beliefs can be justified by using "rules of inquiry."
Stage 6	Knowledge is relative yet justifiable on the basis of rational arguments.
	• Knowledge is personally constructed.
	• Beliefs are justified by comparing evidence.
Stage 7	Knowledge is relative, though some interpretations have greater truth than others.
	• Knowledge is constructed.
	• Beliefs are justified probabilistically.

Source: Adapted from "Reflective Judgment: Concepts of Justification and Their Relationship to Age and Education," by K. S. Kitchener and P. A. King, 1981, *Journal of Applied Developmental Psychology, 2,* 89–116. Adapted with permission.

A second criterion is the *process by which we acquire knowledge.* Individuals in Stages 1, 2, and 3 emphasize the defining role of direct observation or authority figures; that is, knowledge is encoded directly from external sources. Those at Stage 4 rely chiefly on personal, idiosyncratic processes, such as personal opinion. Individuals at higher stages of reflective judgment show an increasing proclivity to rely on objective, consensual processes, such as critical debate and hypothesis testing that are tempered by personal reflection.

A third criterion is the *type of evidence* used to justify one's views of the world. Individuals at Stage 1 typically view justification as self-evident. Thus, a Stage 1 reasoner may assert that evidence that God exists "is all around us." Those at Stages 2 and 3, in contrast, are apt to cite a specific authority, such as an eminent theologian, book, or expert. Individuals at Stages 4 and 6 tend to rely on idiosyncratic evidence. For these individuals, a belief in God would be justified on the basis of the individual's personal beliefs, whereas those in Stages 5 and 7 rely on consensual forms of evidence, such as laws, scientific facts, and the opinions of a diverse body of experts.

The work of Kitchener and colleagues suggests that two primary mechanisms affect the development of reflective judgment (Kitchener, King, & DeLuca, 2006). One mechanism is *experience.* Previous research has found that age, education, and home environment all provide a statistically significant prediction of reflective judgment skills (Kitchener & King, 1981). Related research also suggests that reflective judgment may be affected by the type of intellectual discipline one enters (King & Kitchener, 2002; King et al., 1990). A second mechanism is one's *belief system*. In this regard, Kitchener and King (1981, p. 90) state, "Differences in concepts of justification . . . are derived from different assumptions about reality and knowledge." What these assumptions are and how they differ across individuals remain unclear. No doubt, some are related to epistemological beliefs about the certainty, complexity, and permanence of knowledge; others may be related to a broader set of beliefs that include assumptions about the role of innate ability (Dweck & Leggett, 1988) and the legitimacy of constructivism in the knowing process (Chandler, Boyes, & Ball, 1990).

Stages in Reflective Judgment

Reflective judgment is assumed to develop in a sequential fashion; that is, individuals progress from Stage 1 to higher levels without skipping stages. This does not mean that each person reaches the highest stages or that two people progress at the same rate. Rather, development of reflective judgment is highly idiosyncratic.

Each stage is associated with a unique set of assumptions about reasoning. These assumptions pertain to certainty of knowledge, processes by which one acquires knowledge, and kinds of evidence used to evaluate claims about knowledge. These criteria are shown in Table 7.4.

Individuals in Stage 1 are characterized by the belief that knowledge is certain, absolute, and indistinguishable from one's beliefs. Within this framework beliefs are either right or wrong, but they are never ambiguous. Individuals in this stage are prone to accept apparent truths at face value, without a great deal of scrutiny. Justification of truth or knowledge is not required, owing to the close relationship between knowledge and direct observation. In many

TABLE 7.4   Evaluative Criteria for Each of the Seven Stages of Reflective Judgment

Level	Performance	Certainty	Justification of Conclusions
1	Fixed	Absolute; certain.	Personal beliefs that are self-evident. No justification or evidence given.
2	Fixed	Absolute; certain.	Recognized authorities. Direct observation of world.
3	Fixed	Temporarily uncertain.	Authorities or direct observation when knowledge is uncertain.
4	Changes	Permanently uncertain.	Idiosyncratic beliefs.
5	Changes	Permanently uncertain.	Rules of inquiry for a particular context (e.g., societal norms).
6	Changes	Certain in a context.	Evaluation of objective evidence via personal criteria.
7	Changes	Certain in a context.	Formalized rules of inquiry (e.g., logic). Evaluation of empirical data.

Source: From *The Relationship Between Epistemological Beliefs, Causal Attributions, and Reflective Judgment* by M. F. Dunkle, G. Schraw, and L. Bendixen, 1993, April. Paper presented at the Annual Meeting of the American Educational Research Association, Atlanta, GA.

ways, Stage 1 thinkers lack the ability to make reflective judgments because they believe that knowledge is predetermined and absolute.

Stage 2 reasoners differ from those in Stage 1 in that they believe that knowledge, though assumed to be absolute and predetermined, is limited to authorities and experts. Individuals at this level implicitly live by the motto "When in doubt, ask an authority." Of course, this approach to resolving complex moral and ethical issues can have disastrous consequences because there is no reason to believe that reflective judgment will improve as long as one believes that only experts are capable of skilled reflective reasoning; that is, excessive faith in "omniscient authorities" may undermine the subsequent development of reflective judgment!

Stage 3 differs from either of the stages previously described. Individuals in this stage recognize that even authorities may lack answers to difficult dilemmas. In this view of reflective judgment, individuals may come to the initially disconcerting conclusion that no one is capable of ever reaching the truth about a complex issue. Yet the belief that truth ultimately will be identified empirically typically is still maintained. According to Kitchener and King (1981), beliefs at this level are justified by what feels right to the individual.

Stage 4 represents a dramatic change from the three earlier stages in that knowledge and beliefs now are viewed as fundamentally uncertain. Truth becomes relative within this framework because, as is often the case, different views can be supported or refuted by a variety of incompatible facts. One important advantage to this way of thinking is the recognition that what is true for one person will not necessarily be true for another. A major liability of this stage is that truth and knowledge must be justified on a person-to-person basis; hence, beliefs and assumptions may differ dramatically even between individuals who share otherwise similar worldviews.

Individuals in Stage 5 possess an even greater sense of epistemological uncertainty because objective knowledge is assumed to be nonexistent. Knowledge within this framework becomes completely relative because the ultimate truth or falsity of an argument can be evaluated only within the context in which the information occurs; thus, conclusions about knowledge always are subject to change if a different context is given for interpreting the issues. According to Kitchener and King (1981), choosing between competing interpretations often is resisted during this stage, on the assumption that no single solution can ever be completely validated.

In contrast, Stage 6 reasoners recognize that some arguments are better than others and can be evaluated on their merit. A further assumption by individuals in this stage is that the basic process of evaluating arguments remains unchanged even if the context in which the argument is presented changes. Stage 6 reasoners appreciate the reciprocal relationship between the process and the product of justification; that is, the conclusions one reaches are determined, in part, by the kind of argument one uses to reach those conclusions. Individuals in Stage 6 also recognize that multiple "constructions" of a problem are possible and even desirable.

Stage 7 reasoning differs still further in that although interpretations of truth and knowledge change across different contexts, some interpretations are more justifiable than others on the basis of either evidence or the rigor of one's argument. Knowledge is constructed during this stage on the basis of personal inquiry into the nature of the problem and evidence that supports or refutes one's tentative conclusions. Beliefs are justified probabilistically on the basis of evidence available to the individual. Stage 7 includes recognition that what is currently accepted as the most reasonable solution to a problem may later change to accommodate new information or arguments.

Kitchener and King's model provides a useful framework for understanding the development of reasoning skills as they relate to changes in beliefs about the certainty and verifiability of knowledge. Individuals whose reasoning is typical of earlier stages (Stages 1, 2, and 3) view their world in a rather fixed and limited way on the assumption that knowledge is certain; individuals in later stages (Stages 6 and 7) see the world in a more flexible way on the assumption that knowledge is not fixed.

Reflective Judgment and Education

The work of Kitchener and King raises important questions about the nature of teaching and learning. One question is how the classroom environment affects a student's reasoning. Does greater student autonomy lead to better reflective judgment? How do dispositional characteristics, such as one's degree of efficacy, attribution style, or personal goal orientation, affect one's willingness to engage in or improve one's reflective thinking? How are age, educational background, and home environment related to the development of reflective judgment?

Kitchener and King (1981) investigated some of these issues and reported dramatic differences among individuals in each of the seven stages. One question concerned whether students reasoned about different problems in similar ways. Results of Kitchener and King's initial study with high school and college students revealed that individuals tended to reason about different kinds of problems in a similar way. Style of reasoning typically was confined to the same or adjacent stages, suggesting that people's basic assumptions about knowledge lead to predictably similar conclusions. Subsequent research supports the view that individuals reason at more or less the same level regardless of the problem type (Kitchener & King, 2004).

A second question concerned the relationship among age, educational experience, and reflective judgment. As one might expect, high school students tended to reason at lower stages (the average stage was 2.77) compared with college undergraduates (the average stage was 3.65) or graduate students (the average stage was 5.67). The difference between high school and graduate students was especially strong (three full stages), suggesting that the amount of education that one receives is clearly linked with the sophistication of one's reflective reasoning. These findings are consistent with a number of other studies that indicate that continued education is related positively to relativistic beliefs and more sophisticated reasoning (Brownlee & Berthelsen, 2006; Kitchener & King, 2004; Murphy & Mason, 2006).

Other relationships were tested as well. Although no differences were found between males and females in any of the seven stages, students' verbal ability was highly correlated with reasoning ability. Those with better verbal skills tended to reason at higher stages than those with lower scores. Several tests of formal-operational problem solving revealed that virtually all 60 students participating in the study had achieved some degree of formal reasoning. Apparently, however, the ability to engage in formal-operational reasoning was not a sufficient condition for advanced reflective judgment. Many students capable of such reasoning scored at Stage 3 or lower.

A number of studies have followed students for multiple years in order to track changes in reflective judgment (Kitchener & King, 2004; Kitchener, King, & DeLuca, 2006). One important finding was that students progressed sequentially through adjacent stages rather than skipping one or more stages. Another finding was that some groups progressed faster than others, although differences in the rate of development were attributable, in part, to the fact that some groups started at a very high level. During the 6-year period, high school students progressed the most, moving roughly two full stages—from 2.83 to 4.99. During the same period, college undergraduate students improved slightly more than one full stage—from 3.72 to 4.89. College graduate students showed little improvement at all, moving from 6.15 to 6.27.

A comparison of these stage scores reveals several interesting points. First, high school students progressed two full stages during a 6-year period, reasoning at a level commensurate with college undergraduates. This finding indicates that differences in reflective judgment need not be viewed as permanent. Given adequate instruction and age-related maturation, most students can be expected to improve their reasoning abilities over time. In contrast, college undergraduates failed to bridge the gap between themselves and graduate students after a 6-year follow-up even though the latter group showed no statistically significant improvement. One reason may be that better reasoners go on to graduate school, whereas poorer reasoners do not. An alternative explanation is that graduate school improves one's reflective judgment substantially. Unfortunately, Kitchener and King's (1981) study does not allow us to answer this question with any degree of certainty because none of the original pool of college undergraduates continued on to graduate school.

Education and Thinking

One question left unanswered by Kitchener and King's research is the effect that formal education may have on reflective judgment. Several studies have provided surprising insights into this question (see Pascarella & Terenzini, 1991; and Schommer-Aikins, 2002, for reviews). A number of studies found that college undergraduates hold different epistemological beliefs depending on their academic major (Baxter-Magolda, 2002; Gill et al., 2004; Hofer, 2004; Yang, 2005). Education majors were far more likely than science majors to believe in certain knowledge and quick learning. In general, undergraduate science majors held more sophisticated beliefs about knowledge, which appeared to affect their everyday decision making. Unfortunately, this research does not allow us to determine whether students with less sophisticated beliefs chose an academic major that allows them to persist in those beliefs or whether simple beliefs are the consequence of one's academic major.

A classic study by Lehman, Lempert, and Nisbett (1988), however, found that one's academic major can shape one's way of thinking in important ways. Lehman et al. tested graduate students in four disciplines (medicine, law, psychology, and chemistry) at the beginning of their first and third years. Participants were given four types of conceptual reasoning tests: (1) statistical reasoning applied to everyday life, (2) methodological reasoning that tested one's ability to detect flaws in an argument attributable to lack of a control group, (3) conditional reasoning that required students to establish necessary and sufficient conditions for an outcome to be true, and (4) verbal reasoning designed to evaluate students' ability to evaluate evidence. In one study, first-year graduate students were compared with third-year graduate students in the same program. In a second study, another group of students was compared during their first year and again 2 years later.

Results were similar in both cases. An analysis of first-year students across the four disciplines revealed no differences on graduate school admission tests; that is, all were of roughly the same ability level. First-year students also performed similarly on the four reasoning tests, with the exception of chemistry students, who scored significantly lower on the statistical and verbal reasoning tests. A comparison of verbal reasoning scores between the first- and third-year students revealed no important differences across the four groups. This outcome was expected because students in each of the disciplines were expected to be proficient in this skill prior to entering graduate school. The difference between beginning and advanced psychology students on the statistical reasoning test was that they improved roughly 70%—a rather startling gain. Medical students improved by roughly 25%, whereas law and chemistry students did not improve at all.

One might ask why the psychology students improved so dramatically compared with the other groups. The answer, at least for those who have completed such a program, is rather obvious: Graduate psychology programs typically require students to complete at least three advanced-level statistics classes, as well as several classes on basic research methodology. It should not be surprising that psychology students improved far more than students who were not required to take such courses.

A comparison of conditional reasoning scores led to somewhat different findings, however. In this case, the medical, law, and psychology students improved 30 to 40% during their first 2 years of graduate school, whereas the chemistry students did not improve. Again, the reason for such improvement can be traced to extensive use of conditional reasoning skills in these graduate programs. Students are required on a daily basis to establish the conditions under which legal, medical, or experimental evidence is necessary and/or sufficient to prove a particular hypothesis. Why chemistry students did not improve remains unclear. One likely explanation is that Lehman et al. (1988) did not include a test sensitive to the improvement made by chemists.

Results of the Lehman et al. study answer some of the important questions raised earlier. First, students' reasoning skills are affected by the intellectual training they receive. One example is that students trained in law improve conditional reasoning skills that are not improved by graduate training in chemistry. Second, students do not appear to choose an academic discipline solely on the basis of skills they already possess. None of the students differed initially on any of the reasoning tasks or on intellectual ability. In general, students seem to enter graduate programs with similar types of intellectual skills and develop greater proficiency with some of these skills only as a result of their academic training. Returning momentarily to findings summarized in Schommer-Aikins (2002), it is probable that undergraduate education majors, compared with science majors, subscribe to different beliefs about knowledge for one of two reasons: Either they are seldom required to question these beliefs, and so they do not, or beliefs supporting simple knowledge and quick learning are reflected in the classes they take.

A more recent study by Lodewyk (2007) found that beliefs and attitudes had different effects on different types of problem solving. High school students reported their epistemological beliefs using a measure based on the five beliefs described by Schommer (1990). Simple beliefs were related to lower levels of reflective judgment. In addition, beliefs were related differently to ill-defined (i.e., multiple solutions) versus well-defined (i.e., one clear solution) problems in a problem-solving task. More sophisticated epistemological beliefs were related to performance on the ill-defined task, but not on the well-defined task. One explanation is that beliefs and assumptions may be more important when solving ill-structured problems.

Summary of Beliefs About Knowledge

The research we have described indicates that people's beliefs about the certainty and complexity of knowledge profoundly affect their reasoning. The work of Hofer (2004), Kuhn (1991), Perry (1970), and Schommer (1990) suggests that individuals hold many beliefs about knowledge and that these beliefs constrain information processing. Kitchener and King's (1981, 2004) research further indicates that different epistemological assumptions constrain individuals' level of reflective judgment. In addition, the Lehman et al. (1988) study revealed that epistemological beliefs and reasoning skills are the result of one's intellectual environment rather than the determinants of the type of academic discipline one pursues.

Hope and Attitude Change

At this point, we shift our attention to another kind of belief that has attracted researchers' attention—hope! Investigations by Snyder and colleagues (Babyak, Snyder, & Yoshinobu, 1993; Snyder, 1995; Snyder, Rand, & Sigmon, 2002) have revealed an impressive number of statistically significant relationships between people's expressed hope and academic achievement. Hope consists of two important components that Snyder (1995) refers to as **agency** and **pathways** or, more colloquially, as the "will" and the "ways." The former refers to an individual's sense of self-determination and perseverance when faced with challenges. The latter refers to how well an individual can generate workable solutions to those challenges.

To test the relationship between hope and other outcomes, Snyder (1995) devised a 12-question inventory containing some questions that measure a person's sense of agency and pathways. One example of an agency question is "My past experiences have prepared me well for the future." An example of a typical pathways question is "There are lots of ways around any problem." Snyder and colleagues have used this instrument in a variety of studies that compared performance on the hope inventory with frequently used measures of life orientation, life experiences, self-esteem, hopelessness, depression, stress, optimism, and sense of control. In most cases, the hope inventory is correlated with these measures to a significant degree, although none of these instruments seem to be measuring quite the same dimension as hope.

As one might expect, the two dimensions measured by the hope inventory are highly correlated, suggesting that a greater sense of self-determination usually is associated with the corresponding belief that challenges can be met and overcome. Snyder and colleagues have conducted studies examining how responses to this inventory are related to specific academic and social outcomes. In a study by Yoshinobu (1989), people with high hope scores demonstrated significantly more self-determination in the light of failure. Those receiving high hope scores reported more potentially useful solutions to challenging circumstances than did those receiving low hope scores. Roedel et al. (1994) also reported that the pathways component was correlated strongly with learning goals and controllable attributions but was uncorrelated with performance goals.

Subsequent studies have shown that people scoring high on hope have a greater preference for difficult tasks that cannot be explained by differences in intellectual ability. When confronted with obstacles, high-hope students showed greater self-determination and solution pathways than medium- or low-hope individuals, and greater levels of optimism (Lopes & Cunha, 2008).

People scoring high on the hope inventory also were more likely to have a greater number of specifiable goals across several domains, including job, personal relationships, health, and spiritual development. Hope also correlated with perceived academic goal attainment, indicating that those who score higher on hope expect to get higher grades in college classes. In fact, students with higher hope and academic expectations do receive higher grades even when their academic ability is taken into consideration! Similarly, individuals with higher hope solve problems more effectively and are rated as having higher job performance (Peterson & Byron, 2008).

Other important findings have been found in these studies as well. First, scores on the hope inventory appear to be independent of intellectual ability. Second, a person's tendency to score high or low on hope is unrelated to gender. Third, the degree of hope expressed by people appears to be stable over time, suggesting that some individuals seem predisposed to be more hopeful than others.

Changing Beliefs

One important question raised by Snyder et al.'s research and by the research on goal orientations and epistemological beliefs is whether maladaptive beliefs can be changed. Most research suggests that changing beliefs may be far more complicated than people assume. One reason is that beliefs are formed on the basis of cognitive and affective information (Murphy & Mason, 2006). In this view, cognitive appraisal of information is objective and rational; affective appraisal is subjective and based on emotional reactions to an object. Whether beliefs are changeable may depend, in large part, on how beliefs initially were formed. Those formed on the basis of affective responses may be resistant to change by cognitive means; those formed on the basis of cognitive responses may be resistant to affective means of persuasion.

Several experiments by Edwards (1990) addressed this issue. Individuals in one experiment were asked to examine some fictitious consumer products, such as a high-energy drink and a portable copier. Participants received information about these products in two stages: During the first stage, people received affective information (e.g., tasting the drink), followed by cognitive information (e.g., reading an advertisement for the product), or they received cognitive information first, followed by affective information. In the second stage, Edwards provided participants with additional information designed to conflict with information provided in the first stage. Half of the people received cognitive information first, followed by affective information; half received information in the reverse order. The purpose of the study was to examine whether attitudes that develop through affective and cognitive means are more resistant to change when the conflicting information is presented by using the same or a different means of persuasion.

Edwards (1990) found that beliefs acquired through affective persuasion were easier to change through affective means and that beliefs acquired through cognitive persuasion were easier to change through cognitive means. Of special interest, however, was the magnitude of change. Beliefs acquired through cognitive persuasion were more resistant to change than beliefs acquired through affective means. In addition, neither affective nor cognitive persuasion appears to be very useful when one is attempting to change beliefs that were formed by using another mode of persuasion; that is, beliefs based on affective responses show little change when individuals are presented with contradictory cognitive information.

To further complicate matters, other studies suggest that affective information may alter our beliefs even when we have no conscious awareness of this information (Greenwald, Klinger, & Lui, 1989; Niedenthal, 1990). A study by Niedenthal (1990) asked college students to describe their impressions of cartoon faces after first viewing human faces that were presented below their perceptual threshold (the level at which visual information can be consciously recognized). Some of these slides showed faces marked by disgust; others showed faces expressing joy. As expected, subjective evaluation of the cartoon faces was significantly more negative after viewing faces conveying disgust.

In contrast, more recent studies suggest that cognitive variables may be important precursors to belief change (Cano, 2005; Murphy, Holleran, Long, & Zeruth, 2005). Murphy et al. (2005) examined the extent to which topic interestingness and need for cognition (i.e., a preference to think and reflect on complex issues one faces in day-to-day life) affect belief change. Students read and responded to controversial texts and only the need for cognition was significantly related to belief change.

These studies all seem to suggest that attitudes and beliefs are acquired in complex ways and may be highly resistant to change (Bendixen, 2002; Dole & Sinatra, 1998; Kuhn & Loa, 1998). Appealing to students through use of well-reasoned cognitive arguments may be of little use if beliefs were formed initially by affective means. For example, consider the difficulty that educators or parents face trying, through cognitive means, to dissuade teenagers from drinking alcoholic beverages when these teens are exposed to affective appeals from television commercials showing happy, carefree young adults leading the good life on a sunny California beach, beer in hand.

From a teacher's or parent's perspective, changing beliefs about intelligence, knowledge, or any other complex phenomenon may be a slow process. Changing teachers' beliefs may be equally difficult (Brownlee, 2004; Brownlee, Purdie, & Boulton-Lewis, 2001; Marra, 2005; Olafson & Schraw, 2006). Clearly, special emphasis should be placed on providing environments in which students are given opportunities to reflect on their own beliefs and shift gradually to new modes of thought (Baxter-Magolda, 1999; Reybold, 2001). As discussed in Chapter 14, experts agree that some degree of cognitive disequilibrium is needed to fuel the conceptual change process (Baxter-Magolda, 2002; Dole & Sinatra, 1998; Murphy & Mason, 2006; Patrick & Pintrich, 2001; Sinatra & Pintrich, 2002).

Teachers' Beliefs

Teachers hold a variety of beliefs that affect their attitudes and behavior in the classroom. These beliefs often involve tacit assumptions about students, learning, the material to be taught, and the organization of the class (Kagan, 1992) and are as diverse as perceptions of self-efficacy, subjective attitudes about content knowledge, and how it can be taught most effectively (Borko & Putnam, 1996; Calderhead, 1996; Woolfolk-Hoy, Davis, & Pape, 2006). Teachers' beliefs frequently affect student–teacher interactions and instructional planning. For example, Gibson and Dembo (1984) found that high-self-efficacy teachers provided less criticism and persisted in helping struggling students more than low-self-efficacy teachers. Ashton and Webb (1986) reported similar findings. High-efficacy teachers used more student praise, engaged in more task-oriented instruction, and ran classrooms that led to higher achievement.

Teachers' beliefs about content material also shape in-class pedagogy (Cobb & Bowers, 1999; Hargreaves, Earl, Moore, & Manning, 2001; Hashweh, 1996; Hiebert, Gallimore, & Stigler, 2002). A number of studies have found that teachers' beliefs led to noticeable differences in how the course textbook was used, as well as instructional practices (see Woolfolk-Hoy et al., 2006, for a review). Teachers' beliefs about how learning occurs also affect how teachers teach course content (Holt-Reynolds, 2000; Johnston et al., 2001). In one study, Smith and Neale (1989) compared three teaching orientations and their effect on teacher planning and instruction. "Discovery" teachers provided interesting activities designed to invoke student curiosity and exploration. "Didactic" teachers (those who emphasize structured content, facts, and principles) were more likely to select and organize content material, give tests, and demonstrate key concepts. In contrast, "conceptual change" teachers focused on evaluation of student beliefs, restructuring existing knowledge structures, and providing incongruent data to students.

Surprisingly, preservice teachers tend to leave teacher training programs with many of the beliefs and attitudes they held when they entered the programs (Borko & Putnam, 1996; Kagan, 1992). This alarming fact suggests that some teacher training programs may be ineffective at altering beliefs even though they expose students to different perspectives on pedagogy (see Chapter 14). Overall, studies examining a wide range of teachers' beliefs suggest that these beliefs are quite stable and resistant to change, are associated with a congruent style of teaching, and are affected most directly by practice rather than by continuing education (see Calderhead, 1996; Howard, McGee, Schwartz, & Purcell, 2000). An emerging body of research also suggests that teachers with more experience appear to shift gradually to *less sophisticated* beliefs compared to teachers with 3 to 6 years of experience (Georgiou, 2008). One possible explanation is that teachers may become more entrenched over time because they feel less efficacious and are more inclined to adopt "fixed-ability" beliefs about their students.

Currently, it is unclear how to facilitate change in teachers' beliefs. Research does provide a three-pronged strategy for changing students' beliefs that also may apply to older students who are preparing to be teachers (Brownlee, 2004; Brownlee et al., 2001; Murphy & Mason, 2006). First, students in teacher training programs must experience a classroom environment in which implicit beliefs become explicit. One way is to encourage open discussion and reflection on beliefs about course content and approaches to learning. Second, students should be confronted with the inconsistency of their beliefs. Third, the teacher should provide opportunities for students to weigh conflicting evidence and to restructure their existing knowledge such that it can be accommodated to course content.

Generally, beliefs about three classroom factors affect teachers' behaviors the most (Schraw & Olafson, 2002). One factor is course content. Research indicates that teachers plan instruction in ways that are consistent with their assumptions about class material. Teachers who hold a belief in certain knowledge are more likely to focus on didactic instruction and essential course content while de-emphasizing discovery in the classroom (Pallas, 2001; Rennie, 1989). A second factor is the type of student receiving the instruction. Most teachers form strong opinions about students. These beliefs are based on several factors, including physical characteristics, test scores, class performance, social skills, parental attitudes, and student self-efficacy (Kagan, 1992; Woolfolk-Hoy et al., 2006). A third factor is the teacher's own explicit beliefs about teaching. One of the most consistent findings in the teacher belief literature is that teachers plan and implement instruction in a way that is consistent with their personal epistemologies.

Relatively little is known about how teachers view knowledge and intelligence (Levitt, 2001; White, 2000; Wilcox-Herzog, 2002), but these topics are becoming a focus for more studies. One important question is whether instruction and learning are facilitated when teachers' and students' beliefs match. Dweck and Leggett's (1988) theory, for instance, suggests that learning-oriented students may find it quite difficult to adjust to a classroom run by a teacher with strong performance goals. Similarly, teachers' epistemological beliefs may interfere with learning or create excessive disequilibrium when they do not match students' beliefs. This is not to say that teachers must accommodate students' beliefs; rather, a mismatch in beliefs and assumptions is apt to create disequilibrium in the classroom. As Posner, Strike, Hewson, and Gertzog (1982) have suggested, disequilibrium may be used productively to promote conceptual change, or it may preclude successful student–teacher interactions if handled poorly.

Implications for Instruction

1. *Everyone holds beliefs about intelligence and knowledge.* The beliefs we hold affect the choices we make inside and outside the classroom. Many of these beliefs are implicit. Generally speaking, explicit awareness of one's beliefs makes them easier to identify and change. Beliefs about intelligence affect classroom satisfaction and persistence. Beliefs about knowledge affect reasoning skills and reflective judgment.

We believe that teachers should help students develop an awareness of their beliefs. Many younger and even older students hold implicit beliefs that exert a profound influence on their thinking and behavior. Developing reflective awareness of these beliefs through journals and peer-based discussions gives students the opportunity to change them as they see fit.

2. *Beliefs about intelligence and knowledge affect our behaviors.* Research has demonstrated convincingly that our attitudes about intelligence and knowledge affect our learning. Individuals who believe that intelligence is fixed or who believe in simple knowledge and quick learning are less likely to persist and use helpful learning strategies. Those who adopt an entity theory are more likely to explain their success and failure in terms of different attributional responses.

3. *Beliefs about intelligence and knowledge affect the way we reason.* Thinking does not occur in an intellectual vacuum. The kinds of assumptions we hold about how people think and learn determine, in part, the kinds of educational opportunities to which we expose ourselves and the kind of knowledge we accept as legitimate. Studies by Kitchener and King (1981), Kuhn (1991), and Lehman et al. (1988) all illustrate this important point. For this reason, beliefs about intelligence and knowledge should be an important topic of discussion in classrooms, especially with older students.

4. *Education affects the kinds of beliefs we hold.* Our beliefs about knowledge and intelligence are shaped by our classroom experiences. Teachers model viewpoints that echo views held at home or perhaps conflict with them. The kinds of beliefs modeled in the classroom may change the way students think. This possibility places a special responsibility on educators to carefully analyze the viewpoints they express in their classes and to provide ample time to explore their implications.

5. *Educational experiences affect reasoning skills.* The study by Lehman et al. (1988) is notable in that it illustrates how environmental constraints affect the development of cognitive skills. Recall that even graduate students experienced substantial changes in reasoning skills that were linked with the specific experiences they had in graduate school. This finding suggests that the specific demands of a discipline (e.g., statistical reasoning in the social sciences) help develop certain skills. Whether the intellectual demands of different disciplines also affect the kinds of epistemological beliefs that students hold is uncertain (cf. Jehng et al., 1993; Schommer-Aikins, 2002).

6. *Beliefs are not strongly related to ability.* This statement may seem surprising to you. We often think of "smart" people as those with the most sophisticated (or adaptive) beliefs. The research described in this chapter, however, generally points to the conclusion that beliefs about intelligence and knowledge are far more related to home (e.g., parental beliefs) and school (e.g., performance demands) variables than to one's measured ability. One implication of this conclusion is that adaptive beliefs (e.g., believing in incremental learning) may compensate for average or low ability (Roedel et al., 1994). We are committed to the view that high academic achievement is attainable by virtually all students, provided they develop a belief system that encourages them to use their existing skills and to cultivate more advanced thinking skills, such as metacognition. We are equally committed to the belief that teachers must initiate and facilitate these changes for them to be truly successful. To see a dramatic portrayal of how this might be accomplished, we recommend that all readers view the classic movie *Stand and Deliver* (1988).

Psychological Assessments and Theory Change

Chapter 6 discussed several different types of beliefs, such as self-efficacy, and concluded with a section on the assessment of beliefs and attitudes (i.e., latent constructs). Chapter 7 extended this discussion by reviewing several other types of beliefs such as goal orientations, epistemological beliefs, and hope. Educational research has come a long way over the past 30 years in terms of understanding and measuring different types of beliefs. Ironically, the sheer difficulty of measuring beliefs has helped researchers better conceptualize the structure and importance of these beliefs. Goal orientation theory provides an excellent example.

Dweck and Leggett (1988) originally proposed a theory that suggested students endorsed either a performance orientation or a learning orientation, based on implicit beliefs about learning. The learning orientation subsequently became known as a *mastery orientation.* In its simplest form, this theory could be interpreted to mean that beliefs were *unidimensional,* meaning that beliefs existed along a single dimension with strong mastery beliefs on one end and strong performance beliefs on the other end. In this model, a person could hold a strong mastery worldview, or a strong performance worldview, but not both. Said differently, the two goal orientations were viewed as mutually exclusive.

Researchers tested this assumption in the late 1980s and early 1990s and concluded that goal orientations are *multidimensional,* meaning that there are two independent dimensions: One dimension measured commitment to a mastery orientation and the other independent dimension measured committeemen to the performance orientation. In this model, an individual could be high or low on both dimensions or high on one and low on the other. From a theoretical perspective, these competing models provided very different conceptualizations of the relationship between goal orientations. Ultimately, the data from repeated studies supported the multidimensional model.

But the story did not end there! Subsequent research reported discrepancies suggesting that individuals could adopt either an *approach* or *avoidance* stance to the mastery and performance orientations (Linnenbrink, 2005; Sideridis, 2005). These data led to a further refinement of goal orientation to include four categories of goal orientations: mastery-approach, mastery-avoidance, performance-approach, and performance-avoidance goals (Pintrich, 2000a; Sideridis, 2005). The data from ongoing research appear to fit this four-category theory of goal orientations reasonably well . . . until perhaps additional data call into question the validity of the proposed theoretical structure of goals.

There are at least two important points to be learned from this example. One is that theories change and evolve, in part, due to data used to test the theory. If data are incompatible with the theory, then changes are in order. A second point is that assessments, when used as evidence of unobservable constructs, provide imperfect measures, in part due to the limitations of the theory and in part due to the limitations of the assessment itself. We believe it is vital to provide the most accurate theoretical description of unobservable phenomena as possible and to use theory to create and interpret assessments. Likewise, we believe it is always better to build a better mousetrap! Better assessments mean better tests of theory and perhaps a crucial change to theory.

Summary

This chapter examines the effect that beliefs about intelligence and knowledge have on academic performance. We introduced the topic of implicit theories—that is, tacit belief systems. Dweck and Leggett's theory described two kinds of theories: Entity theorists maintain a belief that intelligence is fixed; incremental theorists believe that intelligence is changeable.

Entity and incremental theories give rise to performance and learning goals, which in turn lead to maladaptive and adaptive behaviors, respectively. Individuals characterized by a performance orientation are less persistent, are less apt to use learning strategies, and attribute their failure to ability and teachers. Individuals characterized by a learning orientation are more persistent, are more likely to use strategies, and attribute their success to strategy use and effort.

Some epistemological beliefs can affect reasoning. Individuals who believe that knowledge is complex and relative, that learning is incremental, and that one's ability to learn is not innately determined are found to engage in more sophisticated forms of thinking.

We examined teachers' beliefs as well. These beliefs tend to change slowly, yet they strongly affect the attitudes that teachers hold about their students. Teachers' beliefs determine what content the teachers cover and how they cover it (e.g., direct lecture vs. a discovery approach). Teachers with mastery orientations and constructivist epistemologies use more strategies in the classroom and frequently have students with higher levels of achievement. Research suggests that some teacher trainees leave education programs with the same beliefs about teaching they had when they entered the programs. Identification and discussion of these beliefs were described as possible belief-changing strategies.

SUGGESTED READINGS

Dweck, C. S., & Leggett, E. S. (1988). A social-cognitive approach to motivation and personality. *Psychological Review, 95,* 256–273.
This influential review article presents Dweck and Leggett's influential theory in a highly readable fashion.

Hofer, B., & Pintrich, P. R. (2002). *Personal epistemology: The psychology of beliefs about knowledge and knowing.* Mahwah, NJ: Erlbaum.
This edited volume provides an excellent overview of theory and research on epistemological beliefs.

Kitchener, K. S., & King, P. M. (2004). Reflective judgment: Theory and research on the development of epistemic assumptions through adulthood. *Educational Psychologist, 39,* 5–18.
This review provides a comprehensive overview of reflective judgment theory and research.

Kuhn, D. (1991). *The skills of argument.* New York, NY: Cambridge University Press.
This book describes a comprehensive study examining argumentative reasoning. Chapter 7 provides an informative discussion of the relationship between epistemological beliefs and reasoning skills.

Murphy, P. K., & Mason, L. (2006). Changing knowledge and beliefs. In P. A. Alexander & P. H. Winne (Eds.), *Handbook of educational psychology* (2nd ed., pp. 305–325). Mahwah, NJ: Erlbaum.
This chapter provides a fine summary of recent theory and practice in conceptual change.

CHAPTER

8 Problem Solving and Critical Thinking

Historical Perspectives on Problem Solving ◼ Expert Knowledge in Problem Solving ◼
Implications for Instruction: Improving Problem Solving ◼ Critical Thinking ◼ Teaching
Wisdom ◼ Assessment of Problem Solving ◼ Summary ◼ Suggested Readings ◼

Every day, we encounter hundreds of problems ranging in difficulty from deciding which breakfast cereal to eat to planning our long-term career goals. Because we face so many types of problems, it is often difficult to say with certainty what problems are or to know how to categorize them. The sheer range of problems we encounter makes it very difficult to approach problem solving systematically. Word problems in algebra, for example, seem to have little in common with the choices and decisions we face when buying a car.

Loosely, a problem exists when our current state differs from a desired state (Lovett, 2002; Mayer & Wittrock, 2006; Novick & Bassok, 2005; Pretz, Naples, & Sternberg, 2003). Thinking of problem solving in this way can be helpful for two reasons. First, it emphasizes the continual process of problem solving, in which we move from an initial state to a more clearly defined end state. Second, thinking about problem solving as a process of change from one state to another helps us understand that virtually every problem we encounter can be solved by using the same general strategy despite apparent surface differences.

Even though most adults possess some form of general problem-solving strategy, it is not the case that all problems are similar. Experts agree that problems differ with respect to how much structure they provide the problem solver (Hayes, 1988). An **ill-defined problem** has more than one acceptable solution and no universally agreed-on strategy for reaching it (Pretz et al., 2003). Worldwide ecological problems, such as global warming and ozone layer destruction, provide good examples of ill-defined problems because scientists disagree about their causes and possible solutions. A **well-defined problem** has only one correct solution and a guaranteed method for finding it. Solving a quadratic equation in algebra class by using the quadratic formula is a good example of a well-defined problem because there is not only a unique solution but also a guaranteed means of obtaining it.

Historical Perspectives on Problem Solving

Thorndike, Dewey, and the Gestalt Psychologists

Interest in problem solving among psychologists and educators developed early in the 20th century. One of the earliest views was proposed by E. L. Thorndike (1911), who conducted a series of experiments in which he observed cats as they attempted to escape from a carefully constructed wooden crate by pressing a lever. Noting that cats typically would try several random behaviors prior to pressing the escape lever successfully, Thorndike concluded that problem solving consists largely of trial-and-error behaviors that eventually lead to a solution. He argued that problem solving (at least in cats) was not intentional but rather occurred one step at a time as unsuccessful attempts were eliminated from a cat's repertoire. Thorndike was to argue in subsequent work that problem solving takes place in humans in much the same way as it does with any other animal: Success occurs incrementally as a function of the trial-and-error attempts to solve the problem.

In contrast with Thorndike, John Dewey (1910) saw problem solving as a conscious, deliberate process governed by a naturally occurring sequence of steps. Dewey's model included five basic steps that he considered to be teachable skills. In Step 1, *presentation of the problem,* students (or teachers) recognize the existence of a problem. In Step 2, *defining the problem,* the problem solver identifies the nature of the problem and identifies important constraints on its solution. In Step 3, *developing hypotheses,* one or more plausible solutions are proposed. In Step 4, *testing the hypotheses,* the most feasible solution is determined. In Step 5, *selecting the best hypothesis,* the best hypothesis is determined, given the relative strengths and weaknesses of each.

A third approach to problem solving was that of the Gestalt psychologists, a group of European psychologists whose views differed widely from those of American behaviorists. One foremost Gestalt theorist was Wolfgang Köhler (1929), who conducted a series of studies on problem solving using chimps. The most famous of Köhler's chimps was Sultan. In one experiment, Sultan was placed in a cage in which a banana was suspended from the ceiling just beyond his reach. Köhler also placed in various parts of the cage wooden crates that could be used to build a platform to reach the banana, but only if Sultan correctly grasped the concept of *using the crates in a tool-like fashion.* After several unsuccessful attempts and some seeming deliberation on Sultan's part, he succeeded in stacking the crates and reached the banana. Köhler argued that Sultan's behavior provided evidence of insight in problem solving in several ways. First, Sultan did not make numerous trial-and-error attempts to reach the banana as Thorndike would predict. Second, the crates bore no ostensible relationship to solving the problem (at least from the chimp's perspective) yet were used without prompting in a purposeful way to achieve the primary goal of reaching the banana. Köhler's findings and interpretation were considered extremely controversial at the time and continue to be debated today, in part because researchers differ as to the nature of insight and in part because they suggested skilled, reflective problem solving in an animal.

Another important concept introduced by a Gestalt psychologist was **functional fixedness,** a condition that arises when we lose the ability to view familiar objects in a novel way (Duncker, 1945). In one experiment, Duncker provided people with a candle, a box of matches, and some tacks. The object of the study was to attach the candle to a wooden door. The problem could be solved only by first attaching the matchbox to the door with the tacks and then using the box as a platform for the candle.

Duncker also added one other constraint: Some people received the matchbox with matches inside, whereas others received the matchbox and matches separately. Although apparently a trivial difference, individuals who received the empty matchbox solved the problem more quickly.

Duncker concluded from this study that individuals in the empty box condition solved the problem more efficiently because they were more likely to view the box as a potential platform rather than as a receptacle for matches. Including the matches in the box induced functional fixedness in that it activated preconceived notions (schemata) of what a matchbox is and what it can be used for. When the matchbox was perceived in a slightly different context (without matches), individuals were better able to imagine alternative uses for it. Duncker's experiment elegantly illustrated the profound impact of preexisting knowledge and how that knowledge inhibits novel solutions or uses of objects during problem solving.

Contemporary Approaches to Problem Solving

Research on problem solving has received a great deal of attention since Thorndike, Dewey, and the Gestalt psychologists. Since the 1950s, computer scientists and cognitive psychologists have attempted to develop a general problem-solving model that can be applied in domains as diverse as physics and medical diagnosis (Hayes, 1988; Lovett & Anderson, 2005; Newell & Simon, 1972). These models generally emphasize two major components: (1) the use of a general problem-solving procedure and (2) a high degree of metacognitive monitoring by the problem solver. Although several models have appeared, most are quite similar to one another and can be summarized into a five-stage sequence (Bransford & Stein, 1984; Hayes, 1988; Pretz et al., 2003): (1) identifying the problem, (2) representing the problem, (3) selecting an appropriate strategy, (4) implementing the strategy, and (5) evaluating solutions. These five stages are quite similar to the five steps described by Dewey. Within each of the five stages, component subskills also have been identified. We consider each of these stages separately and then discuss the relative merits of a general problem-solving model at the end of this section.

Identifying the Problem   Identifying a problem is one of the most difficult and challenging aspects of problem solving because it requires creativity and persistence and a willingness to ponder a problem for a long period of time without committing to a solution too early in the process (Mayer & Wittrock, 2006; Novick & Bassok, 2005). Many problems (and their solutions) that seem obvious in retrospect are not so obvious to begin with. Consider that batting helmets were not used routinely in major league baseball until the early 1950s, despite the fact that several players had been killed over the years by being struck in the head by wild pitches.

Obstacles to effective problem finding have been identified by researchers. One obstacle is that most people are not in the habit of actively searching for problems. Usually, we let the problem "come to us" rather than seek it out. A good argument could be made, however, that virtually all great discoveries are made only after a previously unrecognized problem has been "discovered." A good case in point is the germ theory of disease. Prior to the 19th century, many physicians believed that illnesses originated from such sources as evil spirits, bad air (e.g., malaria), and poisoned blood. These beliefs led to many nonproductive treatments, such as incantations, whipping, and bloodletting. Not until the advent of a germ theory of disease did physicians correctly identify the source of many treatable diseases.

A second obstacle to successful problem finding is the degree to which the problem solver possesses relevant background knowledge. Problems in the development of computer microchips, for instance, cannot be solved or even identified without a great deal of preexisting knowledge about computer circuitry. Similarly, consider how background knowledge affects "problem finding" in a highly familiar activity such as reading (see Chapter 11). Research indicates that prior knowledge facilitates the perception and temporary elaboration of new information. More important, prior knowledge (the use of *content schemata*) enables readers to attend selectively to important information in the text and to encode new information into an existing schematic structure with less effort.

A third obstacle to problem finding is that people do not take as much time as they need to reflect carefully on either the nature of a problem or its solution. In a landmark study of artistic creativity, Getzels and Csikszentmihalyi (1976) found that the time spent investigating objects prior to drawing a still life was a significantly better predictor of originality than was time spent making the drawing! This relationship was found even when the artist's technical ability was taken into consideration. From extensive observations and interviews, Getzels and Csikszentmihalyi concluded that artists who considered more options during the initial stages of problem finding were more original in their solutions. Most surprising of all was the finding that time spent discovering problems during the initial stages of problem solving correlated highly with artistic success 7 years later.

Getzels and Csikszentmihalyi also described other interesting findings in their study. One was that the majority of successful art students listed "problem finding" as the primary goal of their work. These artists were more concerned with finding and coming to terms with a perceived problem than they were in solving it. Successful artists also tended to possess three dispositional characteristics that facilitated problem finding. First, they were more open to the problem; that is, they did not allow first impressions to interfere with discovering alternative approaches to artistic expression. Second, they engaged in more exploratory activities, such as handling objects in a still life or viewing those objects from different perspectives. Third, they permitted the problem and their initial solution to evolve as they worked with it.

Moore (1990) examined the problem-finding behaviors of experienced teachers and university students studying to be teachers. One difference found between these groups was that experienced teachers spent significantly more time planning when placed in a hypothetical classroom setting. In addition, experienced teachers spent more time than novices investigating and manipulating objects found in the classroom and also provided more solutions to potential classroom problems. In many respects, experienced teachers appear to behave in much the same way as successful artists in the Getzels and Csikszentmihalyi study.

Another aspect of time spent identifying problems is the persistence of problem solvers in the face of initial difficulties. Some individuals give up too easily after only a short period of time because they view problem solving as a time-limited activity. In this regard, Schoenfeld (1983) found that students solving mathematical word problems tended to give up after 5 minutes on the assumption that if the solution did not occur during this period, it would not occur at all. Research reviewed by Mayer and Wittrock (2006) and Novick and Bassok (2005) clearly suggests that successful problem solving is related to the amount of time one spends during the initial stages of problem finding, as well as to the number of solutions that are considered. In many situations, expert problem solvers spend more time identifying problems than do novices.

Finally, effective problem finding is strongly related to divergent thinking. **Divergent thinking** occurs when a problem solver explores solutions that are novel or even inconsistent with the problem at hand (Sternberg, Lubart, Kaufman, & Pretz, 2005). Hollowing out a brick so that it can be used as a mug is a good illustration of divergent thinking because it exemplifies one unusual way an object can be used when we see it in a new light. As you might expect, divergent thinking is related to creativity and problem finding, although problem-finding ability appears to be a better predictor of creativity than is divergent thinking (Csikszentmihalyi, 1996; Runco, 1991). The ability to find problems and to think divergently seems to enhance the evaluation of proposed solutions during problem solving. One reason is that problem solvers are better able to plan in advance, which enables them to eliminate poor potential solutions early on. Divergent thinking helps students think more broadly not only when they are generating ideas but also when they are testing them.

Representing the Problem   Representing a problem can occur in several ways. One form of representation is simply thinking about problems abstractly, without committing one's thoughts to paper. Another is expressing the problem in some tangible form, such as a graph, picture, story, or equation. Representing problems on paper has important advantages. One is that many problems are so complex that they impose severe demands on short-term memory unless we find a convenient way to summarize information. Think back to all of the information you needed to consider when applying to college. Some individuals find themselves trying to remember the cost of tuition and housing, distance from home, quality of institution, availability of desirable academic majors, and social opportunities. Perhaps you had to compare this information for 10 to 15 universities. Clearly, this is too much to consider at one time. Using some form of external representation can reduce greatly the amount of information that needs to be remembered in order to identify and solve a problem.

Using external representations of problems can be useful for another reason. Sometimes, problems are just too difficult to solve mentally because we consider so many possible solutions. Using a visual representation can help us keep track of these solutions or reason more clearly. Consider the Monk's Trip problem, in which a monk journeys all day on foot to the top of a mountain, meditates overnight, and then returns by foot again the following morning by way of exactly the same path, making the return trip down the mountain in two-thirds of the time. The problem is to determine whether there is a spot on the trail that the monk crosses at exactly the same time each day. Take a few moments now to think about this problem before you examine Figure 8.1, which provides a visual representation of this problem.

As Figure 8.1 illustrates, it is impossible for the monk to make the return trip without crossing one spot on the trail at exactly the same time of day. Solving this problem pictorially seems to make this point obvious, whereas solving the problem without the benefit of a picture can be rather difficult. One reason for this difficulty is that much of our limited cognitive capacity in short-term memory is exhausted just trying to remember relevant information. Few resources are left over to actually solve the problem!

Representing problems either internally or externally can be made easier when we analyze the component parts of a problem. Most theorists distinguish among four components that are known collectively as the *problem space*: goal state, initial state, operators, and constraints on operators (see Hayes, 1988, for a detailed discussion and examples). The **problem space** refers to all of the operators and constraints on operators involved in the problem. Some

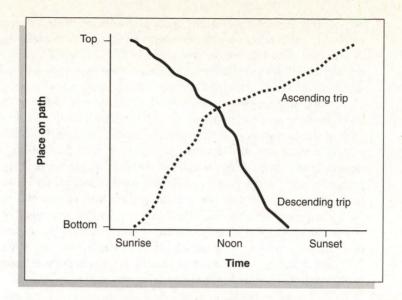

FIGURE 8.1   A Graphic Representation of the Monk's Trip Problem.

Source: Adapted from *Cognitive Psychology,* by J. R. Hayes, 1978, Homewood, IL: Dorsey. Adapted with permission.

problem spaces are small, such as choosing a personal computer that meets your needs and your budget; others are extremely complex, such as finding a vaccine against HIV. Problems that include many possible **solution paths** (more paths from the initial state to the goal state) have larger problem spaces than those with few paths, although the size of a problem space may vary considerably between two people, depending on the way the problem is understood by each person (Mayer & Moreno, 2003; Novick & Bassok, 2005).

The **goal state** refers to what we want to accomplish once the problem is solved. Goals vary in their specificity and complexity, although the clearer the goal, the easier it will be to solve the problem, all things considered. The **initial state** refers to what is known about the problem before one attempts to solve it. How much information do you have about the problem? What information is most important? Is information missing that you will need to consider before proceeding? Can the problem be broken down into smaller subproblems? Have you ever solved a problem like this before? **Operators** refer to objects or concepts in the problem that can be manipulated to reach a solution. Pieces on a chessboard are operators as are variables (e.g., x and y) in an algebraic equation. When taking a test, time and knowledge about the content of the test are operators. **Constraints on operators** refers to restrictions that limit the use of one or more operators. In a game of chess, queens can move in horizontal, vertical, or diagonal directions on the board, whereas bishops can move only diagonally. Knights are restricted to an entirely different set of moves (two spaces in a horizontal or vertical direction, then one step at a 90° angle to the first). On a test, you are limited frequently to 1 hour or less, and you may not use books or notes.

A good deal of research has investigated the importance of operators and constraints on operators (Mayer & Wittrock, 2006; Pretz et al., 2003). One consistent finding is that good problem solvers distinguish relevant from irrelevant constraints on a problem more efficiently than do poor problem solvers, and they use this information to facilitate problem solving. For example, good readers know when to slow down rather than skim a text; that is, they identify relevant information and allocate more attention to it (McCrudden & Schraw, 2007). Being able to identify and focus on relevant information greatly reduces the problem space and enables allocation of resources to understanding the relationship between relevant pieces of information.

Good and poor problem solvers also differ in their ability to categorize problems. Good problem solvers tend to group problems according to "deep structure" principles, such as what kind of solution strategy is required to solve the problem. In contrast, poor problem solvers rely on "surface structure" features, such as the objects that appear in the problem (Novick & Bassok, 2005). When novice problem solvers are taught to categorize by using deep structure principles, their performance usually improves compared with that of other novices. These findings suggest two important conclusions. First, effective problem solving is attributable, in part, to experience; those with more practice solving a particular type of problem can categorize problems more efficiently because of their background knowledge and experience. Second, students can learn to categorize (represent) problems more efficiently by analyzing problems differently. Less attention should be given to surface features of the problem; more attention should be given to the underlying nature of the problem.

Selecting an Appropriate Strategy   People use many kinds of strategies to solve problems. Some of these are highly structured and are referred to as **algorithms.** An algorithm is really just another name for a rule. Using algorithms or rule-based strategies can be very effective because they are guaranteed to work. Finding the roots of a quadratic equation by using the quadratic formula is a good example of a rule-based strategy. But sometimes it is not possible to use a rule-based strategy because either a rule does not exist or the student lacks proficiency at using it. In this case, people rely on **heuristics,** or "rules of thumb," to help them solve problems (Schraw, 2006; Stanovich, 2003). Heuristics are not as efficient as algorithms because they do not always guarantee a solution; in fact, they may even make problem solving more difficult if the student uses the wrong heuristic. Research indicates that experts have a much larger repertoire of algorithms and heuristics that are relevant to a problem. Of greater importance, experts are extremely skilled at identifying which of these strategies is most useful to the problem at hand (Kahneman & Frederick, 2005).

Two of the more common heuristics are **trial and error** and **means–ends analysis.** Trial and error is clearly the least efficient of all the methods because learners have no strategic plan whatsoever. Trial and error may be our only alternative when we are faced unexpectedly with an unfamiliar problem. Often, however, most people will use a trial-and-error approach at the onset of the problem and then switch to a more efficient method after some preliminary information is gained about the problem.

Means–ends analysis differs from trial and error in that the problem solver tries to reduce the distance to the goal by taking a sequence of steps that can be evaluated individually. In essence, means–ends analysis requires the learner to do three things: (1) formulate a goal state, (2) break down the problem into smaller subproblems, and (3) evaluate the success of one's performance at each step before proceeding to the next. One example of means–ends analysis is writing a compare-and-contrast essay on a timed test. The first step is to identify the goal state (the position you want to defend), the second step is to break down the paper into smaller problems (e.g., introduction, comparison of evidence, conclusion), and the third step is to proceed through the paper one section at a time.

Not surprisingly, good and poor problem solvers differ in the kinds of strategies they use to solve problems. Experts tend to use some form of means–ends analysis in which they first categorize the problem on the basis of the kind of solution it requires, and then break down the problem into smaller parts, and finally solve each part in a sequential manner. In contrast, inexperienced or poor problem solvers often resort to trial and error or use a crude form of means–ends analysis based on surface features of the problem. Novice problem solvers also are more likely to break down a problem into fewer meaningful parts and to solve those parts out of sequence.

Another difference between good and poor problem solvers is the ability to plan—a skill that depends on experience, background knowledge, and one's awareness of different kinds of problem-solving strategies. Good problem solvers plan farther in advance and coordinate the entire problem-solving sequence more efficiently. Research in the area of writing suggests that some writers plan "locally," whereas others plan "globally" (Bereiter & Scardamalia, 1987). Global planning seems to contribute greatly to effective writing. As with other types of problem solving, good writing and good planning depend on declarative knowledge about how a text is structured, as well as procedural knowledge about how to compose a text. Global planning also is essential in other cognitive domains and is the bedrock of effective self-regulation (Schunk & Zimmerman, 2006).

Implementing the Strategy   The success one has when implementing a strategy largely depends on how well one identifies and represents the problem and on the type of strategy one adopts. Clear differences exist at each of these levels between good and poor problem solvers. In addition, good problem solvers coordinate the solution phase of problem solving more efficiently. One consistent finding is that experts change strategies more often (strategy shifting), consider more solutions, evaluate solutions more carefully before discarding them, and reach conclusions that are more workable than do novices.

In one study that compared expert and novice teachers, Swanson, O'Connor, and Cooney (1990) found that expert teachers used more strategies while solving classroom management problems than did novices. Experts placed a high priority on defining and representing the problem before deciding on a solution; novices did not. Experts also tended to classify problems at a "deeper" level by carefully evaluating the type and severity of classroom misbehavior; novices tended to categorize problems on the basis of how they would respond to them. As a consequence, experts were more likely to consider different solutions, and to evaluate those solutions, given the larger context of the classroom environment. Novices were more likely to choose a single solution based on the apparent severity of the misbehavior. Another important difference between the two groups was that expert teachers were more likely to choose externally based interventions, such as physically separating children, whereas novices were more likely to select internally based interventions, such as counseling students. These findings have been replicated across different age groups and domains (Dunbar & Fugelsang, 2005; Ellsworth, 2005).

One reason for different problem-solving strategies between expert and novice teachers is that the former possess a great deal of procedural knowledge gained from experience that allows them to focus more of their attention on defining the problem rather than on selecting a strategy to solve the problem. In contrast, novices feel a greater need to reach a solution early, often at the expense of analyzing the problem carefully. One implication of this research is that novice teachers may be poorer problem solvers because they focus too much attention on finding a solution even before they understand the problem. Presumably, novice teachers could benefit by considering problems more carefully or, if that were not possible in a busy class-room, by considering various solutions to problems before they enter the classroom.

Evaluating Solutions   One might think that evaluating solutions is unimportant because it typically occurs after the problem has been solved. This simply is not true. Those who fail to evaluate both the products and the process of problem solving miss an excellent opportunity to improve these skills. An abundance of research in the areas of metacognition (Pressley & Harris, 2006), reflective practice (Schön, 1987), and self-regulation (Schunk & Zimmerman, 2006) suggests that most of the improvement we experience in learning is the result of purposeful evaluation. Evaluation helps us better understand the usefulness and applicability of a particular strategy. Considering why a strategy did not work in one context may enable a learner to use it more efficiently in another. In addition, evaluating solutions permits us to reflect at a deeper level about the process of problem solving.

For these reasons, any complex problem-solving task such as reading, writing, studying, or learning new skills in the classroom should be accompanied by two types of evaluation. The first is an analysis of *products*. Is the end result the best solution available? How does this solution compare with others? Are other solutions likely that were not considered? The second type of evaluation examines the *process*. How well did you do? What did you do right or wrong? How could you improve? Only by asking these types of questions can students be expected to significantly improve their problem-solving skills and their understanding of how to solve problems.

Expert Knowledge in Problem Solving

In the previous section, we described a general model of problem solving that can be applied to any domain. Many researchers have noted that people's ability to solve a problem usually depends on two crucial factors: one is the amount of domain-specific knowledge at our disposal; another is the amount of experience we have in trying to solve a particular class of problems (Taconis, Ferguson-Hessler, & Broekkamp, 2002). Debate continues concerning the most useful way to improve problem solving in the classroom and the workplace, with some researchers emphasizing the development of domain-specific knowledge and others stressing the role of general problem-solving skills (Fuchs et al., 2008; Mayer & Wittrock, 2006). Before we attempt to compare the relative strengths and weaknesses of the two approaches, it may be helpful to consider the role of domain-specific and general knowledge in greater detail.

Domain Knowledge

The realm of knowledge that individuals have about a particular field of study is called domain-specific knowledge, or simply **domain knowledge** (Alexander, 2003). Knowledge domains typically are subject areas (e.g., mathematics and modern art) but also can represent areas of activity (e.g., bicycle mechanics, taxi driving, and gardening). They encompass declarative, procedural, and metacognitive knowledge and can operate at a tacit or an explicit level. For many tasks, including school-related ones, the amount of domain knowledge required to perform successfully is very large indeed. For instance, try to imagine the amount of knowledge needed to make sense out of novels such as *The Color Purple* or *Moby Dick,* a momentum problem in physics, or a description of gene-splicing techniques.

Examples of domain knowledge can be seen all about us every day. Each plays a role in an individual's functioning effectively. Examples of domain knowledge that is more declarative in nature are the knowledge needed to make sense of a road map, the information required to judge what kind of home loan might be best for a person's circumstances, and knowledge of the capitals of Eastern Europe. Examples of domain knowledge that is more procedural also abound—for instance, the knowledge that an office worker reveals as he duplicates a report or runs a spreadsheet program, or that a mechanic exhibits in successfully diagnosing the cause of a poorly running automobile, or the skills an athlete exercises in the course of a volleyball match. Likewise, domain-related metacognitive knowledge is shown as students make the observation that they are "poor in math," find main ideas in a science text, and plan their parts in a class project on the Civil War.

One major goal of schooling is to build all three dimensions of students' domain knowledge (Taconis et al., 2002). By the time students finish formal schooling, we expect them to possess a large and usable body of information in each of several curricular fields, such as history, literature, mathematics, biology, and foreign languages. We also hope that students will have built their domain knowledge in several areas of everyday life, such as jobs, the environment, and community functioning. Students should have experience solving real-life problems in as many domains as possible working alone and in groups (Hmelo-Silver, 2004).

An Example of Domain Knowledge in Cognition

The influence of domain knowledge is tremendous even though we often lose sight of it. Consider, for example, the role of domain knowledge in reading. Typically, we think of differences in what students comprehend and remember from reading as attributable to their basic abilities in reading, not to their domain knowledge. We do know, however, that good readers remember more of what they read and possess more knowledge about the world than poor readers. At the same time, good readers not only remember more about what they read but they also read a great deal more than poor readers. This close relationship between reading ability and knowledge has made research in the area difficult. A now classic study by Recht and Leslie (1988), however, was designed in a way that allowed them to see what effect domain knowledge had on students' memory for what they read.

Recht and Leslie searched for a topic that not only some good readers and some poor readers would know a great deal about but also that some good and some poor readers would know very little about. They settled on baseball. After identifying some junior high school students who were very good readers and some who were poor readers, Recht and Leslie tested all of them about their knowledge of baseball. This procedure allowed the researchers to identify good readers who knew a great deal about baseball, good readers who knew very little about baseball, poor readers who knew a great deal about baseball, and poor readers who knew very little about baseball. Next, the students were asked to read a 625-word passage that described half an inning of a baseball game between a local team and a visiting rival. Then they were tested in several ways for their ability to remember the passage: (1) reenacting the inning with a model field and miniature wooden players while verbally describing what happened, (2) summarizing the passage, and (3) sorting 22 sentences taken from the passage on the basis of how important the sentences were to the happenings of the inning.

Results of Recht and Leslie's (1988) study were striking. On each measure of memory, poor readers who knew a great deal about baseball greatly outperformed good readers who knew very little about baseball. In fact, they performed nearly as well as the good readers who knew a great deal about baseball. Poor readers who knew very little about baseball, however, remembered the least about the passage on all measures. Thus, knowledge in the domain of baseball had a very powerful influence on how much and what was remembered.

The influence of students' domain knowledge on new learning reaches far more broadly than baseball, of course. Remembering information in areas as diverse as chess, art, computer programming, electronics, and biology all have been shown to be related to previous knowledge. In general, the more students know about a specific topic, the easier it is for them to learn and remember new information about that topic.

Not surprisingly, domain knowledge is closely related to problem-solving abilities. Experts, be they artists, mechanics, or nuclear physicists, know that problems in their field are solved most easily when they can be related to other, similar problems. Experts typically think before they act and tend to use a limited but optimal set of problem-solving strategies (Fuchs et al., 2008; Ritchart & Perkins, 2005). They also understand the importance of sketches and diagrams in problem solving. Novices, in contrast, may work very hard at problem solving—even harder than experts—but their strategies are less productive because of their limited domain knowledge and the inefficient ways they go about trying to make their knowledge relevant to problems.

General Knowledge

Although domain knowledge is fundamental for day-to-day problem solving, another kind of knowledge—**general knowledge**—also is needed. General knowledge is broad knowledge that is not linked with a specific domain (Buehl, Alexander, & Murphy, 2002). Think back to our example in Chapter 1, where Kari grappled with the assignment of writing a report. To produce this report, she had to have information, skills, and strategies beyond the specific topic of the paper. For example, she needed a declarative network of concepts and a vocabulary to express her ideas, knowledge of punctuation and grammar to guide her writing, general information about reports and their functions, and procedural skills for operating a word processor. She also needed metacognitive knowledge to organize and carry out all of these activities. None of this general knowledge was related directly to the topic she chose to write about, but it nonetheless was essential for completing this and virtually all problem-solving tasks.

Because it is information that can be applied to almost any task, general knowledge can be thought of as complementary to domain knowledge. Indeed, recent research found that both domain-specific and general knowledge were needed to use problem-solving strategies in an optimal manner (Gugerty, 2007). Of course, what constitutes general knowledge and what constitutes domain knowledge can shift as the task focus shifts. For students reading a novel by Willa Cather and trying to understand her use of certain literary devices, the relevant domain knowledge may be primarily in the realm of English literature. If her descriptions of the native prairie are being studied by a biology class for how they characterized prairie ecology nearly a century ago and the task is to map changes that may be occurring in the prairie environment, the relevant domain knowledge centers on plants, animals, and environment, with literary knowledge becoming general knowledge.

Ordinarily, one can think of general knowledge as knowledge appropriate to a wide range of tasks but not tied to any one task. Examples of general knowledge that is useful for a broad array of activities includes the declarative networks represented by our vocabulary, knowledge of current affairs, and historical knowledge; the procedural knowledge for speaking, for doing mathematics, and for carrying on a conversation; and the metacognitive skills we use across a variety of cognitive tasks. Indeed, the amount of general knowledge necessary for a 15-year-old such as Kari to function on a day-to-day basis at home, in her social world, and at school is almost infinite.

Domain Knowledge and Expertise

Let's turn our attention now to what it takes to become an expert. Researchers studying the development of expertise estimate that it takes about 5 to 10 years or on the order of 10,000 hours to develop true expertise in a domain regardless of intellectual aptitude (Alexander, 2003; Ericsson, 1996, 2003; Lajoie, 2003). In many cases, it may take even longer. It may surprise (or alarm) you to know that beginning radiologists (X-ray specialists) perform far below experienced experts even after completing 4 years of medical school (Lesgold, 1988). Fortunately, the training received during a doctor's internship and as on-the-job training lead to deep expertise that enables doctors to perform with impressive skill and efficiency (Patel, Arocha, & Zhang, 2005).

One reason why expertise develops so slowly is that much of the declarative and procedural knowledge needed to master a domain is acquired *tacitly* over a long period of time (Bereiter & Scardamalia, 1993; Novick & Bassok, 2005). For example, most college students possess a great deal of expert knowledge about their native languages. They read and write fluently, using syntactic (grammar) and semantic (meaning) knowledge to convey complex meanings. They also use language metaphorically to convey nonliteral meaning (e.g., *prisons are junkyards*). Yet, most of them find it very difficult to describe what it is they know about language or how they learned it. Indeed, we often can use what we know but cannot explain it.

Evidence suggests that much of our knowledge is acquired tacitly even when we receive a great deal of formal training in a domain (Buehl et al., 2002; Litman & Reber, 2005). Because of this, even highly skilled experts often find it difficult to describe what it is they know about a body of knowledge and, as a consequence, may be poor decision makers when forced to reflect on their knowledge (Johnson, 1988). Typically, however, experts are better problem solvers than novices for a variety of reasons, including experience, background knowledge, and information processing advantages that are the consequence of expert knowledge (Glaser & Chi, 1988). Figure 8.2 lists seven key characteristics of experts. Experts also are much more likely to be able to articulate complex knowledge and procedures, and to provide explicit models of their problem solving.

Seven Characteristics of Expert Performance

Although our intuition may suggest otherwise, the first characteristic of experts is that they usually are no better able to solve problems in unfamiliar domains than novices; that is, expertise is domain-specific. Consider a brilliant chemist whose car breaks down on a deserted highway. The chances are good that the stranded motorist will walk to the nearest gas station rather than solve the problem herself or himself *unless* she or he also happens to have expert knowledge about auto repair. No evidence suggests that expertise in one domain readily transfers to

1. Experts excel only in their own domain.
2. Experts process information in large units.
3. Experts are faster than novices.
4. Experts hold more information in short-term and long-term memory.
5. Experts represent problems at a deeper level.
6. Experts spend more time analyzing a problem.
7. Experts are better monitors of their performance.

Source: From *Glaser and Chi* (1988).

FIGURE 8.2   Seven Characteristics of Experts.

another. Rather, expertise develops slowly, is highly labor-intensive, and is confined to a particular body of knowledge.

A second characteristic of experts is that they organize information far more efficiently than do novices. Typically, this is accomplished by chunking information into larger recognizable units than a novice might use (see Chapter 4). Chase and Simon (1973a, 1973b) found that one main difference between expert and novice chess players was not the absolute size of their working memories (about seven pieces of information), but rather how much information they could analyze and remember in a single brief exposure (their ability to categorize information). Chess experts were able to view complex chess configurations for as little as 5 seconds yet remember them in remarkable detail; novices remembered very little of what they saw. Surprisingly, when the same experiment was conducted using nonmeaningful chess patterns, no difference was found between the experts and the novices.

A third characteristic is that experts are faster than novices at processing meaningful information because they search and represent problems more efficiently (Pretz et al., 2003). If you ever have had the experience of watching an expert mathematician solve word problems, you observed how easily the expert identified relevant information and selected an appropriate strategy. Although rather disconcerting to the novice, the expert's behavior may be less impressive than it appears because she or he probably has solved hundreds or perhaps thousands of similar problems in the past. The experience gained by solving these problems enables the expert to remember similar problems and solutions and to select appropriate strategies with little effort. These differences even have been observed when comparing expert and novice figure skaters (Deakin & Allard, 1991).

A fourth characteristic that makes experts better (and faster) problem solvers is that their thoughts and actions are highly automatized. Being automatic allows experts to use their short-term memory in a more efficient way compared with novices. Expert mathematicians, for instance, activate and implement appropriate solution strategies so efficiently that they place very few demands on their cognitive resources. These resources can be used to accomplish higher-order cognitive tasks, such as monitoring one's progress and evaluating solutions.

As a fifth characteristic, experts represent problems differently from novices. Experts usually focus more of their attention on the underlying structure of the problem rather than on superficial surface features. Many studies show that expert physicists categorize physics problems on the basis of mechanical principles, whereas novices categorize them on the basis of objects mentioned in the problem (e.g., the angle of a shadow). Experts also are more likely to use means–ends analysis, breaking problems into subgoals and working forward toward the desired end state.

A sixth characteristic is that experts spend more time than novices analyzing the problem at the *beginning* of the problem-solving process. In a large number of studies, experts have been found to spend a greater proportion of their time identifying and representing the problem, compared with novices, even though they spent considerably less time choosing an appropriate solution strategy once the problem had been clarified. Experts also were more apt to rely on complex conditional strategies for reducing a problem into smaller component problems (Clancey, 1988).

The seventh characteristic is that experts are better monitors than novices in most situations *within their domain of expertise*. Experts are more likely to generate alternative hypotheses before solving a problem and are quicker to reject inappropriate solutions during problem solving. Experts also judge the difficulty of problems more accurately than novices and ask more appropriate questions at all stages of the problem-solving process.

The characteristics described here all point to one simple conclusion about the nature of expertise: Experts are faster, more efficient, and more reflective *because of the depth and breadth of their knowledge*. We do not mean to imply by this statement that extensive knowledge guarantees expert performance. Most researchers agree that true expertise represents a complex interaction between general problem-solving strategies and extensive domain-specific knowledge. These two components can best be thought of as complementary processes: Expert knowledge facilitates strategy use, whereas knowledge about general problem-solving strategies enables learners to use their expert knowledge more efficiently (Schraw, 2006).

Some Pitfalls of Expertise

Much has been written about the advantages of expertise. These include the ability to perform quickly and efficiently at very high levels of achievement. However, there are at least three potential costs related to expertise. One is that the amount of time invested in the development of expertise precludes developing expertise in other domains, as well as other casual activities. Typically, an individual will spend 5 to 10 years of concentrated study and practice to become a true expert. For this reason, many people view the time necessary to become an expert as too great a personal sacrifice.

A second and far more serious cost of expertise is conceptual rigidity in which the expert finds it difficult to consider other points of view. Sternberg (2005) suggests that expert scientists may be at risk for confirmation bias because they expect certain outcomes to occur and often have invested years of research and effort in trying to document these outcomes. Stanovich (2003) refers to this phenomenon as *knowledge projection,* in which faulty heuristics are used to reach inadvertently faulty conclusions. Bilalic, McLeod, and Gobet (2008) suggest that experts may be less flexible in their thinking due to their high degree of automation of basic skills and procedures. Ironically, experts may be at greater risk than novices in certain situations because they possess more heuristics that are more automated.

Yet a third problem related to expertise is what Nathan and Petrosino (2003) refer to as the **expert blind spot effect,** in which experts view student problem solving from an expert's perspective rather than a novice student's perspective. The expert blind spot effect may lead expert teachers to overlook the developmental needs of novice students and to select curriculum that is too advanced because it requires students to utilize organizing principles and expert heuristics they do not possess. Debate continues about the frequency with which an expert blind spot occurs. Research generally suggests that experts are not blinded, but perform faster and more accurately than novices (Onkal, Yates, Simca-Mugan, & Oztin, 2003).

Role of Deliberate Practice

Novices do not become experts overnight. As we have said, becoming truly expert typically is a 10-year process. But what is this process like? Is it the same for everyone? And how much does the development of expertise depend on "native talent?" Researchers have become increasingly interested in these questions during the past decade and have generated some rather surprising answers.

The development of expertise occurs in rather predictable stages (Ward, Hodges, Starkes, & Williams, 2007). Bloom (1985), in a landmark study of the development of talent among children and adolescents, identified three stages that he referred to as the early, middle, and late years. Early years are characterized by playful engagement, typically in a highly supportive home environment in which parents stress motivation and effort rather than native ability. Middle years mark a turn in which the novice begins to develop the first true signs of expertise and becomes increasingly dependent on highly skilled mentors. These mentors typically are not parents but rather skilled professionals. The emphasis during this period is on developing a steady regimen of practice, competition, and feedback. Late years are characterized by finding a master teacher who can help the individual develop true expertise. Peer relationships also become increasingly important as developing experts encounter one another on a frequent basis. Total psychological commitment is expected of individuals at this stage.

The process of developing expertise appears to be remarkably consistent across all disciplines. For example, Bloom (1985) concluded that young athletes, musicians, and mathematicians develop in more or less the same way (three stages extending over a 10-year period or more). Research on skill acquisition suggests substages within stages. Ackerman proposed that skill acquisition is characterized by *knowledge acquisition, skill proceduralization,* and *automated application* stages (see Ackerman & Lohman, 2006, for a review). These stages may recur each time a developing expert enters a new level of skill acquisition (e.g., the transition from the early to middle years).

Ericsson and colleagues (Ericsson, 1996, 2005; Ericsson, Krampe, & Tesch-Romer, 1993; Ericsson & Ward, 2007) have conducted studies on the role of **deliberate practice** in the acquisition of expertise. The most important finding of these studies is that skill development and expertise are strongly related to the time and efficiency of deliberate practice. The more one practices, the better one gets *regardless of initial talent and ability* (Ericsson, Roring, & Nandagopal, 2007). A second finding is that initial differences attributable to talent and ability *decrease* over time as a function of practice. This means that highly talented individuals lose their edge over time if they do not practice, compared with less talented individuals. A third finding is that the *quality,* in addition to the *quantity,* of practice is extremely important. The highest quality practice takes place early in the morning before peak resources are allocated to other tasks. It generally is most efficient for 1 to 3 hours, with the ideal being about 2 hours. Practice is associated with informational feedback (knowledge about errors and how to improve performance). The best practice occurs under the watchful guidance of a skilled mentor who helps the developing expert set goals and monitor improvement.

Perhaps the most surprising (and inspirational) finding in this research is that deliberate, extended practice counts much more than native ability (Johnson, Tenebaum, & Edmonds, 2006). Ericsson et al. (1993) are quite emphatic on this point, stating the following:

> In summary, our review has uncovered essentially no support for the fixed innate characteristics that would correspond to general or specific natural ability (in the development of expertise) [emphasis added], and, in fact, has uncovered findings inconsistent with such models. (p. 399)

Bloom (1985) draws a similar conclusion based on extensive longitudinal data, as follows:

> No matter how precocious one is at age ten or eleven, if the individual doesn't stay with the talent development process over many years, he or she soon will be outdistanced by others who continue. (p. 538)

This is not to suggest that native talent and ability are unrelated to skill development and expertise (Ackerman & Lohman, 2006). Talent clearly helps skilled individuals develop faster, and some researchers continue to believe that native talent and the "rage to master" determine one's ultimate success (Winner, 1996, 2000). Recent research suggests that passion to improve and excel is related positively to deliberate practice and performance achievement (Vallerand et al., 2007). Nevertheless, talent alone is not sufficient, and it remains to be seen what level of initial talent is necessary to achieve high levels of expertise. Research reveals that less talented individuals reach higher levels of accomplishment than more talented peers by virtue of guided, deliberate practice. When students are denied the opportunity to develop expertise due to socioeconomic reasons, this may result in substantial talent loss in a society (Plank & Jordan, 2001). In short, there is no easy path to expertise, but there is no reason to believe that the road is blocked for some people more than others, provided all individuals have the time and financial resources to engage in extended, deliberate practice. Those who work the hardest for the longest period of time and have access to skilled mentors usually reach the highest level of skill attainment.

One possibility worth considering is that different individuals reach expert performance through different pathways. Schraw (2006) described three models he referred to as the deliberate practice, talent, and interactive models, which are shown in Figure 8.3. Model 1 suggests that deliberate practice leads to the development of ability and talent that, in turn, leads to expertise. Model 2 shows a reverse process in which ability and talent predispose one to deliberate practice that leads to expertise. Model 3 shows a reciprocal relationship between ability and deliberate practice, which both affect expertise. It may be the case that low-talent individuals reach expertise through an alternative pathway compared to high-talent individuals. This would lend credibility to the models proposed by Ericsson (1996) and Winner (1996).

Problem-Solving Transfer

One important question is the degree to which problem-solving skills in one domain transfer to another. Some researchers believe that transfer occurs very rarely, if ever, because expertise (and expert problem-solving skills) are welded to specific domains (Detterman, 1993) and students may be unmotivated to persist until knowledge and skills transfer (Bereby-Meyer & Kaplan, 2005; Pugh & Bergin, 2006). In contrast, Cox (1997), Halpern (1998), and Mayer and Wittrock (2006) suggest that problem-solving skills may transfer provided educators help students use these skills in a variety of settings and promote the use

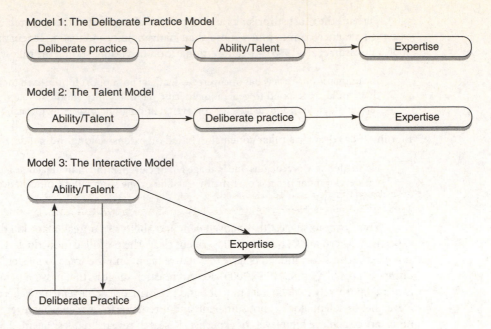

Model 1: The Deliberate Practice Model

Deliberate practice → Ability/Talent → Expertise

Model 2: The Talent Model

Ability/Talent → Deliberate practice → Expertise

Model 3: The Interactive Model

Ability/Talent
Expertise
Deliberate Practice

FIGURE 8.3   **Three Models of Ability, Deliberate Practice, and Talent.**

of metacognitive self-regulation. Some instructional methods appear to work better than others in this regard. One of the most useful is to provide structured practice that promotes automated problem solving (Lovett, 2002; Sweller, 1999). Automated skills appear easier to transfer than nonautomated skills. A second strategy is to relate problem-solving skills in one domain to those in a new domain by using analogies. A third strategy is to provide students with detailed worked-out examples (Paas, 1992) and feedback (Bernardo, 2001). Other methods, such as unstructured discovery, appear to be less productive, although several recent studies indicate that structured discovery promotes deeper learning as well as spontaneous transfer between different types of problems (Chi, de Leeuw, Chiu, & La Vancher, 1994; Kuhn, Schauble, & Garcia-Mila, 1992).

Mayer and Wittrock (2006) describe seven instructional strategies to improve problem-solving transfer. Table 8.1 presents a summary of these strategies. Currently, it is unclear whether any of these methods promote a significant degree of transfer. However, each of these strategies is known to increase efficiency and long-term learning even if it does not directly improve transfer.

Implications for Instruction: Improving Problem Solving

Problem-solving skills can be improved in many ways, some of which require a long-term investment (e.g., accumulating extensive expert knowledge) and some of which lead to more rapid improvement (e.g., mimicking expert strategies). In general, we emphasize the fundamental role of expert knowledge in effective problem solving. Although it is possible to improve problem-solving skills by improving general knowledge about problem solving, there probably is no substitute for the expert knowledge acquired through the 10,000 or so hours of engagement in the domain. With this caveat, we suggest the following steps:

1. *Facilitate the acquisition of expert knowledge.* Years of research indicate that extensive domain knowledge is clearly the most important constraint on effective problem solving (Alexander, 2003; Lajoie, 2003). One instructional strategy is to help students acquire as much expert knowledge as quickly as possible. Educators should seriously consider what constitutes an "expert" body of knowledge in their discipline and attempt to convey this information to all students. This means that teachers must make a special effort to select and organize the core body of knowledge one needs to learn to become an expert.

Another highly effective but often-neglected strategy is for novices to ask an expert for help when they do not understand a problem. One reason to do so is to acquire an expert's "way of knowing" the problem. Indeed, it could be argued that learning what kinds of strategies experts use is less important than understanding why they use them.

2. *Develop an awareness of a general problem-solving strategy.* Everyone, to some extent, can become a better problem solver by understanding the basic process of problem solving (Bransford, Sherwood, Vye, & Rieser, 1986). The five-stage sequence outlined earlier provides an excellent framework for developing component skills (e.g., representing problems externally), as well as for understanding the relationships among component skills. Teaching specific skills such as predicting outcomes (Hurst & Milkent, 1996) and inductive reasoning (Tomic, 1997) also facilitates problem solving.

Studies investigating the value of teaching younger students a general problem-solving method have yielded fairly impressive findings. In one study, King (1991) compared groups of fifth-grade students in which the students solved problems by using or not using a problem-solving prompt card. Those using the prompts solved problems better. Delclos and Harrington (1991) compared three groups of fifth- and sixth-grade students; one group received problem-solving and monitoring training, another received problem-solving training, and a third received no

TABLE 8.1   Instructional Strategies to Improve Problem-Solving Transfer

Instructional Strategy	Description
Load-reducing strategies	Promote automaticity of procedures, reduce unnecessary processing load, eliminate constraints
Structure-based strategies	Provide conceptual structure and physical examples to guide learning
Schema-based strategies	Activate prior knowledge using advance organizers and pre-training
Generation strategies	Promote self-explanation and reflective questioning
Guided discovery strategies	Provide scaffolded assistance to students
Modeling strategies	Modeling by teachers; use of cognitive apprenticeships with advanced students
Teaching thinking skills strategies	Direct instruction of problem-solving and critical-thinking skills

training. Although the combined group (metacognitive and problem-solving training) outperformed all others, the problem solving–only group outperformed the control group.

Together, these studies suggest that problem-solving training has a beneficial effect on younger students. Problem-solving training also is enhanced when it is coupled with other kinds of instruction, such as question answering (King, 1991) and metacognitive training (Delclos & Harrington, 1991). Readers interested in teaching general problem-solving skills may wish to consult the work of Davis Perkins (e.g., Ritchart & Perkins, 2005) for further suggestions.

3. *Focus on discovering and identifying problems.* Many studies reveal that problem discovery is the most crucial stage of the problem-solving sequence. Indeed, to be a good problem finder, one must be highly creative and motivated. Individuals should be encouraged to "linger" on a problem during this stage because of the direct relationship between time spent conceptualizing a problem and the quality of its solution. Those wishing to promote the creative aspect of problem finding may wish to consult Dacey (1989) and Weisberg (1993).

4. *Use external representations whenever possible.* One limitation that most individuals face when trying to solve problems is overloading their cognitive resources. Sensory and short-term memory stores are limited to about seven pieces of information at a time. Many problems greatly exceed this limit, causing an inability to hold all relevant pieces of a problem in working memory. Representing problems in written or graphic form can reduce this cognitive overload and improve problem-solving effectiveness.

5. *Mimic expert strategies.* Sometimes it is possible to teach individuals without expert knowledge to act like experts. Using "expert" fingering techniques when playing the piano, for example, may hasten improvement. At other times, expert strategies are useless without the knowledge needed to use those strategies in a planned way. Consider a chess novice who is taught the Sicilian Defense but who gets into trouble quickly by trying to use it against a skilled opponent. When it comes to problem solving, the saying "A little bit of knowledge is a dangerous thing" often rings true. Using experts' strategies may be helpful in some situations but not others. Professional discretion is advised!

Critical Thinking

A long-standing debate in U.S. education is whether schools should direct their efforts to teaching students *how* to think rather than *what* to think. The fact that such questions continue to be asked (e.g., Ennis, 1987; Halpern, 2003; Kuhn, 1999; Perkins, Jay, & Tishman, 1993; Pithers & Soden, 2000) invites us to consider what it means to "think critically." Most of us would agree that critical thinking is important, that it is complex, and that it encompasses a host of lesser skills, such as identifying and evaluating information. But how does critical thinking differ from problem solving or creativity? In this section, we examine these issues and address three related questions: What skills are necessary to think critically? Is critical thinking constrained by intelligence? And how should one go about designing a critical thinking program?

Toward a Definition of Critical Thinking

For most experts, **critical thinking** differs from problem solving in two ways (Halpern, 2003; Marzano, 1992). One way is that problem solving usually requires an individual to solve specialized problems in a particular domain. These problems typically are well defined and have one or perhaps two correct solutions. Solving word problems in algebra class and replicating a heat-exchange experiment in a science class provide good examples. Performance on such problems has been shown to correlate highly with the amount of domain-specific expertise that learners have.

In contrast, critical thinking usually requires us to consider general issues that cut across several domains. These "problems" frequently are ill defined and have many possible solutions or even may be unsolvable. Consider some issues we must weigh when choosing a president: how to reduce the national debt, the constitutionality of abortion and capital punishment, and whether financial aid should be offered to formerly hostile foreign nations.

Critical thinking also differs from problem solving in the nature of what is being evaluated. Most problems are external states, whereas most critical thinking is directed toward internal states. Choosing a political affiliation, for instance, is part problem solving in that we must choose whom to vote for, but it also is part critical thinking, in that we first need to clarify and evaluate our own beliefs and expectations about each of the candidates.

One definition of critical thinking is *reflective thinking focused on deciding what to believe or do* (Ennis, 1987). We believe that an analysis of some key terms in this definition is helpful for understanding what critical thinking entails. First, critical thinking is a *reflective* activity (Kitchener & King, 2004). Often, its goal is not to solve a problem but rather to better understand the nature of the problem. Critical thinking also is *focused* in that we are not just thinking, but thinking about something we wish to understand more thoroughly. The purpose of thinking critically is to weigh and evaluate information in a way that ultimately enables us to make informed *decisions*. Finally, unlike problem solving, the content of our critical thinking is often a *belief* or a motive we wish to examine more thoroughly.

A second definition of critical thinking is *better thinking* (Perkins, 2001). This view suggests that learning to think critically will improve our ability to gather, interpret, evaluate, and select information for the purpose of making informed choices. We suspect that this is the definition most teachers and parents have in mind when they say, "Students need to think more critically about their lives." Of course, statements such as these require us as parents and professional educators to think more critically about how to improve students' thinking!

A third definition of critical thinking is *distinguishing between thinking that is directed at adopting versus clarifying a goal* (Nickerson, 1987). Adopting is closer to problem solving because it emphasizes a "product" view of decision making, whereas clarifying emphasizes the "process" one uses to reach that decision. We view critical thinking as more than decision making and believe that the process of informed decision making is more important than the decision itself. Let's turn now to some skills involved in critical thinking.

Component Skills in Critical Thinking

Earlier, we described important skills used in problem solving. We now turn our attention to an analogous set of skills used in critical thinking. Ennis (1987) has proposed the most comprehensive set of skills thus far in which he distinguishes between two major classes of critical thinking activities: *dispositions* and *abilities*. The former refers to affective and dispositional traits that each person brings to a thinking task, such as open-mindedness; an attempt to be well-informed; and sensitivity to others' beliefs, feelings, and knowledge. The latter refers to the actual cognitive abilities necessary to think critically, including focusing, analyzing, and judging. A similar set of skills has been proposed by Halpern (2003).

Figure 8.4 lists 12 skills included in Ennis's taxonomy. An inspection of these skills (and selected subskills) suggests that some are appropriate for any type of thinking, whether critical or creative. Others, such as making value judgments, seem to be less important for solving physics problems than when voting for a presidential candidate. According to Ennis (1987), each subskill contributes to critical thinking in its own way, helping us to clarify our goals and objectives, acquire and analyze an adequate knowledge base, make inferences, and interact with others in a rational manner.

Analyzing critical thinking in terms of separate subskills can be somewhat risky because we are apt to lose sight of what critical thinking entails: critical examination of beliefs and courses of action. Instead, some authors suggest that a smaller set of general skills should be used to describe critical thinking (Halpern, 1998; Kurfiss, 1988; Quellmalz, 1987; Swartz & Perkins, 1990). These skills include knowledge, inference, evaluation, and metacognition.

Critical thinking of any kind is impossible without the first of these components—*knowledge*. Knowledge is something we use to think critically and also acquire as the result of critical thinking. As we have seen, expert knowledge enables individuals to solve problems faster, better, and differently than those without such knowledge. Knowledge provides the basis for judging the credibility of new information or points of view; it also helps us to critically scrutinize our goals and objectives. Knowledge in the form of strategies actively shapes the direction we take when trying to resolve a dilemma.

Inference refers to making some type of connection between two or more units of knowledge. Much of successful critical thinking draws on our ability to make simple, insightful inferences between otherwise unrelated facts. In Chapter 6, for example, you learned that each of us makes attributional inferences concerning our success and failure in the classroom. Some of these inferences may be inappropriate under certain circumstances (e.g., beginning algebra students attributing their failure to low ability), whereas others are more appropriate (e.g., poor performance in algebra may be attributable to lack of prior knowledge, domain-specific strategies, and automaticity). Making inferences is an essential step in critical thinking because it enables individuals to understand their situations at a deeper, more meaningful level.

1. Focusing on the question
2. Analyzing arguments
3. Asking and answering questions of clarification
4. Judging the credibility of a source
5. Observing and judging observational reports
6. Deducing and judging deductions
7. Inducing and judging inductions
8. Making value judgments
9. Defining terms and judging definitions
10. Identifying assumptions
11. Deciding on an action
12. Interaction with others

FIGURE 8.4   Twelve Critical Thinking Abilities Described by Ennis (1987).

Several types of inference processes seem to be especially important. One is *deduction,* the process by which we reach specific conclusions from given information. Logicians and mathematicians have identified a variety of deductive reasoning approaches that are useful when solving well-defined problems, such as syllogisms. No matter what the approach, all deductive inferences are similar in that conclusions are based only on the information provided by the problem. In the parlance of Chapter 2, deduction is a data-limited reasoning process. If Josh borrows his mother's car and returns with a dented fender, we can deduce that Josh had an accident with the car. We cannot deduce that he was speeding, legally drunk, or watching a pedestrian while driving, which, in turn, caused the accident.

Another kind of inference process is *induction,* the process by which we reach general conclusions from given, or perhaps inferred, information. Induction is in many ways the opposite of deduction in that conclusions can be reached that go beyond the limits of the data. Inductive inferences tend to be broader and more sweeping than deductive inferences. One of the best examples of inductive reasoning is making up a theory to explain an event before it is investigated (or perhaps even happens). Darwin's theory of natural selection provides a stunning example of inductive inference because it transcends the data described in *On the Origin of Species.*

The third component—*evaluation*—refers to related subskills, including analyzing, judging, weighing, and making value judgments (Perkins & Grotzer, 1997; Zohar, 2008). These skills probably come closest to what we usually think of as critical thinking. *Analyzing* includes activities that enable us to identify and select relevant information. *Judging* requires us to assess the credibility of information or sources of information in an effort to eliminate bias. *Weighing* consists of comparing all information at our disposal, choosing the most appropriate information, and organizing it as logically as possible. *Making value judgments* assumes that we have some moral, ethical, or emotional response to the information that affects our decision making.

The final component of critical thinking is *metacognition* (Halpern, 2003; Kuhn, 1999). As described in Chapter 4, *metacognition* refers to "thinking about thinking." Clearly, an important aspect of critical thinking is our ability to analyze the adequacy of our decisions. Insufficient data or conflicting beliefs and attitudes may require us to postpone an important decision and may limit our ability to construct an informed opinion on a topic. Metacognition is essential to the critical-thinking process because it allows us to monitor the adequacy of the information on which we base our opinions and the reasonableness of our inferences.

Does Intelligence Constrain Critical Thinking?

In the previous section, we described skills necessary for critical thinking. One might ask whether these skills depend on intellectual aptitude. If they do, educators are faced with difficult decisions about grouping students on the basis of ability. Until recently, an ability grouping model formed the backbone of the U.S. educational system. But what if thinking skills are not strongly linked with ability? How, then, should educators go about planning instruction?

Surprisingly, not a great deal of research has been done on the relationship between intellectual ability and critical-thinking skills, although existing research does suggest that normatively high intellectual ability is neither a necessary nor sufficient condition for successful thinking (for further discussion see Stanovich, 2003; and Stanovich & West, 2008). Earlier, we reported that Kitchener and King (1981) found that verbal ability (a correlate of general intellectual ability) was not related to reflective judgment. Swanson (1990) found that metacognitive awareness among children was not constrained by intellectual ability. Stanovich and West (2008) likewise reported that higher-ability persons were just as likely to make biased inferences in their thinking. Nevertheless, up to 40% of middle school and high school teachers in one study reported that instruction on critical-thinking skills was not appropriate for low-achieving students (Zohar, Degani, & Vaaknin, 2001). Based on the rather limited amount of research, we believe it is prudent to promote critical thinking among all students at a level of sophistication that is appropriate for them. Despite prevailing attitudes, there is not convincing evidence that critical thinking instruction is less productive for lower-achieving students.

Many contemporary researchers have adopted a broad view of what it means to be intelligent and how intellectual skills affect critical thinking (cf. Brody, 2000; Gardner, 1983; Sternberg et al., 2005). One view that we find particularly attractive is the model of critical thinking proposed by Perkins and colleagues (Perkins, 1987, 1995; Perkins & Grotzer, 1997). Perkins's model addresses three distinct aspects of intelligence: power, knowledge, and tactics. *Power* refers to the basic level of intellectual aptitude that each of us brings to a task. Clearly, this potential differs from person to person and, in many cases, differs within a single person across a variety of tasks (cf. Gardner, 1983). *Knowledge* refers to the domain-specific and general knowledge at our disposal. Every intellectual activity that we undertake is affected in some way by what we already know. One way in which knowledge helps us is in facilitating the organization of incoming information. Prior knowledge also enables us to construct meaning based on what we already know about a topic.

Unlike power and knowledge, *tactics* can be improved dramatically in only a short period of time (Perkins, Faraday, & Bushey, 1991). Tactics refers to the mental strategies we use to make a cognitive task easier to understand or perform. Perkins and many others place a high premium on tactical knowledge for one important reason: Even a modest repertoire of tactics can compensate for lack of power or knowledge. The compensatory nature of tactics has been demonstrated in many studies (King, 1991; Pressley & Harris, 2006; Swanson, 1990).

The fact that a compensatory relationship exists among power, knowledge, and tactics is of tremendous importance to educators (see Figure 8.5). When developing critical-thinking skills, teachers and students alike should be encouraged to focus less attention on the role of power and more attention on knowledge and tactics. Teachers and students should also bear in mind that some tactics are "welded" to a particular body of knowledge, while others are not (Perkins, 1987; Ritchart & Perkins, 2005). For example, factoring a quadratic equation to find its roots (a tactic) is difficult to separate from knowledge about quadratic equations because the two tend to be learned together. Other tactics, however, such as monitoring one's comprehension, are not specific to any particular body of knowledge. Monitoring is as useful when learning about American history as it is when assembling a sump pump or reading a road map. Some tactics need to be taught within a specific context for knowledge to be mastered; others are far more general and may be used successfully in many domains.

Tactics need not be limited to simple strategies such as skimming a text, factoring an equation, or carrying an umbrella when the weather looks like rain. Perkins (1987) has described a broader tactical approach to learning that he refers to as **thinking frames.** According to Perkins, a thinking frame is a guide or structure that organizes and supports thought processes. One example of a thinking frame is the "scientific method" commonly taught to beginning science students. Another example is the SQ3R (survey, question, read, recite, review) method of study. Other examples encountered in this text are levels of processing (a frame for

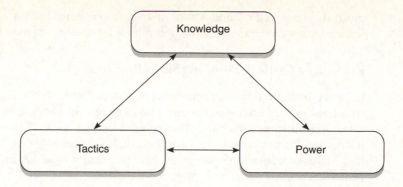

FIGURE 8.5   Components Involved in Learning, Problem Solving, and Critical Thinking.

Source: Perkins, D. N. Thinking frames: An integrated perspective on teaching cognitive skills. From: *Teaching Thinking Skills* by Baron and Sternberg. Copyright © 1987 by W. H. Freeman and Company. Used with permission.

understanding the depth of encoding), epistemological beliefs (a frame for explaining how individuals think about knowledge), and the general problem-solving method described earlier (a frame for attempting to solve any kind of well-defined problem).

One advantage to having thinking frames is that they provide an organizational structure for understanding new information and learning new skills. The Lehman et al. (Lehman, Lempert, & Nisbett, 1988) study described in Chapter 7 indicated that graduate students in different disciplines acquire expertise in reasoning skills that are especially important to their discipline (e.g., statistical reasoning). Acquiring these skills is one way that graduate students learn to "think like" experts. Another way is for graduate students to acquire the thinking frames a discipline holds about the phenomena it studies. For example, medical researchers assume that bacteria and viruses cause disease; thus, the researchers search for cures for these diseases on the basis of external-agent models (they use a germ theory thinking frame).

Perkins (1987) has described three stages in frame development: acquisition, automaticity, and transfer. *Acquisition* refers to learning a thinking frame and, in turn, using that frame to think and reason. Perkins is a strong proponent of teaching frames directly, including extensive modeling. *Automaticity* refers to being able to apply the frame automatically. As with other skills, using a thinking frame automatically is the result of extensive practice; the more practice one gets, the more automatic the frame becomes. *Transfer* refers to using the frame in a new context. Perkins (1987) and Perkins and Salomon (1989) have identified two kinds of transfer. The first kind of transfer, *high-road transfer*, occurs when students make a conscious, reflective effort to abstract the basic principles of the frame in a way that they can be applied in a different content area. High-road transfer requires students to be active, constructive, and reflective. In contrast, the second kind of transfer, *low-road transfer*, occurs spontaneously without awareness, given a narrow range of examples. As a consequence, students may not achieve a thorough (transferable) understanding of the frame. High-road transfer can be promoted by emphasizing reflection, self-monitoring, and extensive practice in a variety of settings (Mayer & Wittrock, 2006).

Perkins strongly advocates the direct teaching and modeling of tactics and thinking frames for several reasons. First, he believes that power (native ability) is extremely difficult to change. Second, he assumes that developing a body of expert knowledge is too time- and labor-intensive, taking perhaps thousands of hours. In contrast, strategy instruction can be accomplished in a much shorter period of time. Although strategies cannot substitute completely for power and knowledge, they often are able to compensate for lower levels of power and knowledge.

Planning a Critical-Thinking Skills Program

Critical thinking experienced something of a heyday in the 1980s. Since then, researchers have continued to be interested in defining and teaching critical-thinking skills, but intact critical-thinking skills programs have experienced a decline, most likely due to funding and the instructional time necessary to teach these skills (Pithers & Soden, 2000). In addition, recent high-stakes accountability movements have put greater emphasis on teaching basic skills and demonstrating adequate yearly progress.

Programs designed to improve thinking, reasoning, and problem-solving skills fall into one of two categories: stand-alone and embedded programs. **Stand-alone programs** focus on the development of thinking skills independent of content area material. **Embedded programs** focus on improving thinking skills in the context of a particular content area, such as history or science.

Most experts suggest that thinking skills be embedded in specific content areas at least some of the time (Halpern, 2003; Ritchart & Perkins, 2005; Swartz & Perkins, 1990). One reason is that content material may increase students' interest in learning in a way that is not possible with stand-alone programs. A second reason is that scant evidence suggests that learning thinking skills is made more difficult when students are asked to learn new content material as well.

This section provides guidelines for designing either a stand-alone or an embedded thinking-skills program. These programs should include the following three goals: (1) identifying appropriate skills, (2) implementing instruction, and (3) evaluating the program. We consider each of these steps separately.

Identifying Appropriate Skills   Program design should begin with questions about the kind of model that will guide instruction (Halpern, 2003). *Descriptive models* explain how good thinking actually happens (Baron, 2008). Often, good thinkers use sophisticated rules, strategies, and heuristics to evaluate information and reach decisions. This does not mean that such thinking is free of errors or is the best way to think in a particular setting. Rather, it describes what good thinkers actually do. *Prescriptive models* explain how good thinking ought to happen. They presume that some forms of thinking are better than others. Educators sometimes design instruction based on a prescriptive model that is too complicated or time-consuming to be used in most everyday settings. An alternative is to approach the teaching of thinking skills from a descriptive standpoint, emphasizing how good thinkers solve problems and reach decisions in everyday life even if their thinking is less than optimal.

Instructors also must decide what kinds of thinking skills they wish to include in their program. Table 8.2 presents a summary of some component skills and assumptions involved in four kinds of thinking programs: critical thinking, creative thinking, decision making, and problem solving. It is important to recall that some of these skills may exceed students' developmental limitations. Some programs also may require more time or resources than others.

Finally, instructors should consider whether *direct* or *indirect* instruction will be used. The former refers to teacher-directed instruction that focuses on clearly identified rules for good thinking. The latter refers to a student-directed approach to instruction that emphasizes

TABLE 8.2   Characteristics of Four Thinking Skills

Type of Skill	Goals	Component Skills
Critical thinking	To evaluate contrasting positions or the clarity of ideas	Identify position or idea, analyze competing views, weigh evidence, gather new information
Creative thinking	To generate new ideas, develop new products	Establish need for idea, restructure existing view of problem, generate possibilities
Decision making	To reach an informed decision	Consider available information, evaluate information, identify options, weigh options, make the decision
Problem solving	To reach one or more adequate solutions to the problem	Identify, represent, select a strategy, implement the strategy, evaluate progress

Source: Adapted from *Teaching thinking: Issues and approaches,* by R. J. Swartz and D. N. Perkins, 1990, Pacific Grove, CA: Critical Thinking Press & Software.

the discovery of meaningful criteria for good thinking. Direct instruction appears to be most effective in situations in which an easy-to-identify strategy exists and problem solutions are limited. Indirect instruction may be most useful when attempting to develop guidelines for thinking about ill-defined problems, such as moral and ethical dilemmas faced in everyday life.

Implementing Instruction   To be effective, teachers must present thinking skills in a clear and meaningful sequence. Instructors should identify this sequence and model it for students. The first part of this chapter described a representative five-step problem-solving sequence. An analogous decision-making sequence might include (1) generating hypotheses about the causes of an event, (2) establishing rules for what constitutes acceptable evidence, (3) accumulating evidence from internal and external sources, (4) assessing the reliability of the evidence, and (5) evaluating the reasonableness of different causal claims.

Several general rules are helpful when considering sequencing. One rule is to start broadly, even in embedded programs. A second rule is to provide ample time to teach the thinking-skill sequence. In general, planning on a 6-month to 1-year time frame seems most reasonable. A third rule is to use what Swartz and Perkins (1990) refer to as bridging. **Bridging** involves grafting a skill previously used in a stand-alone program onto a regular content class, such as history or biology. In essence, bridging refers to embedding previously isolated thinking skills. Bridging is important because eventually students should be able to use general thinking skills in a variety of settings and in a variety of content areas.

Students also must be helped to increase their awareness of new skills. To increase awareness, students should be encouraged to reflect on the acquisition and use of new thinking skills (see Chapter 4). One method is to include in-class discussion of these skills. Other methods are the use of small cooperative discussion groups, journals, and "think aloud" exercises in which a student explains the skill while he or she performs it.

Promoting awareness and discussion of thinking skills, including the component steps involved in each skill, is useful because students are not always as aware as we would like them to be. Along these lines, Swartz and Perkins (1990) have identified four levels of awareness. At the lower end of the scale is the *tacit use of a skill*, which is characterized by skilled performance without awareness. In comparison, *aware use of a skill* occurs when an individual is aware of using it even though the skill cannot be explained. Consider how easily we use grammatical rules and knowledge without explicit knowledge of these rules. *Strategic use* occurs when an individual possesses conscious awareness about the skill and uses this knowledge to regulate the use of the skill. *Reflective use* occurs when an individual reflects on the skill, understands how the skill works, knows how to use it strategically, and can explain it to others.

Effective instruction also must provide varied, extensive practice. The idea of practice as a means for developing automaticity is an important one. Researchers know that automaticity develops faster if a skill is practiced regularly, over a long period of time, and in a variety of settings.

Evaluating the Program   Most experts agree that thinking-skills programs are under- rather than overevaluated (Barrel, 1991; DeCorte & Masui, 2004; Ritchart & Perkins, 2005). Unfortunately, common problems can undermine the evaluation process. One frequent problem is that teachers encounter resistance to teaching thinking skills, as opposed to teaching content. Some students, parents, and administrators may be suspicious of such programs. A second problem is that very few tests reliably measure improvements in thinking. A third problem is that successful thinking-skills programs may take years to achieve their aims.

Notwithstanding these concerns, instructors should evaluate three aspects of every program (Norris & Ennis, 1989; Zohar, 2006, 2008). One aspect is the design adequacy of the program *before* it is implemented. Questions to ask at this stage include: (1) Does the program include the kind of skills you want to improve? (2) Is the program sustainable for long enough to achieve its goals? (3) Are support systems available? (4) Will the criterion skills transfer to new domains? and (5) Does it provide plenty of opportunities to practice the new skills?

A second aspect is the need to evaluate the program *during* implementation. Questions to ask at this stage include: (1) Are the criterion skills being mastered? (2) Are the new skills being used inside and outside the classroom? (3) Do the new skills seem to make a difference in students' thinking? (4) Does the program provide sufficient feedback to students? and (5) Does the instructor have access to evaluative feedback?

A third aspect is the need for evaluation *after* the program has been implemented. Questions to ask at this stage include: (1) Has the program achieved its goals? (2) Did the program improve students' thinking? (3) Was this improvement seen in other areas of thinking or across the curriculum? (4) Are provisions made for maintaining the progress made in the program? and (5) Was the program the most effective use of the students' time?

More recently, DeCorte and Masui (2004) have emphasized the importance of establishing baseline knowledge and skills prior to instruction they refer to as *competence skills*. DeCorte and Masui proposed a four-step model that focuses on competence, learning, intervention, and assessment (CLIA). In essence the CLIA model breaks down critical thinking into four stages. The first stage is a preparatory phase in which students master essential skills and knowledge to think critically within a domain. The second stage focuses on creating an environment in which effective critical thinking may occur, including student collaboration, opportunity for reflection, a focus on learning goals, and use of metacognitive skills. The third stage provides an intervention that helps develop necessary thinking and self-regulation skills.

The fourth stage provides regular formative and summative assessment of instructional quality and students' use of newly developed skills.

Examples of Stand-Alone Programs

Many stand-alone programs designed to teach problem-solving and critical-thinking skills have appeared over the past several decades (see Ritchart & Perkins, 2005, for a review). Typical examples that have been studied are the Productive Thinking Program (Covington, Crutchfield, Davies, & Olton, 1974), the IDEAL Problem Solver (Bransford & Stein, 1984), the CoRT Thinking Materials (de Bono, 1973), and the Feuerstein Instrumental Enrichment (FIE) Program (Feuerstein, Rand, Hoffman, & Miller, 1980). We describe each of these approaches briefly. For a discussion of other thinking-skills programs see Vye, Delclos, Burns, and Bransford (1988).

The Productive Thinking Program   This program includes a set of 15 lessons designed to teach general problem-solving skills to upper-level elementary school children. Each lesson (see Covington et al., 1974, for a more complete description) consists of a booklet describing a basic lesson, accompanied by supplementary problems. The lessons describe two children who face "mystery" situations requiring detective-like activities. Under the guidance of an uncle, the children attempt to solve the mystery (the problem). Presented in a game-like way, the lessons are grounded in a model of problem solving similar to the five-point sequence described earlier. Lessons deal with problem definition, getting the "facts" (knowledge), checking facts, making plans, and rerepresenting problems. The lessons are designed to be completed during a 1-semester period. Evaluation suggests that students of differing abilities all show rather striking improvement on measures of problem-solving skill compared with comparable control groups (see Mansfield, Busse, & Krepelka, 1978; Olton & Crutchfield, 1969).

The IDEAL Problem Solver   The IDEAL Problem Solver describes five stages consistent with the IDEAL mnemonic (Bransford & Stein, 1984). The first, *identifying problems* (I), asks the solver to seek actively some problems requiring solution. The second step, *defining problems* (D), focuses on problem representation. Emphasis is placed on obtaining a clear picture of the problem prior to any solution attempts. The third step, *exploring alternatives* (E), involves generation and analysis of alternatives (operators) that might deal with the problem. The fourth step, *acting on a plan* (A), is closely linked with Step 5, *looking at the effects* (L).

Because it is a general stand-alone model, IDEAL can be adapted to a wide range of age and ability groups. It can also be embedded in many content domains, such as physics, history, and composition. Research on IDEAL and other similar programs has been quite positive, especially when the method is used to improve children's problem-solving skills (Delclos & Harrington, 1991; King, 1991; Vye et al., 1988).

The CoRT Thinking Materials   CoRT (Cognitive Research Trust) materials consist of a 2-year course for improving thinking skills (de Bono, 1973). The lessons include not only problem-solving skills but also the development of interpersonal skills and creative thinking. The lessons are presumed to be appropriate to children of a wide age range. The six units of materials include such topics as planning, generating alternatives, analyzing, comparing, selecting, and evaluating. A unit designed for a 10-week period consists of a series of leaflets, each discussing a single topic.

Also included are examples, practice items, and ideas for further practice on the topic. The leaflets can be used easily in group settings. Games called *Think Links* are designed to facilitate practice with the topics. In the Gestalt tradition (see Chapter 2), de Bono stresses the perceptual aspect of problem solving and tries to teach students effective techniques for breaking loose from ineffective patterns. He also believes that thinking skills are improved by practice; thus, following a brief description of each principle in a leaflet, the bulk of instructional time is spent practicing the principle.

The Feuerstein Instrumental Enrichment Program Feuerstein's Instrumental Enrichment (FIE) system centers on what Feuerstein (Feuerstein et al., 1980) has called *mediated-learning experiences* (MLEs). Mediated-learning experiences provide activities that teach learners to interpret their experience. MLEs are deliberate interventions by teachers, parents, or others designed to help learners interpret and organize events. The basic task of the MLE is to teach the child to play an active role in critical thinking and, ultimately, to think and solve problems independently.

Instructionally, FIE is a series of exercises (called "instruments" by Feuerstein) that provide the context for learning. At present, 14 or 15 instruments, arranged in order of increasing complexity, are available for 10- to 18-year-old students. The program is designed to be taught 3 to 5 times per week for 2 or 3 years. The exercises are paper-and-pencil activities designed to help the student identify problem-solving procedures and permit the teacher to "bridge" from the activities (problems) to subject matter of interest to student and teacher. Most FIE lessons provide "practice" exercises carried out under teacher supervision to provide feedback to students in their attempts to identify and evaluate the strategies used in solution attempts. FIE also provides a language for teaching problem-solving concepts such as *planning, strategy choice, evaluation,* and the like. Each instrument is designed to have wide generality. A special feature of this program is the deliberate focus on instruction of special populations. It has been used with youngsters who have mental retardation, learning disabilities, behavioral disorders, and hearing impairment.

Bransford, Arbitman-Smith, Stein, and Vye (1985) and Savalle, Twohig, and Rachford (1986) have evaluated the effectiveness of FIE. On the basis of a wide range of studies conducted in Israel, Venezuela, the United States, and Canada, students exposed to the FIE program were shown to perform better than control groups on tests such as the Raven's Progressive Matrices and some achievement subtests, such as mathematics. The effects were found with a wide variety of student types. Other studies have shown, however, no significant difference as a result of FIE training. In general, features of successful studies included the presence of well-trained FIE teachers and student instruction that lasted 80 hours or more.

Teaching Wisdom

Many educators and researchers have become interested in the acquisition and development of wisdom (Ardelt, 2004; Baltes & Staudinger, 2000; Halpern, 2001; Perkins, 2001; Sternberg, 2001). **Wisdom,** as Sternberg (2001) defines it, is the willingness to use one's skills and knowledge to act in the soundest manner. Sternberg has developed what he refers to as a *balance theory of wisdom* that includes three main components: tacit knowledge, values, and goals. *Tacit* *knowledge* is procedural in nature and often acquired without direct help from others or through formal learning. *Values* are attitudes and dispositions that enable a person to shape and adapt to his or her environment. *Goals* are desired outcomes that reflect common good. Thus, wisdom is the process of using one's tacit knowledge to adapt to one's environment in a manner that promotes the common good.

Sternberg (2001) and others have argued that wisdom is essential for adaptation and should be included in the school curriculum. One reason is that schools emphasize "book knowledge" that promotes narrow expertise without enhancing day-to-day wisdom. A second reason is that wisdom is an essential part of community involvement and responsible citizenship. Ardelt (2004) argues that wisdom is essential because it bestows upon us a pragmatic knowledge that improves our life and enables us to make better decisions.

Sternberg (2001) has developed 16 principles for teaching wisdom. We summarize the main points of this program as follows: (a) demonstrate how wisdom is essential to a satisfying life, (b) emphasize the relationship between wisdom and practically intelligent action, (c) discuss and model day-to-day adaptive strategies, and (d) teach students to monitor the extent to which they and others make wise choices. Sternberg also has developed a 12-week curriculum suitable for middle school students that promotes wisdom. Several early studies suggest favorable results, although the jury will remain out for at least several more years until the curriculum can be modified, implemented, and evaluated over time.

Research on wisdom and how to improve it in school settings is in its infancy. However, we view this research as promising because it acknowledges the important role of wisdom in our lives. Clearly some people are wiser than others. It behooves us to understand wisdom, how it develops, what aspects of schooling can improve it, and how wisdom trickles down through our lives in helpful ways.

Assessment of Problem Solving

Assessment of unobservable psychological constructs such as intelligence is always difficult, but assessing problem-solving and critical thinking skills is even more difficult for at least two reasons. One problem is the number of skills that a researcher must measure. Most models of problem solving include four or five major steps with a number of subcomponents at each step. Critical-thinking likewise is conceived of as including multiple dimensions, usually in the range of 8 to 12 important skills. A second reason is the complexity of these skills. Historically, understanding and teaching important problem-solving and critical-thinking skills have proven to be quite difficult. Assessing problem-solving outcomes has been even more difficult.

Despite significant measurement challenges, researchers have made great strides in their attempt to assess problem-solving outcomes. Many standardized tests have been developed to assess problem-solving skills in math and science, and tests also have been developed to assess general critical-thinking skills (Mayer & Wittrock, 2006; Ritchart & Perkins, 2005). More daunting, researchers have attempted to measure the underlying processes involved in problem-solving and investigate how these processes are related to important cognitive phenomena such as working memory, metacognitive monitoring, and intellectual ability. For example, researchers interested in mathematical cognition have made important strides in understanding children's mathematical cognition and problem solving. A study by Jitenda et al. (2007)

compared two methods for teaching third-grade students mathematical problem-solving strategies. One method was a single-strategy schema-based method that focused on the mathematical operation necessary to solve the problem, such as *add, take away,* and *change.* The second method focused on a set of general strategies that could be applied to any problem. Both groups made significant progress between pre- and post-tests, but the single-strategy schema group performed significantly better than the general-strategy group. This difference was attributed to the fact that the schema-based strategy activated a specific computational algorithm and provided useful cues about the most appropriate problem-solving strategy to use.

A different team of researchers examined whether problem-solving and computational skills used by third graders were related to each other or separate (Fuchs et al., 2008). Results suggested that problem-solving and computational skills appear to be weakly related in children. In addition, problem-solving skills were related to language skills; language-deficient students performed poorly on the problem-solving task. Computational skill was related negatively to attentional difficulties and information processing speed in working memory. These findings are important because they indicate that problem solving is a somewhat separate skill even in children and that problem-solving and computational skills are related to different individual variables such as attention and working memory.

These findings indicate that even highly complex skills and processes can be assessed and the results used to understand problem solving and critical thinking at all ages. The evidence collected thus far is important in three ways. One is that it supports current theoretical models of problem solving and critical thinking. Second, research has revealed that individual component skills of problem solving like those previously described, and individual critical thinking skills like those in Table 8.2, are related to other important components of cognition such as working memory and relevant background knowledge. A third important finding is that problem solving and critical thinking can be improved significantly through instruction (Halpern, 2003; Ritchart & Perkins, 2005).

Summary

This chapter examined problem solving and critical thinking. Both types of thinking are constrained by two important factors: (1) expert knowledge within a domain and (2) knowledge about a general problem-solving (or critical-thinking) strategy.

Expert knowledge improves problem solving for several reasons, including faster processing, better representation, more effective use of solution strategies, and better monitoring. Knowledge of a general problem-solving strategy also improves performance, even among children. Five stages in this strategy were described: problem finding, representing problems, selecting a strategy, implementing a strategy, and evaluating the solution. We also addressed the role of deliberate practice on expertise and transfer of skills across domains.

We also provided several definitions of critical thinking, a cognitive activity that is assumed to overlap with problem solving but differs from it as well. Critical thinking is related more closely to ill-defined problems, while problem solving often relates to well-defined problems. We described four general skills known to influence critical thinking: knowledge, inference, evaluation, and metacognition.

We next considered whether intellectual ability constrains problem solving and critical thinking. We argued for a compensatory relationship among power, knowledge, and tactics, emphasizing that although native ability affects critical thinking, it can be compensated for through the selective use of knowledge and strategies.

A plan for identifying, implementing, and evaluating a critical thinking program then was presented. Basic components of such programs include defining an instructional sequence, promoting higher-order awareness of critical-thinking skills through the development and use of metacognition, and providing ample time for students to engage in extensive and varied practice of newly acquired thinking skills.

We examined several stand-alone instructional programs designed to improve general problem solving and critical thinking: the Productive Thinking Program, the IDEAL Problem Solver, the CoRT Thinking Materials, and the Feuerstein Instrumental Enrichment Program. Research indicates that all of these programs enhance thinking skills, although each promotes a different pattern of skills.

We also summarized emerging research on wisdom. Wisdom was defined as the use of tacit knowledge and values to act in a reasonable manner for the common good. Researchers currently are developing and testing short-term learning programs designed to increase wisdom.

SUGGESTED READINGS

Baron, J. (2008). *Thinking and deciding* (4th ed.). New York, NY: Cambridge University Press.
This scholarly text considers problem solving, critical thinking, and reasoning from an in-depth perspective. Although it is highly technical and requires some knowledge of cognitive psychology, it is well-written and provides a sweeping view of the field.

Cottrell, S. (2005). *Critical thinking skills: Developing effective analysis and argument.* New York, NY: Palgrave Macmillan.
This book provides guidelines and activities to identify and improve arguments when reading and writing.

Davidson J. E., & Sternberg, R. J. (Eds.). (2003). (Eds.). *The psychology of problem solving.* Cambridge, England: Cambridge University Press.
The volume provides up-to-date review of problem solving in a variety of domains.

Ericsson, K. A. (Ed.). (1996). *The road to excellence: The acquisition of expert performance in the arts, sciences, sports, and games.* Mahwah, NJ: Erlbaum.
This edited volume examines the role of deliberate practice and talent in considerable detail.

Gladwell, M. (2008). *Outliers: The story of success.* Boston, MA: Little, Brown.
This popular and easy-to-read book examines factors that contribute to individual success. Gladwell argues that individuals' outstanding achievements, including problem solving, are not primarily the result of native talent, but of extended practice in environments that nurture their talents.

Holyoak, K. J., & Morrison, R. G. (Eds.). (2005). *The Cambridge handbook of thinking and reasoning.* Cambridge, England: Cambridge University Press.
This edited volume contains comprehensive reviews of varied aspects of thinking and problem solving.

9 Classroom Contexts for Cognitive Growth

Constructivism: The Learner's Role in Building and Transforming Knowledge ■ Social Cognition: Social Factors in Knowledge Construction ■ Assessing Reflective Practice ■ Implications for Instruction: A Portrait of the Reflective Classroom ■ Summary ■ Suggested Readings ■

The evolution of cognitive psychology away from "purely cognitive" variables of memory and thinking to include learners' motivational and belief systems that we described in earlier chapters also has led to another important understanding—the role of social interaction and discourse in fostering cognitive development, motivation, and learning.

It seems obvious to anyone who has ever been a student or a teacher, a child or a parent, that teaching and learning are highly social activities. From the very earliest interactions between parent and child on up to a graduate student's relationship with a graduate advisor, much of our learning is influenced by the larger culture in which we live and takes place through interactions with adults or peers who have greater knowledge.

Despite this seemingly obvious importance of the social context in learning, cognitive development research did not begin to focus in earnest on social processes and their effect on cognition until the late 1970s. The translation and publication in 1962 of *Thought and Language* by the Russian psychologist Lev Vygotsky, and in 1978 of his book *Mind in Society: The Development of Higher Psychological Processes,* began this major shift of focus. Vygotsky's assertion that higher mental functions originate in our social life when children interact with adults or more capable peers (Vygotsky, 1978) resonated with researchers and educators who felt that the information processing approaches to cognitive development had a major weakness in lacking any account of the social context of learning.

Information processing approaches to theories of cognitive development, as described in Chapters 2–5, have focused on describing mechanisms such as encoding, retrieval and strategy choice that operate internally when a learner is participating in a task. These are excellent descriptions of the internal processes occurring during learning, but they fail to describe the social processes often involved—Vygotsky's interactions with adults or more capable peers—and internal processes such as tacit inner speech and reflection. There is now clear evidence that external processes such as scaffolding, peer tutoring, and student collaborations all exert an important influence on the development of internal processes such as self talk, memory and strategy use.

The social context of cognition and its applications to learning and instruction received increasing attention from theorists and researchers through the 1980s and 1990s (Lave, 1988; Moll & Whitmore, 1993; Newman, Griffin, & Cole, 1989; Pressley & Wharton-McDonald, 1997; Rogoff, 1990). The idea of children as active learners, who construct their own knowledge and reflect on their learning with the help of more experienced partners, expanded the way we think about classroom teaching and our ideas of the teacher's role. Teachers moved beyond their roles as information givers, serving in new ones as coaches and guides and facilitating students' knowledge building. This increasing emphasis on the social context and the effects of the wider culture on cognition and learning has led researchers to consider new teaching approaches, such as guided participation (Rogoff, 1990; Rogoff & Angelillo, 2002) and Schön's reflective practitioner model (1987), and to look beyond the classroom to the cognitive effects of the provision and regulation of children's everyday activities (Gauvain, 2001; Loyens, Rikers, & Schmidt, 2008). Our view of the centrality of these ideas to education is reflected in two of the cognitive themes that we outlined in Chapter 1: that learning is a constructive, not a receptive process, and that social interaction is fundamental to cognitive development. If anything, these ideas have continued to increase in relevance since the 1980s and are more viable today among researchers and educators than ever before (Kincheloe, 2005; McCaslin, 2004; O'Donnell, 2006; Wertsch, 2008).

Another of Vygotsky's important contributions to the thinking about cognitive development was the concept of language as one of the most important social and cognitive tools. As researchers have recognized the importance of the social context of cognition, interest has also grown in the role of classroom discussion, or discourse, in building knowledge. A classroom discussion can be seen as the everyday expression of the idea that students are active agents in their own learning, enabling students to construct new conceptions and acquire new ways of thinking. Yet research suggests that classroom discussion often fails to achieve these goals (Chinn, Anderson, & Waggoner, 2001; O'Donnell, 2006). The ideas of Calfee (1994), Chinn and Waggoner (1992), Chinn et al. (2001), O'Flahavan and Stein (1992), and others help define ways that teachers can guide classroom discourse to create a more "reflective" classroom and foster cognitive growth.

The social contexts of cognition and learning have obvious applications to the classroom. As any teacher knows, the classroom is above all a social environment and teaching is a form of social interaction that affects group collaboration (Martin, 2006), motivation (Perry, Turner, & Meyer, 2006), learning (De Jong & Pieters, 2006) and even use of technology (Lajoie & Azevedo, 2006). The challenge to teachers is to provide classroom environments that support knowledge development in all its forms and that encourage students' self-awareness and self-direction. One of the most important perspectives directing how researchers and educators think about the social context of the classroom has its roots in Vygotsky's work: the perspective of *constructivism*.

Constructivism: The Learner's Role in Building and Transforming Knowledge

Constructivism is a broad term with philosophical, learning, and teaching dimensions, but it generally emphasizes the learner's contribution to meaning and learning through both individual and social activity (Fosnot, 2008: Kincheloe, 2005; Packer & Goicoechea, 2000). In the constructivist view, learners arrive at meaning by selecting information and constructing what they know either individually or in collaboration with other learners. Scholars differ in the degree to which they ascribe knowledge construction solely to the learner (see, e.g., Prawat, 1996). Some constructivists view mental structures as reflective of external realities, while others see no independent reality outside the mental world of the individual (Martin, 2006).

Although there are many dimensions of constructivism, most constructivists share four main characteristics (Loyens, Rikers, & Schmidt, 2009). One is that learners are active in constructing their own knowledge by discovering and transforming existing knowledge and experiences into new understandings. A second is that social interactions are important to knowledge construction. In our discussion here, we concentrate most strongly on a form of constructivism—**dialectical constructivism** (Moshman, 1982)—that highlights the importance of social interactions in developing knowledge and thought. In our judgment, this view best helps us identify the elements most likely to create a reflective classroom—one in which teachers and students interact in ways that stimulate both knowledge construction and cognitive growth. A third characteristic is the crucial role of self-regulation and metacognition (Hiekkila & Lonka, 2006), which includes planning, goal setting, strategy selection and coordination, integration, and self-monitoring. A fourth characteristic is using authentic learning tasks in the classroom that reflect how knowledge and skills will be used outside the classroom.

Many key concepts of cognitive psychology, such as *schema theory* and *levels of processing,* represent constructivist thinking. Constructivist perspectives are also shaping significant changes in curriculum and instructional practices in the United States. A constructivist view of learning has provided support for meaning-based approaches to reading instruction, such as those advocated in the *Standards for the English Language Arts* (NCTE, 1996), developed by the International Reading Association and the National Council of Teachers of English. The *Principles and Standards for School Mathematics* (NCTM, 2000) of the National Council of Teachers of Mathematics, though not explicitly constructivist, have a strongly constructivist flavor, as do the *Benchmarks for Science Literacy* (AAAS, 1993) of the American Association for the Advancement of Science and the *National Science Education Standards* (NRC, 1996) of the National Research Council.

The aim of teaching, from a constructivist perspective, is not so much to transmit information as to encourage *knowledge formation* and *metacognitive processes for judging, organizing, and acquiring new information that is student-driven.* The primary reason that constructivist learning is assumed to be superior to other approaches is that the student is active and responsible for meaning-making in the knowledge-construction process. A constructivist approach will manifest itself in the classroom in numerous ways, including the following:

- *Selection of instructional materials:* Employing materials that children can manipulate or use to interact with their environments
- *Choice of activities:* Encouraging students to observe, gather data, test hypotheses, and participate in field trips
- *Nature of classroom processes:* Using cooperative learning and guided discussions
- *Integration of curricula:* Using, for example, long-term thematic projects combining mathematics, science, reading, and writing

In constructivist classrooms, students typically are taught to plan and direct their own learning to some extent. Students are encouraged to take an active role in their learning and teachers adopt new roles as coaches and facilitators rather than serving only as primary sources of information. Typical activities include establishing a safe classroom environment for exploration, fostering an inquiry-based classroom milieu, promoting individual reflection, providing a great deal of opportunity for collaborative discussion, and valuing the importance of the "big picture" as the end result of the knowledge construction process (Kroll, 2004).

Types of Constructivism: A Closer Look

Although some discuss constructivism as if it were a unified philosophical, psychological, and educational perspective, a more differentiated understanding is useful for considering its implications for instruction (Fosnot, 2008: Kincheloe, 2005). Moshman (1982; see also Pressley, Harris, & Marks, 1992; Pressley & Wharton-McDonald, 1997) has distinguished among three types of constructivism: exogenous constructivism, endogenous constructivism, and dialectical constructivism. All involve knowledge construction but reflect different views of how knowledge construction occurs (Ernest, 1995).

In **exogenous constructivism,** knowledge formation is basically a reconstruction of structures, such as cause–effect relationships, presented information, and observed behavior patterns, that already exist in external reality. In this view, our mental structures reflect the organization of the world outside—or *exogenous* to—ourselves. Although they cannot be classified exclusively as examples of exogenous constructivism, important concepts in cognitive psychology such as schemata, network models, and production systems (see Chapter 3), clearly fit within this perspective. Exogenous constructivism emphasizes the strong external influence of physical reality, presented information, and social models on knowledge construction. Knowledge is "true" from this perspective to the extent that it accurately copies the external structures that it ideally represents (Moshman, 1982). A common instructional example of exogenous constructivism is the reciprocal teaching method (see Chapter 4) in which an expert or teacher scaffolds instruction for a novice until the novice can construct sufficient knowledge and regulate her own performance (Webb & Palincsar, 1996).

Contrasted with exogenous constructivism is **endogenous constructivism,** where cognitive structures are created from earlier structures, not directly from information provided by the environment. In endogenous constructivism, according to Moshman, the key process is coordination of cognitive actions; knowledge exists at a more abstract level and develops through cognitive activity within—*endogenous* to—ourselves. Cognitive structures are created from other, earlier structures and follow one another in predictable sequences. Piaget's stages of cognitive development are a prominent example of endogenous constructivism. An intuitively appealing but often-criticized instructional method tied to an endogenous constructivist view is **discovery learning.** Among the criticisms leveled at discovery learning (e.g., see Ericsson, 2003; Kirschner, Sweller, & Clark, 2006) is that studies typically have shown it to be less effective than more structured approaches and that students may lack the knowledge and motivation to construct deep understanding autonomously.

The third category of constructivism represents a point between the extremes of exogenous and endogenous constructivism. Dialectical constructivism places the source of knowledge in the *interactions* between learners and their environments. Knowledge is a "constructed synthesis" that grows out of contradictions that individuals experience during these interactions (Moshman, 1982, p. 375). Dialectical constructivism is linked with yet another philosophical point of view that has become increasingly influential in American psychology—*contextualism*—which holds that thought and experience are inextricably intertwined with the context in which they occur. A common instructional example of dialectical constructivism is the collaborative peer teaching method in which students work together to scaffold instruction for one another (O'Donnell, 2006).

Although these types of constructivism represent divergent views, Moshman argues that each can be useful for understanding different ways in which individuals might construct knowledge. If, for instance, our primary interest is how accurately children perceive the organization of some body of information, such as concepts in biology, we likely would find an exogenous view of constructivism inviting. If our interest is children's cognitive growth from naive to sophisticated mathematical or scientific concepts (see Chapters 14 and 15), an endogenous constructivism is more likely to be useful. In addition, it is important to understand that any individual likely will engage in all three types of constructivism during the development of expertise in a specific discipline. For example, a novice is likely to engage in exogenous constructivism when entering a new domain of learning (e.g., introductory statistics) because she has little prior knowledge. This means that she will depend to some extent on textbooks, teachers, and experts to develop a core knowledge base and basic skills. Similarly, the same individual likely will collaborate with peers at all stages of learning to master material and concepts, and to revise and hone her statistical reasoning skills. Most likely, only after acquiring some degree of expertise will she engage in endogenous constructivism to restructure knowledge in novel ways.

Of the three, dialectical constructivism provides the most general perspective and has become increasingly important in cognitive psychology. A dialectical perspective incorporates both internal and external factors and focuses our attention on the *interaction* between them. For instance, if we are considering instruction aimed at children's *interpretations* of literature or at challenging children's naive conceptions in mathematics or science, we enter the realm of the dialectic. To better understand dialectical constructivism we need to examine the views of its most distinguished proponent, Vygotsky. Although Vygotsky did his pivotal research in the 1920s and died at the young age of 37 in 1934, it wasn't until translation and publication of his monograph *Thought and Language* that his work began to be known in the West. The publication of *Mind in Society* and subsequent translations of his work (e.g., Rieber & Carton, 1987) fueled further interest in Vygotsky's thinking and marked the beginning of an era in which his ideas have had great influence on psychology and education.

Vygotsky's Dialectical Constructivism

The core of Vygotsky's theory is that higher mental functions have their origin in social life as children interact with more experienced members of their community, such as parents, other adults, and more capable peers. Vygotsky emphasizes the integration of internal and external aspects of learning and the social environment for learning (Newman et al., 1989; Wertsch, 2008). In Vygotsky's view, cultures externalize individual cognition in their tools, by which he means not only the shared physical objects of a culture (e.g., a toothbrush, an automobile, and artwork) but also more abstract social-psychological tools, such as written language and social institutions. Physical tools are directed toward the external world, but social-psychological tools are "symbol systems used by individuals engaged in thinking" (John-Steiner, 1997). Cognitive change occurs as children use these mental tools in social interactions and internalize and transform these interactions; that is, they progress from other-regulation to self-regulation (del Rio, 2007; Wertsch, 2008). Contemporary theorists believe that **socially mediated co-regulation** affects a variety of cognitive and social skills and provides the basis for values and expectations that support motivation for learning (Corno & Mandinach, 2004: Hickey & Grenade, 2004; McCaslin, 2004).

Perhaps Vygotsky's most influential concept has been the **zone of proximal development.** The zone of proximal development can be defined as the difference between the difficulty level of a problem that a child can cope with independently and the level that can be accomplished with adult help. In the zone of proximal development, a child and an adult (or novice and expert) work together on problems that the child (or novice) alone could not work on successfully. Both external and internal factors can affect the individual's zone of proximal development (del Rio, 2007).

Cognitive change takes place in the zone of proximal development or, in the phrase of Newman et al. (1989), in the "construction zone." Children bring a developmental history to the zone of proximal development; adults bring a support structure. As children and adults interact, they share values, beliefs, and cultural tools. This culturally mediated interaction, in Vygotsky's view, is what yields cognitive change. The interaction is internalized and becomes a new function of the individual, including cognitive, social, and motivational aspects of one's development.

Vygotsky's colleague Leont'ev (1981) suggested the term *appropriation* to describe how learners internalize cultural knowledge from this process of interaction. Children, Leont'ev suggested, need not, and in fact should not, reinvent the artifacts of a culture. The culture has built up these artifacts over thousands of years, and children can *appropriate* them to their own circumstances as they learn how to use them.

Internalization of knowledge in the zone of proximal development is not an automatic reflection of external events (Wertsch, 2008). Children bring their own understanding to social interactions and make whatever sense they can of exchanges with adults. They can participate in activities beyond their understanding, but still be affected by them; think of a 2-year-old "reading" a book with his or her parent. Likewise, adults may not fully understand children's perspectives but still play an important role in their cognitive change. As children and adults interact, children are exposed to adults' advanced systems of understanding, and cognitive change—learning—becomes possible.

Wertsch (2008) proposed that internalization of external knowledge occurs in four continuous stages, three of which occur in the child's zone of proximal development. The first takes place when a child fails to understand an adult and requires explicit explanation and modeling from the adult. The second occurs when a child understands an adult with limited understanding, which promotes further discussion and explicit other-regulation from the adult to enhance the child's understanding. The third level is characterized by a situation in which the child understands an adult well enough that the child and adult share "co-regulation" of the child's internal thoughts and understanding. The fourth level occurs when the child engages in internalized, self-regulated problem solving and construction of understanding.

Part of the attractiveness of Vygotsky's thinking for cognitive and educational theorists has been his stress on the social influences in cognitive change. Cognitive development, in Vygotsky's view, is not simply a matter of individual change, but results also from social interactions in cultural contexts.

Many educators find the emphasis on adult–child interactions in cognitive growth especially appealing. The concept of **instructional scaffolding,** for example, is closely aligned with Vygotsky's theory of the zone of proximal development. As we see in more detail later in our discussion of classroom discourse, in instructional scaffolding a teacher provides students with selective help, such as asking questions, directing attention, or giving hints about possible strategies, to enable them to do things they could not do on their own. Then, as students become more competent, the support is withdrawn gradually (for a discussion of scaffolding see Beed, Hawkins, & Roller, 1991; Perry et al., 2006).

Some researchers feel that this view of scaffolding tends to focus too much on the adult's contribution to the process and reduces the child to being only a recipient of adult help (Gauvain, 2001). A perspective that focuses more on the learner's contribution is that of *social cognitive theory.*

Social Cognition: Social Factors in Knowledge Construction

Early cognitive research and theory focused on individual memory and thought, with relatively little emphasis on the context in which individuals were functioning. The information processing model we presented in this book's early chapters largely follows this approach. Under the influence of theorists such as Vygotsky, however, cognitive theory now includes a much greater recognition of social influences on cognition. As a consequence, researchers increasingly are turning their attention to children's interactions with parents, peers, and teachers in their homes, neighborhoods, and schools.

The perspective guiding these investigations is *social cognitive theory.* Closely related to dialectical constructivism, social cognitive theory stresses how human skill, activity, and thought develop in the context of specific historical and cultural activities of the community (Fosnot, 2008; Mercer, 2007; Sternberg & Wagner, 1994). Social exchanges between individuals are seen as the primary source of cognitive growth, especially to the extent that they promote talk that enables learners to internalize self-regulation skills via **inner speech** (Jones, 2009). In the next sections, we examine two influential social cognitive models: Rogoff's apprenticeships in thinking model (1990, 1995) and Schön's reflective practitioner model (1983, 1987).

Rogoff's Apprenticeships in Thinking Model

Barbara Rogoff and colleagues (Rogoff, 1990; Rogoff & Angelillo, 2002; Rogoff, Paradise, Arauz, Correa-Chavez, & Angelillo, 2003), following the lead of Vygotsky, have argued that cognitive development occurs when children are guided by adults in social activities that stretch their understanding of, and skill in using, the tools of the prevailing culture. When children are with their peers and adults, they are *apprentices in thinking.* In an apprenticeship, a novice works closely with an expert in joint problem-solving activity. The apprentice also typically participates in skills beyond those that he or she is capable of handling independently. In the manner of an apprenticeship, Rogoff states, development builds on "the internalization by the novice of the shared cognitive processes, appropriating what was carried out in collaboration to extend existing knowledge and skills" (1990, p. 141). Rogoff argues that cognitive development is inherently social in nature, requiring mutual engagement with one or more partners of greater skill.

Other children form one important pool of "skilled partners." For instance, children's play and their dialogues with each other help them think collaboratively and offer a host of possibilities for considering others' perspectives. Play also involves imagination and creativity and so helps children extend themselves into new roles, interactions, and settings. Peers are highly available and active, Rogoff (1990) points out, providing each other with "motivation, imagination, and opportunities for creative elaboration of the activities of their community." Indeed, Kelly (2007) reported higher levels of student engagement in classroom contexts where there was an open dialogue in which student ideas were taken seriously and incorporated into classroom discourse.

For most children, however, adults are the most reliable and important skilled partners, helping them acquire skills through talk and external collaboration and translate these into internal speech and knowledge structures. Parents, relatives, and teachers routinely play many roles with important implications for cognitive development. These include (1) stimulating children's interest in cognitive tasks, (2) simplifying tasks so that children can manage them, (3) motivating children and providing direction to their activities, (4) giving feedback, (5) controlling their frustration and risk, and (6) demonstrating idealized versions of the acts to be performed (Rogoff, 1990).

Adults often engage in **guided participation** (Rogoff, 1995) with children, a process by which children's efforts are structured in a social context and the responsibility for problem solving is gradually transferred. In guided participation, children learn to solve problems in the context of social interactions. Guided participation always involves interpersonal communication and stage setting to build bridges between what children already know and the new information they encounter.

Rogoff argues that mental processes are enriched in guided participation because they occur in the context of *accomplishing something;* that is, cognitive processes direct intelligent, purposeful actions. Participants develop a sense of common purpose through extended dialogue and a shared focus of attention. Children are intrinsically motivated to come to a better understanding of their world and often initiate and guide interactions in which cognitive growth takes place.

Guided participation is not always formal or explicit, however (Kelly, 2007; Leinhardt & Steele, 2005). Events often are shared without participants being aware of efforts at guided participation or intending them to be instructional. A parent may help a child order at a restaurant or trim a tree branch, without thinking of it as teaching. Similarly, a preschool child may learn about what teachers and students do by playing school with an older brother or sister. In addition, participation is guided in part by students' beliefs about their participation. Jansen (2008) found that students with positive attitudes about participation as a means to acquire and internalize knowledge and learning skills were more likely to participate, and in turn, more likely to solicit future opportunities to participate from the teacher. O'Donnell (2006) provides a comprehensive review of classroom contextual factors affecting student participation in collaborative groups.

In summary, Rogoff views cognitive development as a process growing out of interactions with other children and adults. Individual cognition is constructed from the intellectual tools that a particular society has available. Although children's interactions with their peers provide support for building new knowledge, adults play a unique role in helping children move to new cognitive levels. Parents and teachers are reliable expert partners with children in guided participation. These interactions help children build bridges between what they know and what they don't and support children's efforts at acquiring new knowledge.

Schools provide a unique resource for cognitive development, especially for acquiring the more formal tools of language and thought. Schools offer structured opportunities for guided participation with adults and for appropriating adults' knowledge and strategies for problem solving—activities such as acquiring a technical vocabulary for understanding perspective in painting, learning ways to search for information, using cause–effect frameworks for understanding historical events, using algebraic procedures to solve mathematics problems, or applying formal research methods for gathering and categorizing data. Among the most basic challenges for teachers is learning how best to help students acquire effective mental tools. As we discuss later in the chapter, classroom dialogue guided by the teacher can provide important conditions to meet these challenges.

Schön's Reflective Practitioner Model

Like Rogoff, Schön (1983, 1987) also put forward a dialectic constructivist perspective on cognitive development. Schön drew less explicitly from Vygotsky, and his interests were centered mainly on teaching and learning in the professions rather than with children. His perspective on cognitive development nonetheless shares several key elements with Vygotsky's theory and with Rogoff's approach: guided discovery, learning by doing, and the importance of social interactions in building knowledge and understanding. Schön developed his system around three key concepts: knowing-in-action, reflection-in-action, and reflection on reflection-in-action.

Knowing-in-Action   **Knowing-in-action** is tacit knowledge, the sort of knowledge that is unarticulated but revealed in our intelligent actions (Polanyi, 1967; see also our discussion of implicit memory in Chapter 3). We show our tacit knowledge whenever we act in reasonable ways, such as driving a car, greeting a friend, or typing a letter, but are not explicitly aware of the thinking underlying our actions. These actions may be implicit in part because the beliefs they are based on also are implicit (Bendixen & Rule, 2004; Hedberg, 2009; Pirttila-Backman & Kajanne, 2001).

Much of what we know is knowing-in-action and is revealed only as we go about our daily lives. Although it is possible to describe the implicit knowing that underlies your actions, these descriptions will always be *constructions*, "attempts to put into explicit, symbolic form a kind of intelligence that begins by being tacit and spontaneous" (Schön, 1987, p. 25). By describing knowing-in-action, we convert it to **knowledge-in-action,** making it a part of our semantic memory.

Ordinarily, however, knowing-in-action is not verbalized; our actions consist largely of spontaneous, routinized responses. As long as the situation is normal and there are no surprises to our knowledge-in-action categories, our scripts flow smoothly into action. *Surprises*—outcomes that do not fit our scripts—are not necessarily negative events, however.

In fact, they are the key to triggering reflection-in-action, a mechanism Schön argues is crucial for change and cognitive growth.

Reflection-in-Action Reflection-in-action is conscious thought about our actions and about the thinking that accompanies them. Reflection-in-action is a form of metacognition in which we question both the unexpected event and the knowledge-in-action that brought it on. A child entering a new class may tug and pull at the teacher's clothing, an action that brought positive attention from a former teacher but brings a reprimand from the new teacher. A formerly successful routine now is not working, and the surprise forces the child to reflect both on his or her actions and on the reasons for the changed circumstances.

Schön's concept of *reflection-in-action* has a great deal in common with both dimensions of metacognition discussed in Chapter 4: *knowledge of cognition* and *regulation of cognition*. Reflection-in-action stimulates a kind of on-the-spot thought experiment. Depending on the extent of prior knowledge, unexpected failures and successes may lead in various directions: to *exploration,* in which the learner makes no predictions; to *testing moves,* in which different paths are tested for their feasibility; or to *hypothesis testing,* in which competing hypotheses are tested to determine which is valid.

Under a skilled teacher's guidance, a similar process can lead to student learning. The potential for learning lies in the constructive nature of reflection-in-action (Cole & Knowles, 2000; Jay, 2003; Larrivee, 2006). When students are placed in situations that are uncertain and where they are motivated to change, Schön contends, they begin a process of exploration, movement, and hypothesis testing. Research indicates that teacher reflection, especially during preservice training and the early years of teaching, enables them to construct models and theories of their teaching in a manner that improves instruction and student learning (Dinkelman, 2000; Lyons, 2006).

Reflection on Reflection-in-Action All of us construct and reconstruct our cognitive worlds as we experience the events of our lives and reflect on them. By assisting students in constructing new knowledge, skilled teachers can help learners do much more than they could do alone. Schön (1987) refers to this process as **reflection on reflection-in-action.** Skilled teachers can help learners to develop reflection-in-action, that is, to articulate the thoughts guiding their actions and to judge their adequacy. Consistent with Vygotsky's views of the zone of proximal development, the teacher's goal is to be literally "thought-provoking" (Schön, 1987, p. 92). Ideally, the teacher creates an interactive setting in which both the teacher and the students are co-learners, but students' self-discovery has the highest priority.

According to Schön, students cannot be taught what they need to know, *but they can be coached toward self-understanding*—a form of dialectical, social constructivism. Schön advocates creating *practice situations*—relatively low-risk events in which students can learn by doing and receive rich feedback—that motivate learners toward understanding and contain at least some elements that the students themselves have created.

Because of its unfamiliarity, students may initially strongly resist this kind of coaching approach and become unsettled, even angry, when there seem to be "no right answers." They may become frustrated and demand to be told what is "correct." The teacher–coach must keep in mind that he or she is managing a transaction between learners and environment, not offering information. Uncertainty and conflict about values are inevitable. In Schön's view, this uncertainty is among the most powerful motivating forces teachers have available.

In summary, Schön reflects social-cognitive and constructivist points of view by portraying learning as a social-interactive process in which students are helped to create new understandings. The key goal is students' reflection-in-action—metacognitive reflection on unexpected events or variations in phenomena and the thinking that led to them. In Schön's view, students learn when they act and are helped to think about their actions. Learning by doing forces them to make judgments; reflection helps them recognize their assumptions and see what is important. Although students initially may perceive this kind of instruction as threatening, ambiguous, or confusing, clarification comes when students stay with problems and dialogue continues between the teacher–coach and the students.

Schön's reflective judgment model has been investigated in detail in domains such as business management and education and used to develop a model of reflective professional development. Roglio and Light (2009) summarized five key components in high-level reflective practice, including having a repertoire of critical learning skills, reflective instructors who serve as models, well-integrated instructional scaffolding, an interdisciplinary curriculum, and many opportunities for collaboration among students. These five components seem essential to the developmental of reflective practice in any domain (Hedberg, 2009). Not surprisingly, content knowledge seems to be a particularly important requirement for effective reflection (Lee, 2005).

Together, Rogoff's and Schön's models reflect a social-cognitive viewpoint consistent with Vygotsky's. The exchanges between teachers and students create a zone of proximal development in which students construct new knowledge and acquire habits of reflection and increased metacognitive knowledge. These exchanges with teachers and advanced peers are essential to cognitive change and growth and are vital to creating useful situated knowledge and thought. Dialogue between teachers and students is not the only mechanism for building students' understanding and revealing their misunderstandings, but it is among the most potent tools that teachers have available. In the next section, we extend our examination of social cognitive theory by exploring the nature of the discussions that take place in the classroom. We consider the potential of different kinds of classroom dialogue for building knowledge and fostering reflection.

Role of Classroom Discourse in Knowledge Construction

Most people's prototypical classroom images involve language use: teachers asking questions and students answering, class members discussing works of literature or poring over textbooks, and students struggling to write satisfactory answers to test questions. Language is the medium by which concepts are presented and clarified and through which students' knowledge typically is expressed and judged.

Language, as we learned from Vygotsky (1978, 1986), also is one of the most important social and cognitive tools, yet it often is not used effectively as it could be in the classroom. Classroom talk can play a critical role in learning and cognitive growth when it is used effectively. One theoretical perspective on how students can learn from discourse is based on Vygotsky's view that higher mental functions develop through a process by which the learner internalizes and transforms the content of social interaction (Fall, Webb, & Chudowsky, 2000; Wertsch, 2008).

Discourse is a general term referring to structured, coherent sequences of language. In discourse, propositions (see Chapter 3) take on meaning in relationship to one another. Meaning is drawn from the context. Discourse has **coherence,** and references forward or backward give meaning to individual elements (Brophy, 2006; O'Donnell, 2006). A conversation is an example of discourse: as two people discuss an event, the structure builds, each new idea taking meaning from the ones that came before. Essays, short stories, novels, and classroom discussions also are examples of discourse. Here we are interested in **classroom discourse,** which refers to the verbal exchanges in the classroom.

Researchers increasingly consider the quality of classroom discourse to be one of the most critical elements in effective schooling and teacher education (e.g., Calfee, Dunlap, & Wat, 1994; Chinn et al., 2001; Kuhn, Shaw, & Felton, 1997; Nystrand & Gamoran, 1991; Orland-Barack & Yinon, 2007; Wiencek & O'Flahavan, 1994). Classroom discourse, they argue, is a primary vehicle by which teachers guide, organize, and direct their students' activities. Like Rogoff and Schön, these researchers view learning as a constructive process in which social exchanges with others are fundamental to students' construction of meaning. As Hull and her associates (Hull, Rose, Fraser, & Castellano, 1991) have stated, "In the classroom, it is through talk that learning gets done, that knowledge gets made" (p. 318). This view is being translated into research aimed at finding the discourse structures and uses of classroom discourse that best promote learning (e.g., Calfee et al., 1994; Chinn & Waggoner, 1992; Jansen, 2008; Kuhn et al., 1997; Leinhardt & Steele, 2005; Wiencek & O'Flahavan, 1994).

Traditional classroom discourse has not been particularly supportive of student expression and reflection, however. Classroom discourse at all levels, from primary grades through college, tends almost always to be dominated by teacher talk. Students typically say little, and questions are rare. Most classroom talk centers on a single dominant discourse pattern: A teacher asks a question, a student responds, and the teacher gives feedback (Alvermann, O'Brien, & Dillon, 1990; Cazden, 2001; Mehan, 1979). Often simply called the **IRE pattern** (**i**nitiate, **r**espond, **e**valuate), the sequence in slightly more elaborated form is as follows:

1. *Teacher initiates.* The teacher informs, directs, or asks students for information. For example:

   TEACHER: Jen, can you tell me the name of the town where they were going?

2. *A student responds.* Student responses to the teacher's prompt or question can be verbal or nonverbal.

   JEN: Uh . . . I think it was Peatwick.

3. *The teacher evaluates.* The teacher comments on the student's reply or reacts to it non-verbally.

   TEACHER: Right. Peatwick. Good. And what were they . . .

As Cazden and others have pointed out, the IRE is the "default pattern" for classroom exchanges between teacher and student; that is, IRE is what happens unless deliberate intervention is made to achieve some alternative. Although this pattern can support a discussion of sorts, it most often is used for *recitation* in which a teacher quizzes students about content they have just studied. It often is accompanied by mini-lectures—periods of teacher talk that the teacher uses to elaborate on information already being discussed or to present new information. Chinn and Waggoner (1992) and others (e.g., Alvermann & Hayes, 1989; Cazden, 2001) have pointed out that it is extraordinarily difficult for teachers to move away from these patterns and their variations.

It may be, as Chinn and Waggoner speculate, that teacher control and authority are at stake, or it simply may be that teachers stick to this pattern because it is useful for probing student attention and comprehension.

Toward a More Reflective Classroom

We have been building the case in this chapter that cognitive growth is best fostered in a social environment in which students are active participants and where they are helped to reflect on their learning. For teachers to create a reflective classroom in which students build new knowledge and learn to manage their own learning, they almost certainly need to extend classroom discourse beyond the IRE recitations and the IRE-type discussions in which turn-taking rotates between teacher and students.

Calfee et al. (1994) have proposed the idea of **disciplined discussion** as an alternative to the IRE. Disciplined discussion draws on the best features of both *conversation,* which ordinarily is structured informally and student generated, and *instruction,* which typically refers to a more formal and teacher-directed interaction organized around a lesson. In disciplined discussion, a classroom discussion group approaches a text or other information source strategically, with a particular goal in mind. The roles and responsibilities of the participants are defined: Students solve problems by using interactive processes they have learned through modeling, practice, and feedback; a teacher plays several important but not dominating roles, acting as an organizer and participant or simply as an observer.

But what kinds of interactions are most likely to help students build knowledge and reflect on their learning? Chinn and Waggoner (1992) suggest that teachers first need to ensure that students have sufficient knowledge to support the discussion topic, knowledge that may come from personal experience, reading, or other sources. Beyond this are two fundamental criteria, both reflecting a social-cognitive viewpoint: (1) that students share alternative perspectives and (2) that the discourse has an open participation structure.

When students share *alternative perspectives,* they give their personal reactions and interpretations and consider the viewpoints of other participants. Students reading a short story, for instance, are likely to interpret parts of it in different ways. A good discussion provides a forum for determining things they agree on and for building metacognitive awareness. Similarly, children examining a picture of a snail may disagree about whether particular protrusions on its head are antennae or eyes. Discussion can stimulate further inquiry, such as closer observation or consulting other text sources, which will lead to an answer or resolution of the disagreement.

Open participation structure, which refers to the ability of students to talk freely with each other as they would in ordinary conversations, also is vital to building knowledge and reflection. In an open participation structure, both students and the teacher can initiate topics and ask questions (Chinn & Waggoner, 1992), which helps involve students in the discussion. When classroom discourse incorporates both of these functions, it can become *authentic* (Calfee et al., 1994; Graesser, Long, & Horgan, 1988; Nystrand & Gamoran, 1991); that is, organized around genuine questions of interest to the students and eliciting their perspectives.

The CORE Model   What are some ways that discussions can affect the development of knowledge and reflective thought in participating students? Calfee et al. (1994) suggest four possibilities in their CORE (connecting, organizing, reflecting, and extending) model of instruction (Calfee, Chambliss, & Beretz, 1991). First, discussions provide *connections* for learning. Useful knowledge is contextual, grounded in what students already know. Good discussions draw on students' prior domain and general knowledge and allow them to share what they know with their discourse partners. To take part effectively in discussions, students must recall information and use their metacognitive knowledge to link and sequence their ideas. Students learn that good discussions have coherence. By staying on topic and building on the ideas brought up by the participants, together they create a new body of shared information.

Second, discussions help *organize* knowledge. Knowledge construction is not simply a matter of accumulating particular facts or even of creating new units of information. It also involves organizing old information into new forms. Discussions are uniquely suited for these purposes. As participants strive to understand and contribute to discussions, they are forced to relate and organize what they know.

Third, good discussions can *foster reflective thought*. Discussions offer many opportunities for students to become aware of their thinking and to learn skills for regulating their thoughts and actions. Like all forms of discourse, discussions require participants to externalize thought. Presenting, organizing, clarifying, and defending ideas push students' cognitive processes into the open. Reactions of others in the discussion provide feedback on whether they have been persuasive and coherent. The act of explaining their reasoning promotes students' learning, particularly when reasons are elaborated with further evidence (Chinn, O'Donnell, & Jinks, 2000). Teachers, by coaching before and after discussions and adopting roles that allow them to scaffold student thought during discussions, can significantly influence students' abilities to reflect on their interactions and on the substance of their thinking (O'Flahavan & Stein, 1992).

Guthrie (1993) has provided an example of how discussion can stimulate reflection, describing how fifth graders in one of his project classrooms were engaged in a debate about whether life might exist on Mars. One student, John, insisted he had read that life did exist on Mars. He was challenged immediately by other students to identify the book that supported this belief. One student, Patty, proposed that the book in question most likely discussed what it *might be like* to live on Mars but that it did not say life *actually* existed on Mars. After further discussion, she volunteered to go to the school library to try to find more information that would resolve the question. This information did lead to more discussion and finally to resolution of the question (Patty was correct). Discussions like these, involving debate and reaching a conclusion, have a strong reflective component and stimulate students' use of strategic skills (Guthrie, McRae, & Klauda, 2007).

Finally, discussions help *extend* knowledge among students and teachers (Lee, 2005). As students work on long-term projects, their discourse can lead quite naturally into new domains. Guthrie (1993) observed that student discourse on one topic (the moon and its phases) quickly extended into several related topics. Students' declarative and procedural knowledge expanded rapidly as they searched for answers to questions they had posed; metacognitive knowledge increased as they discussed strategies for acquiring information with their peers and with the teacher and as they tried to explain their findings to their classmates.

Using Classroom Discourse to Build Knowledge

It is one thing to assert that high-quality discourse is at the heart of the reflective classroom; it is another to create classrooms in which knowledge construction and reflective thinking are the norm. On the one hand, when the teacher retains too much involvement in discussion, the result often is the IRE pattern, in which classroom discourse more nearly resembles recitation sequences than authentic exchanges. On the other hand, a laissez-faire approach to discussion that totally gives up social and interpretive authority to student groups is an invitation to chaos and deprives students of essential contributions by the teacher (Brown, 2006; Jansen, 2008; Kelly, 2007).

So what is the best way to engage students in authentic, extended discourse with each other and with their teacher? O'Flahavan (O'Flahavan & Stein, 1992; Wiencek & O'Flahavan, 1994) suggests that because discussions are highly complex, it is useful to consider them from a variety of perspectives, each involving a somewhat different form of knowledge construction. In O'Flahavan's view, the most effective classroom discussions are likely to be created when teacher and students work together from the outset to (1) develop the norms for participating in the discussions, (2) determine the interpretive agenda for a group's discussion, and (3) reflect after each discussion about the group's success in achieving both its social and interpretive goals.

O'Flahavan argues that teachers can play two especially important roles in these discussions: *coaching* and *scaffolding*. Although O'Flahavan favors decentralized, student-centered discussions, he considers teacher involvement essential for developing students' cognitive strategies, motivation, and expertise over the long term. In addition to managing some of the discussion, teachers are responsible for other features important to their success: creating the physical context for discussions, including determining group size and composition; devising seating arrangements; and making texts and other materials available.

In general, this work and a variety of recent reviews point toward five general strategies for improving effective learning in classroom discussion (Brophy, 2006; O'Donnell, 2006). The most basic strategy for creating productive discussion groups is to help students construct **group participation norms** (Gureckis & Goldstone, 2006). Most students understand basic social norms for interacting in classroom groups, such as raising their hands and not interrupting. But they may not know how to work well with other students or to listen to them, particularly in decentralized groups in which the teacher is not directing the interactions. One approach is to teach interactive skills directly (e.g., "These will be our rules. We should . . . "). A more effective approach is to allow students to help create their own rules for interaction. O'Flahavan and Stein (1992), for instance, had their students keep running lists of their group's participation norms, which typically included such rules as paying attention, not interrupting, and taking turns. Because these were the students' own norms, they were highly valued, probably more so than if the teacher had devised them. At the same time, the teacher plays an important role in helping the students reflect on whether their participation norms are effective. By serving as a *group process monitor* (O'Flahavan & Stein, 1992), the teacher can help the students periodically evaluate how well their group processes are working.

A second strategy is to help students develop **interpretive norms** for judging their progress (Brown, 2006). Students need to assume considerable responsibility for decentralized discussions to be effective. Assume, for instance, that a high school biology class is preparing a detailed report for local officials on the environmental threats to a nearby wetland. To meet this challenge, the class must make decisions on how it will proceed, such as what data it will gather, how they will be gathered, and the format of the document it eventually will produce. An effective teacher is likely to adopt a stance somewhere between authoritarian determination of the group's intellectual agenda (e.g., "OK, first I want you to study these maps of eastern Douglas County . . . ") and laissez-faire inattention to students' attempts to grapple with this complex and metacognitively demanding task.

A third strategy in helping students develop a reflective stance is **coaching.** In O'Flahavan and Stein's (1992) judgment, students will be most productive when they are allowed to work together in their groups for significant blocks of time—say, 15 to 20 minutes—with the teacher coaching at the boundaries of discussion, before and after discussion blocks. Many recent studies suggest that coaching is an essential component in the acquisition of reflection and is especially effective when used with authentic activities that are relevant to the student (Brophy, 2006).

For O'Flahavan and Stein (1992), coaching takes two major forms: (1) providing students with guidance and direction and (2) helping students reflect on their interactions and achievements. For instance, think of a long-term science project for middle school students in describing the status of a wetlands habitat. Most students would need coaching in basic strategies for gathering information, such as making inferences from texts, determining what is important, and monitoring their understanding while reading about birds, plants, and insects. They also likely would need coaching in such procedural strategies as keeping reflective logs, identifying variables for observation, recording their observations, and planning simple experiments. The teacher also might want to remind students of supplies and resources they are likely to need to complete tasks and to discuss ways these might be obtained. Students who need information about marsh plants and water beetles could be coached in using indexes and tables of contents to search books in the library for relevant information. These kinds of guidance all are effective forms of coaching.

A fourth strategy for creating effective discourse is **scaffolding** (Gijlers, Saab, Van Joolingen, De Jong, & Van Hout-Walters, 2009; Perry et al., 2006; Roglio & Light, 2009), where the teacher enables students to do things they cannot do on their own by helping them articulate what they are thinking, reminding them of assumptions they are making, drawing their attention to information, and providing new perspectives. Scaffolding makes use of Vygotsky's idea of the zone of proximal development, described earlier in this chapter (Gnadinger, 2008). The teacher, as the more expert person, provides frames of reference and modes of interpretation that students are capable of acquiring but do not yet have. In a discussion relating to sources of information about wetlands, for instance, one teacher became aware that her students did not know how to get information about land use and so posed an indirect question about where it might be found, suggesting "Maybe we should think about where we might find information about land use." Students, given this hint and occasional suggestions, soon began to debate the merits of such sources as surveying, aerial photography, satellite images, and landowner reports. Without the teacher's direction, the students likely would have been unable to continue their inquiry. With the scaffolding, they soon began to search library resources and initiated a series of productive contacts with landowners, agencies, and governmental units. The teacher's comment helped move them toward considering new information and frames of reference.

O'Flahavan defines several distinct roles that can be useful for scaffolding student thought. Among these are the role of the *framer,* in which the teacher draws attention to relevant background knowledge or helps students in interpretation; the *elicitor,* in which the teacher focuses the group's thinking on a point by bringing forth elaboration and extension from students; and the *interpretive peer,* in which the teacher is a participant in the group's inquiry.

Finally, *positive motivation* is critical to successful classroom discourse (Perry et al., 2006). Perhaps the most fundamental motivational requirement is that discussions be authentic, accessing the real culture of the students (Calfee et al., 1994; Kelly, 2007). This can be ensured if the group communicates about goals and issues that are meaningful to them. For instance, upper-level elementary students would find activities such as developing a class book about their neighborhoods, writing and directing a play for presentation at "Parents' Night," or creating a mural promoting school safety for younger students meaningful and motivating. In addition to rich topics, other factors important to motivation include the extent of teacher participation (not too much or too little), the teacher's ability to value and take up students' ideas and incorporate them into the ongoing discussion (Nystrand & Gamoran, 1991), and giving students greater control over interpretation, turn taking, and topic selection (Chinn et al., 2001).

Collaboration as a Tool for Learning

It should be clear that all of the strategies previously described involve some degree of collaboration, often between two or more peers, or between an expert and novice. Collaboration in the classroom now is viewed as an essential part of education. Increasingly, sociocultural models of learning such as situated learning theory (Lave & Wenger, 1991), cognitive apprenticeships (Collins, Brown, & Newman, 1989), and the work of Vygotsky (1978, 1986) have played a prominent role in educational research and practice. In the context of the instructional strategies presented here, collaboration can be viewed as a tool much like technology that can encourage an inquiry orientation, utilization of strategies, development and sharing of mental models, and making personal beliefs explicit.

Collaboration in the form of interactions with teachers and students facilitates learning for a variety of reasons. First, teacher and student modeling provide explicit examples of how to perform a task and often provide explicit feedback (Webb & Palincsar, 1996). Second, collaborative supports such as tutors, peer models, or small groups provide an opportunity for explicit discussion and reflection that promotes metacognition and self-regulation. For example, discussion promotes planning and evaluation of whether students met learning goals (Davis, 2001). Students of similar achievement levels may be more effective than teacher-student pairs because the former are able to discuss strategies in the novice's zone of proximal development (Feldman, Campbell, & Lai, 1999). Third, communities of learners have greater knowledge resources than individuals. Fourth, social interactions that cut across gender, economic, and ethnic lines promote social equity in the classroom, which enhances motivation and epistemological awareness (Hogan, 1999).

Collaboration in the classroom may occur among students, teachers, and between students and teachers (Hogan, 1999, 2000, 2002). Student collaboration typically involves tutors or small collaborative work groups. Research suggests that peer tutors who are judged to be of similar ability to their tutees increase the declarative and procedural knowledge and self-efficacy of those students (Pajares, 1996). Sometimes students are paired with expert mentors in what are referred to as **cognitive apprenticeships.** These relationships can help novice students develop expertise quickly and provide many opportunities for reflection that builds metacognitive understanding. Research suggests that tutors and cognitive apprenticeships can help novices achieve a higher degree of in-depth learning in a particular domain (Ramaswamy, Harris, & Tschirner, 2001).

Cooperative learning groups are one of the most common forms of collaboration. For instance, Hogan (1999) developed the Thinking Aloud Together (TAT) program as a means to promote metacognition and self-regulation in a small group collaborative setting. Students in the TAT programs demonstrated greater metacognitive awareness of their learning than students in the control group. Small group collaboration appears to be especially effective when students are engaged in inquiry-based discussion of problems (Meyer & Woodruff, 1998) and when students are given explicit training in how to work effectively in small groups (Bianchini, 1998). One potential problem is that student-centered cooperative groups can be difficult to initiate and manage. Guidelines for managing such groups have been provided by Webb and Palincsar (1996) and O'Donnell (2006).

Collaborations among teachers are necessary as well (Brophy, 2006); two ways to promote them are through cross-level mentoring and co-teaching. Cross-level mentoring refers to an experienced teacher mentoring a less-experienced teacher, usually as part of in-service training (Feldman et al., 1999). Training is typically one-on-one or in a small group and focuses on curricular choices and specific pedagogical strategies for improving student learning. In contrast, co-teaching involves two teachers of similar experience teaching in collaboration (Roth & Tobin, 2001). One advantage to co-teaching is that two teachers are able to make better use of their individual expertise. A second advantage is that one of the teachers can allocate more time to student small-group work while the other teacher directs the ongoing lesson. Co-teaching also helps promote the use of cognitive strategies and better metacognitive monitoring and evaluation, which support higher levels of student self-regulation.

Assessing Reflective Practice

Much of the research cited in this chapter emphasizes the importance of reflection and reflective practice, despite the fact that little work has been done on the assessment of reflection. Larrivee (2008), however, has recently developed such an assessment, which is focused on reflective practice in the classroom. The goal of this 53-item self-report instrument, called the *Survey of Reflective Practice* (SRP), is to identify which level of reflective practice a teacher currently demonstrates in the classroom.

The SRP is based on the work of a number of authors with strong conceptual links to the pioneering work of Donald Schön (Cole & Knowles, 2000; Jay, 2003; Larrivee, 2006). The psychological construct of **reflective practice** was defined as "on the job performance resulting using a reflective process for daily decision making and problem solving" (Larrivee, 2008, p. 342). Larrivee's review of more than 200 research articles suggested a four-level development framework for understanding reflective practice, which included pre-reflection, surface reflection, pedagogical reflection, and critical reflection. Pre-reflection was defined as a situation in which a teacher interprets classroom events without thoughtful analysis. This scale included 14 items such as *Does not see beyond the immediate demands of a teaching episode*. Surface reflection was defined as a situation in which a teacher focuses on tactical issues concerning how to best accomplish classroom teaching standards and objectives. This scale included 11 items such as *fails to connect specific methods to underlying theory*. Pedagogical reflection was defined as a reflective approach in which classroom teaching strategies are guided by an underlying pedagogical theory and the teacher's view of learning transcends the immediate classroom. This scale included 14 items such as *Engages in constructive criticism of one's own teaching*. Finally, critical reflection—the highest level of reflection measured—was defined as a context in which teachers are engaged in ongoing reflection and inquiry about their own teaching and thinking processes. This scale included 14 items such as *Acknowledges the social and political consequences of one's teaching*. Preliminary findings indicate that many teachers are at the surface or pedagogical levels of reflective practice, with relatively few at a critical reflection level.

Although early work on the SRP is promising, there still is much about the relationships among teachers' reflective practices, curricular decisions, and pedagogical choices that remains to be understood. Larrivee (2008), however, has proposed an agenda for future research with the SRP, including examining the developmental timeline of reflective practice in the classroom and across a teacher's career, investigating relationships between teacher effectiveness and reflective practice, and determining how school and professional development programs affect reflective practice. As researchers as well as textbook authors, we look forward to the future development of assessments like the SRP and its use in conjunction with interview methods (Larrivee, 2006; Lee, 2005; Lyons, 2006).

Implications for Instruction: A Portrait of the Reflective Classroom

We return now to our starting point—the goals of building student knowledge and habits of reflection. Building knowledge is not a simple matter. As we know from earlier chapters, there are several kinds of knowledge, each important in its own right. Expertise in any domain requires large networks of declarative knowledge, as well as readily available arrays of procedural skills. It requires metacognitive awareness and the regulatory knowledge of knowing how and when to apply what is known. Because the amount of knowledge we need is very large and the relationships among the knowledge elements so complex, the process of acquiring significant domain knowledge requires motivated, long-term student effort. The challenge to teachers is considerable.

If we succeed in building an ideal reflective classroom, what might it look like? We could begin by imagining a classroom in which the teacher has placed student knowledge construction at its center. To help accomplish this goal, the teacher has organized class activities around long-term, thematic projects in which students can make choices and use knowledge in ways that help them achieve their goals (Calfee & Miller, 2005b, 2007; Corno & Mandinach, 2004; Guthrie et al., 2007). We see a hands-on teacher who makes little use of the IRE pattern and who lectures infrequently. Further, in our reflective classroom, we see a teacher working as a partner with the students and organizing classroom activities around student information seeking and information exchange. One of this teacher's primary roles is guiding and supporting students in becoming self-directed, strategic learners.

A strong sense of purpose is evident in our ideal classroom. As teacher and students work together to reach project goals, activities alternate among whole-class instruction, in which students are coached on how to find and organize information; student reading and writing, in which students search for, find, and organize information and reflect on how they found it; and small-group discussions and collaboration, in which students report what they have learned, discuss their differing points of view, and judge their progress. We see our teacher helping students pick meaningful goals, coaching them on possible strategies for reaching their goals, and scaffolding their thinking as needed. Indeed, three of the 12 core effective teaching guidelines described by Brophy (2006) (i.e., thoughtful discourse, scaffolding student learning and engagement, and cooperative learning) pertain directly to sociocultural support mechanisms in the classroom.

Over time, we see the students in our ideal classroom becoming more and more expert and self-directed. Their growing knowledge is not isolated facts memorized from texts, but is organized and meaningful because it grows from authentic projects in which they have been allowed to choose topics and decide about ways to gather, organize, and present information. Students have learned not only "what" but also "how" and "why." As a consequence, they can readily explain why that information is useful, the strategies they used to find information, and how it is organized. Although our existing classrooms may fall short of this ideal, we still can draw on the basic principles presented that follow to help us move toward a reflective classroom.

1. *Take a broad perspective on knowledge.* Declarative knowledge is a good starting point, as is procedural knowledge—knowing how. Both, however, need to be made useful by being tied to metacognitive awareness and self-regulation. In the long run, these metacognitive dimensions may be the most critical aspects of knowledge acquisition. Because what is known changes rapidly and the amount of information available far exceeds anyone's ability to acquire it, students must develop the capacity to direct their own learning and the motivation to continue to acquire new information and skills.

2. *Develop students' information-seeking skills.* Modern communication technologies provide access to a wealth of information but also require that students learn to search for information, organize it, and judge its reliability. Teaching these skills in the context of long-term projects can be especially effective. Guthrie and his colleagues, for instance (e.g., Guthrie, Bennett, & McGough, 1994; Guthrie et al., 2007; Wigfield et al., 2008), have helped students not only to learn multiple strategies for acquiring information from texts but also to judge the utility of the information they found.

3. *Organize instruction in ways that favor knowledge construction.* One of cognitive psychology's most valuable contributions has been to remind us that learners' activities affect what is learned and how functional it will be. We therefore must help students engage all of their learning capabilities. Rote rehearsal, in which meaning is ignored, tends to generate rote, list-like, fragile learning. In contrast, approaches aimed at student comprehension of the meaning of what is to be learned are much more likely to help students understand, organize, retain, and use the information they encounter (Roglio & Light, 2009). Scaffolded instruction and peer tutoring are particularly effective instructional strategies (O'Donnell, 2006).

4. *Create a "thinking classroom."* Effective knowledge construction and good thinking flourish in classroom cultures organized to support them (Tishman, Perkins, & Jay, 1995). Early cognitive theory tended to portray intellectual growth as a solitary pursuit, but social cognitive theory and research now emphasize family, school, community, and cultural influences on cognitive development (e.g., see Gauvain, 2001; Rogoff & Chavajay, 1995). Rogoff's ideas of guided participation and the child as cognitive apprentice and Schön's concept of reflection on reflection-in-action both emphasize the social nature of cognitive growth.

5. *Use discourse structures that promote reflection and knowledge construction.* Among the most important resources for knowledge construction and reflection are classroom discussions in which students interact freely and grapple with authentic questions. As Rosenblatt argued many years ago in her classic book *Literature as Exploration* (1938), we need to encourage students to express what texts mean to them and then to use discussion to negotiate what they mean. In any subject area, students' initial understandings, though often immature and incomplete, are the only legitimate starting point for learning. As students continue their exchanges with each other and with the teacher about what they are learning, their understanding will deepen.

6. *Use coaching and scaffolding to build student understanding.* Like the guidance provided by the master craftsperson, teachers' coaching and scaffolding are vital to creating new levels of student understanding (Gijlers et al., 2009). As we saw earlier in the chapter, O'Flahavan and Stein (1992) argue for concentrating coaching at the boundaries of discussions. Before discussions, teachers can help students set the agenda for discussion; after discussions, teachers can assist students in reflecting on their successes and failures. Within discussions, scaffolding works effectively as teachers help students clarify their ideas and judge whether they're reaching their goals (Brophy, 2006; McCaslin, 2004).

7. *Consider decentralizing discussions.* Although large-group discussions can be productive (Calfee et al., 1994), the opportunity for individual students to participate always will be limited by group size. Also, some students are reluctant to take part in a full-class setting because of perceived lack of knowledge or shyness. O'Flahavan and his colleagues (e.g., O'Flahavan & Stein, 1992) and Guthrie and his associates (e.g., Guthrie et al., 2007) have shown that groups of four to six upper-level elementary students can carry on long-term inquiry relatively independent of the teacher if they are supported periodically by teacher coaching and scaffolding. Students in such groups can learn both to reflect on their interactions and monitor progress toward their goals.

8. *Make tolerance a basic rule for classroom interaction.* Classroom interaction is a social process and students do not necessarily come to our classrooms with highly refined social skills. They often need to learn rules for classroom and small-group discussion. For instance, the prevailing norms governing whole-class discussions may specify what kinds of replies to questions are considered appropriate, points at which it is acceptable to interrupt, and preferred ways to get others' attention. For a variety of reasons, such as family history or ethnic background, some students' communication styles will not match those of others in the class. Students who interrupt frequently, for example, may have developed this style of communication in their families, have had success with it in other classes, or simply may be extraordinarily eager to do well (see Hull et al., 1991).

Variations in style and skill levels demand that both students and teachers practice basic principles of respect for others' ideas. For the long term, it will be useful for most discussion groups to develop their own participation norms (see O'Flahavan & Stein, 1992; Wiencek & O'Flahavan, 1994). The rules that students themselves generate (e.g., "Take turns," "No putdowns," and "Don't hog the discussion") typically are more effective and will be viewed as less coercive than any the teacher might impose. Also, students can be asked to reflect periodically on whether their rules are creating effective working groups or need to be modified.

Summary

This chapter has described processes for fostering cognitive growth in the classroom. Knowledge acquisition is viewed as a constructive process in which learners build and organize knowledge. Three types of constructivism were outlined: exogenous constructivism, endogenous constructivism, and dialectical constructivism. Of these, dialectical constructivism is the most generally applicable to effective learning, although all three are important components of student learning.

Stimulated by the work of the Russian psychologist Vygotsky and his concept of zone of proximal development, cognitive scientists and many educators now emphasize social processes in knowledge formation. Social interactions between a child and a peer or an adult providing guided participation help build bridges between what children already know and new information they encounter. In effect, children are "apprentices in thinking" whose knowledge and ways of knowing grow out of interactions with others (Rogoff, 1990; Schön, 1983). The child's cognitive development is embedded in their social and cultural contexts.

Classroom discourse is a significant factor in building knowledge and shaping cognitive growth. If discourse is authentic, honors the students' points of view, and has continuity, it will engage students and become a basis for knowledge construction and reflective thinking. The tenor of classroom discourse also shapes students' perceptions of self and learning; it can be supportive or threatening, uplifting or demeaning.

The best discussions allow alternative perspectives and have open participation structures. By providing a forum for expression and feedback, they create opportunities to extend knowledge and to develop reflective thought. Strategies for creating productive discussion groups include having the groups develop and modify their own social and interpretive norms, teacher coaching before and after discussions, and teacher scaffolding during discussions. Such approaches enhance the possibility of knowledge construction and development of self-directed, strategic, reflective approaches to learning.

Collaboration is involved in all of the instructional strategies described in this chapter and is viewed as an essential part of education. In the classroom it may occur among students, teachers and between students and teachers and is a tool that encourages an inquiry orientation, the use of strategies, the development and sharing of mental models, and making explicit personal beliefs.

Because expertise requires organized, flexible knowledge, teachers should help students learn ways to seek and judge information. Ideally, classrooms provide authentic contexts for developing expertise by providing learning that students find meaningful, that builds on prior knowledge, and that allows self-expression. The ideal outcome is for students not only to acquire knowledge but also become independent, self-regulated learners.

SUGGESTED READINGS

Gauvain, M. (2001). *The social context of cognitive development*. New York, NY: Guilford Press.
   This scholarly but readable book examines cognitive development from a social vantage point, arguing that understanding children's learning requires that we not only understand cognitive principles but also the social and cultural contexts for learning.

O'Donnell, A. (2006). The role of peer and group learning. In P. A. Alexander & P. H. Winne (Eds.), *Handbook of educational psychology* (2nd ed., pp. 781–802). Mahwah, NJ: Erlbaum.
   This chapter from the *Handbook of educational psychology* compares several conceptual frameworks for understanding how social processes and classroom contexts affect student learning and development. It also contains a detailed discussion of peer learning strategies such as reciprocal teaching, peer tutoring, and collaborative group work.

Perry, N. E., Turner, J. C., & Meyer, D. K. (2006). Classrooms as social contexts for motivating learning. In P. A. Alexander & P. H. Winne (Eds.), *Handbook of educational psychology* (2nd ed., pp. 327–348). Mahwah, NJ: Erlbaum.
   This chapter, also from the *Handbook of educational psychology*, provides a comprehensive and detailed description of the effect of classroom context on the development of cognition, self-regulation, and student engagement and motivation.

Vygotsky, L. (1986). *Thought and language*. Cambridge, MA: The MIT Press.
   This revised and enlarged edition of Lev Vygotsky's classic work includes an excellent overview of Vygotsky's thinking by Alex Kozulin that explains Vygotsky's influential ideas in easily understandable terms.

Technological Contexts for Cognitive Growth

This chapter is about technologies for learning and teaching. Simply put, a technology is any device or system that we humans use to accomplish our goals. The wheel, an oar, an abacus, a hammer, a toothpick, and a TV set are various examples. In education, some technologies have been with us for hundreds and even thousands of years—items to write with (e.g., a stylus, pen, pencil, and chalk), record ideas (e.g., papyrus, paper, and chalkboards), and preserve and share information in an organized way (e.g., scrolls and books).

When educators refer to technology, however, they almost always are referring to a cluster of continuously evolving electronic hardware (e.g., computers, laptops, handheld devices, MP3 and DVD players), communication networks linking these devices (e.g., wireless networks, cable TV, the Internet), and associated software (e.g., word processing, presentation programs, apps, simulations, games, Web browsers). In this chapter, we focus on these electronic technologies and examine the implications of cognitive psychology for their design and use.

Educators increasingly are aware of technology's potential for changing how learning and teaching take place. Even though education continues to lag behind other segments of society in using technology, having a relatively low level of classroom use compared to its integral part of our daily lives as we bank, shop, search for information and use our cell phones in a growing number of ways, there is hope that technology can improve, and even revolutionize, how students learn and teachers teach.

Our modern era is not the first in which there have been hopes about technology's promise. When movies and television first appeared predictions were made that they would replace most, if not all, classroom instruction. That has not happened. But today's versatile technologies do seem to warrant optimism. With technology an obvious feature in all of our lives and playing an increasing role in schools, where students have access to course-related e-mail communication and Web-based resources such as course syllabi, assignments, reading materials, and practice exams, there is growing interest in how it might be best used. Should students work with technology alone or collaboratively? Can technology facilitate classroom discussions and provide practice opportunities? Can it help promote educational equity? Can online education be effective? Should we spend school resources on handheld devices or are computer labs still a good investment?

The point of this chapter is not to recommend specific new instructional technologies shown by research to produce gains in learning outcomes. There are none. One of the most consistent findings when the educational technology research literature is carefully reviewed is that there are few if any improvements in learning outcomes specifically attributable to the technology alone. That is, when technologies such as online presentation and discussion of teaching case studies by teacher education students are compared with traditional approaches (e.g., the same students reading and discussing teaching case studies in the classroom), there seldom are learning benefits attributable to the technology itself (e.g., see Clark, 1994, 2001, 2003; Salomon, 1984).

What instructional technology research *does* show is that learning is influenced primarily by good instructional methods that *take advantage of what technologies have to offer*. That is, technology *per se* is not what motivates learners and produces learning, but how that technology is used. We will focus on technology in the hands of skilled teachers, teachers who understand cognitive and motivational principles and can turn them into effective instruction. When such teachers guide technology use, what can it do for student learning and cognitive growth?

We begin with an overview of some of the many technology-based resources available to students. Which ones are best suited to different kinds of learning goals? Simultaneously we look at several key cognitive skills and strategies students need to use technology effectively. Taking full advantage of technology's potential requires that students have a repertoire of knowledge, strategies, and beliefs. We highlight several of these that we see as especially important.

In the following four sections we describe some of the theory and research guiding today's instructional technology development. What kinds of cognitive and motivational theories currently inform choices about instructional technology design and use? The first of the four sections describes *cognitive load theory* and multimedia design. Cognitive load theory, which we introduced in Chapter 2, has become a focal point for thinking about instructional multimedia. We present principles based on this theory that will help you make informed judgments about whether media are well designed. The second of our theory sections summarizes the *Four-Component Instructional Design (4C/ID) model,* which provides a blueprint for how technology can be used to develop complex skills. In the third section we explore technology's potential for *scaffolding metacognition and self-regulated learning*. Here we describe how technology-supported learning environments can be used to coach and support learners in becoming more strategic, persistent, and reflective. The fourth section analyzes educational technology's uses from the standpoint of *social cognitive theory,* focusing on computer-supported collaborative learning (CSCL, Schellens & Valcke, 2005; Stahl, Koschmann, & Suthers, 2006), in which technology serves as a hub for learning communities. We conclude our chapter by exploring the growing ties between technology and assessment and the general implications of technology-based approaches for education.

How Can Students Use Technologies?

Technology itself seldom is the driving force behind learning, but it obviously can amplify and extend students' educational experiences. When we look at computer- and Internet-related technologies, we can see many ways they can be used in education. Software is readily available for creating and sharing Web-based resources such as graphics, diagrams, and videos, while wireless classrooms make it feasible to link class members' laptops or smartphones. Table 10.1 presents several ways that students can use educational technology to enhance their educational experience, while Table 10.2 presents key cognitive skills needed to take advantage of them.

The category listed first in Table 10.1—students *receiving information* via technology—is not a new one. It has a history dating back to movies and television and even before. Many teachers now use software such as *PowerPoint,* for example, to present information. This software typically has a number of capabilities for enhancing presentations, such as the ability to use varied type fonts and backgrounds and include features such as clip art, pictures, animations, and sound. These features can make information more attractive and interesting but, if used ineffectively, can distract learners and lead to loss of comprehension.

The second category of technology use, however, has developed more recently. With widening Internet access in U.S. schools and classrooms, technology has opened a significant resource for student learning—*access to information and ways to find it.* Web browsers available on computers and phones link to the Internet, and search engines allow students to find information easily and quickly. In contrast to the problem of lack of information, which many schools and students still face with shrinking libraries and scarce textbooks, technology is creating ironic new challenges—information overload coupled with access to information of dubious quality. As shown in Table 10.2, students need to learn systematic methods of searching for information and recognizing differences in its quality; without these skills, student searches can be derailed by momentary factors (e.g., unusual links turned up by search engines or a succession of interesting-looking links) and result in erroneous or biased information (e.g., from personal Web sites or sites run by unmonitored groups).

Increasingly, technology can help students *organize and present information.* Programs such as *Inspiration* allow students to compile information in formats ranging from semantic maps to outlines. These then can serve as multimedia storyboards or frameworks for essays or stories. To actually present information, many choices are available, including word processing (e.g., Word), desktop publishing (e.g., PageMaker, InDesign), multimedia development (e.g., Flash, Director), and Web design programs (e.g., Dreamweaver). What students produce—papers, multimedia presentations, or Web pages—can range from simple summaries to highly complex productions involving gathering, organizing, refining, and presenting information. The best projects can call on virtually all of a student's cognitive, self-regulatory, and motivational resources.

As students increasingly become involved in complex projects that start with information gathering and lead to information transformation and presentation, teachers should consider the many challenges students will face and devise strategies to help them be successful. Self-regulation skills are critical, as students need to monitor their progress and adjust strategies in order to continue moving ahead. Many will need assistance not only with becoming skillful in using the technology (i.e., developing procedural skills) but also in developing a mastery orientation toward both learning to use the technology itself and completing complex

TABLE 10.1   Selected Student Uses of Technology

Use	Examples of Available Technologies	Examples of Student Use
1. Receive information	• Presentation packages (e.g., PowerPoint)	• Ninth-grade biology students view multimedia presentation that includes video of cell reproduction
2. Search for and find information	• Web browsers (e.g., Firefox, Internet Explorer) • Search engines (e.g., Google, Yahoo!)	• Fourth graders identify keywords to search for information on habitats of foxes, coyotes, and dingos • Eleventh graders find information about the Lewis and Clark expedition on the National Geographic Web site
3. Organize and present information	• Organizing, outlining programs (e.g., Inspiration) • Presentation packages • HTML editors, authoring packages (e.g., Dreamweaver, FrontPage)	• A team of sixth-grade students creates a semantic map to guide their writing on their paper "Life in the Rain Forest" • Teacher education students develop a several-part "philosophy of teaching" that is posted on their class Web site
4. Explore simulated environments	• Simulation games, visualization tools (e.g., SimCity Societies, Geometer's Sketchpad)	• High schoolers use Sketchpad to model a Ferris wheel's motion and graphing activities to learn trigonometry concepts
5. Participate in authentic learning environments	• Communication software (e.g., Thunderbird, Outlook, Gmail) • Databases (e.g., Access, FileMaker Pro) and Web sites • Statistical packages (e.g., SAS, SPSS)	• High school students in several states gather water quality and climate data from their area, send it via the Internet into a database, make hypotheses about trends in data, and compare findings with each other
6. Communicate and collaborate with other students	• Communication and collaboration software (e.g., Skype, iChat, Adobe Connect Pro)	• Graduate students located in several countries taking a school administration distance learning course participate in threaded discussions, work groups, and projects to complete course requirements
7. Practice skills and receive feedback on progress	• DVD or Internet-based programs aimed at skill development • Course management software (e.g., Blackboard, Moodle) for supporting online learning	• First graders practice matching letters to letter sounds using an animated computer program • College students in psychology take several practice quizzes sampling unit objectives, use results to gauge their progress and decide when to take unit mastery tests
8. Use technologies for cognitive support and extending abilities	• Screen readers (e.g., JAWS) that convert on-screen text into speech • Voice recognition systems (e.g., Kurzweil Voice, Dragon Naturally Speaking) allowing computer users to dictate text directly • Word prediction programs (e.g., Co:Writer) that offer likely words after beginning letters are typed	• Visually impaired graduate student explores the Internet from a Windows environment • Eighth grader with poor writing skills dictates words and punctuation into a word processing system • Learning disabled high school student uses word prediction program to find appropriate words and reduce misspellings in an assigned paper

TABLE 10.2   Some Key Cognitive Skills Students Need to Use Technologies Effectively

Key Student Skill	Potential Pitfalls for Students in Using Technology	Strategies Teachers Can Use
1. Locating and judging information	• Following links randomly • Attending to seductive details • Getting "lost" in information searches • Being overwhelmed by too much information • Selecting erroneous or low quality information	• Limit searches to a few questions and limited number of sites (e.g., WebQuest) • Explicitly teach search and summarization strategies • Stress careful preparation for searching • Teach students to self-monitor search and summarize success
2. Communicating effectively using technology	• Lack of effective writing skills • Lack of media design skills • Not understanding purposes of communication • Uncertainty about roles in learning communities • Receiving negative feedback on communication attempts	• Arrange authentic communication opportunities • Explicitly teach writing and media design strategies • Encourage students to use graphic and other organizers to prepare for communication • Create safe environment for online communication
3. Using self-monitoring and self-regulation skills when using technology	• Not understanding overall goals for learning • Failing to monitor progress toward goals • Producing low quality products (e.g., writing, multimedia presentations) • Participating erratically in activities, projects	• Help students select interesting, intrinsically motivating projects • Help students set goals and subgoals for projects • Teach self-regulation skills tied to technology use, including monitoring progress • Create opportunities for students to share products and receive feedback • Provide frequent feedback to students on progress toward goals
4. Proceduralizing knowledge	• Not practicing skills sufficiently • Lack of just-in-time information • Lack of awareness of skills' role in larger tasks	• Give students repeated practice opportunities to proceduralize program knowledge • Engage students in discussions about skills needed to achieve goals • Help students link procedural skills to conceptual understanding
5. Contextualizing knowledge	• Failing to comprehend virtual structures (e.g., organization of word processing programs, browsers, operating systems) • Not applying already-learned skills and knowledge to solving new problems	• Complement development of procedural skills with conceptual instruction • Provide graphic organizers to aid students in linking features
6. Adopting a mastery orientation toward technology-based learning	• Not using alternative strategies when difficulties are encountered • Losing motivation to continue with projects	• Help students set and monitor progress toward intermediate and long-term goals • Remind students of utility of learning • Give frequent feedback on students' progress toward goals

projects utilizing several different kinds of technology (e.g., word processing, multimedia development, and Web authoring programs).

Many educators also recognize technology's growing potential for giving students opportunities to learn in new ways. Students can use *simulated environments* and *visualization tools* to create and visualize things as diverse as mathematical functions, using Geometer's Sketchpad, and a society's workings, using SimCity Societies. Because they require powerful computing, technology-based simulations once were largely confined to higher-end applications (e.g., in film studios, architectural firms). This situation has changed rapidly with development of simulations on personal computers and handheld devices offering high realism and responsiveness. Simulations and games have the potential to offer routes to learning activities students find intrinsically motivating and worthwhile in their own right.

Mirroring our culture's rapidly expanding use of wireless devices and the Internet to communicate, educational *uses of technology for communication and collaboration* are growing. Many students and teachers now routinely interact by e-mail and texting; class Web sites and listservs provide class members with easy access to information, ability to share it with class members, and chances to work together. Success in communication does not happen accidentally, of course; it requires worthwhile issues to communicate about and hinges on students' writing and media skills. While such skills to some extent develop just by working with communication technologies (e.g., sending e-mails and contributing to a discussion on a class discussion board), they often require coaching, feedback, and extensive practice to develop the proceduralized knowledge needed for skilled performance.

Technologies can make *opportunities for practice and feedback* available. Many elementary students use at least some computer-based technology for skill development. While instructional quality can vary tremendously, a host of DVD-based programs, for instance, are available for developing elementary students' literacy (e.g., a program for beginning readers includes practice in picking out rhyming words) and math skills (e.g., a program for third and fourth graders presents practice sets of addition or subtraction problems). Similarly, students in high school and college classrooms now can take repeated Web-based practice quizzes sampling unit content. The feedback they receive allows them to judge how close they are to mastery.

Finally, a cluster of technology-related products and equipment, collectively called *assistive technology,* is now available to support and extend the abilities of learners with disabilities. Assistive technologies continue to multiply, stimulated by developments in fields as disparate as computer hardware and software, robotics, and speech recognition. Some assistive technologies, such as environmental control devices and robots, are primarily aimed at helping individuals who have physical disabilities. Others, more directly related to the cognitive focus of this text, provide significant assistance to individuals with disabilities that interfere with performance of school-related tasks such as reading, writing, spelling, and math.

For example, intelligent word prediction programs for phones, word processors, and e-mail now are available. Users need only to begin to spell a word and likely possibilities are displayed. Sophisticated programs also are available to aid and extend students' cognitive abilities, including systems that read scanned text aloud, browsers that translate Web content into speech, and voice recognition systems that allow users to dictate text directly into computers.

In summary, instructional technology has the potential to provide students with many learning opportunities and extend their cognitive functioning. Some are not new—for example, using technology to receive information from a presentation. Others, however, are opening up entirely new avenues to learning resources and have potential for supporting active, meaningful collaborative learning. Technology uses range from gathering, organizing, and presenting information to interacting with others on group projects. Still other uses are targeted at learners with disabilities, providing technological supports ranging from speech recognition to text-to-speech conversion. Using technology effectively requires many different student competencies (see Table 10.2) ranging from knowing how to search for information to having a mastery orientation that will carry them through the challenges of using technology in complex, long-term projects. To help us think more specifically about productive uses of technology and how students can use it, we now turn to the theory and research on technology, cognition, and education. We begin with cognitive load theory.

Cognitive Load Theory and Multimedia Design

Cognitive load theory, proposed by John Sweller and his associates (Sweller, 1999; Sweller, van Merriënboer, & Paas, 1998; van Merriënboer & Sweller, 2005), focuses on the role of working memory in instructional design. Cognitive load theory increasingly has been applied to the design of educational multimedia, such as computer-based instructional programs and multimedia (Clark, 2003; Mayer & Moreno, 2002; van Merriënboer & Ayres, 2005; van Merriënboer & Sweller, 2005). From a cognitive load perspective, meaningful learning depends on active cognitive processing in learners' working memory. The difficulty is that working memory can only process a few units of information at any given time (see Chapter 2). If learners encounter too many elements in a multimedia presentation—for example, one combining animations, graphics, sounds, printed text, and narrated text—working memory can be overwhelmed. The result of excessive cognitive load, or too many pieces of information being juggled in working memory, is decreased processing efficiency and, at worst, a collapse of the learning process.

Understanding the two types of cognitive load, intrinsic cognitive load and extraneous cognitive load, can help us analyze whether given multimedia presentations are likely to create issues of cognitive load. **Intrinsic cognitive load,** according to Sweller, is a characteristic of the materials themselves in relation to the learner's expertise. Any content being learned creates intrinsic cognitive load in working memory based on its difficulty and complexity. For example, a multimedia presentation for ninth graders on biodiversity will generate a certain amount of intrinsic cognitive load associated with the complexity of the topic of biodiversity and associated concepts. Because it relates primarily to the content itself, intrinsic cognitive load typically cannot be altered. **Extraneous cognitive load,** on the other hand, is affected by the instructional design, such as how a multimedia presentation is organized and the kinds of information included (e.g., clip art, animations, and text). If a presentation contains multiple information sources such as diagrams and texts that need to be mentally integrated, extraneous cognitive load will be generated. In contrast to intrinsic cognitive load, extraneous cognitive load is controllable—better instructional designs create less of it, less effective designs create more.

Intrinsic and extraneous cognitive load are additive; if both are high, working memory capacity can be overwhelmed. Because only extraneous cognitive load is under the control of instructional designers, who can change *how* content is presented but typically cannot change the content itself, the challenge is to design instruction that reduces extraneous cognitive load. To meet this challenge, Sweller and his colleagues have focused on two resources: (1) long-term memory (LTM), with its nearly unlimited capacity and processes of schema formation, and (2) the unique nature of working memory.

First, because LTM has great capacity and many learners possess domain-related knowledge schemas (e.g., a biology student with prior knowledge of cell division processes and a music history student with knowledge about Baroque and Classical composers), multiple elements of information often can be chunked into a single element (see Chapter 3). Chunking reduces the burden on working memory for these learners (Kalyuga, Chandler, & Sweller, 2000). Also, the more automatized schemata are, the more working memory capacity is available for comprehension and problem solving. Thus, multimedia designers (e.g., Merrill, 2000; van Merriënboer & Kirschner, 2007) suggest features targeted at encouraging schema automation.

One approach has been to present *goal-free problems,* in which students practice repeatedly on problem subgoals to attain automaticity, such as calculating many different angles in a geometry program until this skill is very well-learned, *before* they encounter the more complex overall problem-solving task of proving a geometry theorem. Expressed in the terms introduced in Chapter 8, cognitive load is reduced when part of the instruction allows students to use a *goal-free* as opposed to a *mean–ends* strategy. Many times, in trying to solve problems learners are asked to hold and process too much simultaneously in working memory—the current problem state, the goal state, operators to reduce differences, plus a set of subgoals. While Sweller and others (e.g., van Merriënboer, Clark, & de Croock, 2002) caution against overuse, a goal-free approach can be effective because it requires remembering only a specific subgoal and operators applying to it, reducing cognitive load.

A second major way of reducing working memory in multimedia designs is to take advantage of working memory's unique nature. As discussed in Chapter 2, working memory involves two separate channels (Baddeley, 2007; Paivio, 1986a): the visual channel (the *visuospatial sketchpad*) that takes input from the eyes and makes a pictorial representation; and the auditory channel (the *phonological loop*), which produces an auditory representation. As described there, awareness of working memory's visual and auditory channels is important in designing multimedia that avoid cognitive overload problems.

In a series of studies, Mayer and his associates (see Mayer & Moreno, 2002) compared learning outcomes for students receiving computer-presented materials consisting of narration alone to conditions in which narration was paired with an animation. As expected, students having both narration and animation learned better. In further studies, Mayer and his group compared narration and animation presented at the same time (*simultaneous group*) with successive presentation of the same information (*successive group*). In each of the studies (see Mayer & Moreno, 2002), students learned better from simultaneous presentations than from successive presentations. In Mayer and Moreno's view, these results occurred because simultaneous presentation aided learners in making connections between verbal and visual representations in working memory. In these studies, students showed few effects of excessive cognitive load.

In later studies, however, Mayer and his colleagues began to experiment with multimedia conditions calculated to test the capacity of verbal and visual working memory channels. In one set of studies, Mayer's group examined a common practice of multimedia designers—creating highly active screen designs in multimedia presentations by adding interesting explanations or sound effects. Many designers believe that such features make learning more interesting and motivating. What Mayer and his associates found, however, were negative learning outcomes. In an instructional multimedia sequence about lightning, for instance, adding interesting facts (people in swimming pools are sitting ducks!) and sounds to illustrate the steps in lightning formation (e.g., gentle wind, static, and thunder) actually *reduced* learners' problem-solving transfer, as did including instrumental background music. Mayer attributed these results to cognitive load issues. Consistent with predictions from cognitive load theory and contrary to common belief, students learned more deeply when multimedia did *not* include such words and sounds.

A further interesting test of cognitive load theory in multimedia design involved pairing either on-screen or narrated text presentations with animations to test the so-called *modality* (e.g., Mayer & Moreno, 1998; Moreno & Mayer, 1999) or *split-attention* effect (Mousavi, Low, & Sweller, 1995). Cognitive load theory predicts that when animations are used, adding on-screen text can overload working memory because both text and animation must be processed *in the visual channel.* In contrast, when animation is paired with *narrated* text, having the text presented in spoken form should reduce load in the visual channel and increase the chances of deeper cognitive processing. This, in fact, is what these researchers found.

Another common belief among many multimedia designers is that providing multiple sources of the same information (e.g., animation and on-screen text plus narration of the on-screen text) creates useful *redundancy.* From this perspective redundancy should improve learning because learners can choose to learn in their preferred style (e.g., some learn better from animations, others from reading or listening). Generally, it was found that redundancy does not promote deeper learning, but actually diminishes it (e.g., Craig, Gholson, & Driscoll, 2002; Mayer, Heiser, & Lonn, 2001).

In summarizing this research, Mayer and Moreno (2002, 2003; Moreno, 2005) have proposed several principles for guiding multimedia designs that take cognitive load demands into account. Among them is the principle of *contiguity,* which refers to presenting related information simultaneously rather than successively. For instance, when related verbal and visual information (e.g., a diagram and explanatory text) are encountered simultaneously in a multimedia presentation rather than successively, learning and problem-solving transfer will be improved. A second principle is *coherence,* based on research (e.g., Moreno & Mayer, 2000) showing better learning when learners don't have to process extra words, sounds, and pictures. Paralleling cognitively based work in Web design, where "cleaner" designs (e.g., fewer features, minimal words on a page) are seen to be better at guiding attention and memory, the more effective presentations are those that are not embellished and where focus is kept on goal-relevant content.

A third principle, *modality,* refers to taking advantage of working memory's structure by providing information that can be processed through visual *and* verbal modes, such as presenting animations with narrated text. Closely related are the potentially negative effects of *redundancy* in multimedia instruction. Adding redundant information to concise, but effective, explanations usually is unhelpful, especially when redundant information must be processed in the same channel as the primary information. For example, in multimedia materials using animations (processed *visually*), adding on-screen text (also processed *visually*) that duplicates narrated text (processed *auditorily*) is likely to create extraneous cognitive load by placing too many demands on visual working memory.

In summary, cognitive load theory provides much food for thought for those designing or selecting instructional multimedia. Working memory needs to be used effectively if students are to achieve deeper learning such as comprehending scientific principles and transferring problem-solving skills. Learners need to actively process, organize, and link multimedia content in working memory, but we also need to ensure that multimedia learning activities do not overload it. Two ways of avoiding this are drawing on learners' schemas from LTM and helping them automate new ones. Others are connecting information to permit simultaneous processing and not presenting too much information in a single channel. These strategies will help decrease extraneous cognitive load and increase students' chances of success.

The Four-Component Instructional Design (4C/ID) Model and Complex Skill Development

In the previous section, we discussed cognitive load theory and its uses for matching multimedia materials to the characteristics of working memory. But multimedia designers often must also grapple with larger-scale issues of organizing and sequencing whole instructional programs, particularly if they are designing systems for complex cognitive skill development (see, for example, van Merriënboer & Kirschner, 2007). Complex cognitive skills include those that experts perform, such as doctors making a medical diagnosis, architects designing a building, or pilots responding to emergencies.

van Merriënboer's **Four-Component Instructional Design (4C/ID) model** (van Merriënboer, 1997; van Merriënboer et al., 2002; van Merriënboer & Kirschner, 2007), based on work in cognitive psychology and cognitive science, was formulated to guide this kind of complex instructional design. The 4C/ID model rests on the basic premise that complex skills are learned by performing them, so instructional multimedia design based on the 4C/ID model focuses on giving *practice opportunities* rather than just presenting information. The system is designed so that learners acquire skills through practice, with information made available as needed to support skill acquisition.

The first of the 4C/ID model's four components is the *learning task*. As van Merriënboer et al. (2002) point out, complex learning always involves achieving *integrated* sets of learning goals, not learning separate skills in isolation. The 4C/ID model promotes use of learning tasks that are whole, authentic, and concrete. An online course for developing expertise in photography might be organized around the task of creating a black-and-white photo essay, an authentic task. It also would consist of subprograms teaching the required skills and associated knowledge needed to perform the task, such as skills and concepts related to composition, focus and depth of field, lighting, film developing, and making prints.

Learners participating in technology-based instruction based on the 4C/ID model typically would begin work on a cluster of relatively simple, but meaningful tasks called *task classes.* They then progress toward more complex ones. Complexity is determined by the number of skills involved in task classes, how the tasks classes relate to each other, and the amount of knowledge needed to perform them. The lowest level task classes—where instruction of novices would begin—are the simplest versions of whole tasks that experts would encounter in the real world. For example, medical students being asked to make a diagnosis where the symptoms are fairly obvious and the probability of correct diagnosis high. The top-level task classes correspond to the most complex problems that experts would encounter in the real world. High levels of support are given for learning tasks early in a task class; this support would include such techniques as *worked-out examples,* which have been shown to reduce cognitive load (Sweller et al., 1998), or an expert performing a task while simultaneously doing a think-aloud explaining the problem-solving processes behind task performance. By the time learners reach the final learning task, support has been faded out. This pattern of scaffolding and fading support is repeated for each subsequent task class.

One reason for fading support in across task sequences in technology-based training is the so-called **expertise reversal effect** (Kalyuga, Ayres, Chandler, & Sweller, 2003; van Merriënboer & Sweller, 2005). Simply put, supports (e.g., coaching) and instructional methods (e.g., small, incremental steps) that work well for novices can actually have negative effects for more advanced learners. For instance, worked examples, which generally are useful for novices, can become redundant for advanced learners and actually increase cognitive load. Noting the existence of the expertise reversal effect in use of worked examples, Renkl and Atkinson (2003) have recommended a *fading guidance* approach, in which, say, multiple examples might be provided and self-explanations heavily prompted early on in training. These then would gradually yield to activities more suitable for advanced learners, such as imagining solution steps and actual problem solving.

The second and third components of the 4C/ID model are *supportive information* and *just-in-time (JIT) information.* These two types of information play different roles in developing complex skills using technology. To understand these roles, we need to revisit a distinction made earlier in our text between controlled and automatic information processing (see Chapter 2). As you recall, *controlled processes* are effortful, error-prone, easily overloaded, and require focused attention. They basically are equivalent to *schemata* (see Chapter 3). In contrast, *automatic processes* correspond to *procedures* (see Chapter 3); they occur with little or no effort, are data-driven, and require little or no conscious attention. In the 4C/ID framework, the schema-like controlled processes are called **nonrecurrent skills** (van Merriënboer & Kirschner, 2007; see also Chapter 3), and the procedure-like automatic processes are called **recurrent skills.**

Nonrecurrent and recurrent skills together comprise complex cognitive skills; that is, complex cognition consists of both controlled and automatic processes. From the standpoint of the 4C/ID model, the primary challenge in developing complex cognition is to refine and automate *nonrecurrent skills.* Learners need them because schemata represent the powerful generalized knowledge required to solve new, unfamiliar problems (van Merriënboer & Kirschner, 2007). But complex skills also depend on automatically executing production-like recurrent skills. The main instructional goal for these is to automate them as much and as rapidly as possible.

Returning to the second and third components of 4C/ID model, instructional technology systems need to provide *supportive information* to help learners master the *nonrecurrent* aspects of complex cognitive tasks. Supportive information provides a bridge between learners' prior knowledge and the learning tasks. In our example of an online course intended to develop photography expertise, supportive information early in instruction might include analogies between the camera and the eye; between a photo essay and a story; or computer-presented illustrations of high and low-contrast scenes, showing changes in how clearly objects can be viewed against varying backgrounds. Similarly, in a computer-based system for developing novice physicians' diagnostic skills, supportive information might include a computer-presented "guided tour" highlighting key dimensions of a hypothetical patient's lab work and symptoms, or a video clip of an experienced physician talking her way through a diagnosis.

The goal of supportive information is to help learners acquire the kinds of flexible schemata needed to cope with the varied problems of real life. Because schemata are formed and refined through a process of induction, the best route to nonrecurrent skill development is experience with a series of authentic learning tasks. According to van Merriënboer and Kirschner (2007), a series of progressively more complex problems, coupled with supportive information and learner reflection, is likely to achieve this goal.

In contrast to supportive information, *JIT information* is aimed at the *recurrent* aspects of complex skills. JIT information promotes recurrent skill automation. Recall that recurrent skills are performed almost identically in many different problem situations and that automaticity depends heavily on consistent, repetitive practice. JIT information gives learners the step-by-step guidance required to perform recurrent skills and, as the name implies, is provided as needed. It then is quickly faded. For our medical students, for example, JIT information might include specific prompts on how to use a stethoscope to listen for and recognize certain clinical symptoms or to efficiently gather basic clinical data, such as heart rate, blood pressure, and respiration—all recurrent skills. The goal is to make these basic, but critical, skills as automatic as possible as soon as possible, freeing cognitive resources for the nonrecurrent, problem-solving dimensions of medical diagnosis.

The fourth and final component of the 4C/ID model is *part-task practice*. Although computer-based instructional systems can develop both nonrecurrent and recurrent skills, we know that a great deal of practice is needed to achieve automaticity. Experienced photojournalists, for instance, can respond very rapidly to new and changing conditions without attending consciously to subskills (e.g., without thinking about framing shots, depth of field, and lighting). Similarly, we want medical personnel to concentrate on diagnostic problem solving leading to treatment, not thinking about how to perform basic skills.

As described in Chapter 8, expertise is ordinarily a slow-developing process that depends on extended practice to automatize the productions that directly control behavior. Part-task practice is a way of automatizing procedural knowledge more rapidly, while circumventing some of the cognitive load problems resulting when learners try to develop skills while simultaneously trying to solve a problem. In our example of the online photography course, novices might take part in a simulation of the steps involved in making a print, practicing the steps repeatedly. Their practice would be supported by appropriate JIT information until automaticity had been achieved. Medical students might practice listening to heartbeats and respiration sounds using a simulation where they could vary stethoscope placements until they were able to gather information quickly and without error.

van Merriënboer and his associates do not recommend that instructional sequences contain large amount of part-task practice but argue that some part-task practice can help reduce task complexity. If part-task practice is used, they advise relatively short and spaced periods of it intermixed with work on complex, authentic tasks. This pattern provides both the opportunity to practice subskills and relate them to the overall task (van Merriënboer & Kirschner, 2007).

Summary of the 4C/ID Model

The 4C/ID model, which is based on research on cognitive learning and expertise, provides a framework for designing technology systems for developing complex skills. According to the model, learners' primary experiences should be with realistic and increasingly more authentic tasks, such as projects, cases, and scenarios. Instruction should focus on practice, not information giving. The primary goal of training is schema construction and refinement, which are developed by working on varied, authentic tasks. At the same time, training systems need to develop the automated skills essential to any complex cognitive activity. Information provided to the learner must be tailored to the kind of learning taking place. Supportive information, such as coaching and modeling, aids in schema development, while JIT information, such as online help and pop-up menus, promotes automaticity. Research continues on such 4C/ID-related topics as the timing of information presentation, presentation modalities, and optimizing step sizes (see van Merriënboer et al., 2002; van Merriënboer & Kirschner, 2007).

Technology Supports for Metacognitive Development

As educational technologies become more sophisticated, there is increased interest among motivational and cognitive scientists in ways computers can be used to advance students' metacognitive and self-regulatory processes (Azevedo, 2005; Berthold, Nückles, & Renkl, 2007; Graesser, McNamara, & VanLehn, 2005; Moos & Azevedo, 2008; Winne, 2006; van Merriënboer & Kirschner, 2007; Zimmerman & Tsikalas, 2005). This research suggests that well-designed computer programs not only can produce deep learning outcomes but also can scaffold such metacognitive processes as goal setting, elaborating information, and monitoring learning progress. As Graesser et al. (2005) point out, students in normal classrooms or even in one-on-one tutoring sessions seldom spontaneously exhibit deep learning approaches such as inquiry and explanation-centered learning. As a consequence, there are a growing number of attempts to build computer-based environments that scaffold metacognitive processes associated with deep learning.

Examples of these environments include AutoTutor, developed by Graesser and his associates (e.g., Graesser et al., 2005a; Graesser, Person, Lu, Jeon, & McDaniel, 2005b); McNamara and associates' *iSTART* (e.g., McNamara, O'Reilly, Rowe, Boonthum, & Levinstein, 2007); and Betty's Brain from Biswas and associates (Biswas, Leelawong, Schwartz, Vye, and the Teachable Agents Group at Vanderbilt, 2005; Leelawong & Biswas, 2008). These and other programs incorporate multiple sophisticated technical features, such as computational linguistic modules for speech recognition, simulation and animation subprograms, and techniques such as latent semantic analysis (LSA) for representing and evaluating student knowledge. AutoTutor employs animated conversational agents that interact with students in natural language to guide inquiry, metacognition, and deep explanations. The iSTART program, used for developing reading comprehension strategies in high school and college students (Magliano, Todaro, Millis, Wiemer-Hastings, Kim, & McNamara, 2005; McNamara et al., 2007), teaches them to self-explain text meaning and use comprehension monitoring, inferencing, and elaboration strategies. Animated pedagogical agents model reading strategies and offer practice and feedback on self-explanations. Betty's Brain (Biswas et al., 2005; Leelawong & Biswas, 2008) supports student decision making about learning, structured knowledge development, and reflective skills. A unique feature of this program is that it uses teachable agents—that is, computer agents that students teach and, in the process, learn the content themselves.

Research shows that programs like these have considerable promise in their ability to instantiate key conditions of learning. Much like expert human tutoring, which has significant advantages over classroom instruction (Graesser et al., 2005b), they offer individualized coaching that includes modeling, assessment, and feedback on learning strategies. As such programs are further refined, they should become increasingly capable of helping learners acquire both complex content and the effective learning strategies that are the mark of the active, self-reflective learner.

Computer-Supported Collaborative Learning

The previous three sections provide excellent examples of how cognitive principles can inform educational technology design. Good technology design takes into account both the ways our cognitive system works (e.g., attention, working memory, and long-term memory) and how complex cognitive skills develop (e.g., need for supportive and JIT information; coaching and scaffolding for effective learning strategies). Good design works with, rather than against, our cognitive systems, promoting active processing but not overloading working memory.

Understanding how technology can affect individual cognition, however, is only part of the picture. Another area of growing interest is how technology can support learning in groups. Consider, for example, the following questions:

- How can technology be used to help students collaborate?
- What kinds of learner collaborations best promote individual and group learning?
- Can diverse viewpoints shared via technology serve as learning resources?

Questions like these focus on the social dimension of technology use and are closely tied to one of our book's primary themes—that social interaction is fundamental to cognitive growth. They are consistent with the *social cognitive point of view* discussed in Chapter 9, which stresses the key role of social interactions in developing knowledge and thought. Student collaborations and productive exchanges between teachers and students are among the most important of these. But how can technology facilitate such interactions?

Two influential early projects provide good illustrations of classroom-oriented applications of technology to support collaborative learning. These projects have foreshadowed today's strong interest in computer-supported collaborative learning (CSCL). The first, called *Adventures of Jasper Woodbury,* is an instructional series developed by Bransford and his associates aimed at improving the mathematical thinking of middle school students. The second is *CSILE* (Computer Supported Intentional Learning Environment), developed by Bereiter and Scardamalia and their associates at the University of Toronto. Each has been widely used and illustrates innovative uses of a technology system based on cognitive and social cognitive learning principles.

The Adventures of Jasper Woodbury Series

Tapping the growing emergence of social cognitive theory in the early 1990s, the Cognition and Technology Group at Vanderbilt (CTGV) developed an extended problem-based curriculum called the *Adventures of Jasper Woodbury* (the *Jasper* series). Each of a dozen *Jasper* adventures revolves around a complex math-oriented problem requiring extended effort to solve. Because of the problems' complexity (some contain more than a dozen subproblems), they are difficult to solve alone and so students need to work together in problem solving. *Jasper's* primary goals were to develop students' ability to reason, think critically, reflect, argue, and learn independently. Its approach was *anchored instruction* (CTGV, 1997); the "anchors" in *Jasper* were complex, video-based problems for students to solve. Because anchors typically had more than one right answer, students had to evaluate and defend their ideas as they searched for solutions.

For example, one of the *Jasper* adventures, *Rescue at Boone's Meadow,* focuses on concepts of distance, rate, and time. *Rescue* begins with Jasper's friend Larry teaching another friend, Emily, how to fly an ultralight plane. Jasper and his friends also discuss his planned fishing and camping trip to a remote area, Boone's Meadow, which he will reach by hiking in. As the adventure moves ahead, important *embedded data* are introduced—facts and numbers that will become critical later, such as who knows how to fly the ultralight, their weight, the plane's weight, its payload and gas consumption, the location and accessibility of Boone's Meadow, and so on. Having data like these meant that when students were trying to solve problems, they had to engage in reasoned decision making, not just exchange opinions.

The situation unfolds when Jasper, now on his camping trip, hears a gunshot, discovers a wounded eagle, and radios for help. In a complex scenario in which additional embedded data are revealed (e.g., speed limits on nearby highways and the weight of the bald eagle, around 15 pounds!), learners come to the central problem: Emily needs to find the quickest feasible way to get the eagle to Dr. Ramirez, a veterinarian in Cumberland City. Many solutions to this problem are possible, such as various people walking, driving, and flying the ultralight. Obviously, students would have to consider many different kinds of data, estimate such things as fuel consumption and travel time, and solve several subproblems in order to make the best choices about how to reach and transport the eagle.

Anchors like *Rescue at Boone's Meadow* foster many kinds of communication and forms of problem solving. These were expanded by extending *Jasper's* design to include such approaches as a video series to link teachers and students across classrooms and schools, Internet-based feedback, and software tools for representing and visualizing information.

Multiple evaluations have shown that the knowledge of basic mathematical concepts (e.g., figuring area and decimals) of *Jasper* students typically is about the same as matched non-*Jasper* students, which would be expected since *Jasper* does not focus on specific math skills. But students in *Jasper* score better in word problems testing transfer; in identifying what needs to be considered in complex problems (e.g., answering questions like "What does Casey need to think about to figure out how long her trip will take?"); in problem subgoal comprehension (e.g., answering a question like "Why did Casey divide the distance from Broken Bow to Ainsworth by the speed she'll be driving?"); and in their attitudes toward math and its utility (CTGV, 1997).

CSILE/Knowledge Forum: A Collaborative Approach to Knowledge-Building

CSILE (Computer Supported Intentional Learning Environments) was designed by University of Toronto researchers to create a group-based multimedia environment to support inquiry, information search, and collaborative improvement of ideas. The goal was to form a **knowledge-building community,** a group of individuals dedicated to sharing and advancing the group's knowledge. Scientific research teams are good examples of knowledge-building communities; others might be company marketing teams, graduate research seminars, or film societies (Hewitt & Scardamalia, 1998; Scardamalia & Bereiter, 1994).

First developed in the late 1980s and deployed on networked computers, CSILE provided a collaborative environment in which students could enter text and notes, including graphics, about the topic under study. They also could read and comment on each other's notes, in the process building their own and others' knowledge. CSILE's design allowed students to easily generate "nodes" containing ideas, notes, and references tied to whatever topics are being studied and to interact with their classmates about these ideas. This feature basically consisted of a multimedia database containing the ongoing research of the class on a particular topic.

CSILE has been reengineered in recent years as an Internet-based commercial application called *Knowledge Forum* (Scardamalia, 2003, Scardamalia & Bereiter, 2006; Zhang, Scardamalia, Lamon, Messina, & Reeve, 2007). *Knowledge Forum* retains the CSILE's key features—serving as a repository for student ideas and questions and providing a forum for exchanging ideas. As in earlier versions, students build on their classmates' ideas and questions, reference each other's work, and reorganize information in the database. The system's graphics capabilities support structural dimensions of knowledge building; for example, a "views" feature provides graphical organizers for notes. Notes can be added in one or more views, clustered together, and moved around to represent different organizing frameworks. *Knowledge Forum* also provides scaffolds, supports for analysis of texts, theory building, and debating.

Knowledge Forum embodies a number of important **design principles** for collaborative uses of technology, starting with the principle that effective peer interactions can improve inquiry into complex ideas. Another is that requiring students to come to a shared understanding stimulates them to pay attention to each other, answer each others' questions, and clarify their ideas. The technology offers opportunities to see and closely examine other students' work, a relatively rare occurrence in most classrooms. For example, students can see which notes are highly connected and which are not (Zhang et al., 2007). Students also can use a search capability to retrieve and organize their own or classmates' notes. Among the key roles *Knowledge Forum* teachers play are highlighting interesting student work and encouraging them to explore the system's database. They also remind students that, in order to make a real contribution to the group's mission, they need to know what the group knows.

Programs such as *Jasper* and CSILE/*Knowledge Forum* continue to be instructive models for design of computer-supported collaborative learning. Explicitly based on cognitive and social cognitive principles, their goal is student collaboration and deep understanding. Both rest on the assumption that when students interact on issues important to them, deep learning will result. Anchors, which are *Jasper's* focal point, are challenging, complex, multidimensional problems designed to generate problem-solving and communication activities. CSILE/*Knowledge Forum*, in contrast, begins with an empty knowledge base, but seeds it with an issue or issues that become the hub of information gathering, inquiry, and discussion. Both of these systems strongly emphasize learner contributions—the information they have gathered, their perspectives on that information, and their reactions to others' viewpoints. Each uses technology to stimulate individual cognitive growth through the participation and growing sophistication of a community of learners.

As Internet-based technologies continue to improve, CSCL has emerged as an identifiable branch of the learning sciences focused specifically on how people learn together with computer support (e.g., Stahl et al., 2006). New collaborative programs also continue to appear. In Linn's WISE (Web-based Inquiry Science Environment) project (Linn, 2005; Slotta, 2004), for example, students respond to scientific controversies, such as global warming or recycling. With students working together in a Web-based environment and teachers playing a supportive role, WISE provides evidence and hints about the topic; notes, visualization, discussion, and assessment tools; and prompts for collaboration, reflection, and design of solutions.

Although CSCL offers avenues to deep learning, challenges remain. Flexible, theory-based collaboration systems such as *Jasper, Knowledge Forum,* and WISE typically have been developed within large research projects and have been more widely available for research than for general use. Even though commercial course management systems such as *Blackboard* with collaboration-supporting features are used extensively, their collaborative dimensions tend to be underutilized, as instructors typically use them primarily to post information such as syllabi and course resources (Ansorge & Bendus, 2003). In general, online teaching offers excellent opportunities for collaborative learning, but building collaborative dimensions into courses requires both a strong commitment and skillful integration of curriculum, collaborative teaching methods, and technology (Stahl et al., 2006).

Technology and Assessment

Computers have played an important role in assessment for many years, most obviously in standardized testing, which is supported by such technology-dependent activities as automated test scoring, item analysis software, and online applications of item response theory (the basis for automated item selection in computerized test administrations). Technological support for classroom assessment has lagged, however, perhaps because the barriers to it are formidable.

Creating a technology tool to assess and give feedback on student writing, for instance, not only requires highly advanced computer technologies but also deep understanding of the underlying linguistic and cognitive theories. At this point, both domains mostly have been beyond our reach and so we continue, as have generations of educators, to be constrained by time and energy limitations in our desire to provide rich feedback.

Recent research and development, however, give indication that this is likely to change—if not immediately, then in the not-distant future. Techniques such as latent semantic analysis (LSA, Landauer & Dumais, 1997) are being used in testing and computerized tutoring to represent text meanings and gauge comprehension (e.g., Graesser, et al., 2005b; Magliano, Millis, & McNamara, 2003, McNamara, Levinstein, & Boonthum, 2004; Millis, Magliano, & Todaro, 2006; Srihari et al., 2008). Utilizing complex statistical procedures, LSA can provide indices of semantic similarity of texts, for example, between a student's essay and a set of hand-scored essays. LSA-based automated scoring techniques have been shown to match the accuracy of human judgments of such variables as essay grades, text coherence, and document similarity.

In research hinting at future uses of technology to assess complex cognitive processes, Millis et al. (2006) had undergraduates make comprehension-related comments sentence-by-sentence as they read scientific texts (e.g., *The Origin of Coal*). These comments then were matched by LSA to (1) the current sentence being read and (2) other, earlier sentences, previously judged either to be immediate (local) or distant (distal) causes of the current sentence. Millis et al. posited that, because comprehending science texts requires understanding causal relationships, student comments showing ties to distal causes would be evidence for higher comprehension, while comments focused on the current sentence would not. This in fact was what the data showed. Reading comprehension—as measured independently—was highest when students talked more about causal ties to the current sentence than about the sentence itself. In this way an automated technology-based approach can provide an index of whether students comprehend what they are reading.

In research exploring practical uses of technology in assessment, Srihari et al. (2008) assembled a system of advanced technologies to test the feasibility of automated scoring of handwritten student essays. The technologies chosen included some for document imaging and recognition (e.g., to recognize and read children's handwritten words), and others (e.g., LSA) for automated essay scoring. When used on handwritten fifth and eighth graders' essays from a statewide reading comprehension test, the computer-based system provided a good match to human scoring and to scoring based on perfect transcriptions, evidence for the practicality of automated scoring of children's handwritten documents.

As these technologies and their theoretical foundations in cognitive science and linguistics continue to advance, one can envision future conversational computer-based assessment and tutoring systems providing intelligent feedback to students about what they say and write. Other systems can be foreseen that prompt student note taking about what they're reading and give students feedback on the quality of their notes or summaries. Still others might provide students with detailed reactions to their idea development and organization as they write an essay. While classroom and home uses of such systems still lie in the future, it seems highly likely that they will become available to offer students and teachers much needed assistance.

Implications for Instruction

We began this chapter by describing technology's uses in education and outlining key cognitive skills that can help students take advantage of technology. Cognitive theory is essential for judging whether specific uses of technology by either individuals or groups are likely to facilitate learning and cognitive growth. The following implications draw on this discussion, with special emphasis on work of Atkinson and Renkl (2007), Clark (2003), Graesser et al. (2005a), and Merrill (2000):

1. *Use cognitive principles as criteria for judging technology-based instruction.* As technology-based educational applications rapidly multiply, educators increasingly need to make informed decisions about their purchase and use. Market forces will ensure that virtually all educational technologies will be attractively designed and function well. The key questions for educators, however, should be whether programs will produce desired student learning, motivation, strategic behaviors, and metacognitive development. Does a technology-based program targeted at beginning readers, for example, represent a solid literacy curriculum and will its activities produce meaningful learning? Does it scaffold appropriate activities and meaningful student decisions? Are its demonstrations clear and screens designed to avoid excessive cognitive load? Does its content connect appropriately to children's prior knowledge? Questions like these are essential for distinguishing between computer-based instruction of dubious educational value that merely entertains and instruction that will develop important knowledge and skills.

2. *Emphasize technology's sense-making uses.* From a cognitive perspective, technology's best uses are those that produce meaningful learning. Technology provides a resource for achieving such cognitively oriented goals as finding and organizing information, discussing and refining concepts, and presenting ideas. For example, students working on a group project in an eleventh-grade environmental studies class might use Google, Bing, or another search engine to look for the latest information from the Centers for Disease Control and Prevention for a project focusing on Lyme disease, put state-by-state data into a spreadsheet, graph the growth of cases by region since 2007, share this information with other members of their working group to get their reactions, and create pages for the school Web site, perhaps even including some animations. Booklets could be created using publishing software, along with a Keynote presentation for parents' night. Activities like these—each involving significant technology use—are likely to produce deeper learning because students aren't just looking at information, they are making sense of it by using it and communicating it to others.

3. *Support authentic, challenging tasks with technology.* Long-term projects in which technology is used to accomplish project tasks can create many opportunities for extended, motivated intellectual activity. Tasks focusing on learning by doing, with information supporting skilled performance, are most likely to produce complex cognitive skills (van Merriënboer et al., 2002; van Merriënboer & Kirschner, 2007). Having students work on such tasks moves teachers away from the role of information presenter toward coaching and guidance roles, where they can help students develop habits of goal setting, monitoring, and reflection that lead to cognitive growth.

4. *Use technology to create and support collaborative learning communities.* Technology can provide a hub for learner interactions—planning collaboratively, sharing ideas across workgroups and classrooms, building on each other's ideas, getting feedback from classmates, and presenting ideas. These interactions, which focus on important content and data and take place over extended periods, are the building blocks for learning communities and create a context for cognitive growth.

5. *Use technology as appropriate to provide practice and feedback.* Many current commercial instructional programs—especially those designed for students with learning, language, and reading difficulties—focus on skill development through practice. Although there is a legitimate worry about "drill and kill," where students endlessly practice skills of dubious value, the computer actually can be an ideal partner for some kinds of practice (see van Merriënboer & Kirschner, 2007). Technology can present information, prompt responses, and give feedback to learners—all without tiring. For example, in a software application developed by one of the present authors, preservice teachers can practice judging samples of children's writing. As they rate multiple writing samples from different grades on several criteria and receive expert feedback on their ratings, they not only learn to accurately judge the quality of student writing, but also build their self-efficacy for making student writing a part of their future instruction (Dempsey, PytlikZillig, & Bruning, 2005, 2009).

6. *Help disabled students access and make use of assistive technologies.* Assistive technology can provide the critical support many disabled students require to achieve success. While assistive technologies cannot remove the difficulties that come with having a disability, they can assist students in meeting many classroom challenges. A rapidly growing number of versatile and powerful assistive technologies are available, ranging from tools for organizing information to speech recognition and text-to-speech conversion programs that increase opportunities for those with literacy-related disabilities to achieve classroom success.

Summary

This chapter is about new technologies, cognitive psychology's relationship to them, and their utility for learning and teaching. The chapter begins by exploring ways students can use technology and outlines key cognitive skills they need to take advantage of it. Several cognitive theories and sets of related research are discussed in relation to technology design and use. Among them are cognitive load theory, which focuses on working memory; the 4C/ID model, which is a cognitively based design framework for developing complex skills; metacognitive and self-regulated learning theory, which supports designs that scaffold goal setting and monitoring processes; and social cognitive theory, which informs many features of CSCL. Whereas cognitive load theory, the 4C/ID model, and metacognitive theory most directly apply to individual learning, social cognitive theory focuses on interactions among learners and provides a framework for creating technology-based learning communities. The chapter concludes with sections on technology as a growing factor in assessment and a section describing implications aimed at helping teachers and students use technology effectively.

SUGGESTED READINGS

Clark, R. (2003). Research on Web-based learning: A half-full glass. In R. Bruning, C. Horn, & L. PytlikZillig (Eds.), *Web-based learning: What do we know? Where do we go?* Greenwich, CT: Information Age.

Richard Clark, a leading authority on learning outcomes and multimedia, analyzes a number of claims about Web-based learning in light of what research actually shows.

Moreno, R. (2005). Instructional technology: Promise and pitfalls. In L. M. PytlikZillig, M. Bodvarsson, & R. Bruning (Eds.), *Technology-based education: Bringing researchers and practitioners together.* Greenwich, CT: Information Age.

In this chapter, Roxana Moreno presents an expansion of her and Richard Mayer's cognitive-affective theory of learning with media, along with 10 principles derived from their research for guiding the design of instructional multimedia.

van Merriënboer, J. J. G., Clark, R. E., & de Croock, M. B. M. (2002). Blueprints for complex learning: The 4C/ID model. *Educational Technology Research and Development, 54 (1),* 39–64.

This article, which gave wider dissemination to the 4C/ID model, provides a fine overview of how complex skills can be analyzed and how instructional technology systems should be designed for developing complex skills.

van Merriënboer, J. J. G., & Kirschner, P. (2007). *Ten steps to complex learning: A systematic approach to four-component instructional design.* Mahwah, NJ: Erlbaum.

Written to give guidance to designers of complex multimedia training, this book details 10 steps embedded in the 4C/ID model that designers should take to move from a training problem to a technology-based training solution.

11 Learning to Read

At first glance, learning to read seems straightforward. Words have meanings; becoming a reader, therefore, means learning to make straightforward translations from symbols to thought or to speech. Yet when explored more deeply, reading reveals itself to be a complex domain resting on an understanding of language and the world in which linguistic and cognitive factors interact.

Through reading, we can make contact with the thoughts and imaginations of people far removed from us in time and space; we can learn from them and share their feelings. These functional qualities are the reason that reading is so important. Because it gives children entry into the literate world, learning to read marks an important transition point. We begin early, teaching first graders to read, and reading soon becomes instrumental for achievement in other areas of study. Without the ability to read, a child's likelihood of success in virtually any area of the school curriculum is seriously diminished. Reading's importance extends well beyond school, of course. Reading is crucial to most jobs and a significant source of information and pleasure for many adults. In this chapter, the first of three on literacy, we describe the basic linguistic and cognitive processes involved in reading and how these processes interact in beginning reading.

We begin the chapter with an examination of the linguistic and cognitive prerequisites of reading. We show that although reading is complex, its complexity does not make it incomprehensible. We then explore the relatively brief period during which children make the transition to becoming readers. In this section, we describe how children consolidate their growing knowledge about language sounds and print, moving from prereaders to "experts" who can decode unfamiliar words accurately and understand what they have read. Finally, we conclude with a discussion of beginning literacy instruction, highlighting literacy teaching methods and materials and summarizing key issues in the sometimes-heated debates over how best to teach beginning reading.

Literacy's Foundations in Language Development

More than a quarter-century of research on language development has shown it to be an extraordinarily interesting and productive research area. This research not only has given us a fascinating account of children's language acquisition (e.g., see Crystal, 1997) but also revealed how closely language development and literacy are intertwined. As a consequence, to better understand literacy development, literacy researchers now regularly study language-related phenomena as diverse as children's awareness of print's uses and the nature of classroom discussions. This research has shown that literacy is closely linked with children's social uses of language in their homes, communities, and schools (Purcell-Gates, 1996; Purcell-Gates, Duke, & Martineau, 2007; Sulzby, 1991).

By first grade, children's ability to perceive and use language is impressive. Their language skills have been developing rapidly since the second year of their lives; for example, many first graders will have extensive vocabularies of 5,000 or more words (Chall, Jacobs, & Baldwin, 1990). They also have a solid command of the mechanics of their native language and can use it to communicate effectively, but literacy requires them to become explicitly aware of their own and others' language use. Acquiring metacognitive knowledge (see Chapter 4) about language—called **metalinguistic awareness**—is a key to children's transition into literacy.

Although virtually every student has the basic linguistic capacity to learn to read and write, students in most classrooms typically will vary in their language backgrounds and metalinguistic awareness in ways that affect their progress toward literacy. Mixed in with differences in competence and rapid developmental changes are significant variations in the ways children of different social and cultural backgrounds use language. For a growing number of children in the United States, learning to read may take place in a language other than their first one, which presents a significant challenge to teachers teaching children to read. To help in better understanding the nature of language-related factors and how they affect learning to read, we begin with an overview of the major dimensions of language. As children acquire knowledge about each of these, they not only are becoming a part of a language community but also are setting out on the road to literacy.

Dimensions of Language

Human languages are immensely complex systems of conventions that link symbols with meanings for the purpose of communication. In virtually all languages, the primary symbols are speech sounds. Human languages also are structured; they don't just randomly or idiosyncratically collect sounds into words, words into sentences, and sentences into larger units. Instead, at each level of structure, units combine meaningfully according to general organizational principles.

The starting points for most discussions of language are meanings and messages—the ways humans use it. These uses of language, which linguists refer to as **pragmatics,** are its most important feature. Because of their central role in human evolution and behavior, language pragmatics is of great interest to linguists and to a host of other scholars as diverse as geneticists and archeologists. The other major aspect of language is **language structure,** and we describe three important structural levels: (1) **words,** including word meanings (semantics) and how speech sounds are formed into words; (2) syntax, the combining of words into phrases, clauses, and sentences; and (3) discourse, the organizing of sentences into higher order units, such as paragraphs, stories, reports, and conversations (see Figure 11.1; see also Chapter 9 for details on classroom discussion as an example of discourse).

Pragmatics   Language is important to humans. It must be; we have had it for a very long time—100,000 years or more is a common estimate—and every one of the more than 5,000 human cultures has developed a highly complex language system. In contrast, no other species, including the great apes, seems to have more than rudimentary language capabilities. Language gives us a tremendous evolutionary advantage; it allows us to refer to things not directly observable by others ("Do you know what I saw today!?"), to describe the past ("I remember when she'd just started here . . . "), and to imagine and plan for the future ("Wouldn't it be fun to . . . ?"). The fact that language can be separated or *displaced* from events actually observed or experienced gives us the potential for abstract thinking and problem solving. Simply put, language is pragmatic in that it fulfills vital human needs and affects every aspect of our lives.

When we think about language, we often think about using it to communicate information. Virtually everything we're aware of knowing has been transmitted to us by language or interpreted through language, from our family stories to the scientific principles we read in our texts. Some have argued that the social and emotional pragmatic uses of language may be even more important than its cognitive use of communicating information. The everyday language accompanying our daily interactions with others may be far from profound, but it is vital for creating and maintaining our connections with our families, neighborhoods, and society. Talk supports ongoing work and play, and it conveys our feelings and values.

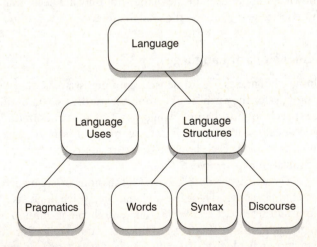

FIGURE 11.1   Language Uses and Structures.

Words: The Building Blocks of Language   Words are a key part of every language. We use a vast number to label, describe, and signal our intentions—as many as 40,000 a day, by one estimate (Locke, 1994). As you can imagine, the study of words and their meanings, called **semantics,** is of great interest to many scholars. For most of us, the most familiar area of semantics is vocabulary. Children seem to come by semantic knowledge naturally; once they start speaking, they acquire new vocabulary words at a remarkable rate—60 or more words a month. As we have seen earlier, the result is that most children enter school with vocabularies numbering in the thousands of words, which provide a tremendous resource for their literacy development.

Spoken words are formed from speech sounds. We humans vocalize an extraordinary variety of them, ranging from clicks, chirps, and babbling to our familiar vowels and consonants. These vocalizations, called **phones,** are the raw material of language. Out of the huge number of possible sounds, however, only a small subset—the **phonemes** of a language—are perceived as meaningful by speakers and listeners in that language. Each phoneme forms a kind of perceptual category that carries meaning (Crystal, 1997). English, for instance, has approximately 44 phonemes, and comprehending English speech depends on an individual distinguishing them from one another (e.g., hearing the difference between /l/ and /r/ lets us tell the difference between *load* and *road*) in order to access the meanings the sounds carry.

Each language has its own distinct set of phonemes, so although phonemes in different languages do overlap, one language's phonemes may not be phonemes in another. For instance, the sound /v/, which is a phoneme (has meaning) in English (e.g., *viper* and *wiper* are distinctly different words), is not a phoneme in the Thai language. As a consequence, native Thai speakers attempting to learn English words containing the sound /v/ (e.g., *divide*) may hear the English /v/ as the familiar phoneme /w/ (/w/ is a phoneme in Thai) and initially perceive and pronounce such words incorrectly (e.g., as *dewide*). They also would experience considerable difficulty distinguishing between two words differing only in these consonants. The tables are turned, of course, when English speakers encounter other languages. For instance, English speakers often experience difficulty perceiving phonemes that are meaningful in Spanish, Chinese, or Russian—differences obvious to native speakers of those languages but initially difficult or impossible for non-native speakers to perceive.

By the time children enter school, most have a sophisticated knowledge of their language's sound system. Recognizing sound patterns and meanings has been essential to their becoming members of a language and social community. Although their abilities to perceive and pronounce sounds are not fully mature, most children can accurately recognize and produce their language's sound segments. Their pronunciation and intonation patterns also are close to those of adults. Yet as we previously stated, learning to read depends on *metalinguistic* capabilities, many of which are only in their beginning developmental stages when children start school.

One of the most important metalinguistic capabilities—**phonemic awareness**—is the understanding that phonemes are individual and separable speech sounds and being able to manipulate them. At age 4, few children know that words can be broken down into phonemic segments; by age 6, most are beginning to show some degree of phonemic awareness (Nation & Hulme, 1997). In alphabetic languages such as English and Spanish, where letters represent sounds, phonemic awareness is crucial to learning how to read and write (e.g., Durand, Hulme,

Larkin, & Snowling, 2005). For instance, phonemic awareness is involved in understanding how sounds are combined to form words (e.g., *"Cuh-ah-tuh . . . CAT"*) and how specific words are similar or different in sound structure (e.g., *How are MAT and SAT alike? How are they different?*).

Learning to read requires connecting this metalinguistic understanding about oral language to written symbols—letters, words, and sentences. Making this connection requires that students also understand the **alphabetic principle**—that written letters and letter combinations represent phonemes and that letter-sound relationships are used in decoding written words. In learning to read, students need to not only identify and label letters and the phonemes they represent, knowing that printed letters and letter combinations represent sounds, but also need to segment, rearrange, and substitute phonemes for each other (Adams, 1990; Byrne & Fielding-Barnsley, 1991, 1993, 1995; Ehri, 2005; Stanovich, 2000; Vellutino, Tunmer, Jaccard, & Chen, 2007).

Although learning English letter–sound relationships is a significant challenge for most children, it is not impossible. The relationship of spelling to sound in English is complex but not arbitrary. Especially for words of Anglo-Saxon origin, which are some of the oldest and most common words in the English language (e.g., *eat, drink, sleep, work, play, nose, mouth, mother,* and *father* all have Anglo-Saxon roots), pronunciations are mostly predictable. For this reason, beginning reading instruction often focuses on this group of words.

Another language concept important for beginning reading is the **morpheme.** Whereas phonemes are the minimal meaningful distinctions in language sounds, morphemes are sounds or combinations of sounds that are the minimal units of meaning (Crystal, 1997). English words are made up of one or more morphemes. For example, the word *cat* is a single morpheme. The word *joyfully,* in contrast, is a combination of three morphemes, joy + ful + ly, each corresponding to the basic units making up the word and each conveying a dimension of the word's meaning. Each of the three morphemes in *joyfully* conveys a dimension of meaning of the word. The root word *joy* has a meaning of itself; adding -*ful* to the noun joy converts it to its adjectival form; and adding-*ly* to *joyful* transforms it to its adverbial form. Only certain combinations of morphemes are possible in a given language; for instance, native speakers of English know immediately that utterances such as *fuljoy, joylyful,* and *joyly* are not real English words. English **morphology** allows only a few of a near-infinite number of possibilities.

Like metalinguistic knowledge about language sounds, metalinguistic knowledge about morphology is vital to literacy (e.g., see Kuo & Anderson, 2006), which requires that children break words into syllables and other meaningful parts in order to comprehend and write them. For example, children have acquired important morphological knowledge when they learn that many English words are made up of chunks that can be combined (RAIN + COAT = RAINCOAT), divided (UNCOVER = UN + COVER), and even redivided (UNCOVER = UN + COV + ER). As is true for each dimension of language, children already have extensive morphological capabilities on which to build a metalinguistic understanding of morphology. They have been using morphological rules from the time they were toddlers—adding markers such as -*s* and -*ed* for pluralization and tense soon after their speech moved beyond the single-word level. In their speech, young children first tend to overapply their growing morphological knowledge (e.g., two *sheepses* and she *goed* home) but gradually move to more mature forms. In literacy, developing morphological awareness is likewise complex and contextual; learning its basics begins early, but mastering its subtleties continues throughout the entire period of formal schooling and beyond.

Words Combined: The Syntax of a Language   At the next higher level of language structure is **syntax**—the organization of words into larger units, such as phrases, clauses, and sentences. The study of syntax (and the related topic of grammar) has long been a major emphasis in linguistics, but especially so after the publication of Noam Chomsky's landmark books *Syntactic Structures* and *Aspects of the Theory of Syntax* (Chomsky, 1957, 1965). These books transformed the way linguists looked at language learning, especially at how syntactical knowledge is acquired and used. Chomsky took a strongly nativist position, arguing that much syntactical knowledge is "hardwired" in human beings and that children only partially acquire syntactic structures through learning processes such as modeling and feedback.

In most languages, syntactic information is vital to comprehension. Syntactic speech is closely linked with propositional thought (see Chapter 3); propositions ordinarily cannot be understood except through their expression in syntactic structures. For instance, the information contained in the syntax of the sentence *The horse kicked Eddie* is essential to knowing what the sentence is saying; that is, to the encoding of the proposition underlying the sentence. Obviously, the sentences *Eddie kicked the horse* and *The horse kicked Eddie* carry very different meanings!

Syntactic regularity appears early in children's speech, even earlier than morphology; children use consistent word order as soon as they begin to use two-word sequences (Brown, 1973; Guasti, 2002). The ability to reflect on and manipulate the internal structure of sentences does not develop until middle childhood, with syntactic development continuing well beyond the middle elementary grades. Because of this and the fact that primary-level students have difficulty comprehending sentences with complex syntax (e.g., *The cat that chased the butterfly around the yard of my Aunt Nellie's sister was orange and black*), most materials used in beginning reading instruction have simple grammatical structures.

Discourse Structure: Frameworks for Comprehension   Children's knowledge about the highest level of language structure—**discourse**—also is vital to their learning to read. In discourse, propositions take on a meaning in relation to one another, with references forward or backward affecting the meaning of individual elements. Even for children just learning to talk, word meanings are shaped by prior and subsequent utterances. Most everyday language is discourse. Classroom discussions are discourse. Writing and reading almost always involve extended discourse sequences; comprehension and building semantic knowledge depend on readers' abilities to tie discourse elements together. To do so, they must recognize, at least implicitly, the structure of stories and informational texts.

Two **discourse structures** of particular importance for literacy development are narratives and exposition. **Narratives** are "stories" structured by a temporal sequence of events. Most children begin to recognize narrative structure not long after they begin to use language (Applebee, 1983; McNamee, 1987) and use this knowledge to understand stories being read or told to them. Most first graders already know quite a bit about narrative structure. Here, for instance, is a story by a first grader that reflects her understanding of a narrative sequence:

> And then she got some ice cream.
> And then she put it in the cone.
> And then he . . . she went outside.

And a . . . the kitty-cat scared her.
And she dropped the cone.
And she looked real mad.

Many narratives, of course, are much more complex than this child's; they can range from a simple recounting like this one to complex plays, novels, and historical accounts. The essential feature of all narratives is a structure based on the temporal sequence of events. Narratives are episodic.

Exposition, in contrast with narratives, reflects the organization of abstract thought about a topic or a body of information. Although expository texts may contain narrative elements (and vice versa), exposition's basic structures are logical and informational, not temporal. Textbooks, essays, and persuasive arguments typically use expository structure. Because expository structure is based more on logical relations than on directly observed temporal associations, the belief that children's ability to comprehend exposition lags well behind their understanding of narratives has been widely held. Perhaps for this reason, the great majority of children's early reading instruction continues to be organized around narratives, not expository texts.

Research has shown, however, that young children actually know a considerable amount about expository text structure and respond positively to learning about that genre (e.g., Donovan, 1996; Duke & Kays, 1998; Pappas, 1993). This has led Duke and her colleagues (e.g., Duke, 2000; Duke, Bennett-Armistead, & Roberts, 2003; Palincsar & Duke, 2004) and others (e.g., Dreher, 2002) to argue for increased attention to informational texts in the early elementary grades. The challenge is considerable. In first grade classrooms that Duke (2000) studied, for example, she found less than 3% of print displayed and 10% of books in classroom libraries were informational. Percentages were even lower in lower social economic status classrooms. The total time per day spent on informational text writing averaged only 3.6 minutes. It may be that knowledge about exposition in the primary grades lags primarily because children are not exposed to it. Given the key role of expository reading to content-area learning (e.g., for understanding concepts and principles in social studies or science) beginning in the upper elementary grades and continuing through all of schooling, a greater emphasis on informational texts in the primary grades seems likely to pay excellent dividends.

Summary of Linguistic Prerequisites for Reading

Becoming literate represents a significant challenge. In reading and writing, children must link their oral language with a new, visual system of symbols. Children's language capabilities are a tremendous resource for literacy. Becoming literate, however, requires them also to develop metalinguistic capabilities—knowledge about the uses of print, how print represents sounds, how words are formed, how sentences are put together, and how sentences become stories or reports. Literacy both requires and enhances readers' knowledge about the abstract properties of language. For literate individuals, language itself becomes an object of awareness and analysis (Olson, 1994). Literacy changes the character of discourse, thought, and problem solving and gives us new ways of representing the world.

Table 11.1 presents a summary of several key metalinguistic abilities related to beginning reading. Most teachers of beginning reading see these abilities as essential. Yet direct skills

TABLE 11.1   **Some Metalinguistic Abilities Underlying Early Reading**

Pragmatic Abilities	
Print awareness	Understanding that print carries meaning; that reading is directional, represents objects or speech, has special words (e.g., *word, letter,* and *pronounce*) that describe literacy's features and activities
Word-Level Abilities	
Graphic awareness	Recognition of letter details (e.g., difference between *d* and *b*) and that words are composed of letters
Phonemic awareness	Ability to hear the separate sounds in words; recognition of words' similarities and differences; knowledge that spoken units can be analyzed and compared (e.g., *sh* and *ch*)
Awareness of grapheme/phoneme correspondence	Knowledge of the alphabetic principle that letters and sounds "go together;" ability to apply that knowledge to decoding unknown words
Morphological awareness	Capability of breaking words into their constituent parts; pronouncing syllables; combining word parts to form new words
Syntactic-Level Abilities	
Syntactic awareness	Recognition and use of clauses and sentence-level patterns; using within-sentence context of words (e.g., correctly pronouncing *read* in the sentence *The girl read the book*)
Discourse-Level Abilities	
Text-structure awareness	Comprehension of relationships between parts of text, including recognition of cohesive elements in text, general knowledge of text structures (e.g., narratives and exposition)

instruction on these and other aspects of reading without connecting them with each other and tying them to a meaningful literacy context does not seem to be a particularly good idea. If children are unable to connect the skills they are learning with the larger context of becoming literate, they can come to view reading as an incomprehensible set of fragmented tasks. A better approach is to teach skills systematically but always related them to the central purposes of reading—understanding and enjoying what is being read.

Becoming literate draws on many kinds of metalinguistic knowledge, but in alphabetic languages like English none is more important to beginning readers than *phonemic awareness,* the ability to notice, think about, and manipulate individual sounds in oral language. Developing students' phonemic awareness is an important goal in most early literacy instruction. A second goal for beginning reading instruction connects this knowledge with print—that students acquire the *alphabetic principle,* learning that individual letters and letter combinations represent speech sounds.

If instruction is poor or incomplete, the challenge of learning to read can be daunting. If all goes well, in the space of a few months children will reliably recognize the unfamiliar and highly abstract representations provided by printed letters and words and map them onto the oral language system they already possess. Researchers may differ on specific instructional methods (e.g., see discussion by Stahl, Duffy-Hester, & Stahl, 1998), but most generally agree that explicit teaching of decoding skills (generally called phonics instruction) is important.

Even though phonemic awareness can develop without instruction and some students will discover the alphabetic principle on their own—through immersion in literacy activities involving books, writing, storytelling, and the like—simple exposure is not enough for most children. Without teaching, acquiring the metalinguistic ability to analyze language sounds and to link them with an abstract symbol system is not a certainty, no matter how rich the linguistic environment. For most students, the process of becoming literate, while having many parallels to first language learning, requires instructional support. In particular, most children need explicit instruction in letter–sound relationships to move them as rapidly as possible to the meaning-making purpose of reading.

Cognitive Prerequisites of Learning to Read

Reading is a language-based activity that also involves constructing meaning from text. In this section, we highlight three cognitive factors on which children's success in learning to read depends: (1) world knowledge, (2) working and long-term memory capabilities, and (3) the ability to focus **attention.** These are not discrete, separable factors, of course; when readers read successfully, all of these dimensions operate at once and interact with linguistic knowledge. In discussing beginning reading, however, it is useful to separate them. Just as is true with children's language experience, some children may be better prepared on some dimensions than others. A beginning reader who has reasonably good skills overall may perform well on certain reading tasks but not on others requiring different knowledge or skills.

World Knowledge

We read to understand. This search for meaning—the process of comprehension—depends on both the writer and the reader. As we have stressed throughout this text, schema theory has had an especially important role in helping us better understand the nature of comprehension processes, including those in reading. To illustrate, let's turn again to a "piggy bank" passage, this one is considerably simpler than the one presented in Chapter 3:

> Toby wanted to get a birthday present for Chris. He went to his piggy bank. He shook it. There was no sound.

As you now recognize, the knowledge a young reader needs in order to comprehend even a brief passage like this is extensive. For instance, the reader must know that getting a birthday present means buying one, that Toby went to his piggy bank to get some money (the passage does not say so), that piggy banks contain money (the passage does not say so), that this money typically is in coin form, that coins in shaken piggy banks make noise, and that no rattling meant no money. For adults, comprehension comes without any special effort; we recognize all of this background information automatically (and mostly without consciously recognizing that we are doing so). Many primary-level students, however, have not had experience with piggy banks; with buying and giving presents; or, for that matter, with birthday parties. If any part of this knowledge is missing, the whole sequence of events in the passage can become incomprehensible. The main point of reading—getting meaning—would not be achieved by these students.

Our knowledge directs attention in reading, guides interpretations, and makes comprehension possible (Anderson, 1984; Ruddell, 1994). The meaning that an active reader constructs is not exactly what the author had in mind as he or she wrote the passage. Neither is it simply the reader's own mental constructions and inferences. As children read, they necessarily interpret words and events in terms of what they know. Children who have helped care for a garden by watering, cultivating, and feeding the plants and gathered produce from the garden, for example, would be much more likely to make sense of a story about, say, a young Chippewa girl who works with her father harvesting wild rice than children who have not had these kinds of experiences.

It is useful for teachers and parents to remind themselves that reading is a constructive process aimed at comprehension. Even when children mispronounce and misidentify words, teachers should continue to direct considerable attention to the meaning of what is being read. Although beginning readers undeniably need decoding skills, such as letter, sound, and word identification, these skills in themselves do not add up to reading. To focus solely on "skills" with beginning readers misses the main point of learning to read—getting meaning from what is read.

Working and Long-Term Memory Capabilities

Because it depends on world and linguistic knowledge, reading is an act of memory. A child fixating on a particular word, for instance, must keep that word in mind long enough to build up the more complex meaning of phrases, sentences, and whole passages. New meaning requires the continuing availability of earlier information; comprehension processes and reading performance depend on linking the meanings of words currently being processed and those processed earlier (Ruddell, 1994; Stanovich, 2000; Swanson, 1992, 2003; Swanson & Jerman, 2006).

As shown in Chapter 2, many studies have shown that human working memory is limited and often quite fragile. Young children's working memory capacity is especially restricted, most likely because they lack well-developed skills for encoding and rehearsal (e.g., Pressley & Schneider, 1997). For example, the number of digits a 5-year-old can recall from a single presentation is only four or so (Dempster, 1981), compared with seven for an adult. If the number of digits presented is greater than this amount, the immediate memory span is exceeded and all or most of the information will be lost.

Yet reading consists of sequential encounters with related, not isolated, elements. Letters are clustered into meaningful words, words into phrases and sentences, and sentences into text. Although it might appear that information encountered while reading would quickly exceed children's immediate memory span (e.g., after they have read five or six words), it ordinarily does not. When words and sentences make sense, readers can use their semantic and syntactic knowledge to "chunk" information or, perhaps more accurately, to convert it into *propositions* (see Chapter 3). In reading, words are part of meaningful patterns, not discrete, isolated units.

Both working and long-term memory processes are needed to make reading meaningful; constructing meaning depends on their interaction. New information must be "kept alive" in working memory while previously encountered information is drawn from long-term memory. With this interaction in mind, some researchers who have examined reading from a memory perspective (e.g., Breznitz & Share, 1992; Swanson, 1992) have argued that slower-than-normal speeds of word decoding may place higher-than-normal demands on working memory and interfere with meaningful reading. When words are decoded slowly, each one's meaning must be held in memory longer in order for the reader to comprehend the meaning of a sentence or paragraph. Some evidence has been presented in support of this position, although conflicting demands on attention for the poor decoder (poor decoders do not comprehend as well because they must concentrate more on decoding, while good decoders decode more automatically, allowing more attention to meaning) also appears strongly involved in poor decoders' inability to comprehend and recall what they have read (Samuels, 1994). Because poor readers' word-level decoding often is not automatic, they need to devote additional attention to it. This puts further stresses on their ability to comprehend (Stanovich, 2000).

Attention

Reading requires attention: children must have a book out, be oriented toward it, and be looking at it in order to read. Reaching even this point with some children is not a trivial accomplishment, but teachers can take advantage of a large array of behavioral management systems (e.g., see Kazdin, 2001) developed to foster attentional skills.

Subtler forms of attention within the act of reading also are critical. Readers must learn to direct their attention to the relevant elements of text in an organized, systematic way (e.g., "Sean, when you look at those two words—*lane* and *cane*—how can you tell that they rhyme?"). Attention is needed for readers to control their eye movements, focus on specific words, and at least in English, move their eyes in left-to-right sweeps. Their attention must move successively from word to word and be directed to important ideas in the text. It must shift appropriately between text and illustrations. During formal instructional periods, the problem of focusing attention becomes even more complex as attention must be allocated, in turn, to the text, to classmates' responses, and to the teacher's directions and feedback. As discussed in the next chapter, acquiring metacognitive strategies for guiding these and related processes is vital to reading comprehension.

Summary of Cognitive Prerequisites for Reading

At first glance, reading seems only to be a matching task in which children learn to link visual cues with their vocabulary. In fact, reading is a highly complex interaction with text, requiring orchestration of a stream of complex graphic input with several levels of linguistic and world knowledge. Reading places demands on working memory and requires children to draw on their long-term memory to understand what they are reading. It also requires extended experience with books and other reading materials and learning to attend to the details of letters, words, and text.

Transition to Reading

As we have just seen, the ability to read rests on many linguistic and cognitive skills, each necessary but not sufficient for learning to read. It also is important to keep in mind that, although reading typically receives by far the most emphasis, it actually is only one among a complementary array of critical literacy-related skills that include not only reading, but writing, speaking, and listening. Young children display a wide array of literacy-related behaviors (e.g., looking at picture books and scribbling) that precede and develop into conventional literacy (Sulzby, 1991). From this standpoint, it seems inappropriate to label children as "readers" or "nonreaders" because literacy-related behaviors are developing in multiple dimensions. Still, it is useful to map the changes that young readers go through in the crucial period when they move from having little or no facility in decoding words to a point where they can do so easily. Making this transition is at the heart of learning to read and is one of its primary accomplishments.

Linnea Ehri (1991, 1994, 1998; Ehri & Wilce, 1985; see also Ehri, 2005) has conducted a series of elegant research studies that has provided a window on how children's decoding skills develop as they first begin reading. Initially, children are pre-readers with little or no skill in decoding words. Then, her work has shown, children typically move next into what she calls a partial alphabetic phase, and finally on to full and consolidated alphabetic phases, in which they use systematic phonemic decoding. We describe each of these phases in the following sections.

Pre-Alphabetic Phase

Our starting point is children who are unable to read any primer or pre-primer words in isolation. Ehri (2005) describes these pre-readers as being in a *pre-alphabetic* phase, in which alphabetic knowledge is not used at all to read words. Given a list containing such words as *bat, hit, go,* and *is,* for instance, these children would be unable to read any of them, even though many already know quite a bit about literacy, such as the fact that newspapers, coupons, and magazines tell people something (Purcell-Gates, 1996). They even may be able to identify the names of products or businesses from signs. What these children are "reading" is more context than print, however. They cannot read any print materials removed from context and pay little attention to the graphic (letter) cues.

A good example of this phenomenon can be seen in an often-cited study by Masonheimer, Drum, and Ehri (1984). Masonheimer et al. located some 3- to 5-year-olds who could identify environmental words (e.g., *Pepsi* and *Wendy's*) in their familiar context (as part of a logo). Most of these children could not read these same words when they appeared in contexts other than the original ones (e.g., simply as printed words). They also were unable to detect alterations in the graphic cues (e.g., *xepsi*). Children at this stage are primarily responding to their environment and not to the print (Mason, Herman, & Au, 1991). To become a "real" reader, skills other than those acquired from simple exposure to the environment are needed (Ehri, 2005; Stanovich, 2000).

Another group of pre-readers in the pre-alphabetic phase pay attention to some characteristics of letters, but not to the sounds represented by the letters. Students in this phase might notice visually distinct word features, such as the "tail" at the end of the word *dog.* For children using this strategy, reading is a kind of paired-associate task that involves linking a word's look with its pronunciation and meaning (Ehri, 1994). Because these associations are arbitrary and words' distinctive visual features are exhausted quickly, visual-cue readers are unable to read consistently. The memory demands of reading in this way soon become overwhelming. As a consequence, this associative strategy soon is abandoned by most readers in favor of one relying more on phonetic information.

Partial Alphabetic Phase Readers

In Ehri's view, the first "real" reading occurs when children begin to process letter-sound relations and to use phonetic cues. They have become **partial alphabetic phase readers.** In this phase (also called *phonetic cue reading*), children are clearly focusing on the characteristics of words themselves, not just on the context in which words are embedded. Their processing is only partial since they read words by forming and storing associations between only some, but not all, of the letters in words' spellings and their sounds in pronunciation (Ehri, 2005). For instance, a child may learn to read the word *fix* by associating the letter names *f* and *x* with the word's sounds or write the word *giraffe* as *jrf.* These letter-sound associations, though incomplete, do convey important information about pronunciation. They also are not arbitrary and so are much easier to remember and more effective in reading than the visual cues of word and letter shape.

Full Alphabetic Phase Readers

In Ehri's judgment, children have unlocked an important key to reading when they use phonemic information to distinguish among similarly spelled words and read them with reasonably high accuracy. They have become **full alphabetic phase readers,** who can learn new words by making complete connections between letters in spelling and phonemes in pronunciation. They understand the alphabetic principle, illustrated by their having learned the alphabet, identifying the separate sounds in words, and understanding that spellings more or less systematically correspond to pronunciations (Ehri, 2005). In an alphabetic language such as English, this means they are mastering a cognitive mapping system linking the 40 or so English phonemes with written letters and letter combinations.

Consolidated Phase Readers

Even though full alphabetic phase readers know the major letter-phoneme correspondences and can match up pronunciations to letters and letter combinations, their skills continue to develop. With increasing experience with letter patterns that appear repeatedly in different words (e.g., *happen, happy*), they begin to consolidate letter-phoneme relationships into larger units. Rimes, syllables, and even whole words become units. For instance, a long word such as *printing* can be learned more easily because it no longer is being processed as many separate letter-sound connections but as two syllable-sized "chunks."

Decoding and Beginning Reading

As children move through Ehri's final phases in learning to read words, they are not yet "expert readers" in a general sense, but definitely have acquired essential reading skills. They have learned to use their knowledge about spoken language to decode print. Virtually all authorities agree that decoding skills are vital to learning to read. Figuring out meanings from context is useful, but cannot substitute for the ability to identify individual words rapidly and accurately (Adams & Bruck, 1995; Perfetti, 1992; Stanovich, 2000). Also, the alphabet system children have acquired is a powerful mnemonic device for helping them learn and remember new words more easily (Ehri, 2005).

At the same time, we should remember that reading is a complex, interactive process focused on comprehension, not just decoding. Decoding is a key to learning to read but is not the only factor and not necessarily even the first thing that should be taught (Calfee & Patrick, 1995). Reading places demands on the full range of a child's linguistic and world knowledge, and reading instruction should draw on all of these dimensions. Agreement is less certain about what to emphasize in beginning reading instruction: decoding or the more global dimensions of literacy. What should be the focus of beginning reading instruction? Following the lead of many reading experts (e.g., Adams, 1990; Calfee & Patrick, 1995; Hiebert & Raphael, 1998; Juel, 1996), we would argue that the answer to this question may be analogous to advice for a healthy diet: varied and balanced fare combining the acquisition of decoding skills with contextual analyses in a meaningful reading activity (McIntyre & Pressley, 1996; Pressley, 2000, 2006).

Consider the passage in Figure 11.2. Take a moment to try to make sense of it. Although the parallel to beginning reading is not exact because of your superior knowledge as an adult, we believe that it is highly instructive. Think especially about the kinds of knowledge you use to understand it. If you are like most other readers, reading a text like this forces you to draw on a variety of information. Letter- and word-level decoding obviously is important. Like partial alphabetic readers, you probably made a rough correspondence between many of the letters and sounds but not all of them. You also used your knowledge of syntax and your pragmatic knowledge that this passage probably has meaning. As soon as you were able to decode your first word or two, your knowledge about the world—in this case, your knowledge about real estate sales—could be brought into play.

dılʌks bʌŋəloz. ɛksepšʌnlǫ prɛstıž lʌkšurǫ lokešʌn. ımidıʌt akypʌnciz ɵri larǰ bɛdrumzz, lɔts ʌv specz, atïčt gʌrɔǰ. əplyʌnsʌz stez. hy ɵrietiz. kal čïd at ʌfɔrdəbl rıʌltiz. 555-1234

FIGURE 11.2   A Short Passage from the *Chronicle*.

Just as it was for you in this "bungalow" passage, beginning readers' reading is not just mapping symbols on phonemes and words, although this is essential. Reading is a meaning-making activity in which all kinds of knowledge are used. Although we know that rapid, automatic word decoding leads to sentence and passage meaning, we also must remember that sentence and passage meaning affect and direct decoding. Thus, instructional methods stressing only a single approach to learning to read may handicap children who will use multiple keys to unlock the meanings of words, sentences, and stories.

Methods of Teaching Reading

Exactly what should be a teacher's focus in teaching beginning readers? Calfee and Henry (1986) have suggested mastery of the following four dimensions as vital to successful reading:

Decoding. Printed words must be translated into their pronounceable equivalents.

Vocabulary. Meaning must be assigned to words and a network of associations activated.

Sentence and paragraph comprehension. Text units need to be "fit" to their functional roles (e.g., as the subject or predicate of a sentence or as topic sentences in paragraphs).

Text comprehension. Complete texts need to be understood as entities—for example, as stories (narratives), as informational (expository) texts, or as dialogues.

If you examine this list closely, you can see that these dimensions correspond closely to categories of language structure we discussed earlier—sounds, words, syntax, and discourse. A sensible curriculum for teaching children to read must address each of these dimensions, and help children to see the uses and benefits of literacy. Unfortunately, the history of reading instruction has not always been one of balanced attention to all factors important to literacy development. Instead, proponents often have advocated one approach over another, sometimes with near-religious zeal. Over the years, numerous controversies have raged about how best to teach children to read.

An important early publication highlighting a major divide in beginning reading instruction that still exists today was Jeanne Chall's 1967 landmark book *Learning to Read: The Great Debate.* As part of a comprehensive analysis, she divided reading methods into two broad categories: **code-emphasis methods** and **meaning-emphasis methods,** terms that remain useful in understanding continuing debates about reading instruction methods. The former refers to approaches that initially emphasize decoding, learning the correspondence between letters and sounds. Prominent among code-emphasis methods is **phonics,** which focuses on acquisition of basic letter/sound relationships and the rules for sounding out words. Contrasted with these code-emphasis methods are meaning-emphasis approaches, which favor meaning over decoding in beginning reading. Included in Chall's meaning-emphasis category were **sight word methods** (sometimes called "*look-say*"), which stress the need for children to acquire at least a limited stock of familiar words (e.g., *ask, fly, when*) they can recognize on sight. Another meaning-emphasis approach is **language experience,** a method in which children's oral language, such as their stories about their experiences and observations, is dictated and written down; what is written then becomes the basis for reading. In this way skills are taught in the context of the child's own direct experience with language and the world.

In a behavioral era that conceptualized learning to read as acquiring a hierarchy of reading skills, meaning-based approaches languished in the 1970s. In some instances, beginning reading instruction followed a pattern dominated by seatwork and skill-development worksheets prescribed by the basal readers. To simplify reading materials, the strategies of restricting vocabulary choices and employing readability formulas (which provide a quantitative estimate of text difficulty typically derived from sentence length and word frequency) often were used. These attempts to control a text's predictability and readability unfortunately sometimes ignored other critical aspects of text that make it comprehensible and interesting. For instance, a good story line contributes to comprehension and interest but is not captured by readability measures. The result of modifying text by using readability indices too often produced text that, though theoretically carefully matched with the student's grade level, was disjointed and not very readable.

By the 1980s, studies of classroom instruction began to reveal the extent to which reading comprehension and the literary value of reading materials were being neglected (e.g., see Durkin, 1978–1979, 1981). Also, the introduction of well-articulated theories of comprehension from cognitive psychology (e.g., Anderson & Pearson, 1984) now gave curriculum developers and writers a theoretical basis for emphasizing comprehension. Schema theory, for instance, provided a foundation for emphasizing factors such as story structure, text organization, and activating prior knowledge. Unfortunately, sensible advocacy for paying attention to meaning and avoiding decontextualized skill-based instruction was framed by some as a call to abandon virtually all teaching of strategies and skills, including decoding instruction. A few individuals purporting to represent whole-language approaches to literacy seemed to be proposing that children would learn to read simply through exposure to good literature, much like they earlier learned to speak in the language-rich environment of home and community (for interesting discussions of these and related issues, see Goodman, 1996; Pressley, 2002; Weaver, 1994).

Most current models of reading (e.g., Adams, 1994; Kintsch, 1988, 1998; Stanovich, 2000) and authorities on reading instruction (e.g., Adams, 1990; Calfee, 1994; Clay, 1991; Pressley, 2000, 2006) stake out a middle ground between code and meaning emphases, arguing for a "balanced approach" in which both are recognized as essential to learning to read. They suggest that reading is not best construed as "either–or"—that is, it is neither an automatic data-driven process or a top-down process dominated by higher level cognitive and language activity. Despite the seeming reasonableness of a balanced approach, controversy has continued.

For example, there is considerable debate about the federal government's strong emphasis on phonics-based reading instruction for beginning readers. Its scholarly basis was a major report by the National Reading Panel (NRP, 2000), which subsequently has shaped federal education policy and research funding. Although the NRP report pointed out that phonics instruction constitutes only part of a total reading program, it recommended the method of systematic phonics, which includes extended sequences of structured, explicit instruction on letter-sound relationships. The primary goals of the systematic phonics approach are familiar ones, including making sure that children understand written letters-spoken sound relationships, can automatically recognize familiar words, and can decode unfamiliar words. As we have discussed, such goals make excellent sense, especially since understanding letter-sound relationships is a primary route to meaning in alphabetic languages such as English. These goals also are supported by a large body of research relating variables such as letter-sound knowledge, automatic word recognition, and phonics training intervention to reading skill growth and comprehension (e.g., Adams, 1990; Conner, Morrison, & Katch, 2004; NRP, 2000; Snow, Burns, & Griffin, 1998).

Although only a few individuals—reasoning by analogy that, like toddlers learning a first language, reading and writing will develop naturally in a context rich in books, writing, reading, and talk—argue against teaching phonics skills, many more have been critical of what they see as an over-emphasis on phonics and a misapplication of phonics instruction as a one-size-fits-all method. In other words, their objection is not to teaching phonics, but to prescriptive teaching methods in which phonics is taught to the exclusion of other critical language dimensions. For example, do all children need extended sequences of phonics, given that it seems mostly effective for children with low initial decoding skills (e.g., Conner et al., 2004)? Are the positive research outcomes, although statistically significant, practically important (e.g., Hammill & Swanson, 2006) and will they have beneficial long-term effects on reading development (e.g., Paris, 2005)? If phonics is the primary focus of beginning reading, will attention be paid to powerful out-of-school factors known to influence early (and later) literacy development, such as the "30 million word gap" documented by Hart and Risley (2003), which represents the difference between the number of words encountered by 3-year-olds growing up in the least favorable home and community environments compared to the number encountered by their most privileged counterparts?

While recognizing that there always will and should be debate about what constitutes effective beginning reading instruction, we emphasize again the desirability of balance and note some encouraging signs. For example, phonics instruction is considerably less likely to be neglected now than when whole language approaches (e.g., Goodman, 1996; Weaver, 1994) were interpreted by some to mean that decoding skills should be taught only incidentally or not at all. Consistent with research evidence that automatic word recognition processes play an important role in skilled reading (see, e.g., Stanovich, 2000), primary teachers recognized for their excellence almost universally make teaching decoding a fundamental part of their literacy instruction (Pressley, 2006; Pressley, Allington, Wharton-McDonald, Block, & Morrow, 2001; Pressley, Rankin, & Yokoi, 1996). On the meaning side, an enormous body of excellent children's literature now is available, giving children added motivation to read and more models of language use. Widely used **basal reading series**—materials for literacy instruction that include coordinated texts, teachers' manuals, and student activities—emphasize comprehension, analysis, and extension as well as decoding. While in the past basal reading series were appropriately criticized for providing a less-than-coherent view of reading (e.g., poorly structured, uninteresting, and stereotypical reading materials; boring worksheet-based practice activities that meant little to children), most current basal series include systematic skill development, but do so in a comprehension-focused context of writing, speaking, and listening. Other positive developments are review processes that have mostly eliminated sexist portrayals of characters and broadened the range of racial and cultural backgrounds represented in trade books and basal series. To us, these changes represent a movement toward the desired "balanced diet" of reading instruction consistent with a broad, multifaceted view of literacy development.

Summary of Beginning Literacy Instruction

Beginning literacy instruction is a varied and sometimes emotion-laden enterprise. The past several decades have seen many shifts in how best to teach reading. Some methods emphasize more code-based approaches that involve teaching skill acquisition related to decoding letters and words. Others stress text meaning and general and linguistic knowledge. Although virtually all authorities agree that attention to both decoding and meaning dimensions is important, there remains considerable debate about how much to emphasize each in beginning reading. Key elements of decoding—including phonemic awareness, letter knowledge, and the alphabetic principle—should be explicitly taught. Reading is more than learning to decode, however, and reading instruction needs to maintain a strong focus on the many other dimensions of literacy, including reading for comprehension and enjoyment.

Assessment of Early Reading Progress

Because learning to read is one of schooling's most important accomplishments, there naturally is great interest in variables that either predict success or provide valid markers of reading progress. Among the most frequently assessed are *phonemic awareness, letter knowledge,* and *oral reading fluency.*

Phonemic awareness, as we have seen, is the ability to notice, think about, and manipulate the phonemic segments of spoken words. Demonstrating this speech-related skill requires conscious attention to individual sounds within a spoken word (Hatcher et al., 2006; Morris, Bloodgood, Lomax, & Perney, 2003). If beginning readers cannot mentally separate a word's meaningful sounds, they cannot perform the critical task of matching these sounds to the letters and words they're trying to read.

Two indicators of phonemic awareness were used in a study of children's reading development from kindergarten through first grade by Morris et al. (2003). The simpler of the two measured children's ability to identify initial consonants in spoken words (e.g., Can you say the first sound in the word *milk*?). A more advanced skill, **phonemic segmentation,** was measured by asking them to create the separate phonemes in a three-phoneme word (e.g., when /bat/ was pronounced, responding with /b/ /ă/ /t/). Whereas almost all of Morris et al.'s children could identify initial consonants by the end of kindergarten, most did poorly on phoneme segmentation. This changed rapidly, and by early the following fall, in first grade, performance of the median (middle) child in Morris et al.'s sample was above 80%. A variety of studies suggest that teaching phonemic segmentation skills to children as young as 4 years of age can help promote later reading success (e.g., Hatcher, Hulme, & Snowling, 2004; NRP, 2000).

A second marker of early reading skills—letter knowledge—typically is measured by children's ability to name upper- or lower-case letters or to state letter sounds. Letter knowledge, like phonemic awareness, plays an obvious role in learning to read in alphabetic languages like English. Children's knowing the alphabet and letter sounds when they begin school is a predictor of reading success (Hulme, Snowling, Caravolas, & Carroll, 2005; Lonigan, Burgess, & Anthony, 2000; NRP, 2000). In the United States, where children learn letter names before they learn letter sounds, children typically use their knowledge of letter names to learn letter sounds (Treiman, Pennington, Shriberg, & Boada, 2008). Not all letters are created equal

in aiding students in learning letter sounds. On letter sound tests, children typically will perform best on letters containing the letter's sound at the beginning of their names, less well on
letters with their sounds at the end of their names, and least well on letters that do not have
their sounds in their names (Treiman et al., 2008).

A third frequently used but controversial measure of early reading progress is **reading
fluency,** the ability to read quickly, accurately, and with expression (Schwanenflugel et al.,
2006). Interest in reading fluency is based on theory and research showing that automatic
word recognition is important to reading comprehension (e.g., Kuhn & Stahl, 2003; LaBerge &
Samuels, 1974; NRP, 2000; Schwanenflugel et al., 2006). Currently, the most widely used reading fluency measures are subtests of the Dynamic Indicators of Basic Early Literacy Skills
assessment (DIBELS, Good & Kaminski, 2002), administered annually to nearly 2 million
kindergarten through sixth-grade students in the United States.

Assessment of early reading progress with tests like DIBELS has been strongly criticized.
Cautioning against over-interpretation of reading fluency scores, Paris (2005) has pointed out
that reading rate is affected by numerous variables *not* related to automatic word recognition,
including text familiarity, complexity, perceived audience, and reading purpose. Other leading
researchers and theorists (e.g., Allington, 2005; Pearson, 2006; Pressley, 2006) have argued that
DIBELS fluency measures and fluency training tied to test results have become a *de facto* curriculum that is poorly connected to the real purposes of reading—understanding and recalling
what has been read. S. J. Samuels (2007), whose early research (e.g., LaBerge & Samuels, 1974)
helped provide the empirical and theoretical basis for automaticity's key role in reading, contends that DIBELS is a poor measure of reading fluency because it emphasizes reading speed
but neglects comprehension. Because DIBELS represents a limited perspective on fluency,
Samuels argues, its widespread use and fluency instruction tied to it will lead many teachers
and students to focus on speed at the expense of comprehension.

We share this concern and, consistent with Paris's (2005) views, would further advise
that researchers and educators gathering data on beginning readers pay close attention both to
the nature and developmental trajectories of all variables being measured. Paris has pointed
out that variables like letter knowledge are "constrained"—in learning the alphabet, for example, the number of elements to be mastered is small (e.g., 26 letters) and the acquisition period
quite brief (e.g., many children will know around half of the letters at the beginning of kindergarten but almost all of them by the end). Phonemic awareness develops somewhat more
slowly than letter knowledge, but most children still master its basics in the primary grades.
Because skills like these are so rapidly acquired, there are only short periods where they predict
progress or future reading success (e.g., in or around kindergarten for letter name knowledge).
Also, although constrained skills are necessary for reading development, they are not sufficient.
They "set the stage for reading development" (Paris, 2005, p. 200), but should not be viewed as
causes of important literacy outcomes such as vocabulary growth and reading comprehension,
which continue to develop throughout school and life.

We would add, finally, that *all* assessments of early reading progress need to be interpreted with considerable caution. Virtually any measure tapping children's cognitive abilities,
language skills, or general well-being (e.g., memory capacity, early speech competence,
SES)—will correlate to some degree with reading success. As a consequence, the fact that a given
variable is associated with current or future reading performance does not necessarily indicate a

direct or even indirect effect on reading. For example, a correlation between letter knowledge or phonemic awareness and reading comprehension also reflects factors such as SES, extent of parent-child interactions, and exposure to books in the home, which may be the actual basis for the observed relationship.

While it is important that researchers and educators continue to assess important dimensions of early reading, they and we should be cautious about drawing inferences. The validity of constrained variables is affected by when they are measured and the distributions of their scores. Correlations, even strong ones, may be due to variables other than those being studied. Even experimental interventions demonstrating measurable training effects (e.g., a rhyming and phoneme awareness instruction treatment that improves phonemic awareness) is not automatically evidence for the treatment's value; outcomes may be short-term and not have lasting effects on important reading skills that continue to develop over a reader's lifetime, such as vocabulary growth or reading comprehension.

Implications for Beginning Reading Instruction

For most children, a skilled teacher's assistance is essential in learning to read. Becoming literate depends on children's ability to link written symbols with their spoken language and draws heavily on their linguistic and world knowledge. In alphabetic languages such as English, children must learn a system that maps letters and letter combinations to language sounds. As we have seen, reading depends on decoding words but also is much more than decoding. Linguistic and cognitive processes ranging from basic perception of letter shapes to the highest levels of thinking and problem solving are involved. Thus, beginning literacy instruction requires teachers to orchestrate the many components of literacy into a meaningful whole. The scaffolding techniques discussed in Chapters 4 and 9 are particularly useful, with teachers helping students use their linguistic knowledge to meet literacy's challenges. Without a skilled teacher's help, many will not succeed. Following are themes that we believe are vital to helping students make successful transitions to literacy.

1. *Approach reading as a meaningful activity.* Reading is a meaning-making act. This fact can be lost in some kinds of literacy instruction. Although decoding skills are essential for reading, decoding needs to be connected to reading's purpose—meaning making. If children begin to equate reading with skill demonstration, such as reading quickly, they can lose track of literacy's overall purposes and come to perceive literacy instruction as skill training. We need to remind ourselves of the basic reasons for literacy—learning, communicating, and enjoyment—and demonstrate them for our students.

2. *Take a broad perspective on literacy.* We believe that "critical literacy" (Calfee, 1994), which refers to the ability to read, write, listen, and speak effectively, is a better goal for early literacy instruction than "learning to read." Critical literacy is achieved by having children use their developing language skills in meaningful tasks and helping them develop their overall linguistic and cognitive competence. Although learning to read is an essential goal for the primary grades, the broader purpose is using language in all its forms to think, reason, and communicate effectively.

3. *Help beginning readers move toward automatic decoding.* One of this text's themes is the role of automatic cognitive processes in complex cognitive skills. Skilled reading, with its ties to rapid, fluent word decoding, is an excellent example. Although beginning readers can and should use context to help them decode words, skilled reading depends on automatic word recognition.

Good readers do decode most words automatically. They rely relatively little on context for their decoding, although they can use it effectively if they need to (Adams & Bruck, 1995; Perfetti, 1992). In contrast, poor readers typically have difficulty in automatic word decoding (Stanovich, 2000). Thus, early, explicit decoding instruction is essential, but it does not follow that all children need extended phonics instruction or that all will benefit equally. Students can move toward more rapid, automatic decoding in a number of ways, including guided meaningful reading, in which the teacher directs students' attention to relevant graphic and phonemic characteristics of words. Rereading passages to improve fluency and automaticity also may be helpful (Samuels, 1994).

4. *Draw on children's domain and general knowledge.* Knowledge underlies virtually all effective cognitive functioning (see Chapters 8 and 9) and the cognitive processes of reading are no exception. Unless reading connects to children's experiences, it can become a meaningless exercise in word calling. All children have knowledge about their worlds that teachers can use in beginning reading instruction. Evoking their frames of reference allows them to understand what they are reading and better regulate their own learning.

5. *Encourage children to develop their metalinguistic knowledge.* A central idea of this chapter, echoing the self-regulation theme of this book, is that becoming literate involves children becoming explicitly aware of new language dimensions. Virtually all children have the basic linguistic capabilities they need to become readers, but most need to develop the metalinguistic abilities that will enable them to understand the roles letters, words, sounds, and text structure play in literacy. Children coming from language traditions other than English face special challenges in American schools. No matter what levels of language skill students may bring, a teacher can increase metalinguistic awareness by building on their current capabilities with language and drawing their attention to its many dimensions.

6. *Expect children to vary widely in their progress toward fluent reading.* Most children move into literacy fairly uneventfully, but some will struggle with learning to read. In any given group of readers, as many as 10 to 15% will fall 1 or 2 years behind their peer group in reading level by third or fourth grade. From 3 to 5% will have more serious problems and will lag two or more grade levels behind their peers.

A Comment on Reading Difficulties

The origins of reading difficulties vary and are a matter of debate. Some students simply are not developmentally ready for reading instruction in the first grade and find it difficult to grasp the abstract linguistic tasks of learning to read. Others come from cultural or language backgrounds that poorly match their experiences in reading instruction. Most or all of these children likely would perform well if reading instruction had been improved or delayed; a significant challenge is avoiding these kinds of problems and, for those who have not yet succeeded, perhaps undoing a false concept of themselves as "poor readers."

A few students will have considerable difficulty in learning to read even with excellent instruction. Some of these students have low general ability; their difficulty is less with reading than with comprehension's cognitive demands. Others, however, will have normal or above-normal intelligence but have a specific handicap or learning disability in the area of reading. These children differ from children who are simply poor readers. Many have notable speech and language deficits, often coupled with difficulty in spelling and writing. In fact, the root problem for many disabled readers often is one of language. A genetic basis seems probable for some reading disabilities (Berninger, 1994; Rayner & Pollatsek, 1989), which tend to occur more among males than females, among more left-handers than right-handers, and to run in families.

Poor reading skills make school achievement difficult. Yet, many children with severe reading disabilities do go on to high levels of accomplishment, both by using their own knowledge and strategies to compensate for lack of reading skill and by drawing on the talents of teachers specially trained in methods designed to help disabled readers learn to read. As teachers, we need to recognize the difficulties that disabled readers face and to help them obtain the specialized assistance they need.

Reading Recovery: One Approach to Reading Difficulties

Reading Recovery, an intervention for first-grade children in the lowest 10 to 20% of their classes, was started many years ago in New Zealand by Marie Clay, who also coined the term **emergent literacy.** Brought to the United States in the mid-1980s, Reading Recovery continues to have strong advocates as an intervention for first-grade children experiencing significant problems in learning to read. Reading Recovery is designed around a comprehensive model of literacy development that includes the following:

1. A diagnostic process in which children are assessed on a variety of literacy tasks, such as their ability to identify letters, read words, write, and do oral reading, as well as on their literacy knowledge and strategies.
2. A series of 30-minute daily tutorials in which a Reading Recovery teacher works one-on-one with an individual student.
3. Standardized sessions that provide a systematic set of activities, including having the child practice letters and words, read from short books, and produce short compositions that are cut up and re-read.
4. A systematic process of staff development in which teachers are trained by Reading Recovery trainers.

The goal of the tutoring is to have the child make faster than average progress (Lyons, Pinnell, & DeFord, 1993) in order to reach the school average for reading ability, when the tutoring program is discontinued. For a typical student, Reading Recovery sessions will span some 12 to 16 weeks and include up to 60 half-hour sessions.

Reading Recovery embodies characteristics of successful beginning reading instruction, including phonemic awareness, systematic observation and teaching, high expectations for achievement, student goal setting and regular review of goals, repeated readings of text, and experimentation with language through writing (Hiebert & Raphael, 1996). Although not explicitly developed from Vygotsky's theory (see Chapter 9), the emphasis is on teacher–student collaboration and on teacher scaffolding, with teachers giving hints and otherwise helping students develop a system of organized strategies that improve their reading. It also gives students considerable instructional time and allows teachers many opportunities to directly assess students' literacy skills. Although Reading Recovery's methods embody a comprehensive theory-based approach and have shown positive results (e.g., Allington, 2005; D'Agontino & Murphy, 2004; Schwartz, 2005), relatively high costs are a concern. With each Reading Recovery teacher serving 16 or fewer students in a school year and with an intensive training period for each teacher, the per-pupil costs are high. Proponents counter that Reading Recovery, though admittedly costly, is less expensive in the long run than special education or other remedial programs.

Summary

Learning to read is a significant linguistic and cognitive achievement that most children accomplish early in their primary school years. Superficially viewed, reading seems to be simply word-by-word decoding, but it is in fact a multifaceted process orchestrating all aspects of language and cognition. Beginning readers' success hinges on developing metalinguistic abilities and on knowledge activation, memory, and attention. Metalinguistic awareness makes it possible for children to map the visual symbols of written language onto oral language and create meaning. Readers' world knowledge underlies comprehension, as they use their working and long-term memory to process information sequentially, hold it in memory, and relate it to existing knowledge and language structures. Managing attention also is essential; readers must focus strategically on key features of letters, words, sentences, and texts in order to read effectively.

Well before they begin to read, most children already know something about the purposes and conventions of reading. They often can "read" environmental cues, such as signs and logos. True reading, however, requires attention to word and text features. In their earliest attempts to read, children often rely on visual cues in text, such as word shapes. Children who know the alphabet and are aware of language sounds can use partial phonetic cues supplied by letter names. Expert decoders can use the entire range of phonemic cues supplied by letters and letter combinations.

Decoding is necessary but not sufficient for learning to read. Literacy also depends on understanding the pragmatic uses of literacy and on knowing vocabulary, syntax, and text structures. Beginning literacy instruction generally includes each of these areas, but different instructional methods vary in their emphasis. Some rely on fluent word decoding to lead to meaning. Others stress meaning, with the expectation that comprehension and context will assist in decoding. Because reading is an interactive process involving simultaneous processing at multiple levels of language and cognition, it is unlikely that any narrow approach will be effective. Each of reading's dimensions contributes to reading success. Successful reading instruction will emphasize reading as a meaningful process, no matter what feature of reading is being developed.

SUGGESTED READINGS

Newman, S. B., & Dickinson, D. K. (2002), *Handbook of early literacy research.* New York, NY: Guilford Press, and Dickinson, D. K., & Newman, S. B. (2005). *Handbook of early literacy research* (Vol. 2). New York, NY: Guilford Press.

These two volumes provide a comprehensive and authoritative resource for beginning reading instruction. Together they contain more than 50 chapters by leading researchers and theorists covering a range of topics important to understanding early literacy development and teaching beginning readers.

Pressley, M. (2005). *Reading instruction that works: The case for balanced teaching* (3rd ed.). New York, NY: Guilford Press.

Michael Pressley makes the case in this volume for a balanced approach to early reading instruction that includes not only whole-language and skills-based components, but also motivation. New chapters in this edition focus on fluency, vocabulary, and writing.

Stanovich, K. E. (2000). *Progress in understanding reading: Scientific foundations and new frontiers.* New York, NY: Guilford Press.

Written by a leading reading researcher, this volume summarizes his own fine work and the progress of research on reading and reading disabilities.

At about the 3rd grade, when most students have acquired basic literacy skills, the emphasis in many classrooms shifts from learning to read to "reading to learn." Elementary school students may read, for example, about pioneer life, the moon, or about animals and their habitats. As they move toward middle school and high school, the emphasis on reading as a primary avenue to learning becomes more pronounced. Eighth graders may be expected to learn basic principles of ecology from a general science textbook; 12th graders routinely are assigned readings in texts or anthologies in preparations for discussions. Many college teachers rely heavily on reading assignments in textbooks as part of their instructional approach. You may, in fact, be reading this chapter as part of an assignment. The assumption, of course, is that at least part of what is important for you to learn can be acquired by reading this text.

Although reading to learn is seen as important, recent assessments by the National Center of Educational Statistics (e.g., Grigg, Donahue, & Dion, 2007; Lee, Grigg, & Donahue, 2007) show that many elementary, middle, and high school students continue to find reading difficult. The latest administration of the National Assessment of Educational Progress (NAEP), for example, showed declines in 12th graders' reading performance compared to previous years (Grigg et al., 2007), with more than one-fourth failing to perform at the Basic level. In the 2007 NAEP reading test, nearly one-third of 4th graders and more than one-fourth of 8th graders were not reading at the Basic level. Given the importance of reading to learn for many school and vocational goals, this relatively low reading performance concerns many educators.

Educational psychologists always have been intensely interested in learning from reading, and their research on this topic has generated a massive literature. Early research tended to focus on acquiring information; more recent research and theory (e.g., see Block & Pressley, 2002; Israel & Duffy, 2009; McNamara, 2007; Rapp, van den Broek, McMaster, Kendeou, & Espin, 2007) have emphasized reading comprehension, factors affecting it, and strategies for improving it. In this chapter, we examine several dimensions of "getting meaning" from texts. To set the stage for our discussion, we begin by describing two important early reading comprehension models, followed by examination of two current models. Then we explore several aspects of comprehending texts. We first focus on a basic but important outcome of reading—learning new vocabulary. We examine both how vocabulary is acquired through reading and methods of teaching vocabulary directly. Next, we shift to a more general outlook emphasizing how organized knowledge is acquired. Here, we first describe several ways in which writers and teachers can make text information more comprehensible and memorable. We then describe approaches to helping students develop reading strategies to support their reading comprehension. Following this is a section on assessing reading comprehension and a concluding section on implications for instruction.

Early Models of Reading Comprehension

Reading comprehension models traditionally have been clustered into three general groups: data-driven, conceptually driven, and interactive (Rayner & Pollatsek, 1989). **Data-driven (bottom-up) processing** refers to processing guided primarily by external stimuli; data flow quickly and mostly automatically through the information processing system. **Conceptually driven (top-down) processing,** in contrast, refers to processing guided heavily by conceptual frameworks stored in memory. **Interactive processing** refers to processing guided by an interaction between automated processes triggered by the data a text provides, on the one hand, and by the reader's knowledge and strategies, on the other.

In this section we examine two early reading models by Philip Gough and Kenneth Goodman that illustrate data- and conceptually driven models of reading, respectively. Most modern models of reading (e.g., Goldman & Rakestraw, 2000; Graesser, 2007; Kintsch, 1988, 1998, 2005; van den Broek, Rapp, & Kendeou, 2005; Zwaan & Madden, 2004) are interactive, incorporating both data-driven and conceptually driven processes. The Gough and Goodman models are instructive because they highlight contrasting processes critical to comprehension. Our description also will aid you in understanding features of current interactive models. We turn first to Gough as an example of a data-driven model of reading.

Gough's Data-Driven Model

Data-driven models of reading emphasize decoding and word meanings. In portraying the comprehension of a passage, for instance, such models identify a starting point, such as word identification. Higher-order structures, such as sentences, then are built up word by word as the reader moves through the text (Rayner & Pollatsek, 1989). In this perspective, information flows from letters and words to syntactic structures to discourse and semantic structures.

Gough's model (Gough, 1972) was an early attempt to describe these processes, but to better understand the model it is useful to review some issues from basic research on reading. Many researchers, Gough among them, have used eye-tracking equipment to follow readers' eye movements as they travel across a page of printed text. Typically, readers' eye movements consist of a series of stops and starts. The eyes focus briefly on one point of text (called a **fixation**) and then move rapidly to another point. The movement is referred to as a **saccade.** Vision is limited during fixations to a visual span of only a few letters (McConkie, 1997; Rayner, 1997).

Gough (1972) used the results of eye-tracking research as a starting point for his model. According to his model, readers proceed through a sentence "letter by letter, word by word" (p. 354). Reading processes begin with an eye fixation at the first segment of text, followed by a saccade, a second fixation, and so on through the text. Gough posited that each fixation places about 15–20 letters into iconic memory. Once information from the fixation is in the iconic store (in raw, unprocessed form), pattern-matching processes begin, moving one letter at a time from left to right. Gough estimated that it would take about 10–20 milliseconds for the identification of each letter. Gough further assumed that the information would remain about 0.25 seconds in the iconic store and that readers could perform about 3 fixations per second. Using these assumptions (which were based on data about readers' eye movements), Gough estimated that reading rates of about 300 words per minute were possible.

Gough envisioned that once pattern-matching processes on each letter were complete, a mapping response occurs as representations of letters' sounds are recalled and blended together to form the representation of the sound of the word. When the representation of a word's sound is complete, the word meaning is retrieved from memory and the process repeats with the next word. The decoded words are held in short-term memory, and the meaning of sentences is determined there. If a clear understanding is obtained, the gist of the meaning passes on to long-term memory.

Although no data-driven reading models totally exclude the role of long-term memory or presume meaning is determined completely by stimulus input, Gough's model is one of the clearest examples of a data-driven approach. It portrays each letter of each word as being processed in serial fashion; meaning is assigned automatically on the basis of stored meanings. Gough himself pointed out several serious shortcomings with such strict data-driven models (also see Andre, 1987b, for a detailed analysis of data-driven models). Among them are the fact that information does not necessarily come from the iconic store serially (i.e., reading off the iconic store from left to right), that strict translations of letters into their sound representations would not allow readers to comprehend homonyms (or words in which spelling–sound correspondences are irregular, such as *through, enough,* and *cough*), and that words' contexts often determine their meaning (e.g., Bob admitted to the judge that he *stole* the fur *stole*).

Goodman's Conceptually Driven Model

In contrast to data-driven models, **conceptually driven models** of reading emphasize the guiding role of knowledge in comprehension. Instead of describing meaning as the product of a sequential, letter-by-letter, word-by-word analysis of text, conceptually driven models are based on the premise that readers' expectations about a text, prior knowledge, and activities while reading determine comprehension processes. In this view, readers use their knowledge and the printed symbols on a page to construct meaning.

A prominent early model emphasizing conceptually driven processing was Kenneth Goodman's. Unlike Gough's model, which was based on analyses of eye movements, Goodman's portrayal of reading grew out of his observations of children's oral reading errors, which he called *miscues.* In Goodman's research (see Goodman, 1982b, 1982c) children were asked to read stories aloud that were somewhat difficult for them. Goodman's analysis of the kinds of mistakes they made indicated to him that they constantly were predicting the contents of upcoming text. Further, Goodman believed that readers used text as a means of confirming or disconfirming their predictions about what it was going to say, describing reading as a "psychological guessing game."

Unlike Gough's model, Goodman's model of reading did not require a sequence of invariant steps. Instead, it posited four cycles of processing occurring simultaneously and interactively: *visual* (picking up the visual input), *perceptual* (identifying letters and words), *syntactic* (identifying the structure of the text), and *semantic* (constructing meaning for the input) (Goodman, 1994). When readers begin reading, they construct an initial meaning for the text. This meaning then provides predictions against which future input is judged. If the reader's prediction is confirmed, reading continues and the constructed meaning is enriched with new information. If the reader's prediction is incorrect, however, the reader will slow down, reread, or seek additional information to construct a more accurate meaning.

Goodman's model suggests that miscues should be fairly common. They are not necessarily the result of poor reading, but instead stem from the same processes as good reading. In fact, the strongest support for Goodman's idea that constructed meanings govern reading comes from his research on reading errors (Goodman, 1982a; Goodman & Goodman, 1982). When the children Goodman observed made errors in oral reading, they spontaneously corrected those that interfered with meaning—typically by rereading and correcting themselves. When children made errors that did not affect meaning, however, these seldom were noticed or corrected (e.g., reading *headlights* for *headlamps*). Generally, if words that children called out fit the meaning they had constructed for the story, they seldom saw them as errors, regardless of whether they were read correctly.

Goodman's model has been useful in highlighting conceptually driven processes, and its base in the analysis of children's reading errors makes it appealing. Although it hasn't been as productive in guiding reading research as some other meaning-based approaches (e.g., schema theory, strategies-based instruction), it nonetheless reminds us of the importance of readers' knowledge and the need to understand what is being read. As we now turn to current models, we see that—while they might place greater emphasis on either data- or conceptually driven processes—they are more interactive. They incorporate both automatized and conceptually driven processes. Some also emphasize variables such as reader goals and their desire to achieve a coherent understanding of what is being read.

Current Models of Reading Comprehension

Modern reading comprehension models continue to reflect early emphases on data-driven and conceptually driven processing, but now fit most comfortably into the category of **interactive models.** Here we present two of the most prominent current models. Kintsch's-Construction-integration model (Kintsch, 1998, 2005), which arguably is the most comprehensive current model of reading comprehension (see Graesser, 2007), is an interactive model that continues to place its strongest emphasis on automatized processes. Contrasted to it are the so-called explanation-based models, or constructionist models (Graesser, 2007; Graesser, Singer, & Trabasso, 1994; Zwaan & Madden, 2004). While automatized processes still are prominent in constructionist models, they tend also to stress meaning-oriented variables such as reader goals, coherence of knowledge representations, and quality of explanations. We begin with Kintsch's model.

Kintsch's Construction-Integration Model

As we have seen, purely data-driven models of reading comprehension have problems accounting for the influence of context and readers' knowledge. Conceptually driven models of text comprehension, on the other hand, focus on knowledge but can be vague and fail to account for data-driven processes such as phonemic and word decoding. Because of these apparent limitations of data-driven and conceptually driven models, interactive models were proposed as far back as the 1970s (e.g., Adams & Collins, 1977; Rumelhart & McClelland, 1981). The most influential of these was proposed originally by Kintsch and Van Dijk (1978; see also Kintsch, 1986) and has been extensively modified over the years. In its current form, the model is referred to as the **construction-integration (CI) model** (Kintsch, 1988, 1998, 2005).

The CI model portrays how text is represented and integrated with readers' knowledge. It focuses on discourse processing (the comprehension of main ideas or themes encountered during reading) and on how meaning is constructed as readers move through texts. In the CI model, the basic meanings of sentences are represented by propositions (see the discussion "The Building Blocks of Cognition" in Chapter 3) and text meanings as hierarchical semantic networks of propositions. As you recall, a single sentence can contain more than one proposition. In early versions of the model (e.g., Kintsch & Van Dijk, 1978), these individual propositions were used as input to the model. The current CI version uses complex propositions as its input; each complex proposition consists of several simple propositions related to a core meaning. Complex propositions include such features as category (whether the proposition represents an action, event, or state), modifiers, and circumstance (time and place).

A key distinction within the CI model is between a text's microstructure and its macrostructure (Kintsch, 1998). The **microstructure** of a text consists of the propositions generated from the sentence-by-sentence information in the text, plus some information from readers' long-term memories. The microstructure consists of all of a text's propositions, linked to each other to the extent that they share common elements, or nodes. In Kintsch's conception, readers automatically link propositions that are embedded in one another or share common elements. Through short cycles of processing words, phrases, and sentences, a microstructure is built up from the basic propositions of the text. Vocabulary repetitions, inferences, and working memory capacity all play important roles in determining the microstructure readers construct.

At the same time readers are building a microstructure, they also are creating a **macrostructure** corresponding to the gist, or overall meaning, of the text. Whereas the microstructure consists simply of the text's propositions, the macrostructure is hierarchical and represents a text's global structure. The macrostructure can be signaled by the text's headings or sections, but often it needs to be inferred by the reader (Kintsch, 1998). The macrostructure thus combines the knowledge and inferences of the individual with the text microstructure. In essence, macrostructure elements are main ideas, higher-level propositions abstracted from the microstructure.

Out of this process, readers form two distinctive types of representations. The first, called the **text base,** is the text ". . . as the author of the text intended it" (Kintsch, 1998, p. 50). Text base representations generally are mostly faithful to the presented passage, consisting of propositions derived from the input sentences plus a small set of basic inferences (Goldman, Varma, & Cote, 1996). The more complete representation of how readers understand texts is the **situation model,** composed *both* of text-derived propositions (the text base) and proposi-tions contributed from long-term memory. The situation model integrates readers' prior knowledge with text information. Situation models are not simply what the text *states:* They reflect both text information and what readers know. Understanding a text, therefore, almost never consists of a pure text base; instead, it is the personal interpretation of readers combining information in the text with information from their long-term memory (Kintsch, 1998).

Early versions of Kintsch's model (e.g., Kintsch & Van Dijk, 1978) included strong assump-tions about top-down, schema-driven processes for forming situation models. As the model has evolved (e.g., Kintsch, 1988, 1998, 2005), however, greater emphasis has been given to automatic processes. The current CI model, while still interactive, highlights automatized processes of con-structing and integrating information within a connectionist framework (see Chapter 3). As Kintsch points out, although prior knowledge plays a crucial role in text interpretation, top-down processes do not dominate; except in rare cases, ". . . what is out there strongly constrains and guides comprehension." (Kintsch, 2005, p. 128). Sequential cycles of processing generate networks of propositions and their associations that then are, in effect, shaped through an integration process that settles on the meaning.

The name for the CI model is based on its representation of comprehension as happening in two phases, a construction phase and an integration phase. In the **construction phase,** readers' propositions and concepts automatically activate networks of associations and simple inferences. Network elements, such as words and propositions, are connected at varying levels of strength. Assume, for example, that readers encounter the sentence we mentioned earlier, "The pilot put the plane into a steep bank" in a passage about near-misses in commercial aviation. A number of relevant associations will be generated (e.g., *flying, turn, danger,* and *wings*) but so will other asso-ciations to *bank* that are valid, but off-target for the passage's meaning, such as *money, tellers,* and *vault.* In this construction phase, however, *all* associations—relevant and irrelevant—simply are created by automatic, context-free associative processes. The result is a connection net consisting of many elements having varying *association strengths* with one another.

In the **integration phase** a kind of pruning occurs as associations are eliminated that do not fit the text's overall discourse structure. As the propositional network is activated and reacti-vated as the reader encounters new phrases and sentences, it begins to stabilize. Propositional nodes related to the meaning of what is being read (e.g., *flying, turn, danger,* and *wings*) continue to be activated and strengthened, whereas others unrelated to passage meaning (e.g., *money* and *tellers*) are not activated and drop out. In the end, what a text means to a reader is represented by a network of highly activated nodes formed through multiple cycles.

The CI model and its earlier versions have generated many predictions and much empirical research (e.g., see Graesser, 2007). The Kintsch models predict, for example, that propositionally complex texts will take longer to read than texts with fewer propositions, even with length held constant. They do. Another set of predictions, based on assumptions about propositions and their importance, is that memory for higher level propositions in microstructure and for gist will be better than memory for lower level information. These predictions also have been supported. Other work with the CI model has focused on the match of learners with texts, based on the assumption that there is a "zone of learnability" (see Kintsch, 1998) when the text is at the right level of difficulty. Too-difficult texts do not provide the necessary overlap between the text infor-mation and learner knowledge to provide necessary activation; too-easy texts fail to stimulate learning because they don't activate anything new.

Overall, the CI model and related models of reading give researchers and teachers an important theoretical framework for understanding how comprehension occurs. The features of the CI model, for instance, in which multiple memory traces for successive sentences are connected with the individual's knowledge structures to create overall text representation, or meaning, plausibly describes a process where meaning is built up out of the basic structure of the text, prior knowledge, and inferences connecting the two.

Constructionist Models

Graesser (e.g., Graesser, 2007; Graesser et al., 1994) has proposed a **constructionist model** of reading comprehension that shares many assumptions with Kintsch's CI model, such as knowledge representation by propositions, knowledge activation, and the role of automatized processes. However, it focuses more on the inferences that are constructed and the coherence of the mental representations that are created when readers comprehend texts (Rapp et al., 2007). As Graesser et al. (1994) point out, constructionist models fit within a tradition in psychology dating back at least to Bartlett (1932).

Three major assumptions guide constructionist models (Graesser, 2007). The first, the *reader goal assumption,* is that readers can be expected to represent text meanings in ways consistent with their goals. Thus a reader skimming a short story in a last-minute attempt to pass a quiz may create a sketchy representation of characters and plots that contrasts dramatically with the "normal" rich-in-meaning text model. A second assumption, the *coherence assumption,* refers to the idea that readers try to construct representations that make sense at both local (e.g., clauses, sentences) and global levels, when local information chunks are fit into higher level chunks. The final assumption, the *explanation assumption,* is that readers can be counted on to generate explanations about events and actions encountered in the text occur (e.g., "Hmmmm—he must have been really desperate to have set out on foot during the storm.")

Constructionist theory has become sufficiently precise that it permits predictions about the types of inferences that readers generate as they read texts, such as *superordinate goals of characters* that motivate their actions (e.g., " . . . he's just trying to look good," in explaining why a character spent time visiting with a particular person) and *causal antecedents* that explain why something is mentioned (e.g., a character's getting drunk being explained by the causal antecedent, "his girlfriend ditched him").

Although, as Graesser (2007) has pointed out, research on constructionist models has not been as extensive as for the CI model, many predictions of constructionist models have been supported, including those about the kinds of interferences readers will generate as they read texts, what information they'll recall, and how they summarize texts. The focus on coherence and explanation also has led to better understanding of what good readers do (Rapp et al., 2007). For example, good readers are active in tying new information to what previously has been read and what they already know (Millis, Magliano, & Todaro, 2006). They usually are focused on the "why" of understanding a story much more than on its details of when and where. Motives and causes of unexpected events typically will be more important than details about characters (e.g., their appearance, how they do things). In other words, readers' self-explanations and understanding why things happen are the keys to comprehension (Graesser, 2007).

Common Assumptions of Current Reading Models

Kintsch's CI model and constructionist models such as Graesser's are excellent examples of current reading models. Many other researchers and theorists, however, have been active in proposing and testing assumptions of a variety of reading models, most of which share many features with either or both of the positions in how they represent the process of reading comprehension. Among such models are those of Goldman (e.g., Goldman & Varma, 1995; Goldman, Varma, & Cote, 1996), Gernsbacher (e.g., Gernsbacher, Robertson, Palladino, & Werner, 2004), van den Broek and Rapp (e.g., Rapp et al., 2007; van den Broek et al., 2005) and Zwaan (Zwaan, 1996, Zwaan & Madden, 2004). The following list of shared assumptions in current reading models is derived from Graesser and Britton (1996), Graesser (2007, 2008), Goldman et al. (1996), and others:

1. *Comprehension involves processing at multiple levels.* In order to comprehend text, readers need to interact with word meanings, syntax, and discourse structures, to name only a few dimensions of language (see Chapter 11). When they read, readers generate associations to words; convert sentences into propositions; link those propositions to information already in their long-term memory; and, if they understand the big picture, get a sense of the overall structure of a text.

2. *Comprehension involves the management of working memory.* One of the assumptions of the CI model is that active processing focuses on the current sentence, plus relevant information from memory. Kintsch (1998) describes the role of working memory in text comprehension as being like a spotlight moving across a text, sentence by sentence, with a mental representation being constructed and integrated in the process. In short, comprehension has to be accomplished within the constraints of a limited capacity working memory (Goldman et al., 1996). Just and Carpenter (1992) have shown, for instance, that if the demands on working memory during reading exceed its limitations, comprehension performance will deteriorate, sometimes dramatically.

3. *Comprehension involves inference generation.* Understanding involves more than interpreting what is explicitly stated in a text. To comprehend, readers must access relevant world knowledge and generate interferences that make a text coherent. Some inferences are generated quickly—for instance, those that address readers' goals ("I don't really need to know this!") and those explaining why actions and events occur in stories ("He wouldn't have acted that way unless he was embarrassed or hurt"). Other inferences may be less automatic, such as inferences by an 8th grader about what information is relevant and what isn't in a math word problem.

4. *Comprehension requires ongoing construction of meaning.* Reading comprehension involves taking in information sequentially, while simultaneously building up a text representation. As each new segment of text is encountered, it immediately needs to be integrated with the text information currently being held in working memory. Comprehension is not a collection of pieces corresponding to sentence meanings; it is a dynamic mental model that continuously is being developed and revised.

Summary of Current Models of Reading

Although reading models continue to evolve, our judgment is that modern interactive models strike a good balance between data- and conceptually driven processes. Kintsch's CI model and a number of other current models propose an extensive foundation of relatively automatic processes for reading, including word recognition and converting sentences to propositions. At the same time, these automatized processes are seen as being guided by the reader's general knowledge and interacting with the reader's purposes. In common with a top-down view and in contrast with a bottom-up model, they emphasize how contact with the text is the basis for meaning construction, with the reader's prior knowledge shaping the meaning that finally results. The models also remind us that the knowledge constructed can take a variety of forms, depending on readers' goals. We now turn to a basic, but vital, kind of knowledge deeply connected to reading—knowledge about words.

Building Vocabulary Through Reading and Instruction

"Words embody power, words embrace action, and words enable us to speak, read, and write with clarity, confidence, and charm" (Duin & Graves, 1987, p. 312). This statement rings true to most educators, who observe firsthand that in many areas **vocabulary knowledge** is linked closely with competence. Understanding words and knowing how to use them—vocabulary knowledge—is an important index of domain and general knowledge. Vocabulary knowledge also influences learning efficiency. Larger vocabularies aid cognitive processing in ways as diverse as more rapid listening and reading comprehension and more precise idea expression in speaking and writing.

The link between vocabulary knowledge and important educational outcomes has been known for many years. In an early but representative study, Conry and Plant (1965) found correlations of .65 and .46 between vocabulary scores and high school rank and college grades, respectively. Correlations between vocabulary scores and intelligence test scores also typically are high, often +.80 or above. Additionally, important literacy-related skills such as reading comprehension (e.g., Stahl & Fairbanks, 1986; Sternberg, 1987) and writing quality (e.g., Duin & Graves, 1987) are linked closely with vocabulary.

Because knowing words is so important, educators have concentrated a great deal of energy on helping students acquire them. Direct instruction has been a common approach, with teachers often having students memorize words and their definitions. Some of the limitations of certain kinds of **direct vocabulary instruction,** however, have been pointed out in research by Nagy and his associates (R. C. Anderson, 1996; Nagy, Anderson, & Herman, 1987; Nagy & Herman, 1987). Their research provides a persuasive case for the important role of reading in vocabulary growth.

The argument for the connection of reading to vocabulary growth is as follows. First, vocabulary growth during the years children are in school is remarkable. Nagy et al. (1987) estimated, for instance, that children add as many as 3,000 words per year to their vocabularies between the 3rd and 12th grades; students may accumulate a reading vocabulary of something like 25,000 words by 8th grade and as many as 50,000 words by the end of high school (Graves, 2006). Second, learning word meanings to a level where they can be accessed quickly and usefully takes considerable time (Beck, McKeown, & Kucan, 2002; Graves, 2006). Because the time that can be devoted to direct vocabulary instruction is limited, only a relatively small portion of vocabulary growth during the school years, just a few hundred words a year, actually can be attributed to direct instruction. Nagy and his associates have contended that reading provides a compelling alternative explanation for students' rapidly growing vocabularies, even though acquiring meanings through reading is a slow, incremental process. A single contact with a word, for instance, typically produces only partial learning, and full comprehension of a new word requires multiple encounters.

Reading does provide numerous opportunities for vocabulary learning. In a series of carefully designed studies examining how words might be learned from context, Nagy and his coworkers showed that, although the absolute amount of learning is quite small in any encounter, incidental learning of word meanings does occur during normal reading. The probability of acquiring significant word knowledge from reading a word once in text is not more than 10% or so. This small increment in word knowledge becomes important, however, when the amount of reading children do in and out of school is considered. Anderson, Wilson, and Fielding (1988), for instance, showed that a typical fifth-grade student reads about 300,000 words from books outside school per year; other print materials, such as newspapers and comic books, increase the total to about 600,000 words. When a conservative estimate of 15 minutes per day of reading in school is added, the number of words read by the typical fifth grader is upward of 1 million a year; avid readers read many times this amount. The strong inference from data like these is that reading is indispensable to vocabulary growth; the words that students learn through reading likely represent a third or more of the words most acquire annually.

This argument that reading is a primary avenue of vocabulary growth was strengthened further by research relating amount of **print exposure** to vocabulary size. Stanovich and his colleagues (Cunningham & Stanovich, 1991; Stanovich, 2000; Stanovich & Cunningham, 1993; Stanovich, West, & Harrison, 1995) measured print exposure through checklists in which respondents indicated whether they were familiar with particular authors, book titles, magazines, and newspapers. The assumption was that the more items respondents checked, the more reading they had done. Real items on the checklists were mixed with foils so that guessing could be controlled; for instance, a list of children's book titles included titles of real books (e.g., *A Light in the Attic* and *Polar Express*), as well as plausible-sounding but nonexistent book titles (e.g., *The Lost Shoe* and *Curious Jim*).

Print exposure as measured by these scales turned out to be a potent predictor of vocabulary knowledge for groups ranging from fourth- and fifth-grade children (Cunningham & Stanovich, 1991) and college students (Stanovich & Cunningham, 1993) to residents of a retirement community (Stanovich et al., 1995). Moreover, the relationship of print exposure to vocabulary holds even when the influence of general ability (e.g., high school grade point average, mathematics ability test scores, and reading ability scores) is removed statistically, suggesting that differential exposure to words through reading is the key factor in vocabulary size no matter what the individual's ability level. Print exposure not only is a unique predictor of vocabulary size but also a better one than intellectual ability measures (e.g., see Stanovich, 2000), which almost always relate significantly to vocabulary.

The Case for Direct Vocabulary Instruction

Although children are learning many more words than we can or would want to teach directly (e.g., direct instruction on the 3,000 or more words students learn each year would require teaching 20 or more words every day throughout the school year, see Graves, 2006) and there is strong evidence for reading's key part in developing students' vocabulary, there still are good reasons to teach vocabulary directly (see Baumann, 2009; Beck et al., 2002; Blachowicz, Fisher, Ogle, & Watts-Taffe, 2006; Graves, 2006). Biemiller and Boote (2006) point out the large differences in vocabulary size between more and less advantaged students. For disadvantaged students, even relatively smaller vocabulary gains are likely to be important, just as English language learners can benefit from acquiring key vocabulary. In content areas, understanding precise meanings of academic vocabulary, such as knowing the meaning of *operation, variable,* and *function* in an algebra class is essential to academic growth. As Graves (2006) has stated, " . . . the fact that we cannot directly teach all the words students need to learn does not mean that we cannot and should not teach some of them." (p. 61).

High-quality vocabulary instruction also can produce effects extending beyond the specific words being taught. Graves (2006), for example, has proposed a four-part framework for comprehensive vocabulary instruction designed to directly develop students' vocabulary, habits of word learning and positive attitudes about words. First, he contends, teachers should provide *rich and varied language experiences.* A starting point for this would be simply encouraging reading of all kinds. During reading-related activities, however, teachers also can draw attention to individual words by repeating them, asking about word meanings, and helping students draw distinctions between related words (e.g., "Do *wet* and *damp* mean the same thing?"). Second, teachers should *teach individual words directly.* Evidence shows that the best vocabulary instruction includes intentional teaching of key words and a variety of opportunities to use them (Baumann, 2009; Blachowicz et al., 2006). Third, students should be taught *word learning strategies.* For example, students who have learned to use morphological information (see Chapter 11) and context to decipher words are better able to infer what new words mean. Finally, Graves argues that students can be helped to develop *word consciousness* by being encouraged to notice words, becoming excited about them, and learning to use them well. Word consciousness, a form of metalinguistic awareness, can be developed by methods as diverse as having students investigate words' origins and playing with idioms and puns (e.g., "She said she had 'a frog in her throat'—hmmm . . . do you think she *really* had a frog in her throat?"). Also, young writers can be encouraged to brainstorm groups of related words (e.g., *happy, contented, cheerful, joyful, overjoyed, ecstatic,* etc.) to increase the variety and richness of what they write.

Word Knowledge: What It Means to Know a Word

It might seem from our discussion so far that vocabulary knowledge is an either-or thing—either you know a word or you don't. Picture for a moment, though, the answers you might get if you asked a group of college students the meaning of a relatively rare word, say, *ascetic.* Some would have no idea at all; some might venture a guess (e.g., "Is it something like 'clean'?"). Others would be more confident (e.g., "I think it means 'austere, self-denying'") and perhaps even add an instance of its use (e.g., "The monk lived an *ascetic* life, denying himself all but the most basic necessities"). Still others might want clues before they ventured a guess (e.g., "Could you use it in a sentence for me?"). Given the example "He looked like a student, thin and *ascetic,*" some of them might propose, "Well, it's got something to do with a student and how he looks. It's either 'pale' or 'poor,' . . . could be either!" Still others just would be confused: "Isn't it something like 'art appreciation'?" "Knowing a word" obviously is not an all-or-none phenomenon!

Graves (2006) has pointed out that learning a word's meaning varies markedly depending on the learner's current knowledge and the depth of understanding required. For instance, first graders often are asked to read words they already have in their oral vocabularies (e.g., *house, car,* and *mother*). It is a different challenge to learn a new meaning for a known word. Many words are *polysemous;* that is, they have multiple meanings (e.g., *run* and *set*). Still another demand arises when the student must learn a new word for a known meaning (e.g., a child understands the idea of "being on time" but does not comprehend the word *punctual* when she reads it). Finally, in some instances, students may not have the concept or the word, as in reading text materials that contain unfamiliar concepts (e.g., *paradigm* and *dysfunctional*). Initially, our goal is for students to understand the words they read. Our ultimate goal is much more ambitious: We hope they learn to use the words flexibly and fluently in writing and speaking.

Definitional Versus Contextual Word Knowledge

In thinking about vocabulary learning goals, researchers have found it useful to distinguish between definitional and contextual word knowledge. **Definitional knowledge** refers to the relationship between a word and other known words, as in a dictionary definition (e.g., an *octroi* is a tax paid on certain goods entering a city). When asked about vocabulary, most people envision definitional knowledge first. A definition places a word within a semantic network of words the learner presumably already knows and can be a way for students to acquire useful knowledge about a word.

The knowledge developed from seeing or hearing words in context may be even more useful, however. For example, a native speaker of English immediately sees the oddity of certain vocabulary choices in sentences like *"She drove her plane to Austin, Texas"; "I hope I have a capable application to your program"; "He initiated his car's engine";* and *"She despaired her hope of ever meeting him again."* When we consider words individually, we are tempted to think of their meanings as independent of their context. Yet with rare exceptions word use in natural language is highly contextual; what words mean often depends on how they are combined with others. Thus, student vocabulary knowledge needs to extend well beyond words' dictionary definitions to **contextual knowledge,** understanding how they actually are used in writing and speaking.

The contextual nature of word meanings has led some authorities (e.g., Nagy, 1988; Nagy & Scott, 2000) to propose that vocabulary knowledge is organized in schema-like structures containing not only the meaning of the word but also a host of temporal, spatial, and grammatical cues. Consider the following sentence:

> As the mechanic tried to tighten the bolt one last turn, the bolt _____ , and his wrench clattered to the concrete.

If we are asked to supply a word for the blank, we immediately draw on our linguistic, metalinguistic, and world knowledge. Choices such as *cried, sensitive,* and *happily* are discarded as either "unboltlike" or grammatically nonsensical, and we rapidly move on to more acceptable possibilities.

In even a short passage, suitable word choices typically are surprisingly constrained by the syntactic and discourse context in which words are embedded. Many clues to a word's meaning come from outside the word itself. In our example, we quickly surmise from the context—without necessarily thinking explicitly about it—that the missing word must be a verb, something that might happen to a bolt when a mechanic tightened it one last time, and that, if it happened to a bolt, would result in the wrench's flying off and clattering to the floor. In this example, a word was missing, but the process is similar when readers encounter any unknown word while reading.

With the actual word present, even an unknown one, within-word **morphological cues** also become available to the reader. Consider this example:

To his dismay, the inventor found that his automatic bed-maker was *unmarketable.*

Readers unfamiliar with the word *unmarketable* also have, in addition to the external cues, several morphological cues available. From earlier instruction or from direct experiences with prefixes and suffixes, many students are able to analyze the parts of the word and recognize *un-* as a prefix, *market* as the stem or root word, and *-able* as a suffix indicating an adjectival form of a word. From contact with other, more frequent words beginning with *un-*, such as *unsafe, unhappy,* and *unclear,* these students should have a sense of *un-* as indicating negation. Knowledge of the root word *market* may enable them to recognize that the word *unmarketable* has to do with buying and selling.

This assortment of internal cues, coupled with those from the external context, make it possible for students to approximate word meanings as they read. Having both within-word and external context cues by no means ensures that they will be able to use or even recognize them as potential clues to figuring out words, however. The less sophisticated the readers, the fewer linguistic and metalinguistic cues they will recognize. Also, some contexts in which new words are encountered are relatively rich, others are not.

Understanding words in context does not necessarily mean consciously "figuring them out." In ordinary reading and as portrayed in most current models of reading such as Kintsch's, fixations on a word simply trigger automatized word-related knowledge. For example, we automatically comprehend the different meanings of the word *left* as we read the following sentences: "He is *left*-handed" and "He was *left* at the altar." Similarly, when we speak, we almost never pay attention to words' dictionary definitions. We just use them, saying things without hesitation like "Ooowww—I think I've broken my *foot!*" "That pitch was outside by a *foot!*" or "My kitten Crouton always wants to sleep at the *foot* of my bed."

In summary, word knowledge is not a simple either-or matter. "Knowing a word" goes far beyond dictionary definitions to subtle understanding of words' meanings and uses. Thus, vocabulary knowledge is an excellent example of this book's theme that knowledge is contextual (see Chapter 1). While vocabulary knowledge can seem to be quite explicit, much of what we know about vocabulary is tacit and unrecognized—knowing what words go with others, for instance. Vocabulary knowledge also is highly automatized and arguably more procedural than declarative (e.g., as in the correct recognition and use of the polysemous words *left* and *foot* in our examples; see Nagy & Scott, 2000). Reading is an ideal way of acquiring this contextualized knowledge about word meanings and uses.

Helping Students Build Their Vocabulary

How best do we help students increase their vocabularies? A starting point, of course, is simply to encourage reading in any way possible. From the work by Nagy and others, we know that vocabulary growth is related to how much students read. Over their lifetimes, students will acquire much of their vocabulary from reading, on their own, without having been taught (Graves, 2006). Thus, reading is one of the most important gateways to this vital dimension of human learning.

Beyond simply encouraging reading there are several strategies teachers can use to stimulate vocabulary growth. Reading provides a rich context for learning vocabulary, but only if students are prepared to use it. In the long run, learning how to figure out word meanings may be even more important than learning specific words. Morphological, syntactical, and context clues are potentially available for students to use, but they will often need encouragement and practice to use linguistic and world knowledge effectively.

The vocabulary knowledge that students acquire through reading should be complemented by direct vocabulary instruction (Baumann, 2009; Beck et al., 2002; Biemiller & Boote, 2006; Blachowicz et al., 2006; Graves, 2006). Functional vocabulary knowledge is built on a solid foundation of understanding word meanings and their relationships to one another. Especially when words are presented around a theme or topic, knowledge structures will develop that make new vocabulary acquisition and reading comprehension more likely.

Direct instruction also can be used to encourage students to notice and learn new words as they read. In an intensive vocabulary instruction condition in Duin and Graves's early (1987) study students were asked to keep track of the times they read, spoke, or heard selected words in outside activities. Because students were actively encouraged to notice new words (which they did), they also became more inclined to learn them and use them on their own.

Building Organized Knowledge Through Reading

There is a long history of educational psychology research focusing on *what is retained* as a result of reading. This research, commonly known as "text learning" or "prose learning" research, primarily has examined ways that text materials—especially informational (expository) text—can be modified to influence how readers read and what they learn. In the following sections, we summarize three major research programs focused on improving learning from text—advance organizers, text signals, and text-related questions. Each continues to be important not only for informing teachers' decisions about how to guide student reading effectively, but also for understanding current views of reading comprehension. As you will see, each is closely tied to important cognitive principles. We begin with advance organizers.

Advance Organizers

Advance organizers are " . . . appropriately relevant and inclusive introductory materials . . . introduced in advance of learning . . . and presented at a higher level of abstraction, generality, and inclusiveness" than subsequent to-be-learned reading materials (Ausubel, 1968, p. 148). Advance organizers provide "ideational scaffolding" that assists in the retention of the more detailed materials that follow. In short, they activate prior knowledge and give readers an organized framework in which to understand what they're reading.

The idea of advance organizers has been one of the most intuitively appealing and long-lived concepts in reading research. Anything that can help learners relate new information to what they already know ought to be valuable. In one of the earliest examples of advance organizer research, Ausubel and Fitzgerald (1961) had students read a passage about Buddhism and tested them for their content mastery under three conditions: (1) a condition in which subjects first read a historical introduction, (2) a condition in which the principles of Buddhism were first set forth in abstract and general terms, and (3) a condition that first used a review of Christianity as an organizer designed to relate what the students already knew about religions to the material they were being asked to learn on Buddhism. Results were clear: On the posttest, students who read the advance organizer relating Christianity to Buddhism outperformed students in the two other conditions.

Although Ausubel and his associates obtained positive results in their research on advance organizers, as time passed findings in the field became less clear. A recurring problem was with the vagueness of the concept *advance organizer.* Text features as diverse as outlines, questions, pictures, graphs, and paragraphs were being defined in one study or another as advance organizers. Coupled with the methodological problems often seen in early research (e.g., not keeping track of how long students studied material, not employing true control groups, and poor posttest development), the lack of specificity for what defined an effective advance organizer limited research progress.

Many of these problems were cleared up as researchers began to use more sophisticated experimental designs and tie their work into schema theory, which provided greater theoretical clarity. Results in this later research showed that advance organizers a paragraph or two long prefacing the to-be-learned content generally produced beneficial effects on readers' memory for materials. In general, as summarized in work by Glover and his associates, advance organizers that give readers *analogies* for upcoming content, that are *concrete* and use concrete examples, and that are *well-learned* by readers will be more beneficial than abstract, general, or partially learned organizers (Corkill, 1992; Corkill, Glover, & Bruning, 1988; Dinnel & Glover, 1985). If properly developed, advance organizers can provide an effective method for teachers and writers to enhance readers' learning from text.

Text Signals

A second important body of text learning research has focused on **text signals,** writing tactics designed to improve the cohesion of reading materials or to indicate that certain text elements are particularly important (Lorch & Lorch, 1995). The assumption behind inserting signals in text is that they can affect comprehension by helping readers discern a text's topic structure and organization. As signals direct attention to a text's topics and its relations, recall of text structure and content should be improved. Several kinds of text signals commonly used by writers include the following:

- Number signals "The three most important points are [1] . . . , [2] . . . , and [3] . . . "
- Headings, such as the heading at the top of this section
- Italicized or bolded text
- Preview sentences "As we will see in chapter 13, . . . "
- Recall sentences "Recall from chapter 4, where we . . . "

Number signals (Lorch, 1989) are exactly what they sound like—numbers used to enumerate a set of points, steps in a process, a list of names, or other reading content. They are useful for identifying important elements of a text that students are to remember (e.g., four causes of the War of the Roses and five steps in readying a lathe for operation). *Headings* break up longer text into segments of thematically related content and reduce the amount of cognitive effort required to comprehend the material. When a set or series of ideas, names, or steps is to be remembered, number signals are useful; when specific elements of reading materials are crucial, they can be *italicized* or **bolded.**

Two other types of useful text signals are *preview sentences* and *recall sentences*. Preview sentences signal upcoming contents. If preview sentences are placed early in a reading passage, they will tend to focus readers' attention on the upcoming material and help students better remember it. Students tend to group together the signaled content and the information in which the signal was embedded when they recall it (Glover et al., 1988). Recall sentences, on the other hand, signal back to previously learned material. They often are used by textbook writers, but they also have uses in shorter assignments by helping students remember information relevant to the content in which the signal is embedded. They also help students cluster information in memory and to assimilate new information with knowledge they already possess.

Inserted Questions

A third way of improving learning from text materials has focused on questions inserted into reading materials. More than 50 years ago, Ernst Rothkopf began an influential research program exploring how such questions, also called **adjunct questions,** affect readers' memory for information in expository text. In one of his initial studies (Rothkopf, 1966), participants read a lengthy section of expository material and were tested on their ability to remember its content. Some participants answered inserted questions every so often while they read; others did not. The positioning of the questions—before or after passages—was varied across the conditions in which participants answered questions. In addition, the adjunct questions were relevant to only some parts of the reading materials. Much of the content was not directly related to answering the adjunct questions. After Rothkopf's participants finished reading, they took a test on the material. Some test items were repeated versions of the adjunct questions; others covered content unrelated to the adjunct questions. Repeated questions were meant to tap *intentional learning*—learning required to answer the adjunct questions. The posttest questions assessing content not relevant to the adjunct questions tapped *incidental learning*—learning not required by the adjunct questions.

Three major findings came from Rothkopf's pioneering study. First, adjunct questions had a strong effect on intentional learning; that is, students' performance on the posttest questions that assessed their knowledge of content required for the adjunct questions was far superior to students' performance on questions assessing incidental learning. Second, when adjunct questions were placed *after* reading materials, they facilitated *both* intentional and incidental learning, although the impact on incidental learning was less. Third, when adjunct questions were placed *before* reading materials, they enhanced intentional learning but did not facilitate incidental learning. Indeed, on measures of incidental learning, a control group that received no adjunct questions but was asked to study hard and to remember the passage's details outperformed the group that received adjunct questions in advance of reading.

Rothkopf's study had important influences, both methodologically and conceptually, on subsequent research on text learning, and was followed by an explosion of studies on questions inserted in expository texts. This research generally painted a consistent picture of the benefits of inserted questions. It also probed ways that questions themselves might be varied and potentially affect learning. One of the most important variations was found to be *level of question*. Of course, research varying *level of question* presupposes some method of reliably classifying the level of learning being tapped by inserted questions.

None of the many question classification methods has been more influential than the hierarchy created by Bloom, Englehart, Furst, Hill, and Krathwohl (1956), variations of which still are widely used in classifying instructional objectives and developing test items. The Bloom et al. ***Taxonomy of educational objectives*** posited six levels of learning that vary based on the sophistication and complexity of the learning required. Ordered from simple to complex, these levels were knowledge, comprehension, application, analysis, synthesis, and evaluation.

Knowledge-level learning merely requires factual retention, such as names or dates. It is akin to rote learning and was the learning tapped by the level of question employed in Rothkopf's initial research. *Comprehension-level* questions require more sophisticated knowledge, as they require students at least be able to paraphrase the to-be-learned material in their own words. *Application-level* learning requires using information in some concrete way. It differs from comprehension-level learning in requiring the implementation of knowledge, such as the distinction between a student being able to explain the concept of *irony* (comprehension) and actually use it in writing a short story (application). *Analysis-level* learning is more complex yet in that learners must be able to break down information into its component parts so that the relationship among all components is clear. For example, the request "Compare and contrast levels of processing with schema theory" requires that students break down both schema theory and levels of processing into their component parts (e.g., encoding and storage) and relate them to one another. *Synthesis-level* learning, as proposed by Bloom et al., demands that students put together old knowledge in new ways. For example, consider the request "Using your knowledge of encoding specificity, construct a test over content you're currently teaching that will enhance your students' test performance." Fulfilling this request requires you to use knowledge you already have (both how to construct tests and the concept of encoding specificity) in a new way. Finally, at the highest level of Bloom's taxonomy is *evaluation-level* learning, which involves students making judgments about the value of methods or materials, based on their knowledge. For example, if you were shown three videotapes of teachers presenting a lesson and asked to judge how well each teacher took into account the limitations of students' working memory, you would be engaging in evaluation-level learning.

In general, findings from inserted questions research have favored use of higher-order over lower-order questions. Lower-order questions tend to facilitate only knowledge-level learning (Andre, 1987a). They also have an unfortunate tendency to produce "posthole" effects, in which students learn only what the questions ask for, ignoring the remainder of the text and sometimes even missing the passage's main point. Higher-order questions, in contrast, tend to enhance both intentional and incidental learning. Although they work when used before and after reading, it typically is better to pose them in advance (Hamaker, 1986; Hamilton, 1985). Presumably, because higher-order questions cannot be answered by locating a specific term or phrase, students need to carefully search and evaluate large segments of text to answer the questions. The result is more elaborative processing and better learning. It also turns out that questions *requiring students to make decisions* are more effective than questions at the same level of Bloom's taxonomy that do not require decisions. The act of making a decision (e.g., "Is X true or not?") about some content appears to result in deeper processing, leading to better memory for the content. If student decision making is a part of a teacher's instructional goals, adjunct questions can be framed to include appropriate decisions about information being read.

Additional Uses of Questions to Promote Comprehension

Another question-based technique, **elaborative interrogation,** has been used to prompt student inferences about texts (e.g., Woloshyn, Paivio, & Pressley, 1994; Wood, Pressley, & Winne, 1990). In the simplest form of elaborative interrogation, learners read a series of sentences, answering "why" questions to clarify the relationship between the subject and the predicate of the each sentence. For instance, if elementary students read the sentence "Cats like to lie in the sun," they would be asked *why*—that is, to generate a reason why this fact might be true (e.g., because the sun warms them up). Recall of sentences processed in this way is increased substantially; similar effects are present when elaborative interrogation is used with expository paragraphs (see Seifert, 1993).

In general, elaborative interrogation seems to help readers not just to recall more facts, but to build more complete mental representations based on the inferences they make. In a study by Ozgungor and Guthrie (2004) college students answered elaborative interrogation questions while reading a 1,500-word passage from *Scientific American* magazine. The elaborative interrogation group was compared to control participants who simply read the passage twice. Ozgungor and Guthrie found that students in the elaborative interrogation group not only recalled more information than control students, but their inferences were more accurate and coherent. They also noted greater benefits for students with less prior topic knowledge than for those who knew more.

King (1994, 2007) has extended the research on inserted questions and elaborative interrogation into classroom methods that use questions to prompt readers' critical reading. We know, for instance, that good readers actively monitor their comprehension, decide which information is important, think about how information might be used, and ask themselves questions. In King's view, teaching students to explain why and how something has occurred and to connect their explanations to what their reading partners know helps all readers improve their understanding of what they read. In several studies, King has shown that higher-order learning activities (e.g., at the application, analysis, synthesis, and evaluation levels) are well within the abilities of elementary school children. When students are systematically taught how to construct inferential questions that prompt deeper thinking, for example, they have better discussions of what they've read and significantly improved performance on comprehension tests (see King, 1994, 2007). Self-questioning also can be extended to include thinking aloud and creating classroom exchanges organized around asking and answering student-generated questions.

Each of the methods for promoting reading comprehension discussed in this section—whether advance organizers, text signals, and or questioning—has close ties to important cognitive principles, especially knowledge activation, knowledge organization, and active processing. They also can be related to key elements of reading comprehension models, such as the ideas of *macrostructure* and *situation model* in Kintsch's CI model. Research on each of these topics suggests that these methods can be effective and useful additions to a teacher's instructional repertoire. In general, the more ways teachers can help students actively process and organize what they learn and relate it to what they already know, the better their comprehension and retention will be.

Building Capabilities for Reading: Reading Strategies

Like cognitive perspectives in general, a cognitive perspective on reading emphasizes helping students develop adaptable strategies for comprehending text and constructing meaning (Baker & Beall, 2009; Block & Lacina, 2009; Dole, Nokes, & Drits, 2009; Graesser, 2007; McNamara, 2007; Rapp et al., 2007; Wharton-McDonald & Swiger, 2009). The goal is to help students acquire metacognitive awareness and control over how they read. Today's strong emphasis on reading strategies was developed out of several early insights: recognition that "strategic" approaches to reading comprehension develop slowly (e.g., Brown, Day, & Jones, 1983), that reading is highly metacognitive in nature (e.g., Baker, 2002), and that skilled reading requires conditional knowledge to apply strategies at the right time and place (e.g., Paris, Cross, & Lipson, 1984). In the next few pages, we examine some important examples of strategies instruction, beginning with a program developed more than a quarter-century ago—reciprocal teaching—that still has considerable applicability today.

Reciprocal Teaching

Dole et al. (2009) have called Palincsar and Brown's reciprocal teaching " . . . arguably the single most important work on cognitive strategies instruction designed to improve reading comprehension" (p. 354). First initiated in the 1980s, **reciprocal teaching** is a broad and flexible program that focuses on four reading comprehension strategies: summarizing, questioning, clarifying difficult parts of text, and predicting (e.g., Brown & Palincsar, 1989; Palincsar & Brown, 1984; see also Rosenshine, Meister, & Chapman, 1996). In Palincsar and Brown's approach, a teacher models reading comprehension strategies and guides students in performing them. At the start of a lesson, the teacher engages the students in a short discussion designed to activate relevant prior knowledge. Both the teacher and the students then silently read a brief passage, and the teacher models how to summarize the passage, develop a question about the main point, clarify difficult ideas, and predict what will happen next. Everyone then reads another passage, with the teacher now asking the students questions that give them clues about what they are thinking and what kind of instruction they need. As the students respond, often haltingly at first, the teacher provides guidance in helping them summarize, ask questions, comprehend, and predict.

Gradually, across sessions, the teacher shifts responsibility to the students so that they are the ones summarizing, asking questions, clarifying, and predicting future happenings. Highlighted in the process is *how* the teacher and the students think as they try to comprehend. Teacher scaffolding may be fairly direct when the teacher guides the process (e.g., a teacher comments, "Try putting yourself in Juan's place for a moment") or indirect (e.g., a comment to a student, "I like to check after each section to see if I can say what it's all about—the main idea, you know"). Reciprocal teaching also includes direct instruction on how to perform comprehension strategies, as well as tips for reading more effectively.

One of reciprocal teaching's key strategies is *summarizing*, which involves not only figuring out which are the most important ideas in a passage but also creating a new text—a summary—representing the original one. Research on teaching students to summarize suggests the utility of continuing to develop this skill. In an extension of the reciprocal teaching approach to at-risk college students, for example, Hart and Speece (1998) had students practice summarizing passages. At first, the teacher used a think-aloud procedure to model summarization, but leadership soon was transferred to the students, who practiced summarization in groups and modeled it for each other. As students developed their summarization skills, the teacher's role shifted to providing feedback, prompts, and praise for good work.

Hart and Speece used the following rules for teaching summarization, drawn from the comprehension model of Kintsch and Van Dijk (1978) and early research on summarization strategies by Brown, Day, and Jones (1983): (1) Delete minor and unimportant information, (2) combine similar ideas into categories and label them as needed, (3) select the main idea if the author provides it, and (4) invent the main idea when the author does not provide it. Overall, summarizing involves integrating materials into coherent, accurate representations. For shorter passages, these may be two or three sentences in length, but for longer passages may be a paragraph or more.

Question–Answer Relationships (QAR)

Another program of reading strategies research that continues to be influential is that of Raphael and her associates (e.g., Raphael & McKinney, 1983; Raphael & Pearson, 1982; Raphael & Wonnacott, 1985). Raphael's research used questions to guide students' attention not only to information directly appearing in text materials themselves, but to what they can infer from their own prior knowledge and the author's approach. Raphael and Wonnacott (1985), for example, contrasted fourth graders in a control condition with students of similar ability levels who received training in finding the answers to reading-related questions. Three types of questions were used: (1) those for which the answers were *explicit* in the text, (2) those for which the answers were *implicit* in the text (inferences were needed, such as the inference used in determining someone's age from her or his description), and (3) those for which an *integration* of the reader's background knowledge and text information was required (inferences required were similar to those you might make in using the content of this chapter to devise methods for improving your students' reading comprehension). Students in the experimental condition received four days of training and practice in answering the questions. Considerable attention was given to showing students how to answer the questions. Results indicated that the training facilitated students' ability to draw inferences about text materials and significantly improved comprehension. In a follow-up experiment, Raphael and Wonnacott (1985) taught teachers in an in-service program how to train students to answer the three types of questions. Results again were positive. Instruction in how to answer the different kinds of questions, coupled with practice and feedback, resulted in students' significant improvements in reading comprehension.

Subsequently, Raphael and her colleagues (see Raphael & Au, 2005) have shaped methods developed in their research into a comprehensive reading comprehension approach called **question–answer relationships (QAR).** As in the original research, some of the questions teachers and students pose are answerable from the text itself. For example, so-called "Right There" questions can be answered by finding the place in the text where the information is found. "Think and Search" questions, however, entail searching different parts of a text (e.g., across sentences, paragraphs, or even chapters) in order to find the answer. These are text-focused, but require inferences in order to answer them. Two other kinds of questions in QAR—"On my own" and "Author and me" questions—require students to go beyond the text. "On my own" questions can be answered without having read the text at all, but are useful in activating readers' prior knowledge and connections to the text topic. "Author and me" questions require having read and understood the text in order to answer. For instance, they may call for students to predict what will happen, visualize a scene, or make a judgment about a character's motives. While these questions also involve knowledge activation, they require students to relate their knowledge to what they are reading.

Transactional Strategies Instruction (TSI)

As Block and Pressley (2002) have pointed out, successful readers don't just use strategies one at a time or only when instructed. As a result, strategies researchers have moved decisively toward designing and testing comprehensive, classroom-based approaches in which multiple strategies are taught together. These integrated packages include teacher modeling and explanations to encourage students to use reading strategies in self-regulated ways.

Among the best known of these comprehensive approaches is **transactional strategies instruction (TSI)** (Brown, Pressley, Van Meter, & Schuder, 1996; Pressley et al., 1992). TSI strategies include summarizing, using context clues, visualizing, making connections to prior knowledge, and making and verifying predictions. Strategies are taught explicitly, with extensive training continuing minimally over a semester or school year. Typically, strategies will be introduced one at a time, with extensive instruction on learning the strategy and how and when to use it. Then, as the strategies are mastered successively, they are gradually integrated so they can be used flexibly and effectively. In general, results for use of TSI have been positive, with elementary, middle, and high school students trained in TSI increasing their comprehension of text (see Block & Pressley, 2002; Pressley & Schneider, 1997).

Although it is possible to acquire reading comprehension strategies implicitly or by trial and error, strategy use is more likely when they are taught explicitly (Dole et al., 2009; Duffy, 2002; Pressley, 2002). By describing the purpose of strategies, modeling their use, and explaining how each can be implemented, teachers gradually shift more and more responsibility to the students. As students gain confidence, they can model strategy use for each other. Teachers can assume the role of coach, encouraging students to use and self-evaluate their strategies, and giving them feedback.

Like any complex, long-term instructional approach, TSI is not necessarily easy to implement. Acquiring a flexible repertoire of reading strategies and cognitive skills is a long-term process requiring a great deal of practice and feedback (Dole et al., 2009; Pressley & Harris, 2006). Instruction needs to be continued throughout the school year and even across years. Specific obstacles include finding classroom time to model and practice the strategies, integrating strategies with content-area instruction, and producing consistent strategy instruction from year to year. In the end, however, teachers are likely to feel that time spent teaching reading strategies is time well spent (Hilden & Pressley, 2007).

Concept-Oriented Reading Instruction (CORI)

Since the early 1990s, Guthrie and his colleagues have been testing and refining a model of reading development, **concept-oriented reading instruction (CORI).** CORI combines an emphasis on content-area learning, primarily in science, with a strong emphasis on reading comprehension. CORI provides systematic, explicit instruction in six reading comprehension strategies: (1) activating background knowledge, (2) questioning, (3) searching for information, (4) summarizing, and (5) organizing information graphically (e.g., through concept maps, matrices), and (6) identifying story structures.

Like other comprehensive approaches to reading strategy instruction, CORI uses systematic, explicit methods to teach its strategies. For example, in studies reported by Wigfield et al. (2008), the strategies were taught over a 6-week period, one strategy per week. Each strategy was modeled by the teacher, scaffolded for individual students, and practiced extensively. Then, in a second 6-week period, the strategies were integrated with each other (an exception was story structure, which was integrated throughout) and utilized increasingly in classroom activities. This approach, as Wigfield et al. (2008) noted, is similar to the recommendations of the National Reading Panel Report (NRP, 2000). The result of this kind of careful instruction is that students learn each of the strategies well, along with the conditional knowledge to integrate them effectively into their reading.

One of CORI's distinguishing features is that it combines reading strategies with methods and materials designed to build motivation for both reading and science learning. A key concept is **reading engagement**—students becoming intrinsically motivated to read (Guthrie, McRae, & Klauda, 2008; Wigfield et al., 2008). Strategies are important, but students must be motivated to use them. They also need to put forth effort in their reading, persist when they encounter obstacles to their learning, and read frequently, both for learning and for pleasure. To reach these goals, CORI emphasizes five instructional practices tied closely to motivational theory (see Chapters 6 and 7).

First, CORI instruction stresses *relevance,* calculated to foster intrinsic motivation. For example, numerous real-world observations, ranging from bird watching to monitoring the phases of the moon, are used to prompt and energize student investigations, including searching for information in books. Second, CORI stresses *student choice,* which relates to the concept of autonomy. Third, the program uses *success* to build students' self-efficacy, both in their ability to read successfully and investigate topics in depth. Fourth, *collaborative classroom structures,* such as group projects and discussions, tap social sources of motivation for reading. Finally, *thematic units* representing "big ideas" are used to build mastery goals and to make materials more organized and meaningful.

A particular strength of the CORI model, in our view, is that strategies and content-area instruction with strong motivational components are integrated into a single instructional approach. Multiple analyses (e.g., see Guthrie et al., 2007; Wigfield et al. 2008) have shown

CORI, when compared to traditional and strategy-only instruction, to produce superior outcomes on reading comprehension, strategy use, and reading engagement. Reading strategies instruction, which is delivered according to best practices developed over the past 20 years or more, is enhanced by being embedded in instruction in which students are strongly motivated to read and use reading strategies. Students who are excited about becoming "experts" on birds, butterflies, turtles, or planets will be highly motivated to seek and find the information they need from books or online. Similarly, students who are highly engaged in learning will be motivated to learn and practice the reading strategies (e.g., summarizing, placing information into graphical organizers, integrating information from multiple sources, etc.) that will help them reach their learning goals.

Assessing Reading Comprehension

For most of us, the typical processes of reading assessment look familiar and sensible—readers read a passage, chapter, or book, and then complete a test over what they've read. But many problems lurk just beneath the surface of this seemingly reasonable approach. One of these is the basic question of what, exactly, are most reading comprehension tests really measuring? At this time, the answer to that question still is mostly unknown.

Most current reading comprehension tests are based on general, commonsense notions about reading comprehension, but have little demonstrated relationship to any theories of reading comprehension, such as those discussed in this chapter. This issue has been known for many years (see Pearson & Hamm, 2005), but mostly has not impacted test development. For instance, an analysis of several popular reading comprehension tests by Keenan, Betjemann, and Olson (2008) has shown that supposedly comparable tests differ in what they measure, with some even measuring different qualities at different ages. The result of such ambiguity about what tests are measuring is that they provide little in the way of practical feedback to either teachers or students. Similarly, differences in test formats, such as multiple-choice, cloze, or retellings of content (Francis et al., 2006), and even in text structure (Deane, Sheehan, Sabatini, Futagi, & Kostin, 2006) can have significant effects on reading test performance, further confusing the meaning of test results.

Another unknown in reading comprehension assessment is how to factor in students' prior domain knowledge. Obviously, there can be no "pure" measure of reading comprehension, where prior knowledge plays no role. But it's clear that there almost certainly will be differences in "reading comprehension" for students who are highly knowledgeable about a passage's content, compared to those who aren't. Ideally, readers would be assessed on a wide range of topics and formats such that test outcomes could be related to content-area knowledge, reading comprehension subskills, and writing genre. In this vein, Leslie and Caldwell (2009) have proposed more context-sensitive assessments and aggregating across multiple assessments to gain a more complete picture of reading comprehension. Unfortunately, because of time limitations and the high reliability required in high-stakes testing, most current reading comprehension measures continue to provide a fairly narrow range of passages and possible responses, even though the wider-ranging assessments would yield more useful information.

Two Alternative Approaches to Reading Comprehension Assessment

With most standard "read and then answer questions" comprehension assessments clouded by problems like those previously mentioned, some have attempted devise other approaches to measuring reading comprehension. One of these is the Dynamic Indicators of Basic Early Literacy Skills (DIBELS), a widely used battery of tests given to a very large number of U.S. students annually. A key measure in DIBELS that is viewed as reflecting reading comprehension is oral reading fluency—how *fast* students can read passages aloud in a fixed amount of time, most typically a minute or so. In contrast to most reading comprehension measures, connections can be made between DIBELS and reading theory—specifically, the hypothesized connection between automatized word decoding and reading comprehension. DIBELS is valid, its developers contend, because faster decoders have fewer demands on their attention and working memory and therefore more resources to devote to comprehension. Slow decoders, in contrast, not only are likely to spend more energy on decoding than comprehension, but to overload their working memory. Thus, reading speed provides an indicator of reading comprehension.

In spite of DIBELS seeming tie to theory, criticism of it as a valid reading comprehension measure by reading authorities has been extraordinarily sharp and widespread (e.g., Goodman, 2006; Pearson, 2006; Pressley, Hilden, & Shankland, 2005). As discussed in the previous chapter, S. J. Samuels, one of the leading authorities in reading fluency theory, has argued that DIBELS mostly measures reading speed. In Samuels' view (Samuels, 2007), the theoretical base for DIBELS is not nearly as strong as claimed—the key to reading comprehension is *simultaneous* decoding and comprehension, not just the decoding speed tapped by DIBELS. As a personal illustration, Samuels has written that, although he can read a passage in Spanish orally with accuracy and speed, he wouldn't comprehend it, because he isn't fluent in Spanish. By analogy, simply reading a DIBELS test passage with speed and accuracy may or may not represent reading comprehension. At worst, he worries, rapid reading may be nothing more than "barking at print"—reading aloud without comprehension.

In their analyses of reading comprehension development, which also bear on questions of DIBELS's validity, Paris and Hamilton (2009) have shown that the decoding speed-comprehension relationship changes as readers develop. In their view, oral reading speed measures may be useful within a larger framework of assessment for beginning readers because decoding speed and comprehension are more closely connected at that point in readers' development. For older readers, however, oral reading speed and comprehension are much less clearly linked. While automatic decoding still is important to reading comprehension, the reading speed-comprehension connection becomes tenuous; good readers may read more slowly or quickly depending on the passage and their goals. Furthermore, as silent reading becomes the norm in the upper elementary grades, using an oral reading measure becomes even more suspect.

In a very different approach to measuring reading comprehension, other researchers have begun studies of readers' verbal responses to what they are reading. Their method uses a statistical method called **latent semantic analysis (LSA)** to analyze these responses. LSA is a technique for representing meanings contained in a particular text or knowledge domain (Landauer & Dumais, 1997). It makes estimates of similarity between text units, such as words or sentences, by calculating how often they co-occur within documents. Through LSA's analysis and representation of all such co-occurrences, the correspondence between two sets of text-based information can be calculated. One of LSA's current uses is in grading essays on standardized tests, where LSA's indicators of how well test-takers' responses match information in a target domain are compared to scores assigned by human graders.

In LSA's use for reading comprehension assessment, LSA analyses of readers' protocols are related to other, more traditional measures of reading comprehension. Millis et al. (2006), for example, had college students type their thoughts sentence-by-sentence into the computer as they read scientific texts. LSA then was applied to these protocols to gauge their similarity to (1) the current sentence being read and (2) prior sentences that were linked causally to the current sentence. Reading comprehension theory previously had predicted (Graesser et al., 1994) and prior research had shown (e.g., Magliano, Millis, & McNamara, 2003) that verbal protocols of good readers tended to focus more on the *prior* causal sentences than on the current sentence. In Millis et al., students also were tested on three more traditional "after-reading" measures of student comprehension: (1) "text base" questions, requiring recall of specific content, (2) "situation model" questions, requiring inferences from multiple sentences to answer, and (3) the comprehension subtest of the Nelson-Denny Test of Reading. Overall, the relationship between the LSA scores and these traditional reading comprehension measures was positive when what the student typed was semantically similar to prior causal antecedents and negative when what they typed was tied to the current sentence. In other words, comprehension was best when students thought back about prior information.

This kind of work, although still in early stages and currently focused on adult readers, provides an interesting new perspective on comprehension assessment that hints at the possibility of assessment based on what students say or write as they read. It also seems to have the potential for helping us understand in more detail the role of memory processes, reading strategies, and causal reasoning during reading, and the extent to which readers try to achieve coherent mental representations of what they're reading.

Implications for Instruction

This chapter focused on the processes of reading to learn—"getting meaning" from text materials. The importance of reading to learn is difficult to overestimate; it is a key to school learning, a significant part of effective living, and an unparalleled source of enjoyment. Most educators would endorse readily the goal of reading engagement goal advanced by Guthrie and his associates (Guthrie et al., 2007; Wigfield et al., 2008) of students choosing to read frequently for a variety of reasons and having the requisite cognitive skills for comprehending what they read. This chapter has highlighted key dimensions of reading that are important in this quest. The following implications for instruction draw on these dimensions.

1. *Help students become active readers.* Current models of reading show with increasing certainty that comprehension involves an array of processes. Some are highly automatized processes of perception and association, while others are more top-down and directed consciously by readers. None can be ignored if reading comprehension is the goal. The more active readers are—asking questions about what is read, relating what is read to what they already know, thinking of implications, putting ideas into their own words—the more likely comprehension and learning become. Both result from active readers interacting with text materials.

2. *Build on what readers already know.* Virtually all reading theorists view learning from reading as a result of interaction between readers and the materials being read. When information is tied to readers' prior knowledge, understanding will be increased. One method—*advance organizers*—involves giving materials to readers in advance of reading to serve as scaffolding for what is to be learned. These serve as a known framework for new, unfamiliar material. Other methods such as *questioning techniques* and *reading strategies* rely more on helping readers themselves make what they read meaningful. No matter which path is taken to meaningful reading, the effect will be to increase both comprehension and recall.

3. *Encourage students to become active vocabulary learners.* Having a large, flexible vocabulary is a major part of what it means to be educated. Reading is the primary avenue to vocabulary growth. The more readers read, the larger their vocabularies and the richer the networks of knowledge underlying these words will be. Voracious readers tend to have very large vocabularies; moderate readers, moderate vocabularies; and infrequent readers, small ones. Although vocabulary growth from reading can occur without intervention, teachers also should assist students in acquiring vocabulary from reading by teaching them strategies for using context effectively. Direct instruction also is important for supplementing vocabulary growth, particularly if its effects are augmented by encouraging students to notice new words and use strategies for learning them (Graves, 2006).

4. *Teach comprehension strategies explicitly.* A generation of research has shown the value of reading strategies for promoting comprehension. Students need, for example, to tell the difference between important and unimportant information and to summarize large chunks of information into more manageable ones. They need to make appropriate inferences from what they read and to monitor whether they understand. Students who generate imagery and questions as they read are likely to comprehend better and learn more. Each of these strategies has been shown to help students read more effectively and adaptively. If they are taught such strategies systematically with modeling, coaching, and extended practice, almost all children can become expert strategy users.

5. *Encourage wide reading.* Read, read, read! Teachers need to take the lead in encouraging students to read. Reading is linked strongly with success in school and in the workplace. Even with the current emphasis on a variety of media, reading remains the primary source for the information underlying deep understanding in almost every field of endeavor. Many students today at all ages still are not reading effectively. For too many of them, comprehension is literal and not at needed levels. We need to work hard to develop engaged readers—readers who not only are motivated to read for a variety of purposes but who also have the skills to comprehend the materials they read.

Although this is far from a trivial challenge, it is not an impossible one. For instance, teachers and schools can establish school–home reading programs that encourage reading at home and library use. Being read to and having the chance to read to others can form values and habits that last a lifetime. In school, teachers can make reading more rewarding by selecting interesting reading materials and tying reading to learning goals that students find meaningful and functional. Teachers also can help students read more effectively by modeling comprehension strategies and systematically teaching their use. As students' motivations to read increase and their abilities to comprehend improve, reading becomes a more productive and pleasant experience.

Summary

We began this chapter by describing examples of three types of reading comprehension models: data-driven, conceptually driven, and interactive. Data-driven models primarily emphasize automatized processes of perception and association to explain reading. Conceptually driven models, in contrast, emphasize meaning construction based on readers' background knowledge. Interactive models envision both data-driven and conceptually driven processes interacting in the construction of meaning. A prominent example of such interactive models—Kintsch's CI model—portrays reading comprehension as resulting from automatic processes generating multiple associations, which are linked to one another in an associative network. What a passage means to the reader is represented by the associations remaining after the network stabilizes. One important outcome of reading is vocabulary acquisition, a process that occurs naturally as students read. Contact with words during reading appears to be a major source of vocabulary growth, which proceeds at a phenomenal rate during the school years. Although acquisition of word meanings during reading occurs in small increments, the vocabulary knowledge acquired is particularly useful because it includes information about context. In general, the more students read, the larger their vocabularies. Students' vocabulary knowledge and their effectiveness as vocabulary learners can be enhanced by direct vocabulary instruction, encouraging them to notice new words, and teaching them to use morphological and contextual information to figure out what words mean.

Some methods for improving comprehension, such as advance organizers, signals, and inserted questions, are closely tied to the reading materials themselves. *Advance organizers* are overviews students read in advance to help them relate new information to what they already know. *Text signals* focus readers' attention on specific segments of text and make reading materials more coherent. *Questions* inserted in text can be more or less effective depending on the level of the questions and where they are placed. Generally, comprehension is best aided by a few higher-order questions prefacing text.

A second set of methods for comprehension improvement is based on student use of strategies that help them read more actively and deeply. Reading strategies can be taught individually, but more often they are taught together in comprehensive programs, such as reciprocal teaching, question–answer relationships (QAR) transactional strategies instruction (TSI), and concept-oriented reading instruction (CORI).

SUGGESTED READINGS

Block, C., & Pressley, M. (Eds.). (2002). *Comprehension instruction: Research-based best practices.* New York, NY: Guilford Press.
>   This volume, edited by two noted scholars, contains more than 20 readable chapters on reading comprehension and comprehension strategies instruction.

Graves, M. F. (2006). *The vocabulary book: Learning and instruction.* New York, NY: Teachers College Press.
>   This practical book, by a leading vocabulary researcher, provides a valuable guide to helping students develop their knowledge and utilization of words. It contains suggestions not only on how to teach words directly, but also about ways to build students' excitement about learning words and their ability to learn words on their own.

Israel, S. E., & Duffy, G. G. (Eds.). (2009). *Handbook of research on reading comprehension*. New York, NY: Routledge.
This handbook consists of a set of more than 30 authoritative chapters authored by a wide-ranging set of experts. Topics range from historical and theoretical perspectives on reading comprehension to methods for teaching and assessing comprehension.

McNamara, D. S. (Ed.). (2007). *Reading comprehension strategies: Theories, interventions, and technologies*. New York, NY: Erlbaum.
This edited volume provides an excellent overview of current perspectives on reading strategies. Its chapters provide insights into how experts view reading comprehension and how strategies can be utilized to improve reading comprehension.

Ruddell, R. B., & Unrau, N. J. (Eds.). (2004). *Theoretical models and processes of reading* (5th ed.). Newark, DE: International Reading Association.
This book, the latest update of a volume first published in the 1970s, includes an outstanding collection of chapters—classic and current—by leading reading authorities. Sections on comprehension processes, reader response, metacognition, and theoretical models of reading relate particularly closely to the topics of reading comprehension and learning from text.

13 Writing

A Cognitive Model of Writing ▪ Individual Differences in Writing ▪ Improving Students' Writing ▪ Assessing Writing ▪ Implications for Instruction: Encouraging the Writing Process and Building Writing Skills ▪ Summary ▪ Suggested Readings ▪

Excellent writing always has been admired, but it seems that now, more than ever, writing well is viewed as an essential skill. In a survey of U.S. adults (National Commission on Writing, 2007) almost 75% of those surveyed agreed that writing well was more important for success than it had been 20 years earlier. More than 8 in 10 believed that knowing how to write well should be required for high school graduation; only basic math and reading skills were more frequently chosen. Two-thirds saw writing skills as essential for college success. Virtually all of those surveyed (97%) rated writing as essential or important. And not only adults think writing is valuable. In a recent survey (Pew Internet and American Life Project, 2008), 86% of teens agreed that good writing was important or essential to success.

While believing in the importance of writing skills is good, many problems still exist with student writing and how writing is taught. Although there are some signs of improvement (e.g., Salahu-Din, Persky, & Miller, 2008), our students mostly do not write nearly as well as we would like. The poor writing of many students causes concern about their future job and educational success. Many students also have less-than-positive attitudes about writing, ranging from low confidence in their own ability to apprehension and anxiety when they are asked to write. Another problem is the frequency and quality of writing instruction, which has been called "the neglected R." Compared to reading and math, writing has received relatively little emphasis in either recent federal legislation or in the development of performance standards. Student writing and writing instruction occupy only a small part of most students' days. The overall quality of writing instruction also is suspect. Preservice teachers typically receive little if any instruction on how to teach writing. As a consequence, writing instruction can range from outstanding to poor.

While adequately addressing issues like these across our society may be a decades-long challenge, there is cause for optimism. There is an increasing focus on writing in schools, especially at the elementary level, as both educators and researchers heed concerns about the amount and quality of writing. Writing now is more often integrated with reading within language arts instruction, and is being incorporated into science, social studies, and math instruction. Research on the cognitive and motivational processes of writing is increasing (e.g., see Bruning & Horn, 2000; Graham, 2006b; Kellogg, 2008; McCutchen, 2006; Zimmerman & Kitsantas, 2002), and as a consequence, we are learning more about the writing process. Researchers are applying cognitive and motivational theory to writing instruction with good effect, showing that such techniques as modeling writing strategies, encouraging planning and revision, providing schemata for revision, and creating supportive writing environments can significantly improve student writing quality and attitudes (e.g., Bereiter & Scardamalia, 1987; Boscolo & Gelati, 2007; Graham, 2006a; Graham, Harris, & Mason, 2005).

In this chapter we describe a cognitive approach to writing and writing motivation. We begin by examining a model by Flower and Hayes that has had great influence in guiding research on writing. We then explore individual differences in writing, comparing qualities of more sophisticated writers with those of less-developed writers. Next, we examine important issues in writing assessment. In the final major section of the chapter, we describe the implications of cognitive and motivational research for classroom writing instruction. We end with some thoughts on the topic of creative writing.

As you read this chapter, you will see that the writing process vividly illustrates several of our cognitive themes for education (see Chapter 1). Constructive learning processes, mental structures, automatized skills, motivation and beliefs, and social interactions all play major roles in successful writing.

A Cognitive Model of Writing

Writing can take many forms. Novels, letters to the editor, poetry, and grocery lists all are forms of writing. Writing tasks also can differ dramatically in intent, length, and the amount of creativity expected. Writing also varies in complexity and quality according to topic, the writer's goals, and the student's age—just compare a third grader's narrative about his vacation with a college student's paper on the history of peace initiatives in the Middle East.

One feature of a good theoretical model is that it can take variations such as these into account, highlighting components and processes that remain stable regardless of the type of activity under consideration. A good model also helps researchers think productively about a phenomenon and guides the design of research. Probably more than any other model of writing, the one proposed by Linda Flower and John Hayes (e.g., Carey & Flower, 1989; Flower & Hayes, 1984) has served these important purposes. Flower and Hayes's model (see Figure 13.1) portrays writing as a problem-solving activity with three major components: the task environment, long-term memory, and working memory. Each major component contains subcomponents representing specific writing processes.

The Task Environment

The task environment, for Flower and Hayes, essentially "defines the writer's problem." It consists of two major components: the writing assignment (the writing task faced by the writer) and external storage (the writing a writer produces and the external aids she or he may use).

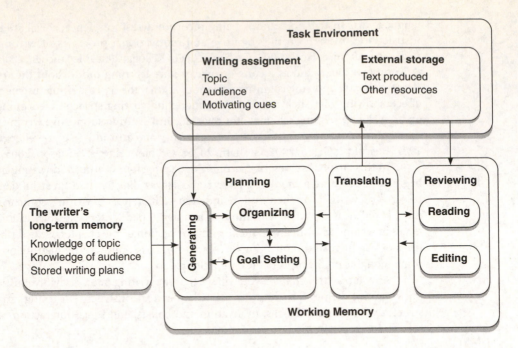

FIGURE 13.1   Flower and Hayes's Model of Writing.

Source: From *Cognitive Processes in Writing* (p. 11), by L. W. Gregg and E. R. Steinberg, 1980, Mahwah, NJ: Erlbaum. Copyright 1980 by Erlbaum. Adapted with permission.

The Writing Assignment   In Flower and Hayes's model, *writing assignment* is a generic label referring to the external conditions that provide a framework for a writer's initial representation of the writing task. School writing assignments, for instance, often furnish such a framework. They usually describe a topic and its scope, imply an intended audience, and often contain motivating cues. Take, for instance, an assignment that asks students to write a two-page essay on political issues involved in curtailing global warming. Such an assignment clearly specifies the topic and scope of the essay. Although audience is not mentioned, students typically would know whether it is for the teacher's consumption, or for judges in an essay contest. Motivating cues, such as grades (e.g., "This essay is worth one hundred points") or other outcomes (e.g., "Five winners will receive scholarships to the university's Summer Institute of Environmental Sciences"), are also often significant aspects of a writing assignment.

As with other forms of problem solving, how the writing task is initially represented has an effect on ultimate performance. Assignments vary in how effective they are in helping students represent their writing goals. Unclear assignments can result in writers creating poor or incomplete representations of their goals, with likely outcomes of low-quality writing or writing mismatched to its audience.

External Storage   The second part of the task environment in Flower and Hayes's model is *external storage*—the text the writer is creating and other materials that serve as resources to the writer. For example, a student working on an essay has the partially completed essay itself to look back on. She also may have notes she has written to herself about the assignment (e.g., "Be sure to mention how auto emissions contribute to global warming"). For longer assignments, such as term papers, students often have several forms of external storage to consult as they write, including note cards, drafts of the paper, summaries of sources they have read, and their own evaluations of different parts of what they have written.

External storage of information drastically reduces memory load as the writer creates new information. Compared with speakers, who typically have no external records of what they have said, writers can consult their work multiple times. Flower and Hayes's model shows the writer drawing on external storage as she rereads, evaluates, and revises her writing.

Long-Term Memory

The second major component in Flower and Hayes's model is **long-term memory,** which affects all the processes of writing. Bereiter and Scardamalia (1987) divide the knowledge that writers can access in long-term memory into two major groupings: *knowledge about content* (knowledge about the topic itself) and *knowledge about discourse processes* (knowledge about audiences and metalinguistic knowledge about the structures of different writing genres). This knowledge continually changes as the writer reads and writes. In fact, it is useful to think of an ongoing interaction between the external environment and long-term memory; reading materials, notes, and the writing itself constitute external resources for writing, and memory provides internal resources.

Cognitive processes interact continually in working memory and long-term memory as writers think about their goals, search for ideas and vocabulary, and evaluate and review text they have written. Writers do not simply check with long-term memory at the outset of their writing; rather, long-term memory is a continuing resource throughout the writing process.

No matter how well-developed a writer's composing abilities are the ultimate quality of the writing produced depends on the writer's ability to apply both content and discourse knowledge to the task (Kellogg, 2008; Olinghouse & Graham, 2009; Saddler & Graham, 2007). Lacking content knowledge, even Shakespeare might have written poorly had he been assigned an essay on a subject like nuclear physics. Conversely, it seems likely that few nuclear physicists could produce a literary work of the highest quality, in part because most would lack substantive expertise in the more sophisticated features of literary discourse.

Working Memory

Information from the environment and from long-term memory are combined in the third major component of Flower and Hayes's model, **working memory.** Working memory is where the major cognitive activity of writing takes place. Flower and Hayes envision three major processes occurring in working memory: *planning, translating,* and *reviewing.* Writers do not necessarily go from planning to translating to reviewing, however. Instead, most move back and forth between processes as the need arises. More complex arrangements, in which a writer accesses the external task environment and long-term memory, also are likely. We begin our discussion of working memory processes with planning.

Planning   The planning process includes three subprocesses: goal setting, generating, and organizing. These subprocesses interact vigorously and may be initiated at any time during writing. *Goal setting* refers to establishing objectives for writing. Goals may be long term (e.g., "I'll write an A+ paper," and "This chapter has to fit into the rest of the book") or short term (e.g., "Here I need to give a few examples" and "I probably should do a summary that will lead into the next section"). Goals are a part of the writer's preparation but also may be set after an initial writing session has been completed (e.g., "I think I'd better add something about the Adirondacks"). Goal setting is not a one-time activity but rather occurs many times during the course of writing.

Goal setting is especially critical in certain kinds of writing, such as the persuasive compositions often included in assessment tests. In this type of writing, setting specific subgoals is necessary. This can be a difficult task for students, but Ferretti, MacArthur, and Dowdy (2000) found that giving an elaborated goal that included explicit subgoals helped students produce much more persuasive, well-reasoned essays.

The *generating* subprocess refers to the development of the ideas and content used in writing. Ideas may be generated from long-term memory (e.g., "Let's see, didn't we talk about that in class?") or from the external environment ("I know it's in my notes here somewhere. Oh, great, here it is!"). Generation is an ongoing process influencing all other parts of the writing model. For example, suppose you are responding to an essay question about presidential elections. At first, you may plan to analyze the choice of the last three vice presidents. Soon, however, you discover that you cannot remember all their names. To continue, either you will need to consult some source for this information or your goals must be altered. Goals may also change as a result of generating unanticipated ideas, as when you hit on a good example or unexpectedly recall facts about an event.

The *organizing* subprocess of planning is closely related to both generating and setting goals. In organizing, writers create sensible, coherent structures out of their goals and ideas. Although organizing also typically is seen as happening early in writing, writers return to it again and again as writing proceeds. Each new paragraph and sentence requires attention to organization, as do any changes in goals or in the ideas available to a writer.

Translating   In Flower and Hayes's model, *translating* is a second process in working memory. Translating involves transforming one's ideas into written text. It requires accessing semantic memory, finding vocabulary to express ideas, putting words into sentences, and reading off words as they are written. Like planning, translating can put a strain on the capacity of writers' working memories (McCutchen, 2006). As many translating activities become automatic or nearly so in good writers, the load is reduced greatly (Berninger & Winn, 2006; Kellogg, 2008). The performance of experienced writers is a good example of how automaticity can decrease cognitive load on working memory, as discussed in Chapter 2.

Reviewing   The reviewing process in working memory involves reexamining what has been written and comparing this product with the writer's internal standards for acceptable writing. Although we think of reviewing occurring when writing is finished, it happens at any time during writing, even when the initial plans for a passage are being created.

Reviewing consists of two subprocesses: evaluating and revising. *Evaluating* is basically rereading the text and judging its quality. Obviously, evaluating what has been written depends not only on writers' general content knowledge but also on their sophistication with the particular form of writing they are attempting to produce (Kellogg, 2008; McCutchen, 2006).

Good and poor writers differ dramatically in how well they evaluate writing. For example, given samples of poor writing, good writers are apt to point to flaws in the writer's construction, coherence, and choice of words. Poor writers, in contrast, tend to blame their own inability to decode the text as the source of the problem. In other words, good writers understand what good and poor samples of text are like. They further understand that good writing involves a writer's need to blend both content and discourse knowledge. Poor writers do not readily identify these features; instead, they tend to believe that their reading is at fault. This general pattern also is seen when writers critique their own products. Good writers often identify problems in their own work, but poor or immature writers are less likely to see shortcomings and often miss potential comprehension problems for readers (Beal, 1996).

Revising, the second subprocess involved in reviewing, refers to the rewriting and restructuring of text. In Hayes's reformulation of the original Flower and Hayes model (see Hayes, 1996, 2006), he argues that revision is guided by writers' schemata for what revision means. For example, many writers, including adults, think of revising writing mainly as changing surface features of what they've written (e.g., correcting punctuation or misspellings, retyping a paper to make it neater) rather than making changes at the conceptual level (e.g., in organization, style, or emphasis). Such differences in how revision is viewed will have important consequences for how effective revision will be.

In general, as McCutchen (2006) points out, skilled writers are more likely to revise for meaning. Less skilled writers often have great difficulty even seeing that a first draft might benefit from additional editing (Graham & Harris, 1993), and the editing they do is often limited to minor changes of wording or adding content. Accomplished writers are much more likely to revise materials they have written, viewing almost any sample of their work as preliminary and subject to editing (Bereiter & Scardamalia, 1987; Britton, 1996).

Struggling writers often have difficulty regulating the planning and revising processes when writing. Directly teaching these processes to older elementary students can improve how much and how well they write (e.g., see Graham, 2006b). The benefits of planning and revising strategies are examples of how self-regulation is critical to cognitive development and learning—one of the cognitive themes outlined in Chapter 1.

An Example of the Writing Model

Perhaps the best way to capture the flavor of Flower and Hayes's model is to follow a hypothetical individual through the task of completing a writing assignment. Let's try to keep up with Emma. She is enrolled in a high school journalism class and has been assigned the task of writing an article for the school newspaper.

"Hmmm," reflects Emma, "I need to write a 250- to 275-word article describing the three candidates for senior class president. Well, I do have a file of the candidates' descriptions of themselves. It'd make sense to look at those first."

Emma pulls out a folder and begins flipping through it until she comes to the set of candidate descriptions. She examines them carefully, tapping her pencil on her desk. "Some of these are pretty fancy and use big words. But everybody in school has to be able to read the article.

I won't try to impress anybody with my vocabulary. Also, when Mr. Barker says, 'Keep it brief,' he means 'keep it brief.' Think 250 words, Emma, not 300 words!"

Emma turns on her computer and glances at a handout Mr. Barker gave out that day. On a yellow pad, she begins to scratch together an outline and thinks, "I'll just start by putting down their names and listing the honors and awards they've won so far in high school. That should be pretty easy to do. Next, I'll take their responses to the candidate survey they filled out and try to summarize how each person feels about the 'issues,' using his or her own words, of course. I also need to find one special thing to say about each person. Mr. Barker will like that."

Emma's reaction to the assignment is not especially unusual or striking, but it does allow us to see some elements of the model in action. The initial *task environment* (the assignment, the questionnaire, and Mr. Barker himself) seemed quite clear to Emma. She immediately began using her long-term memory in planning at least a rough framework for the whole writing task. Note that in her planning Emma used both *content knowledge* (her knowledge of the candidates) and *discourse knowledge* (e.g., knowledge that her audience was both Mr. Barker and the students at her school, that she was writing a journalistic-style article, and that her writing could be guided by the handout describing the candidates' responses to the issues). Emma's brief thoughts also allow us to see that she was busy organizing the material she was going to write as she began to form, at least loosely, her goals for writing.

Later, as we look back in on Emma, we see that she has begun actually writing and is working in short bursts, stopping now and again to stare at the computer screen. "Oh, what a horrible sentence!" she mutters. She deletes the line and starts again. "I don't want to make it sound like Susan doesn't like sports at all," she muses, "just because she thinks sports shouldn't be so important. Let's try this instead: 'Susan Smith believes that sports are....'"

Emma writes several more lines and then stops, leaning closer to the screen: "... want...," she mutters to herself. "No, it's 'The group *wants*...,' because group is one thing—singular. But can I say that a *group* wants something ... doesn't it have to be a *person* who wants something?"

This little segment of Emma's thinking lets us in on the *translating process,* in which she turns her ideas into words. We also can see that she is reviewing her work as she goes along. She evaluated a sentence, found that it did not convey the meaning she wanted, deleted it, and revised it. She then made another attempt at translating, this time producing a better sentence, but still was considering whether she'd gotten it the way she wanted.

Looking back at Emma one last time, we find that she finally has completed her article and is rereading it, making changes as she moves along. "OK. That sounds pretty decent. But this doesn't. Wow, not so good, Emma! Gotta fix that! ... Mmm. I think a comma goes there and, well, I'd better cut out that *which* ... capitalize *Kappa.* ... Hey, this isn't too bad, if I say so myself."

In this final observation, we see that Emma's reviewing was typical of most skilled writers' reactions to their work: She carefully evaluated the material and made revisions where needed, some of them fairly substantial. Finally, she made a last check of the mechanics of writing (punctuation, capitalization) after the task was complete.

Even a small sample of a writer's work, such as Emma's, tells a great deal about the dynamics of the writing process. *What is written is linear, but the process of writing is not.* As mentioned earlier, writers do not move from planning to translating to reviewing in a neat, orderly progression. Instead, they cycle back and forth among writing subprocesses. In fact, some of the most important individual differences among writers seem to be in their abilities to shift rapidly from operation to operation.

Individual Differences in Writing

Over the years, much research has focused on how individual writers differ in ways other than the obvious differences in ability to write. Some surprising and not so surprising differences have been documented. In terms of traditional measures, good and poor writers at the same grade level do not differ widely in measures of intelligence or academic achievement (Benton, Glover, Kraft, & Plake, 1984) but do differ in reading ability (Benton et al., 1984; Shell, Colvin, & Bruning, 1995).

Generally, good readers are better writers than poor readers. Correlational studies have indicated that measures of reading comprehension are positively related to writing ability (+.50 or above) and to students' beliefs about their ability as writers (Shell et al., 1995). These relationships are not surprising when we consider that frequent reading exposes students to many more samples of writing, most of which, we would assume, are of reasonably good quality. At least indirectly, reading can teach students about good writing. It likely also helps develop students' abilities to detect errors in text and monitor comprehension, which relate to revision and writing quality (Beal, 1996; McCutchen, 2006; McCutchen, Francis, & Kerr, 1997).

Better writers also have done more writing (Mazzie, 1987). This fact makes sense because writing is a complex cognitive skill and, like any other skill, improves with practice and feedback (Beach & Friedrich, 2006). In general, we would expect that as students are asked to write more and are given feedback on their writing, their writing ability will improve. As an editor once put it to one of the authors: "If you want to write, you have to write, write, write. No person ever mastered writing by talking about it."

Information Processing Differences

Beyond reading ability and time spent writing, writers differ in several other cognitive dimensions. One of these is how individual writers process information. In an often-cited study, Benton et al. (1984), contrasted better and poorer college student writers (defined on the basis of how samples of their writing were scored by a panel of judges) on a series of information processing tasks. They found no significant differences in the students' grade point averages or achievement test scores, which confirmed earlier work, and also no differences between the groups in short-term memory; however, they did find differences in how individuals in the two groups manipulated information in working memory.

In one task, Benton et al., exposed subjects to a series of letters randomly generated by computer. After the last letter was presented, subjects were instructed to reorder the letters they were holding in working memory into alphabetical order. All subjects completed several trials to allow reliable estimates of their abilities to reorder the letters. The results indicated that better writers were both faster and more accurate on this task than poorer writers.

Although letter reordering might be seen as a somewhat trivial activity not closely related to writing skills, other information-manipulation tasks closer to those required in actual writing showed comparable results. On a word-reordering task (presumed to be similar to actually forming a sentence from memory), subjects were given sets of 9 to 14 words in random order. Their task was to reorder the words into the one order that made a sentence for each string of words. Across several trials, the better writers again proved to be faster and more accurate than the poorer ones. They also were better on a task that required them to put sets of randomized sentences into a well-formed paragraph (presumed to be similar to assembling a paragraph during actual writing) and one that required organizing sets of 12 sentences into three different paragraphs (presumed to be similar to organizing information for writing).

Benton et al.'s first experiment then was replicated with a sample of high school students. On each of the information-manipulation tasks, better writers again were significantly more rapid and accurate than poorer writers. This finding supports the conclusion that better writers are superior at manipulating information; they can reorder letters, words, sentences, and paragraphs more efficiently than less skilled writers.

Directly related to the information processing differences just described are the ways different writers allocate their attention. Young writers often need to focus on the mechanics of writing, such as manipulating a pencil and forming letters. For very young writers, especially, the motor skill demands of writing can be so high that they mouth each letter and word as they write it. With practice, children begin to gain automatic control over writing motor skills and no longer need to devote as much of their attention to making letters. In work with beginning writers with and without a handwriting disability, Graham, Harris, and Fink (2000) found that handwriting is causally related to learning to write. They theorized that handwriting instruction improved the quality of students' writing because difficulty with handwriting is such a drain on the student's attentional capacity that it limits their use of other writing processes.

Overall, it seems likely that many information processing differences observed by Benton et al. (1984) and others result from better writers more successfully automatizing a number of cognitive processes required by writing. For example, less skilled writers often have not yet become fluent in key writing subskills, such as punctuation, capitalization, spelling, or even transcription of letters. As a result, more cognitive resources are needed to execute these skills, reducing writers' ability to concentrate on meaning and effective communication. However, as writing subskills become more automatic—and specific training can be highly effective in developing them (e.g., see Berninger et al., 2002; Graham, 2006b; Graham & Perin, 2007)— novice writers can concentrate their attention more fully on what they are trying to express.

Idea Generation Differences

As one might suspect, considerable differences are found in the number and quality of ideas for writing assignments generated by students of different ages and abilities (Graham, 2006a). One of the most persistent problems for young writers is finding enough to say. Older children generally will have more ideas than younger ones, and adults more than either. Development is only one of several factors affecting idea generation, however. Other factors are knowledge about the topic and audience (Carey & Flower, 1989), knowledge about story elements (Olinghouse & Graham, 2009; Saddler & Graham, 2007), and availability of writing strategies (Graham, 2006b). The extent to which writers have acquired tools for idea generation seems to be at least as important as development.

One of the more interesting studies examining the idea-generation phenomenon in writing was conducted by Root (1985), who surveyed the idea-generation techniques of professional expository writers who wrote magazine and newspaper articles. Most focused their efforts on developing a wide range of marketable stories similar to those seen in general-interest magazines (e.g., "The Great Northern Line," a story about railroading; and "Three Mile Island Revisited," a story about the aftermath of an accident at a nuclear power plant); a few emphasized book-length projects. Because these people made their living from writing, idea generation was critical.

Results of Root's survey were at once commonsensical and fascinating. These professional writers spent a great deal of their time reading. Although they read about specific topics primarily while working on particular stories (e.g., reading about nuclear power when preparing a story on the dangers of nuclear reactors), their general tendency was to read widely and to look for ideas in varied places. These professional writers also typically kept newspaper and magazine clippings along with their own notes about ideas for later use, even when they had no idea whether the notes would ever be helpful.

Root's study results parallel one major thesis of this volume: *Knowledge is key to effective cognitive functioning.* Knowledge has no substitute if idea generation is the goal. For most young children and even for many older ones, this knowledge comes from their own experiences, but having strategies for finding and comprehending text materials can greatly expand their knowledge base for writing (Bruning & Schweiger, 1997; Guthrie, Wigfield, & Perencevich, 2004; Pressley, 2002).

Our students usually are relative novices at writing and will not have the broad range of knowledge possessed by professional writers. We can, however, increase the number of ideas on which they can draw by simple techniques in which they brainstorm vocabulary and writing topics either prior to or during writing. These kinds of strategies can be learned by students of almost any age and ability level and have significant effects on the amount and quality of writing produced (see Englert, Raphael, Anderson, Anthony, & Stevens, 1991; Graham, 2006a, 2006b; Graham & Harris, 1996). Encouraging students to generate ideas and inferences even before they know a subject well helps them elaborate and reflect on their ideas, producing better writing and more meaningful learning (Tynjala, Mason, & Lonka, 2001). With careful teacher attention, students can learn idea generation strategies and will realize that they are essential to writing effectively.

Planning Differences

Writers exhibit important differences in what they attempt to accomplish with their writing. Effective writers almost always concentrate on *expressing meaning* as their primary goal. In Bereiter and Scardamalia's framework, their focus in planning will be more on **knowledge transforming,** such as working out the communication goals being sought and thinking about the strategies likely to achieve them. These goals then are used to guide the construction of content and to evaluate the writing that has been produced (Torrance & Galbraith, 2006). This is not to say that these writers ignore writing mechanics such as grammar, spelling, and punctuation, but most monitor them because they understand that mechanical errors will interfere with their goal of communicating meaning.

In contrast, more novice writers spend less time planning and tend to write associatively. That is, they perform mostly as **knowledge tellers,** for whom the act of writing one idea simply prompts the next (Bereiter & Scardamalia, 1987). Faced with a writing task, novice writers often stick literally to their text sources and may write down what they know about a topic with little apparent monitoring of the structure or coherence of what they've written. Also, concern with mechanics and avoiding errors tends to dominate the writing of less effective and experienced writers.

In general, writing guided by planning will be of higher quality, both in terms of content and organization. However, some experts (e.g., Elbow, 1981; see also Hayes, 2006) have argued that a form of associative writing called free writing can be useful as an antidote to many students' obsession with mechanics and fear of making mistakes. In **free writing,** students are encouraged to quickly produce as many ideas as possible without worry about organization, correctness, or precision. The goal is to create ideas during the writing process free from self-editing and inhibition, so editing and even looking back during the free writing process is discouraged. Instead, writers are encouraged to write and edit in cycles, with editing following separately on the "voyage home," where students are helped to select, organize, and revise what they have written.

Differences in Organization

Good writing is organized. Organized writing has a variety of dimensions, including well-formed sentences, paragraphs that express ideas clearly, and arguments that flow logically. It also differs by the type of text being created. As we have seen in the previous chapters on reading, stories (narratives) have certain forms, reports (expository texts) others, and persuasive documents still others. One dimension of organization that appears in all texts and that varies considerably across writers, however, is a property of texts called cohesion.

Cohesion refers to writers' and speakers' use of linguistic devices to link ideas (Crystal, 1997). These linguistic devices, called **cohesive ties,** come in many forms. *Referential ties* may employ pronouns (e.g., Enrique fell asleep. *He* was tired.) and definite articles (e.g., Three writers were there: a hack, a poet, and a playwright. *The* hack made the most money.). *Conjunctive ties* employ conjunctions to connect ideas (e.g., Kesia ate the pizza *and* Quinn's french fries), to show causation (e.g., Felicia tossed and turned all night *because* she ate too much pizza), and to show the obverse of ideas (e.g., Edward had heard about pineapple pizza *but* couldn't really imagine it). *Lexical cohesion* binds together ideas through word choice. A simple form of lexical cohesion employs the same word or phrase on more than one occasion (e.g., Royce found himself a *sunny* spot in the bleachers. He thought that 2 hours of *sun* would be perfect).

Good writers use both more and more varied cohesive ties. Consider the following sample of a child's writing lacking these connections:

> Lynette and Marissa went to town. She saw a store with glasses and marbles in the window. She bought some from the woman. She was happy.

The reader of this paragraph has no idea whether Lynette or Marissa saw the store or which item was purchased. Beyond not knowing who made the purchase, the reader also does not know who went away happy—the buyer or the seller.

As writers develop, they become more sensitive to the need for cohesion in texts. Cohesion-related skills also can be taught. Saddler and Graham (2005) have shown positive effects on writing quality when students practice the technique of **sentence combining,** which involves using referential and conjunctive ties to join related sentences. Many other cohesion-related skills are acquired informally. For instance, more experienced writers often use transition sentences between paragraphs (notice how the first sentence in this paragraph ties it back to previous material). Experienced writers also use text signals to direct readers back to materials encountered earlier (e.g., "As you recall . . .", "see Chapter 12") and to alert them to coming content (e.g., "As you will see in the next chapter, . . ."). They also periodically insert summaries of information. Teachers can help students improve their writing by teaching them how to guide readers' attention and monitor the clarity of their writing.

Improving Students' Writing

In the first two sections of this chapter, we examined Flower and Hayes's model of writing and reviewed differences in writers' cognitive processes. We now turn to frameworks for improving student writing. Like other areas to which cognitive psychology has been applied, research on methods for helping writers improve their skills has drawn on a social cognitive perspective (see Chapters 1 and 9; see also Harris et al., 2008a). In this section, we review three elements of effective programs for improving student writing and their beliefs about writing. We first describe features of a literacy community—a classroom focused on literacy. Next we discuss the kinds of interactions that are desirable in a writing-oriented classroom, which include teacher–student writing conferences and peer–peer interactions. Finally, we describe a system that has been used effectively to build writing skills and attitudes—self-regulated strategy development (SRSD).

Creating a Context for Writing: The Literacy Community

A **literacy community** refers to a group of individuals in a setting organized around reading, writing, speaking, and listening. In schools, members of a literacy community are the students and the teacher. Like reading, speaking, and listening, writing is a tool for learning and communication. Students are encouraged to use writing to learn (e.g., making notes about observations, journaling, etc.) and to express their ideas (e.g., by writing descriptions, summarizing what they've learned, creating stories, etc.). Teachers, who guide the overall functioning of this community, work to create an environment in which writing is motivated by the desire to communicate and valued as an expression of what students want to say. Social interactions are key to this context, because students need to share what they think, know, and learn through talking and writing.

As members of literacy communities, students discuss their writing plans and writing, read their own and others' writing, and reflect on their own writing. The scope of writing activities typically is broader than the individual, as pairs or groups of students engage in collaborative projects and reports (Englert, Mariage, & Dunsmore, 2006; Tynjala et al., 2001). The social interactions occurring in the literacy community create a context for students to write effectively and pleasurably (Alvermann, 2002; Dyson, 1993; Dyson & Freedman, 1991; Freedman, 1992).

Teachers play a vital leadership role in literacy communities, orchestrating an environment in which all dimensions of literacy—speaking and listening, as well as writing and reading—occur productively. An initial challenge is finding stimulating writing tasks that will challenge students to be thoughtful and inventive. One way to do this is through in-depth student projects in which students work on a topic or theme over several days or weeks (e.g., see Guthrie et al., 2004). Another challenge is adopting new teaching roles that may be quite different from traditional ones. In literacy communities, teachers are much more likely to function as coaches or facilitators than as authorities and information sources, working in students' zones of proximal development, as described by Vygotsky (1978) and discussed in Chapter 9. Instruction often is individualized, with teachers providing collaborative support to students as they write. This support often includes teacher–student dialogue aimed at helping the student better define writing tasks, identify information sources, think of ways to express ideas, and decide what revisions are needed.

Interactions in the Literacy Community

Peer–Peer Interactions   When implemented effectively, literacy communities are highly interactive. Talking with peers, for example, helps students consider different perspectives, more clearly formulate their ideas, and consider their audience. Working with peers, students can give and receive advice, ask and answer questions, and learn and teach (Cazden, 2001; Freedman, 1992). Such activities are highly consistent with social constructivist views that modes of thinking result from internalizing social interactions and that interacting with others is a source of cognitive growth (see Chapters 1 and 9).

Peer editing provides another important set of interactions in the literacy community. In its simplest form, students are paired with writing partners. Each student in a pair edits the other's writing, gives feedback on what he or she likes about the writing, and talks about ways it might be improved. Peer editing can include editing prewriting activities, such as plans for writing or oral versions of a story or report, reading papers aloud to one another, collaborating on revisions, trading papers, and revising each other's work. Peer editing need not be limited to pairs of students; groups of up to four or five students can work together effectively. Although peer editing requires training students in how to provide helpful feedback and work cooperatively (see Beach & Friedrich, 2006), it has been used successfully with writers of all ages, ranging from primary level to college age, with positive outcomes ranging from enhanced quality of writing to improved student attitudes toward writing (e.g., Englert et al., 1991; Graham, Harris, & Mason, 2005; Graham & Perin, 2007).

Our analysis suggests several reasons for the effectiveness of peer editing. One is that peer editing puts a premium on audience awareness, which you will recall is an important element in Flower and Hayes's model. In Englert et al.'s (1991) words, peers "silently but effectively represent the needs of the audience and make the concept of audience visible" (p. 340). By reading other students' drafts, students learn directly how their writing communicates or fails to communicate meaning to another person.

Another reason for its effectiveness is the immediate feedback peers can provide. While a teacher might need several days to comment on 100 or more essays, students can readily share writing plans with their partners, write brief segments, trade with their partners, and react to their partners' materials, all within the space of a class period. A third reason for peer editing's success is that editing skills generalize to the planning, evaluation, and revision of one's own writing. Improved editing is likely to lead to establishing and using personal standards for writing, especially when read-aloud techniques are stressed.

Our judgment is that, with appropriate student preparation and teacher guidance of the peer interactions, peer editing can be used successfully in almost any writing program. Beyond the instructional emphasis we described, the technique also has the advantage of freeing the teacher for teacher–student writing conferences in which teachers can help individual students develop their ideas and motivate them to acquire the specific skills they need.

Teacher–Student Conferences   The **teacher–student conference** is one of the most widely used and time-tested techniques for interacting with students about their writing (Sperling, 1990). In some teacher–student conferences, students simply seek and receive guidance and feedback. In others, however, the dialogue seems more like conversation than instruction, with interactions between teacher and writer aimed at developing ideas and strategies for writing. In this latter kind of conference, there is good deal of negotiation and meaning making, where students gradually acquire the knowledge about what it means to be a good writer (Englert et al., 2006).

In general, teacher–student writing conferences should emphasize such things as purposes of the writing activity, processes students need to use to write effectively, and the relationships between them. During such conferences, usually held individually, the teacher can pose questions about students' goals, the meanings they want to convey, and the cognitive and strategic processes they are using during writing. These interactions can help the teacher single out important aspects of writing for discussion. Teacher–student conferences also can tie the act of writing with *talking* about writing. Having students write while the teacher observes and interacts with them can be an effective way to teach skills in a personalized manner. Consider, for example, the following exchange from a 10th-grade composition class:

TEACHER: I like how you described Fiver, but let me read the sentence about Hazel aloud. You listen critically.

STUDENT: OK.

TEACHER: "Hazel was leader material but he didn't know yet."

STUDENT: It doesn't sound so good, does it?

TEACHER: No, but I think you can do much better. Here [points at note pad], write another sentence and share your thinking as you do.

STUDENT: OK. Let's see . . . "Hazel had" . . . I mean a word that says he didn't know about . . . "undiscovered"?

TEACHER: That'd work.

STUDENT: "Hazel had undiscovered leadership."

TEACHER: OK, but not just leadership.

STUDENT: I see. It doesn't fit just . . . Mmmm. "Hazel had undiscovered leadership abilities."

TEACHER: That's a good sentence!

STUDENT: Yeah. You don't just have it. It's like a skill or something, so you have to say "abilities."

As you can see, the teacher was acting like an informal editor and gently nudging the student along as he constructed a clear sentence. The teacher also was careful to praise the student's efforts when positive change occurred. Modeling can be seen in an excerpt drawn from a conference the teacher had with another student.

STUDENT: "Sir Holger fought the followers of the evil mage."

TEACHER: That's a pretty good sentence. The meaning you want to share is very clear. I don't like the structure as well as I could, though. I prefer to avoid the way you've used *of*. I like possessives instead. They save words. For example, "Sir Holger fought the evil mage's followers." It flows a little better.

STUDENT: It does sound better that way.

TEACHER: Some teachers might disagree, but I've always thought that if you can eliminate unnecessary words, you've helped your writing. Look here [points to an assigned reading]. I thought of this last night. Instead of "Bring me the swords that are sharpest," I'd say, "Bring me the sharpest swords."

When students see writing samples of differing quality, they can begin to distinguish between them and to internalize standards for their own writing. "Internalizing standards," of course, is a shorthand way of describing students' growing metalinguistic awareness about writing's complexities and the ability to use that knowledge to regulate their own writing.

Self-Regulated Strategy Development

Over the past quarter century, Steve Graham, Karen Harris, and their associates have developed a broad program of research focused on helping students become more successful and confident writers. Their approach, called **self-regulated strategy development (SRSD),** combines explicit teaching of writing strategies with many features of literacy communities. SRSD focuses on three major goals: (1) helping students learn about writing genres (story, persuasion) and strategies (e.g., brainstorming ideas, planning, revising), (2) teaching students strategies for managing and directing their own writing, and (3) building positive writing attitudes and motivation to write (Harris, Santangelo, & Graham, 2008). The impetus for developing SRSD was observations that many children struggle tremendously with writing and that the failure to write successfully can contribute to a host of problems, ranging from poor academic performance and writing anxiety to low self-efficacy and motivation to write. In Graham and Harris's view, successful writing programs need to build both students' writing skills and their writing-related motivations and beliefs.

SRSD strategy instruction is embedded in a supportive and positive classroom environment. For example, SRSD includes many features known to promote motivation: having students write for real purposes, giving them writing choices (e.g., about topic, how their writing space is arranged, how they organize their writing), discussing writing goals at teacher–student conferences, interacting with peers about writing, and receiving frequent, constructive feedback. Instruction is long term and ends when students can use strategies and self-regulation procedures effectively.

Positive attitudes and motivations are developed in several ways in SRSD. Learning is collaborative, with instruction shifting between whole group, small group, and individual approaches. Teachers initially model and describe strategies, but students ultimately are responsible for applying and monitoring strategy use. Active, collaborative learning is used to enhance students' motivation, sense of ownership, and attributions of success to effort (see Chapter 6). In general, teachers model an enthusiastic, positive view of writing.

Teaching a particular strategy—for example, SCAN, a strategy for revising previously written persuasive or opinion essays—involves multiple stages. These include activating prior knowledge, discussing the strategy (e.g., talking about its goals and benefits), modeling its use, having students memorize it, helping them to apply it, and finally use it on their own. As students learn a strategy and how to apply it, they are aided by various forms and checklists (e.g., "Six steps for revising checklist"). Acronyms for the strategy being taught, such as SCAN, provide an easy-to-remember label for the strategy and highlight its key elements (S—does it make *sense*? C—Is it *connected* to my belief? A—Can you *add* more? and N—*Note* errors). Lessons typically last 20 to 40 minutes and are taught several times a week. According to Harris et al. (2008), most elementary students can learn to use a strategy effectively and independently in 3 to 5 weeks.

Harris, Graham, and their associates have conducted several extensive analyses of studies testing the effectiveness of strategy instruction (including SRSD) for students in grades 2 through 12 (e.g., Graham, 2006a, 2006b; Graham & Perin, 2007; Rogers & Graham, 2008). One of their evaluation techniques has been meta-analysis, which is a statistical procedure for determining whether effects of a particular treatment occur across multiple studies. Results typically are reported as effect sizes, which in group comparisons are roughly equivalent to standard deviation units. An effect size of .50 (an average difference across studies between treatment and control groups of roughly half a standard deviation) is usually considered a medium effect and .80 a strong one.

In studies analyzed by Graham (2006b), strategies were taught to many different groups of students, including high and low achieving students in grades 2 through 12 who either had or did not have learning disabilities. In these studies, strategy instruction showed highly positive effects on writing-related outcomes, with a mean effect sizes of 1.15 at posttest, of 1.32 at maintenance, and of 1.74 for generalization across genre. When key elements of writing—such as writing quality, elements, length, and revisions—were considered separately, effect sizes were 1.21, 1.89, 0.95, and 0.90, respectively. When SRSD was compared to other strategy-based methods, effect sizes were almost twice as large. Thus, the impact of strategy instruction—and especially SRSD instruction—is impressive, especially since positive results are present for a variety of strategies, several writing genres, and many types and grade levels of students.

Assessing Writing

Assessments of writing now are appearing more and more on standardized tests. Solid arguments can be put forward for including writing on such measures. As we have indicated, writing well is an important, highly valued outcome of education. Writing also captures qualities other test formats do not, such as the ability to organize and communicate information. As a result, assessments of writing now are a factor in decisions ranging from program admission and placement (e.g., entry to college or graduate school, participation in special programs or classes) to program completion (e.g., graduation from high school).

But there are growing criticisms of formal writing assessment. One of these is that assessing writing, especially as part of "high stakes" measures, can begin to control how writing is taught. Over time, it is argued, writing instruction inevitably starts to mirror its assessment. Because writing well on the assessment has important consequences, doing well on the assessment begins to be viewed as the goal of writing instruction. Teachers begin to "teach to the test" by sharing criteria by which writing will be judged and having students practice sample writing assessments (e.g., Gallager, 2007; Hillocks, 2002; Mabry, 1999). Another criticism of writing assessments is that, on tests, writing is done under conditions that not only are artificial, but at odds with good writing instruction. On most assessments, students typically respond to a single narrow prompt, have no real audience, aren't allowed to collaborate, and write under strict time limits—all conditions far from ideal for successful writing instruction.

Many of these issues are traceable to the need for efficiency and high reliability on standardized tests. Although most test experts would agree that sampling many writing styles and genres is ideal, it isn't generally considered to be feasible. Varied prompts create greater response variability and scoring difficulties. As a result, test makers strongly favor precisely crafted **writing prompts** targeted at standard genres (e.g., narrative for young students, description for middle grades, argumentation for older students).

Because writing tests typically are narrowly focused, the ways schools prepare students to write successfully also become formulaic. For example, the widely taught five-paragraph theme or "academic essay"—which includes an introductory paragraph stating an argument, three middle paragraphs supporting that argument, and a concluding paragraph—may help students write a competent response to an argumentation-related writing prompt, but as Pirie (1997) put it, overlearning and overapplying this format can force students, much like the hopeful ladies in Cinderella, to try to " . . . make unwilling material fit into three obligatory body paragraphs" (p. 77).

A final criticism of current writing assessments is that students typically receive almost no relevant feedback from them. Helpful, constructive feedback on student writing, if obtained at all, comes mostly from teachers. In the early grades, teachers' responses to writing most commonly are given in writing conferences which, as we've seen, can be highly valuable to students. As students enter middle and high school, feedback more typically will come from teachers' written comments on student papers, and occasionally from peers. These exchanges and comments also can give students information about factors ranging from their content mastery to whether their writing is authentic and effective.

Providing good feedback on writing still can still be challenging—even for the best-intentioned and most capable teachers. For example, feedback focused on editing or "correcting" errors on final student papers—which remains a favored approach of many teachers (e.g., Matsumura, Patthey-Chavez, Valdes, & Garnier, 2002)—is likely to direct student attention to surface-level changes and mechanical aspects of writing (e.g., sentence structure). Written comments on student papers are too often vague or inconsistent (Beach & Friedrich, 2006).

The kinds of feedback students prefer, however, may provide important clues about effective feedback. According to Beach and Friedrich (2006), students judge two kinds of comments to be most helpful—those suggesting ways to improve what has been written and those explaining why features of their writing are good or bad. Clear revision directions, such as asking for additional information or specific changes, are preferred to more global, general comments. Critical feedback about students' ideas also can be useful, according to Beach and Friedrich, but should be framed in a constructive, nonpunitive way.

In our view, some of the more promising current approaches to writing assessment are those where assessment is embedded within integrated, problem-oriented instruction (e.g., Beach & Friedrich, 2006; Calfee & Miller, 2005a, 2005b; Cervetti, Pearson, Barber, Hiebert, & Bravo, 2007; Guthrie et al., 2004). Such approaches can stimulate many different kinds of writing and provide multiple opportunities for feedback, including feedback from peers. Calfee and Miller's Read-Write-Science project (Calfee & Miller, 2005a, 2005b), for instance, emphasizes the role of reading and writing in science learning. Early in a unit students are asked to write down and share their prior knowledge. As they read in trade books or textbooks, they do "thinkalouds" for new concepts they encounter, making and organizing their notes using their choice of graphic structures and justifying their organizational approach to their peers and teachers.

These informal writing products then serve as bridges to formal composition, done in response to writing prompts introduced by the teacher. The writing prompts—in contrast to those for formal writing assessments—explicitly draw students' attention to writing goals, intended audiences, and use of varied writing forms. As students write, they can draw on all the information they've previously written down and organized. When finished, they share what they've written in small groups or whole-class interactions, which exposes them to peers' points of view (Calfee & Miller, 2005a, 2005b). After revision, final drafts then are scored using rubrics tied not only to standard dimensions of writing (e.g., vocabulary, organization) but also to content knowledge (Miller & Calfee, 2004).

Finding inventive ways of using projects and group processes, perhaps modeled after those employed by Calfee and Miller and others, will widen the range of writing students do and provide new avenues for feedback to them. For the foreseeable future, however, high stakes writing assessments seem likely to continue to influence teachers and students' conceptions of what constitutes "good writing." Although it is true that novice writers, especially, need to learn the basic criteria for high-quality writing that are reflected in current assessment systems, such as choosing appropriate words, creating good sentences, and organizing ideas, we need to assure students that writing assessments are not the only or the best examples of good writing. We also must help students value and practice the rich array of informal (e.g., jotting notes, captioning pictures, organizing ideas) and expressive (e.g., journaling, writing short stories, creating poetry, etc) modes of writing that typically are not formally assessed.

Implications for Instruction: Encouraging the Writing Process and Building Writing Skills

Today writing is recognized as a window to cognitive activity and important tool for cognitive growth. It has been shown to be a multifaceted process with many important cognitive elements, including those of problem solving. Writers use their goals, sense of audience, and knowledge about discourse to transform content knowledge. When students plan their writing, try to express themselves, and examine their own and other students' writing, they are engaging in constructive processes likely to lead to cognitive growth.

Writing can be a useful learning tool in math, science, social studies, and other classrooms, but its effectiveness varies according to how writing assignments are structured. Tynjala et al. (2001) suggest that teachers structure writing assignments to meet certain conditions. They point out that writing tasks should make use of students' prior knowledge and existing conceptions and beliefs, encourage students to reflect on their own experiences and theorize about them, involve students in applying theories to solving practical problems, and be integrated with classroom discourse and other schoolwork.

Incorporating writing into the classroom does not have to be complicated. The following implications, drawn from both the basic cognitive literature on writing and the work of applied writing researchers (Englert et al., 2006; Graham, 2006b; Kellogg, 2008; Tynjala et al., 2001) suggest some straightforward strategies for effective classroom writing.

1. *Have students write frequently.* Almost 50 years ago, McQueen, Murray, and Evans (1963) performed a still-impressive study of factors leading to proficient writing performance of entering college freshmen. Their findings pointed to one factor as the most important determinant of writing skill—how much the students had written in high school.

Many teachers still do not have students write as much as they should, possibly because frequent student writing requires an extensive commitment of time and changes in teaching style. Yet few school activities are more productive of cognitive growth than having students write often and receive thoughtful feedback on their writing. As we have discussed, one way to include more writing without drastically increasing the teacher's workload is to use peer editing. Peer editing and other student interactions about writing offer the benefit of creating meaningful interactions among students, which as you will recall from our themes in Chapter 1 is vital to cognitive development.

2. *Create an informal, supportive climate for writing.* Traditional writing instruction, particularly at the secondary level and above, has tended to follow a teacher-centered course in which students write in response to teacher assignments and instructions. Until relatively recently, writing also has tended to be viewed as a solitary activity, evaluated primarily by grades and teacher written comments.

Newer conceptions of writing, however, are based on the social constructivist assumption, as outlined in Chapter 9, that learning about writing will be greatly enhanced by meaningful interactions with teachers and other students. If this assumption is correct, and we believe that it is, then productive writing environments will involve students and teachers talking to each other about writing. Students will be generating a great deal of written language and dialogue about what has been written. They will talk about their plans for writing, they will write and revise, and they will receive positive confirmation for their writing efforts, even those that are only partly successful. Creating these kinds of environments is within the reach of every teacher and every school, but to establish them teachers may need to adopt new, possibly unfamiliar roles as a coach, conversation partner, and facilitator of discussions.

3. *Emphasize prewriting strategies.* Some of writing's most important activities are those that take place before any words are actually written. Identifying goals for writing, for instance, motivates writing, gives students a basis for decisions about content and writing strategies, and allows them to determine whether they have been successful. Brainstorming ideas for writing improves its quality. Thinking about audience also shapes and improves students' writing. As Bereiter and Scardamalia (1987) recognized, the time spent in advance of writing not only is evidence of the writer's level of sophistication, but is tied to writing quality.

4. *Stress knowledge transforming, not knowledge telling.* One of the most useful distinctions made by writing researchers continues to be Bereiter and Scardamalia's (1987) contrast between writing as knowledge telling and writing as knowledge transforming. As we have seen, in knowledge telling, planning and goal setting are minimal; writers recall what they know and basically write their ideas down until the supply is exhausted. Knowledge transforming, however, is a generative process involving active reworking of thoughts and how to express them (White & Bruning, 2005). In knowledge transforming, thinking affects composing and composing affects thinking. Instead of writing being a process of individuals telling what they know, the writing act transforms and develops writers' knowledge. In writing, knowledge is constructed, reflecting one of our major cognitive themes in education. Viewed as a form of knowledge construction, writing clearly involves higher-level cognitive processes—elaborating ideas, problem solving, and reflective thinking—and becomes a tool for learning in any subject area.

Students of all ages can become knowledge-transforming writers. Several teaching approaches have been shown to be effective in helping students use writing to transform knowledge. One approach is to teach planning, writing, and revision strategies directly (Beal, 1996; Graham, 2006a, 2006b). Bereiter and Scardamalia (1987) noted that knowledge-transforming writers spend considerably more time planning before they begin writing than do knowledge-telling writers. During this time, they are engaged in such activities as making notes, thinking about their audience, and mentally "trying out" various discourse structures. Even very young writers can be helped to acquire variations on these skills.

Interacting with peers is an equally important approach for developing knowledge-transforming writers. Writing-to-learn tasks need to involve more than just writing; they should be integrated with social interaction and classroom discussion (Tynjala, 1998). When students talk with others about their writing, read others' work, or even just write with others around, they learn to envision the content, form, and audience for what they're writing (Calfee & Miller, 2005a, 2005b). The external dialogue or checklist of the novice gradually becomes the metalinguistic awareness and self-regulation of the mature writer.

Teachers are a final important key to developing knowledge-transforming writers. By their choice of writing tasks and through their interactions with students, teachers can set expectations for high-quality writing. One way of doing this is to provide students with excellent models of specific kinds of writing, such as reading and discussing short stories as part of learning to write short stories. Similarly, students' essay writing may be facilitated by having them read excellent essays and identify features they can incorporate into their own writing. Teachers provide the vital bridge between the novice writer's ability and the level of performance required to solve the problems of writing. Teachers' scaffolded instruction helps students think of strategies for attaining their goals and developing fragile new skills and abilities (Englert et al., 2006).

5. *Encourage students to develop productive revision strategies.* One of the surest signs of novice writers is their belief that once something has been written, no change can or should be made. When these writers do make revisions, they tend to be "cosmetic," focused on such things as neatness and spelling. Expert writers, however, have learned that substantive revision is the key to real improvement. For them, editing and revising are integral parts of the writing process.

Several avenues lead to better revision strategies. First, students need an appropriate schema for revision (Hayes, 1996). Many student writers believe revision involves only changes in words or sentences and will limit their revision efforts accordingly. When they are prompted to think more globally about revision to include reorganizing text or adding or deleting whole sentences while considering audience needs, their revisions can improve significantly (Wallace et al., 1996).

Second, dialogue with peers can lead to improved revision strategies. Peers can serve as an important audience for student writing and make the concept of audience real. Peer interactions also help build the foundation for the internal dialogue of the accomplished writer (Englert et al., 2006).

Third, revision strategies can be taught directly and produce positive effects on writing quality. Graham and Harris's SRSD program, for example, is a comprehensive system of strategy instruction that has been shown to successfully teach revision strategies.

A final avenue to revision is to have students read their writing aloud to peers, parents, or siblings. Tell the students to trust their ears and to revise awkward-sounding sentences. Our experience has been that students often overlook mistakes when reading silently to themselves, but reading their writing aloud often makes errors (e.g., missing or extra words, mismatches of tense and number) obvious. Children quickly find that some writing "sounds wrong" and that good writing is pleasing to the ear. Reading aloud to others also provides students with immediate feedback on the quality of their writing. Just reading aloud is not enough, of course; students need to rewrite the awkward places until they "sound right."

6. *Take advantage of technology.* As student access to technology grows in our schools, more of their writing is being done on the computer. Some of this writing plainly can be impressive. Consider the following essay written by a first grader near the end of the school year:

> ### The Little Bear Goes Camping
> Once there was a little bear. She had a mom and a dad. It was summer and little bear had nothing to do. Then her mother and father desited maybe to let little bear go camping with her big cousen. So they asked little bear if she wanted to. So they asked little bear and she said yes she thoaght that was a great idia. So little bear got all packed. Then her cousen came. So they went to the woods and started to camp. They had a wunderful time. They went fishing and they did a hole bunch of stoff When they got home they started to talk all about what they did when they went camping. They had a wunderful time. Little bear broaght back flowers for her faimly pretty ones i mean it!!!! THE! END!!!

There really is no doubt that a story of the quality and length of "The Little Bear Goes Camping" would have been less likely for this first grader to write with paper and pencil rather than with a computer. We know that for many young children just learning to write, transcription processes such as handwriting can generate significant demands on cognitive resources (Berninger et al., 2002; Graham, 2006a), demands that may be reduced when transcription difficulties are eased by technology.

As students gain facility in word processing and can begin to more easily add and delete words, insert sentences, and rearrange a text, much less effort is required than when the entire product must be rewritten by hand or retyped. Energy once devoted to transcribing and recopying can now be focused on the content, quality, and creative design of the writing. Yet technology is not a miracle cure for problems in writing instruction. The basics still apply—students still need to write often and receive good feedback. Also, because student access to technology in U.S. schools remains uneven, writing instruction that depends heavily on it will miss many children.

7. *Keep grammar and language mechanics in perspective.* We believe that students need to acquire the orthographic, morphological and syntactic skills fundamental to writing (e.g., spelling, punctuation, capitalization). Also, a shared classroom vocabulary about grammar and

other features of language is essential (e.g., students and teachers need to have a common understanding of what adjectives and adverbs are). However, developing students' writing requires "putting first things first." Students need to understand that the basic reason for writing is to communicate—stating one's ideas, expressing feelings, and persuading others. Communicating meaning, not acquiring grammar facts, should be the central focus of writing instruction.

Basic language skills nonetheless are still important. Misspelled words, misplaced commas, and poor sentence structure confuse and frustrate readers and detract from communication. For writing teachers, the challenge is to encourage students' skill development within the framework of the meaning they are trying to convey.

A Final Note: Creative Writing

Thus far in this chapter we have emphasized using writing for expressing ideas and developing thinking. We have not focused specifically on creative writing, nor have we examined instructional procedures designed to make writing more creative. Still, creative writing is a topic of great interest and several important issues are worth reviewing.

Creativity and the Evaluation of Writing   One issue related to creative writing is evaluation. Some have argued that creativity in writing and evaluation of writing are antithetical; that is, writers cannot be creative if they are constrained by the possible evaluation of their work. The arguments supporting this position are based on reasoning that writers will not be willing to take risks and to explore new paths if they are worrying about evaluation. From this perspective, the way to foster creative writing is to withhold all forms of evaluation from writing and form a safe environment in which writers feel free to express themselves.

But encouraging creativity and evaluating writing need not be mutually exclusive. Most published work requires an expression of creativity, yet most editors would be unlikely to bother to read a manuscript unless it is mostly error-free. To write creatively in the world of editors and publishers, one must first be able to write correctly. Just as in creatively playing a musical instrument, a certain level of technical competence is necessary for creative writing.

At the same time, care should be taken to avoid quashing new ideas or attempts to be creative. Your feedback should make it clear that you are not trying to discourage students from being creative, but rather are helping them express their ideas more effectively. We advise that teachers always provide students with feedback designed to improve their writing quality without being needlessly critical. Teachers' expectations are important. Students are far more likely to strive for creativity if teachers expect it.

Carey and Flower (1989) have pointed out that creative writing cannot occur without a great deal of knowledge about both the topic and the processes of writing. Building students' knowledge about the writing topic and teaching them about writing will increase their chances of writing creatively. Our argument is similar to what writers and editors long have said to beginning writers: "To write well, you need to write about what you know."

One highly successful writer who followed the dictum of writing about things he knew was James Michener. Michener, author of *Caravans, Tales of the South Pacific, Centennial, Space,* and many other novels, spent years of his life acquiring the knowledge he needed to write. Michener took months and even years to learn about the areas and cultures he wanted to write about. In fact, as he became more successful, he hired an entire staff of researchers to travel with him and help him learn enough to write knowledgeably. Although one can argue about Michener's creativity, an examination of his habits and the results of research on other writers (e.g., Root, 1985) shed light on a seldom-mentioned issue related to creativity: Gathering information, an important part of planning for writing, is an integral part of creative writing.

Summary

Most people regard writing as important to educational and occupational success. It is also highly valued as a means of self-expression but has not been emphasized as much as some other dimensions of schooling. Nonetheless, a great deal has been learned about writing, how to improve it, and how to promote positive attitudes toward it. One especially useful model of the writing process, developed by Flower and Hayes, describes how writing brings together thought and language. This model portrays writing as a problem-solving activity involving three interacting components: task environment, long-term memory, and working memory. The major cognitive processes of writing—planning, translating, and reviewing—occur in working memory.

There are several differences between more and less effective writers. Among these are the ability to manipulate information, generate ideas, plan, and organize. Creating a supportive environment for writing is a key to effective writing instruction and assessment. Procedures such as peer–peer discussions, peer editing, and teacher–student conferences can be used to create a literacy community that will enhance the quality of students' writing and their enjoyment of writing activities. Although an excessive focus on writing mechanics can divert students away from the main purposes of writing, a good approach seems to be to provide feedback on grammar and punctuation as students engage in meaningful writing activities. Creativity in writing can be facilitated by a supportive, nonthreatening environment that gives students many opportunities to write and helps them learn firsthand about the processes of writing.

SUGGESTED READINGS

Bazerman, C. (Ed.). (2008). *Handbook of research on writing*. New York, NY: Erlbaum.
  This handbook, containing a diverse set of chapters on topics ranging from the history of writing to writing's functions in society, provides a broad range of perspectives on writing and its many dimensions and uses.

Bereiter, C., & Scardamalia, M. (1987). *The psychology of written composition*. Mahwah, NJ: Erlbaum.
  This classic work by Carl Bereiter and Marlene Scardamalia clarified our understanding of the writing process. Their research concentrated on the distinction between knowledge telling and knowledge transforming in writing. Results of that research, summarized in this book, have helped us appreciate the nature of writing and how it develops, and pointed the way to strategies that educators use widely for developing student writing ability.

MacArthur, C. A., Graham, S., & Fitzgerald, J. (Eds.). (2006). *Handbook of writing research*. New York, NY: Guilford Press.
  This edited volume contains authoritative chapters on a variety of topics, including theories and models of writing, how writing develops, and methods of teaching writing. A related book for practitioners by the same authors, *Best practices in writing instruction* (Guilford Press, 2007) provides specialized advice from writing experts on topics ranging from assessing writing to building motivation to write.

14 Cognitive Approaches to Mathematics

Teaching mathematics is a complex task involving many factors. Students need to acquire procedural skills for solving mathematics problems and to understand the concepts and principles to which the skills relate. For too long, however, mathematics has been viewed and taught in the United States as a skill set best learned through repetitive practice. One result is that students don't really grasp what they are doing and why. They may be able to perform mathematics computations, but still not actually understand the underlying principles. Lacking understanding, they are unlikely to apply their skills to math problems that differ from those they've studied or to use mathematics knowledge effectively in their lives.

Many U.S. students' beliefs about mathematics also have tended to be negative and unproductive. One widely held and especially damaging belief of many of them, for instance, is that mathematics skill is innate (see Chapter 7) and that ordinary students cannot be expected to understand what they are being asked to learn. At least partly as a consequence of beliefs like these, many students do not take enough mathematics to prepare them for advanced study or for entry into many occupations. Although the number of U. S. students taking more advanced math courses is trending upward (Dalton, Ingels, Downing, & Bozick, 2007), still only a little more than half take more than two basic algebra courses, and only about 15% enroll in calculus, a key to entry in many occupations. Dropping out continues to be heavily disproportional by ethnicity; far fewer African American, Hispanic, and Native students than White and Asian students take classes beyond algebra. Although recent data for all groups show encouraging trends toward improvement in all ethnic groups in course-taking (Dalton et al., 2007) and math performance (Lee, Grigg, & Dion, 2007), gaps in numbers taking more advanced math courses (e.g., precalculus and calculus) continue to be substantial.

At the same time, it is heartening that much current attention is focused on finding more effective methods for mathematics teaching and learning (e.g., Kilpatrick, Swafford, & Findell, 2001; National Mathematics Advisory Panel [NMAP], 2008; Newcombe et al., 2009; RAND Mathematics Study Panel, 2003; Schoenfeld, 2006). Like many other subject areas, mathematics has been "reinvented" within a cognitive and social constructivist framework. National statements of goals, such as the *Principles and Standards for School Mathematics* (National Council of Teachers of Mathematics [NCTM], 2000), offer a much different perspective on how math is learned and should be taught. Statements like these stress the goal of students making sense of mathematics. For example, primary-level students are expected to understand common fractions such as $1/4$ and $1/2$; by the end of elementary school, they should be able to use fractions, decimals, and percentages to solve problems. During middle and high school, students are expected to learn to use algebra to represent and analyze mathematical relationships and acquire an understanding of exponential, logarithmic, polynomial, and periodic functions. The overall aim could be called "quantitative literacy," in which students are able to interpret data and use mathematics in their everyday lives. Mathematics is envisioned as a subject of ideas and mental processes. In this new cognitive conception of mathematics learning, students are encouraged to construct mathematical knowledge by formulating conjectures, exploring patterns, and seeking solutions rather than merely memorizing procedures and formulas and practicing problem sets repetitively.

The knowledge base supporting this new conception of mathematics is expanding constantly, as both researchers and practitioners use the theories and methods of cognitive science to study mathematics learning and teaching (e.g., NMAP, 2008; Newcombe et al., 2009). The growing body of cognitive research in mathematics, though strongly domain specific, is built on the basic model of cognition we outlined in the early chapters of this book.

As described in Chapter 8, a major characteristic of advanced problem solving is having specialized and organized knowledge. Mathematics is no different. Students must acquire a large body of conceptual and procedural knowledge in mathematics to support their problem-solving strategies. They need to know how to understand and represent problems in mathematical terms (Mayer & Hegarty, 1996) and to generalize their mathematical knowledge and skills to other school subjects and outside the school setting. They must acquire positive beliefs and attitudes about themselves and their mathematical knowledge and the self-regulatory skills to use their knowledge in flexible and adaptive ways (Hoffman & Spatariu, 2008; Usher, 2009; Usher & Pajares, 2009).

As you have seen throughout this text, cognitive research on instruction emphasizes the value of meaning-based approaches to learning. In this chapter, we describe the learning and teaching of two illustrative and important components of the mathematics curriculum: arithmetic and algebra. Each topic is examined in detail to demonstrate its complexity, as well as the usefulness of cognitive approaches for understanding the mathematical processes that students acquire. In contrast with the judgments of many that arithmetic is a rote skill and algebra more "conceptual," we portray both as problem-solving processes.

The thrust of much cognitive research in mathematics has been to search for clearer understanding of the mental processes students use to solve mathematics problems. Early in the "cognitive revolution," for instance, Riley et al. (1983) and Kintsch and Greeno (1985) proposed that representing mathematics problem solving as schemata provides a framework for such an understanding. A *set schema,* for instance, represents the idea of parts and a whole; the concept of *addition* can be understood as the presentation of two or more sets (parts) mathematically combined to form a whole (the superset). In addition to a set schema, addition also requires a *change schema* to show how parts may be combined. Much of arithmetic, and potentially much of other mathematics, can be described by using these two schemata. In general, we argue that mathematics requires the acquisition of networks of mental representations. Understanding grows as networks become larger and more organized. The class of operations we collectively call mathematics is built on the understanding these networks represent.

For mathematics knowledge to be utilized effectively, conceptual understanding must be tied to a set of procedures. These procedures, commonly called **algorithms,** guide the actions necessary to solve problems. As you remember from Chapter 8, algorithms are procedures (rules) that apply to a particular type of problem and that, if followed correctly, guarantee the correct answer. In arithmetic, for example, children use various counting algorithms, whereas in algebra students perform various algebraic operations. Algorithms are important to mathematics, but sometimes teachers and students have confused algorithmic skills with problem solving itself. Executing algorithms is not problem solving, but when students create an algorithm and apply it to a problem, they have engaged in problem solving (Mayer & Hegarty, 1996).

A key goal in mathematics problem solving is flexible knowledge, where students have acquired multiple strategies and can choose the most efficient ones. Allowing students to create their own strategies helps them link conceptual knowledge with the procedures they select. Also, as they try out various strategies, successes and failures of certain procedures often will result in changes in the conceptual framework. This iterative process of feedback between conceptual and procedural knowledge and comparing how well strategies work leads to improved problem representation and increasingly sophisticated mathematics proficiency (Clarke, Ayres, & Sweller, 2005; Rittle-Johnson, Siegler, & Alibali, 2001; Star & Rittle-Johnson, 2009).

Knowledge Acquisition

As students acquire a larger conceptual base and procedural skills in mathematics and tie them together, they become more efficient and flexible problem solvers (Rittle-Johnson & Star, 2007; Star & Rittle-Johnson, 2008, 2009). Expert mathematicians use the semantic (meaning) aspects of a problem to encode its relevant features. Many mathematics students, however, fail to grasp problems' underlying meanings and instead often rely on problem form—the syntactic, or surface, features of problem presentations. For example, they may look for key words in word problems (e.g., "some," "more Xs than Ys") and use these words to try to solve the problem, without necessarily comprehending the problem itself and being able to specify the relationships among the variables. Consider the following arithmetic word problem:

Bill has six marbles and gives two to Joe. How many marbles does Bill have left?

If students are reacting only to keywords, they would identify the two numbers in the problem and a keyword—in this case, *left*—that elicits schemata for subtraction. In this case, focusing on keywords will give the correct response. Schoenfeld (1985) observed that, in one major textbook series, the "keyword method" gave the right answer for virtually all problems (97%). But what if the problem were stated in the following "inconsistent" manner?

Bill gave two marbles to Joe. He has four left. How many marbles did Bill have to begin with?

Students typically find this version more difficult, both for language-related and problem-representation reasons. Real-life mathematical problems, of course, most often aren't neatly packaged either. In general, any teaching strategy that lets students solve problems without requiring them to form meaningful problem representations is unlikely to develop flexible problem-solving strategies. Only if this information is meaningful will students develop strategies appropriate to a wide variety of mathematical tasks.

As Mayer and Hegarty (1996) pointed out, mathematics in many ways is an ideal area in which to study cognition. Mathematics' structure provides a clear base for examining problem solving in elementary and secondary school students. Mathematics also is well-suited for illustrating cognitive processes (see Chapter 3) and our cognitive themes in education, particularly those of learning as a constructive process; the role of mental structures in organizing memory and guiding thought; and the contextual nature of knowledge, strategies, and expertise. We examine cognitive approaches to mathematics problem solving by first focusing on arithmetic and then on algebra.

Arithmetic Problem Solving

Historically, an assumption shared by most mathematics educators and teachers has been that basic skills are the foundation for conceptual understanding. One outcome of this assumption is that elementary-level mathematics instruction traditionally has been aimed at mastery of arithmetic facts and computational procedures. Only after these basics were acquired and as students progressed through the grades could the emphasis gradually shift to a more conceptual understanding of mathematics and its uses in actual problem solving. More advanced mathematics topics such as algebra and probability needed to wait until basic skills had been fully mastered.

Newer conceptions of mathematics view this traditional approach of "skills first, concepts later" as artificially separating two complementary aspects of understanding and using mathematics (Carraher, Schliemann, Brizuela, & Earnest, 2006; Newcombe et al., 2009). A wealth of theory-driven research with young children, for example, has shown that their knowledge about numbers and about operations of addition and subtraction (e.g., strategies for adding or subtracting two numbers), far from being purely procedural, involves integrating a succession of increasingly complex and efficient conceptual structures with language-based skills (e.g., Baroody, Li, & Lai, 2008; Canobi & Bethune, 2008; Condry & Spelke, 2008; Siegler, 1996; Zur & Gelman, 2004). Although the computational operations for addition and subtraction are habitual for most adults and might seem to be only procedural, our near-automatic performance obscures their deeply conceptual nature.

Whether adult or child, we need flexible ways to respond effectively in the many situations that require mathematical competence. If our conceptual understanding is lacking or too rigid, procedural skills will be applied by rote and transfer of learning will be poor. Conceptually based mathematics instruction, particularly in addition and subtraction, can be successful in teaching students more adaptive ways of thinking (Blote, van der Burg, & Klein, 2001). Consequently, we take the perspective that all mathematics, perhaps most especially the early stages of children's acquiring knowledge about arithmetic, should be viewed as a problem-solving activity with both conceptual and procedural dimensions.

What "Bugs" Can Teach Us

Studying children's addition and subtraction errors has contributed greatly to our understanding of the nature of arithmetic problem solving. In an early examination of the subtraction errors of a large number of children, J. S. Brown and Burton (1978) discovered that a sizable number consistently used one or more incorrect versions of the general subtraction algorithm. Many of the incorrect algorithms gave correct solutions some but not all of the time. For example, some children consistently applied a faulty subtraction algorithm "Take the smaller number from the larger in each column," which led them to subtract smaller numbers from larger ones regardless of which number was on top:

$$
\begin{array}{cccc}
8 & 23 & 47 & 52 \\
-3 & -16 & -35 & -17 \\
\hline
5 & 13 & 12 & 45
\end{array}
$$

Note that this incorrect, or "buggy," algorithm as Brown and Burton called it, does give the correct answer in the first and third problems; in those problems, children's getting the correct answer only makes it *seem* that they understand the operations of subtraction. Yet, using this same algorithm throughout these four problems yields the wrong answer in the second and fourth problems, where the numbers on top in the second columns (3, 2) are smaller than the numbers on the bottom (6, 7).

A teacher seeing the four problems in sequence could easily dismiss the mistake in the second problem as carelessness and the one in the fourth as a difficulty with borrowing, not recognizing that the child is using the same defective subtraction algorithm for all of the problems. The ability to diagnose errors like these can help teachers isolate conceptual difficulties children are having and help them acquire the correct understanding for groups of problems (Hill, Rowan, & Ball, 2005).

By analyzing the performance of thousands of schoolchildren, Brown and Burton (1978; Burton, 1981) identified and classified more than 300 different subtraction bugs. This impressive array of bugs in subtraction led to closer examination of the processes children use in both addition and subtraction, including classification of different types of addition and subtraction errors.

Problem Typologies

Finding the best way of organizing the many kinds of addition and subtraction situations that exist in the real world has been the subject of much research. One organizational possibility is to treat addition and subtraction problems as open "sentences." By varying the unknown, six addition and six subtraction sentences (e.g., $a + b = ?$ or $a - ? = c$) can be created (Carpenter & Moser, 1983). These deceptively simple tasks, in fact, provide the content for much of early elementary school arithmetic. For elementary school students, these sentences can yield whole-number solutions drawn from the basic arithmetic facts. These sentence types are not of equal difficulty to early elementary school children, however. In general, subtraction sentences typically are more difficult than addition sentences. Sentences of the form $a + b = ?$ or $a - b = ?$ are mostly easier than sentences of the form $a + ? = c$ or $a - ? = c$, and sentences with the operation to the right of the equal sign (e.g., $c = ? - b$) are more difficult than parallel problems with the operation to the left of the equal sign. Exactly why differences like these exist still has not been determined with certainty. One possibility is that teachers and texts present problems in one form much more frequently than in the others. This means that students get much more practice with $a + b = ?$ structures than those with operations on the right of the equal sign. Another possibility is that some structures map better than others on the addition and subtraction strategies that children are constructing (Fuson, 1992).

Baroody and Standifer (1993) classified addition and subtraction into five basic situations: change-add-to, change-take-from, part-part-whole, equalize, and compare. Both *change-add-to* and *change-take-from* involve beginning with a single collection and changing it by adding to or removing something from it. This results in a larger or smaller collection. For instance:

> CHANGE-ADD-TO: Heather had six apples. Chris gave her five more apples. How many apples does Heather have altogether?
> CHANGE-TAKE-FROM: Chris has five apples. He gave away two apples. How many apples does he now have?

Part-part-whole, equalize, and *compare* all begin with two quantities, which are either added or subtracted to find the whole of one of the parts. Two numbers are operated on to produce a unique third number. For example:

> PART-PART-WHOLE: Heather had six red apples and five green apples. How many apples does she have?
> EQUALIZE: Heather has six apples. Chris has three apples. How many more apples does Chris have to buy to have as many as Heather?
> COMPARE: Heather has twelve apples. Chris has five apples. How many more apples does Heather have than Chris?

Each of these problem types also can be presented in different ways; for instance, the compare problem above has an unknown *difference* but also could be stated as having an unknown second part (e.g., Heather has twelve apples. She has seven more than Chris. How many apples does Chris have?) or unknown first part (e.g., Heather has some apples. She has seven more than Chris, who has five. How many apples does Heather have?).

Because young children use counting as a main means of adding and subtracting, determining how children solve these problems and their various forms requires an examination of counting strategies. Most U.S. children come to kindergarten with some counting skills, and many can count sets up to 10 objects (Van de Walle & Watkins, 1993), perhaps because 4-year-olds are often taught by parents, older siblings, or others to count to 10. Early on, however, number words and number concepts are not well connected with each other (e.g., Canobi & Bethune, 2008); children do not yet understand the crucial idea of a one-to-one correspondence between a collection of objects and a particular number. But they soon begin to integrate counting to cardinal meanings of number words (e.g., that the word *three* corresponds to three things) and to use counting strategies for solving problems (Canobi & Bethune, 2008; Condry & Spelke, 2008; Zur & Gelman, 2004).

Examination of protocols of young children solving addition problems such as those outlined previously reveals three levels of counting strategies for solving problems. A description of these situations follows.

Counting All with Model   Carpenter and Moser (1982) have shown that, in carrying out the simplest addition strategy, children use physical objects or their fingers to represent each number or set to be combined, after which the combination of the two sets is counted. So, to add 4 and 7, a child represents each addend (set to be added) with a model of blocks or other objects (4 and 7, respectively) and then counts the combination of the two [in this case, 1, 2, 3, 4 (pause), 5, 6, 7, 8, 9, 10, 11].

Counting On from First   As children gain experience with numbers, their strategies change. In this more efficient addition strategy, the child recognizes that it is not always necessary to begin from 1, but begins with the first addend and then counts forward the number of the second addend. So, the child counts as follows: 4 (pause), 5, 6, 7, 8, 9, 10, 11.

Counting On from Larger   Later, an even more efficient strategy appears: The child begins with the larger addend. In our example, the child counts as follows: 7 (pause), 8, 9, 10, 11. This strategy often is used when children are asked to add numbers greater than 10, which are difficult to represent with their fingers.

During their first 4 years in school, children invent increasingly abbreviated and abstract strategies to solve addition and subtraction problems (Fuson, 1992; Fuson & Fuson, 1992). Instruction can help students learn specific strategies in the developmental sequence. Fuson and Fuson (1992), for instance, examined students' acquisition and use of *counting on* and *counting up* strategies in a project aimed at giving first and second graders opportunities to solve a wide range of addition and subtraction word problems. Children were taught to use a *counting up* strategy for subtraction. This strategy involves beginning with the first addend and then keeping track of the *number of words* said after the first addend word. For instance, to solve $10 - 7$, a child would say, "7 (pause), 8, 9, 10," while keeping track of the number of words after the pause. Fuson and Fuson showed that children learned both to count on and count up accurately. They also were as accurate and fast at counting up for subtraction as they were at counting on for addition. According to these researchers, an important benefit of using counting up for subtraction is that counting up uses ordinary forward counting and avoids the much more difficult backward counting that is part of the usual *take away* meaning of subtraction. Thus, children acquired a reliable method for subtracting, an important developmental achievement in becoming competent in solving such problems. At the same time, they also were acquiring a broader conceptual understanding of different meanings of subtraction and the minus sign.

Counting on and counting up do eventually drop out, and children move on to other strategies. The majority of first graders use some form of counting strategy. In second grade, about one-third of such responses appear to be based on number facts, and by the third grade, almost two-thirds of the responses are based on number facts (Carpenter & Moser, 1983). Many children continue using counting strategies for a long time because these strategies yield reliable results. Counting methods do not appear to be crutches that interfere with more complex problem solving. In Fuson and Fuson's study, children were observed to use them productively in addition and subtraction as complex as four-digit problems with regrouping.

Careful observation of adult addition and subtraction also suggests that counting strategies are not limited to children! Studying the seemingly simple operations of single-digit addition and subtraction reveals their true complexity; we can easily imagine the extent of conceptual knowledge and associated algorithms needed to add and subtract two-, three-, and four-digit numbers. Although most children acquire the necessary algorithms for solving these more complex problems, research in this area provides persuasive evidence that children need to integrate conceptual and procedural knowledge to use their problem-solving skills flexibly.

Language: Another Factor

Simple problems in arithmetic can be made more or less difficult, depending on the language used in the problem statement. In another early study, Hudson (1980) gave children problems similar to the one shown in Figure 14.1 and asked them one of the following questions: (1) How many more dogs than cats are there? (2) Suppose the dogs all race over and each one tries to chase a cat! Will every dog have a cat to chase? How many dogs won't have a cat to chase? Kindergarten children answered 25% of such problems correctly in response to the first question but answered 96% correctly in response to the second question. Clearly, the form of the question affects problem representation and ability to apply an appropriate solution schema. Question 1, cast in a more abstract manner, seems to lead to more problem-representation errors.

The question of level of abstraction of problem statement leads naturally to an issue of long-time concern in mathematics—word problems. Many children encounter difficulty with word problems. Comprehending the problem statement (which Hudson's study touched on) as well as generating the appropriate mathematical schema can make such problems difficult. Text comprehension as it relates to arithmetic problem solving continues to be the topic of careful study.

Text Comprehension and Arithmetic Problem Solving

Word problems are among the most common types of mathematics problems encountered at all levels of schooling. They can range from simple "combine" problems (e.g., Sophia had 3 marbles. Olivia has 2 marbles. How many marbles do they have altogether?") to highly complex ones requiring understanding not only of mathematics but also of a discipline (e.g., a problem in engineering might require not only algebra and calculus, but also knowledge of such concepts as *angular momentum, vector, inertia* and of multiple principles relating these concepts).

Even simply stated problems such as the earlier "combine" problem, however, are surprisingly complex. Stated only in numerical form (i.e., $3 + 2 = 5$), combine problems like this can be solved by counting or, if memorized, by retrieval from LTM (Fuchs et al., 2009). When a problem is stated in word form, however, learners need to identify key concepts and values (e.g., Sophia has *3* marbles), form a representation or set for the problem, select the correct algorithm for solving the problem (*addition*), and then apply it to get the correct answer (i.e., adding 2 to the original 3 to get 5). Even here, more is required than just translating key words into computations. Students must form accurate mental representations that encode a problem's key relationships and goals (e.g., Jitendra et al., 2007; Jonassen, 2003).

FIGURE 14.1   Dogs and Cats. Hudson (1980) used problems such as this one to determine children's difficulty with "How many more_____than_____are there?" problems.

How word problems are represented continues generally to be portrayed within the framework of schema theory. As you recall from Chapter 12, Kintsch and Van Dijk's theory of text processing (Kintsch, 2005; Kintsch & Van Dijk, 1978; Van Dijk & Kintsch, 1983) proposes that readers comprehend text by segmenting sentences into propositions and relating these propositions to one another. In applying this perspective to word problems, Kintsch and Greeno (1985) posed this general question: How does text processing affect understanding semantic information in the problem and generation of appropriate mathematical schemata for problem solution? In other words, how are text comprehension and mathematics problem solving related? Kintsch and Greeno's response was that solving word problems is a two-step process. In the first step, the student creates schemata for comprehending the text of the word problem. Simply put, when students encounter a word problem, they first need to make sense of it. In the second step, these text-generated schemata activate *mathematics* schemata. In Kintsch and Greeno's view, comprehending a word problem means constructing a series of conceptual representations, or set schemas, from the text. As each of the propositions in a word problem is processed, new sets are formed and previous ones displaced. A final set correctly representing the problem in mathematical terms is the one leading to problem solution.

A schema-based perspective is reflected in a number of currently used instructional approaches designed to improve children's success with arithmetic word problems. In work by L. Fuchs and D. Fuchs and their colleagues (e.g., Fuchs et al., 2005; Fuchs et al., 2006; Fuchs et al., 2009), word problem comprehension and computational abilities are viewed as distinct aspects of mathematical cognition. From this perspective, different schemata are tied to different word problem types. For instance, a *total* problem type (in which two or more amounts are combined) encompasses word problems such as "There are 42 boys and 46 girls in fifth grade at Rousseau School. How many fifth graders are there at Rousseau School?" Variations in this problem would have missing information in different spots (e.g., There are 98 fifth graders at Rousseau School. Forty-two (42) of them are boys. How many girls are there at Rousseau School?). Two other types of problems are *difference* and *change* problems. An example of a difference problem, which involves two amounts being compared, is: "Ella has 16 marbles. Jack has 9 marbles. How many more marbles does Ella have than Jack?" An example of a change problem, in which an initial amount increases or decreases, is: "Trevor is 52 inches tall this year. He grew 4 inches in the last year. How tall was he a year ago?"

The word problem intervention of Fuchs et al. (2009) focused first on learning to recognize and name these three problem types. When this was accomplished, students were taught to generate algebraic sentences (e.g., $20 + x = 31$) for solving the problem. This schema-based intervention was compared to tutoring focused mostly on numeric calculations, and both were compared to a control group that received no special tutoring. Problem types were introduced as a unit in the word problem condition. For instance, for *difference* problems students were taught to identify the larger and then the smaller amount in the problem, while in *change* problems students were taught to find starting, change, and ending amounts. They also were taught to cross out irrelevant information.

Fuchs et al. found that both tutored groups were superior to controls in their procedural skills (e.g., accuracy and speed of addition and subtraction), which is important since procedural skill deficits can be a bottleneck hindering mathematics achievement (e.g., Geary, Hoard, Byrd-Craven, Nugent, & Numtee, 2007). Only the schema-based instruction, however, helped students become better generally at word problems, suggesting that learning to tie the language of the word problems to correct schemata is crucial. Schema-based instruction also improved the performance of students of varied skill levels, indicating that it can be useful for all students.

Fuchs et al. (2009) have described their instruction, which focuses on recognition and utilization of relationships embedded in word problems, as "schema-broadening." As children encounter multiple examples of each problem type and are guided in their analysis, they acquire understanding of both different kinds of problems and the procedures for solving them. When tied to foundational calculation skills, schema-based approaches seem promising for promoting mathematical growth.

The Role of Memory in Arithmetic Problem Solving   One advantage of looking at arithmetic problem solving through a schema theory lens is that it reveals why children might have difficulties with word problems. If a schema theory account is correct, children continually form and revise schemata as they attempt to solve problems. With each revision, however, previous schemata presumably are being displaced, which places a high demand on children's attention and working memory.

In early work anticipating current research on the relationship between working memory and arithmetic performance, Case (1978, 1985) conducted multiple studies of the short-term memory capacity of young children, defining what he called **M-space** (memory space or memory capacity, in chunks). As you recall (see Chapter 3), adults' short-term memory capacity has been estimated to be approximately seven, plus or minus two chunks of information. Case's work suggested that young children's capacity is far below this adult level.

Utilizing Case's concept of M-space, Romberg and Collis (1987) carried out a systematic evaluation of short-term memory capacity in young children, describing situations such as the following, in which 6- and 7-year-olds were asked to find a sum:

TEACHER: What number equals $2 + 4 + 3$?

CHILD: $2 + 4 = 6$, now what was the other number?

TEACHER: What number equals $2 + 4 + 3$?

CHILD: Now, 2 plus, uh, what are the numbers?

As you can see, this conversation is quite revealing. It would seem that the request for the other number in the child's first response implies a memory failure, not an operational one. The child's second response suggests that the child's effort to remember the third number has resulted in a capacity overload prompting the request to repeat the numbers. Using a series of memory tests, Romberg and Collis showed that the average M-space directly increases with grade level, although, as might be expected, within-grade variability was large. On their best measure of M-space, Romberg and Collis found that kindergarten children had M-space scores of almost exactly 1, whereas first grader M-spaces were about 1.23, and the M-spaces of second graders averaged just over 3. These data suggest considerable memory-related issues for younger children that can inhibit even simple abstract arithmetic problem solving.

Recent work by Fuchs and Fuchs (e.g., Fuchs et al., 2006), Geary (Geary et al., 2007), and Swanson (2006) has further illuminated the relationship of working memory capacity to arithmetic, especially in solving word problems. The so-called "executive" component of working memory seems most critical, especially the ability to control attention. Studying mathematics growth in the primary grades, Swanson (2006) found that measures of executive functions in working memory predicted changes in children's ability to solve math problems. Likewise, Fuchs et al. (2006) found consistent relationships between teachers' ratings of children's attention (distractibility) and the children's math performance. Ability to focus and recall information in working memory may be especially critical for success in arithmetic tasks, which typically require sequential attention to problem features.

Findings like these should remind us that many elementary-level children will face processing and retrieval challenges in doing mathematics tasks. For some young children at least, arithmetic success may have as much to do with attention and working memory as it does with understanding mathematics concepts and principles. Different aspects of mathematics also involve different cognitive abilities (Geary, Hamson, & Hoard, 2000), which may cause children difficulty with certain topics in mathematics. Some children might have weaknesses in math fact retrieval, for instance, but understand counting principles and mathematical concepts; others might have strong computational skills but weaker understanding of concepts (Jordan & Hanich, 2000).

Problem Solving in Algebra

Our discussion so far has been dominated by how younger children build conceptual and procedural knowledge in mathematics. We now turn to algebra to examine these processes at a different level. Understanding algebra's cognitive processes and procedural knowledge also is important from a practical standpoint: student success is crucial because algebra continues to be a dividing point beyond which many students do not venture (Dalton et al., 2007).

In algebra, just as in arithmetic, it is critical that students acquire integrated conceptual and procedural skills. To be flexible problem solvers, students need both to reliably identify different kinds of problems and apply more than one solution method (e.g., Jitendra et al., 2009; Rittle-Johnson & Star, 2007, 2009; Star & Rittle-Johnson, 2008). For word problems, especially, adequate problem representations are essential because only a good representation will lead to a solution (Mayer & Hegarty, 1996; Rittle-Johnson et al., 2001). Solving word problems is likely to be a barrier for many students unless they are given extensive guided practice both in comprehending and representing mathematics problems stated in word form (Jitendra et al., 2009).

In a landmark early study, Mayer (1981) analyzed algebra word problems in high school algebra textbooks. He found more than 100 problem types, including a dozen kinds of distance/rate/time problems alone! He also discovered that problems differed in how often they appeared in the texts. When he asked students to read and then recall a series of eight story problems, they remembered high-frequency problems more successfully (Mayer, 1982). These findings suggest that students store schemata for common types of algebra problems in long-term memory. In another early study, Silver (1981) asked seventh graders to sort story problems into piles and then compared the sorting performance of good and poor problem solvers. Good problem solvers tended to sort the stories on the basis of an underlying *algebra schema*—what the problems required mathematically. Poor problem solvers, however, tended to group stories on the basis of the problems' *surface structure*.

One may conclude from studies like these that successful problem solving is related to the formation of a variety of problem schemata types. However, Mayer also found multiple problem types within problem categories, suggesting that mastering algebra might require developing and storing as many schemata as there are varieties of problems within categories—as many as 100 subtypes. To represent them all, students likely need to learn how to represent problems in many ways, including diagrams, pictures, concrete objects, equations, number sentences, and verbal summaries.

Explaining Algebra Errors in Terms of Schemata

The implication that students must acquire a very large number of schemata for solving word problems seems disconcerting. If algebra problems demand a new schema for each subtype, then sheer numbers make it likely that many won't be adequately formed. Also, as the pool of schemata increases, the chances of learning and storing faulty schemata also must increase. Reed's work on algebra errors suggests that this may indeed be the case.

Using Inappropriate Schemata   Just as appropriate schemata are needed to successfully represent and solve word problems, so too can inappropriate schemata lead to incorrect problem representation and solution. Reed and his colleagues (Reed, 1984, 1987; Reed, Dempster, & Ettinger, 1985) carried out several studies of students' ability to estimate answers to algebra word problems. Consider the following problem from Reed (1984, p. 781):

> Flying east between two cities that are 300 miles apart, a plane's speed is 150 mph. On the return trip, it flies 300 mph. Find the average speed for the round trip. (Answer: 200 mph)

Reed found that 84% of college students estimated 225 mph as the average speed. Only 9% gave the correct response. Why the high error rate? Students' responses clearly showed that they understood the problem in terms of an "average speed" schema, but the overwhelming majority saw the problem as one of a *simple* average (find the sum of the two speeds and compute the mean; 450/2 = 225 mph) rather than as a *weighted* average. In other words, for many students the problem description did elicit a schema ("find the average") but one that yielded an incorrect response. Note that the problem implies that the plane flew twice as long at the slower speed, taking 3 hours to fly 600 miles, giving an average speed of 200 mph. Many students, unfortunately, apparently failed to make that inference.

As the work of Kintsch and Greeno (1985) suggests, the need to make inferences from the written text of the word problem may activate inappropriate schemata. To test that hypothesis, Reed gave another version of the same problem to a group of students:

> A plane flies 150 mph for 2 hours and 300 mph for 1 hour. Find its average speed.

Note that, in this version, the fact that the plane flew slowly for 2 hours is made explicit. This time, 40% of students gave the correct response, and only 19% chose the incorrect 225 mph response. Although a substantial number still failed to solve the problem correctly, making it more explicit apparently evoked the appropriate schema for "estimating a weighted average" in many more students.

Making Faulty Estimates   One of the positive outcomes of this early research has been a strong emphasis in current mathematics education on evaluating whether answers are reasonable. For mathematics teachers and tutors, checking to see whether an answer makes sense is almost axiomatic. Yet, Reed's data suggests that students often fail to make useful estimates of whether an answer is correct. This failure is illustrated clearly in the following example:

> It takes Bill 12 hours to cut a large lawn. Bob can cut the same lawn in 8 hours. How long does it take them to cut the lawn when they both work together?

Thirty percent of students estimated the simple average—10 hours. But think about this answer for a moment. It contains a serious inconsistency, implying that it takes *longer* for Bill and Bob to mow the lawn together than for Bob to do it alone! These students apparently lacked not only an intuitive sense for when and how to compute weighted averages, they also lacked an "estimation" schema for evaluating the reasonableness of their answers. Reed has pointed out estimation's value as a tool for detecting what schema a student has used intuitively and further argued that students need to develop schemata for particular types of algebra problems that translate into solution algorithms. If a student lacks number sense and does not estimate well (e.g., Van de Walle & Watkins, 1993), then this is evidence that an algorithm is being applied by rote and is not based on understanding.

In general, looking at mathematics through a schema theory lens can be helpful for both explaining learning and diagnosing errors. Of course, learners may or may not use schemata effectively. Although students do seem to create schemata as they interact with algebra problems, schemata by themselves often are not sufficient for problem success. As discussed earlier, one likely issue is the sheer number of schemata to be learned. Another is that students can easily be misled by problems' surface features—how they are stated—and form the wrong conceptions of what the problem is asking.

Common Errors in Constructing Equations from Word Problems

Reed (2006b) has pointed out that when students try to construct equations for algebra word problems, their equations often incorrectly match things being referred to in word problems (referents) to units in their equations. For example, in a problem in which one person walks more quickly to catch up with another after starting a few minutes later (e.g., 6 minutes after the first person) and their respective speeds are expressed in miles per hour (e.g., 2 mph for person 1, 3 mph for person 2), students often will not realize that the time difference (here, 6 minutes) needs to be expressed in hours (i.e., as .1 hour instead of 6 minutes) in order to yield a meaningful answer (that is, the time for person 1 to overtake person 2) based on walking rates expressed in miles per hour (2 mph and 3 mph).

One strategy for rectifying mistakes like these is to guide students repeatedly through writing equations for many different kinds of word problems. The difficulty with this approach, however, is that constructing equations can generate high cognitive load. Equations include numbers, symbols, and units—all of which need to be correctly assigned—meaning that a large number of things need to be kept in mind simultaneously during the problem solving process. Instead of doing this, Reed designed targeted training focused specifically on choosing correct units. This training was based on the method of "contrasting cases," in which students were asked to judge which of two examples represented a meaningful quantity. Consistent with Sweller and his associates (e.g., Ayres, 2006; Sweller, et al., 1998), Reed argued that the simpler task of distinguishing between an appropriate and inappropriate quantity produces less cognitive load than the more complex one of constructing equations, and may be a more effective instructional strategy. Following is an example of contrasting cases much like those used by Reed. Which is more meaningful, a or b?

a. 9 ft $\times$ 10 ft   b. 9 lbs $\times$ 10 lbs

Note that the operations in a produce a meaningful answer, 90 square feet, whereas those in b produce a nonsensical product, "90 square pounds."

Now consider a different example related to currency exchange, where the dollar is valued at .70 euros. Which choice, a or b, produces a meaningful answer?

$$\text{a. } 20 \text{ euros} \times \frac{.70 \text{ euros}}{\$1.00} \qquad \text{b. } 20 \text{ euros} \times \frac{\$1.00}{.70 \text{ euros}}$$

Here a produces an answer of 14 euros^2, which is not meaningful, whereas b produces a meaningful answer of $28.57, the value in dollars of 20 euros. Reed (2006b) found that although many college students will have difficulty with problems like these, using contrasting cases training with feedback helped them identify which mathematical expressions match real-world referents. It also significantly increased a training group's ability to construct equations for algebra word problems compared to a control group that only practiced constructing equations. In Reed's view, skills like these (e.g., connecting units to referents) are one key to making a successful transition to algebra. Like reading comprehension, which depends heavily on highly automatized skills (e.g., for letter, word recognition, see Chapter 12), mastering algebra requires that students learn to quickly and easily connect referents in word problems to parts of equations.

Are Algebra Word Problems Always More Difficult Than Equations?

Most people, including many algebra teachers, believe that algebra word problems are an especially difficult form of problem. This belief is reflected in shared lore about the horrors of word problems and perhaps our recollection of some of them (e.g., a plane left Chicago's O'Hare airport at exactly 3:30 P.M., while a second one left St. Louis 47 minutes later, both bound for San Francisco . . .). It also is implied in algebra teaching methods in which new topics first are introduced to students in equation form and only later do they encounter word problems.

There is a logic underlying this sequence, of course. As we have already discussed, when problems are stated in words, text comprehension issues will play a part in determining problem difficulty. A related requirement is that correct mathematical relationships need to be constructed based on the text-based inputs of the word problem. Seemingly, only when these challenges are mastered and word problems translated into algebraic equations can such problems be solved.

At least some research has shown that there are certain conditions in which word problems actually can be *easier* to solve than matched equations. Koedinger and Nathan (2004) tested three hypotheses about the relative difficulty of word problems and algebra equations. The first, a *symbolic facilitation* hypothesis, reflected the common belief that word problems create extra difficulty because of their language comprehension requirements. It predicted superior performance for equations over matched story problems. A *situation facilitation* hypothesis predicted a different outcome—that students, because of their familiarity with certain contexts, should do better on word problems referring to familiar contexts (e.g., money) than those not referring to a specific situation. Finally, a *verbal facilitation* hypothesis predicted that students would make fewer errors on (1) word problems and (2) equations stated in words (called *word equations,* e.g., "Starting with 21, if I subtract 3 and then divide by 6, I get a number. What is it?) than they would on (3) the same problem stated symbolically (e.g., $(21 - 3)/6 = x$). The reasoning behind the verbal facilitation hypothesis was that, especially for those new to algebra, problems represented algebraically require using unfamiliar symbolic language that actually may be more difficult than verbally stated problems. For instance, algebraic language adds new lexical items (e.g., x, *) and new syntactic and semantic rules (e.g., order of operations, sides of an equation) with which students need to become fluent.

Koedinger and Nathan's results were intriguing. Participants in their first study, high school algebra students, performed significantly better on (1) word problems (66% correct) and (2) word equations (62%) than they did on matched (3) symbolic equations (43%). The difference between word problems and word equations was not significant overall, contradicting the situation facilitation hypothesis. Thus, the common assumption that word problems invariably are more difficult did not hold. As Koedinger and Nathan report, the better performance of conditions 1 and 2 as compared to condition 3 probably was the result of differences between verbal and symbolic representation, not between situational context (word problems, condition 1) and abstract description (word equations, condition 2). Analysis that combined data from a second study yielded a further interesting result. When the content of the word problems and word equations conditions involved whole numbers, there were no significant differences between these two groups. However, when the content involved decimals, a significant difference appeared (64% vs. 47%), indicating that context can play an influential role in certain instances.

In a detailed analysis of problem-solving strategies, Koedinger and Nathan observed that participants often used informal approaches that didn't seem to rely on symbolic representation at all! For instance, a number of participants effectively used a *guess and test* approach, in which they would guess at the unknown value, work out the arithmetic, and check the result. Then, if the outcome differed, they would try again. Other students used an *unwind* strategy to find an unknown start value by working backward from the final result step by step. These approaches, while far from ideal in the long run, can be reasonably effective when students have experience with the situation described in the problems (e.g., dividing up a bag of candy), since information from episodic memory can be utilized.

Koedinger and his associates have been careful to note that they do not advocate eliminating equation solving from the algebra curriculum. Algebraic symbols obviously are a language of complex problem solving and an essential part of all mathematics. In later work with college students, Koedinger, Alibali, and Nathan (2008) demonstrated that a "symbolic advantage" can emerge when more complex problems are being solved (e.g., when there are two references to the unknown, instead of only one). With such problems, students are better at solving equations than analogous story problems. In other words, although verbal representations may have advantages for simple problems, abstract symbolic representations are better suited for complex ones.

In general, we can conclude that students need to be skilled with both verbal and symbolic representations. In real life, problems appear in a huge variety of forms. Instead of trying to teach students first to solve equations and only later moving to word problems or vice versa, an integrated approach may be helpful in which students can utilize their prior knowledge and strengths in verbal processing, especially at the outset. The ultimate aim, of course, acquiring a solid conceptual understanding tied to symbolic and verbal representations.

Algebra and Arithmetic: An Artificial Distinction?

Many authorities in mathematics education (e.g., Blanton & Kaput, 2004; Greeno & Collins, 2008; NCTM, 2000; Thompson, 2008) have grown increasingly uneasy with the idea that there is a distinct division between arithmetic and algebra—a transition point where arithmetic "ends" and algebra "begins." Instead, they see arithmetic and algebra having much in common and find their separation in the curriculum to be artificial and harmful to students' mathematical development. From this standpoint, many of the difficulties students currently encounter in algebra have more to do with the failure to introduce algebra to them earlier as a natural partner of arithmetic than with students' developmental status (i.e., that algebra is beyond their cognitive capabilities).

Taking this perspective, Carraher and his associates (e.g., Carraher et al., 2006; Carraher, Schliemann, & Schwartz, 2007) have advocated for what has been called **early algebra** (also called *algebrafied arithmetic*). They contend, for instance, that algebraic notation can be used even among primary grade students to help them reason mathematically and learn mathematical concepts that some might think were beyond their reach. Arithmetic obviously involves number facts, but also has an inherently algebraic character when its ideas are generalized. In other words, the algebraic meaning embedded in arithmetical operations is an "essential ingredient," not an optional one.

Carraher and his associates have used a variety of methods to expose the algebraic character of elementary mathematics. For instance, primary-grade students are encouraged to explore topics in mathematics by using multiple forms of representation, including language, tables, graphs, and algebraic notation. In one study (Carraher et al., 2006) students in four elementary classrooms were followed from the middle of second grade through the end of fourth grade. As they moved through their curriculum, they learned to represent a series of open-ended problems in various ways. One of these was by using *number lines,* which were introduced by stringing twine around the room to which numbers from −10 to +20 were attached. Changes in measured and counted quantities students represented on this number line ranged from money and height to distance and temperature. Another concept was negative numbers, for example, where students used the number line to show the difference between having no money at all ($0) versus owing 5 dollars (−$5). Some problems that included numbers greater than those available on the number line led to discussions of where the number line might end and even to the concept of infinity.

In one of Carraher et al.'s (2006) problems, two children, Mary and John, were described as each having the same (unknown) amount in their piggy bank on Sunday. On Monday, their grandmother came to visit and gave them each $3. On Tuesday at the bookstore, Mary spent $3 and John $5, while on Wednesday, John made $4 washing a neighbor's car and Mary an identical amount babysitting, which they put in their piggy banks. The students then learned that on Thursday Mary opened her piggy bank and found that she had $9.

In grappling with this problem under the teacher's guidance over a period of time, students learned to represent an unknown amount with a symbol (*N*), to represent changes in unknown amounts in algebraic terms (e.g., $N + 3, N - 3$), to operate on unknowns (e.g., $N + 3 - 3 = N + 0 = N$, showing how Mary had returned to her original amount after spending the $3 that her grandmother had given her) and, when the final amount in Mary's piggy bank became known, to use their algebraic reasoning to determine how much money both Mary and John had ($5 for Mary and "$2 more," or $7, for John). The children then were able, again with their teacher's guidance, to generalize both number line strategy and use of algebraic notation to quite a different problem—representing heights of individuals who were a certain number of inches taller or shorter than others. Over time, students learned to use these methods in solving new problems.

Those taking an early algebra perspective generally would argue that to focus only on the concrete in arithmetic is to give a superficial view of mathematics, an approach Reed (2006b) has described as a *calculational orientation*. Certainly data like those just discussed would seem to show that children, even in the early grades, are able to take a *conceptual orientation* and reason algebraically. Early algebra instruction, of course, needs to be tied closely to direct experience and background knowledge and algebraic notation only gradually introduced. As notational skills are acquired, however, they seem to become valuable for helping children begin to generalize their thinking and understand functional relationships (Blanton & Kaput, 2004; Carraher et al., 2007; Humberstone & Reeve, 2008). This approach, coupled with additional forms of representation such as tables, graphs, and objects can establish important foundations for later mathematical reasoning.

Assessing Self-Efficacy in Mathematics

As you saw in Chapter 6, self-efficacy is a significant factor in determining motivation to engage with tasks and keep going when challenges are encountered. Mathematics self-efficacy is no exception. Whether it is a primary-grade student confident in his ability to subtract two-digit numbers or a graduate student who believes she can solve a set of simultaneous equations as part of an engineering problem, confident students are more likely to engage with mathematics, stay with math-related tasks when things get difficult, and ultimately succeed.

We typically think of conceptual knowledge and procedural skills as the key instructional goals in mathematics. They are essential, but they aren't all we should think about. We know from our own experience and from many studies of student attitudes toward mathematics that many students lack confidence for doing math. The consequences of this low confidence often are significant. Students may delay enrollment in mathematics-oriented courses or experience anxiety when they take them. They may procrastinate in completing assignments. They may even choose courses of study in order to try to avoid mathematics entirely. Thus, if you work with students in math-related subjects, you may want to better understand their mathematics self-efficacy. Knowing how confident your students are can give you valuable information both before and after instruction.

Measures of self-efficacy actually can be constructed quite easily. First, you need to identify a performance domain of interest (e.g., students' ability to complete their homework, multiply two-digit numbers, figure areas of triangles, make up word problems, write equations in slope-intercept form). The next step is to create items that map onto that domain. Following Bandura's (1997) prescription for constructing self-efficacy items, these should be written as first-person

Please rate each of the following items on a scale from 0 to 100, where 0 indicates that you have absolutely no confidence in doing this and 100 indicates complete confidence. You can use any number between 0 and 100 (e.g., 38, 75) to indicate your level of confidence.

1. _____ I can find the slope of a line, given its rise and run.
2. _____ I can graph equations like $4x + 5y = 15$ or $3.5x + 7y = 14$.
3. _____ I can explain to a classmate how a line's slope relates to changes in x and y.
4. _____ From a graph of my state's population in 1990, 2000, and 2010, I can estimate the rate of change for each decade.
5. _____ I can look at two equations in slope-intercept form and decide whether their lines are parallel.

FIGURE 14.2   Sample of Items and Instructions for Assessing Self-Efficacy in the Area of Linear Equations.

statements (e.g., ; "I can finish my math homework on time each day," "I can do word problems correctly," "I can get the right answers when I multiple two-digit numbers," "I can graph the equation $4x + 5y = 15$"). You then have students rate how true or false each item is for them. There are no "correct" answers, of course. Bandura has suggested using a scale ranging from 0 to 100 (in this case, 0 would be definitely false for me and 100 definitely true; students can assign any number they wish between 0 and 100). Scores on a set of items (7 or 8 typically are enough to create a reliable scale) can be summed to yield a self-efficacy score for each student.

Figure 14.2 contains sample self-efficacy items for performing on a topic in beginning algebra, linear equations. The items represent some of the subskills that might be taught in a series of lessons focusing on linear equations.

Summing a student's scores across items (e.g., $100 + 72 + 0 +$ etc.) will give you an estimate of how confident the student is in the domain represented by the items. You can then use your students' scores to check whether their self-efficacy generally is high or low in this domain, or whether it might be higher for one group than another (e.g., for girls than boys). Self-efficacy scores also can be compared to students' actual performance in the domain (e.g., to their unit quiz on linear equations); you likely will see considerable correspondence, but not a perfect relationship. For example, a few students who report high confidence might not actually be good performers, while others with relatively low self-efficacy may perform quite well. But because you know that students' self-efficacy affects their math-related behavior and the decisions they make about mathematics, you may want to use the information to think about ways to increase their self-efficacy.

Bandura has proposed that self-efficacy can be increased in four major ways. The first and most straightforward way is by students' experiencing success in a task, or as Bandura (1997) has called it, *mastery experience.* When we succeed at something, our confidence for doing it again will go up. So it is with mathematics—successful student performance in an area of mathematics will build confidence for performing in that domain next time. The second source is *vicarious experience.* Simply put, we become more confident when we observe others like ourselves succeeding. When students see peers completing a challenging math problem, for instance, their own confidence is likely to go up. The third source is *social persuasion,* which refers to encouragement by teachers, parents, and peers. The message "you can do it!" coming from a teacher may be just enough to get a student to try one more time and achieve success. The fourth source of self-efficacy beliefs is *emotional and physiological states.* Students' physiological reactions to a situation are interpreted in ways that affect their confidence. For example, a student might believe that her being nervous when she is called on in math class and the anxiety she feels while taking math tests are signs that she's not good at math. In fact, these feelings may have nothing to do with her competence, only her anxiety. The way to build self-efficacy through this route is to increase students' comfort with math in as many ways as possible and to help them reinterpret their feelings in more positive ways.

Usher and Pajares (2009) recently have developed a scale to measure these four sources of self-efficacy in middle school students. Their research shows that mastery experiences in math (e.g., doing well on math assignments, making good grades, etc.) have a strong relationship to mathematics self-efficacy, a finding consistent with prior research in many other areas. Vicarious experiences (e.g., seeing other students do well in math), social persuasion (e.g., being praised for doing well in math), and physiological states (reporting low levels of anxiety about math) also are tied to student confidence.

Usher and Pajares' work suggests several strategies mathematics teachers can use in their classrooms to build student confidence. The first and probably the most important is creating a classroom environment where students feel that they are mastering mathematics skills and completing challenging assignments. As one experienced mathematics teacher interviewed by Usher (2009) put it:

> "How many times do you hear people say, 'I was never good at math. I don't understand it.' If you can get them to think, 'Hmmm. I can understand this,' then you've probably raised their confidence level by 50% just by thinking they can." (p. 299)

Whatever methods you can use to raise students' mathematics self-efficacy—starting with making sure they achieve success and conveying your beliefs that they can and will succeed—almost certainly will pay important dividends in their enjoying mathematics and making good decisions about it.

Cognitive Psychology and Mathematics Instruction

Current conceptions of mathematics teaching and learning emphasize the goal of building conceptual understanding. At the same time, procedural skills in mathematics should not be neglected—without reliable algorithms, problems cannot be solved—but these skills need to be grounded in a flexible knowledge base containing linked conceptual, procedural, and strategic knowledge. Our view of mathematics learning and teaching is in keeping with this perspective. We believe a cognitive perspective provides insights into the conceptual basis of both arithmetic and algebra. We take the position that all of mathematics instruction should be treated as a predominantly cognitive, problem-solving enterprise.

Prior to formal instruction in arithmetic, we know that children exhibit sophisticated and appropriate mathematics problem-solving skills, including attending, counting, modeling problems, and inventing more and more efficient procedures. Pushing students only toward computational skill mastery, however, seems to cause them to abandon earlier, more flexible problem-solving approaches in favor of application of rote skills and more compartmentalized numeric thinking. The calculational approach critically evaluated by Reed (2006b) can have the result of teaching children that mathematics is primarily an exercise in symbol manipulation unrelated to problem solving. In contrast, versatile mathematics performance combines conceptual, procedural, and strategic knowledge.

As we have pointed out, most authorities on mathematics teaching and learning (e.g., NCTM, 2000; NMAP, 2008) now argue for making problem solving the focus of mathematics instruction. A growing body of research and trends in mathematics curricula reflect the impact of this argument on mathematics research and practice. Seeing the algebraic basis for arithmetic operations such as addition and subtraction is a case in point. The challenges many students face as they encounter algebra suggest, however, that the perspective of seeing all of mathematics as involving reasoning, problem solving, and creative thinking still needs to be fully translated into instruction.

Accurate and flexible performance in algebra, like competence in arithmetic, comes only from acquiring a web of conceptual understandings. This conceptual structure includes declarative, procedural, and conditional knowledge from which solutions can be derived. As is true for younger children's experiences with arithmetic word problems, algebra instruction must help students develop a semantic understanding and ability to represent word problems in mathematical terms. Only when problem representation is based on understanding can students apply their knowledge to a wide variety of problems. Highly specific approaches aimed primarily at identifying keywords or memorizing solution algorithms will yield predictable results—a focus on surface features of problems and sometimes failure to solve even slightly different problems.

Implications for Instruction

Cognitive approaches to learning mathematics imply teaching methods that promote deep understanding. The following suggestions are based on current cognitive perspectives on mathematics instruction.

1. *Mathematics should be taught from a comprehension-based, problem-solving perspective.* As much as possible, specific facts and concepts, procedures, algorithms, and schemata should be learned in the framework of meaningful problem solving. Just as readers construct an understanding of what they read, mathematics students need to construct their knowledge about mathematics. They are most likely to do so when they are allowed to use mathematical knowledge in solving problems that are interesting and meaningful to them (Bransford et al., 1996).

Students also need to be encouraged to reflect on their own thinking and activities (see Chapter 9). Problems should be structured so that students are not just searching for right answers, but for *reasons* why an approach might or might not be useful in a particular situation. Comparing alternate solution strategies (e.g., Star & Rittle-Johnson, 2009) can be quite helpful for prompting this kind of reflection. Flexible mathematics knowledge not only includes conceptual and procedural knowledge but also strategic knowledge related to how and when to use concepts and procedures.

2. *Build on students' informal knowledge.* In any domain, students extract meaning from their experience. Although the goal of mathematics instruction may be the ability to use a

system of abstract symbols and operations, student experiences almost always are a good starting point. Brown, Collins, and Duguid (1989), for instance, argued that mathematics instruction should not immediately attempt to abstract mathematics concepts and procedures from the contexts that originally give them meaning. The implication is that, at least initially, learning should be linked with real problems that students understand well. When procedures are built on comprehension, students will be able to apply their knowledge more flexibly.

3. *Teachers should provide models for mathematics problem-solving behavior.* Students can benefit greatly from hearing teachers think aloud while solving sample problems. Talking through solution strategies details the procedural and strategic processes of problem solving and shows their importance. Also made explicit in teacher thinkalouds are the relationships between the information the problem contains and the strategies the teacher is considering. Even showing paths that lead to incorrect solutions can be productive; doing so illustrates that errors are a natural part of mathematics reasoning and shows where and how such errors can occur.

4. *Assist students in verbalizing and visualizing processes used in solution attempts.* A key goal of mathematics reform is creating classroom environments that support multiple representations of mathematical ideas. One way to do this is by "math talk," which can be effective even at the preschool level for building children's mathematics capabilities (e.g., Klibanoff, Levine, Huttenlocher, Vasilyeva, & Hedges, 2006). For older students, class discussions, group work, and individual or group presentations on math-related topics all help students better understand mathematics concepts and principles and represent mathematical content in multiple ways (Hyde, 2008; McCrone, 2005). Acquiring the symbolic language of mathematics is important, but so is the ability to represent mathematical relationships through verbal explanations, drawings, graphs, tables, spreadsheets, and objects. As students try to express their understanding, teachers can ask them to reflect on what they are doing and to look for errors or new approaches. Also, instead of providing correct answers when students get stuck, teachers can ask questions and function as coaches and facilitators.

5. *Use students' errors as sources of information about their understanding.* Teachers can acquire a great deal of valuable information by examining how students think about mathematics problems. Errors provide especially rich clues to misunderstandings students may have. Close examination of student problem-solving processes may reveal errors attributable to a student's lack of conceptual, procedural, or metacognitive knowledge. Errors should not be taken lightly; superficial examination of error patterns may lead teachers to inappropriate conclusions about why students are making particular mistakes.

6. *Provide a mixture of problem types.* The practice of grouping all problems solvable with a particular approach generally seems ill-advised. A better way is to provide a variety of problems or settings in which students can apply various kinds of mathematics knowledge. Students need practice in recognizing different problem types and exposure to a variety of problems leads to both discrimination among problem types and better generalization of their mathematical knowledge.

7. *Use teaching methods that build student confidence and positive attitudes about mathematics.* Many students have relatively low confidence in their ability to do mathematics and less than positive attitudes about it. Although these beliefs and attitudes can be deep-seated because of their origins in family or culture, teachers can have a great impact on improving

them. Higher self-efficacy for mathematics can be produced by increasing student success, exposing them to successful models, and offering timely words of encouragement. Reducing anxiety by changing procedures (e.g., by changing classroom interactions or how assessments are done) can also help create environments more likely to generate confidence and positive attitudes.

8. *Teachers themselves should have appropriate levels of mathematics skill.* Implicit in carrying out any of the preceding suggestions is the need for teachers who are well prepared and comfortable with mathematics. Children enter elementary school with well-developed mathematics problem-solving skills that can be enhanced by skilled teachers. Many current teachers, however, especially at the elementary level, lack adequate levels of preparation and understanding of mathematics teaching methods.

The National Assessment of Educational Progress (2000) found that eighth graders whose teachers majored in mathematics or mathematics education scored higher, on average, than did students whose teachers didn't major in these fields. Similarly, work by Ball and her associates (e.g., Hill et al., 2005) has shown relationships between teachers' mathematical and pedagogical content knowledge and student achievement. In recognition of findings like these, there is a growing emphasis both in agencies such as the National Science Foundation (NSF) and in teacher education (e.g., Derry, Wilsman, & Hackbarth, 2007) on improving teachers' mathematics preparation. The goal is to help them acquire not only deeper, more flexible knowledge of mathematics but the ability to apply cognitive and motivational principles as they carry out mathematics instruction.

Summary

The major purpose of this chapter is to describe a cognitive perspective on learning and teaching mathematics. An extensive body of research on arithmetic operations, such as counting, addition, and subtraction, has shown that success in arithmetic depends on the acquisition of an increasingly organized body of conceptual knowledge. Procedures for solving problems need to be linked closely with this conceptual knowledge. Students also need metacognitive or strategic knowledge for knowing when and how to apply their mathematical knowledge. Treating the content of addition and subtraction and other arithmetic operations as problems to be solved, rather than as sets of facts to be stored in memory, appears to be a productive approach to the learning of arithmetic content.

An examination of how students solve algebra word problems suggests that difficulties stem from students' failures to learn flexible and powerful strategies based in conceptual knowledge. Students often develop procedures applicable to only a very narrow range of problems. Faced with problems beyond that range, they have little basis for understanding the task. Some authorities have argued that traditional mathematics instruction, focused more on skill acquisition than on problem solving, can turn productive, problem-solving primary-grade children into rigid, unproductive middle school and secondary school students. Although this position may be somewhat overstated, there is little doubt that focusing on developing mathematical understanding and problem solving provides a better foundation for effective mathematics instruction than concentrating exclusively on learning procedures and algorithms.

SUGGESTED READINGS

Kelly, A. E. (2008). Reflections on the National Mathematics Advisory Panel Final Report. *Educational Researcher, 37,* 561–564.

> This overview by Anthony Kelly, editor of a special issue of the *Educational Researcher* on "Foundations for success: The final report of the National Mathematics Advisory Panel," introduces articles that include reactions to the NMAP final report and a rejoinder to them by the report's authors. These articles reflect a wide variety of perspectives about what should be emphasized in future mathematics instruction and research.

Kilpatrick, J., Swafford, J., Findell, B. (Eds.). (2001). *Adding it up: Helping children learn mathematics.* Washington, DC: National Academy Press.

> This accessible volume explores how students in pre-K through eighth grades learn mathematics and recommends changes in teaching, curricula, and teacher education that will improve mathematics learning during these critical years.

Usher, E. L. (2009). Sources of middle school students' self-efficacy in mathematics: A qualitative investigation. *American Educational Research Journal, 46,* 275–314.

> Usher's study, based on interviews with middle school students, provides a rich description of the factors that are related to low or high mathematics confidence in the critical middle school years when students are making up their minds about their future directions in mathematics.

CHAPTER

15 Cognitive Approaches to Science

Naive Science Conceptions ■ Expert–Novice Differences in Science ■ A Model for Teaching Science ■ A Model of Science Achievement ■ Assessing Science Learning ■ Implications for Instruction ■ Summary ■ Suggested Readings ■

As our world grows increasingly technological and complex, knowledge and understanding of science becomes a necessity for all students. Although only an estimated 2% of students actually will become scientists, the need to be able to analyze scientific information and understand scientific concepts will pervade all students' lives. *Before It's Too Late: A Report to the Nation from the National Commission on Mathematics and Science Teaching for the 21st Century* (2000) outlined four key reasons for increased science and mathematics competency: the rapid pace of change in the global economy and the workplace, the role of math and science in everyday decision making, its close ties to our national security, and its intrinsic role in shaping and defining our common life, history, and culture.

These remain compelling reasons. As science knowledge and discovery, as well as the number of issues demanding science-based responses, have continued to accelerate, the concern over the adequacy of science education also has grown. Publications outlining the national science standards, including the National Science Education Standards (National Research Council [NRC], 1996), Benchmarks for Science Literacy (American Association for Advancement of Science [AAAS], 1993), and Inquiry and the National Science Education Standards (NRC, 2000), all advance the perspective that the goal of science teaching should be *scientific literacy* for all children.

The goal of scientific literacy extends far beyond the rote memorization of facts and definitions. Its particular emphasis is on students' thorough understanding of the scientific method and scientific concepts. To fully appreciate the scientific method, especially the development and testing of hypotheses, students must learn science as a problem-solving process—as inquiry based and constructivist in nature (Limon & Mason, 2002; Martin, 2006; Tobin, Tippins, & Gallard, 1994). Unfortunately, some science instruction still places a greater premium on acquiring science-related vocabulary rather than on scientific problem solving. For students to become scientifically literate, they must move beyond memorizing definitions of scientific terms. They need to learn to use scientific concepts and principles to *solve problems*, not only in the classroom and laboratory but also in real life.

How can we foster scientific literacy? Much of what we have discussed in previous chapters comes into play when we think about the cognitive basis for scientific literacy: memory, declarative and procedural knowledge, encoding and retrieval, and other cognitive processes all play a part. But certain factors that play pivotal roles in all learning are especially relevant to the learning and teaching of science. In *How People Learn* (2000), Bransford, Brown, and Cocking distill a broad review of learning research down to three key findings, all of which relate to the cognitive perspective of this text:

- Students come to the classroom with preconceptions about how the world works, and if their initial understanding is not engaged, they likely will fail to grasp new concepts and information, or not retain them once they leave the classroom.
- To develop competence in an area of inquiry, students must (a) have a deep foundation of factual knowledge, (b) understand these facts and ideas in a contextual framework, and (c) organize their knowledge in ways that facilitate retrieval and application.
- A metacognitive approach to instruction can assist students in taking control of their own learning by helping them define learning goals and monitor their progress in achieving them.

These three findings are especially applicable to developing science literacy and structure much of our thinking about how to foster science learning in the classroom.

Perhaps more than in any other discipline, students bring many preconceptions to science instruction that strongly affect their learning. We begin this chapter by examining how these preconceptions evolve and what educators can do to change them. Much of this research draws on pioneering studies of naive theories conducted during the 1980s and on later studies of **conceptual change** that have elaborated on these findings. The first section of this chapter deals with the effects of such preconceptions and how they can be confronted and changed.

Many of the important ways that students can develop competence in science can be illustrated through research contrasting the ways that experts and novices learn. One key assumption is that differences in problem-solving processes are related to expertise (Anzai, 1991; Taasoobshirazi & Carr, 2008). Much research on problem solving, which arguably is the core competency of science learning, has compared the performance of experts (e.g., college physics instructors) and novices (e.g., undergraduate physics majors). As you recall from Chapter 8, it is the *way* experts learn and use their knowledge, not simply their general memory or intellectual abilities, that makes them expert (Bransford et al., 2000; Feist, 2006). Experts differ from novices in the depth of their knowledge and in the ways that they organize and transform their knowledge. They also have well-developed metacognitive strategies.

The third part of this chapter describes a model for teaching science based on current research and practice that focuses on inquiry and scaffolding scientific thinking and metacognitive skills—applying to the science classroom many of the techniques for fostering cognitive growth discussed in Chapter 9. In the last part of this chapter, we consider a model of science achievement that describes the effects of family, prior learning, instructional time, and instructional quality on students' science achievement.

Naive Science Conceptions

Young children are intuitively scientific. From an early age, they constantly observe and question their world. From their observations and questions, they develop hypotheses and ideas about how the world works. By the time children enter school they already have many well-formed, strongly held, yet often scientifically incorrect, scientific conceptions. Children and many adults hold these **naive theories.** Such theories of scientific phenomena, developed on the basis of everyday experiences, are often well-articulated and, even though they are incorrect, provide people with causal explanations for how the world operates (Duit & Treagust, 2003; Limon & Mason, 2002; Murphy & Mason, 2006).

In a now-classic experiment, McCloskey, Caramazza, and Green (1980) asked college students to respond to situations like that shown in Figure 15.1. They then used students' reactions to these situations to determine the extent to which they understood classic Newtonian physics. Students examined the two drawings of a coiled tube shown in the figure. Each drawing shows a marble leaving the exit of a coiled tube. The students' task was to determine which line (straight or curved) better depicted what would happen if someone rolled a marble through the tube. The straight line represents both what the laws of physics indicate will happen and what happens when this experiment actually is conducted.

Surprisingly, McCloskey et al. found that even students who had taken a course in high school physics gave answers that showed naive conceptions of physical laws. One-third of the students indicated that the ball would continue in a curved line, an outcome that violates Newton's first law, the law of inertia, which states that any object continues either in a state of rest or in uniform, straight-line motion unless acted on by another force.

The errors observed by McCloskey et al. and those reported in a similar study that used gravity problems (Champagne, Klopfer, & Anderson, 1980) reveal that incorrect responses represent people's naive, intuitive conceptions of physics. The ordinary experiences of everyday life, and even prior schooling, are sources of data that seem to support naive theories. Consequently, the presence of well-developed, but incorrect, theories, coupled with everyday experiences that seem consistent with these theories, leads to beliefs about how the world operates that can be quite difficult to change. Many students find their naive concepts superior to the abstract and often seemingly counterintuitive principles of Newtonian physics.

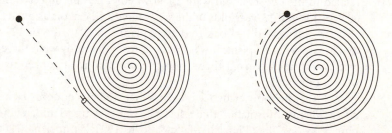

FIGURE 15.1   **Balls Leaving Coiled Tubes.** McCloskey, Caramazza, and Green (1980) used figures like this one to determine students' understanding of Newtonian physics.

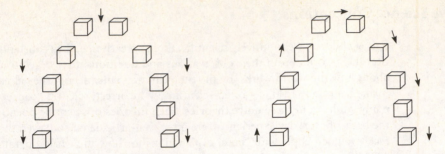

FIGURE 15.2   Conception of the Force Acting on a Block Tossed into the Air (arrows indicate direction of force). An expert's conception of the force acting on a block tossed into the air is presented on the left. The right side is a novice's response. This task is similar to that used by Clement (1983).

To illustrate, Clement (1983) presented data on **naive beliefs** about motion. In this problem, an object, such as the block in Figure 15.2, is tossed into the air and is caught by the tosser. The problem solver is asked to draw a diagram and to use arrows to show the direction of the force acting on the block at any particular point. The left side of Figure 15.2 shows an expert's response; the right side shows a typical incorrect response.

The "simple" expert drawing (see Figure 15.2) appears to ignore (and contradict) the intuitive, and incorrect, "upward motion" illustrated in the right part of the figure—what students call the "force of the throw." Clement (1983) reported that only 12% of engineering students responded correctly to this question prior to taking a college physics course. He then gave the same problem to two more experienced groups of students. Only 28% of a group who had completed the introductory course in mechanics, in which motion is a prominent topic, responded correctly. And only 30% of a second group that had completed two semesters of physics solved the problem correctly. Although these data suggest that instruction improves class performance somewhat, more than 70% of students continued to give naive responses. Teaching effectiveness aside, these data suggest the difficulty that teachers may have in overcoming naive beliefs (Clement, 1991, 1992).

Another example of the naive concepts that students have about the workings of the world can be seen in Osborne and Freyberg's (1985) study in which, among other questions related to biology, children were asked whether certain objects were plants. Amazingly, only 60% of 12- and 13-year-olds in the study identified carrots as plants, and only 80% of 14- and 15-year-olds agreed that oak trees were plants. In fact, 10% of 12- and 13-year-olds thought that grass was not a plant. It was not clear from the study what these children thought carrots, oaks, and grass were, but there is no question that their conceptual systems related to plants were rudimentary

Overwhelming evidence indicates that students not only lack scientific information but also bring misinformation that affects the way they try to understand problems (Limon, 2003; Linn & Eylon, 2006; Pintrich, Marx, & Boyle, 1993; Zimmerman, 2007). Students' misconceptions tend to be very powerful—in some areas, negating direct evidence they observe in experimental and classroom settings. Some researchers (see Bahar, 2003, for a review) contend that this misinformation is more than simply holding a set of false beliefs. Instead, they argue that most students lack a coordinated and consistent conceptual system for understanding the world. Students appear to have a variety of incomplete and uncoordinated schemata that arise primarily from unguided experience—that is, uncontrolled observation. Other researchers have taken an even stronger position—that many students' conceptual systems, while incorrect, are in fact highly organized. Carey (1985) and Carey and Smith (1993), for instance, argued that even elementary students do have very rich conceptual frameworks, not just fragmentary, unconnected false beliefs. Though these frameworks are incorrect, they are coherent conceptual systems that are consistent with many real-life observations.

One thing that is clear to experienced science educators is that students bring considerable erroneous information to science classes. Recent research also continues to support the view that learners do not enter the classroom as blank slates, but arrive with a great deal of erroneous information and misconceptions that interfere with learning new information and constructing accurate mental models of complex scientific phenomena (Limon, 2001; Linn & Eylon, 2006; Vosniadou, 2002). These must be unlearned before appropriate conceptual systems can be acquired. Because students' incorrect conceptual systems are the result of a life's worth of personal, unguided observations of the world, these systems may be strongly held and difficult to change. Teachers must expect children to have incorrect conceptions and seek them out. Children are not likely to abandon these beliefs unless they are presented with instruction that shows new ideas are "more intelligible, more plausible, and more fruitful" than old, incorrect beliefs (Osborne & Freyberg, 1985, p. 48).

To summarize, as a consequence of accumulating knowledge informally through early childhood and beyond, many students have misconceptions about science that may be difficult to change through classroom instruction. Before students can learn new and more appropriate scientific concepts they often need to reconceptualize these deeply held misconceptions—a process that is likely to be slow and require more than simply correcting errors (Bransford, Brown, & Cocking, 2000). Individuals of all ages who do not understand the power of a scientific approach will continue to trust their intuitions, even in light of scientific observations and experiments that contradict them. Teachers must be aware of students' intuitive (and often incorrect) science knowledge, draw out existing misconceptions, and use these as starting points for new learning (Bransford et al., 2000). Substantial instructional time must be used to present students with situations that expose and confront their naive beliefs.

Confronting Naive Beliefs

Unlike mathematics, where much of the formal content is taught first in school settings, children have been accumulating scientific knowledge based on their everyday observations. Children learn physical "laws" as they run, hop, throw a ball, play on a slide, or open a door. They see the sun "come up" and "go down," forming with it a strong sense (a naive theory) that the sun circles the earth each day, rather than the correct (scientific) conception of a rotating planet Earth. While these ideas provide knowledge that children need to negotiate their worlds, they also lead to inadequate and often incorrect conceptions of how the world operates. Much of this knowledge is tacit, unarticulated information embedded in the child's actions and experiences (Kuhn, 1989; Vosniadou, 2002). These conceptions are stored in memory and, quite naturally, provide the basis for explanations when children are faced with science problems.

The best way to eliminate naive beliefs is to expose them and confront them directly (Gregoire, 2003; Limon, 2003; Pintrich et al., 1993). Merely teaching basic science facts (or *cold* conceptual change, as Pintrich et al. refer to it), is unlikely to succeed. Instead, experience-based science instruction is needed that provides a motivational incentive for change. Recent research suggests that *hot* conceptual change based on active engagement and motivation to change beliefs can help students transcend naive beliefs and construct accurate mental models of scientific phenomena (Duit & Treagust, 2003; Linn & Eylon, 2006).

In summarizing a comprehensive review of studies in conceptual change, Pintrich et al., identified four necessary conditions for meaningful conceptual change to occur. One condition is *dissatisfaction* with current conceptions. Unless students (and teachers) have sufficient reason to abandon naive beliefs, it is unlikely that a change will occur. For instance, what strategies could a teacher use to interest students in alternative explanations of the sun's daily path across the sky? A second condition is that new conceptions must be *intelligible.* Clearly, students will feel little need to replace existing beliefs with new ones that seem to have even less explanatory power than those they already hold. A third condition is that new conceptions must be *plausible.* In essence, plausibility increases the chances that new beliefs can be meaningfully related to existing knowledge structures and used during scientific problem solving. The final condition is that new frameworks must appear *fruitful* to facilitate further investigation.

Other researchers have investigated the extent to which conceptual restructuring is necessary (Chinn & Brewer, 1993; Murphy & Mason, 2006). Special emphasis has been put on two kinds of conceptual change. The first is *weak restructuring,* in which existing knowledge in a specific domain, such as physics, is reorganized but not added to. This kind of conceptual change may be appropriate when students possess relevant expert knowledge that nevertheless leads to erroneous conclusions. The second kind of conceptual change is *radical restructuring,* which is appropriate when students possess naive theories that are deficient compared with those of experts. In this case, students "do not simply have an impoverished knowledge base compared to that of an expert; the novice has a different theory, different in terms of its structure, in the domain of the phenomenon it explains, and in its individual concepts" (Vosniadou & Brewer, 1987, p. 54). Radical restructuring may be necessary when students possess relevant knowledge but lack relevant conceptual structure to that knowledge. Only by redefining what they already know (and perhaps adding new knowledge) can these students hope to understand important scientific concepts adequately.

A Model for Changing Naive Beliefs

Nussbaum and Novick (1982) proposed a threefold strategy for changing naive beliefs: (1) reveal and understand student preconceptions, (2) create conceptual conflict with those preconceptions, and (3) encourage the development of revised or new schemata about the phenomena in question. We examine each step in the following sections.

Revealing Student Preconceptions   Teachers must first engage students in activities that reveal their naive beliefs (Demastes, Good, & Peebles, 1996; Limon, 2001; Vosniadou, 2002). Figure 15.3, based on the work of Nussbaum and Novick (1982), presents the responses of some elementary students at a laboratory school to an exposing event dealing with the particle theory of gases. Students were shown a flask and a vacuum pump and told that half of the air in the flask had been drawn out with the pump. The students were asked to imagine that they

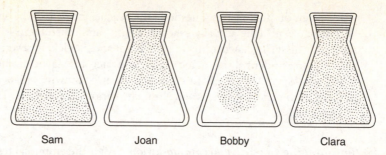

FIGURE 15.3 **Children's Depictions of a Science Problem.** These depictions are representative of those made by elementary students at a university laboratory school when they were told half the air in the flasks had been pumped out.

possessed magic spectacles that permitted them to see the air remaining in the flask and to draw a picture of the air remaining in the flask. On completing the drawings, students were asked to describe and explain them. Thus, both verbal and pictorial accounts of student preconceptions were generated.

Figure 15.3 shows that students had a wide range of conceptions about the nature of gases. Obviously, all members of the class did not share the same view of their properties! The teacher's major role in this first stage of changing naive beliefs is to help students express their ideas clearly and concisely and encourage them to respond to each other's ideas, but refrain from judging the adequacy of their responses. As students exchange views they not only learn their peers' ideas, they clarify their own thinking. These activities help move students to the next phase.

Creating Conceptual Conflict The drawings and explanations generated by the class are posed as alternatives to whatever view each student holds. If it happens that students don't pose a "correct" or "scientific" view, the teacher may supply it as one given by a student in another class. The teacher also may need to resist students' appeals for "which is the right one?"

Student-to-student discussion in itself can change some students' conceptions. After allowing substantial time for discussion, the teacher leads the students to see the need for an empirical test (e.g., an experiment or demonstration) to determine the merits of the alternatives. Teacher questions such as "How can we decide which is better?" or "What can we do to decide?" will help students see the need to gather evidence for decision making.

An experiment or demonstration then must be chosen that will, after careful examination, eliminate all but the scientifically correct alternative. In the example from Nussbaum and Novick, the teacher diverted the children to a different task altogether. She took a syringe and pushed the plunger halfway into the barrel. When asked to describe the nature of the contents of the apparently empty syringe, the class responded, "air." The teacher then asked what happened to the air when she pushed the syringe halfway home. Students readily generated answers that included some version of "squeezing" or "compressing" the air. To generalize the meaning of the concept of *compression,* the teacher reminded the students of earlier work with liquids and solids that had demonstrated compressibility and asked them to speculate about the special characteristics of air that permit it to be compressed.

After discussing this question, the teacher returned the children's attention to the "exposing event" (the partially evacuated flask) and asked them to think about the air in the flask and the syringe. According to Nussbaum and Novick, in several replications of this experience, some student always made a comment such as "Maybe the air is made up of little pieces with empty space between." The class then reviewed drawings made during the exposing event and began to make inferences and eliminate various alternatives. This process led students to the final phase.

Encouraging Cognitive Accommodation   After the empirical test has been completed and discussed, the teacher needs to give students support and to provide additional information and perspectives as needed that will help them restructure their ideas about the exposing event. In the gas example, students frequently asked "What holds the particles apart?" This question brought up another property of gases—the inherent motion of the particles. To complete the teaching example, the teacher drove the plunger still farther into the syringe and asked the students to comment. Finally, she asked whether she could compress the air to zero volume, reminding the students that a limit of compressibility is reached when no space is left between the particles.

The air example provides some sense of the complexity of obtaining student explanations of physical phenomena and how their naive explanations can, through skillful use of the students' own observations, comments, and questions, lead them toward more scientifically sound reasoning. When students' discussions are followed by empirical tests that let them discover more valid scientific explanations, students will acquire more accurate science schemata.

Expert–Novice Differences in Science

Few elementary or secondary school students will achieve the expertise of professional physicists, chemists, or biologists and it is unreasonable to think that they should. Researchers study experts and the ways they solve problems not in the belief that every student should become one, but because the study of expertise shows what successful learning looks like (Bransford et al., 2000; Feist, 2006). But just what are the characteristics of expert problem solvers in science?

Differences in Problem Solving

Experts solve problems much more quickly than novices in part because they possess a variety of relevant problem solving schemata and in part because they have automated many aspects of the problem-solving process. This suggests that experts are much more efficient at searching a particular solution space. They also possess substantially more information than novices (Ericsson, 2003; Glaser & Chi, 1988) and their information retrieval is more automatic. Retrieval fluency is important because it reduces the demands on the problem solver's conscious attention and frees up more attention for other parts of the task (Dunbar & Fugelsang, 2005).

Studies of solution time patterns reveal that experts' superior recall can be explained in terms of their ability to *chunk* information. You may recall from Chapter 3 that chunks are schema-like structures for storing declarative knowledge. For example, in solving a problem an expert may recall a number of equations that are tied to a particular physics principle as a single configuration, or "bundle"; this is followed by a pause and then the recall of another bundle of equations appropriate to another relevant principle. Novices, in contrast, don't show such chunking patterns. The presence of bursts of recall among experts suggests, consistent with our discussion of mathematics problem solving, the presence of meaningfully related schemata elicited as bundles when appropriate problem demands are encountered.

This ability to chunk information and to organize it into schemas underlies another trait of experts—the ability to recognize meaningful patterns of information. Studies of chess masters (Chi, 1978; DeGroot, 1965) and expert mathematicians (Hinsley, Hayes, & Simon, 1977) have revealed that these experts can quickly recognize patterns of information, such as successful chess moves and particular problem types, and know the implications of the patterns.

Another major difference between experts and novices is that experts organize their knowledge around the important ideas in their domain. Novices, in contrast, tend to organize their thinking around the surface structure of the problems (e.g., around kinds of equations and how to use them). Typically, experts will begin with fundamental science principles (e.g., Newton's laws) that often only are implied by problem statements. In general, they will engage in deeper and more complete problem representation than do novices and solve problems faster and better because of it (McNeill & Krajcik, 2008; Pretz, Naples, & Sternberg, 2003).

Research contrasting experts and novices in science also has revealed some differences that are harder to describe. One of these is experts' use of what Larkin (1977) referred to as "qualitative analysis" and what Simon and Simon (1978) called "physical intuition." In both cases, the authors were referring to the development of rather elaborate problem representations, often including sketches or other physical representation of problems. Such elaborate problem representations, whether visual or verbal or both, typically are constructed in the early stages of problem solving. They apparently serve to identify ambiguity in problem descriptions and to clarify specific aspects of problems that must be deduced or inferred. Once constructed, experts' task representations help them generate succeeding solution steps, such as particular solution equations.

Still another difference between experts and novices is their choice of strategies. As described in Chapter 8, experts consistently use a *working-forward* (or means–ends) strategy, whereas novices mostly use a *working-backward* approach (Ericsson, 2003; Kotovsky, 2003). Experts usually will first identify problem variables and then move forward to generate and solve equations that use existing information. Novices, in contrast, often begin the solution process with an equation that contains the problem unknown (the desired end product). If the equation contains a variable that was not given, novices work backward from that equation, searching for one that yields (they hope) the variable they need.

For example, suppose the solution to a physics problem required solving the equation $V = mgh$, where the several values in the equation are unknown but h is the unknown the question asks for. The novice will typically work backward from that equation, seeking to generate other equations that will give the values of m, g, and V so that ultimately the equation can be solved for h. The expert, in contrast, apparently understanding the problem in a more fundamental way, works forward from a set of equations generated from the problem statement, concluding the solution sequence with the equation $V = mgh$ in a fashion so that all relevant values are known and placed in the equation, and the solution to h is calculated. It seems that experts' rich network of information is organized into schemata incorporating key concepts from problem statements and from their own knowledge base. These science schemata seem very similar to the algebra schemata described in Chapter 14.

Once schemata related to fundamental principles are activated, experts use stored procedural knowledge to generate solution attempts that then are tested against what the problem statement requires. Experts also possess substantially more procedural knowledge than novices, which may account for the differences in problem-solving strategies chosen by experts (working forward) and novices (working backward).

Differences in Understanding Theories

Profound differences exist between experts and novices in their understanding of science (diSessa, 1993, 2002; Linn, Songer, & Eylon, 1996). Kuhn and colleagues (e.g., Kuhn, 1989; Kuhn, Amsel, & O'Loughlin, 1988; Kuhn, Iordarnou, Pease, & Warkala, 2008) examined some of these differences among three groups—children, lay adults, and practicing scientists—and proposed that children experience more difficulty with science for three reasons. One is that they lack adult experts' domain-specific knowledge and strategies, as described earlier. A second reason is that children fail to understand how theories are structured and used. A third is that novices fail to coordinate theory and evidence and so fail to use evidence effectively to evaluate theories.

Formal scientific theories have at least two distinguishable parts; a *formal aspect* (postulates about how a phenomenon occurs) and an *empirical aspect* (a test of those postulates, usually in the form of data or mathematical proofs). Kuhn (1989) found that most children and many lay adults (e.g., young adults who did not attend college) failed to distinguish between these two aspects of a theory. As a consequence, they either adjusted experimental data to fit the theory or changed the theory to fit the data even when the data were ambiguous or unreliable. Both of these adjustment strategies are faulty for one important reason— they prevent children and nonexpert adults from coordinating data and theory. In contrast, educated adults and especially practicing scientists are quite skilled at coordinating data and theory.

Kuhn (1989) identified three essential skills in scientific reasoning: (1) having explicit awareness of what a theory states, (2) distinguishing between evidence that supports or refutes the theory, and (3) justifying why the data support one theory but not another. It turns out that many children and adults often don't understand the theories they are expected to work with (skill 1 above) and therefore find skills 2 and 3 impossible to carry out (Carey & Smith, 1993; Zimmerman, 2007). Ample evidence also indicates that children and many adults fail to distinguish between different kinds of evidence (Kuhn et al., 2008).

Kuhn has proposed some strategies for improving scientific reasoning. One of these is to help students recognize and compare alternative theories. A second is to provide practice in relating a given set of data to competing theories and a third is to increase metacognitive awareness of the scientific reasoning process itself. Studies have reported that teacher modeling coupled with guided discovery can improve each of these dimensions significantly (Kuhn et al., 2008; Schauble, 1990).

Carey and Smith (1993) have suggested a fourth strategy for improving scientific reasoning that addresses the relative sophistication of students' epistemological beliefs (see Chapter 7). Children often fail to distinguish between theories and to coordinate evidence within a theory because they adopt a *commonsense* rather than a *critical* epistemological worldview. The former assumes, often tacitly, that a theory is a collection of facts based on unequivocal data. The latter assumes that a theory is a constructed approximation to reality that may or may not be supported by the data or rational analysis. As a consequence, students adopting a critical epistemology place a great deal more emphasis on evaluating the quality of data and coordinating it with the formal postulates of the theory.

Carey and Smith designed a scientific thinking curriculum that focused on two important skills: theory building and explicit reflection on the theory-building process (see Chapter 9). Carey, Evans, Honda, Jay, and Unger (1989) tested this approach by asking junior high students to conduct a research program that was aimed at discovering why yeast, sugar, and water produced a gas when combined. Results were mixed in that awareness of scientific reasoning improved but not enough to suggest that real conceptual change had occurred. A similar study by Kuhn, Schauble, and Garcia-Mila (1992), however, indicated that guided discovery can significantly improve scientific reasoning.

A Model for Teaching Science

The major goal of science education is for all students to achieve scientific literacy (see Linn et al., 1996; Linn & Eylon, 2006). Scientific literacy isn't just knowing the "big ideas" of science—its major concepts and principles. It also includes using science-related knowledge in our everyday lives, analyzing scientific issues by asking relevant questions and proposing evidence-based explanations, and having sufficient scientific understanding to be informed citizens (AAAS, 1993; National Commission on Mathematics and Science Teaching for the 21st Century, 2000).

How students can best learn science has been the focus of much research in the past 2 decades (Bransford et al., 2000; Bybee, 1997; Dunbar & Fugelsang, 2005; NRC, 2000). As we discussed earlier, this research suggests that science classrooms need to emphasize developing understanding through inquiry-based instruction and through scaffolded, cooperative learning. But the first challenge to teachers is to draw out students' existing misconceptions about science and engage them in tasks that reveal their thinking. These tasks must be chosen carefully, first to confront the naive beliefs, and to then cause conceptual change by showing students multiple examples of the same concept at work (Kuhn, 1989; Linn & Eylon, 2006; Murphy & Mason, 2006).

To develop scientific competence, students need to begin to think more like experts than novices, which means moving beyond science content to a more sophisticated stage in which they evaluate scientific theories and use them to test scientific claims and evidence. Although students obviously need a foundation of factual knowledge, they also must understand those facts in a sound conceptual framework and organize them in ways that lead to fluent retrieval and application (Bransford et al., 2000). Teachers need to help students not only acquire declarative knowledge and science-related procedural skills, but think about problems in terms of a discipline's underlying scientific principles. Research indicates that novices need a great deal of support in integrating knowledge and skills into scientific ways of thinking, such as making inferences from problem statements. Knowledge, independent of well-organized schemata and procedures, is not sufficient to generate procedures for successful problem solving. For experts, such inferences lead to the activation of schemata that trigger solutions.

Science instruction, according to this view, should be directed at building schemata that allow learners to react to problems with appropriate solution procedures. The trick is to help students organize their knowledge into schemata that are both productive and based in sound scientific concepts. Students also need to develop better scientific reasoning skills, which include argumentation and evidence-based rebuttal of unsupportable claims (Gorman, Kincannon, Gooding, & Tweney, 2004). Ideally, students will learn to move from learning science content to organizing that content into schemata and conceptual theories that can be tested, and then on to revising their understanding via critical scientific reasoning. For example, Blank (2000) proposed a model of critical thinking in science called the *metacognitive learning cycle* (MLC). The MLC emphasizes the systematic use of discussions and reflection to promote explicit metacognitive understanding of critical thinking and problem solving. The MLC consists of four interrelated steps—concept introduction, concept application, concept assessment, and concept exploration. Students are asked to reflect upon their progress at each step either individually or in small groups. In comparison with groups that did not use explicit reflection, the MLC group experienced greater conceptual restructuring and understanding of course content.

Another key to effective science instruction is that subject matter is taught in depth. Fewer topics should be covered in more detail, allowing better understanding of key concepts (Bransford et al., 2000). One way to achieve this is extending integrated science instruction over multiple years rather than devoting 1 year to a single science topic (e.g., chemistry) and the next to another (e.g., physics). Aldridge (1992) has argued that using this kind of "layer cake" approach in which students study a single topic and then move on to other topics without ever returning to the first will fail to provide sufficient depth. In contrast, another effective method is to adopt a "spiral" of instruction, one in which students return to important issues in chemistry or physics on a yearly basis. Using strategies like these, of course, requires a high level of curricular coordination across school years.

Using a metacognitive approach to science instruction helps students define their learning goals and monitor their own progress in achieving goals, which lead to much greater self-regulation and learning. Direct instruction in reflective thinking and self-assessment skills, combined with formative assessment that provides feedback to students, has been shown to increase the degree to which students transfer learning to new situations (White, Frederiksen, & Collins, 2009). Students additionally can benefit from instruction in self-regulated learning strategies in both face-to-face or computer administered formats (Lajoie & Azevedo, 2006).

Much of the research appearing in science education journals in the past decade has focused on two broad topics—curriculum change in science education and use of multiple instructional strategies to improve learning (Hurd, 2002). The next section focuses on several instructional strategies for improving self-regulation and learning. Although there is debate about the relative effectiveness of specific teaching strategies, science educators agree that multiple approaches to learning not only improve overall science achievement, but help students develop the life-long learning skills needed to succeed at higher levels of science (Anderson & Hogan, 2000; Duggan & Gott, 2002).

Inquiry-Based Instruction

If there is a consensus in the research in any area of science teaching and learning, it is about the importance of inquiry. The documents outlining national standards for science education, supported by a large body of educational research, all stress the need for inquiry-based instruction to develop the critical-thinking and problem-solving skills that are at the heart of scientific literacy.

What is inquiry? The inquiry-based classroom grows from a constructivist viewpoint and has many of the characteristics we outlined in Chapter 9. In inquiry-oriented classrooms, students are active learners who learn with the teacher's support. Students participate in varied hands-on activities, pose scientifically oriented questions, collect and use evidence to answer questions, evaluate their explanations, and communicate their methods and findings to others. Inquiry is not only a hands-on process; reading, writing, and discussion play key roles in helping students construct new knowledge.

Authentic inquiry takes years of practice and is not attainable in most science classrooms in the short run (Anderson, 2002; Bell & Linn, 2002; Kuhn, 1989). Nevertheless, it is possible to improve inquiry teaching such that students learn to engage in complex, long-term projects based on inquiry. Anderson (2002) has summarized key components of inquiry teaching for the teacher and student. Teachers facilitate student thinking through scaffolded instruction and explicit reflective thinking. They also demonstrate how theoretical models are used to construct and test scientific arguments (Kuhn, 1989). Students take an active role in their learning by constructing hypotheses and working alone and collaboratively to test them and interpret findings. In addition, they are able to explain their problem-solving strategies verbally or in writing. Doing so promotes reflection, an essential component of metacognitive understanding and self-regulation (Davis, 2001).

In addition to these activities, the National Research Council, in *Inquiry and the National Education Standards* (2000), has emphasized the need for students to use scientific thinking. Students with scientific-thinking skills go beyond learning facts or doing a hands-on activity and become able to use logic and reasoning skills to develop scientific knowledge and an understanding of scientific processes. Inquiry-based learning can help students develop these skills.

Before we define in more detail how teachers can effectively put this model into action, we discuss the learning strategies—both dysfunctional and functional—that students often bring to science classrooms.

Learning and Conceptual Change Strategies

One goal of science education is to teach students new learning strategies that help them acquire and organize information. This goal is not always met. Because students come to instructional settings with learning strategies acquired both in and outside of school, some students will have acquired learning strategies that actually interfere with learning new science material.

In one study, Roth (1985) asked middle school students to read science materials written at their grade level and examined how they thought about it. She identified five learning strategies these students used. Only one of these, unfortunately, resulted in their restructuring and refining naive schemata. The following paragraphs briefly describe these five strategies.

Overreliance on the Sufficiency of Prior Knowledge   Students who exhibited the strategy of overreliance on prior knowledge read the assignment and then reported that they understood what they had read. In fact, many reported that they had "known this stuff" before they even read the material (Limon, 2003). One student, after reading a passage that used milk as an example of how all food ultimately can be traced back to green plants (the food producers), reported the passage was "about milk." The point of the reading—that plants make food that cows convert to milk—was missed entirely. In this student's view, he already knew the content. Instead of using knowledge just acquired from the text to answer questions, some students tended to associate the new material with their prior knowledge and report simply that the text was repetitious.

Overreliance on Text Vocabulary   In this strategy, students isolated new words or phrases in the assignment, often out of context. They felt that they comprehended the text if they could state that it was about a specific word—for example, "photo-something" (photosynthesis). According to Roth, students reported feeling confused about the text only if they could not decode the new words. For these children, understanding the text simply meant recall of new or big terms and a phrase or sentence about each. Of course, this strategy can pay off if the teacher's questions about text materials are mostly requests for definitions or identifications of new words. Such performance doesn't, however, represent deep understanding or construction of new knowledge.

Overreliance on Factual Information   Many students have adopted a view of science as the accumulation of facts (e.g., air expands when heated, water boils at 212°F at sea level). These students see science learning as consisting of recall of facts about a variety of natural phenomena. In Roth's study, such students displayed quite accurate recall of these bits of information, but their ideas were not linked into meaningful schemata, nor were major points distinguished from trivial ones. As you might expect, these students did best with teachers who employed a vocabulary-oriented view of science.

Overreliance on Existing Beliefs   Many students in Roth's studies relied on naive beliefs (Murphy & Mason, 2006; Pintrich et al., 1993), as discussed earlier in the chapter. For these students, new topics were understood in terms of naive beliefs tied to their prior knowledge. These students sought to link text knowledge with existing prior knowledge, a good thing, but their goal was not to modify the structure of existing ideas about how things work. Instead, they were trying to confirm the correctness of their existing beliefs. In many cases, students distorted or even ignored information inconsistent with existing knowledge. In contrast with the overreliance on the sufficiency of prior knowledge learning strategy, these students realized that the information was new but did not appear to understand that it might challenge their existing beliefs.

Conceptual-Change Strategy   Conceptual-change students see text materials as a vehicle for changing existing schemata (Duit & Treagust, 2003; Limon & Mason, 2002). In Roth's study, they worked to reconcile old ideas with new material. As a result, they not only identified and learned the key ideas in the text but also were able to state where the text or other materials conflicted with their existing schemata. They also saw the text as a source of new knowledge and were willing to revise their old schemata in the light of new information. Interestingly, but not surprisingly, this group of students was most often likely to admit to being confused or puzzled by what they were reading.

Exactly why student acquire these different learning strategies is unclear. Nonetheless, teachers need to anticipate them. If students describe encounters with new material as "old stuff," the teacher probably should be creating a classroom environment that shows how the new material challenges old beliefs. Students need to understand that the material is, in fact, new. Similarly, students who view science learning basically as vocabulary or fact acquisition may be presented with situations (e.g., experiments, demonstrations, or field investigations) that require them to link words and facts into schemata that help them better understand and explain the world. The teaching strategies that follow provide methods for addressing these different learning strategies and moving students toward scientific literacy.

Teaching Strategies

According to the National Science Education Standards, the most direct way to improve science achievement for all students is through better science teaching. The general model for teaching science outlined at the beginning of this section can be put into action through two general teaching strategies: (1) confronting and changing naive beliefs and (2) inquiry-based teaching focused on constructing new knowledge and developing metacognitive and scientific thinking skills. The emphasis in this approach is helping students acquire science content that leads to the construction of scientific models and theories for testing scientific claims (Dunbar & Fugelsang, 2005).

Confronting and Changing Naive Beliefs   As described earlier in this chapter, teachers need to draw out students' naive beliefs and misconceptions and then move them toward conceptual change (Vosniadou, 2002). Two ways to uncover students' misconceptions are by discussing their beliefs about the nature of science (Linn & Eylon, 2006) and engaging them in tasks that reveal their thinking. Determining students' initial beliefs about science—their prior knowledge—and using this knowledge as a starting point for new instruction creates a sound basis for the learning of science (Bahar, 2003; Limon, 2003).

Having exposed naive beliefs and preconceptions, teachers then must show students multiple examples of the target concepts at work and provide clear scientific explanations of these concepts. This step requires that teachers have a good understanding of scientific inquiry and fundamental scientific facts and concepts. Unfortunately, many science instructors are not as knowledgeable as they should be regarding all aspects of the science curriculum. This is especially problematic because we know that low-knowledge teachers tend to provide less cohesive explanations, ask fewer questions, and provide a smaller number of opportunities for students to test their scientific wings by theorizing and empirically testing their theories (Linn & Eylon, 2006; Murphy & Mason, 2006).

Once students have a firm basic understanding of a concept, they can be moved toward conceptual change by comparing and contrasting competing viewpoints. One way to accomplish this goal is by through cooperative learning. Research reviewed by Tobin et al. (1994) suggests that cooperative learning environments are effective for increasing elaboration and evaluation of scientific ideas.

Promoting Constructive Learning   The second general teaching strategy is to provide inquiry-based learning, cooperative learning environments focused on developing scientific thinking and metacognitive skills (Pea, 1993; Tobin et al., 1994).

The teacher plays a crucial role in *inquiry-based classrooms,* especially in promoting learning via guided, scaffolded participation in activities (Collins, Brown, & Newman, 1989). Because good science inquiry provides many ways for students to approach a new topic and a wide variety of student activities (Kluger, 1999), teacher direction is vital for launching inquiry, focusing students' attention on methods and topics, and modeling inquiry-related investigative skills. The teacher also plays a major role in structuring the classroom discourse (see Chapter 9). Much of scientific inquiry centers on the asking and answering of questions, a special form of discourse. Effective science teachers have been found to ask more and better questions, pose questions with higher cognitive demand, and ask more follow-up questions. They begin lessons with thought-provoking questions and focus on student understanding rather than looking for right or wrong answers. In effective classrooms, both small- and large-group discussions are common, questioning encouraged, and feedback frequent.

Cooperative learning environments are almost always a part of effective inquiry-based classrooms. Small cooperative groups in which each student develops a particular area of expertise have been found to promote learning via "distributed cognition," as students learn from one another (Campione, Brown, & Jay, 1992). Linking students to mentors and learning centers and utilizing computer learning environments (Demastes et al., 1996) also can expand inquiry-based classroom environments and promote self-efficacy.

Inquiry-based teaching also is closely tied to the teaching of *scientific thinking skills.* Inquiry-based projects can be used to engage students in asking scientific questions and give them hands-on opportunities to explore such questions and collect meaningful data. Through inquiry, teachers can help students interpret data, develop explanations, and evaluate and communicate what they have learned. Most authorities (e.g., McNeill & Kracijk, 2008) argue that active engagement in the scientific process is necessary for students to develop a deep understanding of science and progress toward scientific literacy.

In recent years there has been growing evidence of the importance of metacognitive skills in learning and student achievement (see Chapter 4). This also is true in science learning. Teachers should stress development of reflective thinking and self-assessment skills. Directly teaching students metacognitive strategies such as predicting outcomes, evaluating why some methods work and others don't, and planning ahead all have been shown to increase science learning. Writing tasks seem especially valuable for encouraging students to reflect on their own learning (Scardamalia, Bereiter, & Steinbach, 1984). Assignments that require communication of results from experiments and projects not only are excellent vehicles for teaching metacognitive strategies but they can also increase understanding of the subject. Science journaling, which helps create a dialogue between teacher and student, is yet another method for helping students reflect on their knowledge and beliefs.

Formative assessments that give feedback to students also can help them reflect on their learning and guide their learning processes. Tobin et al. (1994) reported that assessment strategies such as creating and maintaining portfolios of personal work encourage metacognitive skills of reflection and self-assessment. Such portfolios also give students more control over their own learning and build self-awareness.

Focus on Integrated Science Instruction

Linn and Eylon (2006) developed an integrated approach to science instruction that examines the role of design processes and design patterns. *Design processes* refer to four core activities in knowledge integration: eliciting ideas, introducing new ideas, evaluating ideas, and synthesizing ideas. This general sequence of activities is intended to draw out student ideas, add new ideas from other students or the teacher, develop collective criteria for evaluating the adequacy of ideas, and organize ideas into a coherent explanation of the phenomenon being investigated.

The core activities of design processes can be applied strategically to a variety of *design patterns,* including making predictions, conducting experiments, collecting evidence, and reflection. Linn and Eylon (2006, see Figure 22.2) discuss 10 different design patterns that each play an important role in science learning. Optimal instruction is viewed as using each of the design patterns in a meaningful, iterative sequence that enables students to explore ideas and reach integrated solutions through collaborative discussion and reflection.

Although the Linn and Eylon (2006) framework provides many instructional options, there are at least three general aspects that are germane to classroom instruction. One is focusing on methods that promote knowledge integration and conceptual understanding. A second is targeting improvement in students' basic scientific inquiry processes such as hypothesis testing and evaluating evidence. A third is carefully planning how science knowledge and processes should be introduced to students, modeled for them, and systematically developed.

Supporting Teacher Development

As you have seen in the preceding sections, providing excellent science instruction is demanding. The depth of a teacher's science and pedagogical knowledge are the strongest indicators of effective science teaching, implying that teachers need to be lifelong learners in both of these areas. Preservice teacher education and professional development thus are paramount concerns in creating learning environments that foster scientific literacy. We recommend three changes involving teacher education institutions, the public schools, and the schools' relationships with the public.

First, science requirements for new elementary school teachers generally need to be increased. Many colleges and universities still allow preservice elementary education teachers to complete their undergraduate degrees only one or two "real" science courses. Elementary teachers need to attain a level of scientific literacy in biological, physical, and earth sciences that will allow them to model the kind of expert conceptions excellent science instruction requires. In many cases, this will require new college-level science curricula.

Several obstacles exist, however, to improving teacher preparation in science (Anderson & Mitchener, 1994). One of these, which we have just described, is the inadequate subject matter preparation that many science teachers, but especially those at the elementary school level, receive. The resulting lack of content and pedagogical content knowledge in science restricts what science topics they teach and the methods used to teach them. A second obstacle is that, despite an emerging consensus about the value of an inquiry-oriented, constructivist approach in science, viewpoints about how best to prepare science teachers still differ. Not all teacher preparation programs promote the student-centered "construct and understand" methods that most experts today advocate; some instead continue to emphasize a teacher-oriented "learn and practice" approach. A third obstacle is the fact that up to 40% of science educators leave teaching after their first 2 years, which greatly limits the possibility that students will receive science instruction from a well-seasoned expert. A related consequence of this high turnover is that skilled science mentors are unavailable to many students.

A second direction for change focuses on the schools and their relationships to their communities. Essentially, the schools, including the faculty, administration, and school boards, must educate their communities about the importance of science and work to build a solid base of intellectual and economic support for excellent science instruction. Inquiry- and laboratory-based educational experiences are expensive and the monies to support them must come from taxpayers. If they do not have the laboratory facilities and materials needed for instruction, even the best prepared teachers will come up short.

A third direction for change also has a clear school orientation. Surveys (e.g., Dorph et al., 2007; Fulp, 2002) have shown that time allocated to science instruction in elementary classrooms is often grossly inadequate. In Dorph et al.'s survey of K–5 teachers in the San Francisco Bay Area, for instance, 80% of teachers reported spending an hour or less a week on science; 16% reported spending no time at all! As is well known, time on task has been shown to be one of the major determinants of achievement, and if science remains only a small part of the school day, the chances for students achieving a high level of scientific literacy will remain low.

Benefits of Effective Instruction

As we have discussed, a critical factor in high-quality science instruction is the teacher's knowledge of science. For example, teachers' knowledge is related to the quality of teacher–student interactions (Tobin & Fraser, 1990). Less knowledgeable teachers interact less often and less successfully with their students. Teacher knowledge also is related to the amount and quality of teacher questions, with high-knowledge teachers asking deeper level questions that are more likely to promote constructive scientific thinking among students.

High-quality instruction changes students' cognitive structures (Dunbar & Fugelsang, 2005; Linn & Eylon, 2006). In a study of fifth- and sixth-grade students, for example, Kuhn et al. (1992) asked a group of 10 students to investigate why using some balls led to better tennis serves than using others, and a similar group of 10 students to investigate what led to better performance among three cars. Both groups participated in seven 30-minute discussions over a 2-month period. Students were asked to generate a theory about either the balls or the cars and to support that theory by using available evidence.

The longitudinal nature of this study allowed Kuhn et al. (1992) to draw inferences about several important behaviors. One conclusion was that scientific reasoning improved over time in similar ways even though the two groups solved different problems. This finding suggested that guided discovery improves scientific thinking at a level beyond the specific domain of the problem. A second conclusion was that students revised and improved the strategies used to solve the problem over time. This finding suggested that students discover, revise, and delete solution strategies on a continuous basis if they have the chance for extended experimentation on a single problem (see Siegler & Jenkins, 1989, for a similar finding). As discussed earlier in this chapter, students typically need several examples of a single concept and more depth of coverage of topics for effective learning.

Last, but certainly not least, high-quality instruction increases student motivation, which increases learning. Bruning and Schweiger (1997) identified several ways that quality learning environments motivate students to learn more science. These settings typically include scaffolded instruction combined with opportunities to experience science on a firsthand, participatory basis. One benefit of authentic participation is that it increases observation of natural phenomena. Participation also increases student interest, which in turn is closely linked with student engagement and learning (Hidi & Renninger, 2006). Students who are given the chance to participate also experience greater autonomy, which is strongly linked with higher achievement (Deci & Ryan, 1987) and mastery of goals (Dweck & Leggett, 1988) (see Chapters 6 and 7). In addition, active participation increases the level of classroom discourse among students, which has been linked with knowledge restructuring and metacognitive awareness (see Chapter 9).

Researchers also have found that science instruction leads to important changes in the way students represent and think about science concepts when the emphasis is on *coordinating knowledge* and *how* one thinks about science problems rather than on *what* one thinks about (Kuhn et al., 2008; Linn & Eylon, 2006). Consistent with this perspective, the most effective science teachers will have developed a wide repertoire of methods for helping students think about science in new ways. Most of these methods, however, will fit into one or more of the basic approaches described earlier: exposing naive beliefs, creating conceptual conflict, and encouraging cognitive accommodation to more mature views of science.

A Model of Science Achievement

What factors above and beyond expert knowledge and problem-solving strategies lead to science achievement? Reynolds and Walberg (1991, 1992) and Young, Reynolds, and Walberg (1996) conducted a program of research involving more than 5,000 students across the nation to answer this question. Their research considered potential influences among middle school and high school students, including home environment, prior science achievement, motivation, instructional time, and instructional quality. The relative contribution of each variable was considered by using a complex statistical procedure called structural equation modeling. Statistical procedures such as this allow researchers to investigate the interrelationships among many variables simultaneously.

One advantage of this approach is that the direct and indirect effects of a variable can be separated. A direct effect occurs when one variable directly causes a change in another variable. For example, Reynolds and Walberg (1991) found that instructional time was related directly to science achievement in eighth grade; that is, more instructional time led to higher achievement regardless of other variables. In contrast, an indirect effect occurs when the relationship between two variables is mediated by another. In the Reynolds and Walberg studies, home environment affected prior science achievement (in seventh grade), which in turn affected eighth-grade science achievement. Thus, home environment did not have a direct effect on eighth-grade science achievement even though it had a substantial indirect effect.

The Reynolds and Walberg studies of middle school and high school science achievement reported similar findings, so the results of both studies are summarized in the single model shown in Figure 15.4 (on page 354). This type of model is referred to as a path diagram. Measured variables are represented as boxes; the relationships among these variables are shown by arrows. The number beside each arrow is the correlation between variables. The absence of an arrow indicates that a meaningful statistical relationship was not found between variables.

Figure 15.4 suggests some important conclusions that also have been supported by more recent studies (Byrnes & Miller, 2007; O'Reilly & McNamara, 2007). One of these is that prior science achievement is strongly related to current science achievement. This finding highlights the vital role of prior knowledge and distributed practice in learning and scientific problem solving (see Chapter 5). Another conclusion is that the amount of instructional time is related

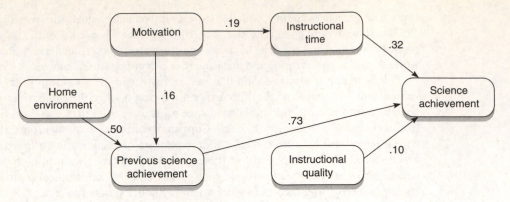

FIGURE 15.4   A Model of Science Achievement.

Source: Adapted from "A Structural Model of Science Achievement and Attitude: An Extension to High School," by A. J. Reynolds and H. J. Walberg, 1991, *Journal of Educational Psychology, 84,* 371–382. Copyright 1991 by the American Psychological Association. Adapted by permission.

to current science achievement (Johnson, Kahle, & Fargo, 2007). This finding indicates that the amount of science instruction makes an important contribution to learning. One possible reason is that students are given a greater diversity of training. An alternative may be that students spend more time delving into a small number of problems but do so in detail. A third conclusion is that home environment plays an important role in current science achievement by facilitating prior achievement. One interpretation of this outcome is that the parents' and siblings' beliefs and attitudes about science affect a student's involvement in science throughout her or his early school career.

The model shown also is noteworthy in that several intuitively obvious relationships were *not* found. For example, no relationship was found between instructional time and instructional quality, nor was a strong relationship found between instructional quality and current science achievement. At face value, these findings suggest that the amount of instruction is more important than the quality of instruction. Caution is needed when interpreting these results, because it is quite possible that instructional quality was uniformly high (or low) across this sample—a condition that would tend to reduce the observed magnitude of the correlation.

Results of these studies are consistent with the main themes of this book—namely that prior knowledge and time on task lead to higher levels of academic achievement, whether in reading, mathematics, or science. Home environment and motivation (Chang, Singh, & Mo, 2007) also were found to be important determinants of science achievement, a finding that strengthens the argument for a global approach, involving parents and siblings, to improving science education. This does not mean that other variables included in the Reynolds and Walberg studies were unimportant, only that they affected current achievement far less than prior knowledge, instructional time, and home environment.

In summary, even though the end goals of science achievement are expert conceptual knowledge, a flexible repertoire of problem-solving strategies, and working effectively with both theory and data, the path to these goals begins with a motivating home environment and a school environment providing equal access for all students. The acquisition of knowledge and skills necessary to excel at science clearly is a complex process that transcends the schoolroom.

Assessing Science Learning

Assessment of reading, mathematics, and science is important as well as challenging. Science may be the most difficult content area to assess, however, primarily because there are so many subdomains that must be considered. Patz (2006) listed eight core science content areas based on the National Science Education Standards that must be assessed:

- Unifying concepts
- Science as inquiry
- Physical science
- Life science
- Earth and space science
- Science and technology
- Science in personal and social perspectives
- History and nature of science

Several problems occur due to the sheer volume of information that must be assessed. One is that there often is insufficient time to teach and assess all relevant information. Patz (2006) estimated that the eight general content areas above lead to 23 to 100 individual content areas that could be evaluated, which is impossible in most assessment settings. Assuming that a minimum of five test items are necessary to assure reliable and valid coverage of a content strand, the eight broad strands seem to be the maximum number that a high-quality test could assess.

A second problem is that it is easier to assess "knowledge" associated with each of the eight content strands than to assess performance-based skills such as theory testing, experimentation, or those that are essential in day-to-day scientific field work. Krajcik (2006) has argued that few performance standards are reflected in science assessment, and of those that are, most are superficial compared to relevant but complex performance skills, such as analyzing and interpreting complex data sets.

A third concern is that current accountability models such as No Child Left Behind (2002) emphasize measures of academic proficiency rather than academic excellence, tending to focus on basic academic requirements at the expense of more sophisticated science content and performance skills. From this perspective, NCLB is seen as lowering the national expectations for math and literacy (Zvoch, 2006). In contrast, entities such as the National Research Council (2006) have called for a rigorous set of science standards focusing on higher level thinking and problem solving.

These concerns are highlighted by results of international testing programs such as TIMSS (Third International Mathematics and Science Study), in which the United States has performed poorly compared to many other nations, especially Asian nations such as Singapore, Japan, and Taiwan. Some critics argue that science content and performance standards have been lowered to the point of harming U.S. economic interests (Shen, 2005). Possible reasons for poor American science scores compared to Asian nations include lower perceived utility regarding scientific knowledge, a shorter school year, higher student mobility, more TV viewing after school, and even overconfidence among students.

There are no easy solutions to the quantity and quality dilemmas we have described. Most state high school assessments use 60 to 80 multiple-choice items to assess the cumulative science skills of high school juniors and seniors. One possibility is that deeper, finer-grained science assessment be conducted by classroom teachers, but unfortunately few science teachers are trained to develop high-quality assessments. Some have argued that such training should be a key component of reform in science education (Roberts & Gott, 2006).

Implications for Instruction

1. *Teach science as a problem-solving process.* The ambitious goal of creating scientific literacy provides great challenges to teachers. Cognitive perspectives on science learning imply teaching it more as a problem-solving process than as a knowledge (vocabulary or facts) acquisition process. Inquiry-based approaches to science teaching have been shown to be highly effective in developing scientific thinking and problem-solving skills.

2. *Identify students' naive beliefs.* Students bring to science a wealth of preconceptions, many of which will be incomplete or incorrect. These preconceptions must be brought to light before effective instruction can occur. The identification process often is slow and uncertain, however, and requires considerable teaching time. The process will be enhanced by a careful choice of instructional materials that elicit the student's own thinking, rather than just reiteration of information the student thinks the teacher wants.

3. *Confront naive beliefs immediately.* Most science educators argue that science curricula should begin with the ideas that students bring with them and then provide students with experiences that ask them to confront their preconceptions in ways that lead to more informed conceptions. The magnitude of this task should not be underestimated. Historically, science curricula have been written from the perspective of the expert, not the novice. Writing materials that challenge students' naive beliefs in productive ways and that ultimately lead them to more expert-like knowledge structures requires careful attention.

Techniques that effectively confront student's naive beliefs include introducing exposing and discrepant events, generating a range of conceptual responses to these events, and practice extending new conceptual responses to a broad range of situations. These activities are most valuable when accompanied by direct student involvement with science materials and with each other.

4. *Use hands-on demonstrations.* Because scientific schemata often are in conflict with experience-based schemata (naive beliefs), experiments or demonstrations usually are necessary to challenge preconceptions. These demonstrations must be chosen thoughtfully so that

they require children to examine their own views in ways that lead them to consider and adopt more scientific views. Hands-on activities should also promote more opportunities for students to engage in metacognitive self-questioning of their learning strategies and conclusions. Substantial teacher patience and openness are necessary so that students feel free to use their own language to come to grips with inconsistencies or inadequacies in their thinking. Although students can memorize correct explanations, observations of explanatory behavior following such memorization suggest that students frequently return to explanations consistent with earlier preconceptions. As pointed out previously, knowledge alone is insufficient to change habits of thought. Students must have experience-based activities that encourage them to construct more expert, mature views of science.

5. *Give students adequate time to restructure knowledge.* Conceptual change in science is a long-term process. Students need opportunities to see for themselves why science-based views of the world are sounder and more useful than their own. Changes in thinking also need to be assessed over relatively long periods of time. This is not to say that teachers shouldn't evaluate the effectiveness of their instruction frequently, but rather that expecting rapid changes in student thinking is unrealistic. If expectations are too high, both student and teacher may become discouraged.

Some studies also suggest that restructuring and strategy development are most effective when students work through complex problems repeatedly. Doing so may help students generate, test, and discard old problem-solving strategies as they discover newer, more efficient strategies that match their developing conceptions of the problem. Jumping from unit to unit may be counterproductive even though it exposes students to a wider range of materials and problems. Covering fewer topics in more depth is more likely to produce greater understanding of scientific concepts and principles.

6. *Monitor the use of dysfunctional strategies.* Even older students often rely on dysfunctional strategies when reading science texts (Roth, 1985). The most common of these are overreliance on prior knowledge and on acquiring vocabulary and factual information. Better goals are re-examining prior knowledge and learning to look to relationships that exist in data. Interviewing and questioning are good techniques for sounding out students' strategies and beliefs.

7. *Help students learn about the nature of scientific theories.* Research indicates that few students prior to high school have a deep understanding of the distinction between theory and data, which makes it difficult if not impossible to really understand the processes of scientific inquiry. Students must be helped to comprehend what theories are, what their uses are, how they differ from data, and how theory and data are coordinated.

8. *Involve parents and siblings.* Research by Reynolds and Walberg (1991) suggests that effective long-term science instruction needs to involve parents and siblings. Views expressed about science at home are crucial. In addition, the kind of epistemological worldview (e.g., commonsense vs. critical) modeled at home will play an important role in a student's acceptance of scientifically based evidence. For older students, teachers may need to address problems that arise because of conflicts between their developing views of science and differing parental views.

Summary

Scientific literacy has become the major goal of science education. Students who are scientifically literate have an understanding of science concepts and principles, along with the scientific method. They can apply their understanding of science not just in the laboratory and classroom, but also in their daily lives. The first step in effective science instruction is helping students realize their preconceptions or naive beliefs. Exposure to carefully chosen empirical and scientific events can lead them to examine their preconceptions and revise them in the direction of more scientific, expert conceptions. The process of confronting naive beliefs and moving students toward conceptual change will usually be slow. Teachers not only need to present challenging experiences to students, but allow them enough time to examine their beliefs. Carefully scaffolded instruction is one strategy for helping students acquire more mature, scientifically based perspectives.

Studies of differences in problem-solving behavior between novices (beginning students in a science) and experts (usually Ph.D.-level practitioners) have revealed that experts not only have deeper factual knowledge, but different strategies and conceptual frameworks than novices. Their ability to recognize meaningful patterns, chunk information in a scientific domain into schema-like packages, and retrieve the information fluently all contribute to successful learning. Experts' schemata include both procedural and declarative information, while most novices appear to lack useful procedural components. Experts and novices also differ in important ways with respect to distinguishing formal and empirical aspects of theories. In reconciling theory and data, novices often "adjust" either the theory itself or the data in a way that obscures genuine scientific understanding.

Teachers must expect many students to possess dysfunctional learning strategies, which often are tied to their naive theories. Some of these strategies are overreliance on vocabulary and prior knowledge. Demonstrations, followed by carefully guided and constructed discussions and questions, can help students confront misconceptions and change poor learning strategies.

Science classrooms should emphasize developing student understanding through inquiry-based instruction and the teaching of scientific thinking and metacognitive skills. The teacher plays a critical role in inquiry learning, especially in promoting learning via guided, scaffolded participation in hands-on activities. Another important role is the structuring of classroom discourse by effective questioning. Direct instruction in metacognitive skills, such as reflective thinking and self-assessment, has been shown to improve learning. Alternative methods of assessment, such as having students create personal portfolios, also have been shown to increase reflective thinking. A final classroom strategy for improving science understanding is an integrated science instruction framework focusing on promoting conceptual understanding, improving basic scientific inquiry processes such as hypothesis testing and evaluating evidence, and carefully introducing, modeling, and developing new scientific information and procedures.

Research suggests that the factors having large effects on science achievement include prior science achievement, amount of instructional time, and the home environment. These findings reinforce other research suggesting that more time spent studying science and including parents and siblings in science activities can result in greater science achievement.

SUGGESTED READINGS

Bransford, J. D., Brown, A. L., & Cocking, R. R. (Eds.). (2000). *How people learn: Brain, mind, experience, and school*. Washington, DC: National Academy Press.

This easy-to-understand, comprehensive overview of educational research and practice is a widely cited publication on learning and teaching that gives excellent insight into current perspectives on science teaching.

Ericsson, K. A. (2003). The acquisition of expert performance as problem solving. In J. E. Davidson & R. J. Sternberg (Eds.), *The psychology of problem solving* (pp. 31–83). Cambridge, UK: Cambridge University Press.

This chapter provides a comprehensive update on the development of expertise related to scientific problem solving.

Kuhn, D. (1989). Children and adults as intuitive scientists. *Psychological Review, 96,* 674–689.

This classic article reviews important differences among children's, lay adults', and scientists' thinking about theories and the process of coordinating theory with data.

GLOSSARY

4C/ID (Four-Component Instructional Design) Model: An instructional design model formulated by van Merrienboër and his associates focusing on complex cognitive skills (Chapter 10)

Action Control: The ability to control actions (e.g., motivation and concentration) that help an individual self-regulate (Chapter 4)

Activating Prior Knowledge: Methods for evoking what students already know in preparation for learning (Chapter 4)

Adjunct Questions: Questions inserted in text materials that readers answer as they read (Chapter 12)

Advance Organizer: Brief prefatory material written at a high level of abstraction that serves as a framework for materials to be learned (Chapters 4 and 12)

Agency: An individual's sense of self-determination and perseverance when faced with challenges (Chapter 7)

Algorithm: A procedure in mathematics or computer science that applies to a particular kind of problem and that, if followed correctly, guarantees the correct answer (Chapters 8 and 14)

Alphabetic Principle: The idea that letters or letter combinations represent phonemes and that letter-sound relationships can be used to decode written words (Chapter 11)

Assignment of Meaning: A stage of perception in which meaning is given to a stimulus (Chapter 2)

Attention: Mental energy used in perception and thought; the focused allocation of resources to a stimulus (Chapters 2 and 11)

Attribute: A feature shared across the examples of a concept (e.g., water is an attribute of the concept of ocean); attributes essential to defining the concept and shared across all examples of a concept are called defining attributes (Chapter 3)

Attribution: A causal interpretation of an event or outcome (e.g., that academic success is attributable to ability) (Chapter 6)

Attribution Theory: A theory proposed by Weiner to explain the attributional process (Chapter 6)

Attributional Retraining: Programs designed to change the attributional responses that individuals make in specific settings (Chapter 6)

Automaticity: Performing of any cognitive skill automatically; automated procedures require very few resources (Chapter 2)

Basal Reading Series: Packages of published materials for literacy instruction that include coordinated texts, teachers' manuals, and student exercises (Chapter 11)

Bridging: Activities designed to promote transfer of knowledge from one domain to another (Chapter 8)

Buggy Algorithm: In mathematics, an incorrect version of an algorithm that, if followed, will yield wrong answers (Chapter 14)

Cerebral Cortex: The gray matter of the brain that can be divided into four functional areas: the frontal, temporal, parietal, and occipital lobes (Chapter 2)

Chunk: A stimulus, such as a letter, number, or word, that becomes unitized; the concept of chunk was proposed by Miller as a unit against which short-term memory capacity could be calibrated (Chapter 2)

Classroom Discourse: Verbal exchanges in a classroom (Chapter 9)

Coaching: Providing scaffolded assistance to a novice to illustrate strategies and feedback that improve performance (Chapter 9)

Code-Emphasis Methods: As used by Chall, beginning reading instruction methods that emphasize learning the correspondence between letters and sounds (Chapter 11)

Cognitive Apprenticeship: Novices learning new concepts and skills through discussion and modeling provided in a long-term, intensive relationship with a more-skilled expert (Chapter 9)

Cognitive (Informational) Feedback: Specific information that links information about performance with the nature of the task (Chapter 6)

Cognitive Load Theory: A theory proposed by John Sweller and his associates focusing on working memory's role in instructional design (Chapters 2 and 10)

Cognitive Modeling: A procedure for developing students' performance that involves giving a rationale for the performance, demonstrating the performance, and providing opportunity for practice (Chapter 6)

Cognitive Neuroscience: A branch of cognitive psychology that focuses on the structure and workings of the *brain* to better understand the human *mind* and cognition (Chapter 2)

Cognitive Science: The multidisciplinary study of how information is represented and processed, incorporating perspectives from psychology, linguistics, computer science, and neuroscience (Chapter 2)

Coherence: A property of discourse in which individual elements derive their meaning from earlier or later elements (Chapter 9)

Cohesion: Relations of meanings that exist within a text and that define it as a text (Chapter 13)

Cohesive Ties: Instances of cohesion, such as repetition of words and anaphoric reference, that link a pair of cohesively related items in a text (Chapter 13)

Concept: One of the fundamental building blocks of cognition, a concept is a mental structure that represents a meaningful category and enables us to group objects or events together on the basis of perceived similarities (Chapter 3)

Concept-Oriented Reading Instruction (CORI): A method for developing reading comprehension created by Guthrie and his associates that combines project-oriented content-area learning, strategies instruction, and ways of building intrinsic motivation (Chapter 12)

Conceptual Change: A major reorganization in memory of the conceptual framework for a domain of knowledge (Chapter 15)

Conceptually Driven Model: A model of reading comprehension that stresses the guiding role of the reader's knowledge and expectations (Chapter 12)

Conceptually Driven (Top-Down) Processing: Cognitive processing guided, in large part, by prior knowledge and predictions, rather than external data (Chapter 12)

Conditional Knowledge: Knowledge about when and why to use strategies (Chapters 3 and 4)

Conjunctive Rules: In concept identification, rules for identifying concepts that require two or more attributes to be present (Chapter 3)

Connectionist Model of Memory: A memory model that represents memory as the strength of connections between units (Chapter 3)

Conservative Focusing Strategy: In concept acquisition, an approach in which learners concentrate on selecting new examples of a concept that differ in only one attribute from the first (Chapter 3)

Constraints on Operators: Restrictions that limit the use of objects or variables used to solve a problem (Chapter 8)

Construction-Integration (CI) Model: A model developed by Kintsch and his associates that represents the reading comprehension process (Chapter 12)

Construction Phase: In Kintsch's CI model, the initial stage of reading comprehension in which propositions and concepts automatically activate readers' associations and simple inferences (Chapter 12)

Constructionist Models: Models of reading that focus on readers' goals, attempts to create representations that make sense, and explanations of why events and actions occur (Chapter 12)

Constructive Memory: The memory that is created by learners interacting with new information and situations (Chapter 1)

Constructivism: A point of view that holds that what individuals learn and understand is constructed through their mental processes and social interactions (Chapter 9)

Contextual Knowledge: A part of vocabulary knowledge that includes understanding how words are actually used in written and spoken language; see also Definitional Knowledge (Chapter 12)

Controllability: In attribution theory, a causal dimension that defines the degree to which the cause of an outcome can be controlled (Chapter 6)

Controlled Processes: Cognitive processes (e.g., allocation of attention) that are under the conscious control of the learner (Chapter 2)

Controlling Action: An action that individuals engage in for extrinsic reasons, such as expectation, reward, or punishment (Chapter 6)

Controlling Reward: A reward used to control students' behavior or performance (Chapter 6)

Criterion-Referenced Evaluation: An evaluation in which an individual's performance is evaluated with respect to preestablished criteria that are unaffected by other students' performance (Chapter 6)

Critical Thinking: Reflection and evaluation of evidence and arguments to draw the most reasonable and valid conclusion from a variety of different alternatives (Chapter 8)

Data-Driven Model: A model of comprehension that emphasizes "bottom-up" processes, such as those involved in decoding and understanding word meanings (Chapter 12)

Data-Driven (Bottom-Up) Processing: Cognitive processing guided, in large part, by external information versus prior knowledge (Chapter 12)

Data-Limited Task: A cognitive activity that is limited because of insufficient or degraded stimuli or information (Chapter 2)

Declarative Knowledge: Systematically organized factual knowledge; "knowing what" (Chapters 3 and 4)

Defining Attribute: An attribute of a concept that is essential to defining it (Chapter 3)

Definitional Knowledge: In vocabulary knowledge, an understanding of the relationship between a word and other words, as in a dictionary definition; see also Contextual Knowledge (Chapter 12)

Deliberate Practice: Repeated practice of a skill with feedback over a long period of time in order to develop high levels of automaticity and expertise (Chapter 8)

Design Principles: Rules guiding how instructional programs are structured (Chapter 10)

Dialectical Constructivism: A form of constructivism that places the source of knowledge in the interactions between learners and their environments; dialectical constructivism represents a midpoint between the extremes of endogenous and exogenous constructivism (Chapter 9)

Direct Vocabulary Instruction: A formal method of teaching vocabulary in which meanings of words are taught explicitly (Chapter 12)

Disciplined Discussion: Calfee's term for classroom discourse that combines the features of informal conversation and formal instruction; in disciplined discussion, students use interactive processes they have learned to reach goals they have set (Chapter 9)

Discourse: Structured, coherent sequences of language in which sentences are combined into higher order units, such as paragraphs, narratives, and expository texts; conversations and extended sequences of writing are examples of discourse (Chapters 9 and 11)

Discourse Structure: A feature of discourse; common discourse structures include narratives (stories) and exposition (expository text) (Chapter 11)

Discovery Learning: Self-guided learning in which students generate and test hypotheses about an idea (Chapter 9)

Disjunctive Rules: In concept identification, rules for identifying concepts that are "either/or" in nature; that is, an object would be an example of a disjunctive concept with two defining attributes if it contained either of the two attributes (Chapter 3)

Distal Goal: A long-term goal (Chapter 6)

Distinctiveness of Encoding: A view that information is memorable to the extent that it is made distinctive (Chapter 4)

Distributed Practice: Practice completed at regular intervals (Chapter 5)

Distributed Representation: A feature of connectionist models of memory in which information is stored in the connections among a very large number of simple processing units, not in the units themselves (Chapter 3)

Divergent Thinking: Thinking characterized by the generation and testing of multiple and diverse solutions (Chapter 8)

Domain Knowledge: Knowledge that individuals have about particular fields of study, such as subject areas and areas of activity (Chapter 8)

Dual Coding Theory: Paivio's theory of memory that proposes that information is encoded within one or both of two distinct memory systems, one specialized for verbal information and the other for images (Chapter 3)

Dual Process Model of Recall: The view that recall requires two steps—generation and test—whereas recognition requires only the latter (Chapter 5)

Early Algebra: An instructional approach (also called *algebrafied arithmetic*) that involves introducing algebra-related concepts and notations to elementary students as an integral part of arithmetic instruction (Chapter 14)

Elaboration of Processing: The idea that memory episodes are encoded as a set of propositions and that the greater the number of propositions activated at encoding, the more likely recall becomes (Chapter 4)

Elaborative Interrogation: An instructional method in which, in its simplest form, learners are asked to read sentences and to answer "why" questions to clarify the relationship between the subject and the predicate of the sentence (Chapters 5 and 12)

Elaborative Rehearsal: Techniques, such as mnemonics, used to elaborate information in short-term memory (Chapter 4)

Embedded Program: A program that teaches critical thinking skills as part of a regular content class, such as history (Chapter 8)

Emergent Literacy: The concept that reading is only one dimension of an array of language-related skills and a natural extension of children's knowledge about language to the print medium (Chapter 11)

Enactive Learning: Learning that occurs by performing a task (Chapter 6)

Encoding: The process of transferring information from short-term to long-term memory (Chapter 4)

Encoding Specificity: The research finding that one's ability to retrieve information depends on the degree to which conditions at encoding are reinstated at retrieval (Chapters 5 and 12)

Endogenous Constructivism: A form of constructivism that portrays cognitive structures as developing out of other, earlier cognitive structures, not created directly from information provided by the environment; see also Dialectical Constructivism and Exogenous Constructivism (Chapter 9)

Entity Theory: The assumption that one's intellectual ability is fixed (Chapter 7)

Episodic Memory: Memory that individuals have for events in their lives; the storage and retrieval of personal, autobiographical experiences (Chapters 3 and 5)

Epistemological Belief: A belief about the nature and acquisition of knowledge (Chapter 7)

Exogenous Constructivism: A form of constructivism in which knowledge formation is considered a reconstruction of structures that exist in external reality and is seen as reflecting the inherent organization of the world; see also Endogenous Constructivism and Dialectical Constructivism (Chapter 9)

Expert Blind Spot Effect: The inability of experts to understand the difficulties novices face or the strategies they use when solving difficult problems that experts solve easily (Chapter 8)

Expertise Reversal Effect: In technology-based instruction, an outcome in which coaching and other scaffolds that work for novices actually have negative effects on more advanced learners (Chapter 10)

Explicit Memory: Memory that we recognize as corresponding to some past event; explicit memory involves conscious recall or recognition of previous experiences (Chapter 3)

Exposition: Written discourse organized around abstractions about a topic or body of information; textbooks, essays, and persuasive arguments are common examples of expository text (Chapter 11)

Extraneous Cognitive Load: Cognitive load that is related to features of instructional design (Chapters 2 and 10)

Extrinsic Motivation: Motivation in which behaviors are motivated by an external reward (Chapter 6)

Feedback: Information that learners receive about their performance (Chapters 6 and 10)

First-Letter Method: A mnemonic in which the first letters of to-be-learned items are used to generate an acronym, such as FACE (for the spaces on the treble clef) (Chapter 4)

Fixation: In reading, the brief period between eye movements during which eyes focus on a point in the text (Chapter 12)

Flashbulb Memory: Graphic memory about a specific, important event (Chapter 5)

fMRI (Functional Magnetic Resonance Imaging): A noninvasive neuroimaging technique that is sensitive to ongoing neurological activity in the brain and may be used to make inferences about human cognition (Chapter 2)

Focus Gambling: A concept-acquisition strategy in which learners vary more than one attribute of a stimulus at once (Chapter 3)

Focus Unit: The starting point for activation in network models (Chapter 3)

Free Writing: A method of writing instruction in which students are encouraged to write as many ideas as possible without worrying about organization or precise expression (Chapter 13)

Full Alphabetic Phase Readers: Readers who, as they conclude the early stages of reading, can identify the separate sounds in words and understand that spellings correspond to pronunciations (Chapter 11)

Full Processing Model: A model of attention that postulates that full, parallel processing is allocated to two channels simultaneously (Chapter 2)

Functional Dissociation: An instance in which implicit and explicit memory performances are unrelated; to some memory theorists, functional dissociations imply separate memory systems; others propose differences in information processing (Chapter 3)

Functional Fixedness: The inability to use familiar objects in a novel way (Chapter 8)

Functional Significance: A subjective impression of why an action or event takes place (Chapter 6)

General Knowledge: Knowledge appropriate to a wide range of tasks but not linked with a specific domain (Chapter 8)

Generation Effect: A finding that verbal material that people generate at encoding is better remembered than material merely read (Chapter 5)

Goal State: The terminal objective when solving a problem (Chapter 8)

Group Participation Norms: In classroom discussions, rules that students follow as they participate in the discussion; see also Interpretive Norms (Chapter 9)

Guided Participation: A process of structuring children's efforts in a social context and gradually releasing responsibility to them; see also Instructional Scaffolding and Zone of Proximal Development (Chapter 9)

Guided Peer Questioning: A classroom procedure in which students are trained both to ask and answer thought-provoking questions about what they're learning (Chapters 4 and 5)

Hedge: A statement that qualifies rules for identifying concepts, required because most natural concepts are ambiguous or "fuzzy" (Chapter 3)

Heuristic: A general problem-solving strategy, or "rule of thumb," that often is helpful when solving a problem, but does not guarantee a solution (Chapter 8)

Icon: Another name for the visual sensory register (Chapter 2)

Ill-Defined Problem: A problem with more than one acceptable solution and no guaranteed method for finding the solution (Chapter 8)

Imaginal Coding System: A long-term memory system in dual coding theory that processes visual information such as pictures and other images (Chapter 3)

Implicit Beliefs: Beliefs that affect one's behavior without any explicit awareness of the beliefs themselves (Chapter 7)

Implicit Memory: A nonconscious, tacit form of retention in which we do not recognize the operation of memory but behave in ways that clearly show that our earlier experiences are affecting current ones (Chapter 3)

Implicit Theory: A theory about some phenomenon or set of events that has not been formalized explicitly (Chapter 7)

Incremental Theory: An assumption that one's intellectual ability is changeable (Chapter 7)

Inert Knowledge: Domain-specific knowledge that does not transfer to other domains (Chapter 4)

Information-Oriented Feedback: Specific information that emphasizes how one's performance can be improved (Chapter 6)

Information Processing Model: A computer-like model of memory that portrays humans as acquiring, storing, and retrieving information (Chapter 2)

Informational Reward: A reward that provides useful feedback to students (Chapter 6)

Initial State: What is known about a problem at the beginning of the problem-solving process (Chapter 8)

Inner Speech: Covert, internalized self-talk that helps students reflect on an activity or knowledge and to regulate their learning (Chapter 9)

Inquiry-Based Instruction: Instruction in science and other content areas that is characterized by posing broad, challenging questions and having students answer them through investigation (Chapter 15)

Instantiation: Linkage of a particular configuration of values with the representation of the variables of a schema; a schema, which is a mental structure, is instantiated by patterns of experience that fit the schema (Chapter 3)

Instructional Scaffolding: Selective help provided by a teacher and gradually withdrawn that enables students to do things they could not do by themselves; see also Zone of Proximal Development (Chapter 9)

Integration Phase: In Kintsch's CI model, the stage in which readers arrive at the final meaning of a text through a process of strengthening relevant associations and pruning nonrelevant ones (Chapter 12)

Interactive Model: A model of comprehension that blends conceptual and data-driven elements and portrays comprehension as a product of their interaction (Chapter 12)

Interactive Processing: Processing guided both by external stimuli and by conceptual frameworks and strategies stored in memory (Chapter 12)

Interpretive Norms: In classroom discussions, judgments that students make about whether they have achieved their intellectual purposes for the discussion (Chapter 9)

Intrinsic Cognitive Load: Cognitive load that is due to the materials themselves (Chapters 2 and 10)

Intrinsic Motivation: Motivation in which behaviors are performed solely for personal satisfaction (Chapter 6)

IRE Pattern: A pattern of classroom discourse in which a teacher initiates a discourse segment by asking a question, the student responds, and the teacher evaluates the student's response; the IRE pattern is the "default pattern" for most classroom exchanges (Chapter 9)

Keyword Method: A mnemonic in which a distinctive sound is identified from a to-be-learned word and then that sound is associated with a distinctive image (Chapter 4)

Knowledge-Building Community: A set of individuals dedicated to advancing the group's knowledge (Chapter 10)

Knowing-in-Action: In Schön's theory, implicit knowledge that is unarticulated but is revealed in our intelligent actions (Chapter 9)

Knowledge-in-Action: Knowing-in-action that has been described and put into explicit, symbolic form (Chapter 9)

Knowledge of Cognition: Knowledge about cognitive processes and how they can be controlled (Chapter 4)

Knowledge Telling: Bereiter and Scardamalia's term for writers simply writing what someone else has said or written with little transformation (Chapter 13)

Knowledge Transforming: Bereiter and Scardamalia's term for writers constructing new knowledge by combining their topical knowledge with knowledge about discourse processes and goals (Chapter 13)

Language Experience: As used by Chall, a method of reading instruction in which children's own oral language, written down, becomes the basis for their initial reading instruction (Chapter 11)

Language Structure: How language is organized, including words, syntax, and discourse (Chapter 11)

Latent Semantic Analysis (LSA): A statistically based technique for representing meanings of a text or knowledge domain (Chapter 12)

Learned Helplessness: A state in which individuals have learned that any behavior they try will fail; thus, they refuse to engage in tasks because they assume they cannot succeed (Chapter 7)

Learning Goal: A strong desire to improve one's performance and achieve mastery in a domain; also called mastery goal (Chapter 7)

Levels of Processing: The view that information is processed at increasingly deeper levels of sophistication (Chapter 4)

Lexical Network: A memory network in which the names of concepts are stored (Chapter 3)

Link: In network models of memory, relations between cognitive units (Chapter 3)

Link Method: A mnemonic in which elaborative links are generated among unrelated items that one must remember (Chapter 4)

Literacy Community: A group of individuals in a setting that is organized around reading, writing, speaking, and listening (Chapter 13)

Locus of Control: In attribution theory, a causal dimension that defines whether the cause of an outcome is under internal or external control (Chapter 6)

Long-Term Memory (LTM): Memory over long periods of time, ranging from hours to days and years; long-term memory is the permanent repository for the information we have acquired (Chapters 2, 3, and 13)

Macrostructure: In Kintsch and Van Dijk's discourse processing model, the reader's representation of the main idea or gist of the text; the macrostructure combines the prior knowledge of the individual with the microstructure of the text (Chapter 12)

Maintenance Rehearsal: Techniques, such as repetition, used to hold information in short-term memory without elaborating it (Chapter 4)

Massed Practice: Practice completed at irregular intervals, but especially in short, concentrated bursts (Chapter 5)

Meaning-Emphasis Methods: As used by Chall, beginning reading instruction methods that favor meaning over decoding (Chapter 11)

Means–Ends Analysis: A method of learning and problem solving in which a large problem is broken into subgoals that are solved sequentially (Chapter 8)

Mediated Response: A subjective, internalized interpretation of an event prior to a response (Chapter 6)

Mediation: An encoding strategy in which to-be-learned information is related to knowledge in memory (Chapter 4)

Metacognition: Knowledge about cognition; knowledge used to regulate thinking and learning (Chapters 4 and 8)

Metalinguistic Awareness: Metacognitive knowledge that children acquire about language and how language is used (Chapter 11)

Metamemory: Knowledge about the contents and functioning of one's memory (Chapter 4)

Method of Loci: A mnemonic in which to-be-learned information is associated with points in a familiar location (Chapter 4)

Microstructure: In Kintsch and Van Dijk's discourse processing model, a knowledge structure that readers build by linking common elements in the text's propositions; the microstructure directly represents the propositions in the text (Chapter 12)

Mnemonics: Techniques (e.g., mental images) used to elaborate factual information to make it more memorable (Chapter 4)

Modal Model: A model of memory that combines the common features of information processing models (Chapters 2 and 3)

Modeling: Demonstrating and describing the component parts of a skill to a novice (Chapter 6)

Modularity: A theory in which important cognitive processes such as speech, vision, and domain-specific reasoning skills are seen as encapsulated within separate physiological modules in the brain that are devoted to that specific type of cognitive activity (Chapter 2)

Morpheme: A sound or combination of sounds that is a minimal unit of meaning in a language; words are made up of one or more morphemes (Chapter 11)

Morphological Cues: Within-word cues, such as prefixes, root words, and suffixes, that provide information on a word's meaning (Chapter 12)

Morphology: A set of principles that describe how sound-based units of meaning are combined into words in a given language (Chapter 11)

M-space: Case's concept of memory space or memory capacity, in chunks (Chapter 14)

Naive Beliefs: Inaccurate beliefs about a phenomenon, acquired through uncontrolled observation (Chapter 15)

Naive Theories: Partial or incorrect conceptual frameworks for understanding a domain and important processes within that domain (Chapter 15)

Narrative: A form of discourse that is structured by a temporal sequence of events; a "story" (Chapter 11)

Network Models: Models of memory, such as J. R. Anderson's ACT, that represent memory as large networks of knowledge (Chapter 3)

Neuropsychology: A branch of psychology that is focused on the relationship between brain functioning and cognitive processes such as memory and language (Chapter 2)

Node: A cognitive unit, usually a proposition or schema, in network models of memory (Chapter 3)

Nonrecurrent Skills: Schema-like controlled processes in complex cognitive skills (Chapter 10)

Norm-Referenced Evaluation: Evaluation in which an individual's performance is evaluated with respect to the group average (Chapters 6 and 7)

Operators: Objects or variables that can be manipulated to solve a problem (Chapter 8)

Outcome (Performance) Feedback: Feedback that provides specific information about performance (Chapter 6)

Paired Associate Learning: A learning task in which learners must associate one member of a pair of things, usually words, with the second member of the pair (Chapter 1)

Parallel Distributed Processing (PDP) Model: A cognitive model that assumes no central processor, only simple processing units dedicated to specific processing tasks; stored in memory are connection strengths among these simple processing units (Chapter 3)

Parallel Processing: Simultaneous, rather than sequential, processing of information in a cognitive system (Chapter 3)

Partial Alphabetic Phase Readers: Readers who, in the early stages of reading, read by associating some but not all of words' letters with sounds (Chapter 11)

Pathways: How well an individual can generate workable solutions to challenges (Chapter 7)

Pattern Recognition: Identification of a perceptual stimulus (Chapter 2)

Peg Method: A mnemonic in which to-be-learned objects are associated with familiar "mental pegs," such as numbers or a rhyme (Chapter 4)

Perception: The process of sensing, holding, recognizing, and making meaning of sensory information (Chapter 2)

Performance Goal: A strong desire to demonstrate one's performance and to achieve normatively high success in a domain (Chapter 7)

Performance-Oriented Feedback: Specific information about the correctness of one's performance (Chapter 6)

Personal Teaching Efficacy: The belief that a teacher can produce significant positive change in students (Chapter 6)

Phonemes: The subset of speech sounds (phones) that are perceived as meaningful by speakers and listeners in a particular language (Chapter 11)

Phonemic Awareness: The ability to recognize phonemes as individual, separable speech sounds; this type of metalinguistic knowledge is critical to learning how to read (Chapter 11)

Phonemic Segmentation: An indicator of phonemic awareness in which children identify the separate sounds that make up a spoken word (Chapter 11)

Phones: The range of vocalizations of which humans are capable; the "raw material" of spoken languages (Chapter 11)

Phonics: A form of reading instruction in which letter–sound relationships are taught explicitly (Chapter 11)

Pragmatics: The meanings, messages, and uses of language (Chapter 11)

Print Exposure: The extent to which a person has had contact with written materials through reading (Chapter 12)

Problem Space: All the operators and constraints on operators involved in a problem (Chapter 8)

Procedural Knowledge: Knowledge that enables an individual to perform certain activities; "knowing how" (Chapters 3 and 4)

Proceduralize: To transform declarative knowledge into condition-action relationships that can be applied across a variety of situations; proceduralization is a function of practice (Chapter 3)

Production Rules: A sequence of specific rules or steps that describe how to implement a strategy, complete an action, or solve a problem (Chapter 3)

Production Systems: Networks of productions; in production systems, multiple productions can be active at the same time (Chapter 3)

Productions: Condition-action rules in an "if/then" form that represent procedural knowledge; they state actions to be performed and the conditions under which the action should be taken (Chapter 3)

Proposition: The smallest unit of knowledge that can stand as a separate assertion and be judged as true or false; propositions are fundamental units in many network theories of memory (Chapter 3)

Propositional Networks: Arrays of propositions in which propositions sharing one or more elements are linked with one another, often in hierarchical fashion (Chapter 3)

Prototype: The "most typical" instance of a concept that best exemplifies the concept (Chapter 3)

Proximal Goal: A short-term goal (Chapter 6)

Pruning: The process in which those neurons that are utilized in cognitive activities thrive, whereas others that are not used do not (Chapter 2)

Question–Answer Relationships (QAR): A reading comprehension method that uses questions (e.g., about the author) to prompt students to engage in tasks (e.g., making predictions) that promote comprehension (Chapter 12)

Reading Fluency: The ability to read materials orally with only minimal pauses or hesitation; tied to automatic word recognition (Chapter 11)

Reading Readiness: The idea that a given level of mental maturity is required before reading instruction can begin; contrasted with the concept of emergent literacy (Chapter 11)

Reading Span Task: A method of measuring working memory that requires individuals to perform two tasks simultaneously (e.g., reading a list of sentences and remembering the last word from each one at recall); this task measures both basic storage and central executive processing mechanisms in working memory (Chapter 2)

Recall Threshold: The minimal level of cuing needed to recall information (Chapter 5)

Reciprocal Determinism: A term used by Bandura to highlight the causal relationships among self-beliefs, experience, and external feedback (Chapter 6)

Reciprocal Teaching: A method of sequenced instruction, developed by Palincsar and Brown, in which teachers model comprehension strategies and guide students in their use; reciprocal teaching initially relies on scaffolding students' responses; responsibility then is shifted gradually to the students (Chapters 6 and 12)

Recognition Threshold: The minimal level of cuing needed to recognize information (Chapter 5)

Reconstructive Memory: The assumption that information is reconstructed at recall on the basis of an incomplete record rather than remembered verbatim (Chapter 5)

Recurrent Skills: Procedure-like automatic processes portrayed in the 4C/ID model that are a part of complex cognitive skills (Chapter 10)

Reflection-in-Action: In Schön's system, conscious thought about our actions and about the thinking that accompanies our actions (Chapter 9)

Reflection on Reflection-in-Action: According to Schön, what skilled teachers do to stimulate students' reflective thinking about their actions and the thought processes accompanying those actions (Chapter 9)

Reflective Judgment: The degree to which one evokes epistemological assumptions and reasoning skills that lead to informed conclusions (Chapter 7)

Reflective Practice: Critical reflection on teaching performance, utilizing methods such as discussion with others, written logs, and analysis of teaching practices (Chapter 9)

Regulation of Cognition: Knowledge that enables one to control and regulate cognitive activities (Chapter 4)

Rehearsal: See Elaborative Rehearsal and Maintenance Rehearsal (Chapter 4)

Relational Links: In network models of memory, the connections between cognitive units (Chapter 3)

Resource-Limited Task: A cognitive activity that is limited because of insufficient attentional resources (Chapter 2)

Retrieval: The process of transferring information from long-term to working memory (Chapters 4 and 5)

Saccade: In reading, the rapid movement of the eyes from one fixation to the next (Chapter 12)

Scaffolding: External support provided to a novice learner by a tutor or teacher with expert knowledge (Chapter 9)

Scanning Strategy: A strategy for concept acquisition in which learners attempt to test several hypotheses at once, which can overload their ability to remember information they are processing (Chapter 3)

Schema (pl. Schemata): A hypothesized mental framework that helps us organize knowledge, directs perception and attention, and guides recall; schemata provide scaffolding for organizing experience (Chapters 2 and 3)

Scripts: Schema-like representations that provide mental frameworks for proceduralized knowledge (Chapter 3)

Self-Determination Theory: A theory based on the assumption that personal autonomy and control affect motivation and academic achievement (Chapter 6)

Self-Determined Action: An action that an individual chooses to engage in for intrinsic reasons (Chapter 6)

Self-Efficacy: The degree to which individuals feel confident that they can perform a task successfully (Chapter 6)

Self-Regulated Learning: The ability to control and explicitly understand all aspects of one's learning (Chapter 6)

Self-Regulated Strategy Development (SRSD): A widely used approach to teaching writing designed to help students acquire writing strategies, learn about different writing genres, and build positive attitudes (Chapter 13)

Semantic Memory: Individuals' memories for general concepts and principles and for the relationships among them; unlike episodic memory, semantic memory is not linked with a particular time and place (Chapters 3 and 5)

Semantics: The study of words and their meanings (Chapter 11)

Sensory Memory: Holding systems in memory that maintain stimuli briefly so that perceptual analysis can occur; most is known about visual and auditory sensory memory (Chapter 2)

Sensory Register: A buffer where perceptual information is momentarily stored until it is recognized or forgotten (Chapter 2)

Sentence Combining: A writing instruction technique that focuses on syntactical and propositional knowledge in which students combine simple sentences into more complex ones (Chapter 13)

Serial List Learning: A learning task in which a series of things, often a list of words, must be learned in order (Chapter 1)

Serial Processing: Information processing in which activation proceeds from one step to the next in a fixed, sequential order (Chapter 3)

Short-Term Memory (STM): Memory over short periods of time, ranging from seconds to minutes (Chapter 2)

Sight Word Methods: As used by Chall, beginning reading instructional methods that stress the need for children to acquire a stock of familiar words they can recognize on sight (Chapter 11)

Situation Model: In Kintsch's CI model, readers' representations of meaning that includes both their prior knowledge and text information (Chapter 12)

Slot: An informal term in schema theory referring to a variable in a schema; if slots in a schema match data in the environment (e.g., a particular word problem is recognized as a subtraction problem), specific data values are assigned to appropriate slots in the schema (Chapter 3)

Socially Mediated Co-Regulation: External supports provided by interactions with others that help novices acquire values and expectations and learn to regulate their own learning (Chapter 9)

Solution Paths: A set of potential solutions to a specific problem (Chapter 8)

Spreading Activation: In network models such as ACT-R, the process of input units causing other units to be activated via their connections, with activation eventually spreading to response units (Chapter 3)

Stability: In attribution theory, a causal dimension that defines whether the cause of an outcome is temporary or enduring (Chapter 6)

Stand-Alone Program: A program that teaches critical thinking skills in isolation (Chapter 8)

State-Dependent Learning: The ability to remember information only in the state (e.g., in a drug-induced condition) one learned it in (Chapter 5)

Storage: The process of holding information in long-term memory in some organized fashion (Chapters 2 and 4)

Story Mnemonic: A mnemonic in which a meaningful story for aiding recall is generated from unrelated words that one must learn in order (Chapter 4)

Syntax: Ways words in a language are grouped into larger units, such as in phrases, clauses, and sentences (Chapter 11)

Taxonomy of Educational Objectives: A framework proposed by Bloom and his associates for classifying learning objectives into a six-level hierarchy (Chapter 12)

Teachable Language Comprehender (TLC): Collins and Quillian's early network model of semantic memory (Chapter 3)

Teacher–Student Conferences: In writing instruction, a widely used technique in which students and teachers meet to talk about student writing (Chapter 13)

Teaching Efficacy: The belief that the process of education generally affects students in positive ways (Chapter 6)

Testing Effect: The influence that taking tests or quizzes over materials being studied can have on their learning and retention (Chapter 5)

Text Base: An ordered list of propositions created by analyzing the propositional structure of an expository text (Chapters 3 and 12)

Text Signals: Words, phrases, and other devices used in reading materials to indicate that certain elements of a text are more important than others or to improve the text's cohesion (Chapter 12)

Thinking Frame: A framework for organizing knowledge and guiding thought processes; see also Schema (Chapter 8)

Transactional Strategies Instruction (TSI): A method of teaching reading strategies in which multiple strategies are developed one at a time through explicit instruction and extended practice (Chapter 12)

Trial and Error: A method of learning and problem solving in which one attempts different solutions randomly (Chapter 8)

Verbal Coding System: A long-term memory system proposed in dual coding theory that processes verbal information such as speech or printed words (Chapter 3)

Vicarious Learning: Learning that occurs through observation of a skilled model (Chapter 6)

Vocabulary Knowledge: Understanding of words and knowledge of how to use them (Chapter 12)

Well-Defined Problem: A problem with only one acceptable solution and a guaranteed method for finding it (Chapter 8)

Wisdom: Willingness to use one's skills and knowledge to act in the soundest possible manner (Chapter 8)

Working Memory: A portion of memory that contains the "current contents" of consciousness; as models of memory have shifted from a storage to a processing emphasis, the concept of short-term memory has been largely replaced by the concept of working memory (Chapters 2 and 13)

Writing Prompt: A question or instructions that set expectations for what students should produce on a writing assessment (Chapter 13)

Zone of Proximal Development: In Vygotsky's theory, the difference between the difficulty level of problems children can cope with independently and the level they can accomplish with the help of older or more expert individuals; child-adult interactions in the zone of proximal development are primary sources of cognitive growth (Chapter 9)

REFERENCES

Ackerman, P. L., Beier, M. E., & Boyle, M. O. (2005). Working memory and intelligence: The same or different constructs. *Psychological Bulletin, 131,* 30–60.

Ackerman, P. L., & Lohman, D. F. (2006). Individual differences in cognitive function. In P. A. Alexander & P. H. Winne (Eds.), *Handbook of educational psychology* (2nd ed., pp. 139–162). Mahwah, NJ: Erlbaum.

Adams, M. J. (1990). *Beginning to read: Thinking and learning about print.* Cambridge, MA: MIT Press.

Adams, M. J. (1994). Modeling the connections between word recognition and reading. In R. B. Ruddell, M. R. Ruddell, & H. Singer (Eds.), *Theoretical models and processes of reading* (4th ed., pp. 838–863). Newark, DE: International Reading Association.

Adams, M. J., & Bruck, M. (1995). Resolving the "Great Debate." *American Educator, 20,* 9–20.

Adams, M. J., & Collins, A. (1977). *A schema-theoretic view of reading* (Tech. Report No. 32). Urbana, IL: University of Illinois, Center for the Study of Reading.

Ainley, M., Hidi, S., & Berndorff, D. (2006). Interest, learning, and the psychological processes that mediate their relationship. *Journal of Educational Psychology, 94,* 545–561.

Alba, J. W., & Hasher, L. (1983). Is memory schematic? *Psychological Bulletin, 93,* 203–231.

Alderman, M. K. (2004). *Motivation for achievement: Possibilities for teaching and learning* (2nd ed.). Mahwah, NJ: Erlbaum.

Aldridge, B. G. (1992). Project on scope, sequence, and coordination: A new synthesis for improving science education. *Journal of Science Education and Technology, 1,* 13–21.

Alexander, J. M., Carr, M., & Schwanenflugel, P. J. (1995). Development of metacognition in gifted children: Directions for future research. *Developmental Review, 15,* 1–37.

Alexander, P. A. (2003). The development of expertise: The journey from acclimation to proficiency. *Educational Researcher, 32,* 10–14.

Allington, R. L. (2005). How much evidence is enough evidence? *Journal of Reading Recovery, 4,* 8–11.

Alvermann, D. E. (2002). Effective literacy instruction for adolescents. *Journal of Literacy Research, 34,* 189–208.

Alvermann, D. E., & Hayes, D. A. (1989). Classroom discussion of content area reading assignments: An intervention study. *Reading Research Quarterly, 24,* 305–335.

Alvermann, D. E., O'Brien, D. G., & Dillon, D. R. (1990). What teachers do when they say they're having discussions of content area reading assignments: A qualitative analysis. *Reading Research Quarterly, 25,* 296–322.

American Association for the Advancement of Science. (1993). *Benchmarks for science literacy.* New York, NY: Oxford University Press.

Ames, C. (1992). Classrooms: Goals, structures, and student motivation. *Journal of Educational Psychology, 84,* 261–271.

Ames, C., & Archer, J. (1988). Achievement in the classroom: Student learning strategies and motivational processes. *Journal of Educational Psychology, 80,* 260–267.

Anderman, E. M., & Wolters, C. A. (2006). Goals, values, and affect: Influences on student motivation. In P. A. Alexander & P. H. Winne (Eds.), *Handbook of educational psychology* (2nd ed., pp. 369–389). Mahwah, NJ: Erlbaum.

Anderson, C. W., & Hogan, K. (2000). Preface: Designing programs for science learning. *Journal of Research in Science Teaching, 37,* 627-628.

Anderson, J. R. (1976). *Language, memory, and thought.* Mahwah, NJ: Erlbaum.

Anderson, J. R. (1983a). *The architecture of cognition.* Cambridge, MA: Harvard University Press.

Anderson, J. R. (1983b). A spreading activation theory of memory. *Journal of Verbal Learning and Verbal Behavior, 22,* 261–295.

Anderson, J. R. (1993). Problem solving and learning. *American Psychologist, 48,* 35–44.

Anderson, J. R. (1996). ACT: A simple theory of complex cognition. *American Psychologist, 51,* 355–365.

Anderson, J. R. (2000). *Cognitive psychology and its implications* (5th edition). New York, NY: Worth.

Anderson, J. R., Bothell, D., Douglass, S., Lebiere, C., & Qin, Y. (2004). An integrated theory of the mind. *Psychological Review, 111,* 1036–1060.

Anderson, J. R. (2005). *Cognitive psychology and its implications* (6th ed.). New York, NY: Worth.

Anderson, J. R., & Bower, G. H. (1973). *Human associative memory*. Washington, DC: Winston.

Anderson, J. R., Douglass, W., & Qin, Y. (2004). How should a theory of learning and cognition inform instruction? In A. F. Healy (Ed.). *Experimental cognitive psychology and its applications* (pp. 47–58).Washington, DC: American Psychological Association.

Anderson, J. R., Fincham, J. M., Qin, Y., & Stocco, A. (2008). A central circuit of the mind. *Trends in Cognitive Psychology, 12,* 136–143.

Anderson, J. R., & Reder, L. M. (1979). An elaborative processing explanation of depth of processing. In L. S. Cermak & F. I. M. Craik (Eds.), *Levels of processing in human memory* (pp. 385–404). Mahwah, NJ: Erlbaum.

Anderson, R. C. (1984). Role of the reader's schema in comprehension, learning, and memory. In R. C. Anderson, J. Osborn, & R. J. Tierney (Eds.), *Learning to read in American schools: Basal readers and content texts* (pp. 243–258). Mahwah, NJ: Erlbaum.

Anderson, R. C. (1996). Research foundations to support wide reading. In V. Greaney (Ed.), *Promoting reading in developing countries* (pp. 55–77). New York, NY: International Reading Association.

Anderson, R. C., & Pearson, P. D. (1984). A schematheoretic view of basic processes in reading comprehension. In P. D. Pearson (Ed.), *Handbook of reading research* (pp. 255–291). New York, NY: Longman.

Anderson, R. C., Spiro, R., & Anderson, M. C. (1978). Schemata as scaffolding for the representation of information in connected discourse. *American Educational Research Journal, 15,* 433–440.

Anderson, R. C., Wilson, P. T., & Fielding, L. G. (1988). Growth in reading and how children spend their time outside of school. *Reading Research Quarterly, 23,* 285–303.

Anderson, R. D. (2002). Reforming science teaching: What research says about inquiry. *Journal of Science Teacher Education, 13,* 1–12.

Anderson, R. D., & Mitchener, C. P. (1994). Research on science teacher education. In G. L. Gabel (Ed.), *Handbook of research on science teaching and learning* (pp. 3–44). New York, NY: Macmillan.

Andre, T. (1987a). Processes in reading comprehension and the teaching of reading comprehension. In J. A. Glover & R. R. Ronning (Eds.), *Historical foundations of educational psychology* (pp. 259–296). New York, NY: Plenum.

Andre, T. (1987b). Questions and learning from reading. *Questioning Exchange, 1,* 47–86.

Ansorge, C., & Bendus, O. (2003). The pedagogical impact of course management systems on faculty, students, and institution. In R. Bruning, C. A. Horn, and Lisa M. PytlikZillig. *Web-based learning: What do we know? Where do we go?* Greenwich, CT: Information Age.

Anzai, Y. (1991). Learning and use of representations for physics expertise. In K. A. Anders & J. Smith (Eds.), *Toward a general theory of expertise* (pp. 64–92). New York, NY: Cambridge University Press.

Applebee, A. N. (1983). *The child's concept of story.* Chicago, IL: University of Chicago Press.

Ardelt, M. (2004). Wisdom as expert knowledge system: A critical review of a contemporary operationalization of an ancient concept. *Human Development, 47,* 257–284.

Ashcraft, M. H. (1994). *Human memory and cognition* (2nd ed.). New York, NY: HarperCollins.

Ashton, P. T., & Webb, R. B. (1986). *Making a difference: Teachers' sense of efficacy and student achievement.* New York, NY: Longman.

Atkinson, R. C. (1975). Mnemotechnics in second-language learning. *American Psychologist, 30,* 821–828.

Atkinson, R. C., & Raugh, M. R. (1975). An application of the mnemonic keyword method to the acquisition of a Russian vocabulary. *Journal of Experimental Psychology: Human Learning and Memory, 104,* 126–133.

Atkinson, R. C., & Shiffrin, R. M. (1968). Human memory: A proposed system and its control processes. In K. W. Spence & J. T. Spence (Eds.), *The psychology of learning and motivation: Advances in research and theory* (Vol. 2, pp. 89–195). San Diego, CA: Academic Press.

Atkinson, R. K., & Renkl, A. (2007). Interactive example-based learning environments: Using interactive elements to encourage effective processing of worked examples. *Educational Psychology Review, 19,* 375–386.

Ausubel, D. P. (1960). The use of advance organizers in the learning and retention of meaningful verbal material. *Journal of Educational Psychology, 51,* 267–272.

Ausubel, D. P. (1968). *Educational psychology: A cognitive view.* New York, NY: Holt, Rinehart & Winston.

Ausubel, D. P., & Fitzgerald, D. (1961). The role of discriminability in meaningful verbal learning and retention. *Journal of Educational Psychology, 52,* 266–274.

Ausubel, D. P., & Youssef, M. (1963). Role of discriminability in meaningful parallel learning. *Journal of Educational Psychology, 54,* 331–336.

Ayres, P. (2006). Impact of reducing intrinsic cognitive load on learning in a mathematical domain. *Applied Cognitive Psychology, 20,* 287–298.

Azevedo, R. (2005). Computer environments as metacognitive tools for enhancing learning. *Educational Psychologist 40*, 193–197.

Baars, B. J. (1986). *The cognitive revolution in psychology*. New York, NY: Guilford.

Babyak, M. A., Synder, C. R., & Yoshinobu, L. (1993). Psychometric properties of the hope scale: A confirmatory factor analysis. *Journal of Research in Personality, 27*, 154–169.

Baddeley, A. D. (1978). The trouble with levels: A reexamination of Craik and Lockhart's framework for memory research. *Psychology Review, 85*, 139–152.

Baddeley, A. D. (1986). *Working memory: Theory and practice*. London, UK: Oxford University Press.

Baddeley, A. D. (2001). Is working memory still working? *American Psychologist, 56*, 851–864.

Baddeley, A. D. (2007). *Working memory, thought, and action*. New York, NY: Oxford University Press.

Baddeley, A. D., & Hitch, G. (1974). Working memory. In G. H. Bower (Ed.), *The psychology of learning and motivation* (Vol. 8, pp. 47–90). San Diego, CA: Academic Press.

Baer, D. M., Wolf, M. M., & Risley, T. R. (1968). Some current dimensions of applied behavior analysis. *Journal of Applied Behavior Analysis, 1,* 91–97.

Bahar, M. (2003). Misconceptions in biology education and conceptual change strategies. *Educational Sciences. Theory and Practice, 3,* 27–64.

Baker, L. (2002). Metacognition in comprehension instruction. In C. Block & M. Pressley (Eds.). *Comprehension instruction: Research-based best practices* (pp. 77–95). New York, NY: Guilford.

Baker, L., & Beall, L. C. (2009). Metacognitive processes and reading comprehension. In S. E. Israel & G. G. Duffy (Eds.), *Handbook of research on reading comprehension* (pp. 373–388). New York, NY: Routledge.

Baltes, P. B., & Staudinger, U. M. (2000). Wisdom: A metaheuristic (pragmatic) to orchestrate mind and virtue toward excellence. *American Psychologist, 55*, 122–136.

Balzer, W. K., Doherty, M. E., & O'Connor, R. (1989). Effects of cognitive feedback on performance. *Psychological Bulletin, 106*, 410–433.

Bandura, A. (1969). *Principles of behavior modification*. New York, NY: Holt, Rinehart & Winston.

Bandura, A. (1986). *Social foundations of thought and action: A social cognitive theory*. Upper Saddle River, NJ: Prentice Hall.

Bandura, A. (1993). Perceived self-efficacy in cognitive development and functioning. *Educational Psychologist, 28*, 117–148.

Bandura, A. (1997). *Self-efficacy: The exercise of control*. New York, NY: Freeman.

Barker, G. P., & Graham, S. (1987). Developmental study of praise and blame as attributional causes. *Journal of Educational Psychology, 79*, 62–66.

Baron, J. (2008). *Thinking and deciding* (4th ed.). New York, NY: Cambridge University Press.

Baroody, A. J., Li, X., & Lai, M. (2008). Toddlers' spontaneous attention to number. *Mathematical Thinking and Learning, 10*, 240–270.

Baroody, A. J., & Standifer, D. J. (1993). Addition and subtraction in the primary grades. In R. J. Jensen (Ed.), *Research ideas for the classroom: Early childhood mathematics* (pp. 72–102). New York, NY: Macmillan.

Barrel, J. (1991). *Teaching for thoughtfulness*. New York, NY: Longman.

Barrett, H. C., & Kurzban, R. (2006). Modularity in cognition: Framing the debate. *Psychological Review, 113*, 628–647.

Barrett, L. F., Tugade, M. M., & Engle, R. W. (2004). Individual differences in working memory capacity and dual process theories of mind. *Psychological Bulletin, 130*, 553–573.

Bartlett, F. C. (1932). *Remembering: A study in experimental and social psychology*. Cambridge, UK: Cambridge University Press.

Baumann, J. F. (2009). Vocabulary and reading comprehension: The nexus of meaning. In S. E. Israel & G. G. Duffy (Eds.), *Handbook of research on reading comprehension* (pp. 323–346). New York, NY: Routledge.

Baxter-Magolda, M. B. (1999). The evolution of epistemology: Refining contextual knowing at twentysomething. *Journal of College Student Development, 36*, 205–216.

Baxter-Magolda, M. B. (2002). Epistemological reflection: The evolution of epistemological assumptions from age 18 to 30. In B. Hofer & P. R. Pintrich (Eds.), *Personal epistemology: The psychology of beliefs about knowledge and knowing* (pp. 89–102). Mahwah, NJ: Erlbaum.

Beach, R., & Friedrich, T. (2006). Response to writing. In MacArthur, C. A., Graham, S., & Fitzgerald, J. (Eds.), *Handbook of writing research* (pp. 222–234). New York, NY: Guilford.

Beal, C. (1996). The role of comprehension monitoring in children's revision. *Educational Psychology Review, 8*, 219–238.

Bechtel, W., & Abrahamsen, A. (2002). *Connectionism and the mind: Parallel processing, dynamics, and evolution in networks* (2nd ed.). London: Blackwell.

Beck, I. L., McKeown, M. G., & Kucan, L. (2002). *Bringing words to life: Robust vocabulary instruction.* New York, NY: Guilford.

Beed, P. L., Hawkins, E. M., & Roller, C. M. (1991). Moving learners toward independence: The power of scaffolded instruction. *Reading Teacher, 44,* 648–655.

Bell, P., & Linn, M. C. (2002). Beliefs about science: How does science instruction contribute? In B. Hofer & P. R. Pintrich (Eds.), *Personal epistemology: The psychology of beliefs about knowledge and knowing* (pp. 321–346). Mahwah, NJ: Erlbaum.

Bendixen, L. D. (2002). A process model of epistemic belief change. In B. K. Hofer & P. R. Pintrich (Eds.), *Personal epistemology: The psychology of beliefs about knowledge and knowing* (pp. 191–208). Mahwah, NJ: Erlbaum.

Bendixen, L. D., & Rule, D. C. (2004). An integrative approach to personal epistemology: A guiding model. *Educational Psychologist, 39,* 69–80.

Bendixen, L. D., Schraw, G., & Dunkle, M. E. (1998). Epistemic beliefs and moral reasoning. *Journal of Psychology, 132,* 187–200.

Benton, S. L., Glover, J. A., Kraft, R. G., & Plake, B. S. (1984). Cognitive capacity differences among writers. *Journal of Educational Psychology, 76,* 820–834.

Benton, S. L., Glover, J. A., Monkowski, P. G., & Shaughnessy, M. (1983). Decision difficulty and recall of prose. *Journal of Educational Psychology, 75,* 727–742.

Bereby-Meyer, Y., & Kaplan, A. (2005). Motivational influences on the transfer of problem solving strategies. *Contemporary Educational Psychology, 30,* 1–22.

Bereiter, C., & Scardamalia, M. (1987). *The psychology of written composition.* Mahwah, NJ: Erlbaum.

Bereiter, C., & Scardamalia, M. (1993). *Surpassing ourselves: An inquiry into the nature and implications of expertise.* Chicago, IL: Open Court.

Bernardo, A. B. I. (2001). Principle explanation and strategic schema abstraction in problem solving. *Memory & Cognition, 29,* 627–633.

Berninger, V. W. (1994). *Reading and writing acquisition: A developmental neuropsychological perspective.* Dubuque, IA: Brown & Benchmark.

Berninger, V. W., Vaughan, K., Abbott, R., Begay, K., Coleman, K., Curtin, G., Hawkins, J., & Graham, S. (2002). Teaching spelling and composition alone and together: Implications for the simple view of writing. *Journal of Educational Psychology, 94,* 291–304.

Berry, D., & Dienes, Z. (1993). Toward a working characterization of implicit learning. In D. Berry & Z. Dienes (Eds.), *Implicit learning: Theoretical and empirical issues* (pp. 1–18). Mahwah, NJ: Erlbaum.

Berthold, K., Nückles, M., & Renkl, A. (2007). Do learning protocols support learning strategies and outcomes? The role of cognitive and metacognitive prompts. *Learning and Instruction, 17,* 564–577.

Bianchini, J. A. (1998). Where knowledge construction, equity, and context intersect: Student learning of science in small groups. *Journal of Research in Science Teaching, 34,* 1039–1065.

Biemiller, A., & Boote, C. (2006). An effective method for building meaning vocabulary in primary grades. *Journal of Educational Psychology, 98,* 44–62.

Bilalic, M., McLeod, P., & Gobet, F. (2008). Inflexibility of experts—Reality or myth? Quantifying the Einstellung effect in chess masters. *Cognitive Psychology, 56,* 73–102.

Biswas, G., Leelawong, K., Schwartz, D., Vye, N., & the Teachable Agents Group at Vanderbilt. (2005). Learning by teaching: A new agent paradigm for educational software. *Applied Artificial Intelligence, 19,* 363–392.

Bjork, R. A. (1999). Assessing our own competence: Heuristics and illusions. In D. Gopher and A. Koriat (Eds.), *Attention and performance XVII. Cognitive regulation of performance: Interaction of theory and application* (pp. 435–459). Cambridge, MA: MIT Press.

Blachowicz, C., Fisher, P., Ogle, D., & Watts-Taffe, S. (2006). Vocabulary: Questions from the classroom. *Reading Research Quarterly, 41,* 524–539.

Black, A. E., & Deci, E. L. (2000). The effects of instructors' autonomy support and students' autonomous motivation on learning organic chemistry: A self-determination perspective. *Science Education, 84,* 740–756.

Blank, L. M. (2000). A metacognitive learning cycle: A better warranty for student understanding. *Science Education, 84,* 486–506.

Blanton, M., & Kaput, J. (2004). Elementary grades students' capacity for functional thinking. *Proceedings of the 28th Conference of the International Group for the Psychology of Mathematics Education, 2,* 135–142.

Block, C., & Lacina, J. (2009). Comprehension instruction in kindergarten through grade three. In S. E. Israel & G. G. Duffy (Eds.), *Handbook of research on reading comprehension* (pp. 494–509). New York, NY: Routledge.

Block, C., & Pressley, M. (2002). *Comprehension instruction: Research-based best practices.* New York, NY: Guilford.

Bloom, B. S. (1985). *Developing talent in young people.* New York, NY: Ballantine.

Bloom, B. S., Englehart, M. D., Furst, E. J., Hill, W. H., & Krathwohl, D. R. (1956). *Taxonomy of educational objectives: The classification of educational goals: Handbook I. Cognitive domain.* New York, NY: McKay.

Blote, A., van der Burg, E., & Klein, A. (2001). Students' flexibility in solving two-digit addition and subtraction problems: Instruction effects. *Journal of Educational Psychology, 93,* 627–638.

Bobrow, D. G., & Norman, D. A. (1975). Some principles of memory schemata. In D. G. Bobrow & A. M. Collins (Eds.), *Representation and understanding: Studies in cognitive science.* San Diego, CA: Academic Press.

Boekaerts, M., Pintrich, P. R., & Zeidner, M. (Eds.). (2000). *Handbook of self-regulation.* San Diego, CA: Academic Press.

Boggiano, A. K., Main, D. S., & Katz, P. A. (1988). Children's preference for challenge: The role of perceived competence and control. *Journal of Personality and Social Psychology, 54,* 134–141.

Boltwood, C. R., & Blick, K. A. (1978). The delineation and application of three mnemonic techniques. *Psychonomic Science, 20,* 339–341.

Borko, H., & Putnam, R. T. (1996). Learning to teach. In D. C. Berliner & R. C. Calfee (Eds.), *Handbook of educational psychology* (pp. 673–708). New York, NY: Macmillan.

Boscolo, P., & Gelati, C. (2007). Best practices in promoting motivation for writing. In S. Graham, C. A. MacArthur, & J. Fitzgerald (Eds.), *Best practices in writing instruction* (pp. 202–221). New York, NY: Guilford.

Bourne, L. E. (1982). Typicality effects in logically defined categories. *Memory & Cognition, 10,* 3–9.

Bower, G. H. (1970). Organizational factors in memory. *Cognitive Psychology, 1,* 18–46.

Bower, G. H. (1981). Mood and memory. *American Psychologist, 36,* 129–148.

Bower, G. H., & Clark, M. C. (1969). Narrative stories as mediators for serial learning. *Psychonomic Science, 14,* 181–182.

Bransford, J. D., Arbitman-Smith, R., Stein, B. S., & Vye, N. J. (1985). Improving thinking and learning skills: An analysis of three approaches. In J. W. Segal, S. F. Chipman, & R. Glaser (Eds.), *Thinking and learning skills: Relating instruction to basic research* (Vol. 1, pp. 133–206). Mahwah, NJ: Erlbaum.

Bransford, J. D., Barclay, J. R., & Franks, J. J. (1972). Sentence memory: A constructive versus interpretive approach. *Cognitive Psychology, 3,* 193–209.

Bransford, J. D., Brown, A. L., & Cocking, R. R. (Eds.). (2000). *How people learn: Brain, mind, experience, and school.* Washington, DC: National Academies Press.

Bransford, J. D., & Franks, J. J. (1971). The abstraction of linguistic ideas. *Cognitive Psychology, 2,* 331–350.

Bransford, J. D., & Johnson, M. K. (1972). Contextual prerequisites for understanding: Some investigations of comprehension and recall. *Journal of Verbal Learning and Verbal Behavior, 11,* 717–726.

Bransford, J. D., & Johnson, M. K. (1973). Considerations of some problems of comprehension. In W. G. Chase (Ed.), *Visual information processing.* San Diego, CA: Academic Press.

Bransford, J. D., Sherwood, R., Vye, N., & Rieser, J. (1986). Teaching thinking and problem solving. *American Psychologist, 41,* 1078–1089.

Bransford, J. D., & Stein, B. S. (1984). *The IDEAL problem solver.* New York, NY: Freeman.

Bransford, J., Vye, N., Stevens, R., Kuhl, P., Schwartz, D., Bell, P., Meltzoff, A., Barron, B., Pea, R., Reeves, B., Roschelle, J., & Sabelli, N. (2006). Learning theories and education: Towards a decade of synergy. In P. A. Alexander and P. H. Winne (Eds.), *Handbook of educational psychology* (2nd ed., pp. 209–244). Mahwah, NJ: Erlbaum.

Bransford, J. D., Zech, L., Schwartz, D., Barron, B., Vye, N., & the Cognition and Technology Group at Vanderbilt. (1996). Fostering mathematical thinking in middle school students: Lessons from research. In R. J. Sternberg & T. Ben-Zeev (Eds.), *The nature of mathematical thinking* (pp. 203–250). Mahwah, NJ: Erlbaum.

Braten, I., & Stromso, H. I. (2005). The relationship between epistemological beliefs, implicit theories of intelligence, and self-regulated learning among Norwegian postsecondary student. *British Journal of Educational Psychology, 75,* 539–565.

Breznitz, Z., & Share, D. L. (1992). Effects of accelerated reading rate on memory for text. *Journal of Educational Psychology, 84,* 193–199.

Britton, B. K. (1996). Rewriting: The arts and sciences of improving expository instructional text. In C. M. Levy & S. Ransdell (Eds.), *The science of writing: Theories, methods, individual differences, and applications* (pp. 323–345). Mahwah, NJ: Erlbaum.

Brody, N. (1992). *Intelligence* (2nd ed.). San Diego, CA: Academic Press.

Brody, N. (2000). History of theories and measurement of intelligence. In R. J. Sternberg (Ed.), *Handbook of intelligence* (pp. 16–33). Cambridge, UK: Cambridge University Press.

Brophy, J. (2006). Observational research on generic aspects of teaching. In P. A. Alexander & P. H. Winne (Eds.), *Handbook of educational psychology* (2nd ed., pp. 755–780). Mahwah, NJ: Erlbaum.

Brousseau, B. A., Book, C., & Byers, J. L. (1988). Teacher beliefs and the cultures of teaching. *Journal of Teacher Education, 39,* 33–39.

Brouwers, A., & Tomic, W. (2001). The factorial validity of the Teacher Interpersonal Self-Efficacy Scale. *Educational and Psychological Measurement, 61,* 433–445.

Brown, A. L. (1980). Metacognitive development and reading. In R. J. Spiro, B. C. Bruce, & W. F. Brewer (Eds.), *Theoretical issues in reading comprehension* (pp. 458–482). Mahwah, NJ: Erlbaum.

Brown, A. L. (1987). Metacognition, executive control, self-regulation, and other more mysterious mechanisms. In F. Weinert & R. Kluwe (Eds.), *Metacognition, motivation, and understanding* (pp. 65–116). Mahwah, NJ: Erlbaum.

Brown, A. L., Day, J. D., & Jones, R. S. (1983). The development of plans for summarizing texts. *Child Development, 54,* 968–979.

Brown, A. L., & Palincsar, A. S. (1982). Inducing strategic learning from texts by means of informed, self-control training. *Topics in Learning and Learning Disabilities, 2,* 1–18.

Brown, A. L., & Palincsar, A. S. (1989). Guided, cooperative learning and individual knowledge acquisition. In L. Resnick (Ed.), *Cognition and instruction: Issues and agendas* (pp. 117–161). Mahwah, NJ: Erlbaum.

Brown, J. S., & Burton, R. B. (1978). Diagnostic models for procedural bugs in basic mathematical skills. *Cognitive Science, 2,* 155–192.

Brown, J. S., Collins, A., & Duguid, P. (1989). Situated cognition and the culture of learning. *Educational Researcher, 18,* 32–42.

Brown, R. (1973). *A first language: The early stages.* Cambridge, MA: Harvard University Press.

Brown, R. (2008). The road not yet taken: A transactional strategies approach to comprehension instruction. *The Reading Teacher, 61,* 538–547.

Brown, R., Cazden, C., & Bellugi, U. (1968). The child's grammar from 1 to 3. In J. P. Hill (Ed.), *Minnesota symposia on child psychology* (Vol. 2, pp. 70–126). Minneapolis, MN: University of Minnesota Press.

Brown, R., & Kulik, J. (1977). Flashbulb memories. *Cognition, 5,* 73–99.

Brown, R., Pressley, M., Van Meter, P., & Schuder, T. (1996). A quasi-experimental validation of transactional strategies instruction with low-achieving second-grade readers. *Journal of Educational Psychology, 88,* 18–37.

Brown, S. A. (2006). Investigating classroom discourse surrounding partner reading. *Early Childhood Education Journal, 34,* 29–36.

Brownlee, J. (2004). Teacher education students' epistemological beliefs. *Research in Education, 72,* 1–17.

Brownlee, J., & Berthelsen, D. (2006). Personal epistemology and relational pedagogy in early childhood teacher education programs. *Early Years, 26,* 17–29.

Brownlee, J., Purdie, N., & Boulton-Lewis, G. (2001). Changing epistemological beliefs in pre-service teaching education students. *Teaching in Higher Education, 6,* 247–268.

Bruner, J. S., Goodnow, J. J., & Austin, G. A. (1956). *A study of thinking.* New York, NY: Wiley.

Bruning, R., & Horn, C. (2000). Developing motivation to write. *Educational Psychologist, 35,* 25–37.

Bruning, R., & Schweiger, B. (1997). Integrating science and literacy experiences to motivate student learning. In J. T. Guthrie & A. Wigfield (Eds.), *Reading engagement: Motivating readers through integrated instruction* (pp. 149–167). Newark, DE: International Reading Association.

Bryne, B., & Fielding-Barnsley, R. (1991). Evaluation of a program to teach phonemic awareness to young children. *Journal of Educational Psychology, 83,* 451–455.

Byrne, B., & Fielding-Barnsley, R. (1993). Recognition of phoneme invariance by beginning readers: Confounding effects of global similarity. *Reading and Writing, 6,* 315–324.

Byrne, B., & Fielding-Barnsley, R. (1995, September). Evaluation of the program to teach phonemic awareness to young children: A 2- and 3-year follow-up and a new preschool trial. *Journal of Educational Psychology, 87,* 488.

Buehl, M. M., Alexander, P. A., & Murphy, P. K. (2002). Beliefs about schooled knowledge: Domain specific or domain general? *Contemporary Educational Psychology, 27,* 415–449.

Bugelski, B. R., Kidd, E., & Segmen, J. (1968). Image as a mediator in one-trial paired-associate learning. *Journal of Experimental Psychology, 76,* 69–73.

Bunce, D., & Macready, A. (2005). Processing speed, executive function, and age differences in remembering and knowing. *Quarterly Journal of Experimental Psychology, 58A,* 155–168.

Burton, K. D., Lydon, J. E., D'Alessandro, D. U., & Koestner, R. (2006). The differential effects of intrinsic and identified motivation on well-being and performance: Prospective, experimental and implicit approaches to self-determination theory. *Journal of Personality and Social Psychology, 91,* 750–762.

Burton, R. B. (1981). DEBUGGY: Diagnosis of errors in basic mathematical skills. In D. H. Sleeman & J. S. Brown (Eds.), *Intelligent tutoring systems* (pp. 62–81). San Diego, CA: Academic Press.

Butler, D. L., & Winne, P. H. (1995). Feedback and self-regulated learning: A theoretical synthesis. *Review of Educational Research, 65,* 245–281.

Byrnes, J. P., & Miller, D. C. (2007). The relative importance of predictors of math and science achievement: An opportunity-propensity analysis. *Contemporary Educational Psychology, 32,* 599–629.

Cain, K. M., & Dweck, C. S. (1989). The development of children's conceptions of intelligence: A theoretical framework. In R. Sternberg (Ed.), *Advances in the psychology of human intelligence* (Vol. 5, pp. 47–82). Mahwah, NJ: Erlbaum.

Calderhead, J. (1996). Teachers: Beliefs and knowledge. In D. C. Berliner & R. C. Calfee (Eds.), *Handbook of educational psychology* (pp. 709–725). New York, NY: Macmillan.

Calfee, R. C. (1994). Critical literacy: Reading and writing for a new millennium. In N. J. Ellsworth, C. N. Hedley, & A. N. Baratta (Eds.), *Literacy: A redefinition* (pp. 19–38). Mahwah, NJ: Erlbaum.

Calfee, R. C., Chambliss, M., & Beretz, M. (1991). Organizing for comprehension and composition. In R. Bowler & W. Ellis (Eds.), *All language and the creation of literacy* (pp. 79–93). Baltimore: Orton Dyslexia Society.

Calfee, R. C., Dunlap, K., & Wat, A. (1994). Authentic discussion of texts in middle grade schooling: An analytic-narrative approach. *Journal of Reading, 37,* 546–556.

Calfee, R. C., & Henry, M. K. (1986). Project READ: An inservice model for training classroom teachers in effective reading instruction. In J. V. Hoffman (Ed.), *Effective teaching of reading: Research and practice* (pp. 199–299). Newark, DE: International Reading Association.

Calfee, R. C., & Miller, R. G. (2005a). Breaking ground: Constructing authentic reading-writing assessments for middle and secondary school students. In R. Indrisano,
& J. Paratore. (Eds.), *Learning to write, writing to learn: Theory and research in practice* (pp. 203–219). Newark, DE: International Reading Association.

Calfee, R. C., & Miller, R. G. (2005b). Comprehending through composing: Reflections on reading assessment strategies. In S. Paris and S. Stahl (Eds.), *Children's reading comprehension and assessment* (pp. 215–236). Mahwah NJ: Erlbaum.

Calfee, R. C., & Miller, R. G. (2007). Best practices in writing assessment. In S. Graham, C. A. MacArthur, & J. Fitzgerald (Eds.), *Best practices in writing instruction* (pp. 265–286). New York, NY: Guilford.

Calfee, R. C., & Patrick, C. L. (1995). *Teach our children well.* Stanford, CA: Stanford Alumni Association.

Cameron, J., & Pierce, W. D. (1994). Reinforcement, reward, and intrinsic motivation: A meta-analysis. *Review of Educational Research, 64,* 363–423.

Cameron, J., Pierce, W. D., Banko, K. M., & Gear, A. (2005). Achievement-based rewards and intrinsic motivation: A test of cognitive mediators. *Journal of Educational Psychology, 97,* 641–655.

Campbell, D., & Stanley, J. (1963). *Experimental and quasi-experimental designs for research.* Chicago, IL: Rand McNally.

Campione, J. C., Brown, A. L., & Jay, M. (1992). Computers in a community of learners. In E. DeCorte, M. C. Linn, H. Mandl, & L. Verschaffel (Eds.), *Computer-based learning environments and problem solving* (pp. 163–188). Berlin: Springer–Verlag.

Cano, F. (2005). Epistemological beliefs and approaches to learning: Their change through secondary school and their influence on academic performance. *British Journal of Educational Psychology, 75,* 203–221.

Canobi, K. H., & Bethune, N. E. (2008). Number words in young children's conceptual and procedural knowledge of addition, subtraction and inversion. *Cognition, 108,* 675–686.

Caprara, C. G., Barbaranelli, G., Steca, P., & Malone, P. S. (2006). Teachers' self-efficacy beliefs as determinants of job satisfaction and students' academic achievement: A study at the school level. *Journal of School Psychology, 44,* 473–490.

Carey, L., & Flower, L. (1989). Cognition and writing: The idea generation process. In J. A. Glover, R. R. Ronning, & C. R. Reynolds (Eds.), *Handbook of creativity* (pp. 305–321). New York, NY: Plenum.

Carey, S. (1985). *Conceptual change in childhood.* Cambridge, MA: MIT Press.

Carey, S., Evans, R., Honda, M., Jay, E., & Unger, C. M. (1989). "An experiment is when you try it and see if it works": A study of grade 7 students' understanding of the construction of scientific knowledge. *International Journal of Science Education, 11,* 514–529.

Carey, S., & Smith, C. (1993). On understanding the nature of scientific knowledge. *Educational Psychologist, 28,* 235–251.

Carmichael, L., Hogan, H. P., & Walter, A. A. (1932). An experimental study of the effect of language on the reproduction of visually perceived forms. *Journal of Experimental Psychology, 15,* 73–86.

Carney, R. H., & Levin, J. R. (2000). Mnemonic instruction, with a focus on transfer. *Journal of Educational Psychology, 92,* 783–790.

Carney, R. H., & Levin, J. R. (2003). Promoting higher-order learning benefits by building lower-order mnemonic connections. *Applied Cognitive Psychology, 17,* 563–575.

Carpenter, T. P., & Moser, J. M. (1982). The development of addition and subtraction problem-solving skills. In T. R. Carpenter, J. M. Moser, & T. A. Romberg (Eds.), *Addition and subtraction: A cognitive perspective* (pp. 42–68). Mahwah, NJ: Erlbaum.

Carpenter, T. P., & Moser, J. M. (1983). Acquisition of addition and subtraction concepts. In R. Lesh & M. Landau (Eds.), *Acquisition of mathematical concepts and processes* (pp. 106–113). San Diego, CA: Academic Press.

Carraher, D., Schliemann, A., Brizuela, B., & Earnest, D. (2006). Arithmetic and algebra in early mathematics education. *Journal for Research in Mathematics Education, 37,* 87–115.

Carraher, D., Schliemann, A., & Schwartz, J. (2007). Early algebra is not the same as algebra early. In J. Kaput., D. Carraher, & M. Blanton (Eds.), *Algebra in the early grades* (pp. 235–272). Mahwah, NJ: Erlbaum.

Carver, S. M., & Klahr, D. (Eds.). (2001). *Cognition and instruction: Twenty-five years of progress.* Mahwah, NJ: Erlbaum.

Case, R. (1978). A developmentally based theory and technology of instruction. *Review of Educational Research, 48,* 439–463.

Case, R. (1985). *Intellectual development, birth to adulthood.* San Diego, CA: Academic Press.

Cazden, C. B. (2001). *Classroom discourse: The language of teaching and learning.* Portsmouth, NH: Heinemann.

Cazden, C. B., & Beck, S. W. (2003). Classroom discourse. In A. C. Graesser, M. A. Gernsbacher, & S. R. Goldman (Eds.), *Handbook of discourse processes* (pp. 165–197). Mahwah, NJ: Erlbaum.

Ceci, S. J., & Bruck, M. (1993). Suggestibility of the child witness: A historical review and synthesis. *Psychological Bulletin, 113,* 403–439.

Cervetti, G. N., Pearson, P. D., Barber, J., Hiebert, E., & Bravo, M. (2007). Integrating literacy and science: The research we have, the research we need. In M. Pressley, A. K. Billman, K. Perry, K. Refitt, & J. Reynolds (Eds.), *Shaping literacy achievement.* New York, NY: Guilford.

Chall, J. S. (1967). *Learning to read: The great debate.* New York, NY: McGraw-Hill.

Chall, J. S., Jacobs, V. A., & Baldwin, L. E. (1990). *The reading crisis: Why poor children fall behind.* Cambridge, MA: Harvard University Press.

Champagne, A. B., Klopfer, L. E., & Anderson, J. H. (1980). Factors influencing the learning of classical mechanics. *American Journal of Physics, 48,* 1074–1079.

Chan, J. C. K., McDermott, K. B., & Roediger, H. L. III. (2006). Retrieval-induced facilitation: Initially non-tested materials can benefit from prior testing of related material. *Journal of Experimental Psychology: General, 135,* 553–571.

Chan, K., & Elliott, R. G. (2004). Relational analysis of personal epistemology and conceptions about teaching and learning. *Teaching and Teacher Education, 20,* 817–831.

Chandler, M., Boyes, M., & Ball, L. (1990). Relativism and stations of epistemic doubt. *Journal of Experimental Child Psychology, 50,* 370–395.

Chang, M., Singh, K., & Mo, Y. (2007). Science engagement and science achievement: Longitudinal models using NELS data. *Educational Research and Evaluation, 13,* 349–371.

Chase, W. G. (1987). Visual information processing. In K. R. Boff, L. Kaufman, & J. P. Thomas (Eds.), *Handbook of perception and human performance: Vol. 2. Information processing* (pp. 28–1 to 28–60). New York, NY: Wiley.

Chase, W. G., & Simon, H. A. (1973a). The mind's eye in chess. In W. G. Chase (Ed.), *Visual information processing* (pp. 215–281). San Diego, CA: Academic Press.

Chase, W. G., & Simon, H. A. (1973b). Perception in chess. *Cognitive Psychology, 4,* 55–81.

Chen, E., & Darst, P. W. (2002). Individual and situational interest: The role of gender and skill. *Contemporary Educational Psychology, 27,* 250–269.

Chi, M. T. H. (1978). Knowledge structures and memory development. In R. Siegler (Ed.), *Children's thinking: What develops* (pp. 73–96). Hillsdale, NJ: Erlbaum.

Chi, M. T. H., de Leeuw, N., Chiu, M., & La Vancher, C. (1994). Eliciting self-explanations improves understanding. *Cognitive Science, 18,* 439–477.

Chi, M. T. H., & Ohlsson, S. (2005). Complex declarative learning. In K. Holyoak & R. Morrison (Eds.), *The Cambridge handbook of thinking and reasoning* (pp. 371–400). Cambridge, UK: Cambridge University Press.

Chi, M. T. H., Slotta, J. D., & de Leeuw, N. (1994). From things to processes: A theory of conceptual change for learning science concepts. *Learning and Instruction, 4,* 27–43.

Chinn, C. A., Anderson, R. C., & Waggoner, M. A. (2001). Patterns of discourse in two kinds of literature discussion. *Reading Research Quarterly, 36,* 378–411.

Chinn, C. A., & Brewer, W. F. (1993). The role of anomalous data in knowledge acquisition: A theoretical framework and implications for science instruction. *Review of Educational Research, 63,* 1–49.

Chinn, C. A., O'Donnell, A. M., & Jinks, T. S. (2000). The structure of discourse in collaborative learning. *Journal of Experimental Education, 69,* 77–97.

Chinn, C. A., & Waggoner, M. A. (1992, April). *Dynamics of classroom discussion: An analysis of what causes segments of open discourse to begin, continue, and end.* Paper presented at the Annual Meeting of the American Educational Research Association, San Francisco.

Chomsky, N. (1957). *Syntactic structures.* The Hague, Netherlands: Mouton.

Chomsky, N. (1965). *Aspects of the theory of syntax.* Cambridge, MA: MIT Press.

Church, M. A., Elliot, A. J., & Gable, S. (2000). Perceptions of classroom context, achievement goals, and achievement outcomes. *Journal of Educational Psychology, 93,* 43–54.

Clancey, W. J. (1988). Acquiring, representing, and evaluating a competence model of diagnostic strategy. In M. Chi, R. Glaser, & M. Farr (Eds.), *The nature of expertise* (pp. 261–287). Mahwah, NJ: Erlbaum.

Clark, J. M., & Paivio, A. (1991). Dual coding theory and education. *Educational Psychology Review, 3,* 149–210.

Clark, R. E. (1994). Media will never influence learning. *Educational Technology Research and Development, 42,* 21–29.

Clark, R. E. (2001). *Learning from media: Arguments, analysis and evidence.* Greenwich, CT: Information Age.

Clark, R. E. (2003). Research on Web-based learning: A half-full glass. In R. Bruning, C. Horn, & L. PytlikZillig (Eds.), *Web-based learning: What do we know? Where do we go?* (pp. 1–22). Greenwich, CT: Information Age.

Clarke, T., Ayres, P., & Sweller, J. (2005). The impact of sequencing and prior knowledge on learning mathematics through spreadsheet applications. *Educational Technology Research and Development, 53,* 1–24.

Clay, M. M. (1991). Child development. In J. Flood, J. M. Jensen, D. Lapp, & J. R. Squire (Eds.), *Handbook of research on teaching the English language arts* (pp. 40–45). New York, NY: Macmillan.

Clement, J. (1983). A conceptual model discussed by Galileo and used intuitively by physics students. In D. Gentner & A. L. Stevens (Eds.), *Mental models* (pp. 206–251). Mahwah, NJ: Erlbaum.

Clement, J. (1991). Nonformal reasoning in experts and in science students: The use of analogies, extreme cases, and physical intuition. In J. F. Voss, D. N. Perkins, & J. W. Segal (Eds.), *Informal reasoning and education* (pp. 345–362). Mahwah, NJ: Erlbaum.

Clement, J. (1992). Students' preconceptions in introductory physics. *American Journal of Physics, 50,* 66–71.

Cobb, P., & Bowers, J. (1999). Cognitive and situated learning perspectives in theory and practice. *Educational Researcher, 28,* 4–15.

Cognition and Technology Group at Vanderbilt. (1997). *The Jasper Project: Lessons in curriculum, instruction, assessment, and professional development.* Mahwah, NJ: Erlbaum.

Coladarci, T., & Breton, W. (1997). Teacher efficacy supervision and the special education resource-room teacher. *Journal of Educational Research, 90,* 230–239.

Cole, A. L., & Knowles, J. G. (2000). *Researching teaching: Exploring teacher development through reflective inquiry.* Boston, MA: Allyn & Bacon.

Collins, A. F., Brown J. S., & Newman, S. E. (1989). Cognitive apprenticeship: Teaching the crafts of reading, writing, and mathematics. In L. B. Resnick (Ed.), *Cognition and instruction: Issues and agendas* (pp. 453–494). Mahwah, NJ: Erlbaum.

Collins, A. F., Gathercole, S. E., Conway, M. A., & Morris, P. E. (1993). *Theories of memory.* Hove, UK: Erlbaum.

Collins, A. M., & Loftus, E. F. (1975). A spreading activation theory of semantic processing. *Psychological Review, 82,* 407–428.

Collins, A. M., & Quillian, M. R. (1969). Retrieval time from semantic memory. *Journal of Verbal Learning and Verbal Behavior, 8,* 240–248.

Collyer, S. C., Jonides, J., & Bevan, W. (1972). Images as memory aids: Is bizarreness helpful? *American Journal of Psychology, 85,* 31–38.

Condry, K. F., & Spelke, E. S. (2008). The development of language and abstract concepts: The case of natural number. *Journal of Experimental Psychology, 137,* 22–38.

Conner, C. M., Morrison, F. J., & Katch, L. E. (2004). Beyond the reading wars: Exploring the effect of child-instruction interactions on growth in early reading. *Scientific Studies of Reading, 8,* 304–336.

Conry, R., & Plant, W. T. (1965). WAIS and group test prediction of an academic success criterion: High school and college. *Educational and Psychological Measurement, 25,* 493–500.

Corkill, A. J. (1992). Advance organizers: Facilitators of recall. *Educational Psychology Review, 4,* 33–68.

Corkill, A. J., Glover, J. A., & Bruning, R. H. (1988). Advance organizers: Concrete vs. abstract. *Journal of Educational Research, 82,* 76–81.

Corno, L., & Mandinach, E. B. (2004). What have we learned about student engagement in the past twenty years. In D. McInerney & S. Van Etten (Eds.) *Sociocultural influences on motivation: Big theories revisited* (pp. 299–328). Greenwich, CT: Information Age.

Covington, M. C., Crutchfield, R. S., Davies, L. B., & Olton, R. M. (1974). *The Productive Thinking program: A course in learning to think.* New York, NY: Merrill/Macmillan.

Cowan, N. (2005). *Working memory capacity.* New York, NY: Psychology Press.

Cox, B. D. (1997). The rediscovery of the active learner in adaptive contexts: A developmental-historical analysis of transfer of training. *Educational Psychologist, 32,* 41–45.

Craig, S. D., Gholson, B., & Driscoll, D. M. (2002). Animated pedagogical agents in multimedia educational environments: Effects of agent properties, picture features, and redundancy. *Journal of Educational Psychology, 94,* 428–434.

Craik, F. I. M. (1979). Human memory. *Annual Review of Psychology, 30,* 63–102.

Craik, F. I. M. (2000, August). *Human memory and aging.* Paper presented at the Proceedings of the 27th International Congress of Psychology, Stockholm.

Craik, F. I. M. (2002). Levels of processing: Past, present . . . future? *Memory, 10,* 305–318.

Craik, F. I. M., & Lockhart, R. S. (1972). Levels of processing: A framework for memory research. *Journal of Verbal Learning and Verbal Behavior, 11,* 671–684.

Craik, F. I. M., & Lockhart, R. S. (1986). CHARM is not enough: Comments on Eich's model of cued recall. *Psychological Review, 93,* 360–364.

Craik, F. I. M., & Tulving, E. (1975). Depth of processing and the retention of words in episodic memory. *Journal of Experimental Psychology: General, 104,* 268–294.

Crossman, E. R. F. (1959). A theory of the acquisition of a speed-skill. *Ergonomics, 2,* 153–166.

Crystal, D. (1997). *The encyclopedia of language* (2nd ed.). Cambridge, UK: Cambridge University Press.

Csikszentmihalyi, M. (1996). *Creativity: Flow and the psychology of discovery and invention.* New York, NY: HarperCollins.

Cunningham, A. E., & Stanovich, K. E. (1991). Tracking the unique effects of print exposure in children: Associations with vocabulary, general knowledge, and spelling. *Journal of Educational Psychology, 83,* 264–274.

Cunningham, J. W., & Fitzgerald, J. (1996). Epistemology and reading. *Reading Research Quarterly, 31,* 36–60.

Dacey, J. S. (1989). *Fundamentals of creative thinking.* Lexington, MA: D. C. Heath.

D'Agonitino, J. V., & Murphy, J. A. (2004). A meta-analysis of Reading Recovery in United States schools. *Educational Evaluation and Policy Analysis, 26,* 23–38.

Dalton, B., Ingels, S. J., Downing, J., & Bozick, R. (2007). *Advanced mathematics and science coursetaking in the spring high school senior classes of 1982, 1992, and 2004* (NCES 2007-312). Washington, DC: National Center for Education Statistics, Institute of Education Sciences, U.S. Department of Education.

Daneman, M., & Carpenter, P. A. (1980). Individual differences in working memory and reading. *Journal of Verbal Learning & Verbal Behavior, 19,* 450–466.

Daneman, M., & Merikle, P. M. (1996). Working memory and language comprehension: A meta-analysis. *Psychonomic Bulletin & Review, 3,* 422–433.

Darwin, G. J., Turvey, M. T., & Crowder, R. G. (1972). An auditory analogue of the Sperling partial report procedure: Evidence for brief auditory storage. *Cognitive Psychology, 3,* 255–267.

Davis, E. A. (2001). Prompting middle school science students for productive reflection: Generic and directed prompts. *The Journal of the Learning Sciences, 12,* 91–142.

Deakin, J. M., & Allard, F. (1991). Skilled memory in expert figure skating. *Memory & Cognition, 19,* 79–86.

Deane, P., Sheehan, K. M., Sabatini, J., Futagi, Y., & Kostin, I. (2006). Differences in text structure and its implications for assessment of struggling readers. *Scientific Studies of Reading, 10,* 257–275.

de Bono, E. (1973). *CoRT thinking materials.* London: Direct Education Services.

Deci, E. L., & Ryan, R. M. (1985). *Intrinsic motivation and self-determination in human behavior*. New York, NY: Plenum.

Deci, E. L., & Ryan, R. M. (1987). The support of autonomy and control of behavior. *Journal of Personality and Social Psychology, 53*, 1024–1037.

Deci, E. L., Vallerand, R. J., Pelletier, L. G., & Ryan, R. M. (1991). Motivation and education: The self-determination perspective. *Educational Psychologist, 26*, 325–346.

DeCorte, E., & Masui, C. (2004). The CLIA model: A framework for designing powerful learning environments for thinking and problem solving. *European Journal of Psychology of Education, 19*, 365–384.

deGroot, A. D. (1965). *Thought and choice in chess*. The Hague, Netherlands: Mouton.

De Jong, T., & Ferguson-Hessler, M. G. M. (1996). Types and qualities of knowledge. *Educational Psychologist, 31*, 105–113.

De Jong, T., & Pieters, J. (2006). The design of powerful learning environments. In P. A. Alexander & P. H. Winne (Eds.), *Handbook of educational psychology* (2nd ed., pp. 739–754). Mahwah, NJ: Erlbaum.

del Rio, P. (2007). Inside and outside the zone of proximal development: An ecofunctional reading of Vygotsky. In H. Daniels, M. Cole, & J. Wertsch (Eds.), *The Cambridge companion to Vygotsky* (pp. 276–302). New York, NY: Cambridge University Press.

Delclos, V. R., & Harrington, C. (1991). Effects of strategy monitoring and proactive instruction on children's problem-solving performance. *Journal of Educational Psychology, 83*, 35–42.

Demastes, S. S., Good, R. G., & Peebles, P. (1996). Patterns of conceptual change in evolution. *Journal of Research in Science Teaching, 33*, 407–431.

Dempsey, M. S., PytlikZillig, L. M., & Bruning, R. (2005). Building writing assessment skills using web-based cognitive support features. In L. M. PytlikZillig, M. Bodvarsson, & R. Bruning (Eds.), *Technology-based education: Bringing researchers and practitioners together* (pp. 83–105). Greenwich, CT: Information Age.

Dempsey, M. S., PytlikZillig, L. M., & Bruning, R. (2009). Helping preservice teachers learn to assess writing: Practice and feedback in a web-based environment. *Assessing Writing, 14*, 38–61.

Dempster, F. N. (1981). Memory span: Sources of individual and developmental differences. *Psychological Bulletin, 89*, 63–100.

Dempster, F. N., & Corkill, A. (1999). Interference and inhibition in cognition and behavior: Unifying themes for educational psychology. *Educational Psychology Review, 11*, 1–88.

Denton, P., Madden, J., Roberts, M., & Rowe, P. (2008). Students' response to traditional and computer-assisted formative feedback: A comparative case study. *British Journal of Educational Technology, 39*, 486–500.

Derry, S. J., Wilsman, M. J., & Hackbarth, A. J. (2007). Using contrasting case activities to deepen teacher understanding of algebraic thinking and teaching. *Mathematical Thinking and Learning, 9*, 305–329.

Detterman, D. K. (1993). The case for the prosecution: Transfer as an epiphenomenon. In D. K. Detterman & R. J. Sternberg (Eds.), *Transfer on trial: Intelligence, cognition, and instruction* (pp. 1–24). Norwood, NJ: Ablex.

Deutsch, D. (1987). Auditory pattern recognition. In K. R. Boff, L. Kaufman, & J. P. Thomas (Eds.), *Handbook of perception and human performance: Vol. 2. Cognitive processes and performance* (pp. 1–49). New York, NY: Wiley.

Dewey, J. (1910). *How we think*. Boston, MA: D. C. Heath.

DiLollo, U., & Dixon, P. (1988). Two forms of persistence in visual information processing. *Journal of Experimental Psychology: Human Perception and Performance, 14*, 601–609.

Dinkelman, T. (2000). An inquiry into the development of critical reflection in secondary school teachers. *Teaching and Teacher Education, 16*, 195–122.

Dinnel, D., & Glover, J. A. (1985). Advance organizers: Encoding manipulations. *Journal of Educational Psychology, 77*, 514–521.

diSessa, A. A. (1993). Toward an epistemology of physics. *Cognition and Instruction, 10*, 105–225.

diSessa, A. A. (2002). Why "conceptual ecology" is a good idea. In M. Limon & L. Mason (Eds.), *Reconsidering conceptual change: Issues in theory and practice* (pp. 29–60). Dordrecht, Netherlands: Kluwer.

Dole, J. A., Nokes, J. D., & Drits, D. (2009). Cognitive strategy instruction. In S. E. Israel & G. G. Duffy (Eds.), *Handbook of research on reading comprehension* (pp. 347–372). New York, NY: Routledge.

Dole, J. A., & Sinatra, G. A. (1998). Reconceptualizing change in the cognitive construction of knowledge. *Educational Psychologist, 33*, 109–128.

Donovan, C. A. (1996). First graders' impressions of genre-specific elements in writing narrative and expository texts. In D. Leu, K. Hinchman, & C. Kinzer (Eds.),

Literacies for the 21st century: Forty-fifth yearbook of the National Reading Conference (pp. 183–194). Chicago, IL: National Reading Conference.

Dooling, D. J., & Lachman, R. (1971). Effects of comprehension on retention of prose. *Journal of Experimental Psychology, 88,* 216–222.

Dornisch, M. M., & Sperling. R. A. (2006). Facilitating learning from technology-enhanced text: Effects of prompted elaborative interrogation. *Journal of Educational Research, 99,* 156–165.

Dorph, R., Goldstein, D., Lee, S., Lepori, K., Schneider, S., Venkatesan, S. (2007). *The status of science education in the Bay Area: Research Study e-report.* Lawrence Hall of Science, University of California, Berkeley, California.

Dowd, E. T. (2004). Cognition and the cognitive revolution in psychotherapy: Promises and advances. *Journal of Clinical Psychology, 60,* 415–428.

Dreher. M. J. (2002). Children searching and using information text: A critical part of comprehension. In C. C. Block & M. Pressley (Eds.), *Comprehension instruction: Research-based best practices* (pp. 289–304). New York, NY: Guilford.

Drummey, A. B., & Newcombe, N. (1995). Remembering versus knowing the past: Children's explicit and implicit memories for pictures. *Journal of Experimental Child Psychology, 59,* 549–565.

Duell, O. K., & Schommer-Aikins, M. (2001). Measures of people's beliefs about knowledge and learning. *Educational Psychology Review, 13,* 419–449.

Duffy, G. (2002). The case for direct explanation of strategies. In C. Block & M. Pressley (Eds). *Comprehension instruction: Research-based best practices* (pp. 28–41). New York, NY: Guilford.

Duggan, S., & Gott, R. (2002). What sort of science education do we really need? *International Journal of Science Education, 24,* 661–679.

Duin, A. H., & Graves, M. F. (1987). Intensive vocabulary instruction as a prewriting technique. *Reading Research Quarterly, 22,* 311–330.

Duit, R., & Treagust, D. F. (2003). Conceptual change: A powerful framework for improving science teaching and learning. *International Journal of Science Education, 25,* 671–688.

Duke, N. K. (2000). 3.6 minutes per day: The scarcity of informational texts in first grade. *Reading Research Quarterly, 25,* 202–224.

Duke, N. K., Bennett-Armistead, V. S., & Roberts, E. M. (2003). Bridging the gap between learning to read and reading to learn. In D. M. Barone & L. M. Morrow (Eds.), *Literacy and young children: Research-based practices* (pp. 226–242). New York, NY: Guilford.

Duke, N. K., & Kays, J. (1998). "Can I say 'once upon a time'?" Kindergarten children developing knowledge of information book language. *Early Childhood Research Quarterly, 13,* 295–318.

Dunbar, K., & Fugelsang, J. (2005). Scientific reasoning and thinking. In K. Holyoak & R. Morrison (Eds.), *The Cambridge handbook of thinking and reasoning* (pp. 705–726). Cambridge, UK: Cambridge University Press.

Duncan, T. G., & McKeachie, W. J. (2005). The making of the Motivated Strategies for Learning Questionnaire. *Educational Psychologist, 40,* 117–128.

Duncker, K. (1945). On problem solving (L. S. Lees, Trans.) [Special issue]. *Psychological Monographs, 58*(270).

Durand, M., Hulme, C., Larkin, R., & Snowling, M. (2005). The cognitive foundations of reading and arithmetic skills in 7- to 10-year-olds. *Journal of Experimental Child Psychology, 91,* 113–136.

Durik, A. M., & Harackiewicz, J. (2007). Different strokes for different folks: How individual interest moderates the effects of situational factors on task interest. *Journal of Educational Psychology, 99,* 597–610.

Durkin, D. (1978–1979). What classroom observations reveal about reading comprehension instruction. *Reading Research Quarterly, 14,* 481–533.

Durkin, D. (1981). Reading comprehension instruction in five basal reading series. *Reading Research Quarterly, 16,* 515–544.

Dweck, C. S. (2000). *Self theories: Their role in motivation, personality, and development.* Philadelphia: Psychology Press.

Dweck, C. S., Chiu, C., & Hong, Y. (1995). Implicit theories and their role in judgments and reactions: A world from two perspectives. *Psychological Inquiry, 6,* 267–285.

Dweck, C. S., & Leggett, E. S. (1988). A social-cognitive approach to motivation and personality. *Psychological Review, 95,* 256–273.

Dyson, A. H. (1993). *Social worlds of children learning to write in an urban primary school.* New York, NY: Teachers College Press.

Dyson, A. H., & Freedman, S. W. (1991). Writing. In J. Flood, J. M. Jensen, D. Lapp, & J. R. Squire (Eds.), *Handbook of research on teaching the English language arts* (pp. 754–774). New York, NY: Macmillan.

Ebbinghaus, H. (1885). *Uber das Gedachtnis [Memory].* Leipzig, Germany: Duncker & Humbolt.

Eccles, J. S., & Wigfield, A. (2002). Motivational beliefs, values, and goals. *Annual Review of Psychology, 53,* 109–132.

Edwards, K. (1990). The interplay of affect and cognition in attitude formation and change. *Journal of Personality and Social Psychology, 59,* 202–216.

Egyed, C. J., & Short, R. J. (2006). Teacher self-efficacy, burnout, experience and decision to refer a disruptive student. *School Psychology International, 27,* 462–474.

Ehri, L. C. (1991). Development of the ability to read words. In P. D. Pearson (Ed.), *Handbook of reading research* (2nd ed., pp. 395–419). New York, NY: Longman.

Ehri, L. C. (1994). Development of the ability to read words: Update. (1994). In R. B. Ruddell, M. R. Ruddell, & H. Singer (Eds.), *Theoretical models and processes of reading* (4th ed., pp. 323–358). Newark, DE: International Reading Association.

Ehri, L. C. (1998). Research on learning to read and spell: A personal-historical perspective. *Scientific Studies of Reading, 2,* 97–114.

Ehri, L. C. (2005). Learning to read words: Theory, findings, and issues. *Scientific Studies of Reading, 9,* 167–188.

Ehri, L. C., & Wilce, L. S. (1985). Movement into reading: Is the first stage of printed word learning visual or phonetic? *Reading Research Quarterly, 20,* 163–179.

Eichenbaum, H. (1997). How does the brain organize memories? *Science, 277,* 330–332.

Eisenberg, N., Martin, C. L., & Fabes, R. A. (1996). Gender development and gender effects. In D. C. Berliner & R. C. Calfee (Eds.), *Handbook of educational psychology* (pp. 358–396). New York, NY: Macmillan.

Eisenberger, R., & Cameron, J. (1996). Detrimental effects of rewards: Reality or myth? *American Psychologist, 51,* 1153–1166.

Elbow, P. (1981). *Writing with power: Techniques for mastering the writing process.* New York, NY: Oxford University Press.

Elliott, E. S., & Dweck, C. S. (1988). An approach to motivation and achievement. *Journal of Personality and Social Psychology, 54,* 5–12.

Elliott, A. J., & Thrash, T. M. (2001). Achievement goals and the hierarchical model of achievement motivation. *Educational Psychologist, 13,* 139–156.

Ellsworth, P. C. (2005). Legal reasoning. In K. Holyoak & R. Morrison (Eds.), *The Cambridge handbook of thinking and reasoning* (pp. 685–704). Cambridge, UK: Cambridge University Press.

Engle, R. W., Kane, M. J., & Tuholski, S. W. (1999). Individual differences in working memory capacity and what they tell us about controlled attention, general fluid intelligence, and functions of the prefrontal cortex. In A. Miyake & P. Shah (Eds.), *Models of working memory: Mechanisms of active maintenance and executive control* (pp. 102–134). Cambridge, UK: Cambridge University Press.

Englert, C. S., Mariage, T., & Dunsmore, K. (2006). Tenets of sociocultural theory in writing instruction research. In C. A. MacArthur, S. Graham, & J. Fitzgerald (Eds.), *Handbook of writing research* (pp. 208–221). New York, NY: Guilford Press.

Englert, C. S., Raphael, T. E., Anderson, L. M., Anthony, H. M., & Stevens, D. D. (1991). Making strategies and self-talk visible: Writing instruction in regular and special education classrooms. *American Educational Research Journal, 28,* 337–372.

Ennis, R. H. (1987). A taxonomy of critical thinking dispositions and abilities. In J. Baron & R. Sternberg (Eds.), *Teaching thinking skills: Theory and practice* (pp. 9–26). New York, NY: Freeman.

Ericsson, K. A. (1996). The acquisition of expert performance. In K. A. Ericsson (Ed.), *The road to excellence: The acquisition of expert performance in the arts, sciences, sports, and games* (pp. 1–50). Mahwah, NJ: Erlbaum.

Ericsson, K. A. (2003). The acquisition of expert performance as problem solving: Construction and modification of mediating mechanisms through deliberate practice. In J. E. Davidson and R. J. Sternberg (Eds.), *The psychology of problem solving* (pp. 31–83). Cambridge, UK: Cambridge University Press.

Ericsson, K. A. (2005). An interview with K. Anders Ericsson. *Educational Psychology Review, 17,* 389–412.

Ericsson, K. A., Chase, W. G., & Faloon, S. (1980). Acquisition of a memory skill. *Science, 208,* 1181–1182.

Ericsson, K. A., & Kintsch, W. (1995). Long-term working memory. *Psychological Review, 102,* 211–245.

Ericsson, K. A., Krampe, R. T., & Tesch-Romer, C. (1993). The role of deliberate practice in the acquisition of expert performance. *Psychological Review, 100,* 363–406.

Ericsson, K. A., Roring, R. W., & Nandagopal, K. (2007). Giftedness and evidence for reproducibly superior performance: An account based on the expert performance framework. *High Ability Studies, 18,* 3–56.

Ericsson, K. A., & Ward, P. (2007). Capturing the naturally occurring superior performance of experts in the laboratory. *Current Directions in Psychological Science, 16,* 346–350.

Ernest, P. (1995). The one and many. In L. P. Steffe & J. E. Gale (Eds.), *Constructivism in education* (pp. 459–485). Hillsdale, NJ: Erlbaum.

Ervin, S. M. (1964). Imitation and structural change in children's language. In E. H. Lenneberg (Ed.), *New directions in the study of language* (pp. 163–189). Cambridge: MIT Press.

Eysenck, M. W., & Keane, M. (2005). *Cognitive psychology: A student's handbook* (5th ed.). New York, NY: Psychology Press.

Fall, R., Webb, N. M., & Chudowsky, N. (2000). Group discussion and large-scale language arts assessment: Effects on students' comprehension. *American Education Research Journal, 37,* 911–941.

Farnham-Diggory, S. (1994). Paradigms of knowledge and instruction. *Review of Educational Research, 64,* 463–477.

Feist, J. (2006). The development of scientific talent in Westinghouse finalists and members of the National Academy of Sciences. *Journal of Adult Development, 13,* 23–35.

Feldman, A. I., Campbell, R. L., & Lai, M. K. (1999). Improving elementary school science teaching by cross-level mentoring. *Journal of Science Teacher Education, 10,* 55–67.

Ferretti, R. P., MacArthur, C. A., & Dowdy, N. S. (2000). The effects of an elaborated goal on the persuasive writing of students with learning disabilities and their normally achieving peers. *Journal of Educational Psychology, 92,* 694–702.

Ferster, C. B., & Skinner, B. F. (1957). *Schedules of reinforcement.* New York, NY: Appleton–Century–Crofts.

Feuerstein, R., Rand, Y., Hoffman, M. B., & Miller, R. (1980). *Instrumental enrichment: An intervention program for cognitive modifiability.* Baltimore: University Park Press.

Fisher, D. L., Duffy, S. A., Young, C., & Pollatsek, A. (1988). Understanding the central processing limit in consistent-mapping visual search tasks. *Journal of Experimental Psychology: Human Perception and Performance, 14,* 253–266.

Flavell, J. H. (1992). Perspectives on perspective taking. In H. Beilin & P. Pufall (Eds.), *Piaget's theory: Prospects and possibilities* (pp. 107–139). Mahwah, NJ: Erlbaum.

Flink, C., Boggiano, A. K., & Barrett, M. (1990). Controlling teaching strategies: Undermining children's self-determination and performance. *Journal of Personality and Social Psychology, 59,* 916–924.

Flower, L., & Hayes, J. R. (1984). The representation of meaning in writing. *Written Communication, 1,* 120–160.

Flowerday, T., & Schraw, G. (2000). Teacher beliefs about instructional choice: A phenomenological study. *Journal of Educational Psychology, 92,* 634–645.

Fontana, J., Scruggs, T., & Mastropieri, M. (2007). Mnemonic strategy instruction in inclusive secondary social studies classes. *Remedial and Special Education, 28,* 345–355.

Försterling, F. (1985). Attributional retraining: A review. *Psychological Bulletin, 98,* 495–512.

Fosnot, C. T. (2008). *Constructivism: theory, perspective and practice.* New York, NY: Teachers College Press.

Francis, D. J., Snow, C. E., August, D., Carolson, C. D., Miller, J., & Iglesias, A. (2006). Measures of reading comprehension: A latent variable analysis of the diagnostic assessment of reading comprehension. *Scientific Studies of Reading, 10,* 301–322.

Freberg, L. A. (2006). *Discovering biological psychology.* Boston, MA: Houghton Mifflin Co.

Freedman, S. W. (1992). Outside-in and inside-out: Peer response groups in two ninth-grade classes. *Research in the Teaching of English, 26,* 71–107.

Fuchs, L. S., Compton, D. L., Fuchs, D., Paulsen, K., Bryant, J. D., & Hamlett, C. L. (2005). The prevention, identification, and cognitive determinants of math difficulty. *Journal of Educational Psychology, 97,* 493–513.

Fuchs, D., & Fuchs, L. S. (2007). Increasing strategic reading comprehension with peer-assisted learning activities. In D. S. McNamara (Ed.). *Reading comprehension strategies: Theories, interventions, and technologies* (pp. 175–197). New York, NY: Erlbaum.

Fuchs, L. S., Fuchs, D., Compton, D. L., Powell, S. R., Seethaler, P. M., Capizzi, A. M., Schatschneider, C., & Fletcher, J. M. (2006). The cognitive correlates of third-grade skill in arithmetic, algorithmic computation, and arithmetic word problems. *Journal of Educational Psychology, 98,* 29–43.

Fuchs, L. S., Fuchs, D., Stuebing, K., Fletcher, J. M., Hamlett, C. L., & Lambert, W. (2008). Problem solving and computational skills: Are they shared or distinct aspects of mathematical cognition? *Journal of Educational Psychology, 100,* 30–47.

Fuchs, L., Powell, S., Seethaler, P., Cirino, P., Fletcher, J., Fuchs, D., Hamlett, C., & Zumeta, R. (2009). Remediating number combination and word problem deficits among students with mathematics difficulties: A randomized control trial. *Journal of Educational Psychology, 101,* 561–576.

Fulp, Sherri L. (2002). *Status of elementary school science teaching*. Chapel Hill, NC: Horizon Research.

Furst, B. (1954). *Stop forgetting*. New York, NY: Garden City Press.

Fuson, K. C. (1992). Research on whole number addition and subtraction. In D. A. Grouws (Ed.), *Handbook of research on mathematics teaching and learning* (pp. 243–275). New York, NY: Macmillan.

Fuson, K. C., & Fuson, A. M. (1992). Instruction supporting children's counting on for addition and counting up for subtraction. *Journal for Research in Mathematics Education, 23*, 72–78.

Gagne, R. M. (1965). The analysis of instructional objectives for the design of instruction. In R. Glaser (Ed.), *Teaching machines and programmed learning: Vol. 2. Data and direction* (pp. 32–41). Washington, DC: National Education Association.

Gallagher, C. (2007). *Reclaiming assessment: A better alternative to the accountability agenda*. Portsmouth, NH: Heinemann.

Gardner, H. (1983). *Frames of mind: The theory of multiple intelligences*. New York, NY: Basic Books.

Gardner, H. (1993). *Multiple intelligences: The theory in practice*. New York, NY: Basic Books.

Garner, R., & Alexander, P. A. (1989). Metacognition: Answered and unanswered questions. *Educational Psychologist, 24*, 143–158.

Garner, R., Gillingham, M. G., & White, C. S. (1989). Effects of "seductive details" on macroprocessing and microprocessing in adults and children. *Cognition and Instruction, 6*, 41–57.

Gauvain, M. (2001). *The social context of cognitive development*. New York, NY: Guilford.

Geary, D. C., Hamson, C. O., & Hoard, M. K. (2000). Numerical and arithmetical cognition: A longitudinal study of process and concept deficits in children with learning disability. *Journal of Experimental Child Psychology, 77*, 236–263.

Geary, D., Hoard, M., Byrd-Craven, J., Nugent, L., & Numtee, C. (2007). Cognitive mechanisms underlying achievement deficits in children with mathematical learning disability. *Child Development, 78*, 1343–1359.

Georgiou, S. N. (2008). Beliefs of experienced and novice teachers about achievement. *Educational Psychology, 28*, 119–131.

Gernsbacher, M., Robertson, R., Palladino, P., & Werner, N. (2004). Managing mental representations during narrative comprehension. *Discourse Processes, 37*, 145–164.

Getzels, J., & Csikszentmihalyi, M. (1976). *The creative vision: A longitudinal study of problem finding in art*. New York, NY: Wiley.

Ghaith, G., & Yaghi, H. (1997). Relationships among experience, teacher efficacy, and attitudes toward the implementation of instructional innovation. *Teaching and Teacher Education, 13*, 451–458.

Gibson, S., & Dembo, M. H. (1984). Teacher efficacy: A construct validation. *Journal of Educational Psychology, 76*, 569–582.

Gijlers, H., Saab, N., Van Joolingen, W. R., De Jong, T., & Van Hout-Walters, B. H. (2009). Interaction between tool and talk: How instruction and tools support consensus-building in collaborative inquiry-learning environments. *Journal of Computer Assisted Learning, 25*, 252–267.

Gill, M. G., Ashton, P. T., & Algina, J. (2004). Changing preservice teachers' epistemological beliefs about teaching and learning in mathematics: An intervention study. *Contemporary Educational Psychology, 29*, 164–185.

Gillespie, D. (1992). *The mind's we: Contextualism in cognitive psychology*. Carbondale: Southern Illinois University Press.

Glaser, R., & Chi, M. T. (1988). Overview. In M. Chi, R. Glaser, & M. Farr (Eds.), *The nature of expertise* (pp. 15–28). Mahwah, NJ: Erlbaum.

Glenberg, A. M., & Epstein, W. (1987). Inexpert calibration of comprehension. *Memory and Cognition, 15*, 84–93.

Glover, J. A., Bruning, R. H., & Plake, B. S. (1982). Distinctiveness of encoding and recall of text materials. *Journal of Educational Psychology, 74*, 522–534.

Glover, J. A., & Corkill, A. (1987). The spacing effect in memory for prose. *Journal of Educational Psychology, 79*, 198–200.

Glover, J. A., Dinnel, D. L., Halpain, D., McKee, T., Corkill A. J., & Wise, S. (1988). Effects of across-chapter signals on recall of text. *Journal of Educational Psychology, 80*, 3–15.

Glover, J. A., Harvey, A. L., & Corkill, A. J. (1988). Remembering written instructions: Tab A goes into Slot C, or does it? *British Journal of Educational Psychology, 58*, 191–200.

Glover, J. A., Plake, B. S., & Zimmer, J. W. (1982). Distinctiveness of encoding and memory for learning tasks. *Journal of Educational Psychology, 74*, 189–198.

Glover, J. A., & Ronning, R. R. (Eds.). (1987). *Historical foundations of educational psychology*. New York, NY: Plenum.

Glover, J. A., Timme, V., Deyloff, D., Rogers, M., & Dinnel, D. (1987). Oral directions: Remembering what to do when. *Journal of Educational Research, 81,* 33–53.

Gnadinger, C. M. (2008). Peer mediated instruction: Assisted performance in the primary classroom. *Teacher and Teaching: Theory and Practice, 14,* 129–143.

Goddard, R. D., Hoy, W. K., & Hoy, A. W. (2000). Collective teacher efficacy: Its meaning, measure and impact on student achievement. *American Educational Research Journal, 37,* 479–507.

Godden, D. R., & Baddeley, A. D. (1975). Context-dependent memory in two natural environments: On land and underwater. *British Journal of Psychology, 66,* 325–332.

Goetz, E. T., Sadoski, M., Fatemi, Z., & Bush, R. (1994). That's news to me: Readers' responses to brief newspaper articles. *Journal of Reading Behavior, 26,* 125–138.

Goldman, S. R., & Rakestraw, J. A., Jr. (2000). Structural aspects of constructing meaning from text. In M. L. Kamil, P. B. Mosenthal, P. D. Pearson, & R. Barr (Eds.), *Handbook of reading research* (Vol. 3, pp. 311–335). Mahwah, NJ: Erlbaum.

Goldman, S. R., & Varma, S. (1995). CAPping the construction integration model of discourse comprehension. In C. Weaver, S. Mannes, & C. Fletcher (Eds.), *Discourse comprehension: Models of processing revisited* (pp. 337–358). Hillsdale, NJ: Erlbaum.

Goldman, S. R., Varma, S., & Cote, N. (1996). Extending capacity-constrained construction integration: Toward "smarter" and flexible models of text comprehension. In B. K. Britton & A. C. Graesser (Eds.), *Models of understanding text* (pp. 73–113). Mahwah, NJ: Erlbaum.

Good, T. L., & Brophy, J. E. (2007). *Looking in classrooms* (10th ed.). Upper Saddle River, NJ: Allyn & Bacon.

Good, R. H., & Kaminski, R. A. (Eds.). (2002). *Dynamic indicators of basic early literacy skills* (6th ed.). Eugene, OR: Institute for the Development of Educational Achievement.

Goodman, K. S. (1982a). Miscues: Windows on the reading process. In F. V. Gollasch (Ed.), *Language and literacy* (Vol. 1, pp. 64–79). Boston, MA: Routledge Kegan Paul.

Goodman, K. S. (1982b). Reading: A psycholinguistic guessing game. In E. V. Gollasch (Ed.), *Language and literacy* (Vol. 1, pp. 19–31). Boston, MA: Routledge Kegan Paul.

Goodman, K. S. (1982c). The reading process: Theory and practice. In F. V. Gollasch (Ed.), *Language and literacy* (Vol. 1, pp. 33–43). Boston, MA: Routledge Kegan Paul.

Goodman, K. S. (1994). Reading, writing, and written texts: A transactional sociopsycholinguistic view. In R. B. Ruddell, M. R. Ruddell, & H. Singer (Eds.), *Theoretical models and processes of reading* (4th ed., pp. 1093–1130). Newark, DE: International Reading Association.

Goodman, K. S. (1996). *On reading.* Portsmouth, NH: Heinemann.

Goodman, K. S. (2006). A critical review of DIBELS. In K. S. Goodman (Ed.), *The truth about DIBELS: What it is, what it does* (pp. 1–39). Portsmouth, NH: Heinemann.

Goodman, K. S., & Goodman, Y. M. (1982). Learning about psycholinguistic processes by analyzing oral reading. In F. V. Gollasch (Ed.), *Language and literacy* (Vol. 1, pp. 149–168). Boston, MA: Routledge Kegan Paul.

Gorman, M. E., Kincannon, A., Gooding, D., & Tweney, R. D. (2004). *New directions in scientific and technical thinking.* Hillsdale, NJ: Erlbaum.

Gottfried, A. (1990). Academic intrinsic motivation in young elementary school children. *Journal of Educational Psychology, 82,* 525–538.

Gough, P. B. (1972). One second of reading. In E. Kavanagh & I. G. Mattingly (Eds.), *Language by ear and by eye* (pp. 331–358). Cambridge, MA: MIT Press.

Graesser, A. C. (2007). An introduction to strategic reading comprehension. In D. S. McNamara (Ed.), *Reading comprehension strategies: Theories, interventions, and technologies* (pp. 3–26). New York, NY: Erlbaum.

Graesser, A. C. (2008). Advances in text comprehension: Commentary and final perspective. *Applied Cognitive Psychology, 22,* 425–429.

Graesser, A. C., & Britton, B. K. (1996). Five metaphors for text understanding. In B. K. Britton & A. C. Graesser (Eds.), *Models of understanding text* (pp. 341–351). Mahwah, NJ: Erlbaum.

Graesser, A. C., Long, K., & Horgan, D. (1988). A taxonomy for question generation. *Questioning Exchange, 2,* 3–16.

Graesser, A. C., McNamara, D. S., & VanLehn, K. (2005). Scaffolding deep comprehension strategies through Point&Query, AutoTutor, and iSTART. *Educational Psychologist, 40,* 225–234.

Graesser, A. C., Person, N., Lu, Z., Jeon, M. G., & McCaniel, B. (2005b). Learning while holding a conversation with a computer. In L. PytlikZillig, M. Bodvarsson, & R. Bruning (Eds.), *Technology-based education: Bringing researchers and practitioners together.* Greenwich, CT: Information Age.

Graesser, A. C., Singer, M., & Trabasso, T. (1994). Constructing inferences during narrative text comprehension. *Psychological Review, 101*, 371–395.

Graf, P., & Schacter, D. A. (1985). Implicit and explicit memory for new associations in normal and amnesic subjects. *Journal of Experimental Psychology: Learning, Memory, and Cognition, 11*, 501–518.

Graham, S. (2005). Attributions and peer harassment. *Interaction Studies, 6*, 119–130.

Graham, S. (2006a). Writing. In P. Alexander & P. Winne (Eds.), *Handbook of educational psychology* (2nd ed., pp. 457–478). San Diego, CA: Academic Press.

Graham, S. (2006b). Strategy instruction and the teaching of writing: A meta-analysis. In MacArthur, C. A., Graham, S., & Fitzgerald, J. (Eds.), *Handbook of writing research* (pp. 187–207). New York, NY: Guilford.

Graham, S., & Barker, G. P. (1990). The down side of help: An attributional-developmental analysis of helping behavior as a low-ability cue. *Journal of Educational Psychology, 82*, 7–14.

Graham, S., & Harris, K. R. (1993). Self-regulated strategy development: Helping students with learning problems develop as writers. *Elementary School Journal, 94*, 160–181.

Graham, S., & Harris, K. R. (1996). Self-regulation and strategy instruction for students who find writing and learning challenging. In C. M. Levy & S. Ransdell (Eds.), *The science of writing: Theories, methods, individual differences, and applications* (pp. 347–360). Mahwah, NJ: Erlbaum.

Graham, S., Harris, K., & Fink, B. (2000). Is handwriting causally related to learning to write? Treatment of handwriting problems in beginning writers. *Journal of Educational Psychology, 92*, 620–633.

Graham, S., Harris, K. R., & Mason, L. (2005). Improving the writing performance, knowledge, and self-efficacy of struggling young writers: The effects of self-regulated strategy development. *Contemporary Educational Psychology, 30*, 207–241.

Graham, S., & Perin, D. (2007). A meta-analysis of writing instruction for adolescent students. *Journal of Educational Psychology, 99*, 445–476.

Graham, S., & Weiner, B. (1996). Theories and principles of motivation. In D. C. Berliner & R. C. Calfee (Eds.), *Handbook of educational psychology* (pp. 63–84). New York, NY: Macmillan.

Graves, M. F. (2006). *The vocabulary book: Learning and instruction.* New York, NY: Teachers College Press.

Greene, B. A., & Miller, R. B. (1996). Influences of achievement: Goals, perceived ability, and cognitive engagement. *Contemporary Educational Psychology, 21*, 181–192.

Greene, R. L. (1992). *Human memory: Paradigms and paradoxes.* Mahwah, NJ: Erlbaum.

Greeno, J., & Collins, A. (2008). Commentary on the final report of the National Mathematics Advisory Panel. *Educational Researcher, 37*, 623–628.

Greeno, J. G., & van de Sande, C. (2007). Perspectival understanding of conceptions and conceptual growth in interaction. *Educational Psychologist, 42*, 9–23.

Greenwald, A. G., Klinger, M. R., & Lui, T. J. (1989). Unconscious processing of dichoptically masked words. *Memory & Cognition, 17*, 35–47.

Gregoire, M. (2003). Is it a challenge or a threat? A dual-process model of teachers' cognition and appraisal processes during conceptual change. *Educational Psychology Review, 15*, 147–179.

Grigg, W., Donahue, P., & Dion, G. (2007). *The Nation's Report Card: 12th Grade Reading and Mathematics 2005* (NCES 2007-468). Washington, DC: National Center for Education Statistics, Institute of Education Sciences, Department of Education.

Grolnick, W. S., & Ryan, R. M. (1987). Autonomy in children's learning: An experimental and individual difference investigation. *Journal of Personality and Social Psychology, 52*, 890–898.

Guasti, T. (2002). *Language acquisition.* Cambridge, MA: MIT Press.

Gugerty, L. (2007). Cognitive components of trouble shooting strategies. *Thinking & Reasoning, 13*, 134–163.

Gureckis, T. M., & Goldstone, R. L. (2006). Thinking in groups. *Pragmatics & Cognition, 14*, 293–311.

Guskey, T. R., & Passaro, P. D. (1994). Teacher efficacy: A study of construct dimensions. *American Educational Research Journal, 31*, 627–643.

Guthrie, J. T. (1993, August). *An instructional framework for developing motivational and cognitive aspects of reading.* Division 15 Invited Address at the Annual Convention of the American Psychological Association, Toronto.

Guthrie, J. T., Bennett, L., & McGough, K. (1994). *Concept-oriented reading instruction: An integrated curriculum to develop motivations and strategies for reading* (Reading Research Rep. No. 10). College Park, MD: National Reading Research Center.

Guthrie, J. T., McRae, A., & Klauda, S. L. (2007). Contributions of Concept-Oriented Reading Instruction to knowledge about interventions for motivations in reading. *Educational Psychologist, 42,* 237–250.

Guthrie, J. T., Wigfield, A., & Perencevich, K. C. (Eds.). (2004). *Motivating reading comprehension: Concept-Oriented Reading Instruction.* Mahwah, NJ: Erlbaum.

Hall, N. C., Perry, R. P., Goetz, T., Ruthig, J. C., Stupnisky, R. H., & Newall, N. E. (2007). Attributional retraining and elaborative learning: Improving academic development through writing-based interventions. *Learning and Individual Differences, 17,* 280–290.

Halpern, D. F. (1998). Teaching critical thinking for transfer across domains. *American Psychologist, 53,* 449–455.

Halpern, D. F. (2001). Why wisdom? *Educational Psychologist, 36,* 253–256.

Halpern, D. F. (2003). *Thought and knowledge: An introduction to critical thinking* (4th ed.). Mahwah, NJ: Erlbaum.

Hamaker, C. (1986). The effects of adjunct questions on prose learning. *Review of Educational Research, 56,* 212–242.

Hamilton, R. (1985). A framework for the evaluation of the effectiveness of adjunct questions and objectives. *Review of Educational Research, 55,* 47–85.

Hamilton, R., & Ghatala, E. (1994). *Learning and instruction.* New York, NY: McGraw-Hill.

Hammill, D. D., & Swanson, H. L. (2006). The National Reading Panel's meta-analysis of phonics instruction: Another point of view. *Elementary School Journal, 107,* 17–26.

Handel, S. (1988). Space is to time as vision is to audition: Seductive but misleading. *Journal of Experimental Psychology: Human Perception and Performance, 14,* 315–317.

Haney, J., & McArthur, J. (2002). Four case studies of prospective science teachers' beliefs concerning constructivist practices. *Science Education, 86,* 783–802.

Hansen, L., Umeda, Y., & McKinney, M. (2002). Savings in the relearning of second language vocabulary: The effects of time and proficiency. *Language Learning, 52,* 653–678.

Harackiewicz, J. M., Barron, K. E., Tauer, J. M., Carter, S. M., & Elliot, A. J. (2000). Short-term and long-term consequences of achievement goals: Predicting interest and performance over time. *Journal of Educational Psychology, 92,* 316–330.

Hargreaves, A., Earl, L., Moore, S., & Manning. S. (2001). *Learning to change: Teaching beyond subjects and standards.* San Francisco, CA: Jossey-Bass.

Harris, K. R., & Graham, S. (1996). *Making the writing process work: Strategies for composition and self-regulation.* Cambridge, MA: Brookline.

Harris, K. R., Graham, S., & Deshler, D. (Eds.). (1998). *Teaching every child every day: Learning in diverse schools and classrooms.* Cambridge, MA: Brookline.

Harris, K. R., Santangelo, T., & Graham, S. (2008). Self-regulated strategy development in writing: Going beyond NLEs to a more balanced approach. *Instructional Science, 36,* 395–408.

Hart, B., & Risley, T. (2003, October). The early catastrophe. *Education Review, 17,* 110–118.

Hart, E. R., & Speece, D. L. (1998). Reciprocal teaching goes to college: Effects for postsecondary students at risk for academic failure. *Journal of Educational Psychology, 90,* 670–681.

Hashweh, M. Z. (1996). Effects of science teachers' epistemological beliefs in teaching. *Journal of Research in Science Teaching, 33,* 47–63.

Hatcher, P. J., Hulme, C., Miles, J. N. V., Carroll, J. M., Hatcher, J., Gibbs, S., Smith, G., Bowyer-Crane, C., & Snowling, M. J. (2006). Efficacy of small group reading intervention for beginning reader with reading-delay: A randomized controlled trial. *Journal of Child Psychology and Psychiatry, 47,* 820–827.

Hatcher, P. J., Hulme, C., & Snowling, M. J. (2004). Explicit phoneme training combined with phonic reading instruction helps young children at risk of reading failure. *Journal of Child Psychology & Psychiatry, 45,* 338–358.

Hattie, J., Biggs, J., & Purdie, N. (1996). Effects of learning skills interventions on student learning: A -meta-analysis. *Review of Educational Research, 66,* 99–136.

Hawkins, H. L., & Presson, J. C. (1987). Auditory information processing. In K. R. Boff, L. Kaufman & J. P. Thomas (Eds.), *Handbook of perception and human performance: Vol. 2. Information processing* (pp. 26–1 to 26–48). New York, NY: Wiley.

Hayes, B. K., & Hennessy, R. (1996). The nature and development of nonverbal implicit memory. *Journal of Experimental Child Psychology, 63,* 22–43.

Hayes, J. R. (1988). *The complete problem solver* (2nd ed.). Mahwah, NJ: Erlbaum.

Hayes, J. R. (1996). A new framework for understanding cognition and affect in writing. In C. M. Levy & S. Ransdell (Eds.), *The science of writing: Theories, methods, individual differences, and applications* (pp. 1–27). Mahwah, NJ: Erlbaum.

Hayes, J. R. (2006). New directions in writing theory. In MacArthur, C. A., Graham, S., & Fitzgerald, J. (Eds.), *Handbook of writing research* (pp. 28–40). New York, NY: Guilford.

Haygood, R. C., & Bourne, L. E., Jr. (1965). Attribute- and rule-learning aspects of conceptual behavior. *Psychological Review, 72*, 175–196.

Healy, A. F., & McNamara, D. S. (1996). Verbal learning and memory: Does the modal model still work? *Annual Review of Psychology, 47*, 143–172.

Hedberg, P. M. (2009). Learning through reflective classroom practice: Applications to educate the reflective manager. *Journal of Management Education, 33*, 10–36.

Hennessey, B. A., & Amabile, T. M. (1988). The role of the environment in creativity. In R. Sternberg (Ed.), *The nature of creativity: Contemporary psychological perspectives* (pp. 11–38). New York, NY: Cambridge University Press.

Henson, R. K., Kogan, L. R., & Vacha-Haase, T. (2001). A reliability generalization study of the Teacher Efficacy Scale and related instruments. *Educational and Psychological Measurement, 61*, 404–420.

Herbert, E., Lee, A., & Williamson, L. (1998). Teachers' and teacher education students' sense of self-efficacy: Quantitative and qualitative comparisons. *Journal of Research and Development in Education, 31*, 214–225.

Hewitt, J., & Scardamalia, M. (1998). Design principles for distributed knowledge building processes. *Educational Psychology Review, 10*, 75–96.

Hickey, D. T., & Grenade, J. B. (2004). The influence of sociocultural theory on our theories of engagement and motivation. In D. McInerney & S. Van Etten (Eds.), *Sociocultural influences on motivation: Big theories revisited* (pp. 223–247). Greenwich, CT: Information Age.

Hidi, S., & Renninger, K. A. (2006). The four-phase model of interest development. *Educational Psychologist, 41*, 111–127.

Hiebert, E. H., & Raphael, T. E. (1996). Psychological perspectives on literacy and extensions to educational practice. In D. C. Berliner & R. C. Calfee (Eds.), *Handbook of educational psychology* (pp. 550–602). New York, NY: Macmillan.

Hiebert, E. H., & Raphael, T. E. (1998). *Early literacy instruction.* Orlando, FL: Harcourt Brace.

Hiebert, J., Gallimore, R., & Stigler, J. W. (2002). A knowledge base for the teaching profession: What would it look like and how can we get one? *Educational Researcher, 31*, 3–15.

Hiekkila, A., & Lonka, K. (2006). Studying in higher education: Students approaches to learning, self-regulation, and cognitive strategies. *Studies in Higher Education, 31*, 99–117.

Hilden, K. R., & Pressley, M. (2007). Self-regulation through transactional strategies instruction. *Reading and Writing Quarterly, 23*, 51–75.

Hill, H. C., Rowan, B., & Ball, D. L. (2005). Effects of teachers' mathematical knowledge for teaching on student achievement. *American Educational Research Journal, 42*, 371–406.

Hillocks, G., Jr. (2002). *The testing trap: How state writing assessment control learning.* New York: Teachers College Press.

Hinsley, D. A., Hayes, J. R., & Simon, H. A. (1977). From words to equations: Meaning and representation in algebra word problems. In M. A. Just & P. A. Carpenter (Eds.), *Cognitive processes in comprehension* (pp. 89–106). Hillsdale, NJ: Erlbaum.

Hmelo-Silver, C. E. (2004). Problem-based learning: What and how do students learn? *Educational Psychology Review, 16*, 235–266.

Hofer, B. K. (2000). Dimensionality and disciplinary differences in personal epistemology. *Contemporary Educational Psychology, 25*, 378–405.

Hofer, B. K. (2001). Personal epistemology research: Implications for learning and teaching. *Educational Psychology Review, 13*, 353–384.

Hofer, B. K. (2004). Exploring the dimensions of personal epistemology in differing classroom contexts: Student interpretations during the first year of college. *Contemporary Educational Psychology, 29*, 129–163.

Hofer, B. K., & Pintrich, P. R. (1997). The development of epistemological theories: Beliefs about knowledge and knowing and their relation to learning. *Review of Educational Research, 67*, 88–140.

Hoffman, B., & Spatariu, A. (2008). The influence of self-efficacy and metacognitive prompting on math problem-solving efficiency. *Contemporary Educational Psychology, 33*, 875–893.

Hogan, K. (1999). Sociocognitive roles in science group discourse. *Journal of Science Education, 21*, 855–882.

Hogan, K. (2000). Exploring a process view of students' knowledge about the nature of science. *Science Education, 84*, 51–70.

Hogan, K. (2002). Small groups' ecological reasoning while making an environmental management decision. *Journal of Research in Science Teaching, 39*, 341–368.

Hogarth, R. M., Gibbs, B. J., McKenzie, C. R. M., & Marquis, M. A. (1991). Learning from feedback: Exactingness and incentives. *Journal of Experimental Psychology: Learning, Memory, and Cognition, 17*, 734–752.

Holland, J., & Skinner, B. F. (1961). *The analysis of behavior.* New York, NY: McGraw-Hill.

Holt-Reynolds, D. (2000). What does the teacher do? Constructivist pedagogies and prospective teachers' beliefs about the role of the teacher. *Teaching and Teacher Education, 16,* 21–32.

Horst, S. J., Finney, S. J., & Barron, X. (2007). Moving beyond academic achievement goal measures: A study of social achievement goals. *Contemporary Educational Psychology, 32,* 667–698.

Howard, B. C., McGee, S., Schwartz, N., & Purcell, S. (2000). The experience of constructivism: Transforming teacher epistemology. *Journal of Research on Computing in Education, 32,* 455–465.

Howe, M. L. (2000). *The fate of early memories.* Washington, DC: American Psychological Association.

Hudson, T. (1980, July). Young children's difficulty with "How many more than are there?" questions (Doctoral dissertation, Indiana University, 1980). *Dissertation Abstracts International, 41.*

Hull, C. L. (1934). The concept of the habit-family hierarchy and maze learning: Part 1. *Psychological Review, 34,* 33–54.

Hull, C. L. (1952). *A behavior system: An introduction to behavior theory concerning the individual organism.* New Haven, CT: Yale University Press.

Hull, G., Rose, M., Fraser, K. L., & Castellano, M. (1991). Remediation as social construct: Perspectives from an analysis of classroom discourse. *College Composition and Communication, 42,* 299–329.

Hulme, C., & Mackenzie, S. (1992). *Working memory and severe learning difficulties.* Mahwah, NJ: Erlbaum.

Hulme, C., Snowling, M., Caravolas, M., & Carroll, J. (2005). Phonological skills are (probably) one cause of success in learning to read: A comment on Castles and Colheart. *Scientific Studies of Reading, 9,* 351–365.

Humberstone, J., & Reeve, R. A. (2008). Profiles of algebraic competence. *Learning and Instruction, 18,* 354–367.

Hurd, P. D. (2002). Modernizing science education. *Journal of Research in Science Teaching, 39,* 3–9.

Hurst, R. W., & Milkent, M. M. (1996). Facilitating successful prediction problem solving in biology through application of skill theory. *Journal of Research in Science Teaching, 33,* 541–552.

Hyde, A. (2008). Mathematics and cognition: To help students develop a deeper understanding of mathematics concepts, use reading and thinking strategies adapted for math. *Educational Leadership, 65,* 43–47.

Hyde, T. S., & Jenkins, J. J. (1969). Recall for words as a function of semantic, graphic, and syntactic orienting tasks. *Journal of Verbal Learning and Verbal Behavior, 12,* 471–480.

Intons-Peterson, M. J. (1993). Imagery and classification. In A. F. Collins, S. E. Gathercole, M. A. Conway, & P. E. Morris (Eds.), *Theories of memory* (pp. 211–240). Hove, UK: Erlbaum.

Israel, S. E., Block, C. C., Bauserman, K. L., & Kinnucan-Welsch, K. (2005). *Metacognition in literacy learning: Theory, assessment, instruction, and professional development.* Mahwah, NJ: Erlbaum.

Israel, S. E., & Duffy, G. G. (Eds.) (2009). *Handbook of research on reading comprehension.* New York: Routledge.

Jacobs, J. E., & Paris, S. G. (1987). Children's metacognition about reading: Issues in definition, measurement, and instruction. *Educational Psychologist, 22,* 255–278.

Jacoby, L. L. (1978). On interpreting the effects of repetition: Solving a problem versus remembering a solution. *Journal of Verbal Learning and Verbal Behavior, 17,* 649–667.

Jacoby, L. L. (1983). Remembering the date: Analyzing interactive processes in reading. *Journal of Verbal Learning and Verbal Behavior, 22,* 485–508.

Jacoby, L. L., & Craik, F. I. M. (1979). Effects of elaboration of processing at encoding and retrieval: Trace distinctiveness and recovery of initial context. In L. S. Cermak & F. I. M. Craik (Eds.), *Levels of processing in human memory* (pp. 1–22). Mahwah, NJ: Erlbaum.

Jacoby, L. L., Craik, F. I. M., & Begg, I. (1979). Effects of decision difficulty on recognition and recall. *Journal of Verbal Learning and Verbal Behavior, 18,* 585–600.

Jacoby, L. L., & Witherspoon, D. (1982). Remembering without awareness. *Canadian Journal of Psychology, 36,* 300–324.

Jansen, A. (2008). An investigation between the relationships of seventh-graders beliefs and their participation during mathematics discussions in two classrooms. *Mathematical Thinking and Learning, 10,* 68–100.

Jay, J. K. (2003). *Quality teaching: Reflection as the heart of practice.* Lanham, MD: Scarecrow Press.

Jehng, J. J., Johnson, S. D., & Anderson, R. C. (1993). Schooling and students' epistemological beliefs about learning. *Contemporary Educational Psychology, 18,* 23–35.

Jenkins, J. J. (1974). Remember that old theory of memory? Well, forget it! *American Psychologist, 25,* 785–795.

Jensen, A. R. (1992). Understanding *g* in terms of information processing. *Educational Psychology Review, 4,* 271–308.

Jitendra, A. K., Griffin, C. C., Haria, P., Leh, J., Adams, A., & Kaduvettoor, A. (2007). A comparison of single and multiple strategy instruction on third grade students' mathematical problem solving. *Journal of Educational Psychology, 99,* 115–127.

Jitendra, A. K., Star, J. R., Starosta, K., Leh, J. M., Sood, S., Caskie, G., Hughes, C. L., & Mack, T. R. (2009). Improving seventh grade students' learning of ratio and proportion: The role of schema-based instruction. *Contemporary Educational Psychology, 34,* 250–264.

Johnson, C., Kahle, J. B., & Fargo, J. D. (2007). Effective teaching results in increased science achievement for all students. *Science Education, 91,* 371–383.

Johnson, E. J. (1988). Expertise and decision under uncertainty: Performance and process. In M. Chi, R. Glaser, & M. Farr (Eds.), *The nature of expertise* (pp. 209–228). Mahwah, NJ: Erlbaum.

Johnson, M. B., Tenenbaum, G., & Edmonds, W. A. (2006). Adaption to physically and emotionally demanding conditions: The role of deliberate practice. *High Ability Studies, 17,* 117–136.

Johnson, M. K., Hashtroudi, S., & Lindsay, D. S. (1993). Source monitoring. *Psychological Bulletin, 114,* 3–28.

John-Steiner, V. (1997). *Notebooks of the mind: Explorations of thinking* (rev. ed.). New York, NY: Oxford University Press.

Johnston, P., Woodside-Jiron, H., & Day, J. (2001). Teaching and learning literate epistemologies. *Journal of Educational Psychology, 93,* 223–233.

Jonassen, D. H. (2003). Designing research-based instruction for story problems. *Educational Psychology Review, 15,* 267–296.

Jones, P. E. (2009). From external speech to inner speech in Vygotsky: A critical appraisal and fresh perspectives. *Communication Studies, 29,* 161–188.

Joram, E. (2007). Clashing epistemologies: Aspiring teachers', practicing teachers', and professors' beliefs and knowledge and research in education. *Teaching and Teacher Education, 23,* 123–135.

Jordan, N. C., & Hanich, L. B. (2000). Mathematical thinking in second-grade children with different types of learning difficulties. *Journal of Learning Disabilities, 33,* 567–578.

Juel, C. (1996). What makes literacy tutoring effective? *Reading Research Quarterly, 31,* 268–289.

Jussim, L., & Eccles, J. S. (1992). Teacher expectations II: Construction and reflection of student achievement. *Journal of Personality and Social Psychology, 63,* 947–961.

Just, M. A. & Carpenter, P. A. (1987). *The psychology of reading and language comprehension.* Boston: Allyn & Bacon.

Just, M. A., & Carpenter, P. A. (1992). A capacity theory of comprehension: Individual differences in working memory. *Psychological Review, 99,* 122–149.

Kagan, D. M. (1992). Implications of research on teacher belief. *Educational Psychologist, 27,* 65–90.

Kahneman, D., & Frederick, S. (2005). A model of heuristic judgment. In K. Holyoak & R. Morrison (Eds.), *The Cambridge handbook of thinking and reasoning* (pp. 267–294). Cambridge, UK: Cambridge University Press.

Kalyuga, S., Ayres, P., Chandler, P., & Sweller, J. (2003). The expertise reversal effect: *Educational Psychologist, 38,* 23–31.

Kalyuga, S., Chandler, P., & Sweller, J. (2000). Incorporating learning experience into the design of multimedia instruction. *Journal of Educational Psychology, 92,* 126–136.

Kalyuga, S., Chandler, P., Tuovinen, J., & Sweller, J. (2001). When problem solving is superior to studying worked examples. *Journal of Educational Psychology, 93,* 579–588.

Kang, N. W., & Wallace, C. S. (2004). Secondary science teachers' use of laboratory activities: Linking epistemological beliefs, goals, and practices. *Science Education, 88,* 140–165.

Kaplan, A., & Maehr, M. L. (1999). Achievement goals and student well-being. *Contemporary Educational Psychology, 24,* 330–358.

Kardash, C. M., & Scholes, R. J. (1996). Effects of preexisting beliefs, epistemological beliefs, and need for cognition on interpretation of controversial issues. *Journal of Educational Psychology, 88,* 260–271.

Karpicke, J. D., & Roediger, H. L. III. (2007). Repeated retrieval during learning is the key to long-term retention. *Journal of Memory and Language, 57,* 151–162.

Karpicke, J. D., & Roediger, H. L. III. (2008). The critical importance of retrieval for learning. *Science, 319,* 966–968.

Katzir, T., & Paré-Blagoev, J. (2006). Applying cognitive neuroscience research to education: The case of literacy. *Educational Psychologist, 41,* 53–74.

Kazdin, A. E. (2001). *Behavior modification in applied settings* (6th ed.). Belmont, CA: Wadsworth.

Keenan, J. M., Betjemann, R. S., & Olson, R. K. (2008). Reading comprehension tests vary in the skills they assess: Differential dependence on decoding and oral comprehension. *Scientific Studies of Reading, 12,* 281–300.

Kellogg, R. T. (2008). Training writing skills: A cognitive developmental perspective. *Journal of Writing Research, 1*, 1–26.

Kelly, S. (2007). Classroom discourse and the distribution of engagement. *Social Psychology of Education, 10*, 331–352.

Kendeou, P., van den Broek, P., White, J. J., & Lynch, J. (2007). Comprehension in preschool and early elementary children: Skill development and strategy interventions. In D. S. McNamara (Ed.). *Reading comprehension strategies: Theories, interventions, and technologies* (pp. 27–45). New York, NY: Erlbaum.

Kilpatrick, J. (1985). Doing mathematics without understanding it: A commentary on Higbee and Kunihira. *Educational Psychologist, 20*, 65–68.

Kilpatrick, J., Swafford, J., & Findell, B. (Eds.). (2001). *Adding it up: Helping children learn mathematics.* Washington, DC: National Academies Press.

Kimball, M. M. (1989). A new perspective on women's math achievement. *Psychological Bulletin, 105*, 198–214.

Kincheloe, J. L. (2005). *Critical constructivism primer.* New York, NY: Peter Lang Publishers.

King, A. (1991). Effects of training in strategic questioning on children's problem-solving performance. *Journal of Educational Psychology, 83*, 307–317.

King, A. (1994). Guiding knowledge construction in the classroom: Effects of teaching children how to question and how to explain. *American Educational Research Journal, 31*, 338–368.

King, A. (2007). Beyond literal comprehension: A strategy to promote deep understanding of text. In D. S. McNamara (Ed.). *Reading comprehension strategies: Theories, interventions, and technologies* (pp. 267–290). New York, NY: Erlbaum.

King, A., & Rosenshine, B. (1993). Effects of guided cooperative questioning on children's knowledge construction. *Journal of Experimental Education, 61*, 127–148.

King, A., Staffieri, A., & Adelgeis, A. (1998). Mutual peer tutoring: Effects of structuring tutorial interaction to scaffold peer learning. *Journal of Educational Psychology, 90*, 134–152.

King, P. M., & Kitchener, K. S. (1994). *Developing reflective judgment.* San Francisco, CA: Jossey-Bass.

King, P. M., & Kitchener, K. S. (2002). The reflective judgment model: Twenty years of research on epistemic cognition. In B. K. Hofer & P. R. Pintrich (Eds.), *Personal epistemology: The psychology of beliefs about knowledge and knowing* (pp. 37–62). Mahwah, NJ: Erlbaum.

King, P. M., Wood, P. K., & Mines, R. A. (1990). Critical thinking among college and graduate students. *Review of Higher Education, 13*, 167–186.

Kintsch, W. (1974). *The representation of meaning in memory.* Mahwah, NJ: Erlbaum.

Kintsch, W. (1986). Learning from text. *Cognition and Instruction, 3*, 87–108.

Kintsch, W. (1988). The role of knowledge in discourse comprehension: A construction-integration model. *Psychology Review, 95*, 163–182.

Kintsch, W. (1998). *Comprehension: A paradigm for cognition.* Cambridge, UK: Cambridge University Press.

Kintsch, W. (2005). An overview of top-down and bottom-up effective in comprehension: The CI perspective. *Discourse Professes, 39*(2&3), 125–128.

Kintsch, W., & Greeno, J. G. (1985). Understanding and solving arithmetic word problems. *Psychological Review, 92*, 109–129.

Kintsch, W., & Van Dijk, T. A. (1978). Toward a model of text comprehension and production. *Psychological Review, 85*, 363–394.

Kirschner, P. A., Sweller, J., & Clark, R. E. (2006). Why minimal guidance during instruction does not work: An analysis of the failure of constructivist, discovery, and problem-based, experiential, and inquiry-based teaching. *Educational Psychologist, 41*, 75–86.

Kitchener, K. S. (1983). Cognition, metacognition, and epistemic cognition. *Human Development, 26*, 222–232.

Kitchener, K. S., & Fischer, K. W. (1990). A skill approach to the development of reflective thinking. In D. Kuhn (Ed.), *Developmental perspectives on teaching and learning thinking skills* (pp. 48–62). Basel, Switzerland: Karger.

Kitchener, K. S., & King, P. A. (1981). Reflective judgment: Concepts of justification and their relationship to age and education. *Journal of Applied Developmental Psychology, 2*, 89–116.

Kitchener, K. S., & King, P. M. (2004). Reflective judgment: Theory and research on the development of epistemic assumptions through adulthood. *Educational Psychologist, 39*, 5–18.

Kitchener, K. S., King, P. M., & DeLuca, S. (2006). Development of reflective judgment in adulthood. In C. Hoare (Ed.), *The handbook of adult development and learning* (pp. 73–98). New York, NY: Oxford University Press.

Klein, S. B., Cosmides, L., Tooby, J., & Chance, S. (2002). Decisions and the evolution of memory: Multiple systems, multiple functions. *Psychological Review, 109*, 306–329.

Klibanoff, R., Levine, S. C., Huttenlocher, J., Vasilyeva, M., & Hedges, L. (2006). Preschool children's mathematical knowledge: The effect of teacher "math talk." *Developmental Psychology, 42*, 59–69.

Kluger, B. B. (1999). Recognizing inquiry: Comparing three hands-on teaching techniques. In *Foundations series: Vol. 2. Inquiry thoughts, views, and strategies for the K–5 classroom: A monograph for professionals in science, mathematics and technology education* (NSF Publication No. 99–148, pp. 39–50). Arlington, VA: National Science Foundation.

Kluwe, R. H. (1987). Executive decisions and regulation of problem solving. In F. Weinert & R. Kluwe (Eds.), *Metacognition, motivation, and understanding* (pp. 31–64). Mahwah, NJ: Erlbaum.

Koedinger, K. R., & Nathan, M. M. (2004). The real story behind story problems: Effects of representations on quantitative reasoning. *Journal of the Learning Sciences, 13*, 129–164.

Koedinger, K. R., Alibali, M. W., & Nathan, M. M. (2008). Trade-offs between grounded and abstract representations: Evidence from algebra problem solving. *Cognitive Science, 32*, 366–397.

Köhler, W. (1929). *Gestalt psychology.* New York, NY: Liveright.

Kohn, A. (1996). By all available means: Cameron and Pierce's defense of extrinsic motivators. *Review of Educational Research, 66*, 1–4.

Kolers, P. A. (1975). Memorial consequences of automatized encoding. *Journal of Experimental Psychology: Human Learning and Memory, 1*, 689–701.

Kosslyn, S. M. (1994). *Image and brain: The resolution of the imagery debate.* Cambridge: MIT Press.

Kotovsky, K. (2003). *Problem solving.* In J. E. Davidson & R. J. Sternberg (Eds.), *The psychology of problem solving* (pp. 373–384). Cambridge, UK: Cambridge University Press.

Kozhevnikov, M., Kosslyn, S., & Shephard, J. (2005). Spatial versus object visualizers: A new characterization of visual cognitive style. *Memory & Cognition, 33*, 710–726.

Krajcik, R. (2006). Practical considerations in high-stakes testing and NCLB. *Measurement, 4*, 250–254.

Krasny, K. A., Sadoski, M., & Paivio, A. (2007). Unwarranted return: A response to McVee, Dunsmore, and Gavelek's (2005) "Schema theory revisited." *Review of Educational Research, 77*, 239–244.

Kroll, L. A. (2004). Constructing constructivism: How student–teachers construct ideas of development, knowledge, learning, and teaching. *Teachers and Teaching: Theory and Practice, 10*, 199–221.

Kuhn, D. (1989). Children and adults as intuitive scientists. *Psychological Review, 96*, 674–689.

Kuhn, D. (1991). *The skills of argument.* New York, NY: Cambridge University Press.

Kuhn, D. (1992). Thinking as argument. *Harvard Educational Review, 62*, 155–178.

Kuhn, D. (1999). A developmental model of critical thinking. *Educational Researcher, 28*, 16–26.

Kuhn, D., Amsel, E., & O'Loughlin, M. (1988). *The development of scientific reasoning skills.* San Diego, CA: Academic Press.

Kuhn, D., Cheney, R., & Weinstock, M. (2000). The development of epistemological understanding. *Cognitive Development, 15*, 309–328.

Kuhn, D., Iordarnou, K., Pease, M., & Warkala, C. (2008). Beyond the control of variables: What needs to develop to achieve scientific reasoning? *Cognitive Development, 23*, 435–451.

Kuhn, D., & Loa, J. (1998). Contemplation and conceptual change: Integrating perspectives from social and cognitive psychology. *Developmental Review, 18*, 125–154.

Kuhn, D., Schauble, L., & Garcia-Mila, M. (1992). Cross-domain development of scientific reasoning. *Cognition and Instruction, 9*, 285–327.

Kuhn, D., Shaw, V., & Felton, M. (1997). Effects of dyadic interaction on argumentative reasoning. *Cognition and Instruction, 15*, 287–315.

Kuhn, D., & Weinstock, M. (2002). What is epistemological thinking and why does it matter? In B. K. Hofer & P. R. Pintrich (Eds.), *Personal epistemology: The psychology of beliefs about knowledge and knowing* (pp. 121–144). Mahwah, NJ: Erlbaum.

Kuhn, M. R., & Stahl, S. A. (2003). Fluency: A review of developmental and remedial practices. *Journal of Educational Psychology, 95*, 3–21.

Kuo, L., & Anderson, R. C. (2006). Morphological awareness and learning to read: A cross-cultural perspective. *Educational Psychologist, 31*, 161–180.

Kurfiss, J. G. (1988). *Critical thinking: Theory, research, practice, and possibilities* (Rep. No. 2). Washington, DC: Association for the Study of Higher Education.

LaBerge, D., & Samuels, S. J. (1974). Toward a theory of automatic information processing in reading. *Cognitive Psychology, 6*, 283–323.

Lajoie, S. P. (2003). Transitions and trajectories for studies of expertise. *Educational Researcher, 32*, 21–25.

Lajoie, S.P., & Azevedo, R. (2006). Teaching and learning in technology-rich environments. In P. Alexander & P. Winne (Eds.), *Handbook of educational psychology* (2nd ed.) (pp. 803–821). Mahwah, NJ: Erlbaum.

Lakin, J. L., Giesler, R. B., Morris, K. A., & Vosmik, J. R. (2007). HOMER as an acronym for the scientific method. *Teaching of Psychology, 34,* 94–96.

Landauer, T. K., & Dumais, S. T. (1997). A solution to Plato's problem: The latent semantic analysis theory of acquisition, induction, and representation of knowledge. *Psychological Review, 104,* 211–240.

Larkin, J. H. (1977). *Skilled problem solving in experts* (Tech. Rep.). Berkeley: University of California, Group in Science and Mathematics Education.

Larrivee, B. (2006). *An educator's guide to teacher reflection.* Boston, MA: Houghton Mifflin.

Larrivee, B. (2008). Development of a tool to assess teachers' level of reflective practice. *Reflective Practice, 9,* 341–360.

Lau, S., & Nie, Y. (2008). Interplay between personal goals and classroom goal structures in predicting student outcomes: A multilevel analysis of person–context interactions. *Journal of Educational Psychology, 100,* 15–29.

Lave, J. (1988). *Cognition in practice: Mind, mathematics and culture in everyday life.* Cambridge, UK: Cambridge University Press.

Lave, J., & Wenger, E. (1991). *Situated learning: Legitimate peripheral participation.* New York, NY: Cambridge University Press.

Lee, H. J. (2005). Understanding and assessing preservice teachers' reflective thinking. *Teaching and Teacher Education, 21,* 699–715.

Lee, J., Grigg, W., & Dion, G. (2007). *The Nation's Report Card: Mathematics 2007* (NCES 2007-494). Washington, DC: National Center for Education Statistics, Institute of Education Sciences, U.S. Department of Education.

Lee, J., Grigg, W., & Donahue, P. (2007). *The Nation's Report Card: Reading 2007* (NCES 2007-496). Washington, DC: National Center for Education Statistics, Institute of Education Sciences, U.S. Department of Education.

Leelawong, K., & Biswas, G. (2008). Designing learning by teaching agents: The Betty's Brain system. *International Journal of Artificial Intelligence in Education, 18,* 181–208.

Lehman, D. R., Lempert, R. O., & Nisbett, R. E. (1988). The effects of graduate training on reasoning. *American Psychologist, 43,* 431–442.

Lehman, S., Schraw, G., McCrudden, M. T., & Hartley, K. (2007). Processing and recall of seductive details in scientific text. *Contemporary Educational Psychology, 32,* 569–587.

Leinhardt, G., & Steele, M. D. (2005). Seeing the complexity of standing to the side: Instructional dialogues. *Cognition and Instruction, 23,* 87–163.

Leont'ev, A. N. (1981). *Problems in the development of mind.* Moscow: Progress.

Lesgold, A. (1988). Problem solving. In R. Sternberg & E. Smith (Eds.), *The psychology of human thought* (pp. 188–213). New York, NY: Cambridge University Press.

Leslie, L., & Caldwell, J. (2009). Formal and informal measures of reading comprehension. In S. E. Israel & G. G. Duffy (Eds.), *Handbook of research on reading comprehension* (pp. 403–427). New York, NY: Routledge.

Levesque, C., Zuehlke, A. N., Stanek, L. R., & Ryan, R. M. (2004). Autonomy and competence in German and American university students: A comparative study based on self-determination theory. *Journal of Educational Psychology, 96,* 68–84.

Levin, J. R. (1986). Four cognitive principles of learning-strategy instruction. *Educational Psychologist, 21,* 3–17.

Levin, J. R. (1993). Mnemonic strategies and classroom learning: A 20-year report card. *Elementary School Journal, 94,* 235–244.

Levitt, K. E. (2001). An analysis of elementary teachers' beliefs regarding the teaching and learning of science. *Science Education, 86,* 1–22.

Lewandowsky, S., & Heit, E. (2006). Some targets for memory models. *Journal of Memory and Language, 55,* 441–446.

Lhyle, K. G., & Kulhavy, R. W. (1987). Feedback processing and error correction. *Journal of Educational Psychology, 79,* 320–322.

Lidar, M., Lundqvist, E., & Ostman, L. (2005). Teaching and learning in the science classroom: The interplay between teachers' epistemological moves and students' practical epistemologies. *Science Education, 90,* 148–163.

Limon, M. (2001). On the cognitive conflict as an instructional strategy for conceptual change: A critical appraisal. *Learning and Instruction, 11,* 357–380.

Limon, M. (2003). The role of domain-specific knowledge in intentional conceptual change. In G. M. Sinatra & P. R. Pintrich (Eds.), *Intentional conceptual change* (pp. 133–170). Mahwah, NJ: Erlbaum.

Limon, M., & Mason, L. (2002). *Reconsidering conceptual change: Issues in theory and practice.* Dordrecht, Netherlands: Kluwer.

Linn, M. C. (2005). WISE design for lifelong learning—pivotal cases. In P. Gardenfors & P. Johansson (Eds.), *Cognition, education, and communication technology* (pp. 223–255). Mahwah, NJ: Erlbaum.

Linn, M. C. & Eylon, B.-S. (2006). Science education: Integrating views of learning and instruction. In P. A. Alexander & P. H. Winne (Eds.), *Handbook of educational psychology* (2nd ed., pp. 511–544). Mahwah, NJ: Erlbaum.

Linn, M. C., Songer, N. B., & Eylon, B. (1996). Shifts and convergences in science learning and instruction. In D. C. Berliner & R. C. Calfee (Eds.), *Handbook of educational psychology* (pp. 438–490). New York, NY: Macmillan.

Linnenbrink, E. A. (2005). The dilemma of performance-approach goals: The use of multiple goal contexts to promote students' motivation and learning. *Journal of Educational Psychology, 97,* 197–213.

Litman, L., & Reber, A. S. (2005). Implicit cognition and thought. In K. Holyoak & R. Morrison (Eds.), *The Cambridge handbook of thinking and reasoning* (pp. 431–453). Cambridge, UK: Cambridge University Press.

Lockhart, R. S. (2002). Levels of processing, transfer-appropriate processing, and the concept of robust encoding. *Memory, 10*(5/6), 297–403.

Lodewyk, K. R. (2007). Relations among epistemological beliefs, academic achievement, and task performance in secondary school students. *Educational Psychology, 27,* 307–327.

Lodewyk, K. R., & Winne, P. H. (2005). Relations among the structure of learning tasks, achievement, and changes in self-efficacy in secondary students. *Journal of Educational Psychology, 97,* 3–12.

Loftus, E. F., & Loftus, G. R. (1980). On the permanence of stored information in the human brain. *American Psychologist, 35,* 409–420.

Loftus, E. F., Green, E. E., & Smith, R. H. (1980). How deep is the meaning of life? *Bulletin of the Psychonomic Society, 15,* 282–284.

Lonigan, C. J., Burgess, S. R., & Anthony, J. L. (2000). Development of emergent literacy and early reading skills in preschool children: Evidence from a latent-variable longitudinal study. *Developmental Psychology, 36,* 596–613.

Lopes, M. P., & Cunha, M. P. (2008). Who is more proactive, the optimist or the pessimist? Exploring the role of hope as a moderator. *Journal of Positive Psychology, 3,* 100–109.

Lorch, R. F., Jr. (1989). Text-signaling devices and their effects on reading and memory processes. *Educational Psychology Review, 1,* 209–234.

Lorch, R. F., Jr., & Lorch, E. P. (1995). Effects of organizational signals on text-processing strategies. *Journal of Educational Psychology, 87,* 537–544.

Louca, L., Elby, A., Hammer, D., & Kagey, T. (2004). Epistemological resources: Applying a new epistemological framework to science instruction. *Educational Psychologist, 39,* 57–68.

Lovett, M. C. (2002). Problem solving. In D. Medin (Ed.), *Stevens' handbook of experimental psychology: Vol. 2. Memory and cognitive processes* (3rd ed., pp. 317–362). New York, NY: Wiley.

Lovett, M. C., & Anderson, J. R. (2005). Thinking as a production system. In K. Holyoak & R. Morrison (Eds.), *The Cambridge handbook of thinking and reasoning* (pp. 401–430). Cambridge, UK: Cambridge University Press.

Loyens, S. M., Rikers, R. M., & Schmidt, G. H. (2008). Relationship between students' conceptions of constructivist learning and their regulation and processing strategies. *Instructional Science, 36,* 445–262.

Loyens, S. M., Rikers, R. M., & Schmidt, G. H. (2009). Students' conceptions of constructivist learning in different programme years and different learning environments. *British Journal of Educational Psychology, 79,* 501–514.

Lyons, C., Pinnell, G., & DeFord, D. (1993). *Partners in learning: Teachers and children in reading recovery.* New York, NY: Teachers College Press.

Lyons, N. (2006). Reflective engagement as professional development in the lives of university teachers. *Teachers and Teaching: Theory and practice, 12,* 151–168.

Mabry, L. (1999). Writing to the rubric. *Phi Delta Kappan, 126,* 673–679.

MacDonald, M. C., & Christiansen, M. H. (2002). Reassessing working memory: Comment on Just and Carpenter (1992) and Waters and Caplan (1996). *Psychological Review, 109,* 35–54.

MacLeod, C. M. (1988). Forgotten but not gone: Savings for pictures and words in long-term memory. *Journal of Experimental Psychology: Learning, Memory, and Cognition, 14,* 195–212.

Macklin, C., & McDaniel, M. A. The bizarreness effect: Dissociation between item and source memory. *Memory, 13*(7), 682–689.

Maddux, S. (2002). Self-efficacy: The power of believing you can. In C. R. Snyder & S. J. Lopez (Eds.), *Handbook of positive psychology* (pp. 277–287). London: Oxford University Press.

Magliano, J. P., Todaro, S., Millis, K. K., Wiemer-Hastings, K., Kim, H. J., & McNamara, D. S. (2005). Changes in reading strategies as a function of reading training: A comparison of live and computerized training. *Journal of Educational Computing Research, 32,* 185–208.

Mandler, G. (2002a). Origins of the cognitive (r)evolution. *Journal of History of the Behavioral Sciences, 38,* 339–353.

Mandler, G. (2002b). Organisation: What levels of processing are levels of. *Memory, 10,* 333–338.

Mandler, J. M. (1984). *Stories, scripts, and scenes: Aspects of schema theory.* Mahwah, NJ: Erlbaum.

Mansfield, R. S., Busse, T. V., & Krepelka, E. J. (1978). The effectiveness of creativity training. *Review of Educational Research, 48,* 517–536.

Markman, E. M. (1979). Realizing that you don't understand: Elementary school children's awareness of inconsistencies. *Child Development, 50,* 643–655.

Marra, R. (2005). Teacher beliefs: The impact of the design of constructivist learning environments on instructor epistemologies. *Learning Environments Research, 8,* 135–155.

Martin, J. (2006). Social cognitive perspectives in educational psychology. In P. A. Alexander & P. H. Winne (Eds.), *Handbook of educational psychology* (2nd ed., pp. 595–614). Mahwah, NJ: Erlbaum.

Martin, V., & Pressley, M. (1991). Elaborative integration effects depend on the nature of the question. *Journal of Educational Psychology, 83,* 253–263.

Marzano, R. J. (1992). *A different kind of classroom: Teaching with dimensions of learning.* Alexandria, VA: Association for Supervision and Curriculum Development.

Mason, J. M., Herman, P. A., & Au, K. H. (1991). Children's developing knowledge of words. In J. Flood, J. M. Jensen, D. Lapp, & J. R. Squire (Eds.), *Handbook of research on teaching the English language arts* (pp. 721–731). New York, NY: Macmillan.

Masonheimer, R. E., Drum, P. A., & Ehri, L. C. (1984). Does environmental print identification lead children into word reading? *Journal of Reading Behavior, 16,* 257–271.

Mastropieri, M., & Scruggs, T. (1989). Constructing more meaningful relationships: Mnemonic instruction for special populations. *Educational Psychology Review, 1,* 83–111.

Matsumura, L.C., Patthey-Chavez, G.G., Valdés, R., Garnier, H. (2002). Teacher feedback, writing assignment quality, and third-grade students' revision in lower-

and higher-achieving urban schools. *Elementary School Journal, 103,* 3–25

Mayer, R. E. (1981). Frequency norms and structural analysis of algebra word problems into families, categories, and templates. *Instructional Science, 10,* 135–175.

Mayer, R. E. (1982). Memory for algebra story problems. *Journal of Educational Psychology, 74,* 199–216.

Mayer, R. E. (2008). *Learning and instruction.* Upper Saddle River, NJ: Pearson.

Mayer, R. E., & Chandler, P. (2001). When learning is just a click away: Does simple user interaction foster deeper understanding of multimedia messages? *Journal of Educational Psychology, 93,* 390–397.

Mayer, R. E., & Hegarty, M. (1996). The process of understanding mathematical problems. In R. J. Sternberg & T. Ben-Zeev (Eds.), *The nature of mathematical thinking* (pp. 29–53). Mahwah, NJ: Erlbaum.

Mayer, R. E., Heiser, J., & Lonn, S. (2001). Cognitive constraints on multimedia learning: When presenting more materials results in less understanding. *Journal of Educational Psychology, 92,* 312–320.

Mayer, R. E., & Moreno, R. (1998). A split-attention effect in multimedia learning: Evidence for dual processing systems in working memory. *Journal of Educational Psychology, 90,* 312–320.

Mayer, R. E., & Moreno, R. (2002). Aids to computer-based multimedia learning. *Learning and Instruction, 12,* 107–119.

Mayer, R. E., & Moreno, R. (2003). Nine ways to reduce cognitive load in multimedia learning. In R. Bruning, C. Horn, & L. PytlikZillig (Eds.), *Web-based learning: What do we know? Where do we go?* (pp. 23–44). Greenwich, CT: Information Age.

Mayer, R. E., & Wittrock, M. C. (2006). Problem solving. In P. A. Alexander & P. H. Winne (Eds.), *Handbook of educational psychology* (2nd ed., pp. 287–303). Mahwah, NJ: Erlbaum.

Mazzie, C. A. (1987). An experimental investigation of the determinants of implicitness in spoken and written discourse. *Discourse Processes, 10,* 31–42.

McCann, R. S., Besner, D., & Davelaar, E. (1988). Word recognition and identification: Do word-frequency effects reflect lexical access? *Journal of Experimental Psychology: Human Perception and Performance, 14,* 693–706.

McCaslin, M. (2004). Coregulation of opportunity, activity, and identity in student motivation: Elaborations on Vygotskian themes. In D. McInerney & S. Van Etten (Eds.), *Sociocultural influences on motivation:*

Big theories revisited (pp. 249–274). Greenwich, CT: Information Age.

McClelland, J. L. (1988). Connectionist models and psychological evidence. *Journal of Memory and Language, 27,* 107–123.

McClelland, J. L., McNaughton, B. L., & O'Reilly, R. C. (1995). Why there are complementary learning systems in the hippocampus and neocortex: Insight from the successes and failures of connectionist models of learning and memory. *Psychological Review, 102,* 419–457.

McClelland, J. L., Rumelhart, D. E., & Hinton, G. E. (1986). The appeal of parallel distributed processing. In D. E. Rumelhart, J. L. McClelland, & PDP Research Group (Eds.), *Parallel distributed processing: Explorations in the microstructures of cognition: Vol. 1. Foundations* (pp. 3–44). Cambridge: MIT Press.

McClelland, J. L., & Seidenberg, M. S. (2000). Why do kids say *goed* and *brang? Science, 287,* 47–48.

McCloskey, M., Caramazza, A., & Green, B. (1980). Curvilinear motion in the absence of external forces: Naive beliefs about the motion of objects. *Science, 210,* 1139–1141.

McCloskey, M., Wible, C. G., & Cohen, N. J. (1988). Is there a special flashbulb-memory mechanism? *Journal of Experimental Psychology: General, 117,* 171–181.

McConkie, G. (1997). Eye movement contingent display control: Personal reflections and comments. *Scientific Studies of Reading, 1,* 303–316.

McCrone, S. S. (2005). The development of mathematical discussions: An investigation in a fifth-grade classroom. *Mathematical Thinking and Learning, 7,* 111–133.

McCrudden, M. T., & Schraw, G. (2007). Relevance and goal-focusing in text processing. *Educational Psychology Review, 19,* 113–139.

McCutchen, D. (2006). Cognitive factors in the development of children's writing. In MacArthur, C. A., Graham, S., & Fitzgerald, J. (Eds.), *Handbook of writing research* (pp. 115–130). New York, NY: Guilford.

McCutchen, D., Francis, M., & Kerr, S. (1997). Revising for meaning: Effects of knowledge and strategy. *Journal of Educational Psychology, 89,* 667–676.

McCutchen, D., Teske, P., & Bankston, C. (2008). Writing and cognition: Implications of the cognitive architecture for learning to write and writing to learn. In C. Bazerman (Ed.), *Handbook of research on writing: History, society, school, individual, text* (pp. 451–470). New York, NY: Erlbaum.

McDaniel, M. A., Anderson, J. L., Derbish, M. H., & Morrisette, N. (2007). Testing the testing effect in the classroom. *European Journal of Cognitive Psychology, 19,* 494–513.

McDaniel, M. A., & Einstein, G. O. (1989). Material appropriate processing. *Educational Psychology Review, 1,* 113–145.

McDaniel, M. A., Einstein, G. O., DeLosh, E. L., & May, C. P. (1995). The bizarreness effect: It's not surprising, it's complex. *Journal of Experimental Psychology: Learning, Memory, and Cognition, 21,* 422–435.

McDougall, R. (1904). Recognition and recall. *Journal of Philosophical and Scientific Methods, 1,* 229–233.

McElroy, L. A., & Slamecka, N. J. (1982). Memorial consequences of generating nonwords: Implications for semantic memory interpretations of the generation effect. *Journal of Verbal Learning and Verbal Behavior, 21,* 249–259.

McInerney, D. M. (2000). Helping kids achieve their best: Understanding and using motivation in the classroom. St. Leonards, New South Wales, Australia: Allen & Unwin.

McIntyre, E., & Pressley, M. (Eds.). (1996). *Balanced instruction: Strategies and skills in whole language.* Norwood, MA: Christopher-Gordon.

McKoon, G., & Ratcliff, R. (1986). Inferences about predictable events. *Journal of Experimental Psychology: Learning, Memory, and Cognition, 12,* 82–91.

McNamara, D. S. (2004). SERT: Self-explanation reading training. *Discourse Processes, 38,* 1–30.

McNamara, D. S. (Ed.). (2007). *Reading comprehension strategies: Theories, interventions, and technologies.* New York, NY: Erlbaum.

McNamara, D. S., Levinstein, I. B., & Boonthum, C. (2004). ISTART: Interactive strategy training for active reading and thinking. *Behavior Research Methods, Instruments, & Computers, 36,* 222–233.

McNamara, D. S., O'Reilly, T., Rowe, M., Boonthum, C., & Levinstein, I. (2007). iSTART: A web-based tutor that teachers self-explanation and metacognitive reading strategies. In D. S. McNamara (Ed.). *Reading comprehension strategies: Theories, interventions, and technologies* (pp. 397–420). New York, NY: Erlbaum.

McNamee, G. D. (1987). The social origins of narrative skills. In M. Hickmann (Ed.), *Social and functional approaches to language and thought* (pp. 287–304). San Diego, CA: Academic Press.

McNeill, K., & Krajcik, J. (2008). Scientific explanations: Characterizing and evaluating the effects of teachers' instructional practices on student learning. *Journal of Research in Science Teaching, 45,* 53–78.

McQueen, R., Murray, A. K., & Evans, E. (1963). Relationships between writing required in high school and English proficiency in college. *Journal of Experimental Education, 31,* 419–423.

McVee, M., Dunsmore, K., & Gavelek, J. (2005). Schema theory revisited. *Review of Educational Research, 75,* 531–566.

Medin, D. L., & Rips, L. J. (2005). Concepts and categories: Memory, meaning, and metaphysics. In K. Holyoak & R. Morrison (Eds.), *The Cambridge handbook of thinking and reasoning* (pp. 37–72). Cambridge, UK: Cambridge University Press.

Medin, D. L., Wattenmaker, W. D., & Hampson, S. E. (1987). Family resemblance, conceptual cohesiveness, and category construction. *Cognitive Psychology, 19,* 242–278.

Mehan, H. (1979). Learning lessons: *Social organization in the classroom.* Cambridge, MA: Harvard University Press.

Meichenbaum, D. (1977). *Cognitive behavior modification: An integrative approach.* New York, NY: Plenum.

Mercer, N. (2007). Talk and the development of reasoning and understanding. *Human Development, 51,* 90–100.

Merrill, D. M. (2000). *First principles of instruction* [online]. Paper presented at the annual convention of the Association for Educational Communications and Technology, Denver, CO. Available at: http://www.id2.usu.edu/Papers/5FirstPrinciples.PDF

Meyer, B. J. F. & Rice, G. E. (1984). The structure of text. In P. D. Pearson (Ed.), *Handbook of reading research* (pp. 316–342). New York, NY: Longman.

Meyer, K., & Woodruff, E. (1998). Consensually driven explanation in science teaching. *Science Education, 81,* 173–192.

Midgley, C. (Ed.). (2002). *Goals, goal structures, and patterns of adaptive learning.* Mahwah, NJ: Erlbaum.

Midgley, C., Anderman, E. M., & Hicks, L. (1995). Differences between elementary and middle school teachers and students: A goal theory approach. *Journal of Early Adolescence, 15,* 90–113.

Midgley, C., Kaplan, A., & Middleton, M. (2001). Performance-approach goals: Good for what, for whom, under what circumstances, and at what cost? *Journal of Educational Psychology, 93,* 77–86.

Miller, G. A. (1956). The magical number seven, plus-or-minus two: Some limits on our capacity for processing information. *Psychological Review, 63,* 81–97.

Miller, R. G., & Calfee, R. C. (2004). Making Thinking Visible: A method to encourage science writing in upper elementary grades. *Science and Children, 3*(42), 20–25.

Millis, K., Magliano, J., & Todaro, S. (2006). Measuring discourse-level processes with verbal protocols and latent semantic analysis. *Scientific Studies of Reading, 10,* 225–240.

Minsky, M. (1975). A framework for representing knowledge. In P. H. Winston (Ed.), *The psychology of computer vision* (pp. 211–277). New York, NY: McGraw-Hill.

Mitchell, D. B., & Brown, A. S. (1988). Persistent repetition priming in picture naming and its disassociation from recognition memory. *Journal of Experimental Psychology: Learning, Memory, and Cognition, 14,* 213–222.

Miyake, A. (2001). Individual differences in working memory: Introduction to the special section. *Journal of Experimental Psychology: General, 130,* 163–168.

Miyake, A., & Shah, P. (1999). Toward unified theories of working memory: Emerging general consensus, unresolved theoretical issues, and future research directions. In A. Miyake & P. Shah (Eds.), *Models of working memory: Mechanisms of active maintenance and executive control* (pp. 442–481). Cambridge, UK: Cambridge University Press.

Moll, L. C., & Whitmore, K. (1993). Vygotsky in classroom practice: Moving from individual transmission to social transaction. In E. A. Forman, N. Minick, & C. A. Stone (Eds.), *Contexts for learning* (pp. 19–42). New York, NY: Oxford University Press.

Montague, W. E., Adams, J. A., & Kiess, H. D. (1966). Forgetting and natural language mediation. *Journal of Experimental Psychology, 72,* 829–833.

Moore, M. T. (1990). Problem finding and teacher experience. *Journal of Creative Behavior, 24,* 39–58.

Moos, D. C., & Azevedo, R. (2008). Monitoring, planning, and self-efficacy during learning with hypermedia: The impact of conceptual scaffolds. *Computers in Human Behavior, 24,* 1686–1706.

Moreno, R. (2005). Instructional technology: Promise and pitfalls. In L. M. PyslikZillig, M. Bodvarsson, & R. Bruning (Eds.), *Technology-based education: Bringing researchers and practitioners together.* Greenwich, CT: Information Age.

Moreno, R., & Mayer, R. E. (1999). Cognitive principles of multimedia learning: The role of modality and contiguity. *Journal of Educational Psychology, 91,* 358–368.

Moreno, R., & Mayer, R. E. (2000). A coherence effect in multimedia learning: The case for minimizing irrelevant sounds in the design of multimedia instructional messages. *Journal of Educational Psychology, 92,* 117–125.

Morris, C. C. (1990). Retrieval processes underlying confidence in comprehension judgments. *Journal of Experimental Psychology: Learning, Memory, and Cognition, 16,* 223–232.

Morris, D., Bloodgood, J. W., Lomax, R. G., & Perney, J. (2003). Developmental steps in learning to read: A longitudinal study in kindergarten and first grade. *Reading Research Quarterly, 38,* 302–328.

Morris, C. D., Bransford, J. D., & Franks, J. J. (1977). Levels of processing versus transfer appropriate processing. *Journal of Verbal Learning and Verbal Behavior, 16,* 519–533.

Morrison, R. G. (2005). Thinking in working memory. In K. J. Holyoak & R. G. Morrison (Eds.), *The Cambridge handbook of thinking and reasoning* (pp. 457–474). Cambridge, UK: Cambridge University Press.

Moshman, D. (1981). Jean Piaget meets Jerry Falwell: Genetic epistemology and the anti-humanist movement in education. *Genetic Epistemologist, 10,* 10–13.

Moshman, D. (1982). Exogenous, endogenous, and dialectical constructivism. *Developmental Review, 2,* 371–384.

Mousavi, S. Y., Low, R., & Sweller, J. (1995). Reducing cognitive load by mixing auditory and visual presentation modes. *Journal of Educational Psychology, 87,* 319–334.

Muis, K. R. (2008). Epistemic profiles and self-regulated learning: Examining relations in the context of mathematics problem solving. *Contemporary Educational Psychology, 33,* 177–208.

Muller, H. J., & Krummenacher, J. (2006). Visual search and selective attention. *Visual Cognition, 14,* 389–410.

Mumford, M. D., Costanza, D. P., Baughman, W. A, Threlfall, K. V., & Fleischman, E. A. (1994). Influence of abilities on performance during practice: Effects of massed and distributed practice. *Journal of Educational Psychology, 86,* 134–144.

Murdock, T. B., & Anderman, E. (2006). Motivational perspectives on student cheating: Toward an integrated model of academic dishonesty. *Educational Psychologist, 41,* 129–145.

Murphy, P. K., Holleran, T., Long, J., & Zeruth, J. (2005, October). Examining the complex roles of motivation and text medium in the persuasion process. *Contemporary Educational Psychology, 30,* 418–438.

Murphy, P. K., & Mason, L. (2006). Changing knowledge and beliefs. In P. A. Alexander & P. H. Winne (Eds.), *Handbook of educational psychology* (2nd ed., pp. 305–325). Mahwah, NJ: Erlbaum.

Nagy, W. E. (1988, April). *Some components of a model of word-learning ability.* Paper presented at the Annual Meeting of the American Educational Research Association, New Orleans.

Nagy, W. E., Anderson, R. C., & Herman, P. A. (1987). Learning word meanings from context during normal reading. *American Educational Research Journal, 24,* 237–270.

Nagy, W. E., & Herman, P. A. (1987). Breadth and depth of vocabulary knowledge: Implications for acquisition and instruction. In M. G. McKeown & M. E. Curtis (Eds.), *The nature of vocabulary acquisition* (pp. 19–35). Mahwah, NJ: Erlbaum.

Nagy, W. E., & Scott, J. A. (2000). Vocabulary processes. In M. L. Kamil, P. B. Mosenthal, P. D. Pearson, & R. Barr (Eds.), *Handbook of reading research* (Vol. 3, pp. 269–284). Mahwah, NJ: Erlbaum.

Nathan, M. J., & Petrosino, A. (2003). Expert blind spot among preservice teachers. *American Educational Research Journal, 40,* 905–928.

Nation, K., & Hulme, C. (1997). Phonemic segmentation, not onset–rime segmentation, predicts early reading and spelling skills. *Reading Research Quarterly, 32,* 154–167.

National Assessment of Educational Progress. (2000). *The Nation's Report Card: Mathematics.* Washington, DC: National Center for Education Statistics, U.S. Department of Education.

National Commission on Mathematics and Science Teaching for the 21st Century. (2000). *Before it's too late: A report to the nation from the national commission on mathematics and science teaching for the 21st century.* Washington, DC: U. S. Department of Education.

National Commission on Writing. (2007). *The 2007 survey on teaching writing: American public opinion on the importance of writing in schools.* Washington, DC: National Writing Project.

National Council of Teachers of English (NCTE). (1996). *Standards for the English language arts.* Urbana, IL: National Council of Teachers of English.

National Council of Teachers of Mathematics (NCTM). (2000). *Principles and standards for school mathematics.* Reston, VA: Author.

National Mathematics Advisory Panel. (2008). *Foundations for success: The final report of the National Mathematics Advisory Panel.* Washington, DC: U.S. Department of Education.

National Reading Panel. (2000). *Teaching children to read: An evidence-based assessment of the scientific research literature on reading and its implications for reading instruction.* Washington, DC: NIH.

National Research Council. (1996). *National science education standards.* Washington, DC: National Academies Press.

National Research Council. (2000). *Inquiry and the national science education standards: A guide for teaching and learning.* Washington, DC: National Academies Press.

National Research Council. (2005). How students learn: History, mathematics, and science in the classroom. In M. S. Donovan and J. D. Bransford (Eds.), *Committee on how people learn: A targeted report for teachers.* Washington, DC: National Academies Press.

National Research Council. (2006). Systems for state science assessments. In M. Wilson & M. Bertenthal (Eds.), *Committee on test design for K–12 science achievement.* Washington, DC: National Academies Press.

Neath, I. & Surprenant, A. M. (2003). *Human memory: An introduction to research, data, and theory* (2nd ed.). Belmont, CA: Wadsworth.

Neisser, U. (1967). *Cognitive psychology.* New York, NY: Appleton–Century–Crofts.

Neisser, U. (1982). *Memory observed.* New York, NY: Freeman.

Neisser, U., & Weene, P. (1962). Hierarchies in concept attainment. *Journal of Experimental Psychology, 64,* 640–645.

Nelson, T. O. (1985). Ebbinghaus's contribution to the measurement of retention: Savings during relearning. *Journal of Experimental Psychology: Learning, Memory, and Cognition, 11,* 472–479.

Neves, D. M., & Anderson, J. R. (1981). Knowledge compilation: Mechanisms for the automatization of cognitive skills. In J. R. Anderson (Ed.), *Cognitive skills and their acquisition* (pp. 86–102). Mahwah, NJ: Erlbaum.

Newby, T. J. (1991). Classroom motivation: Strategies for first-year teachers. *Journal of Educational Psychology, 83,* 195–200.

Newcombe, N. S., Ambady, N., Eccles, J., Gomez, L., Klahr, D., Linn, M., Miller, K., & Mix, K. (2009). Psychology's role in mathematics and science education, *American Psychologist, 64,* 538–550.

Newell, A., & Simon, H. A. (1972). *Human problem solving.* Upper Saddle River, NJ: Prentice Hall.

Newman, D., Griffin, P., & Cole, M. (1989). *The construction zone: Working for cognitive change in school.* Cambridge, UK: Cambridge University Press.

Newman, R. S., & Goldin, L. (1990). Children's reluctance to seek help with schoolwork. *Journal of Educational Psychology, 82,* 92–100.

Nichols, J. D. & Miller[0], R. B. (1993). Cooperative learning and student motivation. *Contemporary Educational Psychology, 19,* 167–179.

Nickerson, R. S. (1987). Why teach thinking? In J. Baron & R. Sternberg (Eds.), *Teaching thinking skills: Theory and practice* (pp. 27–38). New York, NY: Freeman.

Niedenthal, P. M. (1990). Implicit perception of affective information. *Journal of Experimental Social Psychology, 26,* 505–527.

Nilsson, L., Law, J., & Tulving, E. (1988). Recognition failure of recallable unique names: Evidence for an empirical law of memory and learning. *Journal of Experimental Psychology: Learning, Memory, and Cognition, 14,* 266–277.

No Child Left Behind Act of 2001; pub. L. No. 107–110, 115 Stat. 1425. (2002).

Noble, C. E. (1952). An analysis of meaning. *Psychological Review, 59,* 421–430.

Norman, D. A., & Bobrow, D. G. (1976). On the role of active memory processes in perception and cognition. In C. N. Cofer (Ed.), *The structure of human memory* (pp. 123–156). New York, NY: Freeman.

Norris, S., & Ennis, R. (1989). *Evaluating critical thinking.* Pacific Grove, CA: Midwest.

Novick, L. R., & Bassok, M. (2005). Problem solving. In K. Holyoak & R. Morrison (Eds.), *The Cambridge handbook of thinking and reasoning* (pp. 321–350). Cambridge, UK: Cambridge University Press.

Nusbaum, H. C., & Schwab, E. C. (1986). The role of attention and active processing in speech perception. In E. C. Schwab & H. C. Nusbaum (Eds.), *Pattern recognition by humans and machines* (pp. 113–157). San Diego, CA: Academic Press.

Nussbaum, J., & Novick, N. (1982). Alternative frameworks, conceptual conflict, and accommodation: Toward a principled teaching strategy. *Instructional Science, 11,* 183–200.

Nystrand, M., & Gamoran, A. (1991). Instructional discourse, student engagement, and literature achievement. *Research in the Teaching of English, 25,* 261–290.

Oakes, J. (1990). *Multiplying inequalities: The effects of race, social class, and tracking on opportunities to learn math and science.* Chicago, IL: Rand McNally.

Oakhill, J. V., Hartt, J., & Samols, D. (2005). Comprehension monitoring and working memory in good and poor comprehenders. *Reading and Writing, 18,* 657–713.

Oaksford, M., Morris, F., Grainger, B., & Williams, J. M. G. (1996). Mood, reasoning, and central executive processes. *Journal of Experimental Psychology: Learning, Memory, and Cognition, 22,* 476–492.

O'Donnell, A. M. (2006). The role of peers and group learning. In P. A. Alexander & P. H. Winne (Eds.), *Handbook of educational psychology* (2nd ed., pp. 781–802). Mahwah, NJ: Erlbaum.

O'Flahavan, J. F., & Stein, C. (1992). In search of the teacher's role in peer discussions about literature. *Reading in Virginia, 17,* 34–42.

Olafson, L., & Schraw, G. (2002, June). Some final thoughts on the epistemological melting pot. *Issues in Education, 8,* 233.

Olafson, L. J., & Schraw, G. (2006). Teachers' beliefs and practices within and across domains. *International Journal of Educational Research, 45,* 71–84.

Olinghouse, N. G., & Graham, S. (2009). The relationship between the discourse knowledge and the writing performance of elementary-grade students. *Journal of Educational Psychology, 101,* 37–50.

Olson, D. R. (1994). *The world on paper: The conceptual and cognitive implications of writing and reading.* Cambridge, UK: Cambridge University Press.

Olton, R. M., & Crutchfield, R. S. (1969). Developing the skills of productive thinking. In P. Mussen, J. Langer, & M. Covington (Eds.), *Trends and issues in developmental psychology.* New York, NY: Holt, Rinehart & Winston.

Onkal, D., Yates. L. F., Simca-Mugan, C., & Oztin, S. (2003). Professional versus amateur judgment accuracy: The case of foreign exchange rates. *Organizational and Human Decision Processes, 91,* 169–185.

O'Reilly, T., & McNamara, D. S. (2007). The impact of science knowledge, reading skill, and reading strategy knowledge on more traditional high-stakes measures of high school students' science achievement. *American Educational Research Journal, 44,* 161–196.

Orland-Barack, L., & Yinon, H. (2007). When theory meets practice: What student teachers learned from guided reflection on their own classroom discourse. *Teaching and Teacher Education, 23,* 957–969.

Osborne, R., & Freyberg, R. (1985). *Learning science.* Portsmouth, NH: Heinemann.

Overton, D. A. (1985). Contextual stimulus effects of drugs and internal states. In P. D. Balsam & A. Tomie (Eds.), *Context and learning* (pp. 357–384). Mahwah, NJ: Erlbaum.

Ozgun-Koca, S., & Sen, A. (2006). The beliefs and perceptions of pre-service teachers enrolled in a subject-area dominant teacher education program about "effective education." *Teaching and Teacher Education, 22,* 946–960.

Ozgungor, S., & Guthrie, J. (2004). Interactions among elaborative interrogation, knowledge, and interest in the process of constructing knowledge from text. *Journal of Educational Psychology, 96,* 437–443.

Paas, F. G. W. (1992). Training strategies for attaining transfer of problem-solving skill in statistics: A cognitive load approach. *Journal of Educational Psychology, 84,* 429–434.

Packer, M., & Goicoechea, J. (2000). Sociocultural and constructivist theories of learning: Ontology, not just epistemology. *Educational Psychologist, 35,* 227–241.

Paivio, A. (1971). *Imagery and verbal processes.* New York, NY: Holt, Rinehart & Winston.

Paivio, A. (1986a). Dual coding and episodic memory: Subjective and objective sources of memory trace components. In F. Klix & H. Hafgendorf (Eds.), *Human memory and cognitive capabilities: Mechanisms and performances* (Part A, pp. 225–236). Amsterdam, The Netherlands: North-Holland.

Paivio, A. (1986b). *Mental representations: A dual coding approach.* New York, NY: Oxford University Press.

Paivio, A., Clark, J. M., & Lambert, W. E. (1988). Bilingual dual-coding theory and semantic repetition effect on recall. *Journal of Experimental Psychology: Learning, Memory, and Cognition, 14,* 163–172.

Paivio, A., & Csapo, K. (1975). Picture superiority in free recall: Imagery or dual coding? *Cognitive Psychology, 5,* 176–206.

Paivio, A., Yuille, J. D., & Madigan, S. A. (1968). Concreteness, imagery, and meaningfulness values for 925 nouns. *Journal of Experimental Psychology, 76* (Suppl.), 1–25.

Pajares, F. (1996). Self-efficacy beliefs in academic settings. *Review of Educational Research, 66,* 543–578.

Pajares, F. (1997). Current directions in self-efficacy research. In M. Maehr & P. R. Pintrich (Eds.), *Advances in motivation and achievement* (Vol. 10, pp. 1–49). Greenwich, CT: JAI Press.

Pajares, F. (2003). Self-efficacy beliefs, motivation and achievement in writing: A review of the literature. *Reading & Writing Quarterly, 19,* 139–158.

Palincsar, A. S., & Brown, A. L. (1984). Reciprocal teaching of comprehension monitoring activities. *Cognition and Instruction, 1,* 117–175.

Palincsar, A. S., & Duke, N. K. (2004). The role of text and text-reader interactions in young children's reading development and achievement. *Elementary School Journal, 105,* 183–197.

Pallas, A. M. (2001). Preparing educational doctoral students for epistemological diversity. *Educational Researcher, 30,* 6–11.

Pappas, C. C. (1993). Is narrative "primary"? Some insights from kindergartners' pretend readings of stories and information books. *Journal of Reading Behavior, 24,* 97–129.

Paris, S. G. (2005). Reinterpreting the development of reading skills. *Reading Research Quarterly, 40,* 184–202.

Paris, S. G., Cross, D. R., & Lipson, M. Y. (1984). Informal strategies for learning: A program to improve children's reading awareness and comprehension. *Journal of Educational Psychology, 76,* 1239–1252.

Paris, S. G., & Hamilton, E. E. (2009). The development of children's reading comprehension. In S. E. Israel & G. G. Duffy (Eds.), *Handbook of research on reading comprehension* (pp. 32–53). New York, NY: Routledge.

Paris, S. G., & Jacobs, J. E. (1984). The benefits of informed instruction for children's reading and comprehension. *Child Development, 55,* 2083–2093.

Pascarella, E. T., & Terenzini, P. T. (1991). *How college affects students.* San Francisco, CA: Jossey-Bass.

Patall, E. A., Cooper, H., & Robinson, J. C. (2008). The effects of choice on intrinsic motivation and related outcomes: A meta-analysis of research findings. *Psychological Review, 134,* 270–300.

Patel, V. L., Arocha, J. F., & Zhang, J. (2005). Thinking and reasoning in medicine. In K. Holyoak & R. Morrison (Eds.), *The Cambridge handbook of thinking and reasoning* (pp. 727–750). Cambridge, UK: Cambridge University Press.

Patrick, H., & Pintrich, P. R. (2001). Conceptual change in teachers' intuitive conceptions of learning, motivation, and instructions: The role of motivational and epistemological beliefs. In B. Torf & R. Sternberg (Eds.), *Understanding and teaching the intuitive mind* (pp. 117–143). Mahwah, NJ: Erlbaum.

Patz, R. (2006). Building NCLB science assessments: Psychometric and practical considerations. *Measurement, 4,* 199–239.

Pea, R. D. (1993). Learning scientific concepts through material and social activities: Conversational analysis meets conceptual change. *Educational Psychologist, 28,* 265–277.

Pearson, P. D. (1984). Guided reading: A response to Isabel Beck. In R. C. Anderson, J. Osborn, & R. J. Tierney (Eds.), *Learning to read in American schools* (pp. 21–28). Mahwah, NJ: Erlbaum.

Pearson, P. D. (2006). Foreword. In K. S. Goodman (Ed.). *The truth about DIBELS: What it is, what it does.* Portsmouth, NH: Heinemann.

Pearson, P. D., & Hamm, D. N. (2005). The assessment of reading comprehension: A review of practices— Past, present, and Future. In S. G. Paris & S. A. Stahl (eds.), *Children's reading comprehension and assessment* (pp. 13–69). Mahwah, NJ: Erlbaum.

Pepper, S. C. (1961). *World hypotheses: A study in evidence.* Berkeley: University of California Press. (Original work published in 1942)

Perfetti, C. A. (1992). The representation problem in reading acquisition. In P. B. Gough, L. C. Ehri, & R. Treiman (Eds.), *Reading acquisition* (pp. 145–174). Mahwah, NJ: Erlbaum.

Perkins, D. N. (1995). *Outsmarting IQ: The emerging science of learnable intelligence.* New York, NY: Free Press.

Perkins, D. N. (1987). Thinking frames: An integrated perspective on teaching cognitive skills. In J. Baron & R. Sternberg (Eds.), *Teaching thinking skills: Theory and practice* (pp. 41–61). New York, NY: Freeman.

Perkins, D. N. (2001). Wisdom in the wild. *Educational Psychologist, 36,* 265–268.

Perkins, D. N., Faraday, M., & Bushey, B. (1991). Everyday reasoning and the roots of intelligence. In J. F. Voss, D. N. Perkins, & J. W. Segal (Eds.), *Informal reasoning and education* (pp. 83–106). Mahwah, NJ: Erlbaum.

Perkins, D. N., & Grotzer, T. A. (1997). Teaching intelligence. *American Psychologist, 52,* 1125–1133.

Perkins, D. N., Jay, E., & Tishman, S. (1993). Introduction: New conceptions of thinking. *Educational Psychologist, 28,* 1–5.

Perkins, D. N., & Salomon, G. (1989). Are cognitive skills context bound? *Educational Researcher, 18,* 16–25.

Perry, N. E., Turner, J. C., & Meyer, D. K. (2006). Classrooms as contexts for motivating learning. In P. A. Alexander & P. H. Winne (Eds.), *Handbook of educational psychology* (2nd ed., pp. 327–348). Mahwah, NJ: Erlbaum.

Perry, R. P., & Penner, K. S. (1990). Enhancing academic achievement in college students through attributional retraining and instruction. *Journal of Educational Psychology, 82,* 262–271.

Perry, W. G., Jr. (1970). *Forms of intellectual and ethical development in the college years.* San Diego, CA: Academic Press.

Peterson, L. R., & Peterson, M. J. (1959). Short-term retention of individual verbal items. *Journal of Experimental Psychology, 58,* 193–198.

Peterson, S. E., & Schrieber, J. (2006). An attributional analysis of personal and interpersonal motivation for collaborative projects. *Educational Psychologist, 98,* 777–787.

Peterson, S. J., & Byron, K. (2008). Exploring the role of hope in job performance: Results from four studies. *Journal of Organizational Behavior, 29,* 785–809.

Pew Internet and American Life Project. (2008). *Writing, technology and teens.* Washington, DC: Author.

Pichert, J. W., & Anderson, R. C. (1977). Taking different perspectives on a story. *Journal of Educational Psychology, 69,* 309–315.

Pintrich, P. (2000a). The role of goal orientation in self-regulated learning. In M. Boekaerts, P. Pintrich, & M. Zeidner (Eds.), *Handbook of self-regulation* (pp. 452–501). San Diego, CA: Academic Press.

Pintrich, P. R. (2000b). Multiple goals, multiple pathways: The role of goal orientation in learning and achievement. *Journal of Educational Psychology, 92,* 544–555.

Pintrich, P. R., Marx, R. W., & Boyle, R. A. (1993). Beyond cold conceptual change: The role of motivational beliefs and classroom contextual factors in the process of conceptual change. *Review of Educational Research, 63,* 167–199.

Pintrich, P. R., & Schunk, D. H. (2002). *Motivation in education: theory, research, and applications* (2nd ed.). Upper Saddle River, NJ: Merrill Prentice Hall.

Pirie, B. (1997). *Reshaping high school English.* Urbana, IL: NCTE.

Pirttila-Backman, A. M., & Kajanne, A. (2001). The development of implicit epistemologies during early and middle adulthood. *Journal of Adult Development, 8,* 81–97.

Pithers, R. T., & Soden, R. (2000). Critical thinking in education: A review. *Educational Research, 42,* 237–249.

Plank, S. B., & Jordan, W. B. (2001). Effects of information, guidance, and actions on postsecondary destinations: A study of talent loss. *American Educational Research Association, 38,* 947–979.

Polanyi, M. (1967). *The tacit dimension.* Boston, MA: Routledge Kegan Paul.

Ponterotto, J. G. (2005). Qualitative research in counseling psychology: A primer on research paradigms and philosophy of science. *Journal of Counseling Psychology, 52,* 126–136.

Poole, M. B. G., Okeafor, K., & Sloan, E. C. (1989, April). *Teachers' interactions, personal efficacy, and change implementation.* Paper presented at the Annual Meeting of the American Educational Research Association, San Francisco.

Poplin, M. S. (1988). Holistic/constructivist principles of the teaching/learning process: Implications for the field of learning disabilities. *Journal of Learning Disabilities, 21,* 401–416.

Posner, G. J., Strike, K. A., Hewson, P. W., & Gertzog, W. A. (1982). Accommodation of a scientific conception: Toward a theory of conceptual change. *Scientific Education, 66,* 211–228.

Posner, M. I. (Ed.). (2004). *Cognitive neuroscience of attention.* New York, NY: Guilford.

Prawat, R. S. (1996). Constructivisms, modern and postmodern. *Educational Psychologist, 31,* 215–225.

Pressley, M. (1977). Children's use of the keyword method to learn simple Spanish vocabulary words. *Journal of Educational Psychology, 69,* 465–472.

Pressley, M. (2000). What should comprehension instruction be the instruction of? In M. L. Kamil, P. B. Mosenthal, P. D. Pearson, & R. Barr (Eds.), *Handbook of reading research* (Vol. 3, pp. 545–561). Mahwah, NJ: Erlbaum.

Pressley, M. (2002a). Comprehension strategies instruction: A turn-of-the-century status report. In C. Block & M. Pressley (Eds.). *Comprehension instruction: Research-based best practices* (pp. 11–27). New York, NY: Guilford.

Pressley, M. (2002b). *Reading instruction that works* (2nd ed.). New York, NY: Guilford.

Pressley, M. (2006, April). *What the future of reading research could be.* Paper presented at the annual meeting of the International Reading Association, Chicago, IL.

Pressley, M., Allington, R., Wharton-McDonald, R., Block, C. C., & Morrow, L. M. (2001). *Learning to read: Lessons from exemplary first-grade classrooms.* New York, NY: Guilford.

Pressley, M., Borkowski, J. G., & Schneider, W. (1987). Cognitive strategies: Good strategies users coordinate metacognition and knowledge. In R. Vasta & G. Whitehurst (Eds.), *Annals of child development* (Vol. 5, pp. 89–129). Greenwich, CT: JAI.

Pressley, M., El-Dinary, P. B., Gaskins, I., Schuder, T., Bergman, J. L., Almasi, J., & Brown, R. (1992). Beyond direct explanation: Transactional instruction of reading comprehension strategies. *Elementary School Journal, 92,* 511–554.

Pressley, M., & Ghatala, E. S. (1988). Delusions about performance on multiple-choice comprehension tests items. *Reading Research Quarterly, 23,* 454–464.

Pressley, M., & Harris, K. R. (2006). *Cognitive strategies instruction: From basic research to classroom instruction.* In P. A. Alexander & P. H. Winne (Eds.), *Handbook of educational psychology* (2nd ed., pp. 265–286). Mahwah, NJ: Erlbaum.

Pressley, M., Harris, K. R., & Marks, M. B. (1992). But good strategy instructors are constructivists! *Educational Psychology Review, 4,* 3–31.

Pressley, M., Hilden, K., & Shankland, R. (2005). *An evaluation of end-grade-3 Dynamic Indicators of Basic Early Literacy Skills (DIBELS): Speed reading without comprehension, predicting little* (Tech. Rep.), East Lansing, MI: Michigan State University, Literacy Achievement Research Center.

Pressley, M., Levin, J. R., & Delaney, H. D. (1982). The mnemonic keyword method. *Review of Educational Research, 52,* 61–92.

Pressley, M., Rankin, J., & Yokoi, L. (1996). A survey of instructional practices of primary teachers nominated as effective in promoting literacy. *Elementary School Journal, 96,* 363–384.

Pressley, M., & Schneider, W. (1997). *Introduction to memory development during childhood and adolescence.* Mahwah, NJ: Erlbaum.

Pressley, M., Symons, S., McDaniel, M. A., Snyder, B. L., & Turnure, J. E. (1988). Elaborative integration facilitates acquisition of confusing facts. *Journal of Educational Psychology, 80,* 268–278.

Pressley, M., & Wharton-McDonald, R. (1997). Skilled comprehension and its development through instruction. *School Psychology Review, 26,* 448–466.

Pressley, M., & Woloshyn, V. (1995). *Cognition strategy instruction that really improves children's academic performance.* Cambridge, MA: Brookline.

Pretz, J. E., Naples, A. J., & Sternberg, R. J. (2003). Recognizing, defining, and representing problems. In J. E. Davidson and R. J. Sternberg (Eds.), *The psychology of problem solving* (pp. 3–30). Cambridge, UK: Cambridge University Press.

Pugh, K. J., & Bergin, D. A. (2006). Motivational issues on transfer. *Educational Psychologist, 41,* 147–160.

Purcell-Gates, V. (1996). Stories, coupons, and TV Guide: Relationships between home literacy experiences and emergent literacy knowledge. *Reading Research Quarterly, 31,* 406–428.

Purcell-Gates, V., Duke, N. K., & Martineau, J. A. (2007). Learning to read and write genre-specific text: Roles of authentic experience and explicit teaching. *Reading Research Quarterly, 42,* 8–45.

Pylyshyn, Z. W. (1981). The imagery debate: Analogue media versus tacit knowledge. *Psychological Review, 88,* 16–45.

Quellmalz, E. S. (1987). Developing reasoning skills. In J. Baron & R. Sternberg (Eds.), *Teaching thinking skills: Theory and practice* (pp. 86–105). New York, NY: Freeman.

Quillian, M. R. (1968). Semantic memory. In M. Minsky (Ed.), *Semantic information processing* (pp. 21–56). Cambridge, MA: MIT Press.

Rabinowitz, J. C., & Craik, F. I. M. (1986). Specific enhancement effects associated with word generation. *Journal of Memory and Language, 25,* 226–237.

Radvansky, G. A. (2006). *Human memory.* Boston, MA: Pearson.

Ramaswamy, S., Harris, I., & Tschirner, U. (2001). Student peer teaching: An innovative approach to instruction in science and engineering education. *Journal of Science Education and Technology, 10,* 165–171.

RAND Mathematics Study Panel. (2003). *Mathematical proficiency for all students: Toward a strategic research and development program in mathematics education.* Santa Monica, CA: Author.

Randi, J., & Corno, L. (2000). Teacher innovations in self-regulated learning. In M. Boekaerts, P. R. Pintrich, & M. Zeidner (Eds.), *Handbook of self-regulation.* San Diego, CA: Academic Press.

Raphael, T. E., & Au, K. H. (2005). QAR: Enhancing comprehension and test taking across grades and content areas. *Reading Teacher, 59,* 206–221.

Raphael, T. E., & McKinney, J. (1983). An examination of fifth- and eighth-grade children's question answering behavior: An instruction study in metacognition. *Journal of Reading Behavior, 15,* 67–86.

Raphael, T. E., & Pearson, P. D. (1982). *The effects of metacognitive strategy awareness training on students' question answering behavior* (Tech. Rep. No. 238). Urbana: University of Illinois, Center for the Study of Reading.

Raphael, T. E., & Wonnacott, C. A. (1985). Heightening fourth-grade students' sensitivity to sources of information for answering comprehension questions. *Reading Research Quarterly, 16,* 301–321.

Rapp, D., van den Broek, P., McMaster, K., Kendeou, P., & Espin, C. (2007). Higher-order comprehension processes in struggling readers: A perspective for research and intervention. *Scientific Studies of Reading, 11,* 289–312.

Ratcliff, R., & McKoon, G. (1996). Bias effects in implicit memory tasks. *Journal of Experimental Psychology: General, 125,* 403–421.

Rayner, K. (1997). Understanding eye movements in reading. *Scientific Studies of Reading, 1,* 317–339.

Rayner, K., & Pollatsek, A. (1989). *The psychology of reading.* Upper Saddle River, NJ: Prentice Hall.

Recht, D. R., & Leslie, L. (1988). Effect of prior knowledge on good and poor readers' memory of text. *Journal of Educational Psychology, 80,* 16–20.

Reed, S. K. (1984). Estimating answers to algebra word problems. *Journal of Experimental Psychology: Learning, Memory, and Cognition, 10,* 778–790.

Reed, S. K. (1987). A structure-mapping model for word problems. *Journal of Experimental Psychology: Learning, Memory, and Cognition, 13,* 124–139.

Reed, S. K. (2006). Does unit analysis help students construct equations? *Cognition and Instruction, 24,* 341–366.

Reed, S. K., Dempster, A., & Ettinger, M. (1985). Usefulness of analogous solutions for solving algebra word problems. *Journal of Experimental Psychology: Learning, Memory, and Cognition, 11,* 106–125.

Reeve, J. (2002). Self-determination theory applied to educational settings. In E. L. Deci & R. M. Ryan (Eds.), *Handbook of self-determination research* (pp. 183–203). Rochester, NY: University of Rochester Press.

Reeve, J., Bolt, E., & Cai, Y. (1999). Autonomy supportive teachers: How they teach and motivate students. *Journal of Educational Psychology, 91,* 537–548.

Renkl, A., & Atkinson, R. K. (2003). Structuring the transition from example study to problem solving in cognitive skill acquisition. *Educational Psychologist, 38,* 15–22.

Rennie, L. J. (1989, April). *The relationship between teacher beliefs, management and organizational processes, and student participation in individualized classrooms.* Paper presented at the Annual Meeting of the American Educational Research Association, San Francisco.

Reybold, L. E. (2001). Encouraging the transformation of personal epistemology. *Qualitative Studies in Education, 14,* 413–428.

Reynolds, A. J., & Walberg, H. J. (1991). A structural model of science achievement. *Journal of Educational Psychology, 83,* 97–107.

Reynolds, A. J., & Walberg, H. J. (1992). A structural model of science achievement and attitude: An extension to high school. *Journal of Educational Psychology, 84,* 371–382.

Reynolds, R. E. (1993). Selective attention and prose learning: Theoretical and empirical research. *Educational Psychology Review, 4,* 345–391.

Rich, Y., Smadar, L., & Fischer, S. (1996). Extending the concept and assessment of teacher efficacy. *Educational and Psychological Measurement, 56,* 1015–1025.

Rieber, R. W., & Carton, A. S. (Eds.). (1987). *The collected works of L. S. Vygotsky* (N. Minick, Trans.). New York, NY: Plenum.

Rikers, R. M. J. P. (2006). A critical reflection on emerging topics in cognitive load theory. *Applied Cognitive Psychology, 20,* 359–364.

Riley, M. S., Greeno, J. G., & Heller, J. I. (1983). Development of children's problem-solving ability in arithmetic. In H. Ginsburg (Ed.), *The development of mathematical thinking* (pp. 62–71). San Diego: Academic Press.

Rimm-Kaufman, S. E., & Sawyer, B. K. (2004). Primary grades teachers' self-efficacy beliefs, attitudes toward teaching, and discipline and teaching practice priorities in relation to the Responsive Classroom approach. *Elementary School Journal, 104,* 321–341.

Ritchart, R., & Perkins, D. N. (2005). Learning to Think: The challenges of teaching thinking. In K. Holyoak & R. Morrison (Eds.), *The Cambridge handbook of thinking and reasoning* (pp. 775–802). Cambridge, UK: Cambridge University Press.

Rittle-Johnson, B., Siegler, S., & Alibali, M. (2001). Developing conceptual understanding and procedural skill in mathematics: An iterative process. *Journal of Educational Psychology, 93,* 345–362.

Rittle-Johnson, B., & Star, J. R. (2007). Does comparing solution methods facilitate conceptual and procedural knowledge? An experimental study on learning to solve equations. *Journal of Educational Psychology, 99,* 561–574.

Rittle-Johnson, B., & Star, J. R. (2009). Compared to what? The effects of different comparisons on conceptual knowledge and procedural flexibility for equation solving. *Journal of Educational Psychology, 101,* 529–544.

Roberts, R., & Gott, R. (2006). Assessment of performance in practical science and pupil attributes. *Assessment in Education, 13,* 45–67.

Roedel, T. D., Schraw, G., & Plake, B. S. (1994). Validation of a measure of learning and performance goal orientations. *Educational and Psychological Measurement, 54,* 1013–1021.

Roediger H. L., III. (1990). Implicit memory: Retention without remembering. *American Psychologist, 45,* 1043–1056.

Roediger, H. L. III. (2000). Why retrieval is the key process to understanding human memory. In E. Tulving (Ed.), *Memory, consciousness and the brain: The Tallinn conference* (pp. 52–75). Philadelphia, PA: Psychology Press.

Roediger, H. L. III. (2003). Reconsidering implicit memory. In J. S. Bowers & C. Marsolek (Eds.), *Rethinking implicit memory* (pp. 3–18). Oxford, UK: Oxford University Press.

Roediger, H. L. III, Gallo, D., & Geraci, L. (2002). Processing approaches to cognition: The impetus from the levels-of-processing framework. *Memory, 10,* 319–332.

Roediger, H. L. III, & Karpicke, J. D. (2006a). The power of testing memory: Basic research and implications for educational practice. *Perspectives on Psychological Science, 1,* 181–210.

Roediger, H. L. III, & Karpicke, J. D. (2006b). Test-enhanced learning: Taking memory tests improves long-term retention. *Psychological Science, 17,* 249–255.

Roeser, R. W., Peck, S. C., & Nasir, N. S. (2006). Self and identity process in school motivation, learning, and achievement. In P. A. Alexander & P. H. Winne (Eds.), *Handbook of educational psychology* (2nd ed., pp. 392–423). Mahwah, NJ: Erlbaum.

Rogers, L. A., & Graham, S. (2008). A meta-analysis of single subject design writing intervention research. *Journal of Educational Psychology, 100,* 879–906.

Rogoff, B. (1990). *Apprenticeship in thinking: Cognitive development in social context.* New York, NY: Oxford University Press.

Rogoff, B. (1995). Observing sociocultural activity on three planes: Participatory appropriation, guided participation, and apprenticeship. In J. V. Wertsch, P. D. Rio, & A. Alvarez (Eds.), *Sociocultural studies of mind* (pp. 129–164). Cambridge, UK: Cambridge University Press.

Rogoff, B., & Angelillo, C. (2002). Investigating the coordinated functioning of multifaceted cultural practices in human development. *Human Development, 45,* 211–225.

Rogoff, B., Bartlett, L., & Turkanis, C. G. (2001). Lessons about learning as a community. In B. Rogoff, C. G. Turkanis, & L. Bartlett (Eds.), *Learning together: Children and adults in a school community.* Oxford, UK: Oxford University Press.

Rogoff, B., & Chavajay, P. (1995). What's become of research on the cultural basis of cognitive development? *American Psychologist, 50,* 859–877.

Rogoff, B., Paradise, R., Arauz, R. M., Correa-Chavez, M., & Angelillo, C. (2003). Firsthand learning through event participation. *Annual Review of Psychology, 54,* 175–203.

Romberg, T. A., & Collis, K. E. (1987). Different ways children learn to add and subtract. *Journal for Research in Mathematics Education Monograph, 2.*

Root, R. L. (1985). *Assiduous string-savers: The idea generating strategies of professional expository writers.* Paper presented at the Annual Meeting of the Conference of College Composition and Communication. (ERIC Document Reproduction Service No. ED 258 205)

Rosch, E. (1978). Principles of categorization. In E. Rosch & B. B. Lloyd (Eds.), *Cognition and categorization* (pp. 28–48). Mahwah, NJ: Erlbaum.

Rosch, E., & Mervis, C. B. (1975). Family resemblance: Studies in the internal structure of categories. *Cognitive Psychology, 7,* 573–605.

Rosenblatt, L. (1938). *Literature as exploration.* New York, NY: Noble & Noble.

Rosenshine, B., Meister, C., & Chapman, S. (1996). Teaching students to generate questions: A review of the intervention studies. *Review of Educational Research, 66,* 181–221.

Rosenthal, R., & Jacobson, L. (1968). *Pygmalion in the classroom: Teacher expectation and pupils' intellectual development.* New York, NY: Holt, Rinehart & Winston.

Roglio, K. D., & Light, G. (2009). Executive MBA programs: The development of reflective executive. *Academy of Management Learning and Education, 8,* 156–165.

Roth, K. J. (1985, April). *Conceptual change learning and student processing of science texts.* Paper presented at the Annual Meeting of the American Educational Research Association, Chicago, IL.

Roth, W., & Tobin, K. (2001). The implications of coteaching/cogenerative dialogue for teacher evaluation: Learning from multiple perspectives of everyday practice. *Journal of Personnel Evaluation in Education, 15,* 7–29.

Rothkopf, E. Z. (1966). Learning from written instructional materials: An exploration of the control of inspectional behaviors by test-like events. *American Educational Research Journal, 3,* 241–249.

Rubie-Davies, C. M. (2007). Classroom interactions: Exploring the practices of high- and low-expectation teachers. *British Journal of Educational Psychology, 77,* 289–306.

Ruddell, M. R. (1994). Vocabulary knowledge and compre-hension: A comprehension-process view of complex literacy relationships. In R. B. Ruddell, M. R. Ruddell, & H. Singer (Eds.), *Theoretical models and processes of reading* (4th ed., pp. 414–447). Newark, DE: Interna-tional Reading Association.

Rudolph, U., Roesch, S. C., Greitemeyer, T., & Weiner, B. (2004). A meta-analytic review of help giving and aggression from an attributional perspective: Contri-butions to a general theory of motivation. *Cognition & Emotion, 18,* 815–848.

Rumelhart, D. E. (1975). Notes on a schema for stories. In D. C. Bobrow & A. M. Collins (Eds.), *Representation and understanding: Studies in cognitive science* (pp. 268–281). San Diego, CA: Academic Press.

Rumelhart, D. E. (1981). Schemata: The building blocks of cognition. In J. T. Guthrie (Ed.), *Comprehension and teaching: Research reviews* (pp. 3–26). Newark, DE: International Reading Association.

Rumelhart, D. E. (1984). Schemata and the cognitive system. In R. S. Wyer & T. K. Srull (Eds.), *Handbook of social cognition* (Vol. 1, pp. 161–188). Mahwah, NJ: Erlbaum.

Rumelhart, D. E. (1990). Brain style computation: Learn-ing and generalization. In S. F. Zornetzer, J. L. Davis, & C. Lau (Eds.), *An introduction to neural and electronic networks* (pp. 405–420). San Diego, CA: Academic Press.

Rumelhart, D. E., & McClelland, J. L. (1981). Interactive processing through spreading activation. In A. M. Lesgold & C. A. Perfetti (Eds.), *Interactive processes in reading* (pp. 37–60). Mahwah, NJ: Erlbaum.

Rumelhart, D. E., & Norman, D. A. (1978). Accretion, tun-ing, and restructuring: Three modes of learning. In J. W. Cotton & R. Klatzky (Eds.), *Semantic factors in cognition* (pp. 161–184). Mahwah, NJ: Erlbaum.

Rumelhart, D. E., & Ortony, A. (1977). The representation of knowledge in memory. In R. C. Anderson, R. J. Spiro, & W. E. Montague (Eds.), *Schooling and the acquisition of knowledge* (pp. 99–135). Mahwah, NJ: Erlbaum.

Rumelhart, D. E., & Todd, P. M. (1993). Learning and con-nectionist representations. In D. E. Meyer & S. Korn-blum (Eds.), *Attention and performance XIV: Synergies in experimental psychology, artificial intelligence, and cognitive neuroscience* (pp. 3–30). Cambridge, MA: MIT Press.

Runco, M. (1991). Creativity and the finding and solving of real-world problems. *Journal of Psychoeducational Assessment, 9,* 45–53.

Ryan, M. P. (1984). Monitoring test comprehension: Indi-vidual differences in epistemological standards. *Journal of Educational Psychology, 76,* 248–258.

Ryan, R. L., & Deci, E. M. (2000). Self-determination the-ory and the facilitation of intrinsic motivation, social development, and well being. *American Psychologist, 55,* 68–78.

Saddler, B., & Graham, S. (2007). Knowledge about writing and writing performance: Differences between stu-dents who are more and less skilled writers. *Reading & Writing Quarterly, 23,* 231–247.

Sadoski, M., & Goetz, E. T., and Rodriguez, M. (2000, March). Engaging texts: Effects of concreteness on comprehensibility, interest, and recall in four text types. *Journal of Educational Psychology, 92,* 85–95.

Salahu-Din, D., Persky, H., and Miller, J. (2008). *The Nation's Report Card: Writing 2007* (NCES 2008–468). Wash-ington, DC: National Center for Education Statistics, Institute of Education Sciences, U.S. Department of Education.

Salomon, G. (1984). Television is "easy" and print is "tough": The differential investment of mental effort in learning as a function of perceptions and attribu-tions. *Journal of Educational Psychology, 76,* 774–786.

Samuels, S. J. (1994). Toward a theory of automatic infor-mation processing in reading, revisited. In R. B. Rud-dell, M. R. Ruddell, & H. Singer (Eds.), *Theoretical models and processes of reading* (4th ed., pp. 816–837). Newark, DE: International Reading Association.

Samuels, S. J. (2007). The DIBELS tests: Is speed of barking at print what we mean by reading fluency? *Reading Research Quarterly, 42,* 563–566.

Sansone, C., Sachau, D. A., & Weir, C. (1989). Effects of instruction on intrinsic interest: An examination of process and context. *Journal of Personality and Social Psychology, 57,* 819–829.

Sansone, C., & Thoman, D. B. (2006). Maintaining activity engagement: Individuals differences in the process of self-regulating motivation. *Journal of Personality, 76,* 1697–1720.

Sansone, C., Weir, C., Harpster, L., & Morgan, C. (1992). Once a boring task, always a boring task? Interest as a self-regulatory mechanism. *Journal of Personality and Social Psychology, 63,* 379–390.

Savalle, J. M., Twohig, P. T., & Rachford, D. L. (1986). Empir-ical status of Feuerstein's "instrumental enrichments" (FIE) technique as a method of teaching thinking skills. *Review of Educational Research, 56,* 381–409.

Scardamalia, M. (2003). Knowledge building environments: Extending the limits of the possible in education and knowledge work. In A. DiStefano, K. E. Rudestam, & R. Silverman (Eds.), *Encyclopedia of distributed learning* (pp. 269–272). Thousand Oaks, CA: Sage.

Scardamalia, M., & Bereiter, C. (1994). Computer support for knowledge-building communities. *Journal of the Learning Sciences, 3,* 265–283.

Scardamalia, M., & Bereiter, C. (2006). Knowledge building: Theory, pedagogy, and technology. In R. K. Sawyer (Ed.), *Cambridge handbook of the learning sciences.* (pp. 97–118). New York, NY: Cambridge University Press.

Scardamalia, M., Bereiter, C., & Steinbach, R. (1984). Teachability of reflective processes in written composition. *Cognitive Science, 8,* 173–190.

Schacter, D. L. (1993). Understanding implicit memory: A cognitive neuroscience approach. In A. F. Collins, S. E. Gathercole, M. A. Conway, & P. E. Morris (Eds.), *Theories of memory* (pp. 387–412). Hove, UK: Erlbaum.

Schacter, D. L. (1996). *Searching for memory: The brain, the mind, and the past.* New York, NY: Basic Books.

Schacter, D. L. (2001). *The seven sins of memory: How the mind forgets and remembers.* Boston, MA: Houghton Mifflin.

Schacter, D. L., & Cooper, L. A. (1993). Implicit and explicit memory for novel visual objects: Structure and function. *Journal of Experimental Psychology: Learning, Memory, and Cognition, 19,* 995–1009.

Schank, R. C., & Abelson, R. (1977). *Scripts, plans, goals, and understanding.* Mahwah, NJ: Erlbaum.

Scharf, B., & Buss, S. (1986). Audition I: Stimulus, physiology, thresholds. In K. R. Boff, L. Kaufman, & J. P. Thomas (Eds.), *Handbook of perception and human performance: Vol. 1. Sensory perception and human performance* (pp. 14–1 to 14–71). New York, NY: Wiley.

Scharf, B., & Houtsma, A. J. M. (1986). Audition II: Loudness, pitch, localization, aural distortion, and pathology. In K. R. Boff, L. Kaufman, & J. P. Thomas (Eds.), *Handbook of perception and human performance: Vol. 2. Sensory processes and perception* (pp. 15-1–15-60). New York, NY: Wiley.

Schauble, L. (1990). Belief revision in children: The role of prior knowledge and strategies for generating evidence. *Journal of Experimental Child Psychology, 49,* 31–57.

Schellens, T., & Valcke, M. (2005). Collaborative learning in asynchronous discussion groups: What about the impact on cognitive processing? *Computers in Human Behavior, 21,* 957–975.

Schmidt, S. R. (2004). Autobiographical memories for the September 11th attacks: Reconstruction, distinctiveness, plus emotional impairment of memory. *Memory and Cognition, 32,* 443–454.

Schmuck, R. A., & Schmuck, P. A. (1992). *Group processes in the classroom* (6th ed.). Dubuque, IA: William C. Brown.

Schneider, W., & Pressley, M. (1997). *Memory development between two and twenty* (2nd ed.). Mahwah, NJ: Erlbaum.

Schoenfeld, A. H. (1983). Beyond the purely cognitive: Belief systems, social cognitions, and metacognitions as driving forces in intellectual performance. *Cognitive Science, 7,* 329–363.

Schoenfeld, A. H. (1985). *Mathematical problem solving.* San Diego, CA: Academic Press.

Schoenfeld, A. H. (2006). What doesn't work: The challenge and failure of the What Works Clearinghouse to conduct meaningful reviews of studies of mathematics curricula. *Educational Researcher, 35,* 13–21.

Schommer, M. (1990). Effects of beliefs about the nature of knowledge on comprehension. *Journal of Educational Psychology, 82,* 498–504.

Schommer, M. (1994). Synthesizing epistemological belief research: Tentative understandings and provocative confusions. *Educational Psychology Review, 6,* 293–320.

Schommer-Aikins, M. (2002). An evolving theoretical framework for an epistemological belief system. In B. K. Hofer & P. R. Pintrich (Eds.), Personal epistemology: The psychology *of beliefs about knowledge and knowing* (pp. 103–118). Mahwah, NJ: Erlbaum.

Schön, D. A. (1983). *The reflective practitioner: How professionals think in action.* New York, NY: Basic Books.

Schön, D. A. (1987). *Educating the reflective practitioner.* San Francisco, CA: Jossey-Bass.

Schoon, K. J., & Boone, W. J. (1998). Self-efficacy and alternative conceptions of science preservice elementary teachers. *Science Education, 82,* 553–568.

Schramke, C. J., & Bauer, R. M. (1997). State-dependent learning in older and younger adults. *Psychology and Aging, 12,* 255–263.

Schraw, G. (1998). Promoting general metacognitive awareness. *Instructional Science, 26,* 113–125.

Schraw, G. (2000). Reader beliefs and meaning construction in narrative text. *Journal of Educational Psychology, 92,* 96–106.

Schraw, G. (2001). Current themes and future directions in epistemological research: A commentary. *Educational Psychology Review, 13,* 451–464.

Schraw, G. (2006). Knowledge: Structures and processes. In P. Alexander & P. Winne (Eds.), *Handbook of educational psychology* (2nd ed., pp. 245–264). San Diego, CA: Academic Press.

Schraw, G., Bendixen, L. D., & Dunkle, M. E. (2002). Development and validation of the Epistemic Belief Inventory (EBI). In B. K. Hofer & P. R. Pintrich (Eds.), *Personal epistemology: The psychology of beliefs about knowledge and knowing* (pp. 261–275). Mahwah, NJ: Erlbaum.

Schraw, G., & Bruning, R. (1996). Readers' implicit models of reading. *Reading Research Quarterly, 31,* 290–305.

Schraw, G., Crippen, K. J., & Hartley, K. (2006). Self-regulation in science education: Metacognition as a broader perspective on learning. *Research in Science Education, 36,* 111–139.

Schraw, G., & Dennison, R. S. (1994). The effect of reader purpose on interest and recall. *Journal of Reading Behavior: A Journal of Literacy, 26,* 1–18.

Schraw, G., & Flowerday, T., & Reisetter, M. F. (1998). The role of choice in reading engagement. *Journal of Educational Psychology, 90,* 705–715.

Schraw, G., & Moshman, D. (1995). Metacognitive theories. *Educational Psychology Review, 7,* 351–371.

Schraw, G., & Olafson, L. (2002, June). Teachers' epistemological world views and educational practices. *Issues in Education, 8,* 99.

Schraw, G., Potenza, M., & Nebelsick-Gullet, L. (1993). Constraints on the calibration of performance. *Contemporary Educational Psychology, 18,* 455–463.

Schraw, G., & Roedel, T. D. (1994). Test difficulty and judgment bias. *Memory & Cognition, 22,* 63–69.

Scruggs, T., & Mastropieri, M. (Eds). (2004). *Advances in learning and behavioral disabilities: Vol. 17. Research in the secondary schools.* Oxford, UK: Elsevier.

Schunk, D. H. (1983). Ability versus effort attributional feedback: Differential effects on self-efficacy and achievement. *Journal of Educational Psychology, 75,* 848–856.

Schunk, D. H. (1984). Sequential attributional feedback and children's achievement behaviors. *Journal of Educational Psychology, 76,* 1156–1169.

Schunk, D. H. (1987). Peer models and children's behavioral change. *Review of Educational Research, 57,* 149–174.

Schunk, D. H. (2008). *Learning theories: An educational perspective* (5th ed.). Upper Saddle River, NJ: Pearson.

Schunk, D. H., & Cox, P. D. (1986). Strategy training and attributional feedback with learning-disabled students. *Journal of Educational Psychology, 78,* 201–209.

Schunk, D. H., & Zimmerman, B. J. (1994). *Self-regulation of learning and performance: Issues and educational applications.* Mahwah, NJ: Erlbaum.

Schunk, D. H., & Zimmerman, B. J. (2006). Competence and control beliefs: Distinguishing the means and ends. In P. A. Alexander & P. H. Winne (Eds.), *Handbook of educational psychology* (2nd ed., pp. 349–367). Mahwah, NJ: Erlbaum.

Schwab, E. C., & Nusbaum, H. C. (1986). *Pattern recognition by humans and machines: Vol. 1. Speech perception.* San Diego, CA: Academic Press.

Schwanenflugel, P. J., & Rey, M. (1986). Interlingual semantic facilitation: Evidence for a common representational system in the bilingual lexicon. *Journal of Memory and Language, 26,* 505–518.

Schwanenflugel, P. J., Meisinger, E. B., Wisenbaker, J. M., Kuhn, M. R., Strauss, G. P., & Morris, R. D. (2006). Becoming a fluent and automatic reader in the early elementary school years. *Reading Research Quarterly, 41,* 496–522.

Schwartz, R. M. (2005). Literacy learning of at-risk first-grade students in the Reading Recovery early intervention. *Journal of Educational Psychology, 97,* 257–267.

Schwartz, B., & Reisberg, D. (1991). *Learning and memory.* New York, NY: Norton.

Scruggs, T., Mastropieri, M., McLoone, B., Levin, J., & Morrison, C. (1987). Mnemonic facilitation of learning disabled students' memory for expository prose. *Journal of Educational Psychology, 79,* 27–34.

Segar, C. A. (1994). Implicit learning. *Psychological Bulletin, 115,* 163–196.

Seifert, C. M., McKoon, G., Abelson, R. P., & Ratcliff, R. (1986). Memory connections between thematically similar episodes. *Journal of Experimental Psychology: Learning, Memory, and Cognition, 12,* 220–231.

Seifert, T. L. (1993). Effects of elaborative interrogation with prose passages. *Journal of Educational Psychology, 85,* 642–651.

Selfridge, O. (1959). Pandemonium: A paradigm for learning, *Symposium on the mechanization of thought processes.* London: HM Stationery Office.

Shell, D., Colvin, C., & Bruning, R. (1995). Developmental and ability differences in self-efficacy, causal attribution, and outcome expectancy mechanisms in reading and writing achievement. *Journal of Educational Psychology, 87,* 386–398.

Shell, D., & Husman, J. (2008). Control, motivation, affect, and strategic self-regulation in the college classroom:

A multidimensional phenomenon. *Journal of Educational Psychology, 100,* 443–459.

Shen, C. (2005). How American middle schools differ from schools of five Asian countries: Based on cross-national data from TIMSS 1999. *Educational Research and Evaluation, 11,* 179–199.

Shepard, L. A. (2000). The role of assessment in a learning culture. *Educational Researcher, 29,* 4–14.

Shepard, L. A. (2005). Linking formative assessment to scaffolding. *Educational Leadership, 63,* 66–70.

Shiffrin, R. M., & Schneider, W. (1977). Controlled and automatic information processing, II: Perceptual learning, automatic attending, and a general theory. *Psychological Review, 84,* 127–190.

Shute, V. J. (2008). Focus on formative feedback. *Review of Educational Research, 78,* 153–189.

Sideridis, G. D. (2005). Goal orientation, academic achievement, and depression: Evidence in favor of a revised goal theory framework. *Journal of Educational Psychology, 97,* 366–275.

Siegler, R. S. (1996). *Emerging minds: The process of change in children's thinking.* New York, NY: Oxford University Press.

Siegler, R. S., & Jenkins, E. (1989). *How children discover new strategies.* Mahwah, NJ: Erlbaum.

Silver, E. A. (1981). Recall of mathematical problem information: Solving related problems. *Journal for Research in Mathematics Education, 12,* 55–64.

Simon, D. P., & Simon, H. A. (1978). Individual differences in solving physics problems. In R. R. Siegler (Ed.), *Children's thinking: What develops?* (pp. 40–74). Mahwah, NJ: Erlbaum.

Sinatra, G. M. (2001). Knowledge, beliefs, and learning. *Educational Psychology Review, 13,* 321–324.

Sinatra, G. M., & Pintrich, P. R. (Eds.). (2002). *Intentional conceptual change.* Mahwah, NJ: Erlbaum.

Skinner, B. F. (1938). *The behavior of organisms.* New York, NY: Appleton–Century–Crofts.

Skinner, B. F. (1953). *Science and human behavior.* New York, NY: Macmillan.

Skinner, B. F. (1957). *Verbal behavior.* New York, NY: Appleton–Century–Crofts.

Skinner, B. F. (1968). *The technology of teaching.* New York, NY: Appleton–Century–Crofts.

Skinner, E. A., Wellborn, J. G., & Connell, J. P. (1990). What it takes to do well in school and whether I've got it: A process model of perceived control and children's engagement and achievement in school. *Journal of Educational Psychology, 82,* 22–32.

Slamecka, N. J., & Graf, P. (1978). The generation effect: Delineation of a phenomenon. *Journal of Experimental Psychology: Human Learning and Memory, 4,* 592–604.

Slamecka, N. J., & Katsaiti, L. T. (1987). The generation effect as an artifact of selective displaced rehearsal. *Journal of Memory and Language, 26,* 589–602.

Sloman, S. A., Hayman, C. A. G., Ohta, N., Law, J., & Tulving, E. (1988). Forgetting in primed fragment completion. *Journal of Experimental Psychology: Learning, Memory, and Cognition, 14,* 223–239.

Slotta, J. D. (2004). The web-based inquiry science environment (WISE): Scaffolding knowledge integration in the science classroom. In M. Linn, E. Davis, & P. Bell (Eds.), *Internet environments for science education* (pp. 203–231). Mahwah, NJ: Erlbaum.

Smith, D., & Neale, D. C. (1989). The construction of subject matter knowledge in primary science teaching. *Teachers and Teacher Education, 5,* 1–20.

Smith, S. M. (1986). Environmental context-dependent recognition memory using a short-term memory task for input. *Memory & Cognition, 14,* 347–354.

Smith, S. M., Vela, E., & Williamson, S. E. (1988). Shallow input processing does not induce environmental context dependent recognition. *Bulletin of the Psychonomic Society, 26,* 537–540.

Smylie, M. A. (1988). The enhancement function of staff development: Organizational and psychological antecedents to individual teacher change. *American Educational Research Journal, 25,* 1–30.

Snow, C. E., Burns, M. S., & Griffin, P. (Eds.). (1998). *Preventing reading difficulties in young children.* Washington, DC: National Academies Press.

Snyder, C. R. (1995). Conceptualizing, measuring, and nurturing hope. *Journal of Counseling & Development, 73,* 355–360.

Snyder, C. R., Rand, K. L., & Sigmon, D. R. (2002). Hope theory: A member of the positive psychology family. In C. R. Snyder & S. J. Lopez (Eds.), *Handbook of positive psychology* (pp. 257–276). Oxford, England: Oxford University Press.

Solmon, M. A. (1996). Impact of motivational climate on students' behaviors and perceptions in a physical education setting. *Journal of Educational Psychology, 88,* 731–738.

Spear, N. E., & Riccio, D. C. (1994). *Memory: Phenomena and Principles.* Boston, MA: Allyn & Bacon.

Spence, K. W. (1936). The nature of discrimination learning in animals. *Psychological Review, 43,* 427–449.

Spence, K. W. (1956). *Behavior theory and conditioning.* New Haven, CT: Yale University Press.

Sperber, D. (2005). Modularity and relevance: How can a massively modular mind be flexible and context-sensitive? In P. Carruthers, S. Laurence, & S. Stich (Eds.), The *innate mind: Structure and content* (pp. 53–68). Oxford, England: Oxford University Press.

Sperling, G. (1960). The information available in brief visual presentations [Special issue]. *Psychological Monographs, 74*(498).

Sperling, G. (1983). *Unified theory of attention and signal detection. Mathematical studies in perception and cognition* (Rep. No. 83–3). New York, NY: New York University Department of Psychology.

Sperling, M. (1990). I want to talk to each of you: Collaboration and the teacher–student writing conference. *Research in the Teaching of English, 24,* 279–321.

Squire, L. R. (1987). *Memory and brain.* New York, NY: Oxford University Press.

Srihari, S., Collins, J., Srihari, R., Srinivasan, H., Shetty, S., & Brutt-Griffler, J. (2008). Automatic scoring of short handwritten essays in reading comprehension tests. *Artificial Intelligence, 172,* 300–324.

Stahl, G., Koschmann, T., & Suthers, D. (2006). Computer-supported collaborative learning: An historical perspective. In R. K. Sawyer (Ed.), *Cambridge handbook of the learning sciences* (pp. 409–426). Cambridge, UK: Cambridge University Press.

Stahl, S. A., & Fairbanks, M. M. (1986). The effects of vocabulary instruction: A model-based meta-analysis. *Review of Reading Research, 56,* 72–110.

Stalder, D. R. (2005). Learning and motivational effects of acronym use in introductory psychology. *Teaching of Psychology, 32,* 222–228.

Standing, L. (1973). Learning 10,000 pictures. *Quarterly Journal of Experimental Psychology, 25,* 207–222.

Standing, L., Conezio, J., & Haber, R. N. (1970). Perception and memory for pictures: Single trial learning of 2,500 visual stimuli. *Psychonomic Science, 19,* 73–74.

Stanovich, K. E. (2000). *Progress in understanding reading: Scientific foundations and new frontiers.* New York, NY: Guilford.

Stanovich, K. E. (2003). The fundamental computational biases of human cognition: Heuristics that (sometimes) impair decision making and problem solving. In J. E. Davidson & R. J. Sternberg (Eds.), *The psychology of problem solving* (pp. 291–342). Cambridge, UK: Cambridge University Press.

Stanovich, K. E., & Cunningham, A. E. (1993). Where does knowledge come from? Specific associations between print exposure and information acquisition. *Journal of Educational Psychology, 85,* 211–229.

Stanovich, K. E., & West, R. F. (2008). On the failure of cognitive ability to predict myside and one-sided thinking biases. *Thinking and Reasoning, 14,* 129–167.

Stanovich, K. E., West, R. F., & Harrison, M. R. (1995). Knowledge growth and maintenance across the life span: The role of print exposure. *Developmental Psychology, 31,* 811–826.

Star, J. R., & Rittle-Johnson, B. (2008). Flexibility in problem solving: The case of equation solving. *Learning and Instruction, 18,* 565–579.

Star, J. R., & Rittle-Johnson, B. (2009). It pays to compare: An experimental study on computational estimation. *Journal of Experimental Child Psychology, 102,* 408–426.

Sternberg, R. J. (1986). *The triarchic mind: A new theory of human intelligence.* New York, NY: Penguin.

Sternberg, R. J. (1987). Most vocabulary is learned from context. In M. G. McKeown & M. E. Curtis (Eds.), *The nature of vocabulary acquisition* (pp. 89–105). Mahwah, NJ: Erlbaum.

Sternberg, R. J. (2001). Why schools should teach for wisdom: The balance theory of wisdom in educational settings. *Educational Psychologist, 36,* 227–246.

Sternberg, R. J. (2005). Intelligence. In K. J. Holyoak & R. G. Morrison (eds.), *The Cambridge handbook of thinking and reasoning* (pp. 751–776). Cambridge, UK: Cambridge University Press.

Sternberg, R. J., Lubart, T. I., Kaufman, J. C., & Pretz, J. E. (2005). Creativity. In K. Holyoak & R. Morrison (Eds.), *The Cambridge handbook of thinking and reasoning* (pp. 351–370). Cambridge, UK: Cambridge University Press.

Sternberg, R. J., & Wagner, R. K. (Eds.). (1994). *Mind in context: Interactionist perspectives on human intelligence.* Cambridge, UK: Cambridge University Press.

Sternberg, S. (1975). Memory scanning: New findings and current controversies. *Quarterly Journal of Experimental Psychology, 27,* 1–32.

Stevenson, H. H., & Stigler, J. W. (1992). *The learning gap.* New York, NY: Touchstone.

Stipek, D. J. (1993). *Motivation to learn* (2nd ed.). Boston, MA: Allyn & Bacon.

Stipek, D. J. (1996). Motivation and instruction. In D. C. Berliner & R. C. Calfee (Eds.), *Handbook of educational psychology* (pp. 85–113). New York, NY: Macmillan.

Stipek, D. J., & Gralinski, J. H. (1996). Children's beliefs about intelligence and school performance. *Journal of Educational Psychology, 88,* 397–407.

Sulzby, E. (1991). The development of the young child and the emergence of literacy. In J. Flood, J. M. Jensen, D. Lapp, & J. R. Squire (Eds.), *Handbook of research on teaching the English language arts* (pp. 273–285). New York, NY: Macmillan.

Svengas, A. G., & Johnson, M. K. (1988). Qualitative effects of rehearsal on memories for perceived and imagined complex events. *Journal of Experimental Psychology: Educational Psychologist, 24,* 113–142.

Swanson, H. L. (1990). Influence of metacognitive knowledge and aptitude on problem solving. *Journal of Educational Psychology, 82,* 306–314.

Swanson, H. L. (1992). Generality and modifiability of working memory among skilled and less skilled readers. *Journal of Educational Psychology, 84,* 473–488.

Swanson, H. L. (2003). Age-related differences in learning disabled and skilled readers' working memory. *Journal of Experimental Child Psychology, 85,* 1–31.

Swanson, H. L. (2004). Working memory and phonological processing as predictors of children's mathematical problem-solving at different ages. *Memory & Cognition, 32,* 648–661.

Swanson, H. L. (2006). Cross-sectional and incremental changes in working memory and mathematical problem solving. *Journal of Educational Psychology, 98,* 265–281.

Swanson, H. L., & Jerman, O. (2006, Summer). Math disabilities: A selective meta-analysis of the literature. *Review of Educational Research, 76,* 249–274.

Swanson, H. L., O'Connor, J. E., & Cooney, J. B. (1990). An information processing analysis of expert and novice teachers' problem solving. *American Educational Research Journal, 27,* 533–556.

Swanson, L., & Kim, K. (2007). Working memory, short term memory, and naming speed as predictors of children's mathematical performance. *Intelligence, 35,* 151–168.

Swartz, R. J., & Perkins, D. N. (1990). *Teaching thinking: Issues and approaches.* Pacific Grove, CA: Midwest.

Sweller, J. (1999). *Instructional design in technical areas.* Camberwell, Victoria, Australia: Australian Council for Educational Research.

Sweller, J., van Merrienboër, & Paas, F. (1998). Cognitive architecture and instructional design. *Educational Psychology Review, 10,* 251–296.

Taasoobshirazi, G., & Carr, M. (2008). Gender differences in science: An expertise perspective. *Educational Psychology Review, 20,* 149–169.

Taconis, R., Ferguson-Hessler, M. G. M., & Broekkamp, H. (2002). Teaching science problem solving: An overview of experimental work. *Journal of Research in Science Teaching, 38,* 442–468.

Tal, Z., & Babad, E. (1990). The teacher's pet phenomenon: Rate of occurrence, correlates, and psychological costs. *Journal of Educational Psychology, 82,* 637–645.

Thompson, P. W. (2008). On professional judgment and the National Mathematics Advisory Panel Report: Curricular content. *Educational Researcher, 37,* 582–587.

Thorndike, E. L. (1911). *Animal intelligence: Experimental studies.* New York, NY: Macmillan.

Tishman, S., Perkins, D. N., & Jay, E. (1995). *The thinking classroom: Learning and teaching in a culture of thinking.* Boston, MA: Allyn & Bacon.

Tobin, K., & Fraser, B. J. (1990). What does it mean to be an exemplary teacher in science? *Journal of Research in Science Teaching, 27,* 3–25.

Tobin, K., Tippins, D. J., & Gallrad, A. J. (1994). Research on instructional strategies for teaching science. In G. L. Gabel (Ed.), *Handbook of research on science teaching and learning* (pp. 45–93). New York, NY: Macmillan.

Tomic, W. (1997). Training in inductive reasoning and problem solving. *Contemporary Educational Psychology, 20,* 483–490.

Toth, J. P., Reingold, E. M., & Jacoby, L. L. (1994). Toward a redefinition of implicit memory: Process dissociations following elaborative processing and self-generation. *Journal of Experimental Psychology: Learning, Memory, and Cognition, 20,* 290–303.

Treiman, R., Pennington, B. F., Shriberg, L. D., & Boada, R. (2008). Which children benefit from letter names in learning letter sounds? *Cognition, 106,* 1322–1338.

Treisman, A. (2006). How the deployment of attention determines what we see. *Visual Cognition, 14,* 411–443.

Tschannen-Moran, M., & Woolfolk-Hoy, A. (2001). Teacher efficacy: Capturing an elusive construct. *Teaching and Teacher Education, 17,* 783–805.

Tschannen-Moran, M., Woolfolk-Hoy, A., & Hoy, W. K. (1998). Teacher efficacy: Its meaning and measure. *Review of Educational Research, 68,* 202–248.

Tse, D., Langston, R. F., Kakeyama, M., Bethus, I., Spooner, P. A., Wood, E. R., Witter, M. P., & Morris, R. G. (2007). Schemas and memory consolidation. *Science, 316,* 76–81.

Tulving, E. (1972). Episodic and semantic memory. In E. Tulving & W. Donaldson (Eds.), *Organization of memory* (pp. 381–403). San Diego, CA: Academic Press.

Tulving, E. (1983). *Elements of episodic memory*. Oxford, UK: Oxford University Press.

Tulving, E. (1985). On the classification problem in learning and memory. In I. Nilsson & T. Archer (Eds.), *Perspectives on learning and memory* (pp. 73–101). Mahwah, NJ: Erlbaum.

Tulving, E. (2002). Episodic memory: From mind to brain. *Annual Review of Psychology, 53,* 1–25.

Tulving, E., & Osler, S. (1968). Effectiveness of retrieval cues in memory for words. *Journal of Experimental Psychology, 77,* 593–601.

Tulving, E., & Thompson, D. M. (1973). Encoding specificity and retrieval processes in episodic memory. *Psychological Review, 80,* 352–373.

Turner, M. L., & Engle, R. W. (1989). Is working memory capacity task dependent? *Journal of Memory and Language, 28,* 127–154.

Tversky, A. (1977). Features of similarity. *Psychological Review, 84,* 327–352.

Tynjala, P. (1998). Writing as a tool for constructive learning: Students' learning experiences during an experiment. *Higher Education, 36,* 209–230.

Tynjala, P., Mason, L., & Lonka, K. (2001). Writing as a learning tool: An introduction. In G. Rijlaarsdam (Series Ed.) & Tynjala, P., Mason, L., & Lonka, K. (Vol. Eds.), *Studies in writing: Vol. 7. Writing as a learning tool: Integrating theory and practice*. Dordrecht, Netherlands: Kluwer.

Underwood, B. J., & Schultz, R. W. (1960). *Meaningfulness and verbal learning*. Philadelphia: Lippincott.

Unsworth, N., & Engle, R. W. (2007). The nature of individual differences in working memory capacity: Active maintenance in primary memory and controlled search from secondary memory. *Psychological Review, 114,* 104–132.

Urdan, T. C. (1997). Examining the relations among early adolescent students' goals and friends' orientation toward effort and achievement in school. *Contemporary Educational Psychology, 22,* 165–191.

Urdan, T., & Mestas, M. (2006). The goals behind performance goals. *Journal of Educational Psychology, 98,* 354–356.

Urdan, T., Midgley, C., & Anderman, E. M. (1998). The role of classroom goal structure in students' use of self-handicapping strategies. *American Educational Research Journal, 35,* 101–122.

Usher, E. L. (2009). Sources of middle school students' self-efficacy in mathematics: A qualitative investigation. *American Educational Research Journal, 46,* 275–314.

Usher, E. L., & Pajares, F. (2006). Sources of academic and self-regulatory efficacy beliefs of entering middle school students. *Contemporary Educational Psychology, 31,* 125–141.

Usher, E. L., & Pajares, F. (2009). Sources of self-efficacy in mathematics: A validation study. *Contemporary Educational Psychology, 34,* 89–101.

Valinides, N., & Angeli, C. (2005). Effects of instruction on changes in epistemological beliefs. *Contemporary Educational Psychology, 30,* 314–330.

Vallerand, R. J., Blais, M. R., Briere, N. M., & Pelletier, L. G. (1989). Construction et validation de l'Echelle de Motivation en Education [Construction and validation of the Motivation in Education Scale]. *Canadian Journal of Behavioral Sciences, 21,* 323–349.

Vallerand, R. J., Salvy, S. J., Mageau, G. A., Elliott, A. J., Denis, P. L., Grouzet, P. E., & Blanchard, C. (2007). On the role of passion in performance. *Journal of Personality, 75,* 505–535.

van de Walle, J. A., & Watkins, K. B. (1993). Early development of number sense. In R. J. Jensen (Ed.), *Research ideas for the classroom: Early childhood mathematics* (pp. 127–150). New York, NY: Macmillan.

van den Broek, P., Rapp, D., & Kendeou, P. (2005). Integrating memory-based and constructionist processes in accounts of reading comprehension. *Discourse Processes, 39,* 299–316.

Van Dijk, T. A., & Kintsch, W. (1983). *Strategies of discourse comprehension*. San Diego, CA: Academic Press.

van Merrienboër, J. J. G. (1997). *Training complex cognitive skills: A four-component instructional design model for technical training*. Englewood Cliffs, NJ: Educational Technology Publications.

van Merrienboër, J. J. G., & Ayres, P. (2005). Research on cognitive load theory and its design implications for e-learning. *Educational Technology Research and Development, 53,* 5–13.

van Merrienboër, J. J. G., Clark, R. E., & de Croock, M. B. M. (2002). Blueprints for complex learning: The 4C/ID model. *Educational Technology Research and Development, 54,* 39–64.

van Merrienboër, J. J. G., & Kirschner, P. (2007). *Ten steps to complex learning: A systematic approach to four-component instructional design*. New York, NY: Erlbaum.

van Merriënboër, J. J. G., & Sweller, J. (2005). Cognitive load theory and complex learning: Recent developments and future directions. *Educational Psychology Review, 17,* 147–177.

Vansteenkiste, M., Lens, W., & Deci, E. L. (2006). Intrinsic versus extrinsic goal contents in Self-determination Theory: Another look at the quality of academic motivation. *Educational Psychologist, 41,* 19–31.

Vansteenkiste, M., Simons, J., Sheldon, K. M., & Deci, E. L. (2004). Motivating learning, performance, and persistence: The synergistic effects of intrinsic goal contents and autonomy supportive contexts. *Journal of Personality and Social Psychology, 87,* 246–260.

Vellutino, F. R., Tunmer, W. E., Jaccard, J. J., & Chen, R. (2007). Components of reading ability: Multivariate evidence for a convergent skills model of reading development. *Scientific Studies of Reading, 11,* 3–32.

Von Wright, J. M. (1972). On the problem of selection in iconic memory. *Scandinavian Journal of Psychology, 13,* 159–171.

Vosniadou, S. (2002). On the nature of naïve physics. In M. Limon & L. Mason (Eds.), *Reconsidering conceptual change: Issues in theory and practice* (pp. 61–76). Dordrecht, The Netherlands: Kluwer.

Vosniadou, S., & Brewer, W. F. (1987). Theories of knowledge restructuring in development. *Review of Educational Research, 57,* 51–67.

Vye, N. J., Delclos, V. R., Burns, M. S., & Bransford, J. D. (1988). Teaching thinking and problem solving: Illustrations and issues. In R. Sternberg & E. Smith (Eds.), *The psychology of human thought* (pp. 337–365). New York, NY: Cambridge University Press.

Vygotsky, L. (1962). *Thought and language.* New York, NY: Wiley.

Vygotsky, L. (1978). *Mind in society: The development of higher psychological processes.* Cambridge, MA: Harvard University Press.

Vygotsky, L. (1986). *Thought and language* (rev. ed.). Cambridge, MA: MIT Press.

Wade, S. E., Trathen, W., & Schraw, G. (1990). An analysis of spontaneous study strategies. *Reading Research Quarterly, 25,* 147–166.

Walker, N. (1986). Direct retrieval from elaborated memory traces. *Memory & Cognition, 74,* 321–328.

Wallace, D. L., Hayes, J. R., Hatch, J. A., Miller, W., Moser, G., & Silk, C. M. (1996). Better revision in eight minutes? Prompting first-year college writers to revise globally. *Journal of Educational Psychology, 88,* 682–688.

Ward, J. (2006). The student's guide to cognitive neuroscience. New York, NY: Psychology Press.

Ward, P., Hodges, N. J., Starkes, J. L. Williams, A. M. (2007). The road to excellence: Deliberate practice and the development of expertise. *High Ability Studies, 18,* 119–153.

Watson, J. B. (1913). Psychology as the behaviorist views it. *Psychological Review, 20,* 158–177.

Watson, J. B. (1924). *Behaviorism.* New York, NY: Norton.

Wattenmaker, W. D., Dewey, G. I., Murphy, T. D., & Medin, D. L. (1986). Linear separability and concept learning: Context, relational properties, and concept naturalness. *Cognitive Psychology, 18,* 158–194.

Waugh, N. C., & Norman, D. A. (1965). Primary memory. *Psychological Review, 72,* 89–104.

Weaver, C. (1994). *Reading process and practice* (2nd ed.). Portsmouth, NH: Heinemann.

Webb, N. W., & Palincsar, A. S. (1996). Group processes in the classroom. In D. C. Berliner and R. C. Calfee (Eds.), *Handbook of educational psychology,* pp. 841–873. New York, NY: Macmillan.

Weiner, B. (1986). *An attributional theory of motivation and emotion.* New York, NY: Springer-Verlag.

Weiner, B. (1990). Attribution theory in personality psychology. In L. Pervin (Ed.), *Handbook of personality: Theory and research* (pp. 465–485). New York, NY: Guilford.

Weiner, B. (1995). *Judgments of responsibility: A foundation for a theory of social conduct.* New York, NY: Guilford.

Weiner, B. (2000). Intrapersonal and interpersonal theories of motivation from an attributional perspective. *Educational Psychology Review, 12,* 1–14.

Weinstein, C. E. (1996). Self-regulation: A commentary on directions for future research. *Learning and Individual Differences, 8,* 269–274.

Weisberg, R. W. (1993). *Creativity: Beyond the myth of genius.* New York, NY: Freeman.

Welch-Ross, M. K. (1995). An integrative model of the development of autobiographical memory. *Developmental Review, 15,* 338–365.

Weldon, M. S., & Roediger, H. L. (1987). Altering retrieval demands reverses the picture superiority effect. *Memory & Cognition, 15,* 269–280.

Wertsch, J. V. (2008). From social interaction to higher psychological processes: A clarification and application of Vygotsky's theory. *Human Development, 51,* 66–79.

Wharton-McDonald, R., & Swiger, S. (2009). Developing higher order comprehension in the middle grades. In S. E. Israel & G. G. Duffy (Eds.), *Handbook of research on reading comprehension* (pp. 510–530). New York, NY: Routledge.

White, B. C. (2000). Pre-service teachers' epistemology viewed through perspectives on problematic classroom situations. *Journal of Education for Teaching, 26,* 279–05.

White, B. Y., Frederiksen, J. R., & Collins, A. (2009). The interplay of scientific inquiry and metacognition: More than a marriage of convenience. In D. Hacker, J. Dunlosky, & A. Graesser (Eds.) *Handbook of metacognition in education* (pp. 175–205). New York, NY: Routledge.

White, M. J., & Bruning, R. (2005). Implicit writing beliefs and their relation to writing quality, *Contemporary Educational Psychology, 30,* 166–189.

Wiencek, J., & O'Flahavan, J. F. (1994). From teacher-led to peer discussions about literature: Suggestions for making the shift. *Language Arts, 71,* 488–498.

Wigfield, A., Guthrie, J. T., Perencevich, K. C., Taboada, A., Klauda, S. L. McRae, A., & Barbosa, P. (2008). Role of reading engagement in mediating effects of reading comprehension on reading outcomes. *Psychology in the Schools, 45,* 432–445.

Wilcox-Herzog, A. (2002). Is there a link between teachers' beliefs and behaviors? *Early Education and Development, 13,* 79–106.

Williams, G. C., & Deci, E. L. (1996). Internalization of biopsychosocial values by medical students: A test of self-determination theory. *Journal of Personality and Social Psychology, 70,* 767–779.

Willoughby, T., Waller, T. G., Wood, E., & McKinnon, G. E. (1993). The effect of prior knowledge on an immediate and delayed associative learning task following elaborative integration. *Contemporary Educational Psychology, 18,* 36–46.

Winne, P. H. (2006). How software technologies can improve research on learning and bolster school reform. *Educational Psychologist, 41,* 5–17.

Winne, P. H., & Perry, N. (2000). Measuring self-regulated learning. In M. Boekaerts, P. Pintrich, & M. Zeidner (Eds.), *Handbook of self-regulation* (pp. 531–566). San Diego, CA: Academic Press.

Winner, E. (1996). The rage to master: The decisive role of talent in the visual arts. In K. A. Ericsson (Ed.), *The road to excellence: The acquisition of expert performance in the arts and sciences, sports and games* (pp. 271–302). Mahwah, NJ: Erlbaum.

Winner, E. (2000). The origins and ends of giftedness. *American Psychologist, 55,* 159–169.

Winograd, T. (1975). Frame representations and the declarative-procedural controversy. In D. G. Bobrow & A. M. Collins (Eds.), *Representation and understanding: Studies in cognitive science* (pp. 185–210). San Diego, CA: Academic Press.

Woloshyn, V. E., Paivio, A., & Pressley, M. (1994). Use of elaborative interrogation to help students acquire information consistent with prior knowledge and information inconsistent with prior knowledge. *Journal of Educational Psychology, 86,* 79–89.

Wolters, C. A. (2003). Regulation of motivation: Evaluating and underemphasized aspect of self-regulated learning. *Educational Psychologist, 38,* 189–205.

Wolters, C. A. (2004). Advancing achievement goal theory: Using goal structures and goal orientations to predict students, motivation, cognition and achievement. *Journal of Educational Psychology, 96,* 236–250.

Wood, E., Pressley, M., & Winne, P. H. (1990). Elaborative interrogation effects on children's learning of factual content. *Journal of Educational Psychology, 82,* 741–748.

Woolfolk, A. E., & Hoy, W. K. (1990). Prospective teachers' sense of efficacy and beliefs about control. *Journal of Educational Psychology, 82,* 81–91.

Woolfolk-Hoy, A., Davis, H., & Pape, S. J. (2006). Teacher knowledge and beliefs. In P. A. Alexander & P. H. Winne (Eds.), *Handbook of educational psychology* (2nd ed., pp. 715–737). Mahwah, NJ: Erlbaum.

Wortham, S. (2001). Interactionally situated cognition: A classroom example. *Cognitive Science, 25,* 37–66.

Wyra, M., Lawson, M. J., & Hungi, N. (2007). The mnemonic keyword method: The effects of bidirectional retrieval training and of ability to image on foreign language vocabulary recall. *Learning and Instruction, 17,* 360–371.

Yang, F. (2005). Student views concerning evidence and the expert in reasoning a socio-scientific issue and personal epistemology. *Educational Studies, 31,* 65–84.

Yoshinobu, L. R. (1989). Construct validation of the Hope Scale: Agency and pathways components. Unpublished master's thesis, University of Kansas, Lawrence.

Young, D. J., Reynolds, A. J., & Walberg, H. (1996). Science achievement and educational productivity: A hierarchical linear model. *Journal of Educational Research, 89,* 272–278.

Zhang, Z., & Burry-Stock, J. A. (2003). Classroom assessment practices and teachers' self-perceived assessment skills. *Applied Measurement in Education, 16,* 323–342.

Zhang, J., Scardamalia, M., Lamon, M., Messina, R., & Reeve, R. (2007). Socio-cognitive dynamics of knowledge building in the work of 9- and 10-year-olds. *Educational Technology Research and Development, 55,* 117–145.

Zimmerman, B. (2000). Attaining self-regulation: A social cognitive perspective. In M. Boekaerts, P. R. Pintrich,

& M. Zeidner (Eds.), *Handbook of self-regulation* (pp. 13–39). San Diego, CA: Academic Press.

Zimmerman, B., & Kitsantas, A. (2002). Acquiring writing revision proficiency through observation and emulation. *Journal of Educational Psychology, 94,* 660–668.

Zimmerman, B., & Kitsantas, A. (2007). A writer's discipline: The development of self-regulatory skill. In S. Hidi & P. Boscolo (Eds.), *Writing and motivation.* Oxford, UK: Elsevier.

Zimmerman, B. J., & Martinez-Pons, M. (1990). Student differences in self-regulated learning: Relating grade, sex, and giftedness to self-efficacy and strategy use. *Journal of Educational Psychology, 82,* 51–59.

Zimmerman, B. J., & Tsikalas, K. E. (2005). Can computer-based learning environments (CBLEs) be used as self-regulatory tools to enhance learning? *Educational Psychologist, 40,* 267–271.

Zimmerman, C. (2007). The development of scientific thinking skills in elementary and middle school. *Developmental Review, 27,* 172–223.

Zito, J. R., Adkins, M, Gavins, M., Harris, K. R., & Graham, S. (2007). Self-regulated strategy development: Relationship to the social-cognitive perspective and the development of self-regulation. *Reading and Writing Quarterly, 23,* 77–95.

Zohar, A. (2006). The nature and development of teachers' metastrategic knowledge in the context of teaching higher order thinking. *Journal of the Learning Sciences, 15,* 331–377.

Zohar, A. (2008). Teaching thinking on a national scale: Israel's pedagogical horizons. *Thinking Skills and Creativity, 3,* 77–81.

Zohar, A., Degani, A., & Vaaknin, E. (2001). Teachers' beliefs about low-achieving students and higher order thinking. *Teaching and Teacher Education, 17,* 469–485.

Zur, O., & Gelman, R. (2004). Young children can add and subtract by predicting and checking. *Early Childhood Research Quarterly, 19,* 121–137.

Zwaan, R. A. (1996). Toward a model of literary comprehension. In B. K. Britton & A. C. Graesser (Eds.), *Models of understanding text* (pp. 241–255). Mahwah, NJ: Erlbaum.

Zwaan, R. A., & Madden, C. J. (2004). Updating situation models. *Journal of Experimental Psychology: Learning, Memory, and Cognition, 30,* 283–288.

Zvoch, K. (2006). The challenge of assessing students and evaluating schools in the era of high-stakes accountability. *Measurement, 4,* 267–270.

NAME INDEX

SUBJECT INDEX

Phonics, 250
Phonological loop, 222
Planning
  differences in, 297–298
  local v. global, 167
  problem solving and, 167
  writing and, 292
Positron emission tomography
    (PET), 33
Practice
  cognitive skills developed
      through, 6–7
  deliberate, 174–175
  technology and, 220
Pragmatics, 237, 238
Pre-alphabetic phase, 247–248
Pretraining, 29
Primary memory, 14
*Principles and Standards for School
    Mathematics* (NCTM), 194, 312
Print exposure, 268
Prior knowledge, 62–63, 74–75, 81,
    347–348
Probabilistic theories of conceptual
    structure, 45–46
Problem finding, 162–164
Problem solving
  in algebra, 322–328
  arithmetic, 314–322
  assessment of, 189–190
  contemporary approaches to,
      162–168
  Dewey's model for, 161
  domain knowledge and, 168–170
  expert knowledge in, 168–176
  expert-novice differences in,
      342–344
  general knowledge and, 170–171
  Gestalt psychology model for, 161
  historical perspectives on,
      161–168
  identifying problem in, 162–164
  improving, 176–178
  planning and, 167
  representing problem in, 164–166
  solution evaluation in, 168
  strategy for, 160, 177–178

strategy implementation in,
    167–168
  strategy selection in, 166–167
  text comprehension and, 318–321
  Thorndike's model, 161
  transfer of skills in, 175–176, 177
Problem space, 164–165
Problem typologies, in
    mathematics, 315–318
Proceduralized knowledge, 24, 63
Procedural knowledge, 38, 39
  components of, 43
  distributed practice and, 102
Production rules, 52
Productions, 43, 51–52
Production system models of
    memory, 61
Production systems, 52
Productive Thinking Program, 187
Propositional networks, 48
Propositions, 43, 46–48
Prototypes, 21, 44–45
Prototype theories of conceptual
    structure, 44–45
Pruning, 30
Psychological assessment, theory
    change and, 157–158

QAR. *See* Question-answer
    relationships
Question-answer relationships
    (QAR), 279–280

Radical behaviorists, 3
Reading
  assessment of early, 253–255
  assumptions of models of, 267
  attention and, 246
  beginning, 249–250
  building organized knowledge
      through, 273–278
  building vocabulary through,
      268–273
  cognitive prerequisites of,
      244–247
  conceptually driven models of,
      261, 262–263

consolidated alphabetic phase,
    248–249
  construction-integration model
      of, 263, 264–266
  constructionist models of, 266
  data-driven models of, 261–262
  decoding and, 249–250
  difficulties in, 256–258
  fluency in oral, 253
  full alphabetic phase, 248
  instruction in beginning,
      255–256
  interactive models of, 263
  linguistic prerequisites for,
      242–244
  methods of teaching, 250–253
  partial alphabetic phase, 248
  pre-alphabetic phase, 247–248
  transition to, 247–250
  working/long-term memory and,
      245–246
  world knowledge and, 244–245
Reading comprehension
  arithmetic problem solving and,
      318–321
  assessing, 282–284
  assumptions about, 267
  current models of, 263–268
  early models of, 261–263
  instruction and, 284–285
  questions to promote, 277–278
Reading engagement, 281
Reading fluency, 254
Reading Recovery, 257–258
Reading span task, 33
Reading strategies, 278–282
Reasoning
  educational experience and, 157
  scientific, 344
Recall
  dual process model of, 96
  free, 52
  recognition and, 95–97, 106
  as reconstructive activity, 51
  schemata and, 50–51
  of specific events, 100–101
  threshold of, 95